The Great Utopia

The Russian and Soviet Avant-Garde,
1915–1932

The Great Utopia

The Russian and Soviet Avant-Garde,
1915–1932

Solomon R. Guggenheim Museum
State Tret'iakov Gallery
State Russian Museum
Schirn Kunsthalle Frankfurt

GUGGENHEIM MUSEUM

©The Solomon R. Guggenheim Foundation, New York, 1992
©State Tret'iakov Gallery, Moscow, 1992
©State Russian Museum, St. Petersburg, 1992
©Ministry of Culture of the Russian Federation, 1992

ISBN: 0–89207–096–x

Published by the Guggenheim Museum
1071 Fifth Avenue
New York, New York 10128

Printed in Japan by Toppan Printing Co., Inc.

Cover:
Kazimir Malevich
*Red Square (Painterly Realism: Peasant Woman
in Two Dimensions),* 1915
State Russian Museum, St. Petersburg

Photo credits: Michael Agee, Jorg P. Anders,
Vladimir Babailov, Jacques Befank, Valerii Evstigneev,
Aleksandr Galkin, David Heald, Mariusz Lukawski,
Philippe Migeat, Piermarco Menini, Rudolf Nagel,
Otto E. Nelson, Ivan Nenec, *Sovetskoe foto,* Jim Strong,
Joseph Szaszfai, Sergei Tartakovskii, Vitalii Teplov,
Paolo Vandrasch, Igor' Voronov, John Webb

The Great Utopia
The Russian and Soviet Avant-Garde, 1915–1932

Schirn Kunsthalle Frankfurt
March 1–May 10, 1992

Stedelijk Museum Amsterdam
June 5–August 23, 1992

Solomon R. Guggenheim Museum
September 25–December 15, 1992

Lufthansa German Airlines is
a major sponsor of this exhibition.

 Lufthansa

Prefaces
Thomas Krens, Michael Govan
x

Vladimir Gusev, Evgeniia Petrova, Iurii Korolev
xiii

Jürgen Weber
xiv

Contents

Selection Committee

Vivian Endicott Barnett, Christiane Bauermeister,
Charlotte Douglas, Svetlana Dzhafarova, Hubertus Gassner,
Evgenii Kovtun, Irina Lebedeva, Evgeniia Petrova,
Alla Povelikhina, Elena and Vasilii Rakitin, Jane A. Sharp,
Anatolii Strigalev, Margarita Tupitsyn

Direction

Solomon R. Guggenheim Museum, New York
Thomas Krens, Director
Michael Govan, Deputy Director

State Tret'iakov Gallery, Moscow
Iurii Korolev, Director
Lidiia Iovleva, Deputy Director
Lidiia Romashkova, Chief Registrar and Deputy Director

State Russian Museum, St. Petersburg
Vladimir Gusev, Director
Evgeniia Petrova, Deputy Director

Schirn Kunsthalle Frankfurt
Christoph Vitali, Director

Vuchetich All-Union Art Production Association (VUART)
Pavel Khoroshilov, Former Director
Aleksandr Ursin, Director
Valentin Rivkind, Deputy Director

Ministry of Culture, Russian Federation
Evgenii Sidorov, Minister
Aleksandr Shkurko, Deputy Minister
Vera Lebedeva, Head of Museum Department
Anna Kolupaeva, Assistant to Head of Museum Department

Former Ministry of Culture, USSR
Nikolai Gubenko, Minister
Genrikh Popov, Head of Department of Fine Arts
    and Museums
Lidiia Zaletova, Senior Curator of Exhibitions

The Great Utopia

The Russian and Soviet Avant-Garde,
1915–1932

Guggenheim Museum Project Staff

Project Management
Michael Govan, Deputy Director
Jane A. Sharp, Project Associate Curator

Curatorial Staff
Natasha Kurchanova, Curatorial Assistant
Sabine Lange, Curatorial Consultant
Emily Locker, Administrative Assistant
Katherine Glaser, Administrative Assistant
Nataliya Bregel, Administrative Assistant

Exhibition Design
Zaha Hadid with Patrik Schumacher
Pamela Myers, Administrator for Exhibitions
    and Programming
Ali Hocek, Architectural Design Associate
Cara Galowitz, Graphic Designer

Catalogue
Anthony Calnek, Managing Editor
Jane Bobko, Project Editor
Victoria Ellison, Project Associate Editor (glossary)
Kathleen Friello, Research Assistant
Robert Hemenway (copy editor)
Massimo Vignelli (design)
Charles Davey (design and production)

Russian Project Staff

Coordination of Russian Loans
Vuchetich All-Union Artistic Production Association:
Svetlana Dzhafarova
Faina Balakhovskaia
Zel'fira Tregulova

State Tret'iakov Gallery:
Irina Lebedeva (Paintings)
Natal'ia Sokolova
Elena Zhukova (Graphics)

State Russian Museum:
Evgeniia Petrova
Elena Ivanova (Porcelain)
Natal'ia Kozyreva (Graphics)
Liudmila Vostretsova (Graphics)

Additional Coordination
Ol'ga Kupriashchina, VUART
Natal'ia Pchelkina, Lenin Library
Galina Drezgunova, Central State Archive for
    Literature and Art
Liubov' Rodnova
Ol'ga Zemliakova
Aleksandr Lavrent'ev, A. M. Rodchenko and
    V. F. Stepanova Archive
Dotina Tiurina, State Shchusev Museum
Alla Povelikhina, Museum of the History of the
    City of St. Petersburg
Irina Duksina, State Bakhrushin Museum
Larissa Karogodina, Kuskovo State Porcelain Museum
Marianna Bubchikova, State Historical Museum
Elena Karavaeva, VUART

Russian catalogue material
Coordination:
Svetlana Dzhafarova
Faina Balakhovskaia
Zel'fira Tregulova

Manuscript preparation:
Andrei Sarab'ianov
Irina Sorvina

Albright-Knox Art Gallery, Buffalo, New York
All-Russian Museum of Decorative and Folk Art, Moscow
Art Co. Ltd. (Collection George Costakis)
Astrakhan Kustodiev Picture Gallery
Collection Thea Berggren, Chicago
Collection Merrill C. Berman
La Boetie, Inc., New York
The British Library Board
Central State Archive of the October Revolution, Moscow
Central State Archive for Literature and Art, Moscow
Collection Andrei Chernikhov, Moscow
International Iakov Chernikhov Foundation
Collection Elaine Lustig Cohen
Collection of Prints and Drawings,
    The Federal Institute of Technology, Zurich
College of Architecture and Landscape Architecture,
    University of Minnesota
Dagestan Museum of the Arts, Makhachkala
Dallas Museum of Art
Collection A. A. and E. D. Drevin, Moscow
Collection V. A. Dudakov and M. K. Kashuro, Moscow
Collection Zoia Ender-Masetti, Rome
Rosa Esman Gallery, New York
Eric Estorick Family Collection
Ex Libris Gallery, New York
Galerie Natan Fedorowskij, Berlin
Barry Friedman Ltd., New York
Galerie de France, Paris
Galleria internazionale d'arte moderna, Ca' Pesaro, Venice
Collection Hubertus Gassner, Kassel
Gilman Paper Company Collection
Collection John Githens, New York
Collection Krystyna Gmurzynska-Bscher, Cologne
Galerie Gmurzynska, Cologne
Peggy Guggenheim Collection, Venice
Solomon R. Guggenheim Museum, New York
Wilhelm Hack Museum, Ludwigshafen
Galerie Hoffmann, Friedberg,
    Dokumentation konstruktive Kunst
Houk Friedman, New York
Leonard Hutton Galleries, New York
Collection G. Iu. Ivakin, Kiev
Collection Helix Art Center, San Diego
Historical-Architectural Archive, Moscow
Irkutsk Regional Art Museum
Ivanovo State Museum of History and the Revolution
Annely Juda Fine Art, London
Collection M. L. Khidekel', St. Petersburg
Kuskovo State Porcelain Museum
Collection L. B. Labas, Moscow
Galerie Alex Lachmann, Cologne
Lenin Library, Moscow
Los Angeles County Museum of Art
Luchkovskii Collection, Khar'kov

Lenders to the Exhibition

Maiakovskii Museum, Moscow
Martin Muller Inc. and Modernism Inc., San Francisco
Collection Maslach Family
Collection M. Miturich, Moscow
Mukhina College Museum, St. Petersburg
Collection E. V. Murina and D. V. Sarab'ianov, Moscow
Musée national d'art moderne,
    Centre Georges Pompidou, Paris
Museum Fridericianum, Kassel
Museum für Gestaltung, Basel, Plakatsammlung
Museum für Gestaltung, Zurich
Museum Ludwig (Collection Ludwig, Cologne)
Museum of Art and History, Serpukhov
Museum of Fine Arts, Ekaterinburg
Museum of the Air Force, Monino
The Museum of Modern Art, New York
Muzeum Okręgove, Chełm
Muzeum Sztuki, Łódź
Collection A. Nakov, Paris
Collection Lew Nussberg, United States
Galerie Alice Pauli, Lausanne
Collection A. V. Povelikhina, St. Petersburg
Primor'e Regional Picture Gallery, Vladivostok
Regional Art Museum, Kaluga
Regional Art Museum, Kirov
Regional Deineka Picture Gallery, Kursk
Regional Historical Museum, Slobodskoe
Resource Collections, The Getty Center for the History of Art
    and the Humanities
A. M. Rodchenko and V. F. Stepanova Archive, Moscow
The Rothschild Art Foundation, Baltimore
Collection K. Rozhdestvenskii, Moscow
Collection Rubinshtein and Moroz, Moscow
St. Petersburg State Museum of Theater and Musical Arts
Galerie Dr. István Schlégl, Zurich
Collection Il'ia Sel'vinskii Family, Moscow
Spencer Collection, The New York Public Library,
    Astor, Lenox and Tilden Foundations
Staatliche Galerie Moritzburg, Halle
Staatliche Museen Preussischer Kulturbesitz,
    Nationalgalerie, Berlin
Staatsgalerie, Stuttgart
Städtische Galerie im Lenbachhaus, Munich
State Architecture and Art Museum, Rostov-Iaroslavskii
State Art Gallery, Kursk
State Art Museum, Iaroslavl'
State Art Museum, Nizhnii Novgorod
State Art Museum of Latvia, Riga
State Art Museum, Omsk
State Art Museum, Rostov-on-Don
State Art Museum, Samara
State Art Museum, Ul'ianovsk
State Bakhrushin Museum, Moscow
State Historical Museum, Moscow

State Kasteev Kazakhstan Museum of Arts, Alma-Ata
State Lunacharskii Museum of Fine Arts, Krasnodar
State Museum of Fine Arts, Nizhnii Tagil
State Museum of Russian Art, Kiev
State Museum of the Academy of Arts, St. Petersburg
State Museum of the History of the City of St. Petersburg
State Museum of Ukrainian Art, Kiev
State Mustafaev Azerbaijan Museum of Art, Baku
State Radishchev Art Museum, Saratov
State Russian Museum, St. Petersburg
State Shchusev Museum, Moscow
State Surikov Art Museum, Krasnoiarsk
State Tret'iakov Gallery, Moscow
Stedelijk Museum, Amsterdam
Galerie Stolz, Cologne
Collection F. Syrkina, Moscow
TECTA & Stuhlmuseum Burg Beverungen, Lauenförde
Theatermuseum der Universität zu Köln
Tobol'sk State Historical-Architectural Museum, Tobol'sk
Trekhgornaia Textile Mill, Moscow
Tsaritsyno Museum of Applied Arts, Moscow
Union of Architects, Moscow
University of East Anglia Collection
Uzbekistan State Museum of Fine Arts, Tashkent
Collection Vasil'ev, St. Petersburg
Collection von Bergmann, Dusseldorf
Vuchetich All-Union Artistic Production Association, Moscow
Collection Thomas P. Whitney
Collection Nina Williams, England
Yale University Art Gallery
Collection Dieter Zaha, Kassel
Collection L. Zhadova Family, Moscow
Collection Ziersch, Munich

Anonymous lenders from England, Germany, Italy,
Russia, Switzerland, and the United States

Even on purely stylistic and formal grounds, the Russian and Soviet avant-garde's contribution to Modern art merits the scale and depth of the present exhibition. Kazimir Malevich and Vladimir Tatlin, the avant-garde's leaders, brought Modernism to its logical conclusions even as they first fully internalized and reinvented it in a Russian context. Yet those ideas became starting points. The laboratory of Constructivist and Suprematist experiments yielded visual inventions that still influence art, architecture, and design.

In his *Chernyi kvadrat* (*Black Square,* 1915), Malevich resolved the Modernist struggle to reduce form to its essence; and when, for the *0.10* exhibition (Petrograd, 1915–16), the artist hung the work in the place traditionally reserved for a religious icon, he aspired to replace the existing order with a new artistic ideal. Reinterpreting European Cubism, Malevich applied the abstracting process to reduce the substance of the world to primary forms, revealing an entirely other dimension—an absolute, non-objective world. With his *Kontr-rel'ef* (*Counter-Relief,* 1914–15), Tatlin took the fractured planes of Cubism in a different but still logical direction—into real tangible space.

Somewhere between the absolute spiritual idealism of Malevich's Suprematism and the dramatic reality of Tatlin's reliefs is that utopian sensibility, within a historical context of political and social upheaval, which released Russian art from the studio and onto the street, and which endowed it with a desire to pervade every aspect of life—even to become an agent of social change.

The term "utopia" carries with it the spirit of the avant-garde's project to place art at the service of greater social objectives and to create harmony and order in the chaotic world around them. Given the course history has taken in Russia in the twentieth century, "utopia" also has connotations of impracticality; idealism is good in theory, but not in practice. Few images in the Russian avant-garde are more compelling than Tatlin's construction of an Everyman's flying machine, *Letatlin* (1929–32), intended to be the utilitarian marriage of art, science, and technology—now, as a historical relic, it recalls the legend of Icarus, who flew too close to the sun.

One thing that can be gleaned from the scant but growing critical analysis of the Russian avant-garde—the "Great Experiment," as pioneering art historian Camilla Gray called it—is that single interpretations are impossible to maintain. Essential questions persist, relevant to our own predicament: What is the potential for art—an essential ambition of the avant-garde—to infiltrate and transform everyday life? Have traditional painting and sculpture, as Rodchenko proposed, reached the end of their cultural development in favor of more utilitarian communications media and practical arts? What is the relationship between art and politics? Can an aesthetic pluralism be established and institutionalized?

In planning the exhibition, we identified three primary phases of the avant-garde in Russia:

- First, the hegemony established by avant-garde artists committed to Suprematism and to Tatlin's culture of materials before the 1917 October Revolution, and the impact of their theories in defining cultural policies after the Revolution.

- Second, the development in the 1920s of work by artists who sought to project principles of construction and design into rationalized aesthetic systems through pedagogical programs at Moscow's Vkhutemas/Vkhutein (the Higher Artistic-Technical Workshops/Higher Artistic-Technical Institute) and group shows such as the Obmokhu (Society of Young Artists) exhibitions and the *Pervaia diskussionnaia vystavka ob"edinenii aktivnogo revoliutsionnogo iskusstva* (*First Discussional Exhibition of Associations of Active Revolutionary Art,* Moscow, 1924).

- And third, the pluralism of the 1920s—the emergence of new debates over figuration in the media of photography, photomontage, and painting, and the impact of Constructivist theory upon architectural practice.

Our exhibition, *The Great Utopia,* attempts to map out the vast territory of vanguard artistic production in Russia, beginning in 1915 with the *0.10* exhibition, where Malevich's square and Tatlin's relief were first shown, and ending in 1932 with the competition for the Palace of Soviets in Moscow and the First Five-Year Plan, at which time the "left wing" in art lost credibility in the face of Stalin's stern program to build an industrialized Soviet Union.

At its core, the exhibition emphasizes the utopianism of the vanguard project, the tensions between radical affirmations of the autonomy of art and the projection of aesthetic concerns into daily life through design; the exhibition attempts to contextualize issues of style by emphasizing the institutional and ideological foundations for much of the production of vanguard work.

By representing the plurality of approaches to utopian abstraction, the curators demonstrate the essential continuity of the vanguard project before and after the Revolution, in terms of individual artists' contributions and in their collective (and competitive) struggle to play leading roles in the formation of a new consciousness.

This exhibition presents a nearly complete sample of the artistic documents of the Russian and Soviet avant-garde—laid out in all of their diversity, beauty, and contradictions. The exhibition encompasses almost all media, with the notable exception of film, which it was not possible to exhibit because the renovation of the Guggenheim Museum theater has been postponed. No exhibition on the topic has included such a comprehensive representation of artists and of works drawn from so many collections. Seventy percent of the objects were

Prefaces

borrowed from Russian museums and private collections, as well as from museums in Uzbekistan, Azerbaijan, Ukraine, and Latvia. Many of the works on view are being seen for the first time by American and European audiences.

The scale of the exhibition is a function of an urgent need we felt for the full scope of the period to be presented at once, for the benefit both of the devoted scholars and students of the avant-garde who continue to define its complex history and circumstances and of a larger public that will be able to comprehend the breadth and the uniqueness of this movement in the history of art.

The task of assembling such a broad range of material from such a wide range of sources demanded a unique organizational structure. Obviously, no single curator commands a detailed expertise encompassing all of the works and their myriad locations, many of them obscure. A number of sources had to be combined simply to create a working checklist from which to draw a final selection.

In addition, since the history of the avant-garde in Russia, in comparison to the history of European Modernism, is still in part uncharted, no single interpretation is dominant. From its inception, the exhibition necessarily demanded a variety of perspectives in order to select and shape its content.

The team of curators and experts appointed in June 1989 defined the conceptual guidelines for the exhibition and culled working lists of literally thousands of objects from Western and Russian public and private collections. The team of museum and independent curators from Russia, Germany, and the United States—Vivian Endicott Barnett, Christiane Bauermeister, Charlotte Douglas, Svetlana Dzhafarova, Hubertus Gassner, Evgenii Kovtun, Irina Lebedeva, Evgeniia Petrova, Alla Povelikhina, Elena and Vasilii Rakitin, Jane A. Sharp, Anatolii Strigalev, and Margarita Tupitsyn—was chosen to encompass a variety of specializations and backgrounds. Over a period of almost three years and in meetings in Moscow, St. Petersburg, Frankfurt, and New York, the lists were narrowed down to a group of over 900 works that the curatorial team felt would provide the most comprehensive and coherent overview of the period.

It was also a post-Cold War spirit of collaboration that inspired our effort to structure a project that would be a joint venture of American, European, and Soviet/Russian expertise and organizational foundations. The idea originated in the spring of 1988, when Eduard Shevardnadze, then Soviet Foreign Minister, toured the Guggenheim. That summer in Moscow, a first official protocol was created to initiate the project.

As the exhibition was being organized, the Soviet Union underwent the most dramatic and overwhelming changes since the Bolshevik Revolution. With the emergence of perestroika, a great sense of optimism fueled the establishment of the exhibition as a joint East-West venture. Further changes in Russia meant the reorganization of cultural as well as governmental bureaucracies, which could have halted the project, were it not for the patience, dedication, and

communication of all of the institutions involved, including the continued participation of the Russian (formerly Soviet) Foreign Ministry represented especially by Anatolii Adamishin, now Ambassador to Italy, and by Vladimir Petrovsky, Under-Secretary General of the United Nations, whose deep involvement with international cultural issues dates at least to his attendance at the inauguration of the Guggenheim Museum's Frank Lloyd Wright building in 1959.

The two major Russian museums—the State Tret'iakov Gallery in Moscow, led by Iurii Korolev, and the State Russian Museum in St. Petersburg, led by Vladimir Gusev and Deputy Director Evgeniia Petrova—committed their staffs and their important collections to this exhibition. The Vuchetich All-Union Artistic Production Association (VUART)—under former Director Pavel Khoroshilov, Director Aleksandr Ursin, and Deputy Director Valentin Rivkind—took on the very difficult task of coordinating loans from over fifty provincial and other museums throughout the former Soviet Union. The Ministry of Culture of the Russian Federation—led by Minister Evgenii Sidorov and Head of Museum Department Vera Lebedeva—lent their critical official support and logistical assistance, as had the former Ministry of Culture of the USSR, led by Nikolai Gubenko with assistance from Genrikh Popov and Lidiia Zaletova.

Christoph Vitali, Director of the Schirn Kunsthalle, Frankfurt—one of the most prominent cultural institutions in Germany and also the first host of this exhibition—was the critical link in Europe in all aspects of negotiation and organization.

At the Guggenheim, all of the selection lists, research, loans, and catalogue contents were coordinated over the course of three years by a competent and specialized staff led by Jane A. Sharp, Project Associate Curator. With her curatorial expertise, impressive facility with the Russian language, and thorough approach to the exhibition's organization on every level, Jane Sharp was the hub holding together the project's many spokes. Natasha Kurchanova, Curatorial Assistant, managed the English/Russian database of thousands of objects and provided important research and loan coordination with the further assistance of Sabine Lange, Emily Locker, Katherine Glaser, and Nataliya Bregel. Linda Thacher, Associate Registrar, professionally handled the endless details and logistics of the international transport of objects. Erik Quam, Information Systems Analyst, designed and supported the database related to the works of art.

In Moscow, a parallel organization was coordinated at VUART by Svetlana Dzhafarova, Zel'fira Tregulova, and Faina Balakhovskaia, without whose professional work and tireless effort the exhibition simply would not have been possible. They, in concert with Deputy Director Evgeniia Petrova at the State Russian Museum and Curators Irina Lebedeva and Ekaterina Seleznova at the State Tret'iakov Gallery and representatives of other museums, coordinated the loans of all objects in the former Soviet Union.

The catalogue itself was a monumental and unique project begun over three years ago. The content, determined by the curatorial team, was intended to make the book a comprehensive reference that would be of value for years to come. Authors include not only members of the working group but such well-known scholars as Natal'ia Adaskina, Susan Compton, Nina Lobanov-Rostovksy, Christina Lodder, Aleksandra Shatskikh, and Paul Wood. Managing Editor Anthony Calnek oversaw the production of what is the most ambitious catalogue in the Guggenheim's history. The editing of the book was handled with extraordinary skill and dedication by Jane Bobko. The talented American catalogue team also included Victoria Ellison, Associate Editor for the glossary, Robert Hemenway, copy editor, and Charles Davey, production and design consultant, as well as Research Assistant Kathleen Friello. Massimo Vignelli created the simple and elegant catalogue design in keeping with his new graphic system for the Guggenheim.

A complementary catalogue team worked in Russia, coordinated by Svetlana Dzhafarova, Zel'fira Tregulova, and Faina Balakhovskaia and including editors Andrei Sarab'ianov and Irina Sorvina.

The extraordinary design of the exhibition is due to architect Zaha Hadid, who, with Pamela Myers at the Guggenheim, made the exhibition accessible and provocative in the Frank Lloyd Wright space and new Gwathmey Siegel and Associates tower. The exhibition marks the first occasion on which the two spaces have been used as a single entity.

All in all, the exhibition touched almost every person in each of the organizing institutions in New York, in Russia, and in Frankfurt.

Perhaps most important, the exhibition is the product of the cooperation of lenders—museums and private collections. The State Tret'iakov Gallery and State Russian Museum treasures form the core of the exhibition, surrounded by works from Russia, Europe, and the United States. The central contribution from the collection of the late George Costakis, both from his estate and from the group of works he generously donated to the State Tret'iakov Gallery, deserves special note. Costakis, whose long association with the Guggenheim included the 1981 exhibition of his holdings, acquired and protected the richest collection of its kind at a time when almost no institutional attention was being paid to this revolutionary chapter in the history of art.

The exhibition represents the most complex logistical effort ever undertaken by the Guggenheim, involving more people and institutions around the world than any other of the museum's projects and requiring sponsorship from the start. It can often be simply a formality to acknowledge a sponsor. In this case, Lufthansa German Airlines cannot be identified merely as an exhibition sponsor with a natural regard for culture, although it is one of the most active corporate supporters of cultural events throughout the United States, Europe, and Russia. Rather, Lufthansa served as a collaborator—bringing people together, carrying precious information as well as people and art, and providing assistance (including translation and communications) in negotiations. Jürgen Weber, President and CEO, is dedicated, as was his predecessor, Heinz Ruhnau, to a world linked by the high technology of air travel as well as by the essential fabric of cultural communication. That Lufthansa's dedication to culture is deeply rooted in its mission to connect people is no more evident than in the work of Nicolas Iljine, Director of Public Affairs, who was present with Dr. Heinrich Klotz, Director of the Zentrum für Kunst und Medientechnologie, at the inception of the project. Through his equal dedication to people, culture, and business, Nic Iljine was a source of expertise and inspiration throughout a long and complex process.

In sum, it might be stated that the urgency and importance of this unique project is evidenced by the extraordinary hard work, commitment, and faith it inspired in its participants. Utopia is not at hand, but the art of the Russian and Soviet avant-garde in this exhibition may plainly demonstrate some of its essential components—that a blueprint for the future may be more likely found on the margins of our consciousness than at its center; that it may require the invention of a new starting point (the zero form of Malevich's *Black Square*), the progressive involvement of every stratum of society, and the engagement with a diversity of changing aesthetics that becomes the foundation of a practical system of human communication in the midst of a changing world.

—Thomas Krens, Director
Michael Govan, Deputy Director

The Russian avant-garde is a chapter of art history which demands a higher level of knowledge. While many collections around the world house Russian masterpieces from this period and many worthy publications and important exhibitions have presented the originality of Russian culture in the years before and after the October Revolution, these collections and surveys have only highlighted the many nuances and riches of this culture that remain to be explored. Moreover, most of the exhibitions focusing on the Russian avant-garde have discussed the works of art within the narrow framework of the Revolution. As a result, artistic processes have often been neglected in favor of the political and social implications of the works.

The history and role of Russian avant-garde art are far more complex. These artists, despite being intimately bound by the social and political situation of their country, were absorbed as never before by questions of pure aesthetics. The world of the European Modernists—a world which had opened to Russian artists for the first time and whose development they followed with lively interest—combined with their own artistic, literary, and philosophical heritage to create a unique context for innovative creative experiments.

At the turn of the century, an artistic vocabulary capable of describing all possible experiences seemed unquestionably in place. In Russia, the newly defined world order and life-style required new forms of expression. While the artists central to the vanguard movement—Mikhail Larionov, Natal'ia Goncharova, Vasilii Kandinskii, Kazimir Malevich, Pavel Filonov, and others—did not come fully into their own with the Revolution, the events of 1917 focused their maturation. In the diversity of artistic movements in Russia from 1910 to 1920, two principal trends can be clearly discerned and differentiated. One trend describes the emotional-intuitive penetration of the material world, and the other tries to understand matters through a rational-Constructivist analysis. As a result, the initial working title for the present exhibition was *Construction and Intuition.* Although this title was eventually changed, the two themes helped to define the concept at the heart of the exhibition: the tension within the Russian avant-garde between rational and irrational experiences and representations of the world.

In a political sense, this exhibition comes perhaps too late. Since the early 1980s, the idea of romantic underpinnings to the Revolution has lost popularity. Yet the artistic might of this era, with its gathering of creative energies and investigations, has continued to hold its ground against more short-lived political ideologies and economies. It is therefore that much more important for the public to be able to see for the first time the breadth of Russian avant-garde art without a background of political fervor—to see it in peace and to be able to measure fully its place in the development of art in our world.

Our heartfelt thanks to our partners in this project, Thomas Krens, Director of the Solomon R. Guggenheim Museum in New York and the Peggy Guggenheim Collection in Venice; Michael Govan, Deputy Director of the Guggenheim Museum; and Christoph Vitali, Director of the Schirn Kunsthalle Frankfurt.

American, German, and Russian experts have contributed to extensive research and to developing the complex thematic structure of the exhibition. This was not only a fruitful collaboration for the exhibition but also a personal accomplishment for each individual involved.

Equal thanks are due to the sponsor of the exhibition, Lufthansa German Airlines; to Nicolas Iljine, Director of Public Affairs at Lufthansa, who followed the nearly four years of preparations with great sympathy, involvement, and

patience; to the former Soviet Ministry of Culture and its staff; and to the Vuchetich All-Union Artistic Production Association (VUART), with Valentin Rivkind at the helm.

Finally, we are tremendously grateful to all museums and private lenders for the very generous gift of their works as loans to the exhibition.

—Vladimir Gusev, Director
Evgeniia Petrova, Deputy Director
State Russian Museum, St. Petersburg

Iurii Korolev, Director
State Tret'iakov Gallery, Moscow

Like few other artistic movements of this century, the Russian avant-garde—with its group of young, overwhelmingly enthusiastic, and energetic artists—continues to excite, fascinate, and captivate.

A comprehensive look at this creative period between 1915 and 1932 is dramatically presented for the first time in *The Great Utopia.* The exhibition opened to great acclaim at Frankfurt's Schirn Kunsthalle, and subsequently at Amsterdam's Stedelijk Museum. We are delighted that the show can now be seen at the Solomon R. Guggenheim Museum in New York, the final venue on its international tour. Lufthansa welcomes another opportunity to foster cultural exchange by bringing this monumental work to the handsomely restored and newly expanded Guggenheim.

The Great Utopia brings together both individuals and works of art in an international exchange of culture. Through its support of the exhibition in New York, Lufthansa hopes to demonstrate its commitment to worldwide cultural communications. We feel that it is especially important to establish ties with nations that have recently opened their doors to the rest of the world. That is why our airline has expanded its services to Eastern Europe. And through exhibitions such as *The Great Utopia,* we hope cultural ties with these nations will also flourish, strengthening human relations and furthering mutual understanding.

—Jürgen Weber
Chairman of the Executive Board
Lufthansa German Airlines

Editorial Note

Transliteration of Russian and Ukrainian in this book follows the Library of Congress system, modified by the omission of diacritical marks. With the exception of artists who had substantial careers in the West and whose names would be rendered unrecognizable by transliteration (such as Marc Chagall), the transliterated form of Russian names is used throughout (Vasilii Kandinskii, for example, in place of Vasily Kandinsky). Russian surnames of foreign origin have not been restored to their Western form but transliterated (thus Lancere rather than Lanceray). The names of non-Russian artists whose activity was concentrated in Russia likewise appear in their Russian rather than native form (Gustav Klutsis rather than Gustavs Klucis).

With some exceptions, geographical names and the names of institutions follow the Russian and have not been anglicized. Many of these names, moreover, changed during the period covered herein; since August 1991, in the wake of developments in the former Soviet Union, many have changed yet again. The city founded by Peter the Great, for example, was called St. Petersburg until August 1914, Petrograd until January 1924, and Leningrad until September 1991—when the name St. Petersburg was restored. Such fluctuations are observed in these pages, where the choice among variant geographical and institutional names has been determined by context.

Renderings of the names of individuals, institutions, and places, as well as renderings of Russian words, that appear in citations from published English sources have not been altered to fit the prevailing system of transliteration. Nor have any "corrections" been made, in citations from artists' statements and manifestos, of the nonstandard capitalization often used for rhetorical purposes in such documents.

Dates up to February 14, 1918, are given according to the Julian (or Old Style) calendar, and after that according to the Gregorian (or New Style) calendar. Before 1900, the Julian calendar in use in Russia was twelve days behind the Gregorian; from 1900 to 1918, it was thirteen days behind.

The avant-garde in Russia has a complex history. The two essays in this volume that tackle the chronology of Obmokhu (the Society of Young Artists) are evidence of the scholarly dialogue in progress.

Permission was granted for the essays by Vivian Endicott Barnett, Susan Compton, Charlotte Douglas, Christina Lodder, Jane A. Sharp, Margarita Tupitsyn, and Paul Wood to appear first in English in *De Grote Utopie,* published by the Stedelijk Museum, Amsterdam; they are published here in slightly different form. Vasilii Rakitin's essay appears here in an English translation different from that published in *De Grote Utopie.*

The Politics of the Avant-Garde

Paul Wood

I don't know how radical you are or how radical I am. I am certainly not radical enough; that is, one must always try to be as radical as reality itself.

—Lenin

After many decades of occlusion, the art of the Russian avant-garde is now widely available, presented with a clarity and scope which must once have seemed impossible. There are monographs on each of the major figures, and for some artists more than one. Extensive international exhibitions of their works have been mounted. These have been accompanied by surveys revealing interconnections in the work of major and minor producers alike. Linked to such exhibitions, where once a scrap of misinformation about Constructivism sufficed, weighty catalogues have become indispensable. Certain key documents are available in a variety of collections, frequently standing as monuments in their own right to the ferment of intellectual activity that accompanied the avant-garde practice. Furthermore, the main contours of the institutions both formal and informal which exerted such a decisive influence upon individual production have been filled in to an extent which even a decade ago must have seemed unlikely: reorganizations at Vkhutemas (the Higher Artistic-Technical Workshops), debates at Inkhuk (the Institute of Artistic Culture); we even know how many carriages the agit trains had, not to mention where they ran and what function they fulfilled. Scholarly articles regularly appear in a range of journals, often linked to detailed doctoral investigations. Metaphors of trickles, floods, even avalanches are inadequate to describe a collective enterprise of almost military dimensions to lay bare the trammeled soul of Soviet avant-gardism. If present trends continue, by the end of the century Moscow will be as academically well trodden as Montmartre. Yet this is a century for most of which Russia has been a kind of intellectual dark continent, probed, if at all, by hostile Kremlinologists rather than sympathetic students of a vivid cultural constellation. Are we not lucky, then, that the tenebrous coils of prejudice are finally being parted? And, of course, all this work, from encyclopedic summation to diligently unearthed fragment, *is* valuable, the very stuff of intellectual advance. Why, then, the rustle, the murmur, the thickening, the steady coagulation of the sense of a Problem?

It is, after all, simply put. With notable exceptions, studies of the Russian avant-garde have become, in a Kuhnian sense, "normal science." And yet the work to which it adverts is anything but. This is not an insignificant matter, though it is not a very widely acknowledged one. It is a problem that has always existed and that has never gone away but just seems to have become invisible. Like some otherwise defenseless creature in a hostile environment, the question of the politics of the avant-garde has blended into the tangled undergrowth of facts and names, research grants, footnotes, and scholarly paraphernalia. Yet there are sharp teeth lurking here, and narrow eyes peering through crevices in the piles of documents. And it is precisely these eyes, both menacing and beautiful, which constitute the attraction in the first place. The revolutionary avant-garde is not of interest for its normativity. Aleksandr Blok wasn't joking when he summoned Europe to the "bright feast of peace and brotherhood and labor" with the "strings of a Scythian lyre": "Are we to blame if your rib cages burst / beneath our paws' impulsive ardor?" Blok's warning could doubtless be written off as a romantic evocation of the Revolution's most backward aspects—all slave girls, wild horses, and Asiatic jubilation—when the Revolution was really about tractors and planning. But a revolution is a revolution, and the academic researcher padding noiselessly through carpeted libraries or, indeed, faxing documents from one international center of learning to another would do well to remember that Aleksandr Rodchenko, El Lissitzky, Varvara Stepanova, Vladimir Maiakovskii, Dziga Vertov, Gustav Klutsis, and the rest, working in conditions of privation to begin with and harsh censorship later, were all, without

fig. 1
Simplified model of Tatlin's Monument to the Third International *in a street demonstration, Moscow, ca. 1927.*

exception, explicitly committed to working-class revolution—out of which a new order of international socialism would arise. One should not overlook the paradox that the very research which progressively reveals the contours of the Soviet avant-garde is predicated on the historic defeat of the avant-garde's social vision. By whom, by just which forces, is not quite so easy to say. To echo the sentiments of a thinker little acknowledged in these late days of cultural studies: "What is to be done?"

It is an irony upon a paradox that in setting out to answer the question, in attempting to clarify the politics of the avant-garde, there is no other starting point than this unglamorous one, this place where we are. Our starting point consists of these apparent conclusions, this pile of books, this trail of articles: not, after all, the soul of revolutionary Petrograd but the "soul" of the bourgeois academy. The Russian avant-garde, Constructivism, Socialist Realism even, are what they have been made to mean in these pages, in the play of their silences and their affirmations. To ponder the paradox is, in effect, a question of resistance: resisting various normalizations enforced by the history our own culture is writing.

I

It is quite clear that one of the central factors that has fueled historians' widespread desire to confront the Soviet avant-garde—either positively or negatively—is its proximity to the Russian Revolution. This is so obvious that it sounds almost strange to insist upon it. In the days before such claims lost their vogue, E. H. Carr said that the Revolution had been the source of more profound repercussions than any other historical event of modern times. Be that as it may, the Revolution has been the source of greatest controversy in modern times at the level of interpretation: interpreters range from the inhabitants of the most ethereal superstructures to the state planners and military strategists at the other end of the spectrum. This controversy's sheer scale has increasingly drawn art historians into its orbit, though motives have, of course, varied. On one side there has been what amounts, more or less, to a myth of buried treasure: avant-garde artworks from the heroic period that have lain in attics and basements for decades being led blinking into the light of modern scholarship. For historians of this persuasion, ideology has probably counted for little next to the glamour of the quest, which can range from a tomb-robbing lust for gold in its darker reaches to an honorable desire to shed light on a lost but incontrovertibly significant chapter of twentieth-century art. For other historians, the ideological factor has surely played an important role. Confronted in their own productive lives, within and without the academy, by institutional orthodoxies requiring resistance, they find that the art of the most thoroughgoing of all moments of resistance holds a powerful attraction. Thus for both left-wing and liberal historians, the relation of the avant-garde to the Revolution has, in different ways, been a prime motivator: either to recover the work from burial by the Revolution understood as closure or to restore that work as evidence of the Revolution's heroic challenge to orthodoxy and stasis across the board of human endeavor, before its rapid eclipse.

For all that, the precise nature of the avant-garde's relationship to the Revolution has tended to remain underinvestigated. This is the case despite the increasing detail of particular studies, as well as the enormously deepened understanding of the avant-garde's technical innovations—even when these latter have been read in terms of their significant connection to the revolutionary project of social emancipation. That is to say, as the historical account has developed both extensively and intensively, the question of the politics of the avant-garde has been left relatively underresearched.

This is due, in part, to the simple fact of gaps in the historical record. Until the 1970s, little enough was available empirically. As recently as 1983, what gave Christina Lodder's *Russian Constructivism* its benchmark status was preeminently the fact that nobody had previously brought such information to light. To know who said what at Inkhuk in 1922, let alone be able to fit it into a context of debate on key technical and theoretical issues, marked of itself a qualitative advance. The silence cannot be laid wholly at the door of ignorance, however. It is, to a greater degree, reflexive: it has to do with the ideological commitments and blindnesses, interests and silences (sometimes explicit, more often implicit, if not deeply buried) of the collective academic psyche in the liberal-bourgeois educational institutions of the late-capitalist West. For all its epochal status, outside the ranks of a few specialists the historical shape of the Russian Revolution is little enough known; and for each lacuna in the record there is a pathology of mistrust, uninterest, and fear to account for it.

The manner in which the avant-garde's political alignments have been represented in the literature may be generalized under three headings, though these have changed over time and, obviously, been subject to inflection. The hegemonic response, until recently at least, has paradoxically been to dissociate the avant-garde from involvement with revolutionary politics. This "disengagement" thesis can adopt various forms. Traditionally, Constructivism, in the sense of an avant-garde art practice that was transmuted into a more direct cluster of interventions into daily life under the rubric of "art into production," was simply ignored. What "Constructivism" tended to mean was an international subvariant of abstract sculpture within a broadly Modernist tradition, associated with artists, such as Naum Gabo, who had left Russia shortly after the Revolution. Limited and misrepresentative as this now seems, it is sobering to recall that it was probably the dominant view from the 1930s to the 1970s—let us say, from Alfred Barr's brief and ambiguous homage to Lef (the Left Front of the Arts) in 1928 to Camilla Gray in 1962. Even major figures like Rodchenko were little known, others like Klutsis not at all; and the relations of such work to an intellectual and political program simply fell outside the scope of what passed for the history of modern art. Dark days, then, whose end is not to be regretted. It would, however, be unwise to celebrate a passage into light.

A small selection of quite recent examples will suffice. John Bowlt has established a reputation at the head of his field largely through his efforts to establish the density of this period of Russian artistic culture, the coexistence of a variety of different strands of art practice. The lasting benefit of his enterprise has undoubtedly been to relativize Western art history's tendency to become fixated upon the Soviet avant-garde in a narrow sense, (mis)construing it as a precursor of postwar, principally American, vanguard art; and, by contrast, to place the work of that wing of the avant-garde in a perspective of other trends ranging from the realistic to the fantastic. The price of this pluralism, fueled, one may speculate, by the détente politics of the 1970s, has, it seems, been to bend the stick too far in the other direction and depoliticize the avant-garde *tout court*. "Perhaps the most dangerous rumor concerning the Russian avant-garde has to do with its alleged support of radical politics, and radical political philosophy in general."[1] This was written by Bowlt in 1984. Chapter and verse surely no longer need to be given. Yet for an author deeply familiar with the writings of that avant-garde to advance such a claim at that late date is remarkable and must, one assumes, be motivated by considerations concerning the social relations of art quite discrete from the substance of the historical record itself.

For their part, surely, Rodchenko, Klutsis, Lissitzky, Maiakovskii, and others could not have been clearer about their commitment to the Revolution and to the task of building a new society. Take only the simplest example: the program of Lef itself. Maiakovskii in a letter of 1923 charges his correspondent to remember "the purpose for which we have united our efforts," which he then defines as *communist art* (as part of com-culture and communism in general!)."[2] There is a threefold articulation here: a Communist art—quite a specialized thing, which by Maiakovskii's own admission has not yet been fully developed and which it is the business of Lef to promulgate; the relation of this to a wider Communist culture—which is to say, something akin to Marx's "superstructure," the range of institutions both formal and informal wherein social consciousness organizes itself and in which "art" per se is only a part; and then a relation of this to Communist society, by which Maiakovskii obviously means a social mode of production, the "base," which will underwrite the achievement of the other two. This is highly schematic. But it is also programmatic and not at all incidental to the project of Lef—which is, in its turn, central to what we mean when we speak of the "Soviet avant-garde" at all. Examples could, of course, be multiplied.

All this makes it difficult to entertain claims about the avant-garde's political virginity. Yet the thesis is not confined to American authors, who have, after all, suffered a uniquely depoliticized intellectual tradition. Andrei Nakov offers an example of one European variant in a study of Rodchenko which simply omits mention of factors ranging beyond the formal and technical—an omission which is the more surprising given the artist's own frequent invocation of a sociopolitical dimension to his work.[3] Such exclusions—sins of omission, as it were, rather than commission—might be defensible on grounds of relevance, space, and so forth. Not so the stance of the Russian historian Vasilii Rakitin: "In practice the artists who were practitioners of the 1920s left agit-art, a Rodchenko or Lissitzky, have much less in common with leftist sociological hypotheses than has been supposed."[4] This is not a claim that there is *no* relationship, just that it is not central to the avant-garde project; it is not, however, the simple omission of a set of determinations, as in the previous instance, but an explicit thesis about the relation of the avant-garde to revolutionary politics—and the relation it claims is one of relative disinvolvement. Yet throughout the twenties, Lissitzky's writings are replete with references to the value of art residing in its relationship to the community, and to the requirement that artists abandon a conventional sense of artistic work and participate in the development of new forms of community to achieve the goal of a classless society. This endeavor is held to have serious repercussions, moreover, in that it results in the opposition of other, more conservative, artists to the left project: "New space neither needs nor demands pictures—it is not a picture transposed on a surface. This explains the painters' hostility towards us: we are destroying the wall as the resting place for their pictures."[5] This "new space" is linked to a conception of a modern world, a world whose modernity, furthermore, resides not merely in new technology but in new social relations. "It is to the social revolution rather than to the technological revolution" that the basic elements of Lissitzky's work are tied.[6] In 1930, he published a whole book to this effect with the unambiguous title of *Architektur für eine Weltrevolution* (*An Architecture for World Revolution*). After several years' residence in the West during the midtwenties, and in marked contrast to those like Gabo who could not leave the Soviet Union fast enough after

the Civil War ended and Bolshevik power was consolidated, Lissitzky went back to Russia because, as his wife put it: "There were tasks of a special kind awaiting him. He was needed in his homeland; the Soviet Union needed all his knowledge, his experience, his art."[7]

There is a case, let us put it no more strongly than that, for the partial determination of the avant-garde by the example of the successful Bolshevik Revolution. The argument against this relies almost completely on the Soviet avant-garde's roots in a prerevolutionary avant-garde art movement, on the one hand, and its relationship to postwar West European developments in architecture and design during the 1920s, on the other. The existence of these relations does not, however, refute the specificity of the conjuncture of the avant-garde and the Revolution within the Soviet Union. It is a peculiar kind of history which wants to claim almost as a point of principle that the one set of connections debars the other, yet such has been the disposition of hegemonic art history: to emphasize connections compatible with the overall aegis of notions of art's autonomy—even on this most unpromising terrain—and systematically to disregard theoretical, ideological, political orders of relation. As such, this is more a problem of Western art history and *its* institutional-political conjuncture than anything to do with the historical terrain it claims to conjugate.

That there are powerful motivating factors behind the "severance" thesis does not make it any more robust. What those factors are can be gleaned from Rakitin's argument. He needs to play down the avant-garde's relation to revolutionary politics precisely because of the overarching virtue he attaches to the avant-garde; and, concomitantly, because of the vice associated with Sovietization. Thus, the avant-garde is "an energetic free force"; it requires for its practice "the participation of free active persons." As such, it is "thoroughly alien to the Soviet model of life."[8] Rakitin does, at least, have the excuse of being Russian and, therefore, having been constrained for at least part of his career by the closures of the Stalinist system. The same cannot be said of "liberal" West European and American intellectuals whose work remains within the purview of their own culture's official ideology.

The clear line linking Rakitin and other East European "severance" theorists to their Western liberal counterparts is the identification of the Bolshevik Revolution with the monolithic Soviet system of the Cold War. A simultaneous attraction to an adventurous abstract art and repulsion from a totalitarian political system lead to the strategy of divesting the former of its political commitments. The two most common variations on this strategy are, first, the displacement of the sociopolitical impulse to the margins of a practice seen as primarily determined by formal and technical considerations that it shares with similar practices elsewhere. And, second, when that argument becomes too weak to sustain, the notion of "utopianism." The members of the avant-garde are interpreted as innocents caught up in the revolutionary turmoil, mistaking its motivations for their own, and then being badly burned by the consequences of their mistake once the "real" politicians managed to divert some of their will-to-power to the sphere of culture. Neither of these arguments is completely without foundation: that is precisely what lends them their specious plausibility and accounts for their longevity in a political-intellectual conjuncture which wants them to be true. Thus, to invoke Maiakovskii once again: the reason Maiakovskii offers for forming Lef is indeed that the political leadership's attentions are no longer going to be completely absorbed by the exigencies of War Communism; and the artistic left, as a consequence, has to organize itself and get its version of the cultural task inserted properly into the debate which is about to ensue. This is not in itself "utopian," however; quite the contrary.

Utopianism is a resort of historians who want to ensure there is absolutely no passage between Kazimir Malevich, for example, and—let us say—Leonid Brezhnev, as the symbol of the Soviet order at the moment of production of most cultural-artistic histories of it. For American historians in particular, the potency of this system of passages and disjunctions must have been enhanced by the cultural prestige of the exiled Aleksandr Solzhenitsyn and his emphatic assimilation of the Stalinist dystopia to Bolshevism per se—an endemic trait of liberal thought throughout the period, but given significant reinforcement by the horse's-mouth effect of the wave of post-1960s literary dissidents in general and Solzhenitsyn's American exile in particular. Utopianism itself, it may finally be noted, has been inflected in two different directions according to the demands of the account. Thus, either we have the blissful innocence and otherworldliness of artists whose very openness and suggestibility lead to their being raped by the Marxist politicians as soon as they can find the time (subtext: art should avoid politics, then and now) or, in the case of those who appear to have persisted in their association of art with the Revolution, we encounter a construction of willful naïveté, a tempting of fate, a dangerous kind of utopianism purblind to the true nature of the realpolitik it entertained; these people are paraded as a lesson on the dangers of playing with such fire in the first place, for inviting it, as it were, into the house of art (subtext, of course, the same).

There is probably even today a sense in which this image of a "protean avant-garde," either innocent of or childishly infatuated with revolutionary politics and subsequently crushed by the totalitarian Marxist power which has continued to disfigure the twentieth century almost to its end, remains the most widespread view of the Soviet constellation of the early twenties—with Lenin the ruthless leader whose iron shadow fell across a generation of free spirits, a generation whose eccentric vitality has, however, continued to grace liberal culture even as it was anathematized by Marxism's pathology of control.

Accounts of that stripe have been hegemonic. A second broad category emerged, however, to challenge hegemonic certainties as part of that general contestation trading variously under the titles of critiques of Modernism, the social history of art, and the new art history in the later 1970s and the 1980s. Here for the first time serious investigations not only of the individual arts but of interconnections among them begin to appear, tellingly stimulated more by developments in film and literary theory than in art history per se. The result has been a range of reconceptualizations away from crudely conventional assertions of the autonomy of art—though not, it should be said, thereby away from a necessary focus on the formal. Needless to say, the orthodox account of the avant-garde's distinction from politics and this series of radical re-readings have not evolved neatly, one from the other. Rather, the contestation between them has effectively constituted the field during recent times, setting the register within whose compass our qualitative leap in the understanding of the avant-garde has taken place. The upshot has been a field transformed out of all recognition, dedicated most often to re-reading the extraordinary series of technical radicalizations which fundamentally constituted the revolutionary avant-garde of the 1920s, revealing that avant-garde as an unparalleled site of the committed scrutiny and transformation of all the norms of bourgeois cultural practice. The excavation of the full scope of the work of Rodchenko, Vertov, Klutsis, Vladimir Tatlin, Maiakovskii, and Lissitzky, not to mention the related theoretical perspectives of Osip Brik, Viktor Shklovskii,

Valentin Voloshinov, and others, has achieved that rare thing: the eruption of the historical work into the practical conjuncture of the present. It would not be going too far to say that a culture has been recovered—a culture, moreover, that is still revolutionary with respect to our own. Nothing has more vividly thrown into relief the tragic conjunction of the technically extraordinary and the socially and politically regressive within our own culture than this revealed constellation of practices in the fifteen years or so after the October Revolution.

Despite, or perhaps because of, this concentration, the relation of this spectrum of work *to* the October Revolution has not been the focus of such close scrutiny as the contours of the work itself. Needless to say, the aforementioned ideologically motivated sanitizing of the avant-garde has been eclipsed. But the nature of the avant-garde's revolutionary affiliations has, for the most part, continued to be read at the level of a general platform enabling the plethora of technical innovations. That said, Yve-Alain Bois, for example, has mapped his reading of Lissitzky's geometrical investigations back onto a sociopolitical context.[9] At their best, such readings have aspired to conjoin the semantic and social revolutions of the Soviet avant-garde, at least as a point of principle. In so doing, they are an effective counterweight both to depoliticized accounts of avant-garde art and to orthodox political histories which neglect the dimension of the social production of meaning.

Lodder's account overturned many assumptions about the nature of Constructivism, indeed it started from the premise that "no satisfactory overall account"[10] existed. She was, nonetheless, able to devote little space to siting that avant-garde within the revolutionary process. As might have been expected, the consequence, therefore, was a certain asymmetry in her account: innovatory analyses of the aims of the avant-garde and the organization of its institutions, yet reliance upon conventional assumptions about its context. One of Lodder's premises was the ultimate failure of Constructivism; a tragic, even a grand failure, but a failure, nonetheless. This failure is signaled by a retreat from aspirations to intervene in—even to "organize"—building the new world, to small-scale contributions to the spheres of graphic design and theater. Even the turn to photography in the later twenties is read as an attempt to claw back some ground from the increasingly dominant "Realist" painting groups like AKhRR (the Association of Artists of Revolutionary Russia).

The implicit premises here are three, and they are of course not Lodder's alone but the conventional wisdom. First, "the Party" and its preference for a Realist art. Second, the grounds of this preference in Realist art's supposed popularity and accessibility to the uneducated masses, an accessibility which cuts both ways—as an expression of the people's unschooled interests and as a conduit for the Party's preferred messages. Third, economic scarcity, which underpins this symbiosis between an authoritarian Party and a conservative people. Thus the Vkhutemas experiment was "aborted" because of "the material circumstances in which it operated."[11] More than that, the "principal reason" advanced by Lodder for the failure of Constructivism as a whole is "the material poverty that dominated all Soviet activity in the 1920s."[12] No adequate account of Soviet developments in the 1920s could, of course, avoid the economic aspect. But what tends to be overlooked is the extent to which economic questions did not arise as "brute" facts. This may seem alarmingly to underestimate what it is to lack the equipment to produce goods, or what it is to experience famine. The point remains, nonetheless, that the economic dimension is continually implicated in a process of political direction and decision making. If the economic and social wreckage of the War Communism period could sustain

4

the high levels of activity of the revolutionary avant-garde, there is no specifically economic reason why such activity could not be sustained later in the decade. The reasons for the increasing effectiveness of criticism of the erstwhile avant-garde, ultimately amounting to its marginalization and suppression, are more complex; and the "failure" is not Constructivism's alone.

What is at issue is a far wider "failure": the failure of the October Revolution itself. The failure of Constructivism or, indeed, of the "left front" of art in general is best regarded as a symptom of this larger defeat. It is as well to be clear on this point. In both the foregoing accounts of the avant-garde—explicitly in the depoliticized version and at least implicitly in the qualitatively more sophisticated account wherein the avant-garde is powerfully determined by the Revolution—the tendency is, at bottom, to view the avant-garde as victim of the Revolution's success. The implication is that the avant-garde found a space to operate in the heady days immediately following the Revolution, when a mixture of euphoria, chaos, and the leadership's preoccupation with other matters offered a loophole. Seizing its opportunity, the avant-garde became briefly dominant. Once the revolutionary ship was stabilized, however, the authoritarian Party showed its true colors and, as part of the drive to extend its control, suppressed the avant-garde. The realpolitik of building up an industrial base in a backward country meant that the avant-garde became, at best, a sort of luxury when there was no provision for luxuries and, at worst, a vestige of prerevolutionary bourgeois culture which had to be extirpated from the nascent workers' state. It must be said that, once again, there are elements of truth in this explanation: there *was* suspicion of the avant-garde's bourgeois antecedents, and so forth. But the cumulative effect of such accounts, despite their moments of truth, is misleading—skewed by an interpretation of the Revolution which, it is increasingly evident, is itself an ideological construct. What gives this construct its force is, of course, that it has constituted the ideology of *both* competing world-power blocs. For equal and opposite reasons, the bureaucratic monolith in the USSR and the liberal-capitalist democracies in the West have sought to underwrite a continuity between the October Revolution and the state system that succeeded it. To develop this point here would be to get ahead of the story; suffice to say at present that the three constituents of the avant-garde's failure, as offered even in "revisionist" accounts—the monolithic Party, the backward people, and economic dearth—are themselves in need of considerable investigation and revision.

Even Benjamin Buchloh's compelling account of the avant-garde's evolution "from *faktura* to factography" betrays elements of this questionable perspective—though his argument is somewhat the reverse of Lodder's.[13] While for Lodder economic scarcity set the agenda, Buchloh, if anything, overestimates the extent to which it had been conquered, yet in so doing demonstrates fundamentally the same perception of the Revolution's aims. One of the virtues of Buchloh's account is that it acknowledges the self-consciousness of the Constructivists' transformation out of a bourgeois avant-garde art group in the changed conditions post-October; furthermore, this transformation is treated in terms of a focus upon the audience for their work. That is to say, the revolutionary self-transformation of the avant-garde is not treated as merely the result of some internal dynamic but conclusively presented as determined by a sense of its task: whom it is addressing, and what has to be done to consolidate and encourage that new constituency. It is here, however, that Buchloh seems to go astray. The basic problem is a repeated overemphasis on industrialization as if this were an achieved

condition from the moment of the Revolution. Thus, in a passage clearly referring to the immediate postrevolutionary situation of War Communism (when Lissitzky displayed his Suprematist hoarding *Stanki depo fabrik zavodov zhdut vas* [*The Factory Benches Await You*, 1919–20] outside a factory in Vitebsk), Buchloh speaks of "the new audiences of industrialized urban society in the Soviet Union." Ironically, postrevolutionary society was in the process of becoming considerably less industrialized than it had been even under czarism as production was wrecked and the working class itself bled dry by the Civil War. Elsewhere, this time in a discussion of the NEP (New Economic Policy) period, and specifically of avant-garde responses to the reassertion of tradition under NEP, Buchloh refers to an art production addressing "the needs of a newly industrialized collective society"—this at a time when Russian society, as a matter of policy, was neither industrialized nor collective. Factography as it developed in the late 1920s certainly took place in an atmosphere when industrialization, ultimately in the shape of the First Five-Year Plan, came on the agenda. Yet it did not become enshrined as an absolute until 1928 or even 1929. Thus, in a discussion of *faktura* (density) during the so-called "laboratory period," circa 1918–21, Buchloh's reference to "the introduction of industrialization and social engineering that was imminent in the Soviet Union after the revolution of 1917" certainly seems premature. That industrialization of a certain type—not of the sort which actually came about at the end of the decade—may have been required by Constructivism merely underlines the significance of such a gap between requirement and reality.

There are two possibilities here. One is that Buchloh's wider history is insufficiently differentiated, but of no consequence because it doesn't affect his account of developments within the avant-garde. The other is that a tendency to misread the productive context does indeed have some bearing on an explanation of artistic developments which, after all, sets out with the intention of situating them in a dialectic with society and production rather than treating the latter as a passive backdrop to the art. It is this second possibility which I shall go on to explore below. But first, this schematic survey of characterizations of the sociopolitical alignments of the avant-garde requires completion.

Just as the "severance" thesis of liberal dominance came to be challenged by revisionist accounts which for the first time revealed the extent of the avant-garde's project of participation in the revolutionary process of building the new society, so recently there is evidence that a third kind of account is emerging. This is not so surprising as it might seem. Both of the foregoing accounts have themselves emanated from an academic-institutional conjuncture overdetermined by the conditions of the postwar settlement: the division of the world into two superpower blocs. In terms of a structural logic, if not always of strict chronology, it may be possible to ascribe the "severance" and "revisionist" accounts to distinct moments in that period: in brief, to pre- and post-1968. The reemergence of a second Cold War during the Reagan/Thatcher/Brezhnev period tended to give renewed emphasis to perspectives more at home in the earlier phase, just as it threatened to marginalize the revisionisms which for a period after the radicalizations of the late sixties, and during the period of détente, threatened to become hegemonic at least in the social sciences and the newly sophisticated cultural studies departments of Western higher-educational institutions. Since the mid-1980s, and reaching at least a temporary climax in 1989 (whether this proves to be a plateau before even greater upheavals remains to be seen), this map has been redrawn. A condition which appeared to be—or perhaps more accurately, felt as if it were—permanent, has dissolved into history; and official talk, at least, is of a "new world order." One of the main accompaniments to the sound of the Berlin Wall coming down has been the clatter of intellectuals of a variety of persuasions typing out the obituaries of socialism/Communism/Marxism. One of the darkest stars in this dubious intellectual constellation has been Francis Fukuyama's thesis of the end of history, a kind of right-wing Postmodernism in its evocation of a boring future in which the grand narratives of emancipation have expired, but a thesis which nonetheless offered a rerun of Daniel Bell's "end of ideology" claim from the 1950s.[14] The affirmative side of Fukuyama's elision of Marx, Lenin, Stalin, and the socialist tradition *tout court* was an assertion of the permanent realization of liberalism. In fact, the "end of history" consisted specifically in wall-to-wall liberalism, albeit of a conservative, State Department hue. The foundations of Fukuyama's thesis have, since its publication, been subject to criticism, and in the wake of the Persian Gulf War skepticism has accrued mightily about the credentials of George Bush's "new world order." Notwithstanding this, however, the Fukuyama argument is an indication of the new lease on life which the rhetorical death of Marxism et cetera has given to voices which want nothing to do with revolution—neither English nor French nor, of course, Russian; nor, one might add, cultural.

A side effect of the collapse of the Soviet empire in the field of cultural history has been the opening up of a hitherto largely dormant field: the culture of the Stalin period. Much of this work promises, of course, to be of exceptional value, as it brings to light the complexities of that which has heretofore been written off, for the most part, as the ossified Other of Modernism, unworthy of scholarly investigation, the creature of a totalitarian bureaucracy with no compact or articulated identity—no history—of its own. One contested area which this development places on the agenda, however, is the relationship of the avant-garde of the 1920s to the official art of the Stalin era. The traditional option of a pristine, apolitical avant-garde subordinated to a totalitarian political agenda having been somewhat abrogated by those revisionist histories which revealed the extent of the avant-garde's politicization, the question now poses itself the more starkly: what is the relationship of those politics to the politics of Socialist Realism and Stalinism?

One of the key issues here, which falls beyond the scope of the present essay, concerns the political perspective of revisionist-left histories themselves. Suffice to say that for the majority of the left, Stalinism has presented a major ideological, as well as a moral and political, problem. The glaring discrepancy between conceptions of a "presently existing socialism"—positively or negatively inflected according to the author's devotion to the Communist Party tradition—and the realities of the bureaucratic nightmare that Stalinism actually was, coupled with the fact that the bureaucracy systematically denied access to all kinds of information about its own constitution and history, ensured that the question of Stalinist culture did not get addressed. The demise of that system, combined with the renewed boldness of the ideological wing of the apparently victorious, economically liberal/politically conservative capitalist formation in what E. P. Thompson once called the "Natopolitan" countries, has given a new lease on life to denunciations of Stalinism, while reducing any need to be scrupulous in depicting its antecedents. When even the Western Communist parties are competing to distance themselves from the October Revolution (and the legacy they themselves have systematically misconstrued), what historian of art is going to be in a position to be able—let alone to want—to delve into the occluded byways of Russian politics in

the 1920s? That sense of a loosening of restraint, albeit often for negative reasons, on the scrutiny of Stalinism, plus the fact that a great quantity of historical data on the Stalin era is only now becoming available, means that the question passed over in silence by those histories which gave back to the avant-garde its political dimension is now close to the center of concern. Moreover, the contours of an answer are being provided, too. To borrow a term from media studies, our situation on the threshold of a "new world order" offers a preferred reading of that order's defeated opponents. If "severance" was one motif for the avant-garde's relation to politics, a motif redrawn as *cohabitation* by left-revisionist histories, the new neoconservative perspective can be given in one word: complicity.

Not all such accounts are, of course, of a piece; this "map" is only schematic, and the epithet "neoconservative" may not always be wholly justified. Thus, to take only two authors: Boris Groys in a stimulating and suggestive argument treats Socialist Realism as a sui generis cultural formation, whereas Igor Golomstock in a palpably rebarbative text is concerned to reduce it to the status of merely one manifestation of a "totalitarian art" that also includes the products of Italian Fascism and German Nazism.[15] Both, however, in a diametric reversal of arguments for the political innocence of the avant-garde, are concerned to draw connections between it and the ostensibly very different art of Socialist Realism.

Golomstock's case involves more than a hint of guilt by association. In an ironically symmetrical replay—of all things—of Georg Lukács's denunciation of the Expressionist avant-garde for weakening the resistance of the bourgeois humanist tradition to Fascism, Golomstock despairs of the avant-garde for smoothing the path of totalitarianism. It should be said that this is not Golomstock's main focus—which consists in the claimed isomorphism of Stalinist and Nazi art. But a central plank of such a claim is the assertion of continuity between the Bolshevik Revolution and the Stalinist bureaucracy. As his teleological argument has it: "a totalitarian regime disguises itself in revolutionary garb during its first stage of development." In line with this political claim, a "continuity" thesis is asserted in art. The committed wing of the left avant-garde—Tatlin, Rodchenko, Klutsis, Lissitzky— become totalitarians *in nuce*. "Many features" of the avant-garde's artistic ideology "were later incorporated into the foundations of totalitarian art." Citations from 1920s avant-gardists are deployed to prove that "the first calls for the strict administration and central administration of the arts" came from "the revolutionary avant-garde themselves," and thence that the avant-garde "first elaborated a totalitarian ideology of culture." The slippage in the argument is notable. In fact, Golomstock inserts a disclaimer in his argument to the effect that it would be wrong to overstate the avant-garde's responsibility for totalitarian art, since that is just what Socialist Realist theoreticians themselves claimed about the avant-garde vis-à-vis Nazism, as part of establishing their own distance from it. The disclaimer does, however, ring somewhat tokenistically in the face of the multiplicity of claims to the effect that it would be "illegitimate, however, entirely to deny the role of the avant-garde in the formation of the totalitarian artistic ideology." A supposedly conventional antithesis (our first, "hegemonic" interpretation above) is invoked wherein "these two decades [i.e., the 1920s and 1930s] appear to be antagonistic epochs" according to a list of binary oppositions: "freedom and slavery, dynamism and stasis, development and stagnation, etc." By thus absolutizing the supposed "oppositions," it becomes easier to take a "realistic" step back and claim a "hereditary link" between the revolutionary avant-garde and the Stalinist apologetics of Socialist Realism.

The thrust of this argument in Golomstock's case is clearly grounded in a valorization of Western liberal democracy—not surprising, since he is in voluntary exile after a blighted career within the Stalinist system. The point is not so much to question the allegiances imposed by a trammeled biography as to note that in the present conjuncture of its publication, Golomstock's thesis dovetails with the wider triumphalism of Western official readings of the revolutions of 1989. In this connection, there is, in fact, an explicit sense in which the historical continuity thesis is offered as a dire warning to contemporary artists who evince a renewed openness to art's sociopolitical dimension. Artists inclined to a critique of Modernism may be tempted by a "nostalgia" for "art's lost social role" to "flirt, albeit unconsciously, with totalitarian aesthetics."

Groys's argument differs from Golomstock's in its view of Socialist Realism as a specific formation, as well as in its acknowledgment of the paradoxical defeat of the avant-garde's intentions to transcend bourgeois art practice, which the contemporary interest of art museums and historians represents. Nonetheless, apropos the present argument concerning the politics of the avant-garde, he repeatedly asserts Socialist Realism's "identity with the avant-garde era," the "unity of their fundamental artistic aim." Despite appearances, Socialist Realism "put into effect practically all the fundamental watchwords of the avant-garde." Although it moved away from the avant-garde stylistically, "at the same time it continued, developed and in a certain sense, even implemented its programme." Clearly, these arguments require careful consideration. Outrageous as they might seem at first glance to sensibilities nurtured on the alleged otherworldliness of a Malevich, let alone the straightforwardly anti-Soviet credentials of a Gabo, there is once more a grain, though not a kernel, of truth to them. The issue revolves, of course, precisely around the Soviet avant-garde's self-transformation out of a Modernist-type embrace of the autonomy of art rooted in the narrowing of art to the realm of the aesthetic (where the aesthetic is understood in terms of a conception of the expression of emotion and concomitant distance from the cognitive or critical). It is this basic fact of an art being conceived in terms of a social rather than a purely aesthetic task which engenders the desire to curtail its emancipatory aura by reining it in as a precursor of Socialist Realism. Thus, Bois wants, rightly, to claim of Lissitzky's prouns that they are "abstract models of radical freedom."[16] Any such identification is clearly disrupted by an argument which postulates a one-way street from the avant-garde to the subservient, sometimes brutal, always formulaic art of the bureaucratic system.

Groys's key phrase is that Socialist Realism constitutes the "continuation of the Russian avant-garde's strategy by other means." The whole issue, by which I mean the thesis of continuity between the avant-garde and Socialist Realism *and* between the Bolshevik Revolution and Stalinism, centers on the constitution of "means" and "ends." For Groys, the "means" are, on the one hand, a highly idealized form of figurative painting and, on the other, a rhetoric of materialism. His claim is that the end which the avant-garde and Socialist Realism shared was the aspiration to change people's nature: either through a kind of narrative persuasion or by directly intervening in and changing their environments. Such a comparison is, it must be said, smoothed somewhat by the invocation of hyper-Productivists like Boris Arvatov. The wilder reaches of Soviet Taylorism, as represented by such as Arvatov, Boris Kushner, and Aleksei Gastev, are, it must be conceded, terrifying. They are not, however, truly representative of the left front of the arts as a whole. It is more than a little disingenuous to use them as a stick with which to

beat the avant-garde in general. But the question of shared "ends" runs deeper than this, and care is required.

The basic disposition to change people's habits, even the revolutionary desire to bring about a new kind of person living a new kind of life free from oppression and exploitation is, as it stands, too vague to legitimate the assimilation of the revolutionary avant-garde of the 1920s to the official state art of the 1930s. The question is, rather, whether their conceptions of a "new way of life," of "socialist man," and so forth, are the same. Equally important is whether the philosophical positions stood in the same relation to actual policies, insofar as the question of "ends" has two aspects: what they said *and* what they did. The main issue, nonetheless, is whether the ends of the October Revolution can be said to be the same as the ends of the Stalinist system of the thirties and after. Before debating the historical point, it is worth underlining that, for Groys, they are. In one particularly outspoken instance they are de facto identified: ". . . the October Revolution and its slogan of the total reconstruction of the country according to a single plan." There is obviously an overlap here with the arguments of Buchloh noted earlier. And once again the assumption is mistaken. The Bolshevik intention was not, initially, to build up an industrial planned economy in the national Russian state. It was to stimulate, to act as a bridgehead for, revolution in the already industrialized Western nations. Lenin repeatedly argued that "without such a revolution we are lost," and even that "the final victory of socialism in a single country is of course impossible."[17] Moreover, he also judged that when the international revolution did occur, its Russian component would retreat to the second rank, only then slowly building itself up on the basis of aid from the developed countries. It was in complete opposition to this view—which is to say, the view of Lenin, Lev Trotskii, and the Bolshevik Party as a whole—that Stalin, as Carr has pointed out, as early as 1918 voiced skepticism about the international dimension of the Revolution and viewed it in a primarily Russian national context.[18] Thus, the effect of that one sentence in Groys's history is to collapse the international-socialist Bolshevik October into the Stalinist doctrine of "socialism in one country" and its achievement through the Five-Year Plans. It is worth noting that even this latter is an elision of no small order: the doctrine of "socialism in one country" in fact preceded the adoption of the First Five-Year Plan by the better part of five years and, indeed, was initially promulgated in the conditions of the New Economic Policy in 1924—the very social system which the Five-Year Plan overthrew.

The twin assimilation—of October to the Monolith, of Lef to Socialist Realism—receives a particular fillip from an observation made by both Groys and Golomstock. One of the most Orwellian encapsulations of the task of the Socialist Realist artist is that offered at the First Congress of Soviet Writers in 1934 by Andrei Zhdanov, quoting Stalin himself: writers were to be "engineers of human souls." This almost oxymoronic formulation produces a chilling effect and has come to stand as the hallmark of Stalinism's inhumanity and indifference to the individual. Both Groys and Golomstock argue for a continuity between the Constructivist project and this Stalinist conception of the artist. In Groys's case, the claim is rooted in a general invocation of the avant-garde concept of the "artist-engineer." His argument is that the utopian and unrealizable disposition of artists actually to shape the material form of the environment is nothing less than that which was taken over by Stalin and his cohorts—so that artists could now focus on the more manageable task of mind-fixing. What made the avant-garde's project "utopian" was that artists exceeded their brief by aspiring to affect the "base," an ambition Socialist Realism redressed by its focus on the "superstructure."

This is held to be its realpolitik. Golomstock's argument is essentially the same, except that he musters a quotation: Sergei Tret'iakov's image from the first issue of *Lef* (*Left Front of the Arts*), which Golomstock translates as "psycho-engineer." Tret'iakov's subsequent fate in one of Stalin's prison camps thus becomes a heightened instance of the avant-garde being devoured by the Frankenstein it helped to create, and by implication a grisly warning to any and all who find themselves attracted to the role of the "engaged artist."

The avant-garde notion of the engineer or constructor was part of an attempt to realign the practice of art with the business of socialist construction and to distance it from mysticism. As such, it partook of the central historical-materialist tenet that "social consciousness" is determined by "social being." To conflate this with the Stalinist panoply of repression and, by inference, with its well-known corruption of psychiatry in the treatment of dissidents owes more to Cold War ideology than to history. I would be naïve to claim that there were no points of contact among the avant-garde, the Revolution, and Stalinism. But how such a relation is conceived matters greatly. In marked contrast to the foregoing, Victor Serge wrote: "It is often said that 'the germ of all Stalinism was in Bolshevism at its beginning'. Well, I have no objection. Only, Bolshevism also contained many other germs—a mass of other germs—and those who lived through the enthusiasm of the first years of the first victorious revolution ought not to forget it. To judge the living man by the death germs which the autopsy reveals in a corpse—and which he may have carried with him since his birth—is this very sensible?"[19]

Distinct, on the one hand, from traditional claims of the Soviet avant-garde's relative political "innocence," and quite unequivocally dismissive, on the other, of any virtue attaching to its commitment to revolutionary politics, these arguments add a new dimension to the political meanings ascribed to the avant-garde. Coming when they do, they in a powerful sense complete the continuity thesis about Bolshevism and Stalinism. Long the staple of Western ideologists, this claim has often seemed to find its most vivid and persuasive rejoinder in the transformative élan of the revolutionary avant-garde. The effect of these interpretations, in the climate of the "new world order," is to close off that loophole in liberal-conservative ideology for good.

II

The foregoing survey of existing interpretations of the politics of the postrevolutionary Soviet avant-garde, cursory and schematic though it has been, reveals a deficiency. Only accounts in the second broad category (which I have dubbed the "revisionist" histories, in order to distinguish them both from the previously dominant sanitized or apologetic constructions of an apolitical art movement and from the recently emergent, conservatively inflected histories which play upon a claimed complicity with Stalinism as part of a wider project of burying affirmations of social revolution, the collective, and planning)—only these offer an adequate account of the institutions, debates, and formal and technical strategies of the avant-garde. "Only" is, of course, a relative term here. Such accounts have formed the central ground of interpretation of the avant-garde in recent years. But now that the situation in Russia has changed so fundamentally, there is no guarantee that this will remain the case. The identification of the Stalinist system with socialism has been so prevalent that the system's fall can, and perhaps will, contribute more readily to the displacement of social radicalism from the academic agenda than to the regeneration of such concern, which, in more propitious circumstances, the removal of one of its main

obstacles might have permitted. Even those otherwise fruitful "revisionist" accounts, however, have not, on the whole, tended to place avant-garde developments securely within the wider context of debate and struggle which, in the 1920s, *was* the process of sustaining the Revolution and building the new life. On the other side, it goes almost without saying, the orthodox political histories have, for their part, devoted scant, if any, attention to artistic debates.[20] An obvious question arises, therefore. Is it possible, at present, to offer a more positive interpretation of the politics of the avant-garde which may situate it in a nuanced account of the postrevolutionary political process: more nuanced, that is, than a conception which, for all its detail, tends to see the Revolution as a species of natural force, an eruption whose lava flows into a variety of distinct spheres, only to harden into Stalin's iron realpolitik—another "natural" outcome of revolution in a backward country.

There is no small paradox in the readiness of liberal historians to ascribe a kind of determinism to postrevolutionary political history, as though a hardening of the arteries was the only possible outcome for the Revolution. Yet the 1920s in fact witnessed a contested political process the outcome of which was not certain. It has been argued that one reason why Trotskii failed adequately to oppose Stalin at the Twelfth Party Congress in 1923, when the latter's power was far from established, let alone consolidated, was that Trotskii simply could not bring himself to take Stalin's threat to his own status and the gains of the Revolution seriously: "No contemporary, and he [Trotskii] least of all, saw in the Stalin of 1923 the menacing and towering figure he was to become."[21] If so, the miscalculation itself is dramatic enough. But what it indicates, more generally, is that Stalin*ism* as a system represented a position won from the defeat of other perspectives. Russia in the 1920s witnessed a continuing struggle over the balance of forces, economic, political, and cultural—a struggle intensified by the uncertainties of the international situation—rather than a royal road to the cult of personality.

When speaking of the politics of the avant-garde, it is fundamental to retain this sense of a political process. For the greater part of the period, however, there were no forces that resembled political parties in the contemporary Western sense. The Mensheviks and Right SRs (Social Revolutionaries), having been banned in June 1918 for association with "notorious counterrevolutionaries," had been rehabilitated later that year and early in 1919 and continued to exist throughout the Civil War, though their support eroded and both were effectively harried out of existence by the war's end. This coincided with the banning of organized fractions within the Party at the Tenth Congress in 1921. The situation at this point was grave: the war economy had extended a kind of military discipline over the whole of society, which was now in a pulverized condition; the Kronshtadt revolt had just been put down, at terrible cost; and massive controversy over the adoption of the New Economic Policy was threatening to tear the congress apart. Carr comments that the General Resolution on the Unity of the Party "seemed necessary and reasonable at the time."[22] Nonetheless, this decision came back to haunt the opposition to Stalin during the twenties, the problem being that the very organization of oppositional forces—even if in the cause of democratization—broke the rules and could be claimed, therefore, to violate Soviet democracy. The political process which took place, consequently, comprised more or less illegitimate formations, always subordinate to the state power, and increasingly so as power was concentrated further under the control of the centralized apparatus. This is not to say, however, that these formations were ipso facto marginal, or sectarian, let alone counterrevolutionary. Far from it: the main oppositional grouping's central claim was defense of the legacy of October against increasing deviations and retreats.

Given this state of affairs, one is extremely unlikely to find in the historical record evidence of artists' explicit political commitments in any party or neoparty sense. In fact, any such commitments are, with the exception of a few general references to the Communist Party itself, as rare as they are in the documents of the Western avant-garde. This is presumably the origin, and one reason for the longevity, of claims for the apolitical nature of the Soviet avant-garde: one will search in vain for discussion of the political programs of Nikolai Bukharin or Trotskii, or indeed for extended discussion of specific political doctrines such as "socialism in one country" or even the Five-Year Plans (which do, of course, receive mention, but at most as *faits accomplis* rather than as specific political strategies). It may be useful in this regard to distinguish between a relatively organizational sense of politics and a more diffuse sense of political ideology. For if there is an absence of political commitment in the former sense, the record is saturated with examples of it in the latter.

The major artists and theorists without exception place their formal and technical innovations squarely on the basis of the sociopolitical achievement of the October Revolution. Undoubtedly, most of these figures developed their characteristic technical innovations in the period before the Revolution. From 1912 onward, however, with the Lena goldfield massacre, that period was in some respect itself one of rising political militancy—which contributed to the cultural climate. But more to the point, October gave these artistic developments a political focus and in so doing further transformed them. The result was a specific conjunction, a union even, of the formal and the political: an avant-garde practically transformed by a wider social revolution.[23] Such a conjunction was sustainable only as long as the Revolution itself and its own subsequent existence and prospects bore the marks of the wider restrictions and redefinitions undergone.

The salient feature of the Bolshevik Revolution, in a word, was that it was *extra*ordinary. It is arguable that the 1920s in Russia marked a particularly hideous form—or rather forms, for there were distinct stages—of normalization. It may be objected that there was nothing "normal" about forced collectivization and mass famine. But two things should be remembered. First, collectivization and the parallel industrialization program of the later decade were not the first response of the Soviet government to the need to rebuild the country. And second, however concentrated their particular form in Russia, increasing state interventions in the economy came to constitute the norm for all developed nations in the capitalist crisis of the 1930s: in Germany, Italy, and Japan, obviously, but also in the United States and Great Britain, levels of intervention both domestically and in international trade reached new heights. In the end, the building up of a national economy with its own industrial base was normal in a way that breaking the weakest link in the chain of international capitalism and proceeding to use that bridgehead to stimulate breaks elsewhere, was not.

The two emblematic works of revolutionary art belong to a period when commitment to the revolution was able to be, so to speak, homogeneous. Tatlin's model for the *Pamiatnik III-emu Internatsionalu* (*Monument to the Third International,* 1919–20, fig. no. 1) and Lissitzky's *Klinom krasnym bei belykh* (*Beat the Whites with the Red Wedge,* 1920, plate no. 138) both emanate from circumstances which, if scarcely constituting a "glorious dawn," nonetheless were self-consciously heroic. For Blok, events were epochal on a scale transcending even that of the French Revolution, and bore comparison only with the very beginnings of our tradition—which is to say, the start of the Christian era.

One of these emblematic works is three-dimensional, the other two-dimensional; both, however, transgressed their framing norms, of sculpture and of painting, respectively: one moved from constructed reliefs in the direction of architecture, the other from Suprematist painting in the direction of mass-produced posters. Both construct their primary message—of commitment to the all-transforming international socialist revolution—through an equivalent transformation of norms at the levels of perception and technique. It is this attempted integration on which their emblematic status depends as on nothing else, transcending the failure of either properly to be realized. They were, in fact, perhaps unrealizable. It is what one might call their materialistic idealism, emanating from a situation where the utopian seemed to be ingrained in reality—where heaven seemed to roll up like parchment, as Shklovskii wrote—that confers the resilience they have shown as images of twentieth-century revolution, that connotes so strongly the positive side of socialism, when so much that has been claimed in the name of that concept has been brutal and barren. It is both their success and their failure—and the marker, perhaps, of a wider success and failure than their own—that these unrealizable projects stand at the high-water mark of that union of social and aesthetic transformation toward which they must have seemed, at the moment of their making, only a first step. Both were produced in what later became defined as the "first period": that period of revolutionary upturn caused by World War I and its aftermath. It was marked domestically by War Communism and the struggle to secure the Revolution, and internationally by the founding of the Third, Communist, International to seize the moment and promote the extension of the Revolution on a worldwide basis. These spheres formed the respective contexts of Tatlin's and Lissitzky's interventions.

Perhaps the most noteworthy feature of these and similar works, given the general disrepute into which the Revolution has fallen—as an antidemocratic coup d'etat, for example—is the unproblematic nature of the avant-garde's commitment to the October Revolution. Maiakovskii later wrote: "To accept or not to accept? There was no such problem for me (and other Moscow futurists). It was my revolution. I went to the Smolnyi. I did everything that was necessary. Meetings began."[24] The avant-garde's dominance in the cultural field in these early years was not uncontested, either from within Party ranks or by Proletkul't (Proletarian Culture) or by more conservative artists. It did, however, exist, and the slogans about organization were backed up by action. Tatlin was not one for overextended rehearsals of intent; his record, however, speaks for itself. Tatlin's desire for a unified artists' organization, expressed as early as 1914, could have remained avant-gardist rhetoric. The Revolution, however, as well as putting into circulation the slogan of "building the new life," offered a variety of ways for doing so. Tatlin, in addition to his involvement with Izo Narkompros (the Department of Fine Arts of the People's Commissariat of Enlightenment), organized the Union of New Tendencies in Art, an umbrella organization of left artists in Petrograd. This union, the Academy of Arts, and Ginkhuk (the State Institute of Artistic Culture) were the Petrograd equivalents of the avant-garde's institutional bases and organizations in Moscow, such as Vkhutemas and the First Working Group of Constructivists of Inkhuk. This ground is fairly well trodden. But without overemphasizing the avant-garde's prominence—which then tends to cause problems in accounting for its later tribulations—it is worth recognizing the depth of organizational and institutional, as well as theoretical, commitment to the practice of building the new life. The conditions of War Communism seemed dramatically to draw a line between the new life and what had gone before. Conventional forms of class distinction and the bourgeois individualism connected to them were occluded by the enforced collectivity of the struggle to sustain the Revolution.

These conditions did not, however, last forever; and it is in the moves away from them that it becomes possible to speak of a rather different sense of a politics of the avant-garde. It is worth underlining, though, the way in which War Communism framed the project of Constructivism, of "material culture," and of "art into production." Still more fundamentally, however, War Communism constitutes the siting of the whole ethos of a single-minded bending of effort to one end, of suspicion toward all vestiges of the past— particularly anything related to a discredited sense of opulence, which included, of course, aesthetic contemplation, indeed anything carrying with it the stigma of leisured existence. Heroization of the Red Army, a total commitment to the security of the Revolution against the still extant White threat, and, in consort with those defensive tasks, the positive sense of a new world to be built from the ground up all militated against the toleration of revanchism.[25] The greatest single factor working in favor of the October Revolution was, of course, that it had been successful; audacity and courage broke through the hollowed-out protocols of the old. And now War Communism, apparently against even greater odds, had won again. As such, it was also a victory for the culture of the avant-garde, which, alone among the intelligentsia, had supported the Revolution. To the avant-garde, in the process of thinking its way out of bourgeois art for art's sake and formal experimentation into an integrated program for deploying the lessons of that past toward the building of the Communist future, the message must have been clear: "Press on." In sum, then, the major works of the avant-garde's new project of "art into production," that which defined both its distance from an art of contemplation and its commitment to participation in the wider revolutionary project, were in place by the end of the Civil War. But War Communism was something very like a Pyrrhic victory.

The New Economic Policy was adopted in March 1921 at the Party's historic Tenth Congress. NEP, a government-promoted reintroduction of capitalism in order to restart the shattered economy, could not have been more unlike War Communism. Centralized control of all areas was replaced by the fostering of private entrepreneurship. The working class, though numerically small, had been hegemonic in the worker-peasant alliance that allowed the Bolsheviks to oust the Provisional Government that had replaced the unlamented Romanov dynasty in February 1917. After the Civil War, with not only the bourgeoisie but also the proletariat socially atomized, the peasantry were the only social class to emerge relatively intact. NEP was summed up in Bukharin's advice to the peasantry: "Enrich yourselves." Which is to say, the balance of forces shifted from planning to that which is nowadays usually dubbed "enterprise," but for which the terms "greed" and "self-seeking" often do just as well. The balance shifted from town to country and from proletarians not just to peasants but to the "Nepmen," the new entrepreneurial class of merchants and middlemen which NEP brought into being—or rather, released from the amber into which they had been set by October and War Communism. NEP society was the dominant social formation in the Soviet Union in the mid-1920s, unlike both the heroic revolutionary period which preceded it and the increasing centralization of the Five-Year Plans which followed. In fact, it was out of the political contestation, the victories and defeats of NEP, that the Five-Year Plans were born. It has been convincingly argued, for

example, by Michael Reiman, that what one might call the culture of the Five-Year Plans, rudimentary at first but growing in scope, was an ad hoc response to the eventual crisis of NEP, rather than the result of any long-term strategy, let alone a logical or predetermined outcome of the Revolution itself.[26] By 1927–28, the Revolution was, in any case, pretty much ancient history, there to be deployed behind whichever group was powerful enough to annex it and its prestige to its own particular program. From 1921 to about 1928, the conditions of NEP, not the crucible of War Communism in which it had been formed, were the operating conditions of the erstwhile avant-garde.

The attitude of the avant-garde toward NEP is, therefore, a matter of some importance to clarifying its politics. And, indeed, in a scattered but relatively consistent commentary, a position emerges. This is partly born of antipathy to a way of life in which, as Serge noted, "classes are growing up around us again." Thus Vertov, writing in 1926: "We have not come to cinema in order to feed fairy tales to the Nepman and Nepwoman lounging in the loges of our first-class movie theaters."[27] This was no fantasy. It finds corroboration in the diary kept by Walter Benjamin of his trip to Moscow. On a visit to the theater in December 1926, he notes, "a waft of perfume greeted me as I entered," and he continues: "I did not see a single communist in a blue tunic, but there were several types who would not have been out of place in any of George Grosz's albums."[28] This situation points to a second strand in the avant-garde's response to NEP. For it was the emergence of these new social layers and their considerable emphasis upon consumption that provided one important basis for the reinflation of those traditional approaches to art-making and the social role of art which had been eclipsed in the revolutionary period. The avant-garde was opposed both to NEP's reemergent social stratification and to the opening this afforded to more conservative types of cultural practice.

It is a commonplace of art history that the avant-garde was unpopular due to the "innate visual conservatism" of the population at large.[29] Avant-garde commentators themselves, however, offer a description of a more contested site. Stepanova said that photomontage was popular in workplaces and offices.[30] Brik, while he acknowledged the difficulties experienced by the Constructivists, implied a distinction between the relationship of the new techniques to workers' experience in production and the antipathy of the NEP bourgeoisie, with its preference for conventional notions of art as a luxury good.[31] More explicitly, Vertov remarked upon the new lease on life given to fictional films that "recall the old 'artistic' models just as Nepmen recall the old bourgeoisie."[32] At the same time, however, he also discerned a response along class lines, noting how *Kino-pravda* (*Cinema-Truth*) newsreels "are boycotted by film distributors, by the bourgeois and semibourgeois public" yet "shown daily in many workers' clubs in Moscow and the provinces with great success";[33] and he went on devastatingly to turn the tables on the new societal "normalization": "If the NEP audience prefers 'love' or 'crime' dramas that doesn't mean that our works are unfit. It means the public is." Fit or unfit for what, is the question; and it has only to be raised for the answer to be clear: it was the project of building a new collective society that was foundering under NEP conditions. As Shklovskii put it: "The great passion of Lef . . . was a desire to participate in the making of a new life."[34] Yet Serge repeatedly notes how under NEP "symptoms of bourgeoisification" became prevalent, how "money lubricated and befouled the entire machine just as under capitalism," how "by and large, order was returning"[35]—and whom this suited.

Vertov's advertising films for Mossel'prom (the Moscow

Agricultural Industry) and GUM, the state department store, were echoed in the mid-1920s by the various advertising and packaging projects undertaken by Rodchenko and Maiakovskii. In the light of our own sleek consumer economy, these frequently appear no more than quaint, yet in the context of NEP it is a serious point that Rodchenko, Maiakovskii, and Vertov were committing their expertise to the state sector. There were degrees of emphasis: Vertov, as remarked above, condemned crime films, while Rodchenko successfully designed covers for Marietta Shaginian's "Jim Dollar" detective stories. But this does little more than indicate that there was room for diversity within an overall avant-garde commitment to the legacy of the Revolution and struggle against its perceived betrayal under NEP. The evidence is in the state-sector advertisements, the candy wrappers with little verses promoting industry, and posters for "social responsibility" programs such as Rodchenko's *Knigi* (*Books*) for a literary drive in 1925. These are quite distinct from the emphasis on private enterprise and profit which had gained ground. And, should it need underlining, a *politics* was at stake here.

Politics is not simply a matter of committees. In a revolutionary situation, or during an attempt to sustain a revolutionary perspective, all social activity contains a political dimension, and this includes areas which bourgeois culture fences off as the province of private taste—as, paradigmatically, areas of freedom from politics. In 1936, one of the first things George Orwell noticed when he arrived in revolutionary Barcelona was people's clothes. There were virtually "no 'well-dressed' people at all." Nearly everyone was in "rough working-class clothes."[36] Though it has obviously on occasion been a signifier of political meaning, clothing, at least in this practical sense, has not normally been perceived as a site of political meaning, at least not until very recently. Yet in 1924 Tatlin produced his famous designs for a stove, a coat, and a suit. These are frequently treated as eccentricities, without a hope of going into production, at best an index of utopianism and, as such, evidence of the head-in-the-clouds mentality of "impractical" artists, whatever their Productivist rhetoric. Such an explanation is normative with respect to a cultural division of labor. The situation can, however, be read differently, as intentionally disruptive of such norms—a possibility which the orthodox assumption closes down. Tatlin and his colleagues did attempt to form working relations with organizations for the mass production of goods and textiles, but were generally unsuccessful. Larissa Zhadova quotes a contemporary observer, K. Miklashevskii, to the effect that Tatlin, in a lecture, "expressed his dissatisfaction with authorities who did not really support his endeavors to work in industrial concerns."[37] This is to say, it was the "authorities" who appeared to frustrate the artist-constructors in their attempts to turn art into production, not the sheer impracticality of the projects in the first place. And these were managers of NEP concerns whom it behooved to make a profit rather than build a new society. As Maiakovskii commented in the first issue of *Novyi Lef* (*New Lef*) in 1927: "Market demand has become for many people the measure of value as far as cultural phenomena are concerned."[38] Serge spoke of the sometimes austere morality of Bolshevism, the egalitarianism of early Soviet society.[39] In like manner, the historian Selim Khan-Magomedov has noted as one of the key components of life after the Revolution which framed Constructivism "a marked asceticism in the habits, clothing, and official and social life" of the revolutionaries, as distinct from "the behavior of the social elite that had been reborn with the NEP."[40] Brik noted of Rodchenko's Constructivist design work that "artists turn their back on him. Irritated factory managers reject him. The petit-bourgeois goggles . . ."[41] Tatlin produced a montage contrasting his suit with bourgeois lounge suits, a contrast which is explicitly linked by Zhadova to NEP conditions. His captions claimed the new clothing "satisfies hygienic requirements and lasts long," whereas the other is "unhygienic and they wear it only because they think it is beautiful."[42] The contrast is perhaps a little stark for us. But what it implies is that Tatlin's is a piece of work less the product of unworkable eccentricity than of a refusal of NEP conditions at the level of clothing: a refusal of the reassertion of a bourgeois, market-fixated mechanism of fashion, and a determination to design for "this man [who] is a worker and will use the object in question in the working life he leads."[43]

Constructivist interventions in the field of practical design in the mid-1920s remained on a relatively small scale. There was perhaps more activity in the fields of theater and graphic design, but still it fell far short of the aspiration to frame a new way of life with a "culture of materials" which would dialectically help to precipitate a new consciousness, new kinds of social individuals who would themselves go on to live and, in turn, transform that new life. It is all too easy to see this failure, from the dubious vantage point of our own monopoly-capitalist economies, as a result either of the idealism of the projects themselves or the impatience of those "really" leading the revolutionary process for such luxuries when more basic products were required. There is obviously some truth in this—it has the ring of the way the world works. But the picture is complicated by the specific nature of the social formation which replaced War Communism and which gave renewed breathing space to social stratification and motivations more often associated with the bourgeois past. Small wonder that "building the new life" foundered in a society which powerfully foregrounded the reinstatement of elements of the old one. Constructivism in these conditions, trying to push ahead with the sociopolitical transformation put on the agenda by the October Revolution but subsequently marginalized by the New Economic Policy, had more the quality of a rearguard than an avant-garde action.

Benjamin was frequently drawn to comment on the situation obtaining both in literature and in the society at large. Only a day or two after his arrival in Moscow in 1926, he is noting "the political news: members of the opposition removed from important positions," a situation which he immediately links to "the Party's reactionary bent in cultural matters. The leftist movements which had proved useful during the period of wartime communism are now being completely discarded."[44] The effect of NEP for the Constructivists was obviously mixed. War Communism had saved the Revolution, but the militarization of society had wrecked the revolution's social base. NEP had saved the economy, and offered a more normal framework of legality for everyday civilian life, but at the cost of increasing stratification and the occlusion of the whole vision of a socialist society based in the working class. In such a situation, then, what was it for Maiakovskii to write, in 1925, "To build a new culture a clean sweep is needed. The sweep of the October revolution is needed"? Certainly, the significance of an appeal to October during NEP was far from univocal. For Serge's "fat shopkeeper enriched by the sale at speculative prices of articles manufactured by our socialist industry" it was time to breathe a sigh of relief that order was being restored and the dark days of 1919 put behind for good.[45] It is unlikely he would have apostrophized October's new broom other than to pay lip service to the origins of a new status quo. It was a different matter for the avant-garde. In 1923 Nikolai Aseev commented, "the waves of NEP were already rolling overboard in the revolutionary ship." One had to "hold onto the balustrades in order not to be swept into the sea of obscurantism and philistinism." In particular, "the honesty of those people who were the first artists to have reacted positively to the appeal for the participation of the intelligentsia in the October revolution was considered suspect, and their value was constantly questioned."[46]

In such a situation, the attempt to press ahead with the program of "art into production" took on a specific coloring. Framed in 1921 by Aleksei Gan "in terms of the essential distinctive features and requirements of communism,"[47] when those "features" were extrapolated from the now abandoned War Communism, the very sense of "production" which art was to be directed "into" had undergone significant change. At the very least, rather than a universal rhetoric, "art into production" now connoted a specific view, one with its own history, built out of an acceptance of certain assumptions and a concomitant rejection of others—which latter were, moreover, in play as a new status quo at the level both of a market-oriented economy and an increasingly approved conventional art practice. Under NEP, that is to say, "art into production" signified in a system of differences: it was unlike other assumptions about art and about production. In May 1924, right in the middle of NEP, Tatlin offered a synoptic statement of what was still the task in his lecture on "Material Culture and Its Role in the Production of Life in the USSR": "to shed light on the tasks of production in our country, and also to discover the place of the artist-constructor in production, in relation to improving the quality both of the manufactured product and of the organization of the new way of life in general."[48] To an extent, of course, all shades of opinion spoke of the "new way of life," but for the Constructivists in general and Tatlin in particular this was an assertion of continuity with October and, indeed, with that prerevolutionary work which for them prefigured the social and political revolution. It was a restatement of such a perspective. As Tret'iakov later wrote, Lef had been formed "in the conditions of the New Economic Policy . . . Lef means Left Front, and Left Front implies opposition to any other front."[49] Khan-Magomedov has commented on this period: "Rodchenko's activity in the field of commercial graphic art was closely bound up with straightforward political propaganda . . . Many of the book and magazine covers designed by Rodchenko were really, despite their small format . . . political posters."[50] The question is, therefore: is it possible to be any more specific about these politics?

Dissatisfaction with NEP was not confined to the artistic avant-garde. That is, in fact, one of the central planks of this essay. An avant-garde art group in bourgeois society can, of course, withdraw into a specialized position which does not have any ready political correlation. That is the nub of claims for art's relative autonomy from society. It is not, however, to say that, even then, a politics cannot be legitimately attributed to such a grouping. In the case of the Soviet Union in the 1920s, however, various factors militate against concluding that such was the state of affairs. On the one hand, society was saturated with politics, anyway; on the other, the avant-garde actually aspired to an interventionist role. Their practice was not divorced from the political, or at least can be said to have had compacted into it a political dimension. The latter dimension is unlikely to have been the group's property alone, evolved by extrapolation solely from its own art practice or somehow preserved as a memory trace of the original "big bang" revolution. There is no reason why it should have been. The political process evolved, and different perspectives emerged as time went on. It is relatively improbable that a small-scale cultural grouping could have maintained a stance fundamentally at odds with the political order of the day if that order was otherwise in receipt of homogeneous support. It is far more likely that, in such a situation, its program would

have been marked by retreats into more orthodox forms of artistic activity paralleling the wider sociopolitical retreats. It can, of course, be argued that Constructivism did undergo significant revision, for example, in the use of uncut photographs in factography. But this can be seen more as a modification and adaptation of the program than as a straightforward retreat from it.

There was, anyway, an approach to art-making which came very rapidly to be identified with NEP, with the sponsorship of official bodies such as the trade unions and the army, and the provision of conventional portraits for the new bourgeoisie NEP threw up. This was AKhRR. The position of so-called Realist art in the various groups which sprang up from the end of the Civil War onward is considerably more complex with regard to the relations between its form and its content than is often recognized—even in the case of AKhRR itself, the most "illusionistic" of the groups, let alone others like Ost (the Society of Easel Painters), which offered a kind of combination of avant-garde technique and socially significant depicted subjects.[51] Be that as it may, the fact remains that throughout this period AKhRR was at odds with the avant-garde art-into-production tendency; that *it* tended to be identified with NEP; and that the avant-garde did not significantly retreat to more conventional forms of art practice. This suggests the existence of a countervailing political-ideological force in the culture which could enable and sustain distance from the new status quo.

There were, in fact, two "waves" of such opposition. There had always been small oppositional groups even during the Civil War, but, with the exception of the Kronshtadt mutineers, these had been relatively marginal, and it is doubtful whether they exerted much gravitational pull. Circumstances changed, however, as NEP progressed. For some time, NEP, though apparently reasonably successful in the fundamental task of making the economy move again, had begun to generate its own problems. By 1923, largely because of the concessions to the peasantry, an imbalance arose between industry and agriculture. Industrial prices remained high because of the scarcity of manufactured goods. Conversely, agricultural prices were low, with the result that there was no incentive for peasants to sell their produce to the cities: they stood to make little from the transaction and there was not much in the way of manufactured goods they required to buy, anyway. Because of this "scissors" crisis, so named due to the way these divergent tendencies were represented on a graph, there arose again a serious threat to the worker-peasant alliance which NEP had been intended to bolster. Lenin was effectively inactive at this point (and would continue so until his death in January 1924), and the leadership of NEP fell to the "triumvirate" of Stalin (the Party Secretary), Grigorii Zinov'ev, and Lev Kamenev. An alternative proposal to cure the scissors crisis was put forward by Trotskii in April 1923 at the Twelfth Party Congress, a proposal which hinged on the concept of planning. As Isaac Deutscher has pointed out: "That planning was essential to a socialist economy was a Marxist axiom with which the Bolsheviks were, of course, familiar, and which they had always accepted in general terms. Under war communism, they imagined that they were in a position to establish immediately a fully-fledged planned economy . . . But after the introduction of NEP, when all efforts were directed towards reviving the market economy, the idea of planning suffered eclipse."[52] Faced with a retreat from the goal of a planned socialist mode of production, and with the concomitant decline in the social power of the working class relative to the peasantry, Trotskii now reintroduced the idea of "systematically broadening the scope of planning" with the ultimate aim of "thereby absorbing and abolishing the market."[53] Some sense of the stakes involved can be gained from the argument of Trotskii's later article "K sotsializmu ili k kapitalizmu?" ("Toward Capitalism or Socialism?") of August 1925. NEP is there seen as both a combination of and a competition between these two "scissors" tendencies. Trotskii, however, notes that "if state industry develops more slowly than agriculture; if the latter should proceed to produce with increasing speed the two extreme poles [of] capitalist farmers 'above,' proletarians 'below,' this process would of course lead to a restoration of capitalism."[54]

In the cultural field, Tatlin wrote two reports in November 1924 on the work of his Section for Material Culture at the Petrograd Ginkhuk. That he had to do so, twice, is alone indicative of the pressure the project was coming under as the administration sought more biddable recipients for official funding.[55] But more to the point, Tatlin set his defense of a planned approach to the design of material culture in a context of "anarchy" reigning in production. This is, doubtless, in part an observation about design and production processes and the lack of headway being made by integrated "Constructivist" practice. But it also reads as a reflection on the more general productive conditions obtaining under NEP, and the absence of planning in the economy. Contemporary production, Tatlin noted, "in both town and country in all its manifestations," largely because of the continuing legacy of "industrial and domestic production inherited from the old world," was "in a state of anarchy." Production was "splintered into chance productive units," and experience as a whole was "abnormally individualized."[56] This abnormally individual experience of life and anarchic production process need to be set against the avant-garde's continued assertion of very different priorities. Their consistent appeal was to the notion of a "collective" way of life, a way of life which, moreover, needed to be "organized." Thus, the course which Rodchenko taught at Vkhutemas was envisaged in 1926 as producing a "new type of engineer" who would effect "the organization and rationalization of production."[57] Tatlin likewise viewed his role as that of the "organizer of everyday life" in an article of 1929. Quite contrary to these aspirations, daily life under NEP was, as Maiakovskii described it, a "way of life which has not been altered in almost any respect—the way of life which is now our worst enemy, which makes us bourgeois."[58] These arguments are consistent across the decade, yet under NEP, arguments about the need for organization and planned production would have been difficult for the Constructivists to sustain without examples of more concretely theorized programs in the political-economic sphere. Trotskii's proposals, however, although they came to constitute the cornerstone of a political program, basically went unheeded in 1923 by a Party organization which, in Deutscher's words, "considered NEP almost incompatible with planning," and thought it necessary instead to emphasize the "enterprise" economy's stability and longevity in order "to strengthen the peasants' and the merchants' confidence in it."[59]

Other developments were also afoot in the Soviet system. At the same time as the scissors crisis grew in the economy, the "blades" moving ever wider apart through the autumn, 1923 also saw the consolidation of the bloc of Party bureaucrats owing allegiance more to the central power structure than to the confidence of workers at the base. This led to a qualitatively new situation: an organization in which "alignments were temporary blocs around concrete proposals and issues" was replaced by one of "a permanent power caucus in the highest body of the party, whose purpose was to preserve control in its hands regardless of the issues at stake."[60] As the French socialist Boris Souvarine put it, the "dictatorship of the proletariat" was being replaced by the "dictatorship of the secretariat." In the summer and autumn of 1923, because of the mixture of economic pressure and the lack of adequate avenues of political expression, a wave of industrial militancy struck Moscow and Petrograd, extending even to the possibility of a general strike: overall, the most powerful political challenge to the leadership since Kronshtadt. One result of this changed situation was the formalization and extension of the position broached by Trotskii at the Twelfth Congress in the Platform of the Forty-Six, a statement by a group of leading figures in the Party which criticized the authorities for their handling of the economy and the erosion of democracy. October 1923 is thus usually treated as marking the birth of the Left Opposition.

The pressure was sufficient, despite the ban on other parties and on oppositional groups within the Communist Party itself, to force the leadership to open up a debate in the pages of the press. The effect was swift, measurable not least by the doubling of *Pravda*'s circulation. The greatest effect was felt in the army—which had been Trotskii's base since he reorganized it to defend the Revolution in 1918—but the Left Opposition was also strong in the youth organizations and in the universities and other higher-educational institutions. Despite this considerable support for the opposition at the system's roots, however, the newly functioning bureaucratic apparatus, which had been in gear since the Party Congress in the spring, was able to ensure that by the time the Thirteenth Party Conference came around in January 1924, a support which in terms of voting at district level was running at thirty-six percent (and which was possibly even higher in individual party groups, for which results were not announced) was converted into a mere three delegates at the conference itself. By the time of the Thirteenth Congress a few months later, in May, Trotskii had been effectively isolated—a process which was then repeated in the international organization at the Fifth Congress of the Comintern in June.

This very process of reaction does, however, lend a certain support to the hypothesis of a relationship between the Soviet avant-garde of the 1920s and the political Left Opposition. In the wake of the opposition's decline, 1924 witnessed a major purge of the institutions of higher education. It is well known that Vkhutemas was one of the major institutional sites of Constructivism—though, as Lodder has established, the Constructivist influence was by no means coherent across the institution as a whole. (It is only recently, in the work of Lodder and others, that a clear picture of the scope of Vkhutemas has been offered.) Vkhutemas was not, however, an isolated institution but part of a system of institutions of higher education, the VUZy, and in particular of institutions of higher technical education (the VTUZy).[61] The precise relationship of Vkhutemas, from 1926 reorganized as Vkhutein (the Higher Artistic-Technical Institute), to the other institutions of higher technical education is not clear. A relationship did exist, however, since the original decree by which Vkhutemas was brought into being concerned its role in the reorganization and reconstruction of production in the country at large: a task which was assigned to a wide range of practical and technical specialisms, not something confined to the one institution. (A case in point is the Rabfak [the Workers' Faculty], quite often mentioned in accounts of Vkhutemas as an avenue whereby workers without previous qualification could be brought up to a sufficient standard to allow them to continue with the new art and design education. Rabfaks, however, were part of a system, attached to all the VTUZy, not an egalitarian feature of Vkhutemas alone.) It would be unusual if there were no contact between the students at such institutions, particularly in a period with a high profile of ideological and political activity. One obvious avenue would be through Party meetings, but interaction would also have taken place more informally, not least in cultural pursuits. Thus in Petrograd in May 1923, Tatlin put on a memorial performance of Velimir Khlebnikov's play *Zangezi*. Supporting actors were largely drawn from the student body, and Tatlin's account mentions, in addition to art students from the Petrograd Academy, students from the university and the Mining Institute, one of the VTUZy. These institutions (in marked contrast to the situation in 1917, it should be noted, when being a university student was synonymous with support for the Whites) contained a high proportion of actively involved Communist students, a "large majority" of whom, according to Sheila Fitzpatrick, were for the Trotskiist opposition in 1923–24.[62] In 1924, a surprising ten percent of all Party members were students, and half of them were in institutions of higher technical education. In Moscow, furthermore, students comprised no less than twenty-five percent of the Moscow Party organization. A student himself is recorded as having commented: "It was a golden time for the Trotskyite Opposition."[63] With the defeat of the opposition, however, a tremendous purge took place. Narkompros's own statistics give the figure of 18,000 students expelled, though Fitzpatrick argues that the actual numbers were more than double this. More to the point, most expulsions occurred in "the more sullied and overcrowded artistic, socio-economic and pedagogical VTUZy."[64] Given the scale of this activity, it seems highly unlikely that the avant-garde within Vkhutemas, self-consciously positioned as a "left" within culture at the cutting edge of a new way of life, and against that life's erosion by the bourgeoisifying tendencies of NEP—could have remained isolated from the wider oppositional debate during 1923 and 1924. In fact, far from remaining isolated, it is quite likely to have drawn support from the left-oriented students, beleaguered as its adherents apparently felt in the NEP environment.

Later in 1924, in September, Trotskii's *Uroki Oktiabria* (*The Lessons of October*) was published. His account of the October Revolution and its legacy was clearly intended to be relevant to the struggle in 1924. Having remarked that "up to the present time we lack a single work which gives us a comprehensive picture of the October upheaval," he commented: "It is as if we thought that no immediate and direct benefit for the unpostponable tasks of future constructive work could be derived from the study of October."[65] He obviously thought otherwise. October could be used as a lens to bring into focus the struggle against counterrevolutionary forces in the bureaucracy and conservative aspects of the "worker-peasant alliance," which latter NEP was considered to be. The book's effect was to unleash a second phase of the antiopposition campaign, the cumulative result of which was that by 1925, the opposition which had originated in 1923 had been effectively silenced. The principal marker of this defeat in the period which followed, and one which was to have incalculable effects on the future of socialism, not to mention on the legacy of the October Revolution—and, indeed, on the revolutionary project of "building a new life"—was the formulation at the end of 1924 of the doctrine of "socialism in one country." The Bolshevik Revolution had been international in scope. According to Trotskii's theory of "uneven and combined development," a revolutionary outbreak could easily occur in a backward country, and not just in a major industrialized nation which had gone through its capitalist phase, such as Britain or Germany. There was no question, however, of such a revolution being more than a holding operation to stimulate further revolutions in those advanced countries. There are numerous statements of the implications of this view, but Lenin's argument to the Third Congress of the Comintern in 1921 is particularly clear: "Even prior to the Bolshevik revolution, as well as after it, we thought that the revolution would also occur either immediately or a least very soon in other backward countries and in the more highly developed capitalist countries. Otherwise we would perish."[66]

When the revolutionary wave ebbed after 1921 and the capitalist system managed to stabilize itself, the Russian Revolution was obviously going to have to try to hold out for longer than had been intended. NEP was one response to this development. The central point is that NEP was a temporary measure until the capitalist crisis reasserted itself and the tempo of struggle rose again, yet it also transpired that NEP seemed in its own fabric to be turning away from this perspective. As NEP appeared to accommodate more and more to the norm, it was precisely the formation of the Left Opposition within NEP, as Naomi Allen has argued, which now took on the original project: "The existence of an organized Opposition would resist the free expansion of the bureaucracy, subject it to criticism, and perhaps retard its development long enough to keep intact the roots of the proletarian dictatorship until conditions for its existence improved."[67] Such an awaited capitalist crisis did indeed occur with the Wall Street Crash of 1929 and the entry of the world system into profound slump during the 1930s, a slump which was only definitively terminated by the outbreak of World War II at the end of that decade. But by the time of the onset of the crisis at the close of the 1920s, the revolutionary movement had undergone profound change—and the main symptom was "socialism in one country." The idea of building up an independent industrialized state in Russia had been foreign to the Bolsheviks. It now became the central plan of policy—initially within the scope of the mixed, relatively unplanned, economy of NEP. Later, however, as NEP itself entered its terminal crisis, the stage was set for a "third period," which transformation is also important for understanding the later trajectory of the avant-garde.

For the moment, however, what should be noted is that the Left Opposition of 1923 and 1924, which had been crushed by 1925, began to rise again in a second incarnation in 1926. The paradoxical factor here was that those members of the triumvirate who had sided with Stalin to break the Left Opposition that was centered on Trotskii now began to fear the increasing concentration of power in the hands of the General Secretariat. In an abrupt about-face, Zinov'ev, with his power base in Leningrad, now joined forces with Trotskii to constitute a new and more powerful united opposition. By this time, Bukharin had become the main defender of NEP—of, as he famously put it, "socialism at a snail's pace"—and as such, Stalin's main ally against the opposition. This new opposition reached a peak in 1927, a peak, moreover, much higher than has often been thought. On the basis of new evidence, Reiman has argued that "the importance of the left opposition is often underestimated in the literature. It is considered an important current in Soviet ideological and political life, a kind of 'revolt of the leaders' . . . but many authors doubt that the opposition had any substantial influence on the mass of party members and even less on broader sections of the population. One can hardly agree with such views."[68] Reiman goes on to cite an impressive catalogue of opposition successes in various geographical regions, in sections of the organized working class in the major cities, and, once again, in the army and the higher education institutions. There is an international dimension here as well as a domestic one, which complicates the issue: just as the failure of the German revolution played a part in the formation of the opposition in 1923, so now the disastrous policies of the bureaucracy toward the revolution in China contributed to the force of the opposition in 1927.

Whatever the multiplicity of causes, the result was a rise in mass meetings of industrial workers, underground strike committees, and suchlike. When a leading oppositionist, Ivar Smilga, was being got out of the way by assignment to a remote posting—quite a common tactic by the leadership—a crowd of two thousand people gathered, listened to speeches by Zinov'ev and Trotskii, and cheered Smilga to his train. Although the united/left opposition of 1926–27 aimed principally to promote the workers' resistance to the decline they were suffering under NEP, Fitzpatrick argues that "Opposition condemnation of NEP . . . probably did arouse a response among students."[69] There was also support in youth organizations. Overall, "opposition propaganda steadily grew in intensity. The opposition flooded party units with leaflets, pamphlets and other material contributing to a further decline in the Politburo's authority . . . By the end of July the situation in the party had taken fairly definite shape. The opposition succeeded in increasing its influence; it was beginning to think that a change in the party leadership might be attainable at the forthcoming 15th Party Congress."[70] Trotskii later estimated that in 1927 the opposition had 20,000 to 30,000 active members in Moscow alone.

Despite fierce internal conflicts among the leadership, culminating in the expulsion of Trotskii and Zinov'ev from the Central Committee, the opposition's influence continued to grow throughout the summer, leading to the publication in September 1927 of the *Platform of the Opposition.* This echoed many of the criticisms of NEP of the earlier opposition, citing the growth of money-commodity relations, increasing social stratification, and lack of democracy, and proffered as well a newer condemnation of the policy of economic autarky. The *Platform* runs to twelve chapters in some ninety pages. It notes that "there exist in our society these forces hostile to our cause—the kulak, the Nepman, the bureaucrat" and recommends a continuous struggle "on all sectors of the economic, political and cultural fronts."[71] A week after its publication, the *Platform* was banned. A major shift was necessary to implement the ban, requiring nothing less than that the leadership alter—that is, effectively break—the Party's own rules. The state security forces (the GPU), built up by the bureaucracy, were turned against the Party itself. Reiman comments: "Events quickly approached a climax. The opposition, mobilizing its considerable store of influence, tried to make a show of strength to turn the situation to its favour. During Leningrad's celebration of the 10th anniversary of the October revolution in mid-October 1927, the opposition suddenly received impressive support. Trotsky, Zinoviev and other oppositionists who found themselves by chance on one of the official reviewing platforms as the workers of Leningrad paraded past, found themselves the object of demonstrative greetings and cheers from the crowd of a hundred thousand."[72]

This situation was not allowed to repeat itself on the official anniversary of the Revolution on November 7th. Marches and meetings were broken up, speakers howled down. The GPU had entered fully onto the political stage, in consort with which another massive propaganda campaign was mounted. The October demonstration had proved to be the limit. The last demonstration by the Left Opposition took place on November 19, 1927. At the Fifteenth Party Congress, which opened on December 2nd, Trotskii along with seventy-five other leading members of the opposition was expelled from the Party. Next, Trotskii was informed by the GPU that he was to be deported under article 59 of the criminal code, which dealt with counterrevolutionary activity. But such a large crowd gathered on the proposed date, June 16, 1928—several in the crowd lay down on the railway tracks—that the authorities had to resort to deception. According to Carr's account, the departure was postponed for two days. Within twenty-four

hours, however, Trotskii's apartment was broken into by armed police; he was driven to an outlying, cleared part of the station and forced aboard a special train which then linked up with the express well away from Moscow. After a journey by truck and sleigh conveyed him another 150 miles beyond the nearest railhead, Trotskii arrived in internal exile at Alma-Ata, at "the extreme confines of the USSR," on January 25, 1928. A year later, he was expelled from the Soviet Union altogether. In Reiman's summary, "the basis for the existence of any kind of opposition whatsoever inside the Soviet Communist Party had been destroyed. From then on opposition was an unequivocal political crime bringing stern punishment in its train."[73]

The picture that emerges, then, is of a nearly seven-year period, extending from the Tenth Party Congress in March 1921 to the Fifteenth Congress in December 1927, during which the political direction of the Revolution was in a continual process of negotiation and contestation. The end results were a shift in basic premise from the internationalism of 1917 to the doctrine of building "socialism in one country," and the concentration of power in the hands of a central bureaucracy led by Stalin. There were two great waves of opposition to this from the left, in 1923–24 and again in 1926–27. This opposition stood for a return to those principles of October which it perceived to be undermined by NEP: that is to say, an emphasis on socialism rooted in the working class, a reversal of social stratification, a reassumption of planning in the economy, and increased democracy (as well as a complex international dimension with repercussions for the political policy to be pursued in places like Germany and China, and for the economic relationship of the Soviet Union to the capitalist world).

It had been common for the avant-garde in art at the time of the Revolution, and even before, to be referred to as left artists. Thus Tatlin was a member of the left bloc of the Union of Art Workers in Petrograd in the period between the two revolutions of 1917. He was also involved with the left federation of the Moscow Professional Union of Artists and Painters. The notion of an artistic left was quite prevalent, both as a form of self-description among artists to distinguish themselves from "bourgeois" tendencies and as a form of criticism by those, either close to the Party or laying claim to represent a "proletarian culture," who saw left art with its roots in the bourgeois avant-garde as occupying that space where petit-bourgeois individualism met anarchistic or libertarian "ultraleftism." This latter view must have received succor from Lenin's pamphlet critical of the council Communists and related groups, *Detskaia bolezn' "levizny" v kommunizme* (*Left-Wing Communism: An Infantile Disorder,* 1920.) (It is perhaps worth pointing out that the epithet refers less to the childishness or immaturity of the attitude per se than to the relative youth of the Communist movement which, as such, is given to wild enthusiasms and excesses that need to be stabilized.) The point is, the identification of the avant-garde as an artistic left, in a rather diffuse sense, was commonplace, somewhat after the manner in which the term "Futurist" was deployed.

Things seem to be different, however, in the succeeding period. When Maiakovskii organized the Left Front of the Arts around the journal *Lef,* first published in March 1923, "left" was not a diffuse term but a label for a coherent grouping or, more likely, regrouping of forces intended to intervene in a changing situation. *Lef* lasted for seven issues and drew in most of the literary and artistic avant-garde at the levels of both practice and theory. It was quite a large magazine with a print run for the first issue of five thousand copies. Three thousand copies were printed of the third issue, and there were no less than four issues in 1923. There were only two, however, in 1924, and the final issue, with a print run of only 1,500, came out early in 1925. Maiakovskii had, according to Brik, started to think about a new "organizational grouping" as early as the end of 1921, but the proposal was not worked out until a year later.[74] When the magazine came out in early 1923, the members of Lef referred to themselves as the "Bolsheviks of art" and quite explicitly saw their context as a situation where "now there is a respite from war and hunger," i.e., the New Economic Policy. The authorities' attention had previously been taken up with winning the Civil War. Now this was no longer the case, and time and resources could begin to be devoted to a variety of forms of reconstruction. However, the end of the Civil War and the introduction of NEP had given new strength to other cultural forces, such as figurative painting in the visual arts and a bolstering of more traditional forms (which Trotskii called "Classicism") in literature. The "Bolsheviks of art" needed a platform in order to redress the balance which under NEP seemed to be tilting away from them. Thus it seems that internal and external dynamics came together at the beginning of 1923: respectively, the need to articulate a coherent and believable redescription of the left perspective for a *"communist art* (as part of com-culture and communism in general!)" and a context which offered some hope for that argument finding a resonance. There is no point in dropping pennies down a well; conversely, one does not print five thousand copies of a magazine intended to influence only one's friends. Whatever it was that made the project of a Left Front of the Arts sustainable in 1923 clearly ebbed during 1924 and faded out altogether in early 1925. And there is no question of this being mere exhaustion on the part of Lef's members. Rodchenko and Maiakovskii continued their advertising work for the state stores and organizations. Both flung themselves into work for the *Exposition internationale des arts décoratifs et industriels modernes* (*International Exhibition of Contemporary Decorative and Industrial Art*) in Paris. Rodchenko's reading room for a workers' club clearly embodied Constructivist-leftist principles, and Maiakovskii commissioned a new model of the *Monument to the Third International* from Tatlin—which Tatlin built in record time. It may be that there seemed to be more scope for an impact internationally than domestically, given what the Soviet cultural situation had become by 1925—with the added insurance policy that work celebrated abroad would be less susceptible to suppression at home.

At the end of 1926, Benjamin noted how the regime was "above all trying to bring about a suspension of militant communism, to usher in a period free of class conflict, to depoliticize the life of its citizens as much as possible"; "an attempt," he wrote, "is being made to arrest the dynamic of revolutionary progress in the life of the state."[75] This is not, of course, to say that everything was now lost. In a way, that is precisely the point: the situation was still contested. For all his registration of the changes taking place under NEP to the detriment of the left in both culture and politics, Benjamin was also able to appreciate the vitality which was still present in Soviet society: "Life here [is] so extraordinarily meaningful." He goes on: "The entire scheme of existence of the Western European intelligentsia is utterly impoverished in comparison to the countless constellations that offer themselves to an individual here in the space of a month." In a telling image, he likened life in the Soviet Union to conditions in the Klondike gold rush: "It is as insular and as eventful, as impoverished and yet in the same breath as full of possibilities."[76] When he returned to Berlin, he was moved to comment that, with all its civilization, "for someone who has arrived from Moscow, Berlin is a dead city."[77] Given this situation, one should then ask what it was that made *Lef* seem like a viable proposition again in 1927. And, having asked that question, one has to wonder why

New Lef folded again in 1928. What doors opened, and then closed, in 1927 and 1928? For the timing, again, is crucial. As has been noted earlier, Maiakovskii's *New Lef* editorial spoke of the need to restart publication "because the situation of culture in the sphere of art has been completely messed up," and cited the equation of market demand with cultural value as the main problem.[78] Yet there was nothing new in this. Vertov had been slating the "caste of parasites," the "NEP shopkeepers" who "make drunkards of the proletariat using cinema-vodka" since 1923–24—since, in fact, the heyday of the first *Lef*.[79] What gave the spur to publish in January 1927 was that, despite the lack of a periodical, Maiakovskii perceived that "Lef has won and is winning in many sectors of culture."[80] Which is to say, there appeared to be an upturn in the fortunes of the left, a new audience for a reformulation of Lef's position. Once again, Benjamin notes the contradictory currents. On the one side, showing the weakness of the cultural left, is the fact that Grigorii Lelevich, a prominent figure on the proletarian journal *Na postu* (*On Guard*), was being sent away from Moscow at the Party's behest—as we have seen was also the case with political oppositionists. On the other is Benjamin's record of how Lelevich bemoaned the fact that his departure would cause him to miss a major speech to the Comintern by Trotskii, and how he also claimed that "the Party is on the verge of a turnabout."[81]

Things like magazines and organizations do not ebb and flow arbitrarily. Their rise and fall are the function of a complex dialectic of forces, internal and external dynamics whose confluence *is* the organization or the publication. It seems incontrovertibly to be the case that the need for a defined left front in the arts was fueled by a requirement to contest the threatened hegemony of more conservative cultural forces. These forces, in turn, were fueled by NEP. For its part, Lef was related to the ebb and flow of a wider Left Opposition to NEP. As this Left Opposition fought the growing political influence of "the kulak, the Nepman, the bureaucrat," so the left in the cultural field echoed the slogan with a perception of its own opponents as "rightist social strata, the intelligentsia and petty bourgeoisie."[82]

This is not to say that Lef was in any simple sense a cultural "reflection" of the Left Opposition or, indeed, that the latter's broad programs somehow overarched a more specific platform of the left in art. The *Platform of the Opposition,* all ninety-odd pages and twelve chapters, makes no mention whatsoever of art, literature, film, architecture, or culture generally; it is solely a political, socioeconomic document. Organizations of artists and writers, let alone the substantive beliefs they articulate, do not "reflect" political events. Such is not even an adequate statement of much maligned "vulgar" Marxism. Both political parties and cultural groups are superstructural with respect to an underlying economic mode of production. Nonetheless, a variety of shifting responses do occur between different, relatively autonomous spheres. In one of the many discussions among Asja Lacis, Bernhard Reich, and ordinary Russians in the sanatorium where Lacis was undergoing treatment, Benjamin notes almost wearily, "The issue was once again opposition within the Party."[83] The key phrase is "once again": the opposition was clearly a live issue. Not to relate the ebbs and flows of the left in art to the ebbs and flows of a more broadly constituted left, particularly in a situation such as that which prevailed in the Soviet Union during the 1920s, is to strip that cultural milieu of a whole dimension of its identity. One cannot help feeling that the persistent determination to do so has more to do with ideological shibboleths of our own culture than with any faithfulness to the revolutionary avant-garde. The reality of the Russian Revolution still threatens a capitalist system—a system both moral and economic—and the more insistently it can be restricted in scope, rigidified, and made synonymous with the barbarism that supplanted it, the better, from such a point of view. To relate the avant-garde to a site of complex political (and social and moral) contestation is not, however, to reduce it to a reflex of that political struggle. The debates within the left front of the arts, within the various other institutions the cultural left inhabited, far exceeded in sophistication anything the political left ever generated about art, design, literature, or culture as a whole. Nonetheless, by its very nature that political left was alert to the practicalities of the situation in ways which often bypassed the artists, even though, ultimately, they were affected by them.

In terms, then, of the political spectrum of the Revolution and the NEP period, it appears fruitful to relate the erstwhile avant-garde, the left front of the arts, first of all to the ethos of October itself as this was worked out in the immediately postrevolutionary "heroic" phase of War Communism: planning, classlessness, rejection of the past, an almost tabula-rasa-like sense of building the new life from the bottom up, moving from analysis into synthesis. And then to relate it to the emerging perspective of a Left Opposition in which planning and workers' democracy remained priorities in the face of their erosion by the dominant forces of the New Economic Policy. The avant-garde, the left front, is thus related to the Left Opposition. It is so, however, not as a reflection but as kind of relatively autonomous equivalent. To borrow from a slightly different context Buchloh's felicitous rendering, it was its "historically logical aesthetic correlative." That is the claim of this essay: that on at least four grounds the left front of the arts can be read as the cultural correlative of the predominantly Trotskiist Left Opposition: in terms of hostility to NEP; in terms of a commitment to planning; in terms of a requirement for a level of working-class prosperity to consume the goods produced; and in terms of a requirement for industrial democracy to provide an environment in which the artistic-constructor/engineer might function.[84] Circumstantial evidence, such as the penetration of the institutions of higher education by the ideas and organization of the left, and the peaks and troughs of Lef's own activity, appears to support this argument. The alternatives, conversely, are less persuasive: that the avant-garde, even at the moment of October and in its aftermath, was devoid of a coherent political perspective. Or, if it may be said to have had a politics, that this was compatible with NEP.[85] For the reasons given above, neither seems likely. In addition to which, an opposing artistic grouping appears to have flourished under NEP conditions and to have been able relatively to marginalize the left avant-garde during the NEP period.

III

Two principal questions remain concerning the politics of the avant-garde. I will address them in succession. First: If indeed Lef was a kind of correlate to, or at least can be said to have functioned in respect of some productive relationship with, the Left Opposition, why did not the latter embrace it? The relationship among Formalism, Futurism, and Marxism has been the subject of considerable debate, and the usual view is that the "Marxists" disapproved of the first two—of Formalism vehemently, for appearing to sever the link between art and society, and of Futurism for its roots in the bourgeois avant-garde, its impracticality, and its incomprehensibility to ordinary people.

A reconsideration might begin by arguing that the "comprehensibility" issue has been overstated and does not allow sufficiently for developments in the erstwhile avant-garde's position, notably the prominent role played by

montage and factography. There were also nuances to the avant-garde's concession that something valuable was being lost by abandoning "Art" *tout court* to the past. Distinctions emerged quite early between doctrinaire Productivist theorists and the more flexible members of Lef. Rodchenko exasperatedly remarked in an Inkhuk debate of April 1922 that "if we carry on discussing, there will never be any actual work";[86] endless attempts to clarify the theory, that is, would get in the way of what should be quite pragmatic responses to the demands of a changing productive context. Also, in an extraordinary allegory composed in 1925, Lissitzky wrote: "The term A[rt] resembles a chemist's graduated glass. Each age contributes its own quantity: for example, 5 drams of the perfume 'Coty' to tickle the nostrils of the fine gentry. Or another example, 10cc of sulfuric acid to be thrown into the face of the ruling classes. Or, 15cc of some kind of metallic solution that later changes into a new source of light."[87] This seems to be an elliptical proposition of three stages of art: the history of art since the Renaissance, in the service of the ruling class; art as an engaged, combative form of agitation and propaganda during the revolutionary period, against a class system; and, finally, art as a contribution to building the new world, a transforming element. The "metallic solution" may refer to practical design; the "new source of light" is, however, clearly more. As Lissitzky goes on to say: "This A[rt] is an invention of the mind, i.e. a complex, where rationality is fused with imagination."[88] Offering a different inflection to the continuing validity of a notion of art, Maiakovskii granted his famous "amnesty" to Rembrandt and acknowledged that, after all, the Revolution needed a sonnet as well as a newspaper. For his part, Rodchenko seems increasingly to have sought images produced in a modern, "mechanical" way that would jolt conventional perceptions of the world, rather than seeking simply to design new bits of it. Whether this is seen as a "retreat" or a development from a onesided initial position has much to do with the commentator's own perspective on and sympathy for the problems of a revolutionary art. The October group, formed as an umbrella organization for left artists in 1928, and as such one of the last attempts to frame a modified left position, likewise tried to effect a rapprochement between construction and design, on the one hand, and the production of images, on the other.[89]

It is worth recalling in this connection that the status of painting as a possible locale for radical cultural practice remains hotly contested to this day, and that the assumption that it was irrevocably tied to the past was widespread among the cultural left of the period and not confined to the Constructivists. Benjamin's essay of the mid-1930s, "Das Kunstwerk im Zeitalter seiner technischen Reproduzierbarkeit" ("The Work of Art in the Age of Mechanical Reproduction"), is perhaps the locus classicus of the tendency. The aloofness of modern painting—with its rhetoric of an unlearned aesthetic sensitivity, so easily corrupted into apologetics for a social elite—has won it few friends among socialists. Vasilii Kandinskii's collapsing of socialism and historical materialism into the mire of bourgeois materialism and acquisitiveness is only one particularly glaring and uncontrite example. Painting's reactionary affiliations were not merely traceable to the "aura," as Benjamin termed it, in which unique works of art were bathed. The *institution* of avant-garde art was permeated by haut-bourgeois exclusivity and snobbishness—which is, presumably, what led Maiakovskii on his trip to Paris in the midtwenties to liken French artists, with the exception of Fernand Léger, to "slimy oysters." In such a perspective, the readiness of the left avant-garde to search for ways to democratize art, to render it useful to the revolutionary social project, rather than simply to bury it and have done, takes on a rather different aspect.

Turning now to the central issue of the historical confrontation between the avant-garde and the Left Opposition, we can locate its main site in Trotskii's *Literatura i revoliutsiia (Literature and Revolution)*.[90] This study, written mostly in 1923 and published in 1924, is contemporaneous with the first phase of the Left Opposition's ascendancy; as such, it is as close as one is likely to get to an authoritative Left Opposition theory of art. The text, particularly its passages on Tatlin's Tower, has been subject to cavalier quotation and excerpting, designed to prove how intolerant the Party leadership was of the avant-garde, how the walls were closing in even by 1924, and how the course was set for the final "Marxist" closure on free artistic experiment that was realized in the early thirties. In fact, any even moderately receptive reading of Trotskii's full text cannot fail to register its relative openness. Not the least interesting feature of it is that a figure with Trotskii's commitments should, at that period, devote a full-length treatment to this range of questions at all. As for the views he articulates: he is unequivocally critical of theoretical Formalism (not surprising, since it was unequivocally critical of Marxism), regarding it as a species of Idealism. However, in the spectrum of artistic tendencies reviewed, from aesthetically conservative positions, Symbolism, and the literary "fellow travelers" through advocates of a distinctive "proletarian culture," Trotskii repeatedly gives the benefit of the doubt, and indeed a kind of priority, to the Futurist-Lef nexus. What he will not do is accede to demands that the Party recognize any particular grouping, Lef included, as the authentic voice of Communist art. For Trotskii, socialist, let alone Communist, culture lies in the future. The shape it will take will be derived from a classless society that does not yet exist. In the period of the "proletarian dictatorship," the main criterion to be applied when judging a work of art is the extent to which it helps in the future realization of such a culture. When weighed in these scales, Lef, though found ultimately wanting by Trotskii, nonetheless comes out fairly well.

It has to be remembered that Trotskii was not an art critic and, at this date, was not overly familiar with the products of the European avant-garde, having had other things on his mind for most of the preceding two decades since the "dress rehearsal" of 1905. Given the unfamiliarity of that avant-garde's devices and the threat these must have posed to a consciousness raised on the norms of Enlightenment/classical culture, it is Trotskii's bias in favor of toleration rather than dismissiveness that deserves our attention. His relative openness to Modernist technical devices is marked—compared, for example, to Lukács's positions developed in the later twenties and thirties. Where Trotskii undoubtedly struggles is with post-Cubist techniques, broadly speaking, of collage-montage and construction. The most sustained discussions he offers in this respect are of Maiakovskii's "150,000,000" and Tatlin's *Monument to the Third International*. What is quite clear is that the "flatness" involved in post-Cubist work, literary as well as visual, its relative "all-overness," such that conventional compositional dramatics and focuses are denied, its suspension of narrative developments and climaxes, the abrupt shifts it employs rather than orthodox modulations, violated Trotskii's canon of judgment: "The principal fault of futurist poetry even in its best examples, lies in the absence of a sense of measure . . . [Maiakovskii's images] quite often disintegrate the whole and paralyze the action . . . the whole piece has no climax . . . The parts refuse to obey the whole. Each part tries to be separate," and so on.[91] Trotskii's weak arguments about function in his treatment of Tatlin's Tower are little more than the sculptural equivalent of his difficulties before Maiakovskii's

poem or, indeed, a painting. "What is it for" replaces "what does it represent" as the *cri de coeur* of one whose categories are being brought into question without his having the resources adequately to reply. As ever, the response is to deploy the criteria of the previously accepted paradigm as natural, indexed—according to the author's political disposition—to "competence" or to "popularity."

There is nothing unusual about this kind of critical difficulty, it is one of the effects of specialization in modern culture. (It is interesting that Trotskii adopts approximately the same kind of suspended judgment, underwritten by a fundamental concern for the security of the Revolution, for contemporary scientific developments.) Few enough could, in the early 1920s, write with understanding about Cubist devices. What Trotskii does is to try to rescue the impetus of the work, of which he approves, for a kind of traditional humanism from whose refusal as the stock-in-trade of normative art that "impetus," paradoxically, is derived. Little enough of this was clear at the time. For all his condemnation of "pure" Formalism in 1923–24, it is an intriguing question what Trotskii would have made, given his relative openness to and curiosity about avant-garde art, of the "social Formalism" of Mikhail Bakhtin, Pavel Medvedev, and Voloshinov which emerged in the mid- and late 1920s. This is one of those conjunctions, however, which the history of the twentieth century remaindered before it had chance to be born. As it is, Trotskii's somewhat rotund categories failed to mesh fully with the avant-garde work which came under his review. This is not, however, to place his arguments in a presumed continuum of suppression, an assertion which his status as leader of the political opposition to that "continuum" would contradict. Notwithstanding his critical difficulties with Futurism, some the result of relative ignorance, some fruitful and generative, Trotskii's overall assessment is clear: "Though remaining, in some respects, a Bohemian revolutionary offshoot of the old art, futurism contributes to a greater degree and more directly and actively than all other tendencies, in forming the new art."[92]

Trotskii's text, though authoritative, is not, however, the only one we have which sheds light on the attitude of the political Left Opposition to the avant-garde. Nikolai Gorlov, a prerevolutionary Old Bolshevik, allied in the early 1920s with Trotskii, wrote a reply to him, as well as a pamphlet running to sixty pages and entitled *Futurizm i revoliutsiia (Futurism and Revolution)*.[93] Both were published in 1924, the former in *Lef*. In the words of the editor of a 1975 French compendium, Gorlov's pamphlet "represents an exemplary attempt (albeit an isolated one on the part of a politician)" to clarify the relation between artistic issues and "the new economic and social structures born of the revolution."[94] Gorlov is more perspicacious than Trotskii about the relations of existing art with bourgeois society. In particular, his technical grasp of the avant-garde's innovations exceeds Trotskii's, resulting in prolonged textual analysis of Maiakovskii's poetry based on the claim that "Futurism has emancipated the word."[95] He goes on: "It is time to understand that form and content are one, that the new content will inevitably be cramped in the old form, and that the old form has become for us a barrel organ on which you can play nothing but 'Farewell.'"[96] In Gorlov's compelling image, the left avant-garde, Futurism, constituted "the red army of words."[97]

This is not, of course, to imply that political supporters of the Left Opposition would necessarily be sympathetic to left art. There just is not such a symmetry between politics and aesthetics, then or now. Nonetheless, in the two examples we have of discussions of avant-garde art by Left Opposition figures there is no out-and-out rejection of the avant-garde.

Rather, the converse: there are the beginnings of what could have been a constructive dialogue with it. It is perhaps not irrelevant that Trotskii was to form a more explicit alliance with the leading representative of another left avant-garde over a decade later. André Breton's trajectory may shed an oblique light on what was not possible for the Soviet avant-garde.

IV

The second of the two concluding questions concerns the relationship of the left avant-garde to Stalinism. Of all questions, this is the most insistent at the present time, and is likely to continue to be so as Stalinist culture is opened up to scrutiny. The manner in which conservative accounts are already beginning to elide the differences between the two has been noted above. This dynamic in the scholarship of the present period sharply points up the need for the accurate historical positioning of the avant-garde, not least to recover and sustain its examples for radical positions in the present—positions which are likely to find themselves more rather than less beleaguered amid the liberal triumphs of any "new world order" than heretofore. In a study of Klutsis, Margarita Tupitsyn has recently described this issue as the big "off-limits" question.[98] Likewise, Bois's attention was inescapably drawn to it with regard to Lissitzky, where the question of continuity between the different phases of his career becomes urgent. Bois's answer was to claim significant *dis*continuity: "I therefore propose the following thesis: there is indeed a schism between . . . the 'Brechtian' Lissitzky and the 'Stalinist' Lissitzky."[99] Bois saw this "schism," furthermore, not as one between a formally pure avant-garde and an instrumentalist view of art but, importantly, as one "between two ways of conceiving the relations between art and ideology." I believe that Bois is substantially correct in his suggestive analysis of the way in which technical radicalism can, and was intended to, function not purely aesthetically but as "a radical critique of the social order."[100] His essential point is that Lissitzky was at first able to sustain a radical suspension of alternatives, to destabilize the spectator's spatial assumptions—as analogues for social assumptions—without replacing them with readymade solutions; but that, as the dictatorship grew in power, it overwhelmed this fragile possibility and inserted its own new/old closures into the sphere of graphic and ideological work alike. "As long as Lissitzky kept the utopian force of his (political) desire," the radical project was sustainable; but "as soon as the circumstances closed off his utopian impulse," he was faced with no possibilities other than silence or service.[101]

The foregoing discussion of the Left Opposition may have deepened understanding of the context which helped the avant-garde to sustain the transformative force of its political desire. In similar vein, it may help to know the precise nature of the "circumstances" which finally "closed off" this impulse—not least because such knowledge may suggest why, for some at least, service won out over silence. This is always, one suspects, going to be puzzling to those of a liberal cast of mind: how can avant-garde artists bring themselves to serve a totalitarian dictatorship? The answer can only be coercion! Conversely, to conservatives, that service confirms the iniquity of those who lend their support to violent revolution in the first place.

The preceding account can shed some light on this "inexplicable" transformation by once again situating the left front in art in terms of a wider left in the Soviet political process of the 1920s. The paradox is that the final defeat of the Left Opposition at the end of 1927 quickly seemed to be reversed as the policies of the left apparently rose phoenixlike from the ashes of opposition to become the Party leadership's new official position. There is insufficient space here to dwell on this shift, but, in brief, what happened was twofold. Although some Trotskiists and in particular Trotskii himself remained opposed to the Stalinist bureaucracy—and were cast into outer darkness for it—others, and in addition those behind Zinov'ev, quickly turned around and sought readmission to the fold. Simultaneously with these political shifts, the economic contradictions of NEP finally came to a head. Some of the flavor of the situation comes out in a memorandum from Maksim Litvinov to Russian diplomatic representatives abroad, dated February 9, 1928: "In the last few days the economic situation, contrary to earlier expectations, has deteriorated sharply. Serious breakdowns in supply have already occurred on the food market which will probably force the workers' and peasants' government to start rationing the most important food items within the next few days . . . The situation is to be regarded as extremely serious . . . I repeat once again that the workers' and peasants' government is seriously concerned about the future course of events."[102] Crisis in the countryside was matched by crisis in the cities. Major food shortages forced people onto the private market where prices were higher, which had the effect of producing de facto wage cuts. Consequently, strikes broke out. Added to this, old machinery in the factories was wearing out anyway under the drive to increase production, with the result that the condition of workers deteriorated. The circumstances of those who were unemployed was worse. The result was that "alcoholism, prostitution, 'hooliganism' and crime assumed frightening dimensions, amounting to a veritable social disaster."[103] The leadership's response was to revert to the "extraordinary measures" of War Communism, which in this case essentially amounted to a war on the peasantry in the form of the forced extraction of food for the cities. This process involved the leadership around Stalin turning on its erstwhile NEP ally, Bukharin, who now assumed leadership of a short-lived Right Opposition dedicated to preserving NEP and the system of supports for the peasant. This turn against the right, and against NEP, and the rapid resumption of a rhetoric, if not yet a reality, of planned intervention in the economy—which then led quickly to the adoption of the Five-Year Plan proper and, concomitantly, to a renewed emphasis on industry rather than agriculture, i.e., on the worker rather than the peasant—conspired to convey an impression to only too willing oppositionists that the Party had finally seen the light and adopted the program of the left.

This impression was strengthened by a dramatic increase in propaganda against the new "right deviation," as well as, once again, the pronouncement of a new line in the International. This referred to a "third period," a period of new class antagonisms following on the period of stabilization to which NEP had been a response. The "third period" constituted a lurch to ultraleftism, an assertion of "class against class," according to which, for example, social democrats became, rather than potential allies of Communists against capital, class enemies indistinguishable from Fascists as upholders of international capitalism. The rhetorical madhouse which the international Communist movement became—wherein that movement was effectively reduced to a tool of Russian foreign policy—was accompanied both in the Soviet Union and abroad by a renewed emphasis on "proletarianism."

Many erstwhile Left Oppositionists now became the staunchest defenders of the new "left" turn—of militant proletarianism and, in particular, of the Five-Year Plan. That this allegedly left turn had nothing to do with either Bolshevik internationalism—its basis, after all, was the slogan of "socialism in one country"—or with improved conditions *for* the workers, escaped notice in the welter of propaganda in an increasingly centralized political system which now lacked any place for dissent. Workers occupied center stage for propaganda. The point was, they had to. They were the ones who were making the sacrifices to build up the new autarkic economy: heroes of propaganda on the one (mythical) hand, victims of "primitive socialist accumulation" on the other (all too real) one. Contrary to appearances at the time, what was happening was far from an implementation of the left's policies in favor of a working-class-based socialist democracy; it was the final defeat of such a vision. Carr in his definitive history of the process speaks of a "counterrevolution." Deutscher calls it Stalin's "second revolution." Reiman refers to "a complex break with the meaning and essence of the social doctrine of socialism."[104] Alex Callinicos sums up the situation: "'Socialist' industrialization in the USSR was made possible not simply by the destruction of the peasantry but by the intense exploitation of the very class which in theory ruled the country and was supposed to be the main beneficiary of the changes involved."[105] Even Trotskii was not completely clear about what was going on. For most people, the wave of propaganda about the "third period," the left turn, and the great leap to build up a workers' state before it was crushed by the imperialists carried all before it. As Stalin put it in 1931: "The pace must not be slackened. We are fifty or a hundred years behind the advanced countries. We must close this gap in ten years. Either we shall do it, or they will crush us."[106] If the left front of the arts was indeed influenced by the fortunes of the Left Opposition, it would not be entirely surprising to find committed avant-gardists throwing their technical expertise behind the institution of the Five-Year Plan.

One of the points which needs to be borne in mind here is the class position of artists and designers, not to mention theorists. They were not proletarians. They would not have experienced the sharp end of the exploitation mounting in the factories and mines. Quite the contrary: the misery in the countryside and the superintensification of productivity in industry would all have been mediated through the terms of the very propaganda campaign whose articulation *was* the site of the contribution of the designers. The chance to participate in the great leap revolved around belief in the official image (unless one wants to postulate mendacity of a degree which seems highly unlikely). A hint of the pressures and adjustments involved comes through in a comment by Lacis to Benjamin shortly before he left the Soviet Union in January 1927. She claims he does not understand what is going on, and tells him how, shortly after her own arrival in Russia, she had wanted to return to Europe, "because everything seemed finished in Russia and the opposition was absolutely correct." What Lacis is at pains to impress upon Benjamin, however, is that *she* had been wrong. Now she understands that things are changing. What is happening is "the conversion of revolutionary effort into technological effort." Now, "revolutionary work does not signify conflict or civil war but rather electrification, canal construction, creation of factories."[107] The ideology of "socialism in one country" and the way it was presented, as if a corner had been turned so that practical work on the new society could begin, seeped into the perspectives even of those who had originally been hostile to the turn events were taking. This is not to say that material circumstances did not count for something. At the very time during the First Five-Year Plan when industrial wages were falling by fifty percent, Stalin incorporated into his program systematic differentials in favor of managers and specialists. It is not unknown, after all, even in our own impeccable institutions of higher enlightenment, for hearts and minds to follow wage packets.

One of the key social roles in any system is that of technician-specialist. The notion in a workers' democracy is that these individuals are controlled by the mass of workers through the organs of that industrial democracy. In a capitalist system, as, indeed, in the bureaucratic system operating by that time in the Soviet Union, their functions are, however, managerial. With the so-called Shakhty trial in 1928, which set the pace for the show trials of the thirties, a scare was unleashed against foreign specialists as "saboteurs." Concomitantly, the need for new "Soviet specialists" was proclaimed. It is probably in this context that it becomes possible to understand Rodchenko's enthusiasm for transferring jurisdiction of Vkhutein from Narkompros—which was now seen as hopelessly generalist and tainted with Anatolii Lunacharskii's old-fashioned liberalism—to Vesenkha, the Council of the National Economy and prime mover in the call for new Soviet experts. This is an instance of the way in which the situation in the late twenties, after all the difficulties experienced by the left under NEP, seemed to offer a new lease on life to the erstwhile avant-garde project of the "artist-constructor." When the first groups of Rodchenko's students graduated from Dermetfak (the combined Woodworking and Metalworking faculties) in 1928 and 1929, this was the context into which they fitted. Commentary on the event in the Constructivist-influenced architectural press enthused that "Until today our industry has had no specific core of specialists working on the rational construction of articles used in everyday life . . . Vkhutein has now begun to turn out specialists of this type."[108]

Given this kind of productive locale, it is unlikely that figures such as Rodchenko and Lissitzky saw through to the problems of the working class at the base of the system. Or, to the extent that they did, it is, conversely, very likely that they believed themselves to be involved in the amelioration of the workers' condition rather than the bolstering of the very system which oppressed them. Thus Lissitzky in his 1930 *An Architecture for World Revolution* explicitly accords to the architect the role of leading emancipatory force for the "new life," given the fact that, left to their own devices, the "masses . . . tend to be shortsighted as far as their own growth is concerned."[109] Without this idealization, both of the role of the architect/designer/engineer and of the nature of the society that was actually being built out of the crash industrialization and forced collectivization of the First Five-Year Plan, how could Lissitzky have written that "in our country the factory has ceased to exist as a place of exploitation and as a hated institution," and continue that, under the Five-Year Plan, "the factory has become the real place of education: the university for new socialist man"?[110] The myth by which they were completely carried away could not have been further from the truth. Quite the reverse of crucibles of socialist education, the factories were increasingly places of exploitation of the working class. No less a figure than Lazar' Kaganovich, one of Stalin's closest collaborators on the Central Committee, argued, somewhat at variance with Lissitzky's claim, that "the earth should tremble when the director walks round the plant."[111]

It is extremely difficult to think oneself into a situation of such contradictions, not that the system inhabited by Western academics today is free of its own. Klutsis, a Latvian as well as an Old Bolshevik—a potentially fatal combination in Stalin's Russia—became one of the most powerful graphic voices of the Five-Year Plans and an honored designer involved in work for international exhibitions. None of this prevented him from being arrested in 1938 and shot in a prison camp amid a purge directed not only against national minorities but, tellingly, against remnants of the Left Opposition (some of whom, with unlikely heroism, had continued to organize in the Gulag). Lissitzky survived. So did Rodchenko, who in 1930 documented the building of the White Sea Canal in characteristically dramatic, formally dynamic, photographs. The White Sea Canal has since been revealed as effectively a mobile forced-labor camp in which tens if not hundreds of thousands died. At the time, along with Magnitogorsk and Dneprostroi, it was one of *the* prestige construction projects. The myth was that previously antisocial elements underwent voluntary socialist reeducation, working to the music of their own orchestras and supervised only by a few benign Interior Ministry police. Western enthusiasts such as Louis Aragon were completely bowled over by the project, and in Aragon's case it was instrumental in confirming his break with Surrealism and Trotskiism and accession to an orthodox Communist position which he sustained for the rest of his life. What did Rodchenko see? What could he have done about it, anyway? It was not easy even to stop working in Stalin's Russia without drawing attention to oneself. And again, there is the question of belief.

This takes us a long way from the question of the artistic left front's relation to a political Left Opposition, and the distance doubtless increases as the 1930s go on. Yet such a range of possibilities, posed most starkly by the alternatives of a retreat into silence or an embrace of the official line, did confront the avant-garde at the end of the 1920s. Even the choice of "silence" was a relative one and depended, in part, on the resources an artist or designer needed in order to carry on practicing. Thus disfavor as experienced by the architect Ivan Leonidov did lead to silence. In Tatlin's case, his eccentricity may be thought to have increased with the *Letatlin* project (1929–32). Thereafter, he withdrew into work for the theater and a private—and apparently occasional—return to painting. Klutsis and Lissitzky, on the contrary, seem to have gone about the propaganda task with some enthusiasm. Rodchenko's work appears to have split into "official" graphic design, on the one hand, and his private, melancholy circus paintings, on the other. This resumption of the two wings of bourgeois "fine" and "applied" art stands as fair testimony to the failure of the project of the synthesizer, the artist-constructor, building the new society from a wholly original and specific practical position.[112] The most catastrophic and implacable recognition of that failure was Maiakovskii's. Just days before his suicide in 1930, he used the metonym of a candy wrapper to show how everything had gone wrong. Futurists had fought against Classicism, against the cultural values of bourgeois society. In this spirit, Maiakovskii himself and Rodchenko had worked for Mossel'prom and other state enterprises in an attempt to make new values fundamental to the daily life of the socialist society. Yet even in 1924, that daily life was unregenerated, sustained by the conditions of an economic policy which was allowing, even inviting, the old back in. The revival of the opposition in 1926–27 gave a glimmer of hope—sufficient, at least, to restart *Lef.* The apparent belated recognition of the left's policies by the leadership, and the formulation of the Five-Year Plans, carried many along with it. This conjunction stimulated the formation of the October group. Maiakovskii even tried once again to draw closer to proletarianism by seeking membership in RAPP (the Russian Association of Proletarian Writers), this time to little avail. By 1930, Maiakovskii saw that all had been a mirage. What had happened was not the belated resumption of the values of the left but the final emplacement of a social formation which would bury the left and its revolution for generations. At this moment, in a meeting, as a gesture of friendship, a woman gave Maiakovskii a candy, with a Mossel'prom label on one side and a picture of the Venus de Milo on the other.

The ridiculous little item was like a condenser for everything that had gone wrong: the "twenty years of work," as

well as the October Revolution, which had given that work practical focus, taken it out of the realm of the avant-garde cenacle, and appeared to offer it a world to work with. Maiakovskii's recognition was bleak: "So, the thing you've been fighting against for twenty years has now won."[113] His conclusion had a remorseless logic, matched perhaps only by Benjamin's later strictures about the need for the radical Communist intellectual to "denature" his work if necessary, to render it useless to all rather than usable by the enemy.[114] Maiakovskii was, in fact, used by his enemy when canonized as poet of the Revolution by Stalin in the mid-1930s in a grotesque about-face. Even Boris Pasternak, no friend of the Revolution, commented that this was Maiakovskii's second death, one for which he was not responsible. Not everyone was possessed of Maiakovskii's insight. The ideological power of the dictatorship was colossal. And the Five-Year Plans were, seemingly, successful: the Soviet Union built while the capitalist world largely stagnated. Designers had an important place, and were presumably gratified to serve what Lissitzky in 1930 still saw as the development of "a Socialistic society."[115] No one who has not taken up an oppositional position against the weight of a society's dominant readings should feel legitimated to criticize Rodchenko, Lissitzky, Klutsis, and others who designed for Stalin in the 1930s, particularly after Fascism became the main enemy. It was, though, a long way from October: closer, one might say, to the Berlin Wall than to Tatlin's Tower, both monuments in their own ways to Communism and what became of it. Now that the Wall has come down, international socialism may mean something again. Whether it does so or not is an open, yet concrete question: "open" as the Tower, "concrete" as the Wall; and as real as the relation of art and politics.

Notes

I would like to thank Steve Edwards for encouraging me to complete this essay, and my editor Jane Bobko for her invaluable contribution to improving the manuscript.

Lenin's remark in the epigraph was made in Zurich during the First World War in conversation with a young Romanian Dadaist, Marcu. Quoted in Robert Motherwell, ed., *The Dada Painters and Poets* (New York: Wittenborn Schultz, 1951), p. xviii.

1. John Bowlt, "The Old New Wave," *New York Review of Books,* February 16, 1984, p. 28.

2. Vladimir Maiakovskii, letter to Nikolai Chuzhak, January 23, 1923, quoted in Wiktor Woroszylski, *The Life of Mayakovsky,* trans. Boleslaw Taborski (London: Gollancz, 1972), p. 315. Woroszylski's "biography" consists of a collage of quotations from the writings of Maiakovskii and his contemporaries.

3. Andrei Nakov, "Stylistic Changes—Painting Without a Referent," trans. Susan Spund, in David Elliott, ed., *Alexander Rodchenko,* catalogue for exhibition organized by the Museum of Modern Art, Oxford (Oxford: Museum of Modern Art, 1979), pp. 56–57.

4. Vassily Rakitin, "The Avant-Garde and the Art of the Stalinist Era," in Hans Gunther, ed., *The Culture of the Stalin Period* (London: Macmillan, 1990), p. 185.

5. El Lissitzky, "Proun Space," in *An Architecture for World Revolution,* trans. Eric Dluhosch (London: Lund Humphries, 1970), p. 138.

6. El Lissitzky, "Basic Premises," in *Architecture for World Revolution,* p. 27.

7. Sophie Lissitzky-Küppers, *El Lissitzky: Life, Letters, Texts,* trans. Helene Aldwinckle and Mary Whittall (London: Thames and Hudson, 1968), p. 58.

8. Rakitin, "Avant-Garde and Art," p. 186.

9. Yve-Alain Bois, "El Lissitzky: Radical Reversibility," *Art in America,* April 1988, pp. 161–81.

10. Christina Lodder, *Russian Constructivism* (London and New Haven: Yale University Press, 1983), p. 2.

11. Ibid., p. 140.

12. Ibid., p. 145.

13. Benjamin H. D. Buchloh, "From Faktura to Factography," *October* 30 (Fall 1984), pp. 82–119.

14. Francis Fukuyama, "The End of History?" *The National Interest* 16 (Summer 1989), pp. 3–18.

15. See Boris Groys, "The Birth of Socialist Realism from the Spirit of the Russian Avant-Garde," in *Culture of the Stalin Period,* pp. 122–47, and Igor Golomstock, *Totalitarian Art: In the Soviet Union, the Third Reich, Fascist Italy and the People's Republic of China,* trans. Robert Chandler (London: Collins Harvill, 1990). All quotations that follow are from these two works. On Golomstock, see also Paul Wood, "The Retreat from Moscow," *Artscribe* 88 (September 1991), pp. 48–53.

16. Bois, "El Lissitzky," p. 175.

17. Lenin, in July 1918, quoted in Duncan Hallas, *The Comintern* (London: Bookmarks, 1985), p. 7.

18. E. H. Carr, *Foundations of a Planned Economy, 1926–1929,* vol. 3, pt. 3 (London: Macmillan, 1978), p. 1018.

19. Victor Serge, quoted in Peter Sedgewick, introduction to *Memoirs of a Revolutionary, 1901–1941,* by Victor Serge (Oxford: Oxford University Press, 1967), pp. xv–xvi. The passage is quoted again in Alex Callinicos, *The Revenge of History* (Cambridge: Polity, 1991), p. 25. The opening chapters of this book contain further arguments for the discontinuity of Bolshevik Marxism and Stalinism.

20. A partial exception here is the work of Sheila Fitzpatrick: *The Commissariat of Enlightenment* (Cambridge: Cambridge University Press, 1970); *Education and Social Mobility in the Soviet Union, 1921–1934* (Cambridge: Cambridge University Press, 1979); and Fitzpatrick, ed., *Cultural Revolution in Russia, 1928–1931* (Bloomington, Ind.: Indiana University Press, 1978).

21. Isaac Deutscher, *The Prophet Unarmed: Trotsky, 1921–1929* (Oxford: Oxford University Press, 1959), p. 93.

22. E. H. Carr, *The Russian Revolution from Lenin to Stalin, 1917–1929* (London: Macmillan, 1979), p. 34.

23. On this shift, see Paul Wood, "Art and Politics in a Workers State," *Art History* 8, no. 1 (March 1985), pp. 105–24.

24. Vladimir Maiakovskii, quoted in Woroszylski, *Mayakovsky,* pp. 185-86.

25. In this connection, a word of caution is in order for those who leap to condemn Osip Brik for his probable involvement at this time with the Cheka. Whatever the state security organs later became, it was at that time a privilege to defend the Revolution against its enemies on a "front" which paralleled the actual fighting front of the Red Army. Feliks Dzerzhinskii himself is described by Deutscher (*Prophet Unarmed,* p. 85) as "incorruptible, selfless and intrepid," a complex figure who existed in permanent tension between the sordid demands of the Extraordinary Commission for the Struggle against a Counterrevolution and a "lofty idealism," which made him in his comrades' eyes a Savonarola of the Revolution. A similar austerity seems to have characterized Brik.

26. Michael Reiman, *The Birth of Stalinism: The U.S.S.R. on the Eve of the "Second Revolution,"* trans. George Saunders (London: I. B. Tauris, 1987).

27. *Kino-Eye: The Writings of Dziga Vertov,* ed. Annette Michelson, trans. Kevin O'Brien (London: Pluto, 1984), p. 73.

28. Walter Benjamin, *Moscow Diary,* ed. Gary Smith, trans. Richard Sieburth, *October* 35 (Winter 1985), p. 44.

29. David Elliott, introduction to Elliott, *Alexander Rodchenko,* p. 6.

30. Varvara Stepanova, "Photomontage," in Elliott, *Alexander Rodchenko,* p. 93.

31. Osip Brik, "Into Production," in Elliott, *Alexander Rodchenko,* pp. 90–91, 130–31. See also Osip Brik, "Mayakovsky and the Literary Movements of 1917–1930," in "Osip Brik: Selected Writings Presented by Maria Enzensberger," *Screen* 15, no. 3 (Autumn 1974), pp. 35–118. See especially p. 69. I also discuss this point in my "Art and Politics in a Workers State." See especially pp. 114–15.

32. *Kino-Eye,* p. 13.

33. Ibid., p. 32.

34. Viktor Shklovskii, quoted in Woroszylski, *Mayakovsky,* p. 312.

35. Victor Serge, *From Lenin to Stalin,* trans. Ralph Manheim (New York: Monad Press, 1973), pp. 39–40.

36. George Orwell, *Homage to Catalonia* (London: Penguin, 1977), p. 9.

37. K. Miklashevskii, "Hypertrophy in Art," quoted in Larissa Zhadova, ed., *Tatlin,* trans. Paul Filotas et al. (London: Thames and Hudson, 1988), p. 137 n. 35.

38. Vladimir Maiakovskii, quoted in Woroszylski, *Mayakovsky,* p. 415.

39. Serge, *From Lenin to Stalin,* pp. 57–58.

40. S. O. Khan-Magomedov, *Rodchenko: The Complete Work,* ed. Vieri Quilici, trans. Huw Evans (London: Thames and Hudson, 1986), p. 99.

41. Osip Brik, quoted ibid., p. 171.

42. Vladimir Tatlin, quoted in Zhadova, *Tatlin,* p. 143.

43. Vladimir Tatlin, quoted ibid., p. 268.

44. Benjamin, *Moscow Diary,* p. 11.

45. Serge, *From Lenin to Stalin,* p. 40.

46. Nikolai Aseev, quoted in Woroszylski, *Mayakovsky,* p. 299.

47. Alexei Gan, "On the programme and work plan of the group of Constructivists," quoted in Khan-Magomedov, *Rodchenko,* p. 92 n. 14.

48. Vladimir Tatlin, quoted in Zhadova, *Tatlin,* p. 252.

49. S. Tretyakov, "We Raise the Alarm," in "Documents from *Novy Lef,*" ed. and trans. Ben Brewster, *Screen* 12, no. 4 (Winter 1971–72), pp. 60ff.

50. Khan-Magomedov, *Rodchenko,* p. 146.

51. See Paul Wood, "Realisms and Realities," in *Modern Art: Practices and Debates,* book 3, forthcoming.

52. Deutscher, *Prophet Unarmed,* p. 41.

53. Lev Trotskii, speech to the Twelfth Party Congress, April 20, 1923, quoted ibid., p. 100.

54. Leon Trotsky, "Toward Capitalism or Socialism?" in *The Challenge of the Left Opposition,* ed. Naomi Allen, vol. 1 (New York: Pathfinder Press, 1975), p. 322.

55. Tatlin's old rival, Malevich (at this time director of Ginkhuk), added his voice to the criticism of Tatlin's way of running his department.

56. Vladimir Tatlin, "Report of the Section for Material Culture's Work for 1923–1924" and "Report of the Section for Material Culture's Research Work for 1924," in Zhadova, *Tatlin,* pp. 254–57.

57. Editorial in *Sovremennaia arkhitektura* 5–6 (1926), quoted in Khan-Magomedov, *Rodchenko,* p. 207.

58. Vladimir Maiakovskii, statement in discussion on Futurism with Proletkul't, 1923, quoted in Woroszylski, *Mayakovsky,* p. 317.

59. Deutscher, *Prophet Unarmed,* p. 100.

60. Naomi Allen, introduction to *Challenge of the Left Opposition,* vol. 1, p. 35.

61. Fitzpatrick, *Education and Social Mobility,* p. 3.

62. Ibid., p. 95.

63. Ibid., p. 96.

64. Ibid., p. 100.

65. Leon Trotsky, *The Lessons of October,* in *Challenge of the Left Opposition,* vol. 1, pp. 199–200.

66. Lenin, quoted in Irving Howe, *Trotsky* (London: Fontana, 1978), p. 79.

67. Allen, introduction to *Challenge of the Left Opposition,* vol. 1, p. 29.

68. Reiman, *Birth of Stalinism,* p. 19.

69. Fitzpatrick, *Education and Social Mobility,* p. 103.

70. Reiman, *Birth of Stalinism,* pp. 23–24.

71. *The Platform of the Opposition,* in Leon Trotsky, *The Challenge of the Left Opposition,* ed. Naomi Allen and George Saunders, vol. 2 (New York: Pathfinder Press, 1980), pp. 302–3.

72. Reiman, *Birth of Stalinism,* p. 32.

73. Ibid., p. 35.

74. Osip Brik, quoted in Woroszylski, *Mayakovsky,* pp. 311–12.

75. Benjamin, *Moscow Diary,* p. 53.

76. Ibid., p. 72.

77. Ibid., p. 112.

78. Vladimir Maiakovskii, quoted in Woroszylski, *Mayakovsky,* p. 415.

79. *Kino-Eye,* p. 48.

80. Vladimir Maiakovskii, quoted in Woroszylski, *Mayakovsky,* p. 415.

81. Benjamin, *Moscow Diary,* p. 15.

82. "Declaration of the Constructivists," in "Documents from *Lef,*" ed. and trans. Richard Sherwood, *Screen* 12, no. 4 (Winter 1971–72), pp. 25–58.

83. Benjamin, *Moscow Diary,* p. 60.

84. This aspect is discussed further in Wood, "Art and Politics in a Workers State."

85. This is an area fraught with difficulty. Annette Michelson, in her introduction to *Kino-Eye,* cites Karl Radek's 1931 criticism of Vertov's *Entuziazm* (*Symphony of the Donbass*). Radek had been an oppositionist who, since 1928, had thrown in his lot with the Stalinist bureaucracy. For Michelson, this conservative political turn, which constitutes "the place and position from which he was speaking," makes it "hardly an accident" that Radek was driven to dismiss Vertov's work (*Kino-Eye,* p. lviii). The case of Bukharin is interesting and arguably more complex. He is generally acknowledged to have been, along with Trotskii and Lunacharskii, one of the main Bolshevik figures who evinced an interest in and a sophisticated understanding of artistic developments. Yet Bukharin became an ally of Stalin's in promoting NEP from its outset; in the later 1920s, after the defeat of Trotskii, he was the figurehead of the Right Opposition on whom Stalin next turned. Initially, however, before the emergence of the splits under NEP, Bukharin had indeed been perceived as a leader of the left of the Party. There would be far-reaching implications for an argument that claimed that the ultimate failure of his peasant-oriented road to socialism found some prefiguration in a split between his aesthetics and his politics. Whereas in the case of the Left Opposition and Lef, although that relation is never fully articulated (to the detriment, it must be said, of the political project no less than the artistic one), a passage remained open: a passage through which there have moved such tensioned figures as Benjamin and Bertolt Brecht and

their descendants in the postwar period who have attempted to resist both the complete sundering and the complete implosion of art and politics.

86. Aleksandr Rodchenko, quoted in Khan-Magomedov, *Rodchenko,* p. 115.

87. El Lissitzky, "A. and Pangeometry," in *Architecture for World Revolution,* p. 142.

88. Ibid.

89. A brief discussion of October's significance is offered in Wood, "Realisms and Realities."

90. Leon Trotsky, *Literature and Revolution,* trans. Rose Strunsky (London: RedWords, 1991).

91. Ibid., pp. 181–82.

92. Ibid., p. 50.

93. Nicholas Gorlov, "On Futurisms and Futurism: Concerning Comrade Trotsky's Article" and *Futurism and Revolution,* in *The Futurists, The Formalists, and the Marxist Critique,* ed. Christopher Pike, trans. Christopher Pike and Joe Andrew (London: Ink Links, 1979), pp. 169–80 and 181–242, respectively.

94. Gérard Conio, preface to Section 3 of Pike, *Futurists,* p. 162.

95. Gorlov, *Futurism and Revolution,* in Pike, *Futurists,* p. 211.

96. Ibid., p. 199.

97. Ibid., p. 211.

98. Margarita Tupitsyn, "Gustav Klutsis: Between Art and Politics," *Art in America,* January 1991, pp. 41–47.

99. Bois, "El Lissitzky," p. 167.

100. Ibid., p. 168.

101. Ibid., p. 175.

102. M. M. Litvinov, Deputy People's Commissar of Foreign Affairs, memorandum to diplomatic representatives of the USSR, February 9, 1928, reprinted in Reiman, *Birth of Stalinism,* pp. 138–42.

103. Reiman, *Birth of Stalinism,* p. 55.

104. Ibid., p. 86.

105. Callinicos, *Revenge of History,* p. 32.

106. Stalin, quoted in Hallas, *The Comintern,* p. 123.

107. Benjamin, *Moscow Diary,* p. 82.

108. *Sovremennaia arkhitektura* 3 (1929), quoted in Khan-Magomedov, *Rodchenko,* pp. 212–13 n. 48.

109. El Lissitzky, "The Club as a Social Force," in *Architecture for World Revolution,* p. 44.

110. Ibid., p. 57.

111. Lazar' Kaganovich, quoted in Callinicos, *Revenge of History,* p. 35.

112. I have not been able fully to address the relations of Malevich's work to the political perspective explored in this essay. Although it is, of course, distinct from Constructivism, I see no reason to suspect that his work radically violates the view presented here, at least for the greater part of the period investigated. His later work, however, does appear to pose specific problems. The prevailing tendency has been to dismiss his return to figuration as an oddity or a capitulation to the burgeoning forces of Social(ist) Realism. Major exhibitions such as that at the Stedelijk Museum in 1989 have now surely buried this argument. I address the works briefly in my "Realisms and Realities"; so, too, does Charles Harrison in his "Abstraction," in *Modern Art: Practices and Debates,* book 2, forthcoming. In political terms, a question remains: what did it mean that Malevich turned again to depictions of peasant life at precisely the time of the forced collectivization of agriculture and the "liquidation of the kulaks as a class," as Stalinist rhetoric chillingly has it? Whatever the answer to this question, a recently published letter of April 8, 1932, from Malevich to Vsevolod Meierkhol'd makes clear that for him the return to figuration was not a break with the Revolution but a way of safeguarding it and preventing the return of Classicism and Naturalism:

Painting has turned back from the non-objective way to the object, and the development of painting has returned to the figurative part of the way that had led to the destruction of the object. But on the way back, painting came across a new object that the proletarian revolution had brought to the fore and which had to be given form, which means that it had to be raised to the level of a work of art . . . I am utterly convinced that if you keep to the way of Constructivism, where you are now firmly stuck, which raises not one artistic issue except for pure utilitarianism and in theatre simple agitation, which may be one hundred per cent consistent ideologically but is completely castrated as regards artistic problems, and forfeits half its value. If you go on as you are . . . then Stanislavski will emerge as the winner in the theatre and the old forms will survive. And as to architecture, if the architects do not produce artistic architecture, the Greco-Roman style of Zyeltovski will prevail, together with the Repin style in painting (Kazimir Malevich, "Two Letters to Meyerhold," Kunst & Museumjournaal 6 {1990}, pp. 9–10).

113. Vladimir Maiakovskii, quoted in Christopher Pike, introduction to *Futurists,* p. 19.

114. Walter Benjamin, letter to Gershom Scholem, April 17, 1931, in Gershom Scholem, *Walter Benjamin: The Story of a Friendship,* trans. Harry Zohn (London: Faber, 1982), pp. 231–33.

115. El Lissitzky, "Housing Communes," in *Architecture for World Revolution,* p. 42.

The Artisan and the Prophet: Marginal Notes on Two Artistic Careers

Vasilii Rakitin

Which is worth more: wind or stone?
They're both priceless.
    —*Aleksei Kruchenykh and Velimir Khlebnikov*

The epic literatures of many peoples, in both East and West, feature sagas in which two heroes, equal in prowess, are pitted against each other. Valiant warriors on both sides watch their duel with bated breath . . .

The first of two events that determined the fate of art for a long time to come—and not just in Russia but in many other countries—took place in Moscow in the spring of 1914:

Dear Sirs,
    On the 10th, 11th, 12th, 13th, and 14th of May this year the studio of Vladimir Tatlin (37 Ostozhenka, apartment 3) will be open from 6 to 8 P.M. for a free viewing of his SYNTHETIC-STATIC *compositions. In addition, at seven o'clock on the aforementioned days, the Futurist Sergei Podgaevskii will dynamically declaim his latest poetic transrational records.*[1]

A hand-lettered placard mounted above the entrance to the apartment proclaimed: BEHOLD THE TRICK!

Podgaevskii could not simply read his verses—he had to "dynamically declaim" them. And they were not even verses, either, but "poetic transrational records." The choice of words is indicative of a change of mood in Moscow artistic circles, of a gravitation toward the transrational and the alogical. Toward Dada in place of Futurism.

Tatlin used metallic netting and smoked glass in one of the compositions on display, which people claimed was a depiction of a "tearoom at night."[2] They were, however, hard pressed to say what was represented in the other "synthetic-static" works, which had been hung alongside Tatlin's beautiful and perfectly legible set and costume designs for Mikhail Glinka's opera *Zhizn' za tsaria* (*A Life for the Czar*, 1836). (The 1913–14 Mir iskusstva [World of Art] exhibitions at which these designs had been displayed[3] coincided with celebrations in Moscow and St. Petersburg of the tricentenary of the Romanov dynasty—celebrations which were themselves operatic in their grandeur.)[4] Observers today wish to see a connection between Tatlin's *Les* (*Forest,* 1913) design for Glinka's opera and his first reliefs. But the break between them is obvious. There is no smooth transition. Tatlin took not a step but a leap into the unknown.

Nonetheless, Tatlin, with childlike cunning, continued to try to convince the public that there was no particular difference between his new work and old—although he did fear he would not be believed. In December 1914, he was invited to contribute as a member of World of Art to the *Khudozhniki Moskvy—zhertvam voiny* (*Artists of Moscow for the Victims of the War*) exhibition, where again he showed his designs for *A Life for the Czar.* Yet two or three hours prior to the opening, he arrived with his *Zhivopisnyi rel'ef* (*Painterly Relief,* 1914)—a composition of wire, iron, cardboard, and enamel on board—and proceeded to hang it as if that were nothing out of the ordinary. The organizers endeavored to remove the relief from the exhibition—such an eccentric prank, such an aesthetic curiosity, did not suit a flag-waving, patriotic exhibition! Thanks, however, to the insistence of several other artists—and because spectators had already begun to filter into the exhibition halls—Tatlin's relief was allowed to remain.[5]

The following year, Sergei Shchukin, one of the most significant collectors of the new painting, bought a relief by Tatlin out of the *Tramvai V* (*Tramway V*) exhibition in Petrograd, paying what seemed to Russian artists a fantastic price—three thousand rubles.[6] For that amount of money one could purchase fifteen to twenty landscapes by the enterprising "father of Russian Futurism," David Burliuk, or two or three splendid paintings by one of the most popular and prominent artists of the time, Kuz'ma Petrov-Vodkin. Amazement bordered on shock. What was the secret of a few boards and pieces of iron and wire, all of which could be found in any barn or garbage dump?

In the late autumn of 1915, another artist in Moscow, Kazimir Malevich, was attempting to convince his colleagues in Futurist and Dada happenings to gather "under a new banner."[7] He proposed that the poets of yesterday's Futurism "change the means of battle with thought, content, and logic . . . advance Alogism after Futurism"—in essence, that they learn from the example of his Alogist paintings. Malevich even provided examples of his own of the new poetic structures:

> *Papuans bored, but*
> *Cottage second-class*
> *Ticket. Park. Arch.*

These lines loosely match his painting *Stantsiia bez ostanovki. Kuntsevo* (*Through Station: Kuntsevo*, 1913, fig. no. 2), while another of Malevich's examples brings to mind his *Korova i skripka* (*Cow and Violin*, 1913), sometimes called *Vid s balkona* (*View from the Balcony*):

> *The cow ate a palm*
> *Alma-Tadema*
> *Adam Goat Goose.*[8]

It was evident that all the innovators in painting were "no longer Futurists"[9] and that "Futurism" had survived only as a general notion useful in dealing with a public accustomed to the labeling of everything new and up to the minute as "Futurist." The participants in the *0.10* exhibition, held in Nadezhda Dobychina's gallery in Petrograd in 1915–16, called the show the "last Futurist exhibition"—the last that the artists striving to attain "zero form" wanted. Yet the *Magazin* (*The Store*) exhibition, organized by Tatlin and held in Moscow in 1916, would be called "Futurist." And during the Civil War years, "Futurism" would once again be a synonym for everything new, leading an exasperated Lenin to cry, "Can we not find any reliable anti-Futurists!"[10]

The true manifesto of the new movement in painting—Suprematism—was neither the leaflet with a statement by Malevich distributed at the *0.10* exhibition[11] nor the speeches he gave at debates and lectures nor even his polemical treatise *Ot kubizma k suprematizmu* (*From Cubism to Suprematism*),[12] an eccentric experiment in philosophical prose, but Malevich's *Chernyi kvadrat* (*Black Square*, 1915) itself, his "icon."

The icon is a sign of the other world, of sacred harmony, and a witness to higher spiritual values. But the majority of Malevich's followers, raised on the Futurists' irreverent attacks on the old and obsolete, did not immediately comprehend the iconic meaning of the *Black Square*. Malevich's detractors proved to be more insightful. They intuitively understood the historic importance of Malevich's gesture—he hung the *Black Square* at the *0.10* exhibition in the traditional place of the icon—yet, in their holy terror, they confused the new harmony and new artistic idealism with the march of the "oncoming boor."[13]

"We are all primitives of the twentieth century," announced Ivan Kliun.[14] He used the word "primitive" in reference not to Primitivism, the stylistic tendency prevalent in the early 1910s, but to the beginning of a new era in the evolution of art and to vanguard artists as bearers of a new artistic consciousness, powerful and whole. Tatlin's reliefs and Malevich's Suprematism were the most important stimuli in the self-

determination of other avant-garde artists, who were not troubled by the divergence and even the glaring contradiction between Tatlin's and Malevich's paths. In order to clarify their own tasks, it was important that artists define themselves in relation to the new concepts. Formal innovation acted in and of itself, provoking argument, elucidation, and refutation. It was, that is, an aesthetic provocation, a challenge.

Thus Liubov' Popova and Kliun countered Tatlin with their own variations on the relief, admixing Tatlin's experiments and the "sculpto-paintings" of Aleksandr Arkhipenko and, in Popova's case, the work of the Italian Futurists Umberto Boccioni and Ardengo Soffici, as well; in Petrograd, Lev Bruni made reliefs influenced by Tatlin. What was at stake here, of course, was not the affirmation of the spatial relief as a special new genre—the reliefs of Vladimir Burliuk, Kliun, and Vasilii Ermilov (who produced reliefs in Khar'kov in the early 1920s) were based upon different principles. Rather, Tatlin's reliefs acted as conduits to new spatial concepts and to a gradual recognition of a new attitude toward art in general.

Many artists—such as Ivan Puni, Popova, Aleksandr Rodchenko, and Ol'ga Rozanova (whose works were frequently entitled *Suprematizm* [*Suprematism*] in exhibition catalogues)—experienced Malevich's Suprematism as if it were an inoculation against the disease of illusionism and Naturalism, and then quickly went beyond it. After the February Revolution of 1917, the artists of Supremus—a group centered around Malevich in Moscow in 1916–17, which had planned, but was never able, to publish a journal of the same name—joined the so-called young or left federation of the Moscow Professional Union of Artists and Painters. And by 1920, Malevich's solo show at the Sixteenth State Exhibition in Moscow was essentially the exhibition of a living classic.

No one among Suprematism's "fellow travelers" had any desire, as Malevich wished they did, to develop specifically Suprematist principles further. The independence of each artist from the general rubric was clear to all the participants, bar none, in Suprematist ventures. Thus Varvara Stepanova observed bluntly that "Rozanova's Suprematism is contrary to that of Malevich . . . For Malevich, color exists solely to distinguish one plane from another; for Rozanova, the composition serves to reveal all the possibilities of color on a plane." She took particular note of the "minimalism" of Rozanova's most recent work, where "one color [develops] into a self-sufficient painting."[15] Even the seemingly orthodox Suprematist Kliun quickly changed tack, searching out his own concepts of abstract form and constructing his compositions on the interrelation of color and light (on the change in color wrought by light and contrasts, and the influence of adjacent colors on the alteration of form).

Tatlin's reliefs and Malevich's *Black Square* introduced a new artistic yardstick. Competition with the Paris school, which had been the main engine in the evolution of new Russian art circa 1910, lost its meaning.

In about 1920, it would "suddenly" become evident that changes had taken place or were in the offing in many countries—that the scale of artistic values was shifting. Parisian artists would respond to the crisis with Purism and the aesthetics of Le Corbusier, and later with Surrealism. For the time being, however, the signal events were those occurring to the east of Paris. In Moscow and Petrograd, in Holland and Germany, and in Eastern Europe, artists were not only promoting but in their own way transforming new ideas. The Bauhaus, with a minimum of rhetoric, with "workmanlike efficiency," so to speak, for a time resolved all real and imagined conflicts and contradictions—between "free creative work" and society's claim on the artist's work; between logic and rationalism and spontaneity and intuition; between technology and metaphysics—in its notion of a "total art" in active relation with its surroundings. In the 1920s, the question of "epoch and style" was not merely theoretical. And in the art of this period, Malevich and Tatlin are constantly the twin catalysts.

The world as a sense, independent of the image, of the idea—this is the essence of the content of art. {My} square is not an image, just as a switch or socket are not the current.

—*Malevich*[16]

By the time Tatlin's reliefs and Suprematism appeared, a certain stage in the evolution of the new Russian art had come full circle—a stage that, according to Malevich, was initiated by those now seemingly happy and carefree sensualists, the Impressionists. Vanguard Russian artists especially esteemed Claude Monet, whom they perceived—as they did Cézanne and Van Gogh, and later Picasso—as "more Russian than the Russians." Those in Malevich's circle were always and unreservedly admirers of Fernand Léger, while Tatlin prized the lyrical Impressionism of Mikhail Larionov, which combined virtuosity with sincere feeling.

Cubism taught discipline of form and fostered a taste for analysis. It was, for Malevich, the pivotal—or, better yet, central—event in painting's evolution from Impressionism to Suprematism. Among the slogans of Malevich's students—the members of Unovis (the Affirmers of the New Art)—in Vitebsk were the following:

If you want to study art, study Cubism!
You want to learn painting? Begin with Cubism!
If you don't want to become a fashionable painter, begin by studying Cubism!
If you are an artist and do not work cubistically, then begin working this way immediately!
You want to experience the beauty of the fourth dimension? Begin studying Cubism!
If you want to become a creator, study Cubism!
Do you want to reign over nature? Study Cubism!
If you don't want to be ruled by nature, begin studying Cubism![17]

In other words, there was no way to become a contemporary artist without first passing through Cubism.

For Tatlin, Cubism was something worth knowing, yet he evinced no desire to adopt it. Nor, however, did he feel any need to reject it—he was, of course, far from concurring with Félix Vallotton's celebrated utterance: "Cézanne? I choose, with all due respect, to ignore him." In the studio on Ostozhenka, which Tatlin rented with the artist Nikolai Rogovin, he drew nudes in the style of Cubism (whenever other artists congregated and they were able to hire a model). Many such studies remain, in albums and even on loose sheets of paper.

But no Cubism was allowed into his painting—no variations on the paintings in Shchukin's gallery or those illustrated in magazines. Tatlin's devices for deforming nature (devices as important to Expressionism as to Cubism), his "distortions," had more in common with the violation of perspective in icons (but not in primitive art) than with the canvases of the Parisian painters. (It was precisely in 1911–12 that the "antiquity" of the vanguard art of Tatlin became manifest.)

And Futurism? For Malevich and Tatlin, its reign was a time when artistic life itself became a work of art.

Malevich entertained long and seriously both the idea of dynamism and the linked notion of art as pure energy. "I paint energy, not the soul."[18] Energy and the energetics of tension are subjects ever present in his reflections on art—though he

fig. 1
Vladimir Tatlin
Counter-Relief, *ca. 1916.*

fig. 2
Kazimir Malevich
Through Station: Kuntsevo, *1913.*

invests these concepts with his own meaning, viewing both dynamism and energy from the vantage point of absolute art.

In first describing his reliefs as "synthetic-static compositions," Tatlin emphasized their non-Futurist character.

Alogism formed a sort of neutral zone between the trends of the early 1910s and non-objective art and Constructivism. Tatlin contented himself with hanging the BEHOLD THE TRICK! placard, while Malevich (if one isn't blindly accepting the suggestions embedded in his own writings) found himself at a turning point. A turning point to nowhere, and then to "his" Suprematism, of far greater importance than Cubism. Irony for a time allowed the question, Where next? to remain unanswered; it permitted a second's breathing space in the uninterrupted pursuit of new forms. Alogism offered everything—Cubism's geometric planes, Futurism's strangeness and urban kitsch (lettering from advertisements and signboards)—immediately and simultaneously. It was harmony in disharmony. Not synthesis, not the birth pangs of a *Gesamtkunstwerk* but a backed-up stream of artistic reflexes and utterances vis-à-vis contemporary devices and concepts in art. Today we can trace an entirely logical path from Alogism to the montage of the 1920s.

In Malevich's case it was also significant that the Alogist estrangement of meaning encouraged scrutiny of the structure of the painting; it revealed the "pure element" of form: the surface plane.

Of course, Malevich, in passionately absorbing each *ism,* failed to notice that he was parodying them. The parody evolved from his desire to do everything not only better but absolutely right. He was a born systematist; he had to model everything into his own—and, in his opinion, faultlessly exact—world of Impressionism, Cézannism, and Cubism. And if everything was to be exact and complete, he had to circle back and to reexamine himself again and again. Hence it seemed to him, after he had completed his own series of Cubist experiments, that no one in Russia had yet created a truly Cubist work. But, had he worked in France, would he have found a Parisian artist who had?

Malevich's Alogist works, like things *an sich,* are products of the disengagement of form from the objects of perception. These works operate on two levels, that of abstract planes concealing some unknown world and that of irony vis-à-vis the subject that is possibly depicted.

Suprematism liberated these disengaged planes and endowed them with new meaning. New form engendered, or predetermined, new meaning.

This was the winding-up of the old (although the "old" was not very long out of its infancy) and the beginning of the new.

Tatlin navigated among the various *isms* in art like an icebreaker threading a path among floes that threaten to crush it. His was the most logical and the most unforeseen solution—to make not life but the materials existing in life both the subject of art and art itself.

He saw no need to repudiate anything. The polemical debates about art were of no special interest to Tatlin, and not because he wasn't one for talking—he was, in fact, a first-rate raconteur—but because he discerned no particular sense in them. Tatlin was a naturalist, the keenest of observers, who did reject willful intervention. He proceeded "from the bottom up," not from a general idea—the fourth, fifth, sixth, or whatever dimension—but from the life of materials. From the life of materials, and not from materials as such.

Materials have properties such as elasticity, weight, and tension. Line, tone, and color. Old photographs of the reliefs—without the retouching that each time cancels a little more of the complexity of their structure—reveal a subtlety of *faktura* (density or manipulation of material) and light and shade. The

attainments of painting have not been lost. The refinement and intricacy of the linear-rhythmical relationships of painting are, rather, preserved. The riddle of Tatlin's reliefs, unsolved by those in both East and West who have reconstructed them, is how emptiness became an artistic space, how it acquired a subtle poetic meaning.

Tatlin's reliefs embodied a new artistic methodology: the aesthetics of real materials in real space (naturally, both these concepts change, and constantly, over time and space). Tatlin's conversations with young artists from the Apartment No. 5 studio on Vasil'evskii Island in Petrograd, and with the critics Sergei Isakov and Nikolai Punin, led to the following, entirely logical, formulae:[19]

$$\text{Impressionism} \quad \frac{spectrum}{power\ of\ color}$$

$$\text{Cézannism} \quad \frac{quality\ of\ color}{composition\ of\ form}$$

$$\text{Cubism} \quad \frac{faktura}{consistent\ composition}$$

$$\text{Tatlin (and Tatlinism)} \quad \frac{material}{real\ space}$$

And so, a new sign and a new reality.
Two faces of the age.

More accurately, a new life in art for the real. At the beginning, even Tatlin, it appears, did not fully grasp the significance of what he had discovered. It was no big deal. Every artist loves his material. No mere board but "a lovely little one," Tatlin would say. What unusual discoveries were there here? What art? Even in the booklet *Vladimir Evgrafovich Tatlin,* published at the height of art-world polemicizing, we find no theories—not even their facsimile—no manifesto, no ripostes. Only a decidedly straightforward biographical note and reproductions of his works.[20] An account of work produced between this date and that. Look for yourself and draw your own conclusions. Just as El Lissitzky said later in his *Suprematicheskii skaz pro dva kvadrata (A Suprematist Tale about Two Squares,* 1922): "Construct yourselves."

Vera Pestel', who dedicated her painting *Tatlin s banduroi (Tatlin with Bandura)*[21] to Tatlin, writes ingenuously in her memoirs about how much she, Sof'ia Karetnikova, Popova, and Nadezhda Udal'tsova liked Malevich's bright and cheerful geometric paintings. Pestel' and the others made decorative sketches in the Suprematist style for the Verbovka collective, whose peasant women embroidered scarves, handbags, muffs, and carpets with these designs.[22] And the four artists even decorated the club of the left federation of the Moscow Professional Union of Artists and Painters with Suprematist designs.[23]

Malevich's formation of the Supremus group, which good friends of Tatlin's and former admirers of his art (Udal'tsova and Pestel' again) either joined or associated with, was, of course, a blow to Tatlin's pride as an artist. This despite the fact that both Malevich's formal investigations and his stratagems to inaugurate a movement were foreign to Tatlin, as if from another planet.

The stories recounted by Pestel', Valentina Khodasevich,[24] and Sof'ia Dymshits-Tolstaia,[25] who knew Tatlin well (but not each other), paint a picture—full of sympathy—of a "holy fool of Futurism," a man suspicious to the point of absurdity, to the brink of phobia. He openly suspected Malevich of artistic espionage, though it is difficult today to detect the traces of any crime. Tatlin erected something like a tent, but one that could be locked, in the middle of his studio on Staro-Basmannaia Street in the Nemetskaia sloboda region of Moscow. God forbid Malevich should see what he was up to and get ahead of him.

This is a continuation, as it were, of the old "futurization" of artistic life. What happens in art and the stories told about it are artistic facts of identical interest. History immediately decks itself out as myth.

Tatlin's "phobia" was clearly provoked by Malevich, who derived satisfaction from mystifications and practical jokes. Tatlin, of course, also liked to tell tales. They always contained, it's true, a kernel of truth, yet the accounts of his journeys and adventures changed and were embroidered with each retelling. Did he, pretending to be a blind man, play his bandura at an exhibition of Russian art and handicrafts in Berlin in the winter of 1914? He did. And did he speak with and kiss the hand of the Kaiser's wife? Those who heard his captivating tales did not much care whether, in fact, he had. Had he been in Paris? He had. The sculptor and later art historian Boris Ternovets,[26] the sculptor Vera Mukhina,[27] and Jacques Lipchitz[28] all recalled Tatlin's traveling to France after his "stint" playing the bandura in Berlin. In her diary, Popova recorded Tatlin's story about how, right before his departure from Paris for Moscow, he visited "Pavel" Picasso himself (Russians liked to switch from the Spanish name to its Slavic equivalent).[29] After seeing Picasso's Cubist constructions, Tatlin said, he began to work according to other principles.

Malevich's mystifications were of a different variety. He matched Baron Munchausen in flights of fantasy and inspiration. A simple photograph. The artist with a Polish acquaintance in Germany.[30] Two figures. On the back is the inscription: "Le Corbusier and me in Dessau." Malevich was certainly in danger of being found out, yet the very act of rewriting the history of contemporary art afforded so much pleasure. And why wouldn't Le Corbusier have come and offered a salute to the renowned Kazimir from the city of Petrograd?

As a polemicist, Malevich remained a man of the Futurist era and its romantic mythology. In one of his letters from Vitebsk to David Shterenberg in Moscow—a letter written in 1921, when the organization of the *Erste russische Kunstausstellung* (*First Russian Art Exhibition,* Berlin, 1922) was only beginning to be discussed—Malevich took pains to emphasize that he was an ideological worker in art. And that the Berlin exhibition would be of interest to him only if his "icons"—the *Black Square, Chernyi krug* (*Black Circle*), and *Chernyi krest* (*Black Cross*)—were exhibited. And exhibited only, moreover, under the rubric *Suprematizm. Rossiia. 1913* (*Suprematism: Russia, 1913*).[31]

Nineteen thirteen? By now this date has been quoted any number of times.[32] As if Suprematism's having in fact emerged somewhat later than 1913 could diminish its significance in the history of twentieth-century art and discredit it in its own eyes. To be sure, many such "improved chronologies" have been discovered and will continue to be discovered in accounts of the art of this century. Yet Malevich, who was a genius at hypnosis, convinced not only everyone else but even himself that he had inaugurated Suprematism in 1913—and not in any other year. His account of his own career is full of datings of works according not to the year in which they were produced but the year in which they were conceived.[33]

fig. 3
Vera Pestel'
Composition, *1915–16.*

The opera *Pobeda nad solntsem* (*Victory over the Sun,* 1913) was, of course, a major event in the history of Russian Dadaism. But in the history of Suprematism? All attempts to read the origins of Suprematism in Malevich's fortuitous and rather banal set design for the opera (the square in his sketch of the curtain was a form virtually foreordained by the box shape of the stage) reiterate Malevich's own carefully planted suggestion. He caught a lot of fish with this line. Though that certainly casts no shadow on the historic importance of Suprematism.

Malevich's mystifications not infrequently force one to scrutinize his works and principles more closely.

The young artists in Vitebsk and Smolensk, at the most fifteen to eighteen years old, asked Malevich about the origins of the first Suprematist works and of the *Black Square.* Malevich improvised brilliantly. Using the principle of analogy. According to a famous anecdote in the history of nineteenth-century Russian art, the prominent historical painter Vasilii Surikov could not, no matter how he tried, get the coloring he wanted in his painting *The Boyarina Morozova* (1887) until he saw the solution in life: a black crow on white snow. Thus Malevich told his students this story: one day, following a spate of inclement weather—at the time he was living in Moscow, in the Sokol'niki district, in a house rented by Kliun—he went to the window and was stunned by the contrast between the freshly fallen, blindingly white snow and the black knapsack on the back of a boy leaving the house for school. Even if the story was a complete fabrication, it was spectacularly convincing.[34] Malevich wrote to Mikhail Matiushin to announce his *fevralizm* (Februaryism) in painting.[35] So what if the absurdly (like so many other of his works shown at the *0.10* exhibition) entitled *Zhivopisnyi realizm mal'chika s rantsem* (*Painterly Realism of a Boy with Knapsack,* 1915) is not a black square but a composition of two squares—one large and one small?[36]

Such anecdotes, worthy of Vasari, only confirm the role played by emotional impulse.

Iron, glass, and marble. Malevich, as a man with a refined artistic sensibility, could not have remained oblivious to the originality of Tatlin's works. Yet if Suprematism was the end-all and be-all of contemporary painting's evolution from Impressionism, if it was the single truth, the existence of Tatlin put the problem on a different plane, namely: where is the truth?

Tatlin? It was impossible not to notice him. Just as it was impossible not to recognize his talent. And Malevich—the polemicist and "solipsist" of innovation—asked his students and followers to repeat after him: Tatlin does not transcend the confines of Cubism.[37] He represents only a stage in the evolution of Cubism. Variations rather than repetition, maybe, still not true innovation. You must go forward—follow me—onward to the new harmony. One of Malevich's students in Vitebsk, marching in step with the cult of the great leader promoted from above, even thought up a slogan: "Long live Unovis—the path to a Suprematist future—and long live Kazimir Malevich, the true guide along this path!"[38]

For Tatlin, however, "iron blocked the horizon."[39] And his task was to "rupture the ring of the horizon."

Malevich was born a prophet, mystifier, leader, and artistic dictator. And he was very human; he often endured humiliations[40] and had learned how to find his way out of any situation. In Petrograd in the 1920s, for example, confronted by complete repudiation of his art, he conceived a kind of applied research, the "science of art," to which he summoned vanguard artists now bereft of social standing.

For Tatlin, being an artist was never too complicated. He was not the leader of any movement or group, nor did he yearn

to be such, even if he did enjoy indisputable authority among art professionals, both vanguard and not.[41] He was not overly impressed by the fine artistic intuition that nature had given him. It seemed a given, like a good ear for a musician. And others had the same gift. The sharpness and precision of the eye was the most important thing. Absolutely no approximations or imitations of artistic impression. Visual perception meant the eye's tactile sensation of every portion of a work. Sight, therefore, had to be put under the control of touch.[42]

The eye both sees and touches the work. It sees and feels the painting-like warmth of tone of the wood, the elasticity and tension of the iron, the cable giving under the iron's weight. Every rhythm of form. The light and shadows of every facet of the relief. Aesthetics resides in the "selection of materials," in the fit of their contradictions. Precious mahogany and palisander, for example, are conjoined with an ordinary piece of iron used for roofing and drainpipes. The relief—to quote Vladimir Maiakovskii's verse—is "a nocturne on a drainpipe flute."

In Tatlin's *Doska No. 1* (*Board No. 1*) of the winter of 1916–17, wood and paint combine to create a play of color halftones, interstices, and transitions. In its power and subtlety, this work is comparable to the masterpieces of icon painting.

Tatlin was born to make plastic art, nature, and technology into one great new whole. He was not a man of particularly wide intellectual interests. Malevich's philosophical prose summons numerous associations with the philosophy of writers whom he not only had not read (though he had, for example, read Schopenhauer) but of whom he had not even heard. Tatlin didn't provide such a goldmine of self-sufficient intellectual constructs. But he did have a broad grasp of the problem. In his work, material and space strove to become absolutely perfect categories. Material lives a profoundly organic life, it embraces life in its entirety as a new system of the senses. Everything is perfected. But Tatlin's was not the notion—which had given academic painters no peace—of the masterpiece as such. It was, rather, the idea of absolute plastic harmony, in which artisanry and the senses are inseparable. In this regard, Tatlin—poorly educated, lacking any desire to assert himself through polemical jousting, a classic outsider—had more in common with the brilliant Renaissance intellectual, Leonardo da Vinci, than with any artist of his own time . . .

And yet, why did the outsider Tatlin enter the legendary battle with Malevich? What was at stake?

Let us note: Tatlin, speaking about his Tower—his "dynamo-form"—declared iron and glass the "materials of the new Classicism."[43]

On the one hand, he proceeded, as always, from the nature of materials. And here his reasoning dovetailed with the logic of architects designing industrial structures: "In reinforced concrete we have not only a new material but, of far greater consequence, new constructions and a new method for designing buildings. Therefore, in using [reinforced concrete], we have to renounce the old traditions and concern ourselves with meeting new tasks."[44] Let us also note that Tatlin began to work on his Tower at the same time as construction commenced on the engineer Vladimir Shukhov's radio tower in Moscow. (The radio tower, as originally envisioned, was to reach a height of 350 meters.)[45]

On the other hand, Tatlin invested the phrase "materials of the new Classicism" with an artistic significance. A definition of new canons of form with the aid of new materials.

In Petrograd in 1923, Malevich's student, Il'ia Chashnik, completed a study for the cover of the never-published *Suprematizm kak novyi klassitsizm* (*Suprematism as the New Classicism*).[46] Slogans like "Back to Ingres!" weren't at issue, but rather, once again, a definition of new long-term laws for the construction of form.

We must conclude, returning to the rivalry between Malevich and Tatlin, that theirs was a contest not over leadership but over truth—over which path in contemporary art was the true one. Malevich, otherwise a diplomat and pragmatist, was in no mood for conciliation on this score. While Tatlin, according to the memoirs of Punin (who endeavored in a variety of circumstances to reconcile Tatlin to reality), was incapable of compromise in almost any situation.[47] Tatlin's entire life, as a matter of fact, confirms this assertion.

History does not wait. It lays down an ultimatum.
—*Pitirim Sorokin*[48]

The Civil War presented both vanguard artists with a dramatic dilemma.

The new art had been born of the struggle for a self-sufficient artistic language and a non-objective artistic world. Now the state wanted to make art a mere vehicle for agitprop,[49] to limit it to an educational function—to illustration of the requisite slogans and notions. What was important to the new state was "not to carry out a revolution in art (which is impossible) but to put art at the service of the revolution."[50] These words were repeated by Party cultural functionaries from one year to the next, and almost verbatim.

Malevich and Tatlin had different—yet, in some sense, similar—reactions to this development.

"Decoration of the city for revolutionary festivities"—this neutral bookkeeper's formulation on an invoice fit the superrevolutionary decoration of Vitebsk to a tee, until the authorities understood that the propaganda effect of this work was nonexistent, if not negative. In all honesty, who, finding himself in a strange and joyous world of particolored planes, was about to mull over revolution and counterrevolution? These decorations were experiments in a new mural painting, experiments in Suprematist design, yet the words and agitprop phrases incorporated in them were incidental and ineffective. Why is the beautiful composition of colored planes on Nikolai Suetin's panel accompanied by the slogan "Religion is the opium of the people"? Which religion? What opium? And what people—drug addicts, perhaps? The man on the street could hardly have cared less. Some people were stopped by the vividness of the colors. Others jumped back from the strange combinations of geometric forms out of a textbook. Did people stand before Lissitzky's poster *Klinom krasnym bei belykh* (*Beat the Whites with the Red Wedge,* 1920, plate no. 138) and decipher its symbolism? Only the dynamics of its composition made any impression.

Examining agitprop art from such a "bourgeois," consumerist vantage helps one comprehend the "aesthetic scissors," that is, the divergent blades of the artist's interest in working in an urban space and his obvious (in many cases) indifference to the tasks of abstract propaganda.

As one of the leaders at the Moscow Art Board of Izo Narkompros (the Department of Fine Arts of the People's Commissariat of Enlightenment), Tatlin was privy to efforts to carry out the so-called Plan for Monumental Propaganda—monuments to progressive revolutionary and cultural figures of the past. Several of the names on the list of candidates drawn up by the intellectuals were crossed out "at the top." Without discussion. Case closed. The philosopher Vladimir Solov'ev, for instance, and Cézanne, a classic in the eyes of new artists in Moscow. Documents that might reveal how the Art Board reacted to Cézanne's removal from the list have not, it seems, survived. (In 1920, the art club at Vkhutemas [the Higher Artistic-Technical Workshops] would be named the Cézanne

fig. 4
Nikolai Prusakov
Study for a Stove, *1920.*

Club.) Yet it is clear that this mechanical approach to the task at hand and treatment of monuments as illustrations on an assigned theme did not suit Tatlin at all. "Monumental propaganda" might just as well have been called "sculptural propaganda."[51]

Tatlin's Tower was conceived in direct argument with the Plan for Monumental Propaganda and the manner in which it was slated to be implemented. In order to work on his project, Tatlin had to leave Moscow in 1919 for Petrograd, where, with Punin's help, he managed to get a modest subsidy, materials, and a place to work: the former mosaics workshop of the Academy of Fine Arts. The workshop's former director, the ceramicist Petr Vaulin, protested. Now was the very time to be thinking about "erecting houses and temples of the people, decorated with mosaics."[52] He had no idea that Tatlin was occupied with a similarly impractical project. The Tower was one in a series, stretching far back in history and culture, of architectural constructions that were monuments and icons of their age. A series that began with the legendary Tower of Babel and included, in Russia, the church in the village of Kolomenskoe outside Moscow and (a later addition) the Cathedral of Christ the Saviour in Moscow, erected to mark the defeat of Napoleon.[53]

The spirals of the Tower, like serpentine mountain roads, energetically wound their way up into "Malevich's heavens."

The Tower's abstract, cosmic symbolizing of perception lent its functional intentions a particular cast. It was made "from iron, glass, and revolution," but also from reverie, hunger, and isolation. The Tower might possibly house a cafeteria—a dream in a time when food was scarce—and studios for artists, too. In it, the dynamism of life acquired the solemnity of a chorale. A monument in half-frozen and half-deserted Petrograd, a monument on the banks of the Lethe—built for no specific city, for no specific country. A monument to the ruin of the times and a monument to the spirit of absolute freedom.

The world had collapsed and the world lived.

It was both the creation of the artist and the voice of history.

"An absurd and naïve, monstrous beast with a radio-telegraph horn on its head and the legislative assembly of the Third International in its belly"?[54]

"The Council of People's Commissars would flee from such a building on the first sunny day and, camped out nearby on the grass, would immediately issue a decree that Tatlin's tower is for rent, at public auction, to horticulturists wishing to grow pineapples."[55]

The Tower was a sign and symbol not of revolutionary Russia but of the new era in its entirety.

Tatlin's Tower was immediately perceived and adopted by artists in the 1920s as the sign of a new artistic consciousness, not as a monument to the Third International. What was the connotation of "Third International" for Tatlin? A common phrase of the Civil War period. At the time, Izo Narkompros, for example, was planning to publish (but never did) a multilingual journal entitled *Internatsional iskusstva* (*Art International*). Both Tatlin and Malevich prepared texts for it, Tatlin's contribution consisting of clear, extremely brief "theses."[56] The artists' International denoted not establishment of a Bolshevik dictatorship all over the globe but lifting of the curse of disunion from humanity.

There were few who found the Tower to produce an agitprop effect any more persuasive that of the Suprematist panels. This was no targeted attack of the sort found in Sergei Eizenshtein's films.

When the model of the Tower was first exhibited, in Petrograd in November 1920, the opening—which was called,

as the idiom of the time dictated, a meeting—was attended by stunned representatives of the Petrograd art world, astonished at what they beheld, and—for form's sake; after all, it was a meeting—by a handful of sailors and Red Army soldiers. In December the model was exhibited in Moscow at the Eighth Congress of Soviets; it was displayed among diagrams, posters, and other types of agitprop and didactic production at the former Association of the Nobility. Pavel Mansurov, the young non-objective artist from Petrograd who designed the exhibition, did a good job of "serving up" Tatlin. But the delegates didn't bite. The Tower unleashed a storm at a discussion of the model at Vkhutemas's Cézanne Club. There both Naum Gabo and Lissitzky argued for it as the most concrete of architectural projects, which needed to be realized not so much today as tomorrow.[57] Both would eventually do a great deal to popularize the Tower in the West.

A version of the model was displayed—as if it were a standard agitprop object, like the inevitable bust of Lenin—at the *Exposition internationale des arts décoratifs et industriels modernes* (*International Exhibition of Contemporary Decorative and Industrial Art*) in Paris in 1925. And at the *Voina v iskusstve* (*War in Art*) exhibition in Leningrad in 1930. After which the model was dismantled and stored away somewhere. With time, all of its parts were lost. A section of one of its spirals was used for a brief period as a ladder.

Balanced, "middle-of-the-road" opinions were virtually absent in the first debates about the Tower. Either a work of genius or a nonentity. The years of engagé Realism, it would seem, resolved the impasse in favor of nonentity.

One modest informant about the debate over the Tower reported: "If the idea of the monument is truly new and valuable, then it will never die. Prophets have not always been stoned and imposters have not always succeeded."[58]

Others left {Russia}, but as it turned out, those who stayed on had also left.

—*Vladimir Veidle*[59]

Neither Tatlin nor Malevich was deceived by the turn of phrase. *They* did not believe that "revolution and 'revolution in art' are the same thing."[60] They had an opportunity to join forces, if not in the struggle for the new art, then at least in resisting the advent of engagé art. Punin arranged a temporary truce between the warring sides. He facilitated Tatlin's invitation to Ginkhuk (the State Institute of Artistic Culture). Students held meetings to demand that Malevich and Tatlin teach at the Academy of Fine Arts.[61] At the *Petrogradskie khudozhniki vsekh napravlenii* (*Petrograd Artists of All Trends*) exhibition in Petrograd in 1923, work both by Tatlin and by Malevich's school was displayed. Hardly anyone realized that this was not the beginning but the end of the era of artistic freedom.

Tatlin, as he said, was "bored." He loved his work and materials and did not like to give the impression that he was occupied with anything other than his own work.

Malevich was diverted by the game of art as science. He was living, as it were, a second life in art, from Impressionism to Suprematism, and often appeared already to have gone beyond the boundaries of Suprematism. Where?

The analytical investigations of the Suprematists of Unovis in Vitebsk and at Ginkhuk stimulated new types of creative work: Suprematist architecture, on the one hand (it would be more correct to say three-dimensional Suprematist architectonics), and "painterly-plastic realism," on the other. The latter was no repetition of the Impressionism of Monet or the painting of Léger, of the flickering metallic *faktura* of the Cubism of their teacher, or of exercises on the magnetism of

fig. 5
Konstantin Vialov
Relief, *1919.*

the interrelations of Suprematist forms. The individuality of each person was expressed in the process of experiencing the world in painting. Here there was a certain merger of artists who had been members of Malevich's circle and artists who had passed through Matiushin's school. A preference for the universal gave way to the private. Suetin's paintings juxtaposed the traditions of Suprematism with the mysticism of old Russian art. In his own works, Malevich was not infrequently the exponent of the group's ideas rather than the initiator of the new. At times this led to conflicts, yet his students' respect for their teacher remained unchanged.[62]

Tatlin did not support the beautiful mystification of Malevich. He was "hounded out" of Ginkhuk and left for Kiev. There he worked for two years in the Department of Dramatic, Cinematic, and Photographic Arts of the Kiev Art Institute. His students constructed complicated interiors on the principle of his counter-relief. (This is somewhat reminiscent of Kurt Schwitters.) Clashes among groups and movements in Ukraine? Nothing of the sort interested him.[63]

The rector of Vkhutein (the Higher Artistic-Technical Institute), the sociologizing Pavel Novitskii, invited him back to Moscow to teach. A small circle of attentive students quickly formed around him in Vkhutein's Ceramics Faculty.[64] But in the more "visible" Wood- and Metalworking Faculty, Tatlin was clearly not understood—even though his colleagues there included Gustav Klutsis, Lissitzky, and Rodchenko.[65] Tatlin spoke of his work in the same words as they, yet was plainly unable to draw up a teaching program. That his students produced work not at all similar to that of students in the other workshops went unnoticed.

Tatlin proposed bionic principles for constructing artistic form . . .

The influence of my art is expressed in the movement of the Constructivists, of which I am the founder.

—*Tatlin*[66]

Tatlin's path and that of Suprematism in the 1920s are shaded by their attitude toward Moscow Constructivism—the central phenomenon of Russian art of that decade.

Constructivism attempted to answer all the questions posed by the era. It took into account Tatlin's experience, as well as the Suprematism fiercely rejected by the theorists close to him. It even answered the hopelessly difficult question of how art can function amid the collapse of normal human society by advancing an art that participated directly in the process of building life—that is, production art. The term "production art" was then applied in, as it were, two dimensions: art for life (excluding easel painting and sculpture "needed by no one") and new constructive approaches to the solution of the tasks of this art (or these arts).[67]

Malevich placed an equals sign between Constructivism as a new method in art and the ideas of utilitarianism, which he disparaged as "subsistence art." Constructivism thus meant service—by new devices, in a new style—of the agitprop and utilitarian needs of society.

Rodchenko? Long after Rodchenko had countered Malevich's spiritual meditations in *Beloe na belom* (*White on White*, 1918) with his art of the abyss, of the void—*Chernoe na chernom* (*Black on Black*, 1918, plate no. 240)—Malevich still, among his circle of followers, spoke Rodchenko's name as something absolutely negative.

A certain movement emerged within Unovis. A movement that did not renounce the language of Suprematism, yet worked with the new constructive forms. Lissitzky and Klutsis; Chashnik's tribune and Suetin's architectural designs of 1921. This trend contributed a great deal to the art of the 1920s. In it

we find the working out of, or demand for a solution to, problems of new architectural form, design, and book art. Lissitzky, who thought in categories of an epoch's single style, considered this trend and the activities of Obmokhu (the Society of Young Artists) in Moscow to be the sources of a new international constructive style.

Obmokhu remains one of the myths in the history of Constructivism. It hindered both Gabo, the romantic of a new technological art, and Lissitzky. For a very simple reason. Rarely in the works of Obmokhu do we encounter new methods of strictly artistic thinking—methods that, for example, are obvious in Lissitzky (who, given his striking receptivity to "outside influences," might easily seem on the surface an eternal "eclectic"). Rather, in many works by the members of Obmokhu (Karl Ioganson's simple structuralist constructions are one exception), "engineerism" is advanced as the new, topical, up-to-the-minute theme of art. Not infrequently a construction is not truly constructed but merely depicted. A similar phenomenon can be observed among Obmokhu's contemporaries, the painters of the Electroorganism group.[68]

Tatlin? Well, of course, his Tower did initiate Constructivism as a special trend in Moscow. The Tower was one of the indispensable icons of the international style of the 1920s, figuring in publications on painting and sculpture, on design and architecture. It was as essential to them as it was virtually useless in the concrete context of Moscow artistic life. Of course, the Tower's unseen presence was a very important factor. Yet the Moscow Constructivists invented their own history. Tatlin was not excluded from it, but he was not granted any advantages, either.[69]

The impulse provided by Tatlin and the actual evolution of the idea of Constructivism in Moscow during the 1920s diverged objectively and decisively.

Organic artistic culture, toward which Tatlin was moving during these years, and Constructivism were no less opposed than were Suprematism and Constructivism. (Although many Constructivist projects—at least outwardly, on a stylistic level—preserved an echo of Suprematism.)[70]

The Constructivists recklessly spoke of replacing art with life and wanted to make the object of production the object of art.[71] Tatlin built a stove in his room to keep from freezing, sewed a specially tailored coat to keep from shivering in the wind, and cut himself a comfortable work suit.

Playing with the industrial production of an object was not the last motivation of the design solutions of the Moscow Constructivists. Tatlin's designs are those of a Robinson Crusoe who finds himself on an uninhabited island. And in this sense—given the actual conditions in Russia at the beginning of the 1920s—he was more of a realist than were the Moscow Constructivists creating lovely designs disengaged from real life. This was no utopia, not fantasies of the unrealizable, but the fashion of the day, full of life and energy—had life been normal. Tatlin's designs are the designs of a hunter wintering in the taiga and not counting on any help from anywhere.

The Constructivists affirmed the model of a life which could be—for them, the form of art determined new forms of life. Tatlin criticized the Constructivists—the "so-called Constructivists"—for their imitation, as it appeared to him, of contemporary style.[72]

Letatlin (1929–32) is a flying bird, Tatlin's bicycle, on which one can "sail" through the air.

In artistic circles reactions varied yet all struck basically the same chord: "he's flown out of art," "a move into technology,"[73] "an amazing character, but absolutely no artist."[74]

And in nonartistic circles: "a work of art."[75]

The causes and effects were confused.
Tatlin: "Nature is more clever than mechanics."
His speculative and sincere critics:

In the depths of that worldview, out of which Letatlin *wishes to fly, the heavy reactionary biases of the departing class are thickening. {The accusatory tone of the prosecutor is heard.} And what are they? Worship of nature, hostility to the machine, an adjustment of technology to the feelings of the individual person, naïve faith in the "wisdom" of organic forms, withdrawal from the industrial world.*[76]

This is indeed hard to square with the popular saying of the Stalinist era: "You can't wait for charity from nature! Our task is to take it from her."

It was a true perversion that unwashed and illiterate Russia, the Rus' of Chekhov and Bunin, allowed itself the luxury of Chekhov and Bunin, and, moreover, of Skriabin, Vrubel', and Blok.
—*Mikhail Levidov*[77]

It is not at all surprising that the art of the 1930s ignored both Tatlin and Malevich.

In Moscow's strange and Disneylandish Central Park of Culture and Rest, people jumped from a parachute tower reminiscent of Tatlin's monument.[78]

Suetin created a pylon with the text of the Soviet constitution for the *Exposition internationale des arts et des techniques* (*International Exhibition of Art and Technology,* Paris, 1937) in the shape of an arkhitekton—and no one even noticed.[79]

Tatlin painted landscapes, still lifes, and portraits, but did not exhibit them.

Malevich, with his strikingly developed social instinct, once again attempted to outdo everyone upon his release from jail (after having been arrested in Kiev in 1930). In an ordinary composition of colored stripes he included a row of galloping cavalrymen (plate no. 397). You want a "Soviet" picture—here, take it! Many artists, incidentally, made similar gestures during these years when the "Soviet theme painting" was affirmed as the basis of Soviet art. Malevich did not gain much by such a strategy and he resorted to it extremely rarely. It didn't help at all. One of his students still has a letter to Malevich (it arrived one day after his death) notifying him that his request for a pension had been turned down.[80]

The first steps of Pop Art, the art of *assemblage*, the flying apparatus of Ponamarenko, Joseph Beuys's felt suits . . . Lucio Fontana, Mark Rothko, Minimalism—in which Suprematism and Constructivism were finally reconciled—the Zero group.

Marcel Duchamp, Kazimir Malevich, Kurt Schwitters, Vladimir Tatlin.
—Translated, from the Russian, by Todd Bludeau

Notes

The quotation in the initial epigraph is taken from A. Kruchenykh and V. Khlebnikov, *Slovo kak takovoe* (Moscow: EUY, 1913), p. 3.

1. A copy of this announcement of the exhibition in Tatlin's studio is in the Manuscript Division, State Russian Museum, St. Petersburg, f. 121, d. 117, l. 61.

2. This relief was reproduced in Ivan Puni, *Sovremennaia zhivopis'* (Berlin: Frenkel', 1923), p. 30.

3. The exhibitions were held not only in Moscow and St. Petersburg but in Kiev as well.

4. The festivities—which included fireworks and floats along the Neva River in St. Petersburg and a procession of "boyars" in Red Square in Moscow—were matched in scale only by such mass spectacles as *The Storming of the Winter Palace* in Petrograd in 1919–20.

5. The episode was reported in the Moscow press. See, for example, "Dve vystavki," *Nov'* 152 (December 23, 1914), and "Khudozhniki—zhertvam voiny," *Rannee utro* 232 (December 7, 1914). Malevich was among the "victims" whose works were removed by the jury prior to the opening of the exhibition.

6. Shchukin's "coup" was reported in the morning edition of *Birzhevye vedomosti* 14706 (March 4, 1915).

7. Kazimir Malevich, letter to Mikhail Matiushin, September 24, 1915, Manuscript Division, Pushkin House, St. Petersburg, quoted from E. F. Kovtun, "K. S. Malevich. Pis'ma k M. V. Matiushinu," *Ezhegodnik Rukopisnogo otdela Pushkinskogo doma na 1974 god* (Leningrad: Nauka, 1976), p. 187.

8. Kazimir Malevich, letter to Mikhail Matiushin, January 1916, private archive, Frankfurt.

9. Kazimir Malevich, letter to Mikhail Matiushin, September 24, 1915, in Kovtun, "K. S. Malevich. Pis'ma k M. V. Matiushinu," p. 188.

10. Quoted in *V. Lenin i izobrazitel'noe iskusstvo. Dokumenty. Pis'ma. Vospominaniia* (Moscow: Izobrazitel'noe iskusstvo, 1977), p. 445.

11. Two leaflets were distributed at the exhibition, one with statements by Malevich, Ivan Kliun, and Mikhail Men'kov, the other with statements by Ivan Puni and Kseniia Boguslavskaia. A small booklet containing both leaflets was also published.

12. K. Malevich, *Ot kubizma k suprematizmu. Novyi zhivopisnyi realizm* (Petrograd, 1916). The brochure was in fact printed in December 1915, in time for the opening of the *0.10* exhibition.

13. See, for example, Aleksandr Benua, "Posledniaia futuristicheskaia vystavka," *Rech',* January 9, 1916. The expression "oncoming boor" was Dmitrii Merezhkovskii's (see his "Eshche odin shag griadushchego khama," *Russkoe slovo,* June 29, 1914). See also Jane A. Sharp, "The Critical Reception of the *0.10* Exhibition: Malevich and Benua," in this volume.

14. A. Kruchenykh, I. Kliun, and K. Malevich, *Tainye poroki akademikov* (Moscow, 1916), p. 30.

15. Varst [Varvara Stepanova], "Vystavka Ol'gi Rozanovoi," *Iskusstvo* 4 (February 22, 1919), p. 3.

16. Kazimir Malevich, letter to Konstantin Rozhdestvenskii, April 21, 1927, private archive, Moscow.

17. Unovis slogans, 1920, private archive, St. Petersburg: GIZ.

18. "Khudozhniki na dispute ob AKhRR," *Zhizn' iskusstva* 6 (1924).

19. N. Punin, *Tatlin (protiv kubizma)* (St. Petersburg: GIZ, 1921), pp. 17–18. Lev Bruni devised these formulae in 1916.

20. The booklet, like Malevich's *Ot kubizma k suprematizmu*, was published in time for the opening of the *0.10* exhibition. Sergei Isakov's article "K kontr-rel'efam Tatlina" appeared simultaneously in *Novyi zhurnal dlia vsekh* 12, pp. 46–50; *Novyi zhurnal dlia vsekh* was also the publisher of *Vladimir Evgrafovich Tatlin*.

21. This work is known only from old photographs. Pestel''s family also retains letters of hers from the early 1950s in which she mentions Tatlin.

22. One of the most recent publications on the Verbovka collective is *Ornament and Design. Nadezhda Udaltsowa. Varvara Stepanowa. Alexandr Rodchenko* (Moscow and Frankfurt am Main: Gallery Manege, 1991).

23. This according to Pestel''s memoirs.

24. V. Khodasevich, *Portrety slovami* (Moscow: Sovetskii pisatel', 1987), p. 106. In this publication, her reminiscences about Tatlin have, unfortunately, been severely abridged.

25. S. Dymshits-Tolstaia, "Vospominaniia," 1939–40, Manuscript Division, State Russian Museum, St. Petersburg, f. 700, ed. khr. 249.

26. L. S. Aleshina and N. V. Iavorskaia, comp., *B. N. Ternovets. Pis'ma. Dnevniki. Stat'i* (Moscow: Sovetskii khudozhnik, 1977), p. 242.

27. In Paris, Mukhina saw Popova often, and it is likely that she met Tatlin through Popova.

28. Lipchitz, who had been living in Paris for some time, acted as a translator for Tatlin.

29. See A. Strigalev, "O poezdke Tatlina v Berlin i Parizh," *Iskusstvo* 2 (1989), pp. 39–43, and *Iskusstvo* 3 (1989), pp. 26–30.

30. The photograph has been published in K. S. Malevich, *Essays on Art, 1915–1933*, ed. Troels Andersen, trans. Xenia Glowacki-Prus and Arnold McMillin (London: Rapp & Whiting, 1969), vol. 1, ill. 5.

31. Kazimir Malevich, letter to David Shterenberg, February 16, 1921, private archive, Moscow.

32. The date 1913 appears without caveat in the catalogue, *Desiataia gosudarstvennaia vystavka. Suprematizm i bespredmetnoe tvorchestvo* (Moscow: Otdel IZO Narkomprosa, 1919)—both in Malevich's statement (p. 16) and in Stepanova's (p. 7).

33. This was owing, in part, to Malevich's desire to "improve" his old works in advance of his trip to the West in 1927 and his solo show at the State Tret'iakov Gallery in 1929. The resulting confusion in dating was particularly apparent at the Malevich exhibition held at the Stedelijk Museum, Amsterdam, in 1989.

34. This story evidently had its origins in conversations with his followers in Vitebsk and Smolensk in 1920.

35. The term *fevralizm* is, nonetheless, likely tied to the white, "snowlike" backgrounds of the paintings.

36. A postcard reproducing the painting, with a contemporary inscription on the reverse identifying the work, is reproduced in Angelica Zander Rudenstine, ed., *Russian Avant-Garde Art: The George Costakis Collection* (New York: Abrams, 1981), p. 57. The inscription is in fact Malevich's own.

37. Malevich gave his view of the history of Russian Cubism in the context of European Cubism—and of Tatlin's place in the historical process—in articles published in Ukrainian in the Khar'kov journal, *Nova heneratsiia (New Generation)*, in 1928. Both have been published in English; see "The Constructive Painting of Russian Artists and Constructivism," in K. S. Malevich, *Essays on Art, 1915–1933*, ed. Troels Andersen, trans. Xenia Glowacki-Prus and Arnold McMillin (London: Rapp & Whiting, 1969), vol. 2, pp. 74–84.

38. Unovis slogans, 1920, private archive, St. Petersburg.

39. Quoted in Dymshits-Tolstaia, "Vospominaniia."

40. Malevich was threatened with arrest toward the end of his stay in Vitebsk, but was spared, thanks to the help of Robert Fal'k. In 1927 and in 1930, however, he was arrested.

41. It was owing to his stature that Tatlin became a leading figure in the reform of artistic life after the February Revolution.

42. Tatlin, who attached little importance to dates, gave 1912—and sometimes 1913 and 1914—as the year in which he advanced this slogan.

43. V. Tatlin, T. Shapiro, I. Meerzon, and P. Vinogradov, "Nasha predstoiashchaia rabota," *VIII s"ezd sovetov. Ezhednevnyi biulleten' s"ezda* 13 (January 1, 1921), p. 11.

44. *Zodchii* 19 (1915), p. 198.

45. The Eiffel Tower, by comparison, is 300 meters tall.

46. Private archive, United States.

47. On the relations between Punin and Tatlin, see I. Punina, "N. Punin. Kvartira No. 5," *Panorama iskusstv* 12 (1989), pp. 162–98.

48. P. Sorokin, "Otpravliaias' v dorogu," *Utrenniki* 1 (1922), p. 11.

49. Viktor Shklovskii appealed: "In the name of agitation, remove agitation from art," in his *Khod konia. Sbornik statei* (Moscow and Berlin: Gelikon, 1923), p. 45.

50. These are the words of A. Skachko, one of the most prominent cultural officials of the period, in *Vestnik iskusstv* 5 (1922), pp. 2–3.

51. The monuments erected were chiefly of a traditional variety, with little that was innovative about them. Although the "Anketa profsoiuza skul'pturov-khudozhnikov" ("Questionnaire of the Professional Union of Sculptors") did attempt to draw attention to contemporary forms: "Does the monument meet the requirements of plastic culture? Does it express the law of the deformation of forms?"

52. Quoted from a document in the Izo Narkompros archives.

53. See A. Strigalev, "O proekte pamiatnika III Internatsionala khudozhnika V. Tatlina," in *Voprosy sovetskogo iskusstva i arkhitektury* (Moscow: Sovetskii khudozhnik, 1973), pp. 408–52.

54. N. Radlov, *O futurizme* (St. Petersburg: "Akvilon," 1923), p. 48.

55. K. Miklashevskii, *Gipertrofiia iskusstva* (Petrograd, 1924), p. 59.

56. Typescripts of Tatlin's theses and some of the other articles prepared for the journal are held in both state and private archives in Russia.

57. The discussion is mentioned in N. Khardzhiev, "Pervyi illiustrator Maiakovskogo. K 90-letiiu so dnia rozhdeniia

V. Tatlina," *Moskovskii khudozhnik,* December 18, 1975. Since Maiakovskii—who was present—returned from Petrograd on December 11th and appeared at the Polytechnic Museum on the 12th, the discussion evidently took place on December 13th.

58. *Petrogradskaia Pravda,* December 1920, quoted from an undated newspaper clipping in the collection of A. Korsakova, Moscow.

59. V. Veidle, "Iskusstvo pri sovetskoi vlasti," in *Mosty. Sbornik statei k 50-letiiu russkoi revoliutsii* (Munich: Tovarishchestvo zarubezhnykh pisatelei, 1967), p. 44.

60. Ibid., p. 38.

61. Such a resolution was passed, for instance, at a meeting of Unovis in Petrograd on October 14, 1922.

62. See, for example, Il'ia Chashnik and Nikolai Suetin, letter to Kazimir Malevich, October 4, 1924, published in *Suprematismus* (Zurich: Galerie Schlegl, 1989), pp. 50–51.

63. I. Vrona, "O Tatline," 1967, private archive.

64. Tatlin considered Aleksei Sotnikov exceptional among his students in Moscow, and Moris Umanskii and Iakov Shtoffer among those in Kiev.

65. Central State Archive for Literature and Art, Moscow, f. 680, op. 3, ed. khr. 208, l. 238.

66. Quoted from a biographical note written by Tatlin in 1929, published in *Tatlin* (Weingarten: Kunstverlag Weingarten, 1987), p. 328.

67. Production art is widely discussed in the publications of VNIITE, Moscow, in the 1970s. For a different view, see A. Mazaeva, *Kontseptsiiu "proizvodstvennogo iskusstva" 20-kh godov* (Moscow: Nauka, 1975).

68. On Obmokhu, see Aleksandra Shatskikh, "A Brief History of Obmokhu" and Christina Lodder, "The Transition to Constructivism," and on the Electroorganism group, Irina Lebedeva, "The Poetry of Science: Projectionism and Electroorganism," in this volume.

69. Constructivism began in approximately 1920, with the activities of the group for "mass action" whose members included both Aleksei Gan and Rodchenko.

70. Aleksei Gan's typographical layout of *Sovremennaia arkhitektura (Contemporary Architecture)*—the journal of Constructivism in architecture—is one example.

71. In an effort to reconcile abstraction and production art, Boris Kushner advanced the term *bespredmetnaia khudozhestvennaia kul'tura* (non-objective artistic culture) in a lecture at the House of Publishing, Moscow, on March 20, 1922.

72. Tatlin's text in the catalogue for the exhibition of his *Letatlin* sketches at the Museum of Fine Arts (Moscow, 1932) is particularly contentious vis-à-vis the Moscow Constructivists.

73. E. Kronman, "Ukhod v tekhniku. Tatlin i 'Letatlin,'" *Brigada khudozhnikov* 6 (1932), pp. 19–23.

74. Quoted in A. Efros, *Mastera raznykh epokh* (Moscow: Sovetskii khudozhnik, 1979), p. 547.

75. *Letatlin* was described as "not so much . . . an invention as . . . a sui-generis work of art" in N. Frausek, "Iskusstvo v tekhniku," *Tekhnika,* April 9, 1932, p. 4.

76. K. Zelinskii, "Letatlin," *Vecherniaia Moskva,* April 6, 1932, p. 2.

77. M. Levidov, *Prostye istiny. O chitatele i pisatele* (Moscow and Leningrad, 1927), pp. 154–55.

78. A. Voegeli, *Sowiet-Russland* (Bern: Verlag Hans Huber, 1936), Tafel 3.

79. Nikolai Suetin, letter to Anna Leporskaia, 1937, Collection N. N. Suetina, St. Petersburg.

80. Rozhdestvenskii Archive, Moscow.

fig. 1
Ivan Puni
Poster, 0.10: The Last Futurist
Exhibition, 1915.
Lithograph, 74 x 55.5 cm.
Private collection, Zurich.

The Critical Reception of the *0.10* Exhibition: Malevich and Benua

Jane A. Sharp

The prominent St. Petersburg critic Aleksandr Benua (also known as Alexandre Benois) begins his review of the *0.10* exhibition (Petrograd, 1915–16) and of Kazimir Malevich's latest innovation—Suprematism—with the admission that he is not in a position to judge vanguard art, that it is "absolutely foreign to me." And in a self-reflexive passage of the text he explains why: "But what I see at the exhibitions of our 'ultra-Modernists, as such' simply leaves me cold and indifferent. I do not sense the 'spirit of art' and I just become bored at them. In this [reaction] a certain psychologizing manifests itself: I become interested not in what I see but in the reasons why it leaves me cold. My psychologizing is confused and full of contradictions, bringing forth ever renewed floods of fatigue and, again, boredom."[1]

But these first observations are deceptive; Benua's topos in fact calls attention to the immense significance of Malevich's inauguration of Suprematism. Above all, the review is apocalyptical. Benua articulates his response to Suprematism in terms of the horror of the unknown as well as in terms of a certain horror of uniformity—the possibility of endless repetitions of faceless, figureless canvases. For Benua, the *0.10* exhibition was not simply the "last Futurist exhibition" (as the show was subtitled); it represented the end of painting altogether and not the beginning of a new "national style." Moreover, Benua did not interpret the *Chernyi kvadrat* (*Black Square*, 1915, fig. no. 2) as a sign of radical social engagement or *épatement* as he did earlier vanguard work. Instead, he describes the *Black Square* as a tabula rasa, a "complete zero" that has made representation (as a response to the natural world) irrelevant to a completely decadent "indifferent" society. The review proclaims a watershed moment in the vanguard artist's challenge to and absorption into the status quo: the "boorishness" and "Americanization" of Russian society predicted by Benua (and by Dmitrii Merezhkovskii in an earlier review) has in fact been achieved, and no one has noticed.[2]

This reaction has its reverse parallel in a number of comments by vanguard artists and critics after the Revolution when the *Black Square* came to represent the very face of the ongoing revolution and the new society that it sought to create. Like the earliest theorists of the European avant-garde in the mid-nineteenth century, El Lissitzky understood and valued the dynamic power of the radically new in art to predict or even effect radical political and social change.[3] In his essay of 1920, "Suprematism in World Reconstruction," Lissitzky presents his view of the *Black Square* as the harbinger of a new cosmic era: "for us SUPREMATISM did not signify the recognition of an absolute form which was part of an already-completed universal system. on the contrary here stood revealed for the first time in all its purity the clear sign and plan for a definite new world never before experienced—a world which issues forth from our inner being and which is only now in the first stages of its formation. for this reason the square of suprematism became a beacon."[4] Following the Revolution, Lissitzky cast the aims of Suprematism in political terms by counterpointing parallel descriptions of the successive upheavals brought about through art and Bolshevik Communism: "into this chaos came suprematism extolling the square as the very source of all creative expression. and then came communism and extolled work as the true source of man's heartbeat."[5]

Landmarks in the periodical criticism of the times (such as Benua's review of *0.10*) reveal that the alliance forged between stylistic innovation and radical social politics which we ascribe to the revolutionary era was grounded in earlier perceptions of avant-garde art. Benua's response to Suprematism as the herald/revealer of social and aesthetic cataclysm shows how the reception of avant-garde art before the Revolution determined the artist's paradoxical status as a "leftist" wielding considerable authority after the Revolution. In order better to understand this condition, we must recognize first that both left artists and leftist politicians drew their authority in the new society from the radical contexts of their prerevolutionary activities.

Malevich was sufficiently disturbed by Benua's review to write an angry reply, which he intended to have published in a daily newspaper but instead sent directly to the critic himself.[6] In the letter, Malevich reproaches Benua for dominating a system that has exhausted itself and survives only to impede the new. But his response is more than a complaint lodged against the status quo. In language that abounds with social and political metaphor, the letter threateningly predicts the system's violent demise: "You have deprived the academy and museum of any real significance. You have made them strictly partisan exhibitions and thus a tool, the casemate of a prison, a restraint on freedom of thought. You have set up your commonplace clichés there and built up a reputation for them; and the work of anyone that follows your pattern faithfully can hang alongside yours in your exhibitions . . . You have all the tools to erase everything that is not made in your image, but canvas is strong and the garret serves as the boor's gallery and museum. Your grandchildren will get the canvases out from there and will wring the neck of your system."[7]

Of course, a little over a year later, with the October Revolution, the system that Benua represented for Malevich would be overthrown and, by 1920, with the inception of Unovis (the Affirmers of the New Art) in Vitebsk, Malevich's own collective "system" would be installed. His program, like the statutes designed by a number of artists in the years of War Communism, functioned as a critique of the Imperial academic system by replacing its teacher/student hierarchy with a collective workshop structure. The significance of this inversion of social hierarchy and its synecdochical relation to the birth of Suprematism was articulated even before the formal transformation of the Vitebsk Popular Art School into Unovis. The cover of Malevich's pamphlet *O novykh sistemakh v iskusstve* (*On New Systems in Art*) collapses the primary geometric forms of Suprematism and the admonition that "the overturning of the old world of arts will be etched across your palms" (recto); the notice on the verso reads "Work and edition by the workshop [*artel'*] of artistic labor at the Vitebsk Svomas" (fig. no. 3).[8]

This attack and counterattack between critic and artist epitomizes communication before the Revolution between vanguard artists of Malevich's generation and their critics. The exchange manifests the contradiction inherent in the vanguard's position as a movement of opposition to a dominant social structure and aesthetic system which it essentially seeks to replace. Similarly, Benua's discussion of Malevich's work, like his evaluation of other vanguard artists, particularly Natal'ia Goncharova and David Burliuk, is at once an extended critique and a measure of the avant-garde's impact on prerevolutionary Russian society. Although Benua would periodically claim he was bored by the vanguard artist's posturing, a summary reading of his reviews of any number of avant-garde exhibitions before the Revolution would lead us to attribute to him any reaction but ennui. Indeed, Benua was extremely vocal in his hostility to Russia's fledgling vanguard. A prominent artist himself, cofounder of the journal *Mir iskusstva* (*World of Art*) in 1898, and an art historian, Benua became in 1908 the chief art critic of the daily St. Petersburg newspaper *Rech'* (*Speech*), which published each month his reviews of artistic and theatrical events. He was the among the first critics to isolate and describe the new Primitivism

manifested in vanguard exhibitions beginning with the Golubaia roza (Blue Rose) exhibition of 1907.[9] In 1912 he wrote a blistering critique of avant-garde polemics, "Kubizm ili kukishizm" ("Cubism or *Je-m'en-foutisme*"), which focused on the interpretations of French Cubism by David Burliuk and other artists.[10] He may be credited as one of the critics who defined and named the avant-garde, using the terms *peredovaia molodezh'* (vanguard youth), *levye* (leftists), and *futuristy* (Futurists) somewhat indiscriminately in referring to the artists of Petersburg and Moscow who formed the groups Soiuz molodezhi (Union of Youth), Bubnovyi valet (Jack of Diamonds), and Oslinyi khvost (Donkey's Tail). (In his review of the *0.10* exhibition, he would describe Malevich's group as the *krainii levyi flang* [extreme left flank] of the art world.) Together with Iakov Tugendkhol'd, Sergei Makovskii, and Maksimilian Voloshin, all contributors to major newspapers as well as to the influential art journal *Apollon* (*Apollo*), he was a powerful arbiter of taste among the art-going (and art-buying) public; as Malevich would claim with good reason a few years later, "without the stamp of Benua and his associates, no work of art could receive civil rights and life's benefits."[11] Malevich continued by listing the names of artists who had both suffered from and profited by the attention of Benua and his colleagues: "This was the case with Vrubel, Musatov, P. Kuznetsov and Goncharova, whom they finally recognized after throwing mud at them for a long time; but how many have still not been acknowledged!"[12] Malevich's response, in other words, recognizes that the critics (Benua in particular) who so successfully dominated and controlled the art market played a primary role in defining the avant-garde as a marginal, radical force.

Benua's antipathy to avant-garde art appears to have peaked earlier, in 1912, with his cutting reviews of the Union of Youth exhibitions which took place in St. Petersburg and included members of the Moscow avant-garde as well.[13] His criticisms of vanguard art typically center on the Russian artist's accursed proclivity for assimilating external influences. In Benua's view, Russian art is so assimilative that its history and the vanguard's place in this history must be characterized as nonevolutionary. Vanguard innovations in style do not point toward a movement laying the basis for a new school or "national style"; rather they appear as "nothing else but equilibristic stunts, somersaulting in the air." Benua situates this observation, however, in the context of Russian society. Deprived of social support (a stable, informed audience), contemporary art appears to be "arbitrary" and "impermanent"—it can only reflect the current fashion or trend. He argues that despite the remarkable talents involved, vanguard artists share a common trait: they produce "hurried, unthought-through work— shoddy goods [*deshevka*]. This is the absence of what is called a school."[14] Although this attack was leveled at the vanguard youth in general, in his review of Malevich's Suprematist work Benua uses similar metaphors: "And this is not merely the hoarse cry of the carnival barker [*zazyval'shchik*] but the main 'trick' in the puppet show [*v balaganchike*] of the very last word in culture."[15]

By the end of 1913, however, with the opening of Goncharova's mammoth solo exhibition in Moscow, Benua seemed to have reconciled his wholly negative view of vanguard culture with a new appreciation of the expressive power of Primitivism and even of Cubo-Futurism in Russian art. His comments on this occasion reflect his broader anxiety over the "difficulties" inherent in reading vanguard art, prefiguring his critique of Malevich in 1916. In this respect, Benua's review remains an important record of the process of public and critical acceptance that this exhibition initiated for Goncharova's work and for vanguard art generally. Like his

fig. 2
Kazimir Malevich
Black Square, *1915.*
Oil on canvas, 79.5 x 79.5 cm.
State Tret'iakov Gallery, Moscow.

fig. 3
Kazimir Malevich
Cover for his On New Systems in Art, *1919.*
Lithograph, 23 x 37.2 cm.
Collection of Prints and Drawings,
The Federal Institute of Technology, Zurich.

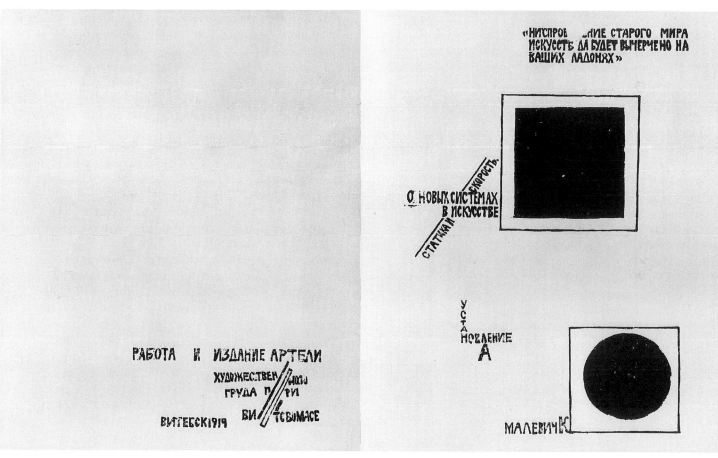

critique of Malevich's work, this earlier review is unusually self-reflexive; it mediates between references to his previously negative evaluation of Goncharova's work and soul-searching examinations of the reasons for his present capitulation:

I went again to Goncharova's exhibition in part to test my first impression, in part simply to delight in it. It turns out I had not gone astray the first time, I was not mistaken. On the contrary, today I sensed even more clearly that this is a great talent and a true artist. Generally speaking, I believed her even more, and consequently I may change completely my whole attitude toward the kind of painting which she represents . . . I saw at this exhibition many old familiar paintings which were in our {World of Art} and other exhibitions. It means a great deal to see them now within the artist's whole oeuvre. Their "talent" was always clear to me and I got into many arguments with close friends over this. But I did not completely "believe in them." Much of her art seemed a pose to me, a distortion and youthful joke. Now I am ready to believe in the complete sincerity of a master and at the same time it is absolutely clear to me that it is not Goncharova who needs to learn but we who must learn from her, as it always follows that one should learn from all the great and strong. No, this is not ugliness or distortion but the very opposite: the intention (accomplished) to become perfectly connected with oneself; to express in the simplest way that which is hidden in the soul and bursts to the surface.[16]

Paradoxically, it is now Benua who comes to the vanguard artist's defense, countering Goncharova's detractors by arguing that much of her work, especially her earliest paintings and pastels, is "completely 'acceptable,' accessible to the comprehension of those who have only an amateurish interest in art."

Benua's acceptance of Goncharova's work, however, like his acceptance of the new trends it represents, does not read as a step toward the commodification of a previously "militant" artistic message.[17] Rather, it is a disruptive, continuously equivocal process for him that requires a complete reevaluation of the whole vanguard tradition which he had dismissed just the year before in his essay "Cubism or *Je-m'en-foutisme*":

As with my experience last year in Sergei Ivanovich Shchukin's gallery, I lived through a lot in the past two days at Goncharova's exhibition. Now I can no longer consider as heresy even the most extreme dislocations {sdvigi}, that nightmarish abracadabra that has issued from Picasso and has infested all of the vanguard youth, here and in the West. These pictures still disturb me, yet I now clearly feel that they exist within the realm of art.

Benua's lengthy discussion of Goncharova's work registers in actuality what Viktor Shklovskii later defined as an aim of *ostranenie* (making strange) in literature—the deliberate impeding of the viewer's perception.[18] Developing his new insights into the pictorial forms of Cubism and Futurism, Benua describes his response to a roomful of Goncharova's latest and most trying Futurist works, her urban machine and factory images:

In accordance with the new formulae of painting: objects are depicted as precisely fragmented and incorrectly reconstituted colors, terrifyingly "raw"; through forms, which only with great difficulty are identifiable with forms in reality, some sort of "half-spoken" signs pass by. One has to look at the painting, and involuntarily read what is said there. One's attention is intensified—even more than that, it is tormented. Looking at such pictures requires suffering.

Benua's appreciation of his dilemma is contingent upon recognizing in Goncharova's language and subject matter signs of the modern age, which he, like so many artists of his generation, transposes into an apocalyptic vision of the future. In this context, the vanguard artist appears as a clairvoyant of the encroaching industrial era—the machine its new god. Benua ultimately finds positive value in Goncharova's work, which he now interprets as a messianic expression of the impending battle with the "philistinism" and "American devilry" associated with developed capitalism in Russia. He concludes that this trend can only be overcome or reversed by "looking for the revelation of God in everything, turning away from superficial stagnation and [instead] constantly penetrating into the essence of things." The difficulty in reading the image has the effect of slowing down perception, allowing the viewer to contemplate the relationship of the fragmented forms to his or her life experience. For Benua, who finds a direct correspondence between the *faktura* (density) of Goncharova's canvases and real perceptual phenomena, her art becomes the "sincere" and "honest" reflection of a world in turmoil. Thus, Benua assures his readers that the "suffering" experienced in viewing Goncharova's work is essentially beneficial, even redemptive.

Two years later, in his review of the *0.10* exhibition, Benua reversed this position. Malevich's *Black Square* cannot redeem society—it is the icon of a cardinal sin: humankind's arrogant elevation of the self (and the machine) above nature and God— the *Black Square* is blasphemy. Benua expresses this view in no uncertain terms, repeating the words *koshchunstvo* (blasphemy) and *koshchunstvovat'* (to blaspheme). It is clear that, with the advent of the *0.10* exhibition, Benua shifted his critique of vanguard art from accusations of epigonism and eclecticism to the hostile recognition that with Suprematism Malevich had truly advanced a coherent new style in painting.

In order to understand Benua's extreme reaction to the first presentation of Suprematism, we must examine his quasi-religious, quasi-social/political rhetoric in more detail. Benua's critique focuses on the way in which the *Black Square* was hung in the exhibition: "high above, right under the ceiling, in the 'holy place'"—in the traditional place of the icon (fig. no. 4). Because of Malevich's choice in hanging the painting, the *Black Square* does not merely constitute an analogue to the icon and thereby acquire similar authority as an image; the *Black Square* actually *replaces* the icon. By usurping the seat of the icon, the *Black Square* diagrams the destruction of one set of values and the installation of a new hierarchy—the dominion of forms over nature. Benua explains: "Without a doubt, this is the 'icon' which the Futurists propose as a replacement for the Madonnas and shameless Venuses [*besstyzhie venery*], it is that 'dominion' [*gospodstvo*] of forms over nature." Malevich's system signals the encroachment of an insidious rationalistic logic into the realm of aesthetic experience, at the base of which lies a "horrific means of mechanical 'renewal' [*mekhanicheskoe 'vosstanovlenie'*] with its machinishness." This act of blasphemy even penetrates Benua's description of the *Black Square*: it is a "Black Square in a white frame" (here Benua uses the term that denotes the setting of the icon— *v belom oklade*—to describe the frame). His language clearly indicates a refusal to acknowledge the evolution of Malevich's art; his concern to expose Malevich's blasphemous act prevents him from taking any notice of Suprematism's own dependence upon the icon (a source for Malevich's Primitivism of circa 1910–12).

Thus, he claims that the *Black Square* issues from and serves only to illustrate Malevich's "sermon of zero and death," his statement (nearly identical to the first paragraphs of *Ot kubizma k suprematizmu* [*From Cubism to Suprematism*]) published in a leaflet which was distributed free at the exhibition.[19] In Benua's view, Malevich's claim to authority, to "dominion" or "supremacy" (whence the term Suprematism is derived), is

fig. 4
View of the 0.10 *exhibition showing Malevich's* Black Square *in the*
"icon's place," center top.

ahistorical, for it is achieved only through pride, by self-assertion. The point and purpose of his essay—to demonstrate the destructive force of Malevich's blasphemous act—are achieved through references to a chief biblical sin, that of vainglory: "[This] is not a chance little episode that occurred on the Field of Mars; it is one of the acts of self-affirmation the source of which has as its name the abomination of desolation. It asserts itself through arrogance, haughtiness, and by trampling over all that is dear and tender; it will lead only to death."[20] Text and review combined, this is an account of "absolute origins"[21] that has no equivalent in Russia's past cultural experience. The force of the disruption that the advent of Suprematism hailed is mirrored in the passion of both the artist's and the critic's language.

A year later, in his review of the *Sovremennaia zhivopis'* (*Contemporary Painting*) exhibition held at Nadezhda Dobychina's gallery (where the *0.10* exhibition had also been held), Benua continues his attack on the ahistoricity of Suprematism, asserting that Malevich's "little circles, squares, and sticks have only given birth to Aleksandra Ekster's exercises."[22] Benua's review is a willful misstatement, since we know that within the year (1916–17) a number of artists—including Nadezhda Udal'tsova, Ivan Puni, Liubov' Popova, Ol'ga Rozanova, Ivan Kliun, and Mikhail Men'kov, among others—had adopted Suprematism as their own and formed the group known briefly as Supremus.[23] Benua's purpose, however, is consistent with his long-standing commitment to exposing the commercial self-interest and "trickery" of avant-garde art.

Malevich's written response is a protracted attack on Benua's system, his authority, and the value which he attaches to mimesis. (Indeed, most vanguard critiques of the art establishment link mimesis with the power obtained by specific artists and critics in the academy and press.) In the first section of the letter, Malevich counters Benua's argument by asserting that mimetic representation, based on the canons of Roman and Greek art, has long ceased to have any value for society. Furthermore, he claims that critics like Benua and Merezhkovskii have failed to see the future in the new; instead, he writes, "Merezhkovsky stands on the new age's square amidst the furious vortex of machines both on earth and in the sky; he stares with blind eyes and continues to hold Caesar's bone above his gray head and to shout about beauty."[24] Contesting Benua's argument that Suprematism is ultimately destructive, he asks, "but how has the World of Art enriched our own times?" and responds with a parodistic description of Benua's own painting: "He has given us a couple of crinoline petticoats and a few uniforms from the time of Peter the Great." Similarly, he matches Benua's biblical rhetoric with his own. His account of the difficulties the avant-garde artist faces in countering Benua's system of "commonplace clichés," which dominates by entrapping unsuspecting young artists desperate to exhibit and attain fame, is a *cri de foi* far more eloquent than his manifesto, *From Cubism to Suprematism*:

I possess only a single bare, frameless icon of our times (like a pocket), and it is difficult to struggle.

But my happiness in not being like you will give me the strength to go further and further into the empty wilderness. For it is only there that transformation can take place.

And I think you are mistaken when you say in reproaching me that my philosophy will destroy millions of lives. Are you not, all of you, like a roaring blaze that obstructs and prevents any forward movement?[25]

Malevich's statement engages one of the principal motifs in Benua's review, that of the vanguard artist as social outcast. Extending his metaphor of the carnival barker, Benua makes an analogy between the cries of the barkers on the streets of Petrograd and the vanguard's claim for legitimation in Russian culture. He writes: "You see that they are artists, that they have the right to a critical evaluation. And yet everything that they say and do rings out with such cries of poverty that pity, which had been verging on respect, yields to some kind of internal panic, and one wants to run away in any direction (even to the lackey-like Petrograd artists) without looking back, only so that one might no longer see those shapes bent by the bitter cold, those painted faces, or hear those horrible cracking voices."[26]

Malevich's dialogue with Benua essentially confirms Benua's analogy—that the vanguard artist acts out in the world of art the experiences of the unenfranchised, the true outcasts in society. This analogy explains, in part, the passion of Malevich's response to Benua—clearly more was at stake in his inauguration of Suprematism than the advancement of a new "style." Malevich's battle was one of empowerment and entitlement in a society which viewed art, politics, and morality as essentially and implicitly integrated.

It is ironic that Benua failed to appreciate the historical evolution of Malevich's work. For there is every indication that Malevich, more than any other vanguard artist of his generation (with the possible exception of Mikhail Larionov), sought to promote a historical context for the inauguration of his movement that would validate his claim for recognition. If Malevich asserted that "the face of my Square cannot become merged with a single master or age," he also affirmed, practically in the same breath, that "I, too, am a stage of development."[27] This statement sets forth the paradox embodied in the avant-garde artist's position, overlaying the values Malevich clearly attached to historical views of his own artistic evolution (and the possibility of engendering a "school") with his desire to create a style that was absolutely unfamiliar to his contemporaries.

Malevich's statement epitomizes the dialectic operating within Modernist discourse on originality and imitation. Inasmuch as Malevich claimed his place in history as the originator of a unique style, his contribution required a context for its interpretation. The desired interpretation (the originality of Suprematism) could be assured only by establishing relationships to preceding artistic trends and by the generation of a following among like-minded artists. Malevich's dual concern echoes in the work and theoretical writings of other left artists throughout the 1920s. The will among vanguard artists to invent or trace their artistic evolution runs up continually against their momentous ruptures with the past and their utopian interest in generating a new origin for the art of the future. Here again, Malevich stands out; the charts which he generated through teaching at Vitebsk and, after 1921, in Petrograd/Leningrad are unique if characteristic. They map the evolution of modern art from Realism to Suprematism and ascribe the generation of a new characteristic form (the "additional element") to a master artist at the head of each new movement. In this way Malevich could diagram his place within an evolutionary model of art history and at the same time point to his unique contribution, the "additional element" contained within Suprematism.[28]

Benua's reaction to the *0.10* exhibition and his analogy between the vanguard artist and the carnival barker provide part of the background for Malevich's historicizing efforts. Like other vanguard artists, Malevich tended to counter critics' misinterpretation of his art, and their authority, by generating his own stylistic history. Evgenii Kovtun and Charlotte Douglas have traced the evolution of Malevich's ideas that led to the development of Suprematism as a style by drawing principally on the remarkably revealing correspondence

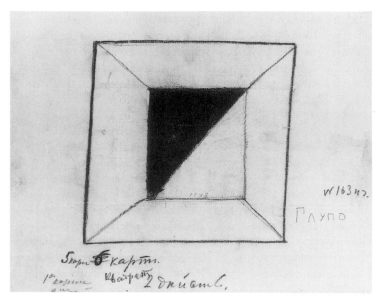

fig. 5
Kazimir Malevich
Set design: Act II, scene 5, for Aleksei Kruchenykh,
Victory over the Sun, *1913.*
Pencil on paper, 21 x 27 cm.
St. Petersburg State Museum of Theater
and Musical Arts.

between Malevich and his close friend and associate, Mikhail Matiushin.[29] References to this correspondence have tended to further Malevich's own interpretive aims: to aggrandize and mystify the creative act of invention (or "self-creation").[30] As this correspondence confirms, by May 1915 Malevich had come to attribute the historical evolution of his new style to a particular origin in his work—to his set designs for *Pobeda nad solntsem* (*Victory over the Sun,* 1913), a performance on which he had collaborated with Matiushin and the poets Aleksei Kruchenykh and Velimir Khlebnikov.[31] Douglas has drawn our attention particularly to the set design for Act II, scene 5 (fig. no. 5) and its "square-within-a-square format" as a design that was "halfway to [the Suprematist square's] realization."[32] Yet Malevich's own intentions *are* realized here—for he had written to Matiushin asking that he include in a new edition of the libretto (planned but never published, according to Kovtun) an illustration of this particular work. Through this publication, the stage backdrop would serve as a testament documenting the origins and evolution of Suprematism. Thus Malevich writes to Matiushin: "I would be very grateful if you would include my drawing of the curtain for the act in which the victory took place . . . This drawing will be of immense significance for painting. That which was done unconsciously now bears unexpected fruit [*neobychainye plody*]."[33]

Malevich's concern to identify a point of origin for Suprematism and at the same time to advance Suprematism as a new origin in a continuous historical evolution of styles explains the tremendous secrecy with which he guarded the work that he painted in this year. In a manner that has no parallel in Russia, Malevich was determined to *author* Suprematism. It was advanced specifically as his signature style. Both Kovtun and Douglas assert that until the autumn of 1915 no one except Matiushin knew what Malevich was working on in his studio, but that on or just before September 25, 1915, Ivan Puni surprised Malevich with an unexpected visit and saw his latest work. Malevich immediately wrote Matiushin, urging him to move ahead with the brochure: "Now, no matter what, I must publish the brochure on my work and christen it and in so doing protect my rights as author."[34] A few days later he informs Matiushin of the aftereffects in the Moscow art world, noting that a bitter debate over the creation of a new direction has arisen, but that "no one knows the how or the what of it," and everyone wants to study his (Malevich's) notes. Still, for the larger public, Malevich's new work remained unknown. As late as November 25th, he could write to Matiushin, "The name everyone knows, only the content no one knows. Let it *remain a secret.*"[35]

The control with which Malevich manipulated the inauguration of Suprematism can also be understood in the light of Benua's frequent reviews or critiques of vanguard epigonism. Two external factors impinged both on Malevich's concern over the historical representation of Suprematism's origin and on Benua's response. First, the rapid pace at which artists were exposed to new trends and producing new work, together with the constant turnover of exhibitions and debates and the flood of reviews, had effected a perceptible acceleration of change in the art world. As early as 1909, Benua characterized this phenomenon as uniquely Russian. In February of that year, he wrote a polemical critique of the Russian art world that begins with the observation: "There is not a day when a new art exhibition does not open. This would be interesting if our groups of artists were organized according to essential [common] features or strivings determined by each group. But nothing of the sort . . . In a provincial manner, divisions occur among artists here for the most absurd reasons . . . and so now simultaneously a mass of exhibitions have opened of a 'midsize type' in which all the same artists participate, and the character of the work from one group to the next is indistinguishable."[36]

Internecine feuds among artists as well as reviews of art exhibitions testify to the spirit of competition which this pluralism of the art world engendered. From the 1911–12 season on, vanguard groups were beset by factionalism, with artists continually realigning themselves. The Donkey's Tail group was formed initially by artists who, with Larionov and Goncharova, broke away from the Jack of Diamonds.[37] Although they exhibited together, Malevich feuded with both Larionov and Tatlin, and Malevich's invention of Suprematism was in part fueled by his long-standing rivalry with both artists.[38] This struggle for ascendancy and legitimation was mapped out in the installation of the *0.10* exhibition, with Malevich and his supporters occupying one room while Tatlin and his group (including Popova, Vera Pestel', and Udal'tsova) were positioned in another; the sign PROFESSIONAL ARTISTS marked the difference between them.

Malevich's efforts during the year preceding the exhibition manifest the profound competitiveness that shaped all aspects of vanguard activities. In this sense his writings conveyed a very clear public message which linked the historical legitimation of his new style with assertions of its superiority over other potential contenders. In 1915, Malevich's letters to Matiushin record Malevich's frustration with the contemporary art scene and with its eclecticism, and articulate the sense among artists that a new coherent movement was needed. As Malevich puts it, "In Moscow they are beginning to agree with me that we must present ourselves under a new banner."[39] Thus, while he asserts the need to present a coherent movement through the *0.10* exhibition, he wonders if anyone else has advanced a rival theory or style and continues by giving the reasons why he finds Suprematism the best name for his: "But it will be interesting to see: will they give [this banner] a new form? I think that Suprematism is the most appropriate [name], since it signifies supremacy [or dominion—*gospodstvo*]."[40] He attached tremendous importance to the text which first bore the name of the style (*From Cubism to Suprematism*) and which had been published by Matiushin in time to be sold at the exhibition. Thanking Matiushin, Malevich writes, "It will advance my position tremendously" and again a few days later, "the brochure is playing an important role for me."[41] In the context of vanguard rivalries, there could be no mistaking the value which Malevich placed on competitive public access to his work and on control over the means and process of its critical reception.

An equally important consideration for Malevich was the changing makeup of the public and the shifts in its reaction to the vanguard debates and exhibitions. Outside of published criticism, the social composition of the urban Russian public is extremely difficult to document. Reviews, however, give a good indication of the turnarounds in the public response to vanguard art. In his "Cubism or *Je-m'en-foutisme*" of 1912, Benua writes that just two years earlier, portions of Burliuk's speech on Cubism would have created a scandal. Benua makes these comments in order to illustrate "how fast we have declined," indicating that by 1912 segments of the public had become inured or even attracted to the vulgarity of vanguard debates and exhibitions. The year 1910 is in fact an appropriate one to mark, since it constitutes the beginning of this generation's series of confrontations with the public in the exhibition space. The first Jack of Diamonds exhibition (which included work by Malevich, Goncharova, Larionov, and Tatlin together for the first time) opened to cries of scandal in December 1910,[42] a year later, at a public debate organized by this group, Larionov announced the platform of the Donkey's Tail group to jeering crowds.[43] By 1912, the public usually attended these debates in

the hope of witnessing a scandal or fight (notorious incidents were always documented in the press). In 1913 Larionov was tried and fined for having punched one artist in the face and thrown the podium into the audience.[44] But in 1913 there were also signs of acquiescence, of public acceptance of provocations and, indeed, of new "radical" painting.

The overwhelming success of Goncharova's solo exhibition in Moscow at the end of 1913 is the first significant measure of public acceptance and critical acclaim for the vanguard artist. Paintings which had been considered radical just a year ago were now appreciated or accepted by the same public and described in the press as "accessible." A reviewer in *Moskovskaia gazeta* (*The Moscow Gazette*) declared: "It seems that Rayist and Futurist art are becoming stylish [*modnyi*]. In a little while, both Goncharova and Larionov will be acclaimed on the level of Korovin and Kustodiev."[45] The same reviewer writes that the success of the opening night was completely unexpected by the organizers and made Goncharova an instant sensation. His summary of the "successful components" of the evening focuses primarily on the appeal her exhibition had as a social diversion, uniting in symbiotic agreement the vanguard artist as *provocatrice* and her receptive audience: "Packed halls, 'chic' public, the incredulous looks and confused smiles of those who were leaving, the ironic 'witticisms' and independent poses of the brave, a couple of Futurist characters persistently competing for attention in orange jackets and with carnations braided in their hair, the blushing-for-joy Goncharova and the magically-appearing-in-twenty-places-at-once Larionov."[46] Thus, the fresh appeal of Goncharova's art is set, within the context of the exhibition space, as that of a new type of urban spectacle— dominated by an elite Muscovite public that now included the vanguard artist.

There are parallel contemporary accounts of the public-debate forum which by 1913 had become an established event. A booklet published in Moscow in 1914 chronicles the reciprocity between the audiences and the organizers of these vanguard debates.[47] Observing that the debates have become increasingly frequent and varied, the anonymous author writes:

If one studies carefully the different lectures, and particularly the debates, one comes to the inevitable conclusion that they are no more than a shameless and open exploitation of popular entertainment. It is frequently so hapless, and crude {an exploitation}, that one has to wonder why the public reacts with such relative calm to these lowbrow transgressions.

By the way, the public, for the most part, gets what it is looking for. And it is usually looking for a scandal.

The participants in debates and lectures have reckoned beautifully with this search for scandal and organize them relatively skillfully. To the naïve person it may seem that the scandal arose suddenly, without warning. Whereas the entrepreneur has invited a particular opponent (especially from among the Futurists), knowing full well in advance that he will create a scandal.[48]

The new reconciliation of the "radical" and the "acceptable" in the public reception of vanguard art and in the forum of the debate explains much about the seemingly contradictory responses to the *0.10* exhibition. Thus, among the reviews of that exhibition, we find a number of wholesale rejections of the work shown there as well as a few of the most subtle positive

fig. 6
Ol'ga Rozanova
Cupboard with Dishes, *1915.*
Oil on canvas, 64 x 45 cm.
State Tret'iakov Gallery, Moscow.

fig. 7
Nadezhda Udal'tsova
Kitchen, *1915.*
Oil on canvas, 66 x 81.5 cm.
State Russian Museum, St. Petersburg.

appraisals. One of the more negative reviewers connected Suprematism with Tatlin, exclaiming that "the audacity of Futurism has given birth to Suprematism, sincerity has turned into a joke at the public's expense. And not a trace of painting remains. Only tinplate."[49] Like Benua in his earlier reaction to Goncharova's Cubo-Futurist work, the reviewer describes his appreciation of the difficulties inherent in looking at the Cubo-Futurist painting, contrasting that perceptual process with the new work on view:

You squint, you blink, you unexpectedly study the corners of the painting on the canvases of the Futurists.
But not with the Suprematists. The work is dry, monotonous, there is neither painting nor individuality. Malevich is like Popova, Popova is like Puni, Puni is like Udal'tsova. You can't distinguish between them.

Negative reviews such as this one are typical of the majority of reviews of avant-garde art and, in their leveling of individualities, rationalize the competitive spirit of vanguard enterprises—both exhibitions and debates. The dialogue between Benua and Malevich is unusual precisely because of the passion and personal nature of the attack. It was in the interest of those in control to underplay the shock of avant-garde transgressions and to neutralize, as the reviewer does above, difference as a function of vanguard innovation. In this context, the positive reviews are more interesting, for they display far more critical sophistication than the negative ones (Benua's aside). And, while reviewers occasionally take sides, they openly refer to artists' concern with their place in history, engaging in a more explicit way the question of originality and *posledovatel'nost'* (succession). For example, Matiushin praises both Malevich's and Tatlin's work and, not surprisingly, asserts that Suprematism gives "the strong impression that it is the oncoming shift [*sdvig*] in art."[50] Regarding Tatlin ("without a doubt, a great artist"), he argues that despite the "intensity of his constructive idea," his earlier reliefs are stronger works of art.[51] Matiushin's review is of greater importance as an indicator of the degree to which the language of criticism and theory had developed by 1915 (he speaks of the "strength of painterly masses," of the "dynamism of colors," of "color planes," and so forth). He notes in closing that the competition among artists for *pervenstvo* (primacy) undercuts the development of their ideas: "Whoever says the last word is king!"[52]

Aleksandr Rostislavov's review, published in the same journal as Benua's, is the strongest positive review of both Malevich's and Tatlin's work.[53] He first notes that the exhibition marks a "difficult shift [*tiazhelyi sdvig*]" in the "changing forms of art." Meanwhile, he argues, this exhibition does constitute the end of a tradition (Cubo-Futurism), whose past has become clearly associated with the work of French artists, primarily Cézanne and Picasso. He observes that the tremendous speed of creative "inventiveness" is underscored by the fact that "yesterday's innovators are today's 'elders'" and are not represented at this exhibition (he probably had Goncharova, Larionov, Vasilii Kandinskii, and Burliuk in mind). He then discusses both Suprematism and Tatlin's counter-reliefs in a way that has no parallel in Russian art criticism before the Revolution. His review of Malevich's paintings concludes with the question: "Doesn't this geometricization have something to say . . . this planar painting of such secretive and appealing complexity and mystery?" He observes of Tatlin's *Kontr-rel'ef* (*Counter-Relief*, 1914–15, plate no. 70) "only an artist could so combine these materials . . . and harmonize the intersecting surfaces and inflections. Moreover, the mechanical work itself is not easy where the materials must strictly serve a preplanned totality."

Likewise, he notes the skill with which Rozanova in *Shkaf s posudoi* (*Cupboard with Dishes*, 1915, fig. no. 6; compare plate no. 46) and Udal'tsova in *Kukhniia* (*Kitchen*, 1915, fig. no. 7; compare plate no. 39) manipulate form and color.

Rostislavov reads an agenda into Malevich's coordination of text (*From Cubism to Suprematism*) and event (the inauguration of Suprematism itself), questioning the linear history the brochure purports to establish. He observes that, from Impressionism to the present day, painting has indeed moved away from mimeticism to "self-contained painterly means of expression." But he notes that others (he names Kandinskii) have reached "non-objectivism" and implies that this path may not lead "in strict sequence to Malevich's Suprematism." By citing both Kandinskii's work and Tatlin's achievement in creating the counter-relief, he essentially challenges the notion of singular stylistic histories, and points instead to the many manifestations of abstract art in Russia. Moreover, he laments the disappearance of Cubo-Futurist "painterly-ornamental perceptibility" and concludes that "the inventiveness and rapid advancements made by new artists cannot be doubted, but the question remains: are not concepts of form in art in a state of chaotic ferment?"[54]

Although diametrically opposed, Benua's and Rostislavov's reviews both register the assimilation of vanguard art to an unprecedented degree. By rejecting Malevich's claims in the first place, Benua demonstrates the extent to which success as an artist was determined by the artist's hegemonic conception of "style." Rostislavov's equivocation reveals, in contrast, a different sense in which "style" could be understood in Russia in 1915: as personal and pluralistic.[55] And significantly, despite Malevich's effort, he remained unconvinced that Suprematism would transform the chaos of today into tomorrow's order. The reception of Suprematism thus points to a broader phenomenon, the transformation of the avant-garde from oppositional strategists and instigators of public scandal into historians of their own recent past. Malevich's affirmation in written texts of his own place in history, like his return in the 1920s to figurative painting of earlier Primitivist themes, continued and extended his quest for legitimacy in a factional and highly politicized cultural environment.

Benua's review of the *0.10* exhibition has been overlooked by most contemporary scholars, even dismissed, no doubt because its tone and content demythologize avant-garde artists' claims to absolute originality. Yet this text, perhaps more than any other, represents the paradoxical status of the Russian avant-garde before the Revolution as outsiders who turned to their advantage concepts of originality and succession which had marginalized them. Malevich's response to Benua, read in the context of his correspondence with Matiushin, reveals both a public and a private creative concern over the legitimation of Suprematism in an art world marked by competition, stylistic eclecticism, and real social and economic disenfranchisement. Both Benua's and Rostislavov's reviews give shape to what might be called the politics of originality. The unique succession of "isms" in the art of the 1910s, documented by published manifestos and often by the press, reveals that the "anxiety of anticipation"[56] among artists in Russia was equal to that experienced by the West European avant-garde. And significantly, in light of the work displayed in the present exhibition, this suggests in turn that the tenor of competition and debate during the critical mid-teens prepared the ground for the combative responses of the same generation of artists to artistic pluralism in the 1920s.

Notes

1. Aleksandr Benua, "Posledniaia futuristicheskaia vystavka," *Rech'*, January 9, 1916, p. 3.

2. Benua (and Malevich as well; see note 6) was responding to an article by the writer Dmitrii Merezhkovskii entitled "Eshche odin shag griadushchego khama," which was originally published in the Moscow daily newspaper, *Russkoe slovo*, June 29, 1914. This article, whose title may be translated "The Oncoming Boor Is One Step Closer," refers to the intelligentsia's anxiety over social philistinism and the commercial exploitation of culture during the period immediately preceding the Revolution in Russia.

3. Several of the earliest of recent studies on the theory of the avant-garde, including Renato Poggioli's *The Theory of the Avant-Garde,* trans. Gerald Fitzgerald (Cambridge and London: Harvard University Press, Belknap Press, 1968), trace the relationship of avant-garde aesthetics and social and political radicalism to the first and second quarters of the nineteenth century in France. Linda Nochlin's exploration of the avant-garde in France, published originally in 1968 in *Art News Annual*, cites the French utopian socialist Henri de Saint-Simon and the Fourieriste art critic Gabriel-Désiré Laverdant. See her essay, "The Invention of the Avant-Garde: France, 1830–1880," in her *The Politics of Vision: Essays on Nineteenth-Century Art and Society* (New York: Harper and Row, 1989), p. 2. Laverdant is also quoted in Poggioli: "Art, the expression of society, manifests, in its highest soaring, the most advanced social tendencies: it is the forerunner and the revealer." *Theory of the Avant-Garde,* p. 9.

4. El Lissitzky, "Suprematism in World Reconstruction," in Sophie Lissitzky-Küppers, *El Lissitzky: Life, Letters, Texts,* trans. Helene Aldwinckle and Mary Whittall (Greenwich, Conn.: New York Graphic Society, 1968), p. 327. The lowercase letters reproduce the style in Lissitzky's original text.

5. Ibid.

6. "A Letter from Malevich to Benois," May 1916, in K. S. Malevich, *Essays on Art, 1915–1933,* ed. Troels Andersen, trans. Xenia Glowacki-Prus and Arnold McMillin (Copenhagen: Borgen, 1968), vol. I, pp. 42–48. Andersen states (p. 243n) that Malevich intended to publish it. Instead, he apparently sent the letter directly to Benua, for it concludes with the postscript: "Since the doors of the press are closed to us I am writing to you personally." The letter is located in the Manuscript Division, State Russian Museum, St. Petersburg, f. 137, d. 1186, l. 1–3. Excerpts were previously published in Russian in Lev N. Diakonitsyn, *Ideinye protivorechiia v estetike russkoi zhivopisi kontsa 19—nachala 20 vv.* (Perm': Permskoe knizhnoe izdatel'stvo, 1966), pp. 214–15. The quotations in this essay are adapted from the published English translation.

7. "Letter from Malevich to Benois," p. 45.

8. K. S. Malevich, *O novykh sistemakh v iskusstve* (Vitebsk: Unovis, 1919). The cover is reproduced in Larissa A. Zhadova, *Malevich: Suprematism and Revolution in Russian Art, 1910–1930,* trans. Alexander Lieven (London: Thames and Hudson, 1982), plate 185. For a full discussion of the "collective" nature of the Vitebsk school (later Posnovis and Unovis), see Aleksandra Shatskikh, "Unovis: Epicenter of a New World," in this volume.

9. A. Benua, "Povorot k lubku," *Rech'*, March 18, 1909, p. 2. Sergei Makovskii was another critic to identify Primitivism as a trend among a new generation of artists. For a summary of and excerpts from Makovskii's writings, see John E. Bowlt, "The Blue Rose Movement and Russian Symbolism," *Slavonic and East European Review* 51, no. 123 (April 1973), pp. 161–81, reprinted in *Russian Art, 1875–1957: A Collection of Essays* (New York: MSS Information Corporation, 1976), pp. 63–93.

10. A. Benua, "Kubizm ili kukishizm," *Rech'*, November 23, 1912, p. 2. It was this review, no doubt, that incited Burliuk to publish his counterattack as a booklet entitled *Galdiashchie Benua i novoe russkoe natsional'noe iskusstvo* (St. Petersburg, 1913). The book took the form of an artificial debate with Benua in which Burliuk quoted long excerpts from Benua's writings interspersed with his own commentary.

11. K. S. Malevich, "Zadachi iskusstva i rol' dushitelei iskusstva," *Anarkhiia* 25 (March 23, 1918). As translated in "The Problems of Art and the Role of Its Suppressors," in Malevich, *Essays on Art, 1915–1933,* vol. I, p. 49. The essay is an important retrospective critique of the power individual critics exercised (both Benua and Iakov Tugendkhol'd are named). Although the essay was published with the signatures of Aleksei Morgunov and Aleksei Gan in addition to that of Malevich, Andersen attributes the text to Malevich. For his discussion of Malevich's participation in this journal, see ibid., p. 244n.

12. Mikhail Vrubel', Viktor Borisov-Musatov, Pavel Kuznetsov, and Natal'ia Goncharova were all major participants in avant-garde exhibitions at different points in time before the Revolution.

13. The organizers of the Union of Youth (1910–14) were Mikhail Matiushin and Elena Guro. Members of the group and participants in their exhibitions were Pavel Filonov, Ol'ga Rozanova, Iosif Shkol'nik, Vladimir Markov (Waldemars Matvejs), David Burliuk, Kazimir Malevich, and Vladimir Tatlin. A number of members of the Muscovite Donkey's Tail group exhibited in Union of Youth exhibitions, notably Natal'ia Goncharova and Mikhail Larionov. See E. F. Kovtun, "K. S. Malevich. Pis'ma k M. V. Matiushinu," *Ezhegodnik Rukopisnogo otdela Pushkinskogo doma na 1974 god* (Leningrad: Nauka, 1976), p. 178 n. 19.

14. Aleksandr Benua, "Sezan i Gogen," *Rech'*, January 27, 1912, p. 2.

15. In the review of the *0.10* exhibition, Benua paradoxically attributes some positive value to these "tricks." He praises Tatlin using the very same terminology with which he criticizes Malevich: "I am familiar with Tatlin's theatrical designs in which there is a charming and original quality of color and an unusual balancing [*ekvilibristika*] of line-[illeg.]. Perhaps this is only trickery, but even trickery is already an art, and for this talent is required." Benua, "Posledniaia futuristicheskaia vystavka," p. 3.

16. Aleksandr Benua, "Dnevnik khudozhnika," *Rech'*, October 21, 1913, p. 4.

17. Goncharova's work had been censored from exhibitions on several occasions, first in March 1910; as a result, she was tried in December 1910 for pornography, but acquitted. See Jane A. Sharp, "Redrawing the Margins of Russian Vanguard Art: Goncharova's Trial for Pornography in 1910," in *Sexuality and the Body in Russian Culture,* ed. Jane Costlow, Stephanie Sander, and Judith Vowles, forthcoming.

18. Victor Erlich translates Shklovskii's term *zatrudnennaia forma* as "deliberately impeded form," but as his analysis of this concept reveals, the term refers both the artist's act of "creative deformation" and to the perceptual process. Citing Shklovskii, he writes: "The act of creative deformation restores sharpness to our perception, giving 'density' to the world around us. 'Density (*faktura*) is the principal characteristic of this peculiar world of deliberately constructed objects, the totality of which

we call art.' . . . Another crucial aspect of the 'deliberately impeded form' . . . is rhythm—a set of contrivances superimposed upon ordinary speech." Victor Erlich, *Russian Formalism: History–Doctrine,* 3d ed. (New Haven and London: Yale University Press, 1981), pp. 177–78.

19. K. S. Malevich, *Ot kubizma k suprematizmu. Novyi zhivopisnyi realizm* (Petrograd, 1916). Although the brochure is dated 1916, a number of reviews document that it was sold at the exhibition when it opened on December 17, 1915. According to Evgenii Kovtun, it was published in two more editions in 1916, the second in Petrograd, the third in Moscow. See Kovtun, "K. S. Malevich. Pis'ma k M. V. Matiushinu," p. 181 nn. 28, 31.

20. Benua's paranoid response also has its precedent in a number of responses to Goncharova's solo exhibitions in both Moscow and St. Petersburg. A self-appointed critic, Valentin Songaillo, published a separate pamphlet on the occasion of her Moscow exhibition. Like Benua in his later critique of Malevich, Songaillo casts his language in quasi-religious terms, labeling Goncharova an "antiartist" in an obvious parallel to the Antichrist. This pamphlet did in fact achieve its intended effect of censoring Goncharova's exhibition. When the show (significantly reduced in size) opened in St. Petersburg in March 1914, police raided the building and seized all of her religious paintings in accordance with a *zapret* (ban) invoked by the "spiritual censorship committee" of the Orthodox Church. On this occasion she was also accused by the press of blasphemy. See Jane A. Sharp, "Primitivism, 'Neoprimitivism' and the Art of Natal'ia Goncharova, 1907–14." (Ph.D. diss., Yale University, 1992), chapter 4.3.

21. I refer to Richard Shiff's seminal writing on the history of this concept, and particularly to his discussion of the "classic" in "The Original, the Imitation, the Copy, and the Spontaneous Classic: Theory and Painting in Nineteenth-Century France," *Yale French Studies* 66 (1984), pp. 27–54, where, referring to Quatremère de Quincy's writings on the classic Greeks, he observes: "They *initiated* a tradition characterized by a system and principle and served as an *absolute* origin, not a mere member, like any other member, of a sequence of copies" (p. 37). His discussion of this concept has extremely important implications for Malevich's view of his own originality, and his anxiety over his success at enlisting followers and having "copyists" who would simultaneously (and paradoxically) both ensure his place in history as an "absolute origin" and devalue his contribution, as will be seen in what follows.

22. Aleksandr Benua, "Vystavka 'Sovremennoi russkoi zhivopisi,'" *Rech',* December 2, 1916, p. 2. Malevich did not exhibit work in this show; among the participants were David Burliuk, Nikolai Kul'bin, Chagall, Kandinskii, Popova, and Udal'tsova.

23. During the course of 1916 the group was formed and a publication planned; Malevich refers to the publication of a journal in his correspondence with Mikhail Matiushin as early as 1915. See Kovtun, "K. S. Malevich. Pis'ma k M. V. Matiushinu," p. 186. Due to the events of war and revolution, the publication was never realized.

24. "Letter from Malevich to Benois," p. 43.

25. Ibid., p. 45.

26. Benua, "Posledniaia futuristicheskaia vystavka," p. 3.

27. "Letter from Malevich to Benois," p. 44.

28. For more details regarding these charts, see Troels Andersen's translations from Russian to English in Troels Andersen, *Malevich,* catalogue raisonné of the Berlin Exhibition, including the collection in the Stedelijk Museum, Amsterdam (Amsterdam: Stedelijk Museum, 1970), pp. 115–36 and Linda S. Boersma's essay, "On Art, Art Analysis and Art Education: The Theoretical Charts of Kazimir Malevich," in *Kazimir Malevich, 1878–1935,* catalogue for exhibition organized by the Russian Museum, Leningrad, the Tretiakov Gallery, Moscow, and the Stedelijk Museum, Amsterdam (Amsterdam: Stedelijk Museum, 1989), pp. 206–23. This linear evolutionary concept of art history was firmly entrenched in Russia by 1914, and the models were primarily West European. Iakov Tugendkhol'd writes, for example, of Matisse and Picasso: "If the work of Matisse represents the extreme and logical conclusion of the prophecies of Gauguin, then Picasso's painting represents the paradoxical completion of Cézanne's." Ia. Tugendkhol'd, "Frantsuzskoe sobranie S. I. Shchukina," *Apollon* 1–2 (January–February 1914), p. 28.

29. Kovtun, "K. S. Malevich. Pis'ma k M. V. Matiushinu"; Charlotte Douglas, "*0–10* Exhibition," in *The Avant-Garde in Russia, 1910–1930: New Perspectives,* catalogue for exhibition organized by the Los Angeles County Museum of Art and the Hirshhorn Museum and Sculpture Garden, Smithsonian Institution, Washington, D.C. (Cambridge, Mass.: MIT Press, 1980), pp. 34–40 and *Swans of Other Worlds: Kazimir Malevich and the Origins of Abstraction in Russia* (Ann Arbor: UMI Research Press, 1980), pp. 35–47.

30. Rosalind Krauss has called the avant-garde artist's discourse on originality (she refers specifically to Marinetti's 1909 manifesto) a "parable of self-creation" and explains: "more than a rejection or dissolution of the past, avant-garde originality is conceived as a literal origin, a beginning from ground zero, a birth." Malevich is one of her sources; she observes, regarding his famous pronouncement "Only he is alive who rejects his convictions of yesterday," that "the self as origin has the potential for continuous acts of regeneration, a perpetuation of self-birth." See Rosalind Krauss, "The Originality of the Avant-Garde: A Post-Modernist Repetition," *October* 18 (Fall 1981), pp. 47–66, reprinted in *Art After Modernism: Rethinking Representation,* ed. Brian Wallis (New York: The New Museum of Contemporary Art in association with David R. Godine, 1984), p. 18.

31. For details regarding the performance and its relationship to Suprematism, see Charlotte Douglas, "Birth of a 'Royal Infant': Malevich and 'Victory over the Sun,'" *Art in America,* March–April 1974, pp. 45–51, and her revised text in *Swans of Other Worlds,* pp. 35–47.

32. Douglas, *Swans of Other Worlds,* p. 46.

33. Kazimir Malevich, letter to Mikhail Matiushin, May 27, 1915, in Kovtun, "K. S. Malevich. Pis'ma k M. V. Matiushinu," pp. 185–86. In his notes, Kovtun quotes from another, unidentified letter from Malevich to Matiushin which clarifies Malevich's image: "The curtain depicts the black square, the embryo [*zarodysh*] of all possibilities—in its development it acquires awesome power" (p. 180). That the correspondence dates to May 1915 suggests that Malevich may indeed have worked to Suprematism through a reexamination of his designs for *Victory over the Sun.* It is clear from the correspondence, at any rate, that his recognition of the historical value of the designs occurred simultaneously with the creation and development of his Suprematist paintings.

34. Kazimir Malevich, letter to Mikhail Matiushin, September 25, 1915, in Kovtun, "K. S. Malevich. Pis'ma k M. V. Matiushinu," pp. 180–81.

35. Kazimir Malevich, letter to Mikhail Matiushin, November 25, 1915, in Kovtun, "K. S. Malevich. Pis'ma k M. V. Matiushinu," p. 189.

36. He names the Soiuz russkikh khudozhnikov (the Union of Russian Artists), Salon, Novoe obshchestvo (the New Society), Obshchestvo peterburgskikh khudozhnikov (the Society of Petersburg Artists), Akvarelisty (the Watercolorists), and the Osennii salon (the Autumn Salon). Aleksandr Benua, "Khudozhestvennye pis'ma. Obilie vystavok," *Rech'*, February 13, 1909, p. 2.

37. The split occurred in November–December 1911 as a result of Larionov's disagreement with the official registration of the Jack of Diamonds group; Larionov and his supporters countered this move by announcing the separate organization of a series of exhibitions beginning with the Donkey's Tail show, which took place in Moscow in March–April 1912. His critique of the Jack of Diamonds group was publicized in the daily press; see "Ssora khvostov s valetami," *Golos Moskvy* 285 (December 11, 1911), p. 5.

38. See Vasilii Rakitin, "The Artisan and the Prophet: Marginal Notes on Two Artistic Careers," in this volume.

39. Kazimir Malevich, letter to Mikhail Matiushin, September 24, 1915, in Kovtun, "K. S. Malevich. Pis'ma k M. V. Matiushinu," p. 187.

40. Ibid.

41. Kazimir Malevich, letters to Mikhail Matiushin, November 22 and 25, 1915, in Kovtun, "K. S. Malevich. Pis'ma k M. V. Matiushinu," p. 189.

42. Gleb Pospelov has documented the reception of the Jack of Diamonds exhibition extensively in his article "O valetakh bubnovykh i valetakh chervonnykh," *Panorama iskusstv 1977* (Moscow: Sovetskii khudozhnik, 1978), pp. 127–35, and more recently in *Bubnovyi valet. Primitiv i gorodskoi fol'klor v moskovskoi zhivopisi 1910–kh godov* (Moscow: Sovetskii khudozhnik, 1990), pp. 98–114.

43. A summary of the debate was published in a daily newspaper: "Moskva. Khudozhestvennyi disput," *Protiv techeniia* 22 (February 18, 1912), p. 3. For an account in English, see Benedikt Livshits, *The One and a Half-Eyed Archer*, ed. and trans. John E. Bowlt (Newtonville, Mass.: Oriental Research Partners, 1977), pp. 81–84.

44. These incidents occurred at a debate organized in conjunction with the *Mishen'* (*Target*) exhibition on March 23, 1913; a summary of the trial was published as "Futuristy na sude," *Golos Moskvy* 240 (October 18, 1913), p. 5.

45. F. M., "Chrezvychaino udavshiisia vernisazh," *Moskovskaia gazeta*, September 30, 1913. In these reviews Goncharova is frequently compared with Konstantin Korovin (1861–1939), a graduate of the Imperial Academy of Arts (who received the title of Academician in 1905) and one of Larionov's teachers at the Moscow School of Painting, Sculpture, and Architecture. Boris Kustodiev (1878–1927), a former student of Repin's at the Imperial Academy, received the title of Academician in 1909.

46. Ibid.

47. "O lektsiiakh i disputakh," *Al'manakh Verbnogo bazara. Moskovskii sezon 1913–14* (Moscow: Levenson, 1914), pp. 12–18.

48. Ibid, pp. 12–13. The author describes the public as being predominantly composed of young women from the provincial intelligentsia.

49. B. Lopatkin, "Futurizm–Suprematizm," reprinted in Herman Berninger and Jean-Albert Cartier, *Les Années d'avant-garde, Russie—Berlin, 1910–1923*, vol. 1 of *Pougny: Catalogue de l'oeuvre* (Tübingen: Ernst Wasmuth, 1972), p. 56.

50. M. Matiushin, "O vystavke 'poslednikh futuristov,'" *Ocharovannyi strannik. Al'manakh vesennii*, 1916, p. 17.

51. Ibid.

52. Ibid.

53. A. Rostislavov, "O vystavke futuristov," *Rech'*, December 25, 1915, p. 3.

54. Ibid.

55. The succession of avant-garde exhibitions in 1915—*Moskva. 1915 god* (*Moscow: The Year 1915*, Moscow), *Tramvai V* (*Tramway V*, St. Petersburg), and *Vystavka kartin levykh techenii v iskusstve* (*Exhibition of Paintings of Left Trends in Art*, St. Petersburg)—must have confirmed the sense of extreme pluralism in vanguard art.

56. This term is borrowed twice: from Richard Shiff's adaptation of Harold Bloom's "anxiety of influence" (*The Anxiety of Influence: A Theory of Poetry* [New York: Oxford University Press, 1973]). See Shiff, "The Original, the Imitation, the Copy, and the Spontaneous Classic," pp. 27–31, 52–54.

Unovis: Epicenter of a New World

Aleksandra Shatskikh

Unovis (the Affirmers of the New Art), though it has been variously labeled a group, a collective, a school, a commune, an organization, and a program, is a phenomenon without parallel in the history of early Soviet art and defies classification. In its origins and day-to-day existence, Unovis betrayed many features of a sui-generis religious fraternity or variety of Masonic lodge. Unovis itself, adopting the revolutionary terminology of the era, preferred the description of a "party in art." This "party" of the artistic avant-garde, so its members believed, was called upon to ensure, through both theory and practice, the emergence of new forms of life via the evolution of new systems in art. The wide range and variety of its endeavors, its broad influence and tangible achievements, do, however, permit one to characterize Unovis as a unique (and largely realized) utopian model—firmly rooted in the ideas of Russian culture of the first decades of the twentieth century—of "art into life."

Kazimir Malevich was Unovis's moving force and architect. Like other leaders of the Russian avant-garde (such as Mikhail Larionov, Mikhail Matiushin, and David Burliuk), Malevich was endowed with exceptional organizational abilities. An irresistible urge to forge artistic alliances marked his career from the beginning; in Kursk at the close of the nineteenth century, for example, he had set up a studio, patterned after the Parisian academies, as a gathering place for artists with common interests. The general situation in European art— where the founding of one's own movement, endowed with a name, theory, and disciples, had become the pinnacle of self-affirmation for the vanguard artist—added fuel to Malevich's organizing efforts. In the mid-1910s, he assembled some ten artists under the banner of the movement he had inaugurated in painting, Suprematism. The group was called *Supremus*, and only the events of World War I prevented the undertaking's achieving its full promise.

Malevich nourished the idea of establishing an authoritative artistic center, which would fulfill multiple functions, over the course of many years. The planning that came to final fruition in the creation of Ginkhuk (the State Institute of Artistic Culture) in Leningrad went back to 1917. In September of that year, Malevich, who had been elected president of the Art Department of the Moscow Council of Soldiers' Deputies, wrote to Matiushin: "I've conceived a number of projects, to wit, organizing the First People's Academy of Arts in Moscow; my idea was warmly received, and the ball's rolling—soon I'll open several small departments of those cells which on a broad scale will constitute the Academy."[1] His work as a teacher in the State Free Art Workshops in Moscow and Petrograd was an additional spur to Malevich's ambitious plans. And the Vitebsk Popular Art School—especially during Malevich's first year and a half there—proved an ideal laboratory for the development of Malevich's ideas.

Malevich, accompanied by El Lissitzky, arrived in Vitebsk from Moscow at the beginning of November 1919[2] and was appointed to a teaching position at the Popular Art School, an institute of higher education founded and headed by Marc Chagall, a Vitebsk native. At the time, workshops were conducted at the school by Vera Ermolaeva, Nina Kogan, Lissitzky, Iurii Pen, Aleksandr Romm, Chagall, and the sculptor David Iakerson. Mikhail Veksler, Ivan Gavris, Evgeniia Magaril, Georgii and Mikhail Noskov, Nikolai Suetin, Lazar' Khidekel', Lev Tsiperson, Ivan Chervinko, and Lev Iudin were among the students. Il'ia Chashnik, who had spent a term at the Popular Art School and in the autumn of 1919 had enrolled with Malevich at the State Free Art Workshops in Moscow, followed his teacher back to Vitebsk.

Malevich was immediately occupied with a number of ventures. A week after his arrival, the *Pervaia gosudarstvennaia*

vystavka kartin mestnykh i moskovskikh khudozhnikov (*First State Exhibition of Paintings by Local and Moscow Artists*)—which included works by Chagall, Malevich, Vasilii Kandinskii, Ol'ga Rozanova, Robert Fal'k, and others—opened in Vitebsk. Lectures and public meetings were held in conjunction with the exhibition, and Malevich's appearances at them attracted large audiences. The chance to publish his theoretical text, *O novykh sistemakh v iskusstve* (*On New Systems in Art*), written in the summer of 1919, had been one of the motivations for Malevich's move to Vitebsk. Now that complex treatise furnished the basis for his lectures and speeches and was augmented by the "Ustanovlenie A" ("Statute A"), written on November 15, 1919. In the new appendix Malevich codified the tenets he presented to his students.

Lissitzky and the students in his graphics workshop printed *On New Systems in Art* lithographically and in an edition of one thousand copies, as specified by Malevich.[3] *On New Systems in Art* was the embryo of the "visual book" subsequently cultivated by Lissitzky. For Malevich's followers and students, the brochure was also painting's "declaration of independence" from objectivity, proclaiming the commandments of a "new testament"—among which the most significant was the injunction to introduce into art a "fifth dimension, or economy."

The zeal and homiletic power of Malevich's lectures—he had entered his prophetic period—worked their influence, above all, on those in his audience primed to apprehend the dizzying transition from figurative, representational art to art that was non-objective. Lissitzky, Ermolaeva, and Kogan were among the first to become fervent supporters of Malevich.

Almost in a matter of days, Lissitzky, an architect by training and until recently under the influence of Chagall, brushed aside figuration and the intricate decorativeness of his earlier work—which had been strongly colored by the traditions of Jewish culture—and plunged, with his native facility and passion, into non-objective art. A vestige of his stormy "romance" with Suprematism and its creator would remain with Lissitzky for the rest of his life: the "transrational" phrase from the opening of *On New Systems in Art*—"U-el-el'-ul-el-te-ka,"* which became a sort of anthem or motto for Unovis— was the inspiration for Lissitzky's adopted name, first El and later El'.[4]

Ermolaeva and Kogan had come to Vitebsk from Petrograd (where their association began with the founding of the City Museum; their assignments to Vitebsk by Izo Narkompros [the Department of Fine Arts of the People's Commissariat of Enlightenment] came one on the heels of the other) and were exponents, as their early works attest, of a figurative art making decorative use of devices of the avant-garde. At the Vitebsk Popular Art School, Lissitzky, Ermolaeva, and Kogan popularized Malevich's theories and formed among themselves a group of "elder Cubists."

The new artistic "party" grew at breakneck speed; as in a fairy tale, events unfolded over the course not of days but of hours. The tempo was set by the receipt, in November 1919, of a significant (and sizable) commission—decorations for the anniversary of the Vitebsk Committee to Combat Unemployment—to be filled in a brief span of time: the anniversary fell on December 17th. Malevich and Lissitzky made the preliminary sketches and plans for the decorations,

fig. 2
El Lissitzky
Cover for Unovis Almanac No. 1, *1920.*
Pencil, india ink, and gouache on paper, 35.5 x 25.5 cm.
Manuscript Division, State Tret'iakov Gallery, Moscow.

---

fig. 1
Malevich (center) and members of Unovis en route from Vitebsk to the First All-Russian Conference of Teachers and Students of Art in Moscow, 1920. Lissitzky, Kogan, Ermolaeva, Chashnik, Khidekel', Iudin, and Magaril are among those pictured.

while teachers and students collaborated on their execution. Intensive labor was required to produce the enormous number of Suprematist decorative panels that adorned the White Army Barracks building, which housed the committee, as well as embroidered banners, slogans, and stage decorations for the committee's festive convocation. Such possibilities of practical application were from the beginning Suprematism's greatest attraction and immediately won over the majority of students at the Vitebsk school. Suprematism's entry into the "utilitarian world of things" would be the cornerstone of Unovis.

The aura in which Malevich and his work were bathed grew tenfold in the wake of a trip by the Vitebsk students and teachers to Moscow to view Malevich's first solo show, open from the end of 1919 through the beginning of 1920 at the Sixteenth State Exhibition. (The architect Moisei Lerman, who was among the Vitebsk students, has described this trip and the exhibition, as well as his vague recollection of encountering Vladimir Maiakovskii there.)[5] Malevich, their new leader, had all the necessary credentials: revolutionary innovation in his work, a fully thought-out theory, clear methods for advancing toward the new, and superior artistic results.

On January 19, 1920, the Vitebsk students organized Molposnovis (the Young Followers of the New Art). Nine days later, they joined forces with their teachers, the "elder Cubists," and Molposnovis was succeeded by Posnovis (the Followers of the New Art).

The members of Posnovis were determined to introduce new forms into all types of creative endeavor, and the celebration of Front Week in 1920 offered them an opportunity to try their hand. They decided to present the legendary opera *Pobeda nad solntsem* (*Victory over the Sun*) on February 6th, the first day of Front Week; the stage and costume designs for this production were created by Ermolaeva under Malevich's general direction (plate no. 152). Nina Kogan contributed the world's first "Suprematist ballet"—a curious and underappreciated venture, astonishing in its conception: Kogan proposed to show the "sequential unfolding of the movement of forms itself," crowned by the "supremacy of the black square" (plate no. 151).[6] (It should be noted that the idea of a "non-objective cinematography" put forward much later by Malevich was to some degree anticipated by Kogan's ballet.) And Mikhail Noskov gave a public lecture on the new art (he, together with his brother, Georgii, played a conspicuous role in the life of the Vitebsk school, Posnovis, and later Unovis; after 1922, unfortunately, all trace of the brothers vanishes).

With these successes, the members of Posnovis grew confident of their powers and resolved to represent themselves henceforth not merely as followers of the new art but as its affirmers. Unovis was born on February 14, 1920.[7] The name, an acronym in keeping with the verbal shorthand and word coining of the times, was greatly to Malevich's liking—he named his daughter Una in Unovis's honor. And the new word spawned others: *unovisets* (Unovist), *unovisskii* (Unovistic), and *unovizm* (Unovism). The ease with which "Unovis" entered the Russian language was an acknowledgment of the reality and vitality of a phenomenon for which no other word existed.

The months from November 1919 through May 1920 may be called Unovis's period of Sturm und Drang. Unovis's problems, working conditions, and the nature of its production are documented in detail in the typewritten *Al'manakh Unovis No. 1* (*Unovis Almanac No. 1*), completed by June 1920 (fig. no. 2).[8] A wealth of material by Malevich himself appears in the *Almanac*, wherein he devotes significant space to the notion of "collective creative work." (It was the precisely the possibilities for "collective creative work" that kept Malevich in Vitebsk for two and a half years.) His article "O 'Ia' i kollektive" ("On the Ego and the Collective")—in

which Malevich expresses the views that served as the theoretical underpinning of Unovis—contains echoes both of the philosophy of "communality" (filtered through the prism of Russian Symbolism) and of the doctrines of the ruling political party, which gave the collective primacy over the individual: "'Collectivism' is one of the paths designated on the road map to achieving the 'world-man,' but it is perhaps still merely one of the necessary crossings restraining on its main highway millions of egos; it offers only an instant of forces converging for the perfection of the creative image of 'being'; in it, each ego preserves its individual force, but in order to move toward perfection the self must be destroyed—just as religious fanatics destroy themselves before the divine being, so the modern saint must destroy himself before the 'collective' and before that 'image' which perfects in the name of unity, in the name of conjunction."[9]

One of the practical consequences of Malevich's theorizing was a conscious striving among the members of Unovis for impersonality and anonymity; they signed their works not with their own names but with "Unovis." Unovis was among the first artists' groups in the twentieth century—if not the very first—to create and exhibit its production under a collective name. (Obmokhu [the Society of Young Artists] was for a long time credited with pioneering this practice. Obmokhu's group signature, however, arose out of entirely different circumstances; it was the result of artel-style practices in the executing of commissions.)[10]

The notion of "collective creative work" has not been a recurring feature of Russian culture alone but has enticed many of the great creative minds of our times. In postrevolutionary Russia, however, the utopian doctrines that had been one wellspring of the state's ideology would be turned upside down through the creation of a totalitarian regime, and the country would pay a heavy price for the attempt forcibly to translate speculative theories into reality. The dark side of a utopia of enthusiasts creating a new way of life according to a single blueprint compulsory for all would very quickly take its toll on Unovis's founder and his followers; Malevich would come to know the oppressive might of the official art that eventually attained power and state support. In 1927—with Ginkhuk, which had in some respects been the successor to Unovis, already closed—Malevich attached a note to the manuscripts he was leaving in the West, explaining, with some distress, the nature of those texts: "[Since I find] myself at the time under revolutionary influence, there may be powerful contradictions with my present form of defending Art, i.e., in 1927. These positions are to be considered genuine."[11] It must be said, to the credit of Malevich and his colleagues likewise "under revolutionary influence," that they never resorted to violent action against the "old guard." The members of Unovis did not regard destruction or abolition as their primary task; they were, rather, creators and cultivators of a new art and a new world. The legendary anecdotes about Malevich's persecution of Chagall prove, upon closer inspection, neither simple nor clearcut.[12] And it is also worth noting that Pen, the academic painter of the Wanderer school who was Chagall's first teacher, remained in his workshop at the Vitebsk school throughout the period that Unovis was based there.

In Malevich's eyes, "collective creative work" greatly expanded the domain of the new art, and the introduction of art into life was to be entrusted to a Council for the Affirmation of New Forms in Art, an elected administrative body that would be affiliated with the Vitebsk Provincial Department of People's Education. The "Plan raboty Soveta" ("Agenda of the Council"), which was published in the *Unovis Almanac No. 1,* contained five lengthy sections.[13] A good portion of the council's mission was realized by Unovis, even though the Vitebsk authorities were, naturally, not inclined to organize such a body.

Unovis went before the Russian art public in June 1920, at the First All-Russian Conference of Teachers and Students of Art. Led by Malevich, the members of Unovis brought to Moscow an exhibition of their work, the *Unovis Almanac No. 1* (which had been hurriedly prepared in time for the conference), and Malevich's *On New Systems in Art.* A specially printed handbill, "Ot Unovisa" ("From Unovis," fig. no. 3), was distributed among the conference participants, who included representatives from all the provincial Free State Art Workshops as well as those in Moscow and Petrograd; the handbill, which opened with an insistent "We want, we want, we want," issued this appeal: "Under the banner of Unovis, let everyone join together to clothe the earth in new forms and meanings." Although the Vitebsk delegates missed the opening of the conference and arrived near its end, their projects and programs—notable for their careful thought, scope, and clarity—their passionate speechmaking, and their exhibition moved Unovis clearly to the fore.[14] It was also in June 1920 that Unovis rose to preeminence among the new art schools and that its influence spread to other cities: direct ties were established between Vitebsk and Perm', Ekaterinburg, Saratov, and Samara (in addition to Smolensk and Orenburg, where followers of Malevich's—Władysław Strzemiński and Katarzyna Kobro in the former, and Ivan Kudriashev in the latter—headed branches of Unovis).

It was with public artistic work—the creation of a "new utilitarian world of things"—that Unovis launched its expansion; during 1920–21, there was no undertaking or holiday in Vitebsk in which Unovis did not have a hand. Streets, buildings, signboards, trams, and even ration cards were decorated with Suprematist designs (plate nos. 127–129, 144, 148–150). Unovis had for the time being to work within the existing environment, and Suprematist designs served, more often than not, as new ornaments for buildings and objects of considerably older vintage. Yet the utopian idea of transforming the world on the basis of the formal potential of Suprematism had brought architecture within Unovis's compass. Architecture, it was generally accepted, was the necessary starting point of a new synthetic style. "Having established the specific plans of the Suprematist system," Malevich wrote in December 1920, "I am entrusting the further development of what is already architectural Suprematism to young architects in the broad sense of the word, for only in Suprematism do I see an era of a new system of architecture."[15]

The European Futurists are well known for their neoromantic schemes for humanity's settlement of the cosmos. Velimir Khlebnikov, Vasilii Chekrygin, and Malevich were their Russian counterparts, whose way had been prepared by Nikolai Fedorov's "philosophy of the Common Cause." In 1918, Malevich had described hypothetical architectural complexes in such articles as "Architecture as a Slap in the Face to Ferroconcrete."[16] The formulation "Suprematism is the new Classicism" would come later, following Unovis's move to Petrograd, but the need to create new architectural forms was first recognized, and the initial planning steps taken, in Vitebsk.[17] The architecture workshop (variously named at different times) was one of the most popular at the Vitebsk school and was headed by Lissitzky from the autumn of 1919 until his departure from Vitebsk in late 1920 (whereupon Chashnik and Khidekel' became the workshop's guiding figures). Lissitzky's talent for "integration" (as Selim Khan-Magomedov has aptly described it) had exceedingly significant consequences for Unovis.[18] Lissitzky fostered a strong utilitarian

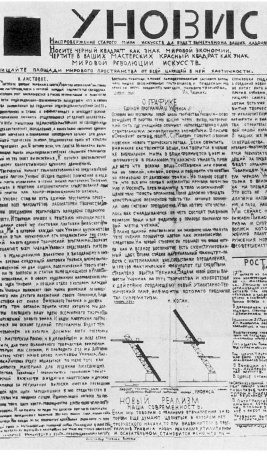

fig. 3
"From Unovis," 1920.
Lithograph, 46 × 37 cm.
Manuscript Division, State Russian Museum, St. Petersburg.

fig. 4
Unovis: Handbill of the Vitebsk Creative Committee *1*
(November 20, 1920), with Chashnik's project in center column.
Lithograph, 58.5 × 51 cm.
Manuscript Division, State Russian Museum, St. Petersburg.

bias, and his professional training and striving for practical results were the bridge that led the innovators of Unovis "out of cold laboratories" and into the real world.

At the end of 1919, Lissitzky introduced three-dimensional elements into his new non-objective compositions. Such forms had, of course, been present in Malevich's earliest Suprematist works: at the *0.10* exhibition (Petrograd, 1915–16), he had shown a canvas incorporating a rectangular parallelepiped and cube. Malevich, however, included three-dimensional forms in his works only rarely, inasmuch as they engendered an illusory space that was at odds with the metaphysical space of the Suprematist canvas. Lissitzky's "bars," "plates," and "cubes," on the contrary, became permanent presences in his work, their execution betraying the practiced hand of the draftsman.

In Lissitzky's elegant works created under the influence of Suprematism, lines, planar shapes, and volumetric elements are combined at will. The "war of opposites," the disharmony that inevitably arose between surface-planarity and spatiality, was further exacerbated by Lissitzky's mixing of perspectives; he constructed almost every form according to a different vanishing point. The result was that each element "flew" into the composition along with the space it occupied and the *sdvig* (dislocation or shift) of colliding spaces provoked frustration in the viewer (the *sdvig*, of course, would become a favorite device of the Constructivists).

Lissitzky devised the name proun (from *proekt Unovisa* [project of Unovis] or *proekt utverzhdeniia novogo* [project of the affirmation of the new]) for these works only following the birth of Unovis; one does not encounter the term before mid-1920. (In Lissitzky's texts in the *Unovis Almanac No. 1*, the word "proun" was not employed once, even though a version of the composition celebrated thereafter as *Proun 1A: Most 1. Eskiz* [*Sketch for Proun 1A: Bridge 1*, 1919–20, plate no. 205] appeared as an illustration to one of his pieces. The formulations Lissitzky did use in the *Almanac*—"projects for new forms of utilitarian structures," "elaboration of tasks of the new architecture," and "projects for monumental decorations"—show him groping for the label that would carry such weight in the future.)

From the beginning, Lissitzky rejected any and all orientations in space for his prouns; he intended them to have neither top nor bottom, hence his use of varying perspectives. It was in the logic of three-dimensional forms, however, that they gradually grew heavy, were pulled "to earth," and demanded a reckoning with the laws of gravity. (It might be noted that Iakerson, also an architect by training—like Lissitzky, he had studied in the architecture and building faculty of the Riga Polytechnic Institute, but his enthusiasm for sculpture won out over his other interests; at the Vitebsk Popular Art School, Iakerson replaced Ivan Til'berg as head of the sculpture workshop[19]—made abundant use of three-dimensional forms in his work during 1920, yet he did so—and from the start—entirely in accordance with the laws of gravity.)

This adaptation of the principles of architectural drawing to Suprematism (a venture similar to that in which Gustav Klutsis was engaged at about the same time as Lissitzky, and perhaps even somewhat earlier) would be a catalyst for Malevich's arkhitektons.

The practical needs of the new state and of Soviet public life, which yielded Unovis commissions for decorations for speaker's rostrums to be used at mass meetings and demonstrations, were another factor in Suprematism's turn toward architecture during the Vitebsk years. Initially, Malevich, Lissitzky, and others confined themselves to decorating the rostrums' façades with Suprematist designs, into which they worked slogans and inscriptions, and did not alter

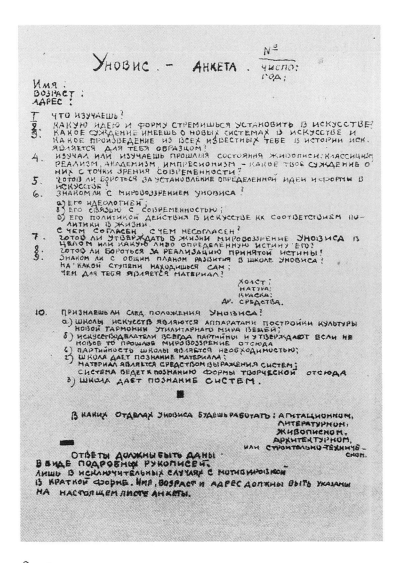

fig. 5
"Unovis Questionnaire," 1920–21.

the basic shape of these primitive structures (plate nos. 130, 147). However, Chashnik—one of the most talented of Malevich's followers and only twenty-six at the time of his death in 1929—created a project for a "tribune under the sign of Suprematism" for a square in Smolensk. Chashnik's project, illustrated in one of Unovis's publications (fig. no. 4), was later developed by Lissitzky (plate nos. 140–141) and served as the basis for his *Leninskaia tribuna* (*Lenin Tribune,* 1924, plate no. 142). Though acclaim for the *Tribune* accrued solely to Lissitzky, he always emphasized that the work was an "Unovis project."

Malevich's Suprematist system was born of the all-embracing *Chernyi kvadrat* (*Black Square,* 1915). The abyss of the *Black Square,* its philosophical ambiguity—it constituted both "all" and "nothing," both "non-objectivity" and "omni-objectivity"—made Malevich's masterpiece a sui-generis "project," a dense nucleus of meanings that Malevich spent his entire life extrapolating. Suprematist paintings—self-sufficient and primary "in the ranks of all the things of the world"—were the first issue of the *Black Square* and its infinitude: "With his brush the artist creates a new sign; this sign is not a form for apprehending what has already been prepared, built, and brought into existence in the world—it is a sign of the new, of what is in the process of being built and appearing in nature through the artist."[20] These Suprematist canvases were, Malevich wrote, sign-projects containing "proto-images of the technical organisms of the future Suprematist [world]."[21] Thus projection—the creation of blueprints or plans of the future Suprematist organization of the world—became the essential hallmark of Unovis's collective work and "project" the chief label for its production (a 1920 Unovis periodical, for example, authored by Chashnik and Khidekel', was entitled *Aero. Stat'i i proekty* [*Aero: Articles and Projects*]).

The "utilitarian world of things" so passionately proclaimed by Unovis did not coincide with the world that, during the same period, the Productivists (the future Constructivists) were seeking to create. Malevich and the members of Unovis wished to comprehend the "real" foundations of the universe and its "organic-natural transformation"—Suprematism acquired an ontological dimension. Malevich devoted virtually all of his time in Vitebsk to the writing of philosophical and theoretical treatises—some of which have yet to be published[22]—which defined the nature of the "utilitarian organisms" that made up the "unified system of the world architecture of the earth." The most advanced among Unovis's members understood and shared Malevich's views. Chashnik, for example, conceived Suprematist works (which he called outright "blueprints" and "plans") as projects for and instruments of a new universe and a new systematization of the world. The aims of the architectural and technical faculty created in Vitebsk in 1921 included, according to Chashnik, "study of the system of Suprematist projection and the designing of blueprints and plans in accordance with it; ruling off the earth's expanse into squares, giving each energy cell its place in the overall scheme; organization and accommodation on the earth's surface of all its intrinsic elements, charting those points and lines out of which the forms of Suprematism will ascend and slip into space."[23]

The differentiation of *real'nost'* (reality) from *deistvitel'nost'* (actuality) was one of the foundations of Malevich's theory. "Reality" lay concealed behind the world's objective envelope, and this envelope had to be torn open and the shackles of *predmetnost'* (objectivity) and *razum* (reason) broken in order to ensure the appearance of a new "Realism"—first in art and subsequently in the world at large. "Actuality," by contrast, was illusoriness incarnate, enslaving man's soul. Malevich and the members of Unovis aspired to create a new "reality," whereas the Productivists and Constructivists remained, in the

fig. 6
Unovis seal, reproduced in Lissitzky's A Suprematist Tale about Two Squares, *1922.*

Unovis view, servants of "actuality" ("lackeys of the factory and of production," as Malevich acerbically described them). The rivalry between Malevich and Vladimir Tatlin—who had taken non-objectivity in such contradictory directions—went back many years[24] and was manifest at the start of the 1920s in the competition between Unovis and Inkhuk (the Institute of Artistic Culture) and between Unovis and Obmokhu. The feud came into the open in December 1921, when more than two hundred Unovis works were exhibited at Inkhuk (members of Unovis were there to elucidate their displays, while Malevich delivered a lecture and participated in discussions).[25] The antagonism between Suprematism and Constructivism was plain to see; the two movements seemed opposite poles in the artistic transformation of the world.

(Lissitzky had been in Moscow from the end of 1920. A member of Inkhuk, he espoused a diluted, compromised version of Suprematism. Lissitzky and Malevich had gone radically different ways, though their personal relations— unlike those between Tatlin and Malevich—remained intact. The title of the journal founded by Lissitzky and Il'ia Erenburg in Berlin in 1922, *Veshch'/Gegenstand/Objet* [*Object*], was a programmatic one, announcing a certain polemic with the "non-objectivity" [or "omni-objectivity"] of Suprematism.)

The tension between the poles of Suprematism and Constructivism that colored numerous areas of early Soviet artistic life existed inside Unovis, as well. It was not Lissitzky alone who integrated impulses from one and the other system. The canvases of Iudin and Tsiperson—who were staunch adherents of Unovis—used layers of paint to achieve relief effects; incorporated sawdust, shavings, sand, and even seeds; and are evidence of the study in Vitebsk of the properties of heterogeneous materials and of attention to *faktura* (density). Moreover, certain members of Unovis—Veksler, Kogan, Georgii Noskov, Suetin, Khidekel', Chashnik, and Iudin— graduated from the Vitebsk Practical Art Institute with the title of "artist-Constructivist."[26]

Unovis's pedagogical system was an integral part of its work. Even while Chagall was still at the helm of the Vitebsk Popular Art School, Unovis proclaimed the creation of a "Unified Painting Audience." When Chagall left in June 1920, Ermolaeva became the school's director; when the school was reorganized as the Vitebsk Practical Art Institute, she became rector and remained in that position until her own departure for Petrograd in the summer of 1922 (Malevich was chairman of the Council of Professors). The Unified Painting Audience was based on the program evolved by Malevich in the Moscow and Petrograd State Free Art Workshops. Ermolaeva and Kogan bore primary responsibility for putting that program into effect in Vitebsk, with Kogan in charge of the introductory course and Ermolaeva supervising students' methodical progress through the disciplines of Cézannism, Cubism, and Cubo-Futurism. (This advancement "from Cézanne to Suprematism" replicated Malevich's own evolution.) Malevich's role was to analyze student assignments and independent work through lectures and conversations intended to "diagnose" a student's talents and possibilities.

The implementation of Malevich's program did not, however, go entirely smoothly, and his analysis of the obstacles and their causes, as well as his careful observation of students' progress in apprehending the different systems of painting, led him to what he subsequently labeled the "theory of the additional element [*pribavochnyi element*] in painting." (In Vitebsk, Malevich used the terms *dobavka* [supplement] and *dobavochnyi element* [supplementary element].) The essence of his theory was that each new trend in painting represented an artistic complex begotten by one specific plastic "gene," a kind of formula-sign from which, as from the nucleus of a cell, the complex organisms of Impressionism, Cézannism, Cubism, and

fig. 7
Members of Unovis, 1921. From left, foreground: Suetin (with black square sewn to his sleeve), Efros, Veksler, Roiak, unidentified, and Chervinko; background: Iudin, Chashnik, Ermolaeva, Khidekel', Kogan, and Malevich.

fig. 8
View of the Unovis display at the Petrograd Artists of All Trends
exhibition, 1923.

fig. 9
Kazimir Malevich
"Unovis (Aff{irmers} of New Forms in Art): Manifesto of the
Suprematists," May 2, 1924.
Malevich Archive, Stedelijk Museum, Amsterdam.

so on evolved. The straight line—the track of a point moving
in space, and Suprematism's fundamental stylistic
component—was declared the Suprematist "gene."
Suprematism's "additional element" was, however, a summit
few of Malevich's followers attained (Malevich critiqued the
work of Ermolaeva and Kogan no less than that of his
students). In 1925, in his article "Vvedenie v teoriiu
pribavochnogo elementa v zhivopisi" ("Introduction to the
Theory of the Additional Element in Painting"), Malevich
would emphasize the Vitebsk origins of his theory and claim
that many of his students had been "ill" from the additional
element of Cézanne's painting, and that they had found the
Cézannist Fal'k more attractive than himself (Fal'k taught in
Vitebsk for several months in 1921, and took a number of
Vitebsk students with him to the Moscow Vkhutemas [the
Higher Artistic-Technical Workshops]; though Fal'k was a

member of the "old guard," Malevich never abandoned his sympathy and respect for him).[27]

To some extent, Unovis's pedagogical practices also embodied Malevich's notions of "collective reason" and "collective creative work." The most advanced students became teaching assistants: they conducted classes, delivered papers and lectures, and discussed and evaluated student work (and each other's). Gavris, Georgii Noskov, Suetin, Khidekel', Chashnik, and Iudin were serving in such a capacity by 1921. Khidekel' and Chashnik were responsible, moreover, for making the architectural and technical faculty the apex of the school. Chashnik wrote in 1921: "The study and apprehension of all systems of the new art in our painting faculties lead to the ultimate real faculty, the architectural and technical faculty . . . The architectural and technical workshop is the crucible of all the other faculties of Unovis, to which all creative individuals, as a unified collective of builders of the new forms of the world, must aspire."[28]

As a thinker, Malevich encouraged reflection and theoretical speculation in his followers, and under his demanding tutelage, Kogan, Khidekel', Chashnik, Iudin, and others gradually revealed a talent for both pedagogical and formal experimentation. And in order to graduate from the Vitebsk school, a student had not only to present the Council of Professors with an art work as his diploma project but to compose a theoretical treatise.[29] Chashnik drew a "Skhema postroeniia Vit[ebskikh] gos[udarstvennykh] khud[ozhestvennykh] tekhnicheskikh masterskikh" ("Structural Plan of the Vit[ebsk] St[ate] Art[istic]-Technical Workshops"), awarding to the student who had completed all courses the title of "consummate learned architect."[30] Iudin recorded his reflections on and experiments with color and form (the latter conducted in close contact with Ermolaeva) in his unique diary full of plans and tables. With the help of his colleagues in Vitebsk, Malevich laid the foundations of the "creative laboratory institute" which had been envisioned in the "Agenda" of the Council for the Affirmation of New Forms in Art and which would become a reality in Ginkhuk.

Malevich was the author of a vast unified oeuvre, in which the plastic and the verbal, works of art and of philosophy, were aspects of a single creative utterance about the world. The same was true of the "collective creative work" of Unovis. The rich and extensive body of writings by Lissitzky, Ermolaeva, Kogan, Chashnik, Khidekel', Iudin, Mikhail Kunin, Gavris, Mikhail Noskov, L. Zuperman, Osip Bernshtein, and others spans a wide range of genres—essays, treatises, explanatory notes, programs, projects, diaries, and letters—and is crowned by the works of Malevich himself, which were published under the Unovis imprint. Unovis's published works are, however, but the tip of the iceberg. One can only hope that the important documents still held in archives will be released and published in the near future.

It had been owing to Chagall's efforts, during his tenure as Commissar of Arts for Vitebsk, that a number of canvases by Russian artists of all movements—from members of Mir iskusstva (World of Art) to left painters—had been sent to the city to form the basis of a museum of contemporary art. Under Malevich's influence—and Malevich had been one of the most active of the museum reformers during the first months of the Soviet state—the Vitebsk museum was quickly transformed from a museum of contemporary art into a museum of painterly culture. The Vitebsk museum housed the fullest and most representative collection of Russian avant-garde works— it had eighteen canvases by Rozanova alone—of any provincial museum with the exception of the Rostov museum (whose collection had been assembled by Liubov' Popova). Space for the collection in Vitebsk was tight, and the majority of the

paintings were stored at the Vitebsk Practical Art Institute. Temporary exhibitions of these works, often installed according to Malevich's instructions, were held at the school and served as material for his lectures and critiques. Malevich, Iudin wrote in his diary, "rendered a diagnosis" on the works of virtually every member of the Russian avant-garde.

Unovis was a "party" that accepted all comers; anyone— poet, musician, actor, or artisan—who wished to promote the "augmentation" of the world with new forms could join. Natan Efros, for example, who would become famous as a professional reader and reciter of poetry, was a member of Unovis's Tvorkom (the Creative Committee) in 1921. (Being a member of Unovis was not, however, generally synonymous with being a Suprematist—the Unovis member had to strive to become a Suprematist.) In the autumn of that year, Unovis, in furtherance of its goal of extending its influence to all creative endeavors, inaugurated the "Unovis Evening," a showcase for contemporary poetry, music, and theater. The first evening in the series, held on September 17, 1921, featured Efros in a solo performance of Maiakovskii's *Voina i mir* (*War and the Universe*), with stage design by Ermolaeva and Tsiperson, and Malevich reading his own poems.[31]

The Unovis "party," like any other, had its own program and bylaws. Applicants were required to complete the highly detailed "Anketa Unovisa" ("Unovis Questionnaire," fig. no. 5). A Working Committee, elected by all members and soon renamed the Creative Committee, supervised all "party" activities. (Once branches of Unovis had been established in other cities, the Vitebsk committee became the Central Creative Committee.) It was a collegial body, with no chairman; Ermolaeva was its secretary, and Bernshtein its clerk until his early death in 1922. Important documents were endorsed with the Unovis seal (fig. no. 6), which had been produced from a drawing by Lissitzky.[32] Malevich, Ermolaeva, and Kogan were permanent members of the Creative Committee during 1920–22; Lissitzky, Chashnik, Khidekel', Gavris, Suetin, Georgii Noskov, Chervinko, Iudin, and Efros all served on the committee at one time or another.

Unovis either organized or participated in a number of exhibitions, the first in Vitebsk in February 1920, when works by members of Posnovis/Unovis were shown as part of the school's student showcase. In June 1920, Unovis exhibited its works at the First All-Russian Conference of Teachers and Students of Art in Moscow. A one-day Unovis exhibition was held in Vitebsk on March 28, 1921. In December 1921, again in Moscow, Unovis exhibited at Inkhuk.[33] At a display in Moscow in March–April 1922 of works by students from the provincial art schools, those by Unovis were pronounced the most interesting.[34] Another exhibition was held in Vitebsk in May 1922. At the *Erste russische Kunstausstellung* (*First Russian Art Exhibition*) in Berlin during the autumn of 1922, Unovis displayed its works in a collective entry. Unovis made its final appearance at the *Petrogradskie khudozhniki vsekh napravlenii* (*Petrograd Artists of All Trends*) exhibition in Petrograd in 1923. Its sixty-odd entries, ranging from Cubism to Suprematism, offered a summation of its work and were exhibited—the paintings of Malevich not excepted—under the group's name (fig. no. 8).

Malevich and the members of his "party" assumed that branches of Unovis would be established throughout the world, and made several efforts at entering on the international stage. Unovis sent materials to Germany in 1921, for instance, and addressed a letter to Dutch artists in February 1922.[35] Suprematism was "exported" to Poland by Strzemiński and Kobro, who moved there in the early 1920s, and it served as the point of departure for Strzemiński's Unizm (Unism)—a Polish term that echoed the Russian "Unovism."

When he established the Bauhaus, Walter Gropius proclaimed a "joyfully creating commune, for which the Masonic lodges of the Middle Ages are the ideal prototype" as his goal. With its own watchword (the "transrational" *U-el-el'-ul-el-te-ka*), bylaws, program, and emblems, Unovis was akin to such a Masonic lodge. The Unovis fraternity's ritual extended even to the clothing of its members—Malevich himself was a prime example: his white apparel and white hat dramatized his passage into white Suprematism, which carried the "white world (world-structure), affirming the sign of purity of man's creative life." And in his diary Iudin mentions sewing a special Unovis red jacket.

Unovis took as its motto Malevich's Suprematist slogan: "The overturning of the old world of arts will be etched across your palms," to which, a short while later, "Wear the black square as a sign of world economy" was appended. And indeed, Unovis's members sewed the black square, their "Masonic emblem," onto the cuffs of their sleeves—the part of their clothing nearest their palms (fig. no. 7). Only Lissitzky employed the red square as an emblem of Unovis (in his design for its seal), and that was in tribute to the prevailing atmosphere in society: "Draw the red square in your workshops as a sign of the world revolution in the arts." Malevich and the true Unovis Suprematists always considered the black square—the "icon" and "zero form" of Suprematism—to be the symbol of Unovis.

The transfer of art-educational institutions from the jurisdiction of Narkompros to that of Glavprofobr (the Chief Administration for Professional Education) in 1921 marked the beginning of difficult times for Unovis. The Vitebsk teachers went unpaid for a considerable period; neither the central nor the local authorities offered the school any support. Unovis's utopian trust in the Soviet government's desire to build a new life on the basis of new forms in art was shattered and revealed as untenable.

Ten students were graduated from the Vitebsk Practical Art Institute in May 1922, after which Unovis ceased its activity in Vitebsk. By the beginning of June, Malevich was in Petrograd, to which Ermolaeva also returned; one after another, numerous members of Unovis—including Suetin, Khidekel', Chashnik, Iudin, Khaia Kagan, Magaril, and Efim Roiak—followed suit. Many among them became associates of the Institute for the Study of the Culture of Contemporary Art at the Museum of Artistic Culture (later Ginkhuk), where Malevich had been named director. Yet even in Petrograd/Leningrad, Malevich was unwilling to part with Unovis. His draft of "Unovis (utv[erditeli] novykh form Iskusstva). Manifest suprematistov" ("Unovis [Aff(irmers) of the New Forms in Art]: Manifesto of the Suprematists," fig. no. 9) dates from May 1924.[36] And at the end of 1924, in an open letter to artists in Holland, Malevich argued the necessity of creating "Unovises" throughout the world.[37]

Malevich's efforts to revive Unovis in new soil did not, however, meet with success. Under the weight of changed living conditions and social patterns, the phenomenon born in Vitebsk vanished. The future will tell us the true worth of the rich legacy that was left behind.

—Translated, from the Russian, by Jane Bobko

Notes

1. Kazimir Malevich, letter to Mikhail Matiushin, September 8, 1917, Manuscript Division, State Tret'iakov Gallery, Moscow, f. XXV/9, l. 21.

2. On the circumstances of Malevich's move to Vitebsk, see A. Shatskikh, "K. Malevich v Vitebske," *Iskusstvo* 11 (1988), pp. 38–43.

3. Kazimir Malevich, letter to Ol'ga Gromozova, 1920, Manuscript Division, State Tret'iakov Gallery, Moscow, f. XXV/9, l. 13–130b. Published in Shatskikh, "K. Malevich v Vitebske," p. 43.

4. The first instances of Lazar' Lisitskii's use of the "article" El, and then El', are to be found in the *Unovis Almanac No. 1*. With the switch to German and the Latin alphabet, he signed his name "El Lissitzky." There are no grounds for the belief that Lissitzky chose *el'* because that is the pronunciation in the Russian alphabet for the letter *l*, his first initial; at the time, the word *liudi* was the guide to pronunciation. There is no question that Lissitzky's unusual name, hardly a pseudonym, was inspired by Malevich's highly musical "transrational" line, which had deep meaning for the members of Unovis; Malevich cited it repeatedly, and Chashnik's 1924 inscription in his fiancée's album called on her to "remember this madman . . . whose way of life is *U-EL-EL*." See *Ilya Grigorevich Chashnik: Lyucite/1902–Leningrad/1929; Watercolors, Drawings, Reliefs*, catalogue for exhibition at Leonard Hutton Galleries (New York: Leonard Hutton Galleries, 1979), p. 11.

5. Moisei Lerman, conversation with author, Moscow, June 15, 1988.

6. N. Kogan, "O suprematicheskom balete," *Al'manakh Unovis No. 1*, l. 21.

7. The date—April 14th—given in Larissa A. Shadowa, *Suche und Experiment: Aus der Geschichte der russischen und sowjetischen Kunst zwischen 1910 und 1930*, trans. Helmut Barth (Dresden: VEB Verlag der Kunst, 1978), p. 309, and in Shatskikh, "K. Malevich v Vitebske" is incorrect.

8. The *Unovis Almanac No. 1* was "constructed" in five typewritten copies. Lissitzky's use of the verb *stroit'* (to construct), an obvious synonym for *konstruirovat'*, is highly revealing of his evolving approach to the "construction of the book." The *Unovis Almanac No. 1* played a significant role in the development of Lissitzky's book design.

Today there are two known copies of the *Almanac*, one in private hands in Moscow, the other in the Manuscript Division, State Tret'iakov Gallery, Moscow, f. 76/9. All references in this essay to the *Almanac* are to the latter copy. A good portion of the contents of the *Almanac* has been published in Shadowa, *Suche und Experiment*, pp. 303–17.

9. K. Malevich, "O 'Ia' i kollektive," *Al'manakh Unovis No. 1*, l. 60b.

10. See Aleksandra Shatskikh, "A Brief History of Obmokhu," in this volume.

11. Kazimir Malevich, note, May 30, 1927, Malevich Archives, Stedelijk Museum, Amsterdam. Reproduced in *Kazimir Malevich, 1878–1935*, catalogue for exhibition organized by the State Russian Museum, Leningrad, the State Tretiakov Gallery, Moscow, and the Stedelijk Museum, Amsterdam (Amsterdam and Moscow: Stedelijk Museum, 1988), p. 52.

12. See Alexandra Shatskikh, "Chagall and Malevich in Vitebsk. History of their relations," *Bulletin AICARC* 1–2 (1989), pp. 7–10.

13. The "Plan raboty Soveta" has been published in Shadowa, *Suche und Experiment,* p. 317.

14. "Materialy I-oi Vserossiiskoi konferentsii uchashchikh i uchashchikhsia iskusstvu," 1920, Central State Archive of Russia, Moscow, f. 2306, op. 23, d. 116. See also G. L. Demosfenova, "K istorii pedagogicheskoi deiatel'nosti K. S. Malevicha," in *Stranitsy istorii otechestvennogo dizaina,* Trudy VNIITE, vyp. 59 (Moscow: Vsesoiuznyi nauchno-issledovatel'skii institut tekhnicheskoi estetiki, 1989), pp. 143–70.

15. K. Malevich, *Suprematizm. 34 risunka* (Vitebsk: Unovis, 1920), p. 4.

16. K. Malevich, "Arkhitektura kak poshchechina betono-zhelezu," *Anarkhiia* 37 (April 6, 1918).

17. See Shadowa, *Suche und Experiment,* pp. 90–94.

18. See S. O. Khan-Magomedov, "L. Lisitskii. Rol' v stileobrazuiushchikh protsessakh i v stanovlenii dizaina," in *Stranitsy istorii otechestvennogo dizaina,* pp. 24–43, and "Novyi stil', ob"emnyi suprematizm i prouny," in *Lazar' Markovich Lisitskii, 1890–1941,* catalogue for exhibition organized by the State Tretiakov Gallery, Moscow, and the Stedelijk van Abbemuseum, Eindhoven (Moscow and Eindhoven: Stedelijk van Abbemuseum, 1990), pp. 35–42.

19. On Iakerson, see A. Shatskikh, "Dereviannaia skul'ptura D. Iakersona," in *Sovetskaia skul'ptura 8* (Moscow: Sovetskii khudozhnik, 1984), pp. 160–69.

20. *Al'manakh Unovis No. 1,* l. 120b.

21. Malevich, *Suprematizm,* p. 2.

22. A number of Malevich's previously unpublished texts appear in D. Sarab'ianov and A. Shatskikh, *Kazimir Malevich. Zhivopis'. Teoriia,* forthcoming.

23. Il. Chashnik, "Arkhitekturno-tekhnicheskii fakul'tet," *UNOVIS* 2 (January 1921), p. 14.

24. See Charlotte Douglas, "Tatlin and Malevich: History and Theory 1914–1915" (Paper delivered at the international symposium, Vladimir Tatlin. Leben. Werk. Wirkung, Städtische Kunsthalle, Dusseldorf, November 25–27, 1989).

25. See Vassilii Rakitin, "Malevich und Inkhuk," in *Kasimir Malewitsch zum 100. Geburtstag,* catalogue for exhibition organized by the Galerie Gmurzynska, Cologne (Cologne: Galerie Gmurzynska, 1978), pp. 284–98.

26. "Spisok okonchivshikh Khudozhestvenno-prakticheskii institut v 1922 godu v mae mesiatse," State Vitebsk Regional Archive, f. 246, op. 1, d. 260, sviazka 17, l. 3900b.

27. K. Malevich, "Sorok piat'. Vvedenie v teoriiu pribavochnogo elementa v zhivopisi," 1925, private archive, Moscow, pp. 21–22. Malevich wrote a brief article on Fal'k in 1924. See K. S. Malevich, "Fal'k," in K. S. Malevich, *The Artist, Infinity, Suprematism: Unpublished Writings, 1913–33,* ed. Troels Andersen, trans. Xenia Hoffmann (Copenhagen: Borgens Forlag, 1978), pp. 125–27.

28. Chashnik, "Arkhitekturno-tekhnicheskii fakul'tet," p. 12, 15.

29. Iudin's diaries for 1922 contain sketches for his diploma work (Manuscript Division, State Saltykov–Shchedrin Public Library, St. Petersburg, f. 1000). For Chashnik's diploma work on "Metod suprematizma" ("The Suprematist Method"), see *Ilya Grigorevich Chashnik,* pp. 20–24.

30. *Ilya Grigorevich Chashnik,* no. 57.

31. *Izvestiia Vitebskogo gubernskogo Soveta krest'ianskikh, rabochikh i soldatskikh deputatov* 208 (1920).

32. Lissitzky's drawing for the Unovis seal was reproduced on the final page of his *Suprematicheskii skaz pro dva kvadrata* (Berlin: Skify, 1922). Chashnik's "Structural Plan of the Vit[ebsk] St[ate] Art[istic]-Technical Workshops" is one of the documents that bear the seal. See *Ilya Grigorevich Chashnik,* no. 57.

33. This information comes from documents in the State Vitebsk Regional Archive, f. 837, op. 1, ed. khr. 59, l. 63, 87, IIIob.

34. *Vestnik iskusstv* 3–4 (1922), pp. 27–28.

35. K. S. Malevich, "A Letter to the Dutch Artists," in K. S. Malevich, *Essays on Art, 1915–1933,* ed. Troels Andersen, trans. Xenia Glowacki-Prus and Arnold McMillin (London: Rapp & Whiting, 1969), vol. 1, pp. 183–87. The fate of the materials sent to Germany is unknown.

36. K. Malevich, "Unovis (utv[erditeli] novykh form Iskusstva). Manifest suprematistov," May 2, 1924, Malevich Archive, Stedelijk Museum, Amsterdam.

37. K. Malevich, "Otkrytoe pis'mo gollandskim khudozhnikam Van-Gofu i Bekmanu," *Zhizn' iskusstva* 50 (1924), pp. 13–14.

1
Kazimir Malevich
Red Square (Painterly Realism:
Peasant Woman in Two Dimensions),
1915.
Oil on canvas, 53 x 53 cm.
State Russian Museum, St. Petersburg.

2
Kazimir Malevich
Suprematist Painting: Eight Red
Rectangles, *1915.*
Oil on canvas, 57.5 x 48.5 cm.
Stedelijk Museum, Amsterdam.

3
Kazimir Malevich
Four Squares, *1915.*
Oil on canvas, 49 x 49 cm.
State Radishchev Art Museum, Saratov.

4
Kazimir Malevich
Suprematist Painting, 1915.
Oil on canvas, 101.5 x 62 cm.
Stedelijk Museum, Amsterdam.

5
Kazimir Malevich
Untitled, ca. 1916.
Oil on canvas, 53 x 53 cm.
Peggy Guggenheim Collection, Venice.

6
Kazimir Malevich
Suprematism: Non-Objective
Composition, *1916.*
Oil on canvas, 80 x 80 cm.
Museum of Fine Arts, Ekaterinburg.

Kazimir Malevich
Suprematism: Non-Objective
Composition, *1916.*
Oil on canvas, 80 x 80 cm.
Museum of Fine Arts, Ekaterinburg.

7
Kazimir Malevich
Dynamic Suprematism (Supremus
No. 57), *1916.*
Oil on canvas, 80.3 x 80.2 cm.
Tate Gallery. Purchased with assistance
from the Friends of the Tate Gallery,
1978.

8
Kazimir Malevich
Suprematism, *1915–16.*
Oil on canvas, 80 x 80 cm.
State Lunacharskii Museum of
Fine Arts, Krasnodar.

9
Kazimir Malevich
Suprematism: Yellow and Black,
1916.
Oil on canvas, 79.5 x 70.5 cm.
State Russian Museum, St. Petersburg.

10
Kazimir Malevich
Suprematist Composition, *1917.*
Oil on canvas, 97.8 x 66.4 cm.
The Museum of Modern Art, New York.

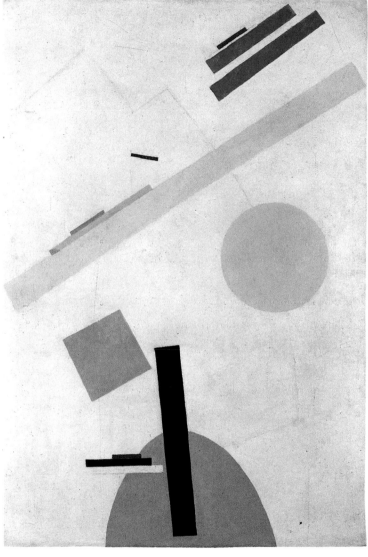

11
Kazimir Malevich
Black Square, *1929.*
Oil on canvas, 80 x 80 cm.
State Tret'iakov Gallery, Moscow.

12
Ivan Kliun
Ozonizer, *1914.*
Oil on canvas, 75 x 66 cm.
State Russian Museum, St. Petersburg.

13
Ivan Kliun
Landscape Rushing By, *ca. 1914–15.*
Oil on wood, wire, metal, and porcelain,
74 x 58 cm.
State Tret'iakov Gallery, Moscow.
Gift George Costakis.

14
Ivan Kliun
Non-Objective, *1914–15.*
Oil on canvas, 71 x 62 cm.
Astrakhan Kustodiev Picture Gallery.

15
Ivan Kliun
Landscape Rushing By, *1914*.
Oil on canvas, 55.5 x 61 cm.
Regional Art Museum, Kirov.

16
Ivan Kliun
Suprematist Composition, *1916.*
Oil on board, 35 x 23 cm.
Wilhelm Hack Museum, Ludwigshafen.

17
Ivan Kliun
Non-Objective Composition:
Suprematism, *1917.*
Oil on canvas, 49 x 44 cm.
State Art Museum, Iaroslavl'.

18
Ivan Kliun
Suprematism, *1915.*
Oil on canvas, 89 x 70.7 cm.
State Tret'iakov Gallery, Moscow.

19
Ivan Kliun
Untitled, *1917*.
Oil on paper, 27 x 22.5 cm.
Collection George Costakis, Germany.

20
Ivan Kliun
Untitled, *1917*.
Oil on paper, x 22.5 cm.
Collection George Costakis, Germany.

21
Ivan Kliun
Untitled, *1917*.
Oil on paper, 27 x 22.5 cm.
Collection George Costakis, Germany.

22
Ivan Kliun
Untitled, *1917.*
Oil on paper, 27 x 22.5 cm.
Collection George Costakis,
Germany.

23
Ivan Kliun
Untitled, *1917.*
Oil on paper, 27 x 22.5 cm.
Collection George Costakis,
Germany.

24
Ivan Kliun
Untitled, *1917.*
Oil on paper, 27 x 22.5 cm.
Collection George Costakis, Germany.

25
Ivan Kliun
Untitled, *1917.*
Oil on paper, 27 x 22.5 cm.
Collection George Costakis, Germany.

26
Vera Pestel'
Still Life, *1915*.
Oil on canvas, 66.5 x 49 cm.
State Art Museum, Nizhnii Novgorod.

27
Vera Pestel'
Still Life, *1917–18*.
Oil on canvas, 78.5 x 70 cm.
State Museum of Fine Arts,
Nizhnii Tagil.

28
Samuil Adlivankin
Still Life: Non-Objective
Composition, *1920.*
Oil on board, 52.5 x 41 cm.
State Art Museum, Iaroslavl'.

Ivan Puni
Suprematist Composition, *1915.*
Oil on canvas, 86.5 x 56.5 cm.
Private collection, Zurich.

31
Ivan Puni
Still Life: Relief with Hammer,
1914, restored 1920 by the artist.
Gouache on cardboard with hammer,
80.5 x 65.5 x 9 cm.
Private collection, Zurich.

32
Ivan Puni
Baths, *1915.*
Oil on canvas, with artist-painted frame,
73 × 92 cm.
Private collection, Zurich.

33
Ivan Puni
Relief with Saw, *1915.*
Wood, sheet iron, cardboard, glass, and
gouache, 76 x 72 x 15 cm.
Private collection, Zurich.

34
Ivan Puni
Suprematist Relief, *1915.*
Oil and gouache on wood, cardboard,
and tin, 70 x 50 x 9 cm.
Private collection, Zurich.

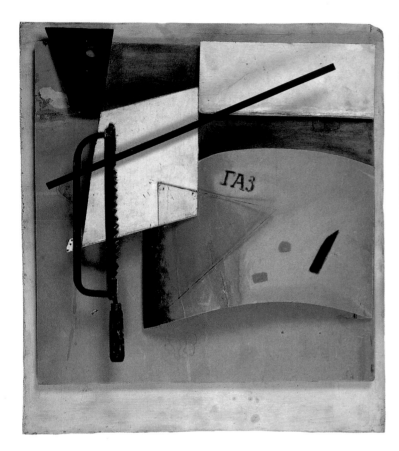

35
Ivan Puni
Suprematist Relief Sculpture, *1915,*
reconstruction 1920s.
Painted wood, metal, and cardboard
mounted on wood panel,
50.8 x 39.3 x 7.6 cm.
The Museum of Modern Art, New York.
The Riklis Collection of McCrory
Corporation (fractional gift), 1983.

36
Aleksei Morgunov
(Non-Objective) Composition,
1916–17.
Oil on canvas, 88 x 65 cm.
Regional Art Museum, Kaluga.

37
Aleksei Morgunov
Composition No. 1, *1916–17.*
Oil on canvas, 71 x 62 cm.
State Lunacharskii Museum of
Fine Arts, Krasnodar.

38
Mikhail Men'kov
Tramway No. 6 (Cubism), *1914.*
Oil on canvas, 82 x 51.5 cm.
State Art Museum, Samara.

Nadezhda Udal'tsova
Kitchen, *1915.*
Oil on canvas, 161 x 135 cm.
Museum of Fine Arts, Ekaterinburg.

40
Nadezhda Udal'tsova
Painterly Construction, *1916.*
Oil on canvas, 106 x 79 cm.
State Tret'iakov Gallery, Moscow.

41
Mikhail Men'kov
Non-Objective, *1919.*
Oil on canvas, 63 x 54 cm.
State Lunacharskii Museum of
Fine Arts, Krasnodar.

42
Mikhail Men'kov
Newspaper, *1918.*
Oil on canvas, 71 x 71 cm.
State Art Museum, Ulianovsk.

43
Mikhail Men'kov
Symphony (Violin), *1918.*
Oil on canvas, 63 x 60.5 cm.
State Art Museum, Samara.

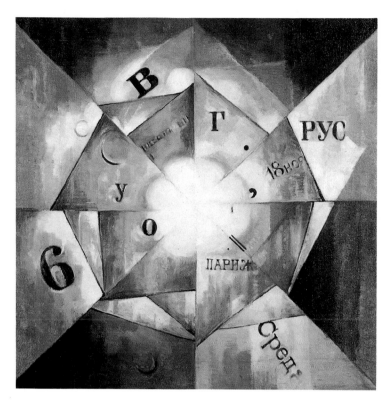

Ol'ga Rozanova
Room, *1915.*
Oil on canvas, 100 x 77 cm.
State Lunacharskii Museum of
Fine Arts, Krasnodar.

45
Ol'ga Rozanova
Non-Objective Composition
(Flight of an Airplane), *1915.*
Oil on canvas, 118 x 101 cm.
State Art Museum, Samara.

46
Ol'ga Rozanova
Cupboard with Dishes, *1915.*
Oil on canvas, 62 x 38 cm.
State Lunacharskii Museum of
Fine Arts, Krasnodar.

47
Ol'ga Rozanova
Non-Objective Composition, *1916.*
Oil on canvas, 78.5 x 58 cm.
State Russian Museum, St. Petersburg.

48
Ol'ga Rozanova
Non-Objective Composition, *1916.*
Oil on canvas, 102 x 94 cm.
Museum of Fine Arts, Ekaterinburg.

49
Ol'ga Rozanova
Non-Objective Composition, *1916.*
Oil on canvas, 71 x 66 cm.
State Tret'iakov Gallery, Moscow.

50
Ol'ga Rozanova
Non-Objective Composition, *1916.*
Oil on canvas, 90 x 74 cm.
Museum of Fine Arts, Ekaterinburg.

51
Ol'ga Rozanova
Non-Objective Composition, *1918.*
Oil on canvas, 62.5 x 40.5 cm.
State Russian Museum, St. Petersburg.

52
Ol'ga Rozanova
Non-Objective Composition, *1917.*
Oil on canvas, 71 x 64 cm.
State Art Museum, Ulianovsk.

53
Aleksandra Ekster
Movement of Planes, *1916–17.*
Oil on canvas, 92.5 x 76 cm.
State Museum of Fine Arts,
Nizhnii Tagil.

54
Aleksandra Ekster
Constructive Still Life, *1917.*
Oil on canvas, 121 x 100 cm.
State Russian Museum, St. Petersburg.

55
Aleksandra Ekster
Non-Objective, *1917.*
Oil on canvas, 71 x 53 cm.
State Lunacharskii Museum of
Fine Arts, Krasnodar.

56

Aleksandra Ekster
Dynamic Composition, *1916.*
Gouache and pencil on paper,
66.7 x 50.5 cm.
Leonard Hutton Galleries, New York.

57
Liubov' Popova
Objects, *1915*.
Oil on canvas, 61 x 44.5 cm.
State Russian Museum, St. Petersburg.

58
Liubov' Popova
Jug on a Table (Plastic Painting),
1915.
Oil on cardboard mounted on panel,
59.1 x 43.3 cm.
State Tret'iakov Gallery, Moscow.
Gift George Costakis.

59
Liubov' Popova
Painterly Architectonic with
Three Stripes, *1916.*
Oil on canvas, 107 x 89 cm.
Collection E. V. Murina and
D. V. Sarab'ianov, Moscow.

60
Liubov' Popova
Portrait, *1916.*
Oil on canvas, 53.5 x 35.5 cm.
Irkutsk Regional Art Museum.

61
Liubov' Popova
Painterly Architectonic, *1917.*
Oil on canvas, 53.5 x 40 cm.
State Surikov Art Museum, Krasnoiarsk.

62
Liubov' Popova
Painterly Architectonic, *1917.*
Oil on canvas, 44 x 35.5 cm.
Tobol'sk State Historical-Architectural
Museum.

63
Liubov' Popova
Painterly Architectonic, *1917*.
Oil on canvas, 106 x 88 cm.
State Lunacharskii Museum of
Fine Arts, Krasnodar.

64
Liubov' Popova
Painterly Architectonic, *1918.*
Oil on canvas, 105 x 80 cm.
Regional Historical Museum, Sloboda.

65
Liubov' Popova
Orange Architectonic, *1918.*
Oil on cardboard, 59 x 39.5 cm.
State Art Museum, Iaroslavl'.

64
Liubov' Popova
Painterly Architectonic, *1918.*
Oil on canvas, 105 x 80 cm.
Regional Historical Museum, Sloboda.

66
Liubov' Popova
Painterly Architectonic, *1918*.
Oil on canvas, 105.5 x 89 cm.
Uzbekistan State Museum of Fine Arts,
Tashkent.

67
Aleksandr Vesnin
Non-Objective Composition,
1917–18.
Oil on canvas, 53.5 x 43 cm.
State Architecture and Art Museum,
Rostov-Iaroslavskii.

68
Aleksandr Vesnin
Composition, *1917–18.*
Oil on canvas, 89.4 x 107 cm.
The Rothschild Art Foundation.

69
Vladimir Tatlin
Complex Corner-Relief, *1915,*
reconstruction no. 5 (edition of five) 1982
by Martyn Chalk.
Paint, iron, aluminum, and zinc,
78.8 x 152.4 x 76.2 cm.
Courtesy Annely Juda Fine Art, London.

**70
Vladimir Tatlin**
Counter-Relief, *1914–15.*
Iron, copper, wood, and rope, 71 x 118 cm.
State Russian Museum, St. Petersburg.

71
Vladimir Baranov-Rossine
Non-Objective, *1918*
Oil on canvas, 71 x 51 cm.
State Radishchev Art Museum, Saratov.

73
Sof'ia Dymshits-Tolstaia
Glass Relief, *ca. 1920.*
Mixed media on glass, steel frame,
24 x 17.5 x 5 cm.
Courtesy Rosa Esman Gallery,
New York.

74
Sergei Sen'kin
Suprematism, *1922.*
Oil on glass, 36.5 x 28 cm.
State Russian Museum, St. Petersburg.

75
Sof'ia Dymshits-Tolstaia
Glass Relief, *early 1920s.*
Oil on glass, 39 x 44.2 cm.
State Russian Museum, St. Petersburg.

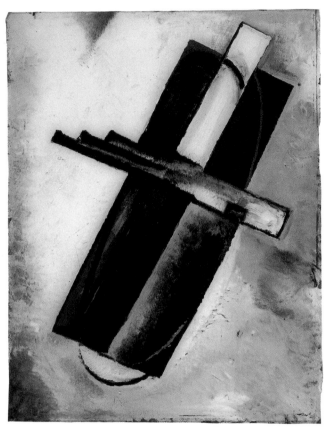

76
Sof'ia Dymshits-Tolstaia
Composition: Compass, *ca. 1920.*
Sand, rope, aluminum paint, and
oil on canvas, 69 x 53 cm.
State Art Museum, Samara.

78
Vladimir Lebedev
Still Life with Saw, *1920.*
Oil, collage, and wood on plywood,
55.5 x 80 cm.
State Russian Museum, St. Petersburg.

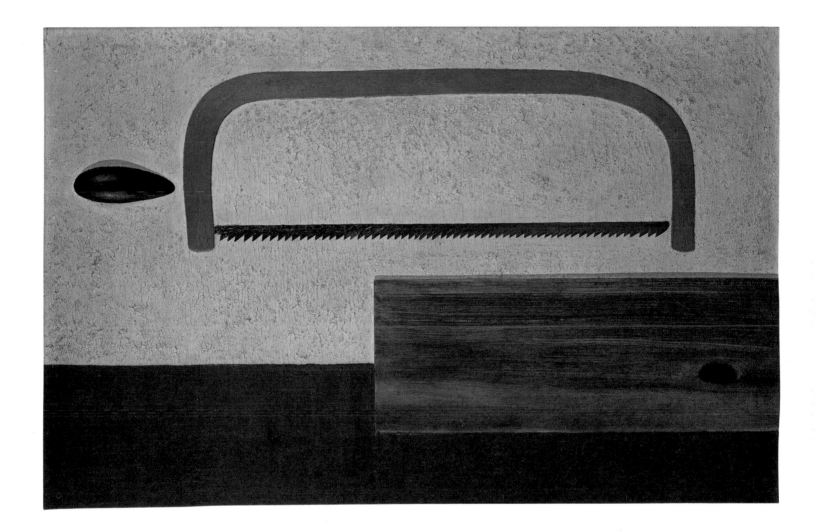

79
Vladimir Lebedev
Still Life with Boot, *1920.*
Oil on canvas, 107 x 77 cm.
State Russian Museum, St. Petersburg.

80
Vladimir Lebedev
Cubism, *1922.*
Oil on canvas, 108 x 62 cm.
State Russian Museum, St. Petersburg.

81
David Zagoskin
Construction, *1921–22.*
Collage and oil on canvas mounted
on board, 60 x 48.5 cm.
State Radishchev Art Museum, Saratov.

82
Władysław Strzemiński
Tools and Products of Industry,
1919–20.
Oil, cork, tinplate, metal, and plaster on
canvas mounted on board, 44.5 x 33 cm.
State Russian Museum, St. Petersburg.

Władysław Strzemiński
Meter, *ca. 1919.*
Cord, ceramic spools, oil, and foil on
board, 81 x 58 cm.
State Art Museum, Samara.

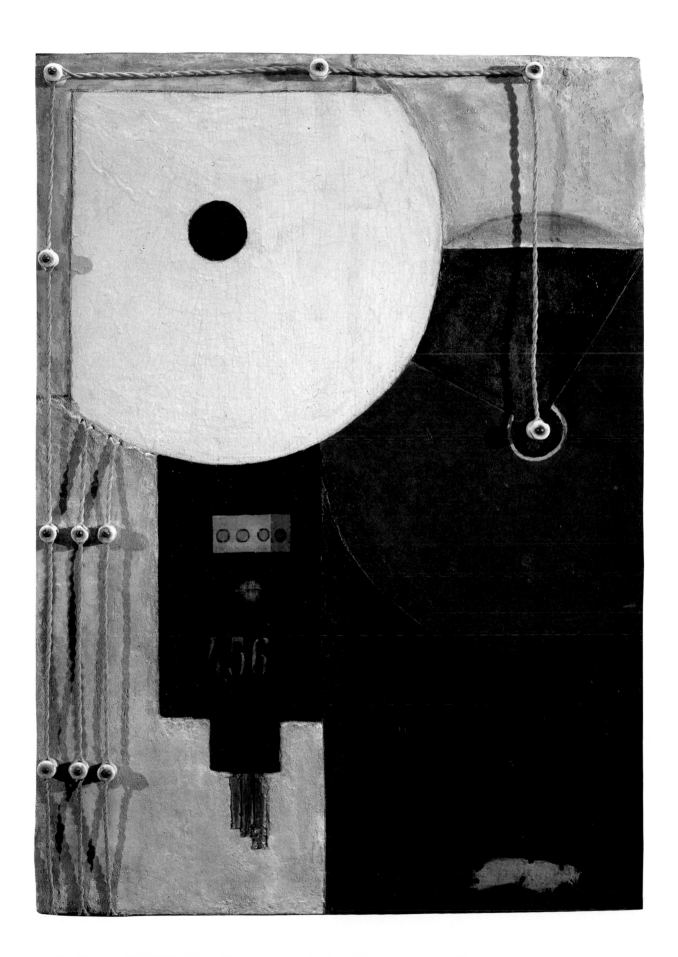

84
Valentin Iustitskii
Painterly Easel Construction, *1921*.
Oil on canvas, 75 x 89 cm.
State Radishchev Art Museum, Saratov.

85
Valentin Iustitskii
Painterly Easel Construction, *1921*.
Oil and wood on board, 46 x 49 cm.
State Radishchev Art Museum, Saratov.

86
Valentin Iustitskii
Painterly Construction with Wire,
early 1920s.
Oil and wire on canvas mounted on
cardboard, 70 x 62 cm.
State Radishchev Art Museum, Saratov.

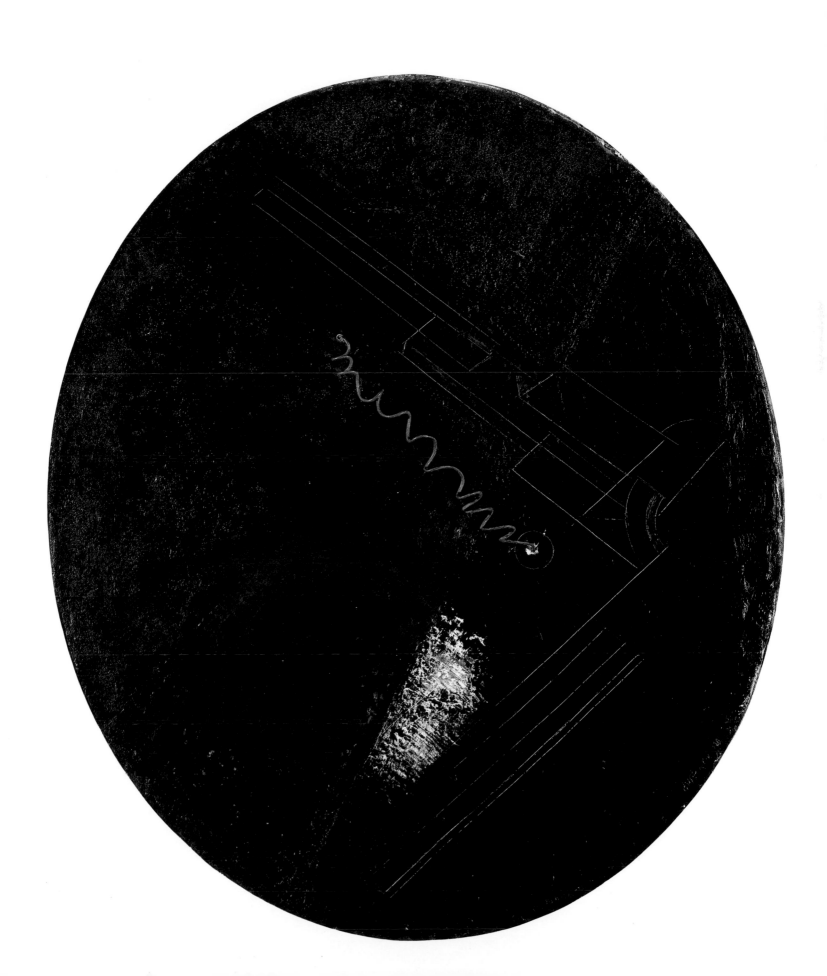

87
Vasilii Ermilov
Composition, *early 1920s.*
Knife, matchbox, wood, and sandpaper,
48.7 x 38.2 cm.
Collection L. Zhadova Family, Moscow.

88
Vasilii Ermilov
Composition No. 3, *1923.*
Construction of wood, brass, varnish, and
paint, 82 x 43 x 7.5 cm.
The Museum of Modern Art, New York.
The Riklis Collection of McCrory
Corporation (fractional gift), 1983.

89
Aleksandr Rodchenko
*Cover for Aleksei Kruchenykh, Tsotsa,
1921.
Collage and pencil on paper,
17.8 x 13.8 cm.
A. M. Rodchenko and V. F. Stepanova
Archive, Moscow.*

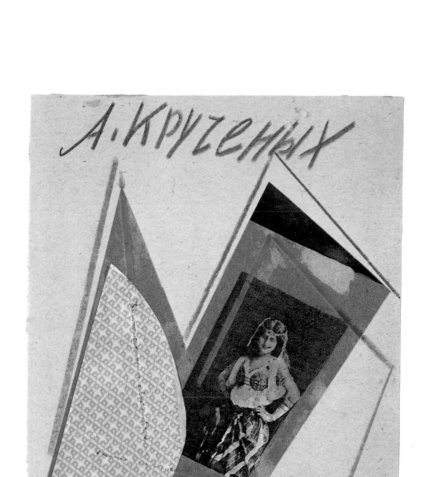

**Ol'ga Rozanova and
Aleksei Kruchenykh**
Illustration for Universal War, *1916.*
Paper and fabric collage on paper,
21.6 x 17.8 cm.
Courtesy La Boetie Inc., New York.

91–96
Olga Rozanova and
Aleksei Kruchenykh
Illustrations for Universal War, *1916.*
Paper and fabric collage on paper, all
approximately 21.6 x 31.5 cm
(dimensions vary).
Cabinet des estampes,
Musée d'art et d'histoire, Geneva.

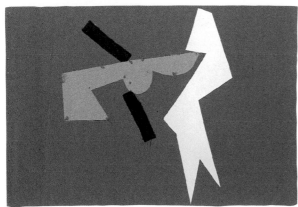

97
Varvara Stepanova
The Third Warrior, *illustration for*
Aleksei Kruchenykh, Gly-gly, *1919.*
Collage and india ink on paper,
15.5 x 11 cm.
A. M. Rodchenko and V. F. Stepanova
Archive, Moscow.

98
Varvara Stepanova
Cover for Rtny kholme, *from the series*
Colored Graphics, *1918.*
Gouache on paper, 23.5 x 18.2 cm.
A. M. Rodchenko and V. F. Stepanova
Archive, Moscow.

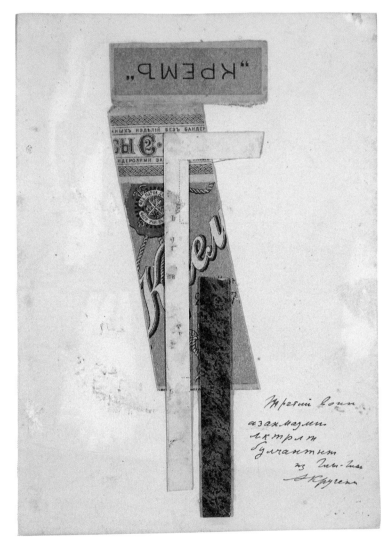

99
Varvara Stepanova
Sketch for Study the Old, but Create
the New, *ca. 1919.*
Gouache on paper, 26.2 x 22.5 cm.
Collection Krystyna Gmurzynska-Bscher,
Cologne.

102
Ivan Puni
Still Life with Letters: "Spectrum,"
"Flight," *1919.*
Oil on canvas, 124 x 127 cm.
State Russian Museum, St. Petersburg.

103
Natan Al'tman
Design for decorations for Palace Square, Petrograd, for the first anniversary of the October Revolution: design for the passage between the Winter Palace and Exerzierhaus, 1918.
Collage, watercolor, and india ink on paper, 20.6 x 39.2 cm.
State Russian Museum, St. Petersburg.

104
Natan Al'tman
Design for decorations for Palace Square, Petrograd, for the first anniversary of the October Revolution, 1918.
Oil on plywood, 52 x 72.5 cm.
State Russian Museum, St. Petersburg.

105
Natan Al'tman
Design for decorations for Palace Square, Petrograd, for the first anniversary of the October Revolution: design for the General Staff Arch, 1918.
India ink, colored paper, and collage on cardboard, 22 x 28.5 cm.
State Museum of the History of the City of St. Petersburg.

106
Natan Al'tman
Design for decorations for Palace Square, Petrograd, for the first anniversary of the October Revolution, 1918.
India ink, pencil, collage, and colored paper on cardboard, 37 x 32.5 cm.
State Museum of the History of the City of St. Petersburg.

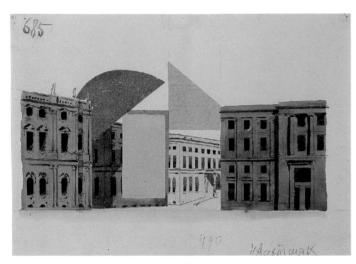

107
Natan Al'tman
Russia: Work, *1921.*
Charcoal on paper mounted on mahogany,
98.2 x 49.3 cm.
State Tret'iakov Gallery, Moscow.

Natan Al'tman
Petrocommune, *1921.*
Oil and enamel on canvas, 104 x 88.5 cm.
State Russian Museum, St. Petersburg.

109
Gustav Klutsis
Workers of the World, Unite!,
design for propaganda kiosk, screen,
and loudspeaker platform, 1922.
Watercolor, ink, and pencil on paper,
32.9 x 24 cm.
Collection George Costakis, Germany.

110
Gustav Klutsis
Project for a construction for the fifth
anniversary of the October Revolution,
1922.
India ink and watercolor on paper,
68 x 49.2 cm.
State Tret'iakov Gallery, Moscow.

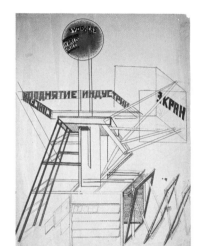

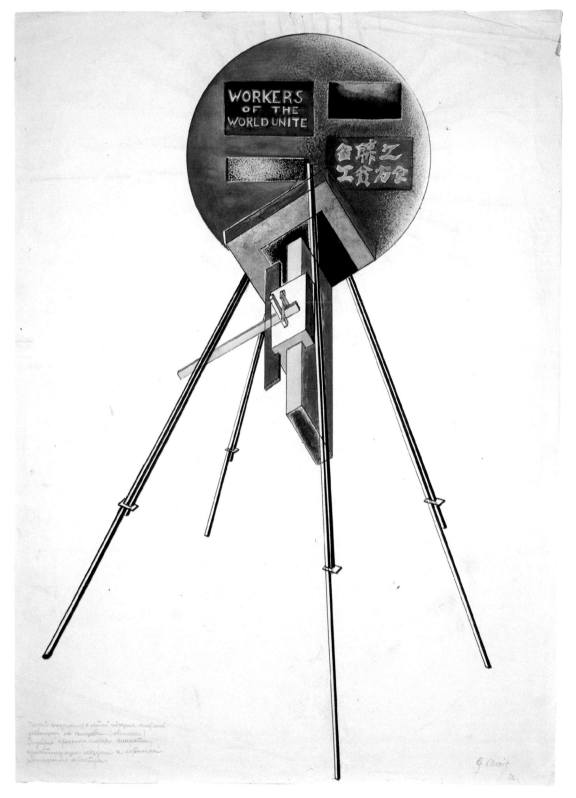

111
Gustav Klutsis
Design for Screen/Radio-Orator No. 5,
1922.
Colored india inks and pencil on paper,
26.6 x 14.7 cm.
Collection George Costakis, Germany.

112
Gustav Klutsis
Design for a screen, 1922.
Watercolor and india ink on paper,
24.6 x 16.5 cm.
Collection George Costakis, Germany.

113
Gustav Klutsis
Design for a stand, 1922.
India ink on paper, 17.5 x 26.7 cm.
State Art Museum of Latvia, Riga.

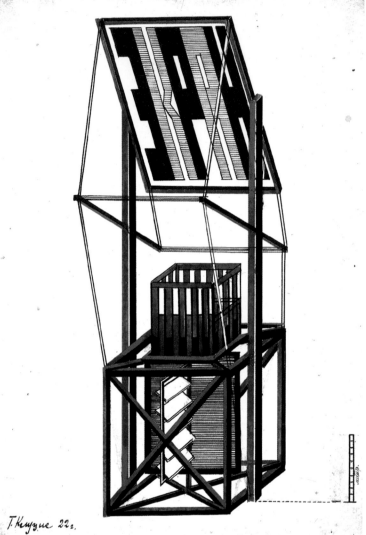

114
Aleksandr Vesnin
Proposal for a Monument to the
Third Congress of the Communist
International, *1921.*
Gouache on paper, 53 x 70.5 cm.
The Museum of Modern Art, New York.
Acquired through the Mrs. Harry Lynde
Bradley and the Katherine S. Dreier
Bequests.

115
Aleksandr Rodchenko
Newspaper Stand, *1919.*
India ink, watercolor, pencil, and varnish
on paper, 53.5 x 35.5 cm.
A. M. Rodchenko and V. F. Stepanova
Archive, Moscow.

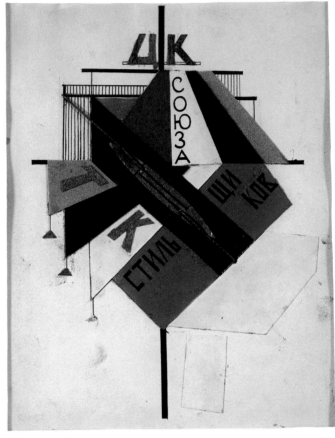

Antonina Sofronova
Study for banner, Central Committee
of the Textile Workers Union,
not dated.
Ink, gouache, and collage on paper,
30 x 20 cm.
Collection Krystyna Gmurzynska-Bscher,
Cologne.

121
Vasilii Ermilov
Exhibition project, Kanatka, *1928.*
Gouache and collage,
38.5 x 27.5 cm.
Museum Ludwig (Collection Ludwig,
Cologne).

122
Vasilii Ermilov
Relief, *1924*.
Wood, metal, and oil on sandcloth,
77.5 x 77.5 cm.
Galerie Dr. István Schlégl, Zurich.

123
Kazimir Malevich
Cover for document folder for the Congress of Committees on Rural Poverty, 1918.
Lithograph, 42.2 x 64 cm.
State Russian Museum, St. Petersburg.

124
Kazimir Malevich
Study for cover for document folder for the Congress of Committees on Rural Poverty, 1918.
Gouache, india ink, and watercolor on paper, 32.7 x 41.3 cm.
Pushkin House, St. Petersburg.

125
Kazimir Malevich
Study for cover for document folder for the Congress of Committees on Rural Poverty, 1918.
Gouache, india ink, and watercolor on paper, 28.9 x 29 cm.
Pushkin House, St. Petersburg.

Kazimir Malevich
Principle of Mural Painting, *1919.*
Gouache, watercolor, and ink on paper,
34 x 24. 8 cm.
State Russian Museum, St. Petersburg.

127
Vera Ermolaeva
Suprematist Construction, *sketch for
festive decoration of Vitebsk, 1920.
Graphite pencil, india ink, and
watercolor on paper, 13.5 x 20.7 cm.
State Russian Museum, St. Petersburg.*

128
Vera Ermolaeva
Suprematist Construction, *sketch for
festive decoration of Vitebsk, 1920.
Watercolor and india ink on paper,
20.5 x 11.4 cm.
State Russian Museum, St. Petersburg.*

129
Vera Ermolaeva
Suprematist Construction, *sketch for
festive decoration of Vitebsk, 1920.
Watercolor and india ink on paper,
17.4 x 11.4 cm.
State Russian Museum, St. Petersburg.*

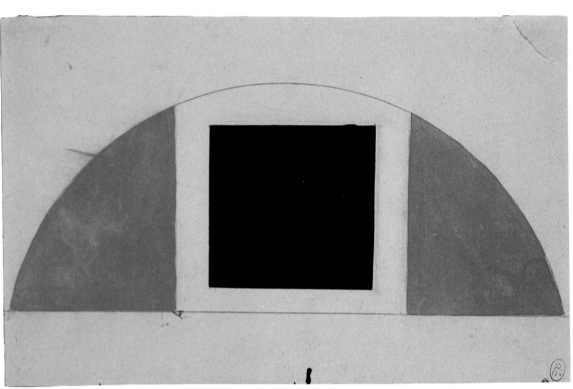

Kazimir Malevich
Speaker's rostrum, 1920.
Watercolor and india ink on paper,
24.8 x 33.8 cm (recto and verso).
State Russian Museum, St. Petersburg.

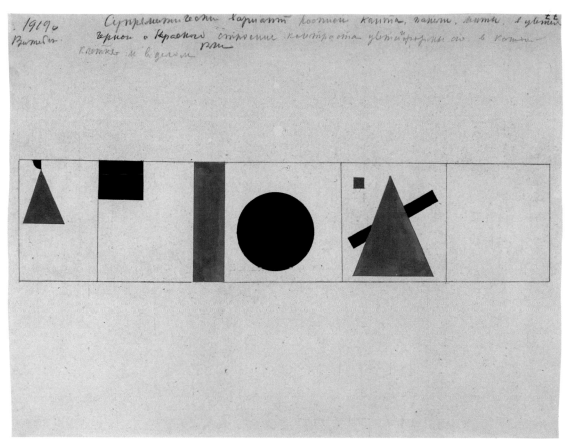

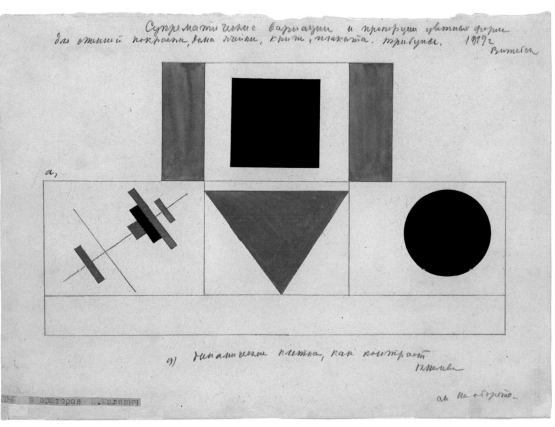

131
Ivan Kudriashev
Design for the First Soviet Theater,
Orenburg, 1920.
Watercolor, ink, and pencil on paper
mounted on board, 21.2 x 53.4 cm.
Collection George Costakis, Germany.

132
Ivan Kudriashev
Design for the First Soviet Theater,
Orenburg, 1920.
Pencil and gouache on paper mounted on
board, 13.3 x 39 cm.
Collection George Costakis, Germany.

133
Ivan Kudriashev
Automobile, *sketch for decoration for the*
first anniversary of the October
Revolution, Moscow, 1918.
Watercolor and graphite pencil on paper
mounted on cardboard, 24.8 x 34.6 cm.
State Tret'iakov Gallery, Moscow.

134
El Lissitzky
Untitled (Rosa Luxemburg), *1919–20.*
Gouache, pencil, and ink on paper,
9.7 x 9.7 cm.
Collection George Costakis, Germany.

135
El Lissitzky
Study for poster (variant), Proletarian
Postal Workers, Remember the Year
1905, *1919–20.*
Gouache, india ink, and graphite pencil
on paper, 18.2 x 22.9 cm.
State Tret'iakov Gallery, Moscow.

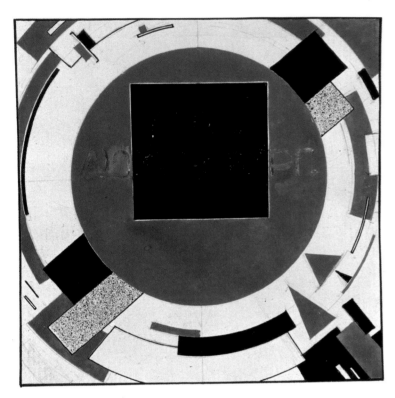

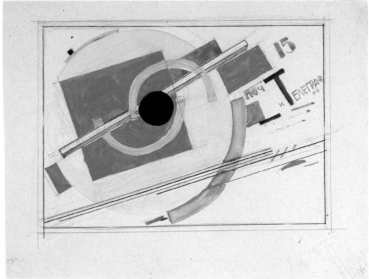

Suprematism, *study for curtains for the
meeting room of the Committee to Abolish
Unemployment, 1919.
Gouache, watercolor, graphite pencil, and
india ink on paper, 49 x 62.5 cm.
State Tret'iakov Gallery, Moscow.*

137
Artist Unknown
Smolensk Rosta poster, Organize a
Week of the Red Gift Here and
Everywhere, *ca. 1920.*
Lithograph, 26.5 x 58.7 cm.
Collection Merrill C. Berman.

138
El Lissitzky
Poster, Beat the Whites with the
Red Wedge, *1920.*
Lithograph, 49 x 69 cm.
Lenin Library, Moscow.

139
Nikolai Kolli
The Red Wedge, *decoration for the first*
anniversary of the October Revolution,
Moscow; perspective, 1918.
Pencil, watercolor, and india ink on
paper, 33 × 20.5 cm.
State Shchusev Museum, Moscow.

140
**Il'ia Chashnik and
El Lissitzky**
*Project for a tribune for a square in
Smolensk, 1920.
Gouache, graphite pencil, and india
ink on paper, 48.2 x 37.8 cm.
State Tret'iakov Gallery, Moscow.*

141
**Il'ia Chashnik and
El Lissitzky**
*Project for a tribune for a square in
Smolensk, 1920.
Gouache, graphite pencil, and india
ink on paper, 33 x 37.8 cm.
State Tret'iakov Gallery, Moscow.*

142
El Lissitzky
Lenin Tribune, *1924.
Gouache, india ink, and photomontage on
cardboard, 63.8 x 48 cm.
State Tret'iakov Gallery, Moscow.*

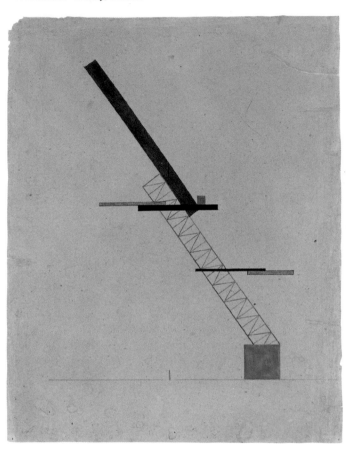

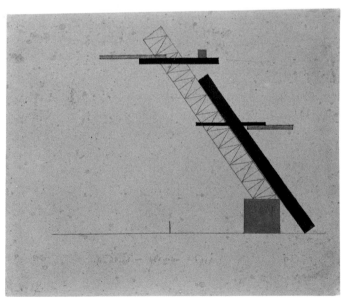

143
El Lissitzky
Tatlin at Work, *illustration for*
Il'ia Erenburg, Six Tales with Easy
Endings, *1921–22.*
Watercolor, pencil, and photomontage on
paper, 29.2 x 22.8 cm.
Eric Estorick Family Collection.

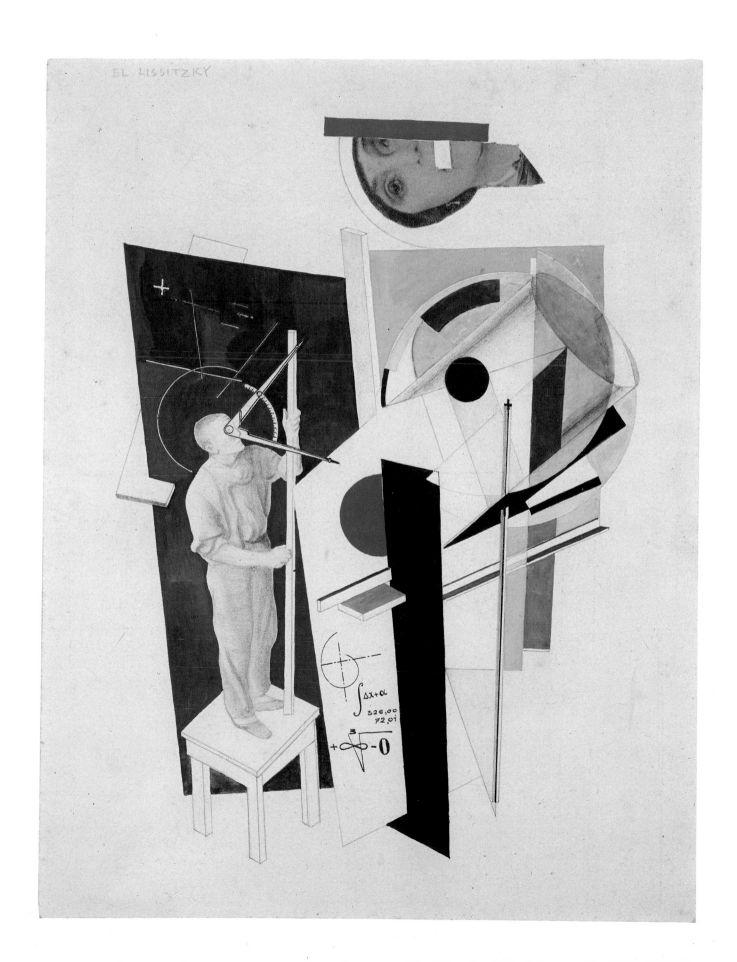

144
Aleksandr Tseitlin
Ration Card, *1920.*
Gouache, india ink, and graphite pencil
on paper, 17.5 x 18.8 cm.
State Tret'iakov Gallery, Moscow.

145
Nikolai Suetin
Study for cover for Maksim Gor'kii,
Vladimir Lenin, *1924.*
Watercolor and ink on paper,
25.1 x 19.3 cm.
State Russian Museum, St. Petersburg.

146
Il'ia Chashnik
Platter, Lenin, *1924.*
Porcelain.
Central Lenin Museum, Moscow.

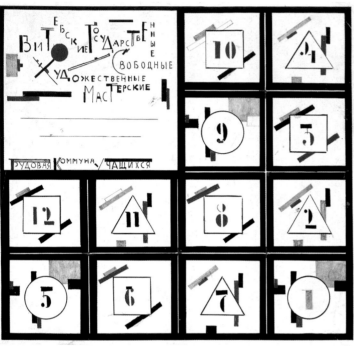

Nikolai Suetin
Project for Unovis Tribune, *1921.*
Gouache on paper, 35. 8 x 26. 7 cm.
State Russian Museum, St. Petersburg.

148
Nikolai Suetin
Train Car with Unovis Symbol en
Route to the Exhibition in Moscow,
1920.
Watercolor, india ink, and gouache on
paper, 27.5 x 43.8 cm.
State Russian Museum, St. Petersburg.

149
Nikolai Suetin
Project: Decoration of a Vitebsk
Tramcar, *1921.*
Colored ink on paper, 43 x 62.3 cm.
State Russian Museum, St. Petersburg.

150
Nikolai Suetin
Project for a Signboard, *1920.*
Gouache on paper, 26.7 x 35.7 cm.
State Russian Museum, St. Petersburg.

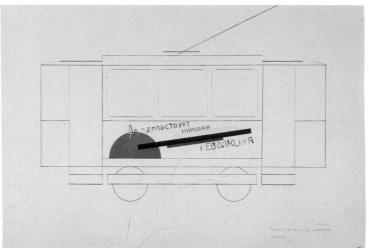

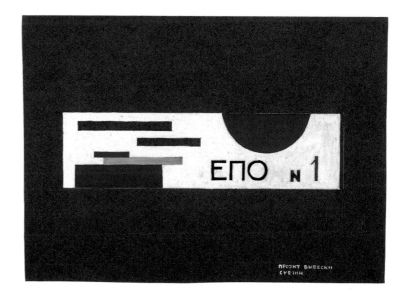

151
Nina Kogan
*Study for set design for a Suprematist
ballet, Vitebsk, 1920.
Gouache, watercolor, and india ink on
paper, 22 x 31.5 cm.
St. Petersburg State Museum of Theater
and Musical Arts.*

152
Vera Ermolaeva
*Set design for Aleksei Kruchenykh,
Victory over the Sun, Vitebsk, 1920.
Woodcut with watercolor additions,
16.7 x 20 cm.
Private collection, Germany.*

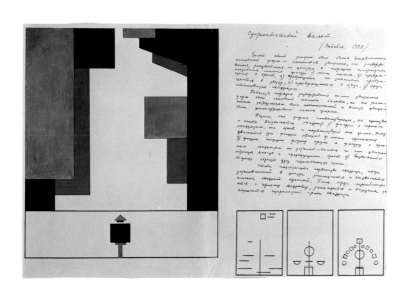

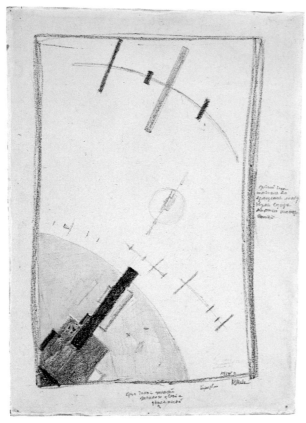

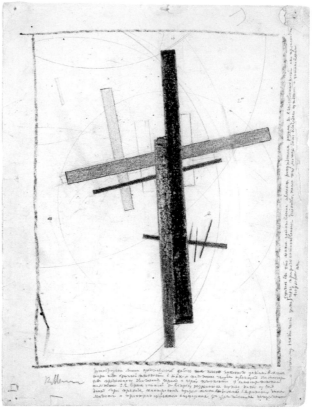

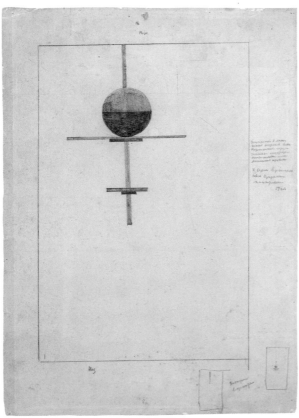

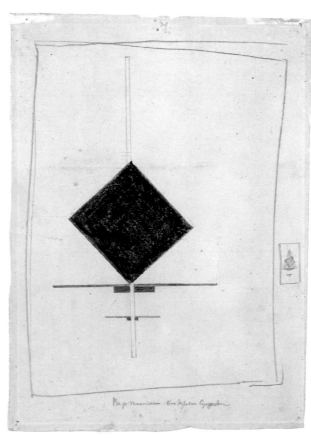

157
Kazimir Malevich
Suprematist Painting, *1921–27?*
Oil on canvas, 84 x 69.5 cm.
Stedelijk Museum, Amsterdam.

158
Kazimir Malevich
Future Planits for Leningrad:
Pilot's House, *1924.*
Graphite pencil on paper, 30.5 x 45 cm.
Stedelijk Museum, Amsterdam.

159
Kazimir Malevich
Modern Buildings: Suprematism,
1923–24.
Pencil on paper, 36 x 53.5 cm.
Stedelijk Museum, Amsterdam.

160
Kazimir Malevich
Arkhitekton "Alpha", *1923–24.*
Plaster, 31.5 x 80.5 x 34 cm.
State Russian Museum, St. Petersburg.

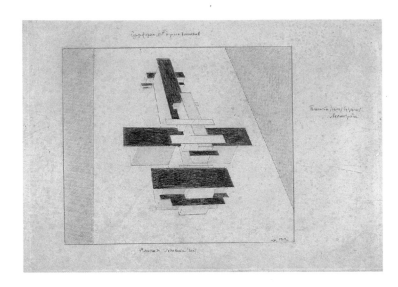

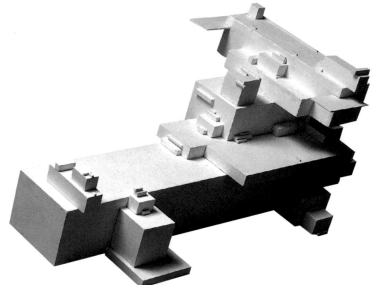

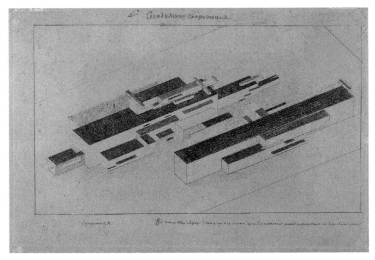

161
Kazimir Malevich
Suprematist Painting, *1921–27?*
Oil on canvas, 72.5 x 51 cm.
Stedelijk Museum, Amsterdam.

162
Kazimir Malevich
Sketch for Fabric Ornament No. 12,
1919.
Watercolor and india ink on paper,
36.2 x 27 cm.
State Russian Museum, St. Petersburg.

163
Kazimir Malevich
Fabric Ornament No. 15 for
Batiste and Cotton, *1919.*
Graphite pencil on paper, 35.6 x 27 cm.
State Russian Museum, St. Petersburg.

164
Kazimir Malevich
Motifs for a Suprematist Fabric, *1919.*
Watercolor on paper, 36.2 x 27 cm.
State Russian Museum, St. Petersburg.

165
Kazimir Malevich
Fabric Ornament No. 10 for Cotton,
1919.
Watercolor on paper, 35.8 x 27.1 cm.
State Russian Museum, St. Petersburg.

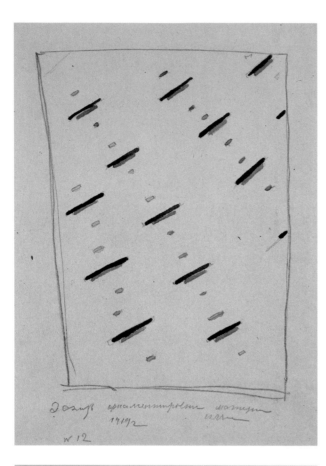

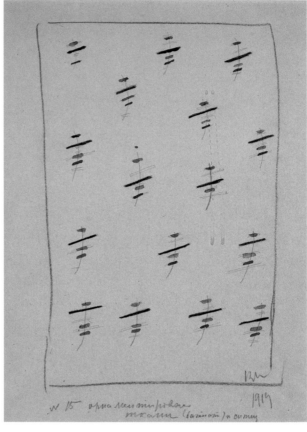

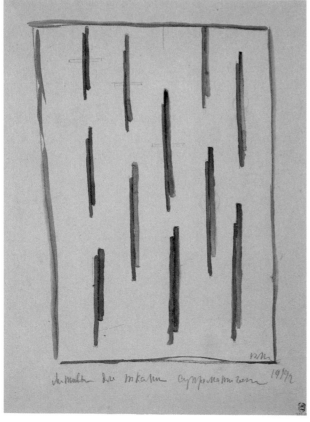

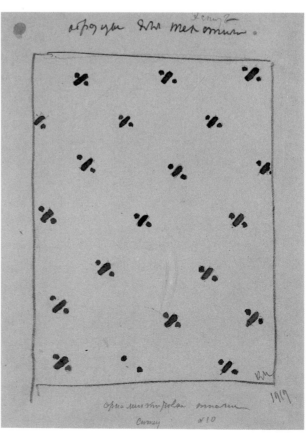

166
Nikolai Suetin
Textile design, 1924.
Watercolor on paper, 18.5 x 28.2 cm.
State Russian Museum, St. Petersburg.

167
Nikolai Suetin
Textile design, 1921–22.
Watercolor and india ink on paper,
19.6 x 28.1 cm.
State Russian Museum, St. Petersburg.

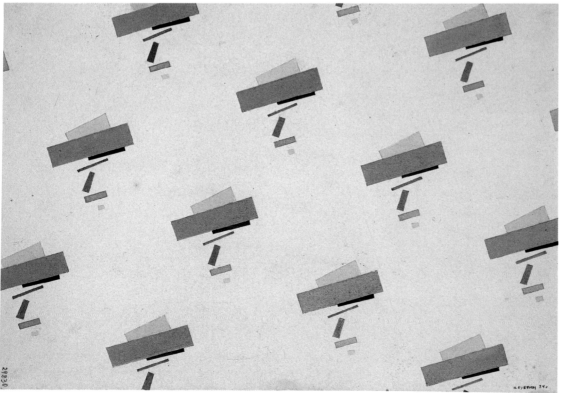

168
Nikolai Suetin
Composition with Yellow Stripe,
early 1920s.
Oil on plywood, 39.8 x 39.5 cm.
State Tret'iakov Gallery, Moscow.

170
Il'ia Chashnik
Design for a cigarette case; three
variations, 1927–28.
India ink and silver paint on paper,
32.8 x 47.6 cm.
State Russian Museum, St. Petersburg.

171
Il'ia Chashnik
Design for applied art, 1926–27.
Colored ink on paper, 47.9 x 33.2 cm.
State Russian Museum, St. Petersburg.

172
Il'ia Chashnik
Design for applied art, 1927–28.
Colored ink on paper, 47.3 x 32.9 cm.
State Russian Museum, St. Petersburg.

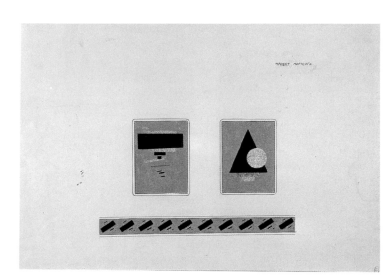

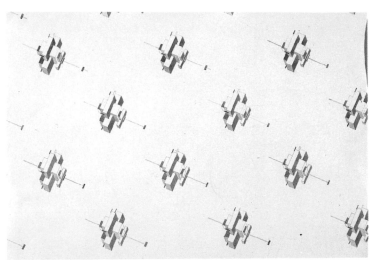

173
Il'ia Chashnik
Suprematism, *1922–23.*
Oil on canvas, 85 x 57 cm.
State Tret'iakov Gallery, Moscow.
Gift George Costakis.

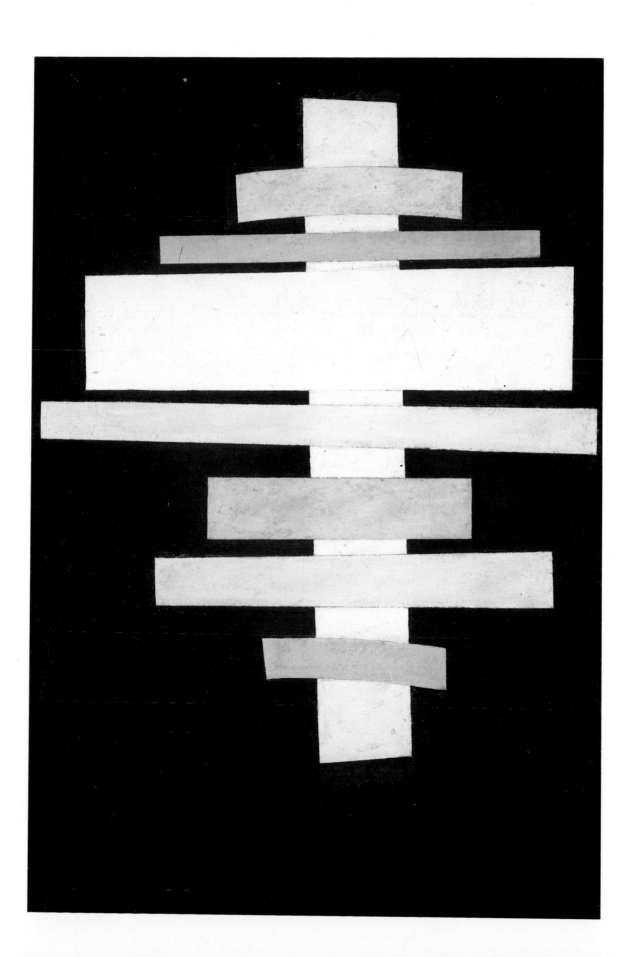

174
Il'ia Chashnik
Vertical Axes in Motion, *1922–23.*
India ink and watercolor on paper,
29 x 21.6 cm.
Leonard Hutton Galleries, New York.

175
Il'ia Chashnik
Red Square (Unovis), *1921.*
Watercolor and india ink on paper,
21.4 x 19.4 cm.
Leonard Hutton Galleries, New York.

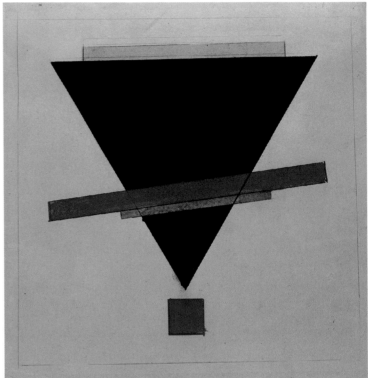

176
Il'ia Chashnik
Color Lines in Vertical Motion,
1923–25.
Watercolor on paper, 35.5 x 25.5 cm.
Leonard Hutton Galleries, New York.

177
Il'ia Chashnik
Circles in a Suprematist Cross, *1926.*
Watercolor, india ink, and pencil on
paper, 29.8 x 20.9 cm.
Leonard Hutton Galleries, New York.

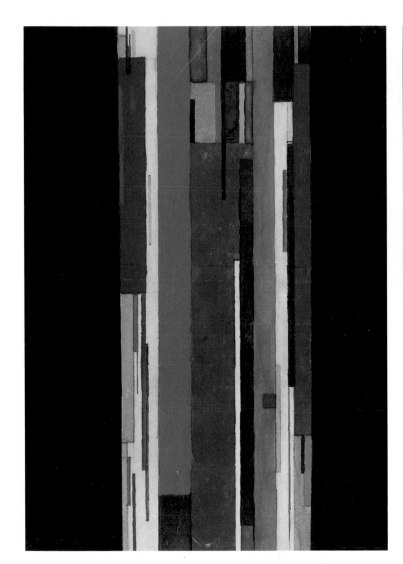

178
Il'ia Chashnik
The Seventh Dimension: Suprematist
Stripe Relief, *1925.*
Painted wood, paper, cardboard, and
glass, 26 x 22.5 x 1.4 cm.
Leonard Hutton Galleries, New York.

179
Il'ia Chashnik
Study for advertising poster, Soviet
Screen No. 4, *1920s.*
Black and red india ink on paper,
98 x 66 cm.
State Russian Museum, St. Petersburg.

180
Il'ia Chashnik
Architectonic Relief, *1926*.
Plaster mounted on board,
16.4 x 18.7 x 2.6 cm.
The Rothschild Art Foundation.

181
Il'ia Chashnik
Suprematist Cross Architecton, *1926*.
Pencil on paper, 22 x 17.5 cm.
Leonard Hutton Galleries, New York.

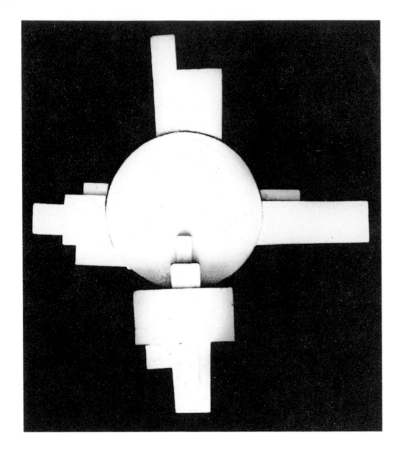

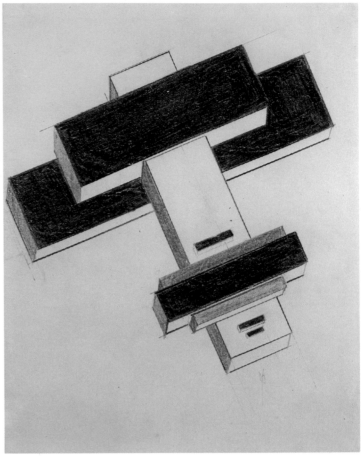

182
Il'ia Chashnik
Cosmos—Red Circle on Black
Surface, *1925.*
India ink and watercolor on paper,
37.2 x 32.8 cm.
Collection Thomas P. Whitney.

Il'ia Chashnik
Supremolet (Suprematist Planit),
1927–28.
India ink on paper, 62.4 x 84.6 cm.
Collection Lew Nussberg, United States.

184
Il'ia Chashnik
Design for Supremolet, *1927.*
Pencil and india ink on paper,
50.9 x 71.9 cm, 62.8 x 84.8 cm matted.
Collection Lew Nussberg, United States.

185
Kazimir Malevich
Teapot, 1923, reproduction early 1970s.
Porcelain, 16.5 cm high.
State Historical Museum, Moscow.

186
Kazimir Malevich
Model for a cup, 1923, reproductions 1984
by Iurii Kraivanov.
Porcelain, Dmitrov Porcelain Factory
(reproduction), 6.5 cm high,
9 cm diameter.
Kuskovo State Porcelain Museum.

187
Kazimir Malevich
Plate with Suprematist design, 1923.
Porcelain, 24.8 cm diameter.
Gilman Paper Company Collection.

188.1
Il'ia Chashnik
Soup bowl, Suprematism, 1920s.
Overglaze and stenciling on porcelain,
State Porcelain Factory, Petrograd,
25 cm diameter.
Kuskovo State Porcelain Museum.

188.2
Nikolai Suetin
Plate, 1923.
Overglaze and stenciling on porcelain,
Lomonosov Porcelain Factory, Leningrad,
23 cm diameter.
Kuskovo State Porcelain Museum.

190
Nikolai Suetin
Cup and saucer, Suprematism, 1923.
Overglaze on porcelain, State Porcelain
Factory, Petrograd, cup 6.5 cm high,
7 cm diameter, saucer 14.5 cm diameter.
Kuskovo State Porcelain Museum.

189
Nikolai Suetin (design) and
Varvara Rukavishnikova
(execution)
Cup and saucer, 1923.
Overglaze on porcelain, State Porcelain
Factory, Petrograd, cup 7.3 cm high,
saucer 15.9 cm diameter.
Kuskovo State Porcelain Museum.

191
Nikolai Suetin and
Il'ia Chashnik
Inkstand, 1923–25.
Overglaze on porcelain, State Porcelain
Factory, Petrograd, 6.5 cm high,
13 x 16 cm base.
Kuskovo State Porcelain Museum.

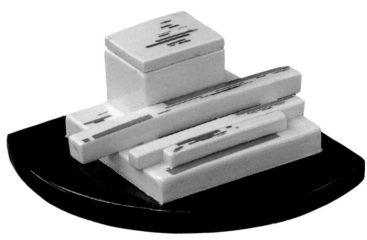

192
Irina Rozhdestvenskaia
Tea service with Suprematist design,
1930–31.
Stenciling on porcelain, creamer 8.8 cm
high, sugar bowl 8.3 cm high, cup 5.6 cm
high, saucer 15.1 cm diameter, cup 5.6 cm
high, saucer 15.1 cm diameter.
State Historical Museum, Moscow.

193
Nikolai Suetin
Tea service with Suprematist design, 1930.
Overglaze on porcelain, sugar bowl 10.2 x
13.2 x 10.6 cm, cup 5.5 x 11.3 x 9.7 cm,
saucer 15 cm diameter, teapot 13.5 x 10.3 x
8.3 cm, creamer 13.5 x 10.3 x 8.3 cm, cup
5.5 x 11.3 x 9.7 cm, saucer 15 cm diameter.
State Russian Museum, St. Petersburg.

194
Nikolai Suetin
Plate with Suprematist design, 1930.
Painting on porcelain, 22.4 cm diameter.
State Russian Museum, St. Petersburg.

195
Nikolai Suetin
Tea service with black-and-green
Suprematist design, 1930.
Porcelain, teapot 15.4 x 21.5 x 12 cm,
cup 7.5 x 9.5 x 7.4 cm, saucer 14.6 cm
diameter, sugar bowl 11.7 x 15.3 x
10.5 cm, tray 35 cm diameter, creamer
11.5 x 13.8 x 9.3 cm.
State Russian Museum, St. Petersburg.

196
Nikolai Suetin
Vase, 1933.
Porcelain, Lomonosov Porcelain Factory,
Leningrad, 23.5 cm high,
7.5 x 6.2 cm base.
Kuskovo State Porcelain Museum.

197.1
Nikolai Suetin
Vase, 1927–early 1930s.
Porcelain, Lomonosov Porcelain Factory,
Leningrad, 25.5 cm high,
9.5 x 9.5 cm base.
Kuskovo State Porcelain Museum.

197.2
Nikolai Suetin
Vase, early 1930s.
Porcelain, Lomonosov Porcelain Factory,
Leningrad, 24.5 cm high,
12 x 12 cm base.
Kuskovo State Porcelain Museum.

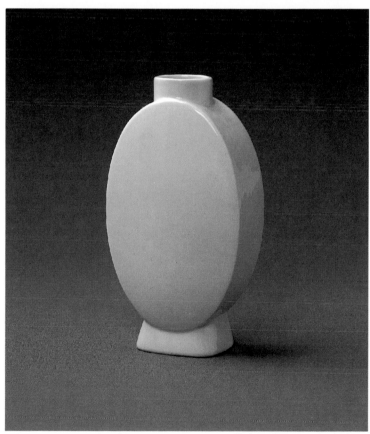

198
Lev Iudin
Composition, *1921.*
Graphite pencil on paper, 9.8 x 7.2 cm.
State Tret'iakov Gallery, Moscow.

199
Lev Iudin
Composition, *1920–21.*
Ink, black and graphite pencil, and
gouache on paper, 21.1 x 12.8 cm.
State Tret'iakov Gallery, Moscow.

200
Lev Iudin
Composition (Head), *1921.*
Graphite pencil on paper, 18.5 x 11 cm.
State Tret'iakov Gallery, Moscow.

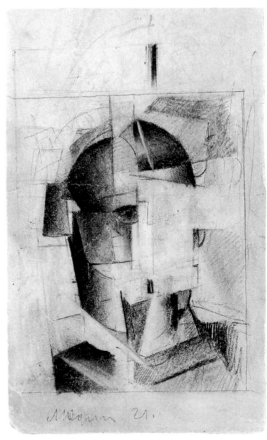

201
Lev Iudin
Cubism, *1920–21.*
Oil on canvas, 42 x 28 cm.
State Lunacharskii Museum of
Fine Arts, Krasnodar.

202
Lev Tsiperson
Cubism, *1920.*
Oil on canvas, 71 x 54 cm.
State Radishchev Art Museum, Saratov.

203
Ivan Gavris
Violin (Cubism), *1920.*
Oil on canvas, 107 x 70 cm.
*State Lunacharskii Museum of
Fine Arts, Krasnodar.*

204
Attributed to El Lissitzky
Composition, *1919*.
Oil on canvas, 71 x 58 cm.
State Museum of Ukrainian Art, Kiev.

205
El Lissitzky
Sketch for Proun 1E: Town, *1919–20.*
Graphite and gouache on paper,
18.1 x 22.8 cm.
Eric Estorick Family Collection.

206
El Lissitzky
Sketch for Proun 1A: Bridge 1,
1919–20.
Gouache on paper, 8.5 x 15 cm.
Eric Estorick Family Collection.

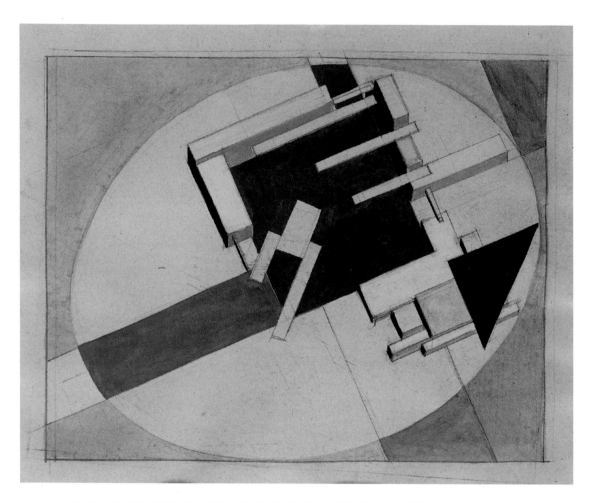

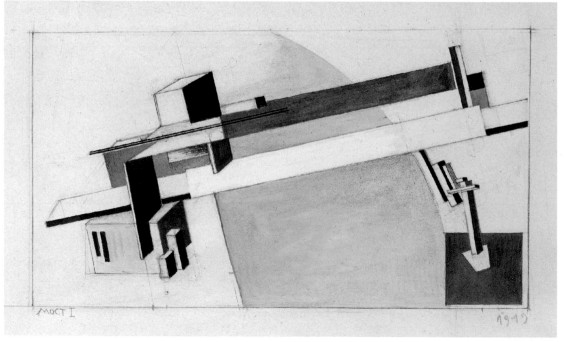

Town, *1919–20.*
Oil and sand on plywood, 47 x 63.5 cm.
State Mustafaev Azerbaijan Museum
of Art, Baku.

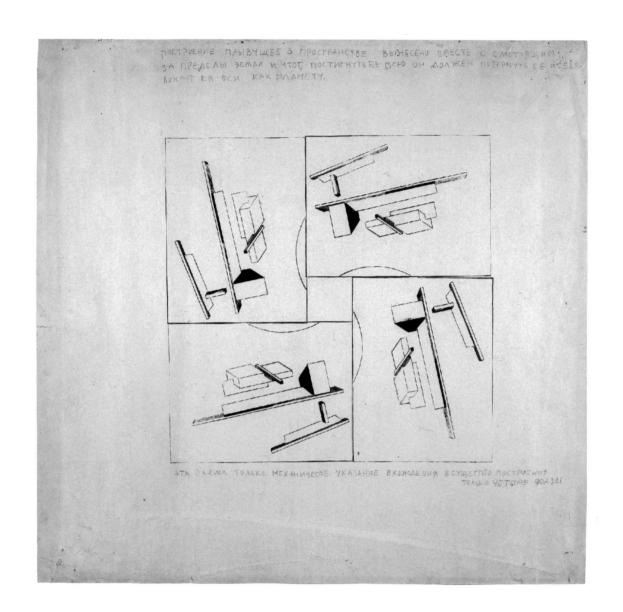

210
El Lissitzky
System of the Theater, *from* Figures
from A. Kruchenykh's Opera
"Victory over the Sun," *1920–21.*
Watercolor, gouache, and graphite and
black pencil on paper, 49.4 x 37.9 cm.
State Tret'iakov Gallery, Moscow.

211
El Lissitzky
Study for cover for Figures from
A. Kruchenykh's Opera "Victory over
the Sun," *1920–21.*
Gouache, india ink, and graphite pencil
on paper, 49.4 x 37.9 cm.
State Tret'iakov Gallery, Moscow.

212
El Lissitzky
The New One, *from* Figures from
A. Kruchenykh's Opera "Victory over
the Sun," *1920–21.*
Gouache, india ink, silver paint, and
graphite pencil on paper, 49.4 x 37.9 cm.
State Tret'iakov Gallery, Moscow.

213
El Lissitzky
Troublemaker, *from* Figures from
A. Kruchenykh's Opera "Victory
over the Sun," *1920–21.*
Gouache, india ink, silver paint, and
graphite and black pencil on paper,
49.4 x 37.9 cm.
State Tret'iakov Gallery, Moscow.

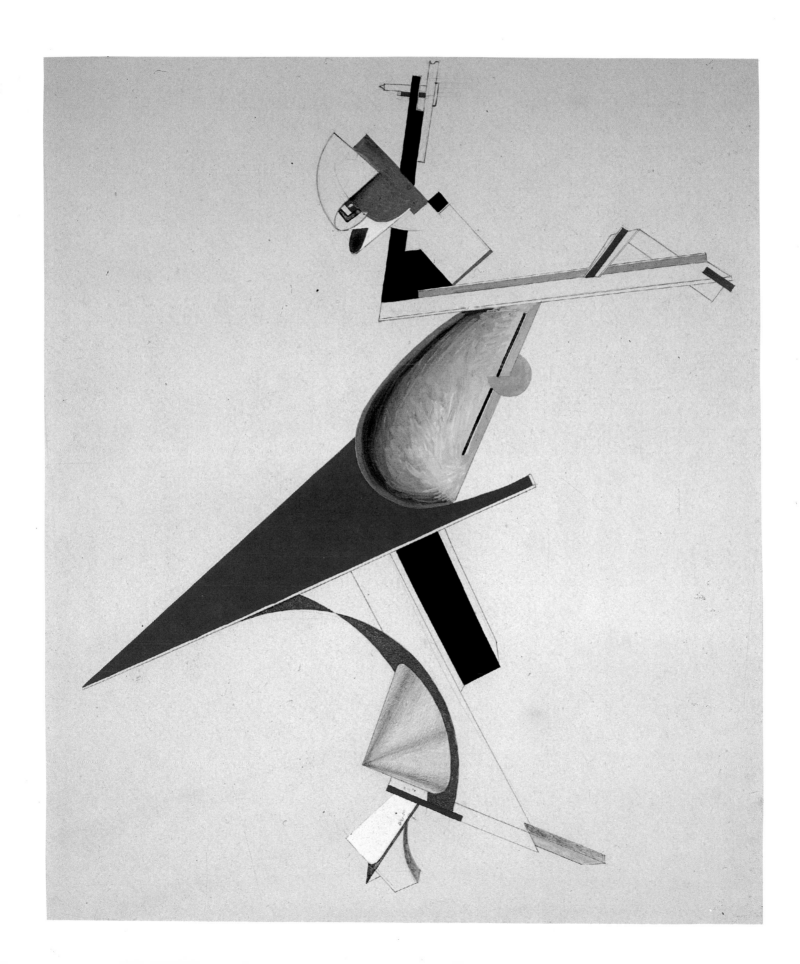

214
El Lissitzky
Cowards, *from* Figures from
A. Kruchenykh's Opera "Victory over
the Sun," *1920–21.*
Gouache, india ink, and graphite and
black pencil on paper, 49.4 x 37.9 cm.
State Tret'iakov Gallery, Moscow.

215
El Lissitzky
Sportsmen, *from* Figures from
A. Kruchenykh's Opera "Victory over
the Sun," *1920–21.*
India ink, gouache, varnish, and
graphite and black pencil on paper,
49.4 x 37.9 cm.
State Tret'iakov Gallery, Moscow.

216
El Lissitzky
Reader, *from* Figures from
A. Kruchenykh's Opera "Victory over
the Sun," *1920–21.*
Gouache, india ink, silver paint,
varnish, and graphite and black pencil
on paper, 49.4 x 37.9 cm.
State Tret'iakov Gallery, Moscow.

217
El Lissitzky
Old-Timer, *from* Figures from
A. Kruchenykh's Opera "Victory over
the Sun," *1920–21.*
Gouache, india ink, varnish, and
graphite and black pencil on paper,
49.4 x 37.9 cm.
State Tret'iakov Gallery, Moscow.

218
El Lissitzky
Futurist Strong Man, *from* Figures
from A. Kruchenykh's Opera
"Victory over the Sun," *1920–21.*
Gouache, india ink, and graphite and
black pencil on paper, 49.4 x 37.9 cm.
State Tret'iakov Gallery, Moscow.

219
El Lissitzky
Gravediggers, *from* Figures from
A. Kruchenykh's Opera "Victory
over the Sun," *1920–21.*
India ink, gouache, varnish, silver paint,
and graphite pencil on paper,
49.4 x 37.9 cm.
State Tret'iakov Gallery, Moscow.

220
El Lissitzky
Proun 93 (Spiral), *ca. 1923.*
Pencil, india ink, ink, gouache, and
colored pencil on paper, 49.9 x 49.7 cm.
Staatliche Galerie Moritzburg, Halle.

221
El Lissitzky
Study for Proun G7, *ca. 1922.*
Collage, watercolor, crayon, and graphite
on cardboard, 47.9 x 39 cm.
Stedelijk Museum, Amsterdam.

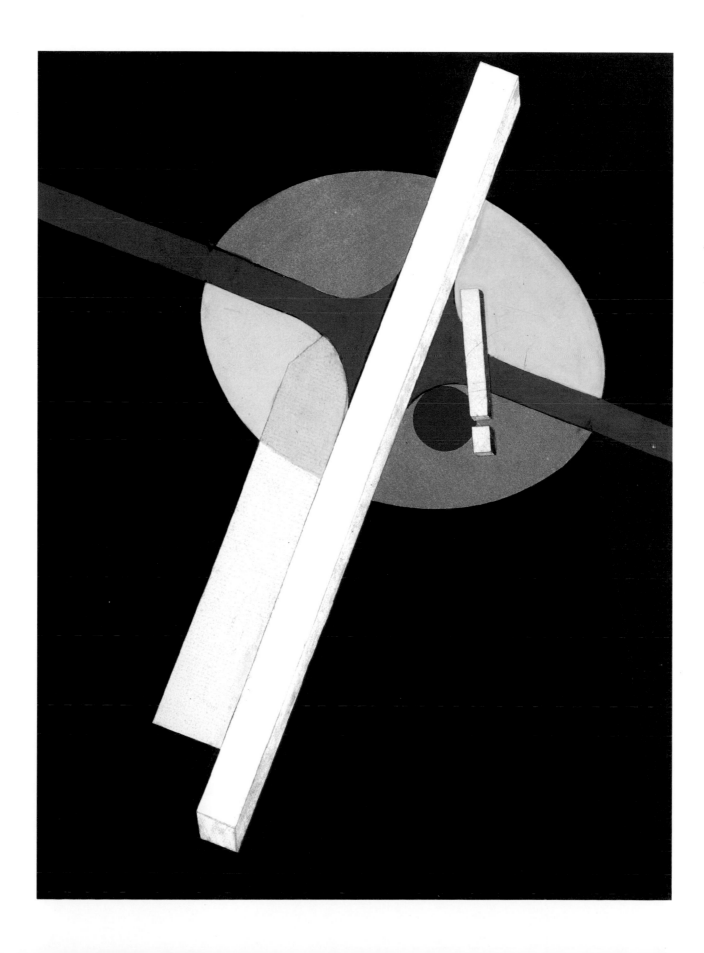

222
Lazar' Khidekel'
Yellow Cross, *1923.*
Oil on canvas, 53 x 62 cm.
Collection M. L. Khidekel',
St. Petersburg.

223
Sergei Sen'kin
Non-Objective Composition, *1920.*
Oil on cardboard, 100 x 81 cm.
Museum of Fine Arts, Ekaterinburg.

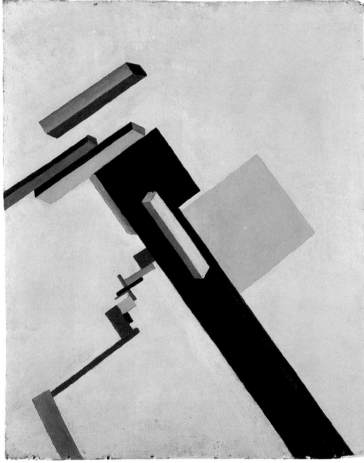

224
El Lissitzky
Proun H333, 1923.
Gouache and collage with multicolored
paper and airbrush on paper,
44.5 × 44 cm.
Private collection, Munich.

225
Khaia (Anna) Kagan
Composition, *1927–28.*
Oil on canvas, 100 x 55 cm.
Collection V. A. Dudakov and M. K.
Kashuro, Moscow.

226
Khaia (Anna) Kagan
Decorative tray, ca. 1925.
Overglaze on faience, 30 cm diameter,
excluding handles.
Collection V. A. Dudakov and M. K.
Kashuro, Moscow.

227
Khaia (Anna) Kagan
Suprematism (Composition), *1928.*
Oil on canvas, 88 x 66 cm.
Museum Ludwig (Collection Ludwig,
Cologne).

Vasilii Kandinskii
Red Spot II, *1921.*
Oil on canvas, 131 x 181 cm.
Städtische Galerie im Lenbachhaus,
Munich.

229
Vasilii Kandinskii
White Cross, *January–June 1922.*
Oil on canvas, 100.5 x 110.6 cm.
Peggy Guggenheim Collection, Venice.

230
Vasilii Kandinskii
Composition: Gray Oval, *1917.*
Oil on canvas, 105 x 133.5 cm.
Museum of Fine Arts, Ekaterinburg.

231
Vasilii Kandinskii
Composition No. 224 (On White I),
1920.
Oil on canvas, 95 x 138 cm.
State Russian Museum, St. Petersburg.

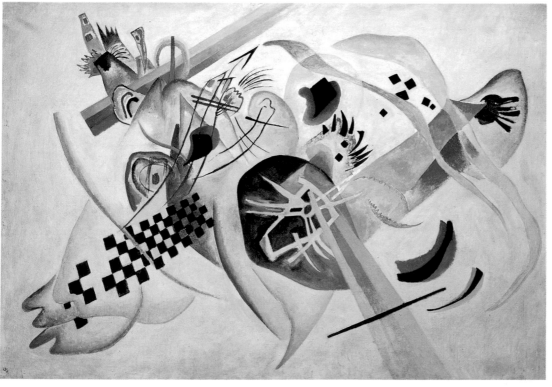

232
Vasilii Kandinskii
White Oval, *1919*.
Oil on canvas, 80 x 93 cm.
State Tret'iakov Gallery, Moscow.

233
Vasilii Kandinskii
Blue Segment, *1921.*
Oil on canvas, 120.6 x 140.1 cm.
Solomon R. Guggenheim Museum,
New York.

234
Vasilii Kandinskii
White Center, *1921.*
Oil on canvas, 118.7 x 136.5 cm.
Solomon R. Guggenheim Museum,
New York. Hilla Rebay Collection.

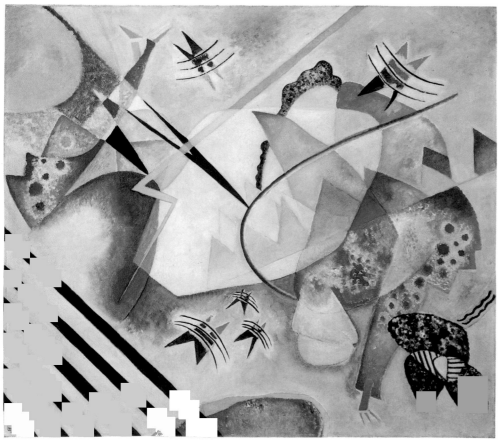

236
Aleksandr Rodchenko
Composition No. 64/84 (Abstraction
of Color: Elimination of the Density
of Color), *1918*.
Oil on canvas, 74.5 x 74.5 cm.
State Tret'iakov Gallery, Moscow.

237
Aleksandr Rodchenko
Black on Black, *1918.*
Oil on canvas, 84.5 x 67 cm.
State Russian Museum, St. Petersburg.

Aleksandr Rodchenko
Points: Composition No. 119, *1920.*
Oil on canvas, 47 x 37.5 cm.
Galerie Gmurzynska, Cologne.

239
Aleksandr Rodchenko
Composition No. 66/86 (Density and
Weight), *1919.*
Oil on canvas, 122.3 x 73 cm.
State Tret'iakov Gallery, Moscow.

241
Aleksandr Rodchenko
Non-Objective Painting (Lines),
1919.
Oil on canvas, 84.5 x 71.1 cm.
The Museum of Modern Art, New York.
Gift of the artist, through Jay Leyda,
1936.

242
Aleksandr Rodchenko
Non-Objective Composition, *1918.*
Oil on board, 53 x 21 cm.
State Russian Museum, St. Petersburg.

243
Aleksandr Rodchenko
Dissipation of a Plane, *1921.*
Oil on canvas, 79 x 70.5 cm.
A. M. Rodchenko and V. F. Stepanova
Archive, Moscow.

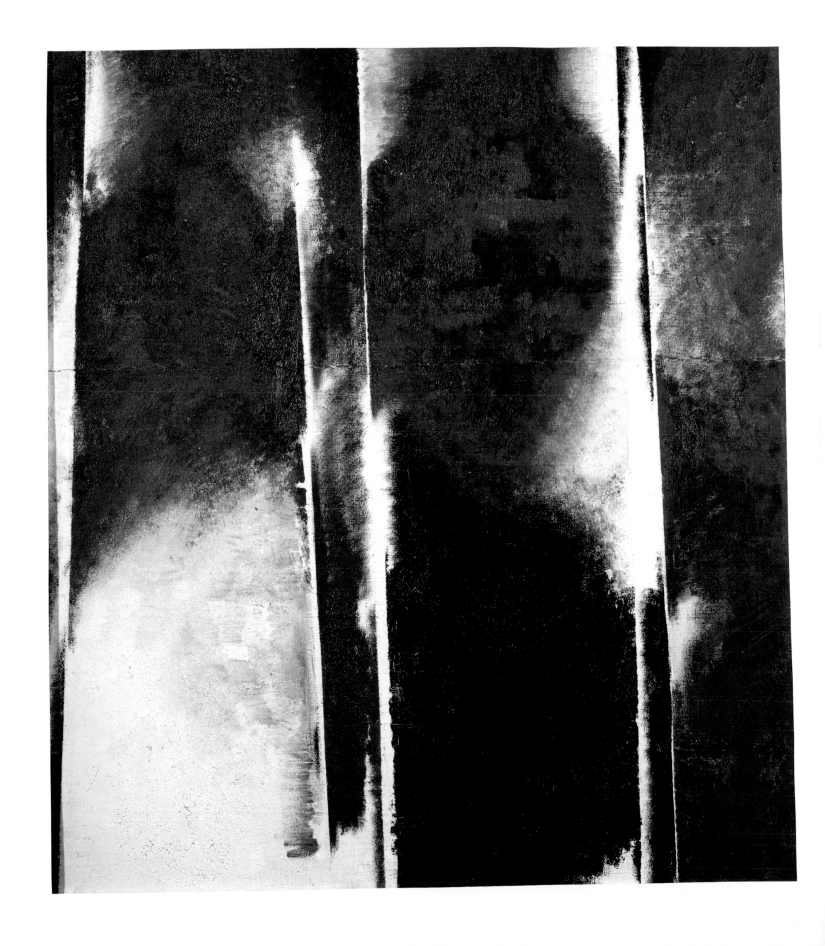

244
Vladimir Stenberg
Composition, *1920.*
Colored pencil on paper, 21 x 13.9 cm.
Collection George Costakis, Germany.

245
Vladimir Stenberg
Construction, *1920.*
Ink on paper, 25.4 x 19.3 cm.
Collection George Costakis, Germany.

246
Konstantin Medunetskii
Composition, *1920.*
Pencil and orange crayon on paper,
26.8 x 23.4 cm.
Collection George Costakis, Germany.

247
Konstantin Medunetskii
Construction, *1920.*
Brown ink on paper, 27 x 19.1 cm.
Collection George Costakis, Germany.

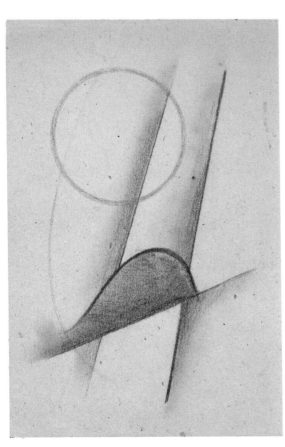

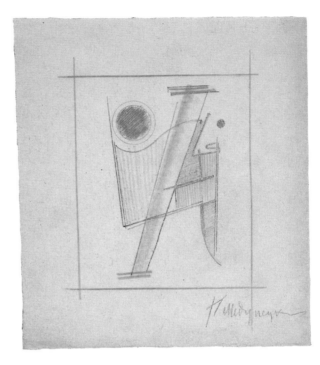

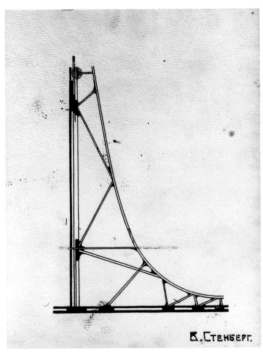

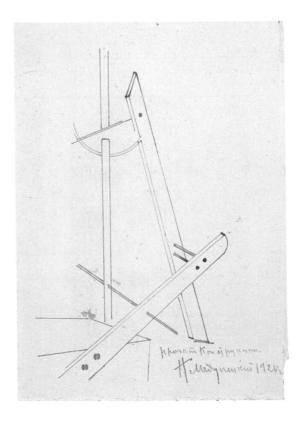

249
Karl loganson
Construction, *1921.*
Colored pencil and pencil on paper,
31.8 x 24.3 cm.
Collection George Costakis, Germany.

248
Karl loganson
Composition, *1921.*
Colored pencil, ink, and pencil on paper,
24.1 x 32.3 cm.
Collection George Costakis, Germany.

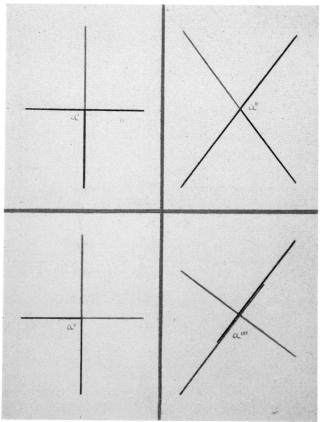

250
Boris Korolev
Construction, *1921*.
Pencil on paper, 35.4 x 25.9 cm.
Collection George Costakis, Germany.

251
Boris Korolev
Composition, *1921*.
Pencil and gouache on paper,
16.1 x 10.6 cm.
Collection George Costakis, Germany.

252
Aleksei Babichev
Composition, *1921*.
Pencil on paper, 49.5 x 34.5 cm.
Collection George Costakis, Germany.

253
Aleksei Babichev
Construction, *1921*.
Ink, gouache, and pencil on paper,
52.1 x 28.2 cm.
Collection George Costakis, Germany.

254
Nadezhda Udal'tsova
Red Nude, *1919.*
Oil on canvas, 70 x 70 cm.
State Architecture and Art Museum,
Rostov-Iaroslavskii.

255
Aleksandr Drevin
Suprematism, *1921.*
Oil on canvas, 107.2 x 86.8 cm.
Yale University Art Gallery.
Gift Société Anonyme.

Aleksandr Drevin
Painterly Composition, *1921.*
Oil on canvas, 124 x 95 cm.
State Tret'iakov Gallery, Moscow.

257
Liubov' Popova
First Half of the Spectrum, *from her*
response to Vasilii Kandinskii's Inkhuk
Questionnaire on color, 1920.
Gouache on paper, 21 x 27 cm.
State Tret'iakov Gallery, Moscow.

258
Liubov' Popova
First Half of the Spectrum, *from her*
response to Vasilii Kandinskii's Inkhuk
Questionnaire on color, 1920.
Gouache on paper, 19.2 x 27.6 cm.
State Tret'iakov Gallery, Moscow.

259
Liubov' Popova
First Half of the Spectrum, *from her*
response to Vasilii Kandinskii's Inkhuk
Questionnaire on color, 1921.
Gouache on paper, 17.5 x 41.3 cm.
State Tret'iakov Gallery, Moscow.

260
Liubov' Popova
First Half of the Spectrum, *from her*
response to Vasilii Kandinskii's Inkhuk
Questionnaire on color, 1920.
Gouache on paper, 17.7 x 42.2 cm.
State Tret'iakov Gallery, Moscow.

261
Liubov' Popova
Untitled, *1920.*
Gouache and paper collage on paper,
30 x 23.2 cm.
Leonard Hutton Galleries, New York.

262
Liubov' Popova
Composition, *1920.*
Gouache and paper collage on paper,
44.4 x 30 cm.
Private collection.

263
Liubov' Popova
Composition, *1921.*
Gouache on paper, 34.3 x 27.5 cm.
Collection George Costakis, Germany.

264
Aleksandr Vesnin
Cover for exhibition catalogue,
5 x 5 = 25, 1921.
Pencil, oil, and whiting on cardboard,
22 x 12.6 cm.
State Shchusev Museum, Moscow.

266.1
Liubov' Popova
Constructivist Composition, *1921.*
Oil on board, 93 x 61.5 cm.
Private collection, England.

266.2
Aleksandr Vesnin
Abstract Composition, *1921.*
Oil on cardboard, 95.5 x 63 cm.
State Shchusev Museum, Moscow.

267
Liubov' Popova
Space-Force Construction, *1920–21.*
Oil with marble dust on board,
112.6 x 112.7 cm.
Collection George Costakis, Germany.

268
Varvara Stepanova
Construction, *ca. 1921.*
Collage on paper, 35.9 x 22.9 cm.
Collection George Costakis, Germany.

269
Liubov' Popova
Study for exhibition catalogue,
5 x 5 = 25, 1921.
Colored pencil and collage on paper,
23.1 x 15.6 cm.
State Shchusev Museum, Moscow.

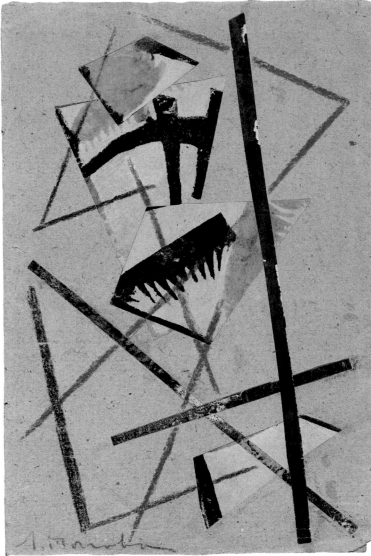

270
Varvara Stepanova
Study for poster for the second part of the
5 x 5 = 25 exhibition, 1921.
Collage and gouache on paper,
28 x 25 cm.
Collection Krystyna Gmurzynska-Bscher,
Cologne.

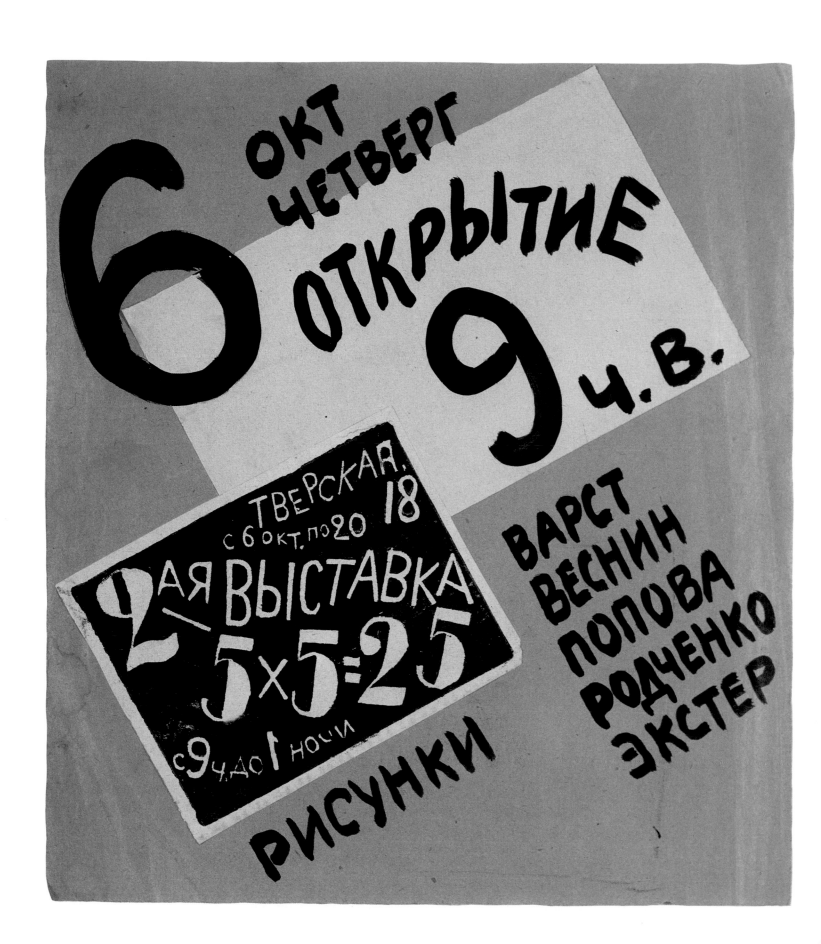

271
Varvara Stepanova
Figure, *1921.*
Oil on plywood, 125 x 71.5 cm.
A. M. Rodchenko and V. F. Stepanova
Archive, Moscow.

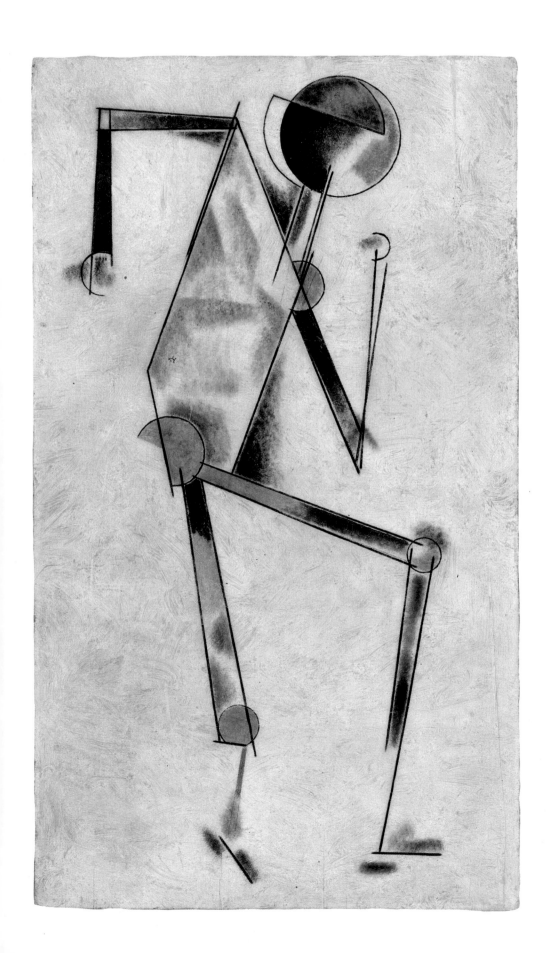

Varvara Stepanova
Five Figures on a White Background,
1920.
Oil on canvas, 79.5 x 97.5 cm.
A. M. Rodchenko and V. F. Stepanova
Archive, Moscow.

273
Aleksandra Ekster
Composition, *ca. 1921.*
Gouache on paper, 42 x 39 cm.
Albright-Knox Art Gallery, Buffalo,
New York. Edmund Hayes and
Charles W. Goodyear Funds, 1974.

274
Aleksandra Ekster
Construction, *1922–23.*
Oil on canvas, 89.8 x 89.2 cm.
The Museum of Modern Art, New York.
The Riklis Collection of McCrory
Corporation (fractional gift), 1983.

Aleksandra Ekster
Color Construction, *1922.*
Oil on canvas, 62 x 66 cm.
Dagestan Museum of the Arts,
Makhachkala.

276
Aleksandra Ekster
Construction of Color Planes, *1921.*
Oil on canvas, 89 x 89 cm.
State Radishchev Art Museum, Saratov.

277
Aleksandra Ekster
Construction of Lines, *1923.*
Gouache and watercolor on paper,
56 x 56 cm.
Private collection.
Courtesy Rachel Adler Gallery.

278
Konstantin Medunetskii
Color Construction, *1920.*
Oil on canvas, 87.6 x 61.5 cm.
State Russian Museum, St. Petersburg.

280
Konstantin Medunetskii
Color Construction No. 7, *1921.*
Oil on canvas, 71 x 62 cm.
State Lunacharskii Museum of
Fine Arts, Krasnodar.

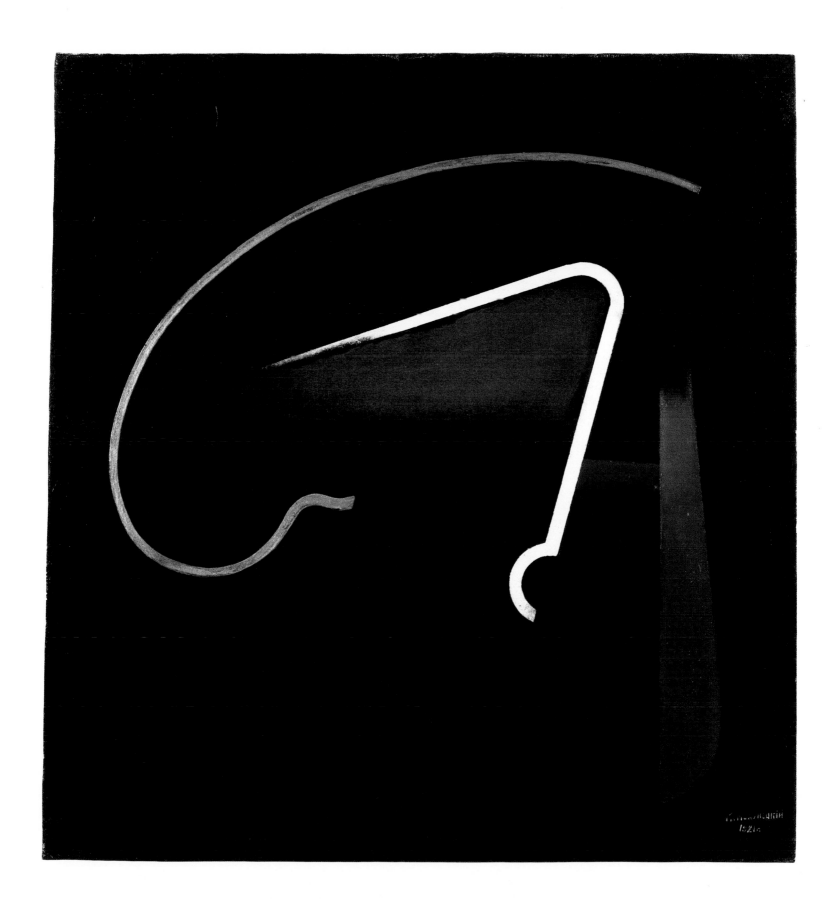

281.1
Konstantin Medunetskii
Spatial Construction, *1921*,
reconstruction 1992 by Michael Duchting.
Steel and wood, 61 x 40 x 13 cm.
Collection Dieter Zaha, Kassel.

281.2
Konstantin Medunetskii
Spatial Construction, *1921*,
reconstruction 1992 by Michael Duchting.
Steel and wood, 84 x 44 x 39 cm.
Collection Dieter Zaha, Kassel.

282
Konstantin Medunetskii
Spatial Construction, *1919–20.*
Tin, brass, steel, and painted iron on
painted metal base, 46 cm high.
Yale University Art Gallery.
Gift Société Anonyme.

283
Vladimir Stenberg
Color Construction No. 12,
1920–21.
Mixed media on canvas, 52 x 45 cm.
State Tret'iakov Gallery, Moscow.

284
Vladimir Stenberg
Color Construction No. 13, *1919–20.*
Mixed media on canvas, 45 x 52 cm.
State Tret'iakov Gallery, Moscow.

285
Vladimir Stenberg
Color Construction No. 10,
1920–21.
Mixed media on canvas, 52 x 45 cm.
State Tret'iakov Gallery, Moscow.

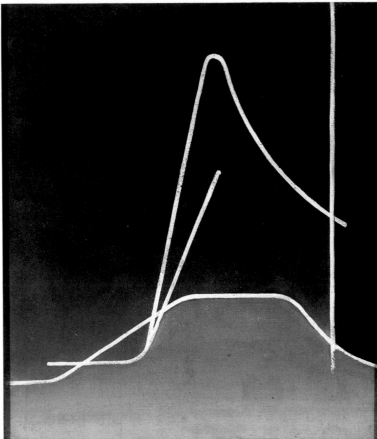

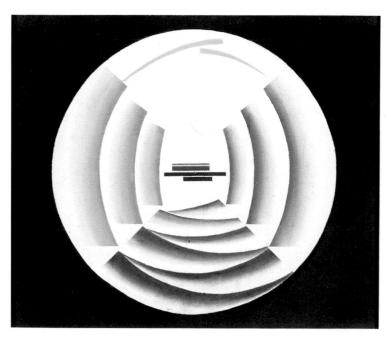

286
Vladimir Stenberg
Color Construction No. 4, *1920.*
Oil on canvas, 75 x 38.5 cm.
State Russian Museum, St. Petersburg.

287
Georgii Stenberg
Non-Objective Composition, *1920.*
Watercolor, india ink, and whiting on
paper, 30.4 x 18.5 cm.
State Russian Museum, St. Petersburg.

288
Georgii Stenberg
Color Construction, *1919.*
Oil and metallic paint on cardboard,
27 x 17 cm.
Albright-Knox Art Gallery, Buffalo,
New York. George B. and Jenny R.
Mathews Fund, 1976.

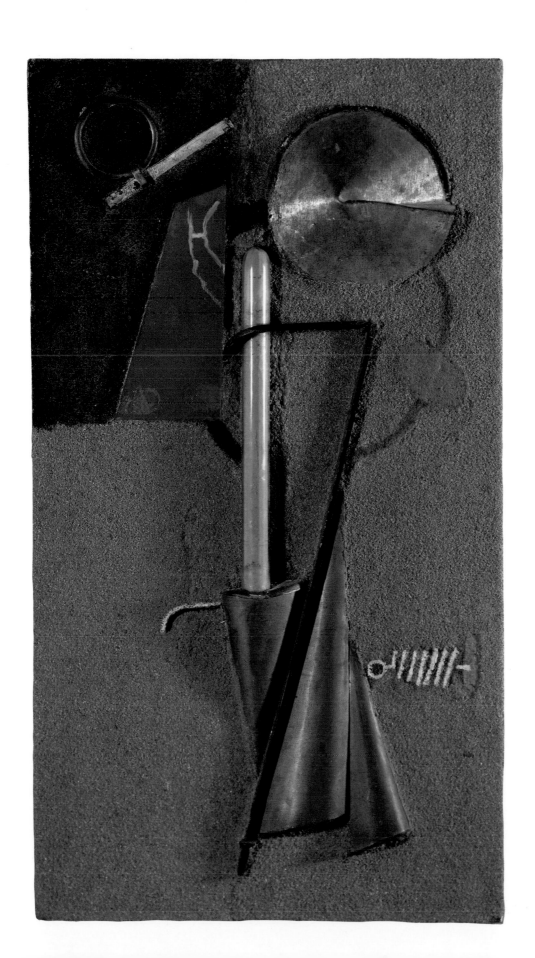

290
Aleksandr Rodchenko
Spatial Construction No. 5, *1918,*
reconstruction.
Painted aluminum, 47.5 x 37.5 x 21 cm.
Wilhelm Hack Museum, Ludwigshafen.

291
Vladimir Stenberg
Spatial Construction KPS 29, *1921,*
reconstruction 1977.
Brass tubes, steel rods, hardwood painted
with black lacquer, and steel wires,
275 x 60 x 52 cm, including base.
Collection Galerie Hoffmann, Friedberg,
Dokumentation konstruktive Kunst.

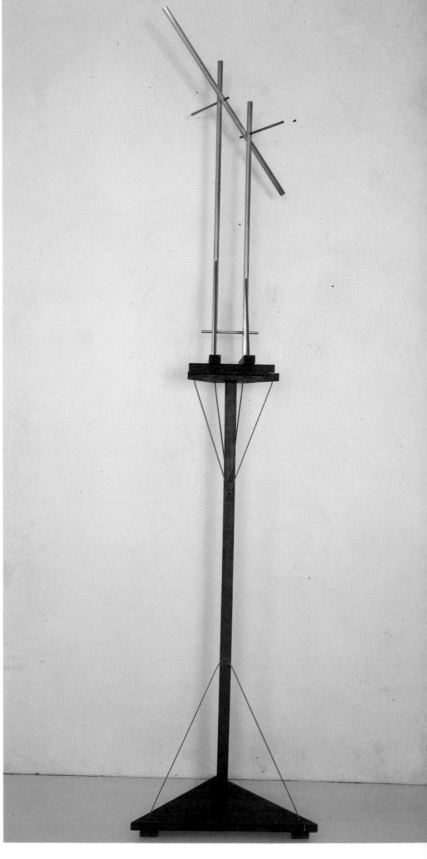

292
Vladimir Stenberg
Spatial Construction KPS 42 N IV,
1921, reconstruction 1973.
Aluminum, 264 x 70 x 130 cm.
Galerie Gmurzynska, Cologne.

293
Georgii Stenberg
Spatial Construction KPS 51 N XI,
1921, reconstruction 1973.
Browned and chromium-plated iron,
glass, and wood, 220 x 100 x 61 cm.
Galerie Gmurzynska, Cologne.

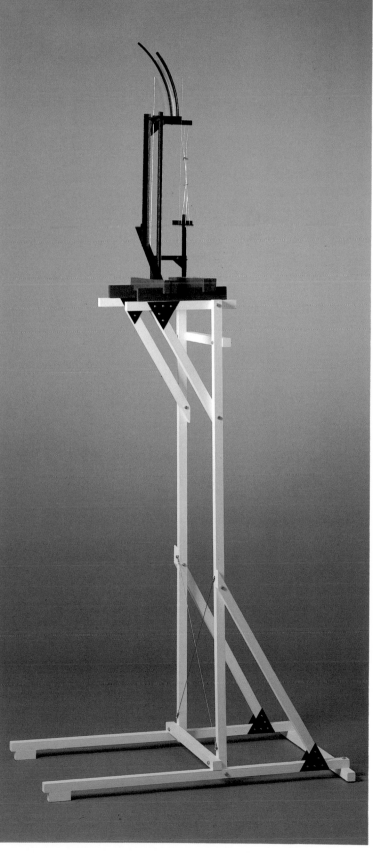

294
Aleksandr Rodchenko
Oval Hanging Spatial Construction
No. 12, *1921, reconstruction by*
Aleksandr Lavrent'ev, 1970.
Varnished plywood, 54 x 80 x 50 cm.
A. M. Rodchenko and V. F. Stepanova
Archive, Moscow.

295
Katarzyna Kobro
Suprematist Construction
(Suspended), *1921.*
Steel, 43 x 28 cm.
Private collection.

296
Aleksandr Rodchenko
Hanging Spatial Construction, *1921,*
reconstruction 1982.
Aluminum, 59 x 58 x 59 cm.
Galerie Gmurzynska, Cologne.

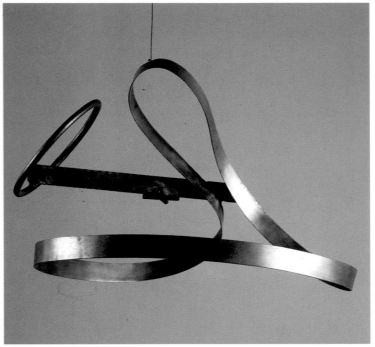

297
Katarzyna Kobro
Abstract Sculpture I, *1924.*
Glass, metal, and wood,
72 x 17.5 x 15.5 cm.
Muzeum Sztuki, Łódź.

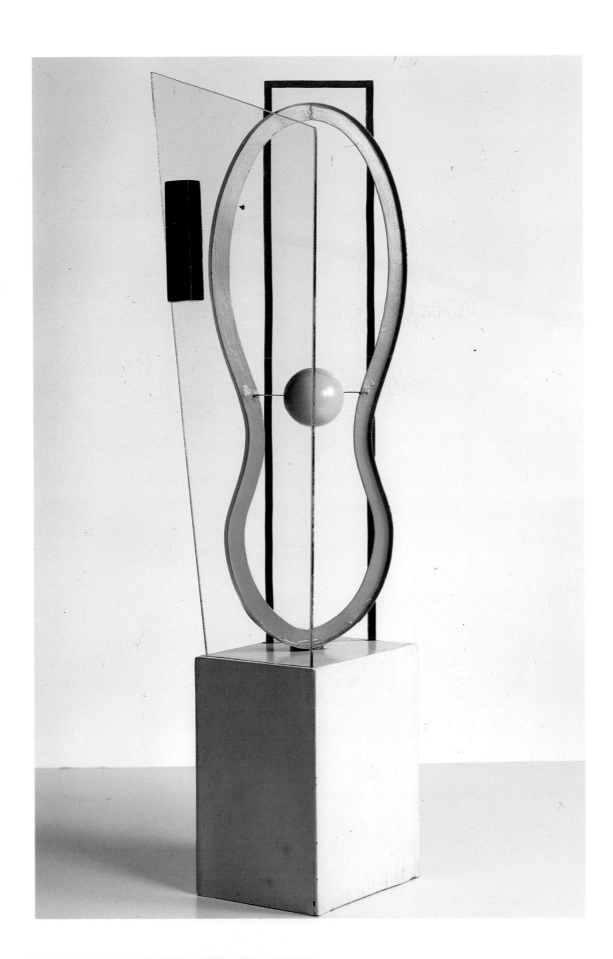

298
Antoine Pevsner
Composition, *1917–18.*
Oil on canvas, 80 x 52 cm.
Musée national d'art moderne,
Centre Georges Pompidou, Paris.
Gift Mrs. Pevsner, 1964.

299
Antoine Pevsner
Still Life: Absinthe, *1922–23.*
Oil on canvas, 75.5 x 49 cm.
State Russian Museum, St. Petersburg.

300
Naum Gabo
Constructed Head No. 2, *1916.*
Steel, 45 x 40.5 x 40.5 cm.
Collection Nina Williams, England.

301
Naum Gabo
Maquette for Constructed Torso,
1917–18, reassembled 1985.
Cardboard, 117 cm high.
Berlinische Galerie, Museum für moderne
Kunst, Photographie und Architektur,
Berlin.

302
Antoine Pevsner
Gray Tone, *1920.*
Oil on canvas, 62 x 49 cm.
Galerie Alice Pauli, Lausanne.

303
Naum Gabo
Design for a Construction, *1918.*
Pencil on paper, 40.5 x 27.3 cm.
Collection Nina Williams, England.

304
Naum Gabo
Study for an Outdoor Construction,
1917.
Pencil on paper, 23 x 23.5 cm.
Galerie de France, Paris.

305
Naum Gabo
Study for a Tower, *1917.*
Pencil on paper, 40.3 x 28.5 cm.
Berlinische Galerie, Museum für moderne
Kunst, Photographie und Architektur,
Berlin.

306
Naum Gabo
Study for a Square in Moscow, *1919.*
Pencil on paper, 42 x 35 cm.
Collection Thomas P. Whitney.

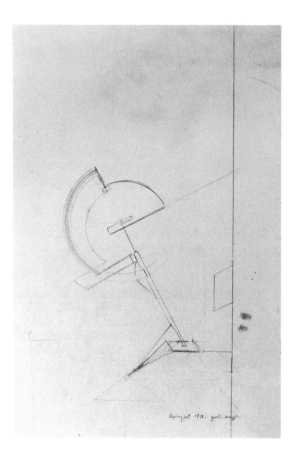

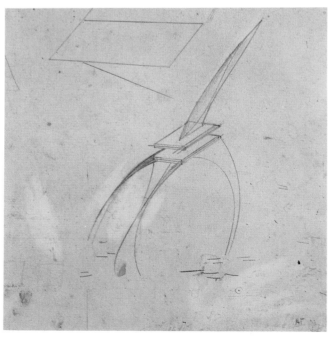

307
Naum Gabo
Column, *ca. 1923, reconstruction 1937 by*
the artist.
Perspex, wood, metal, and glass,
105.3 x 73.6 x 73.6 cm.
Solomon R. Guggenheim Museum,
New York.

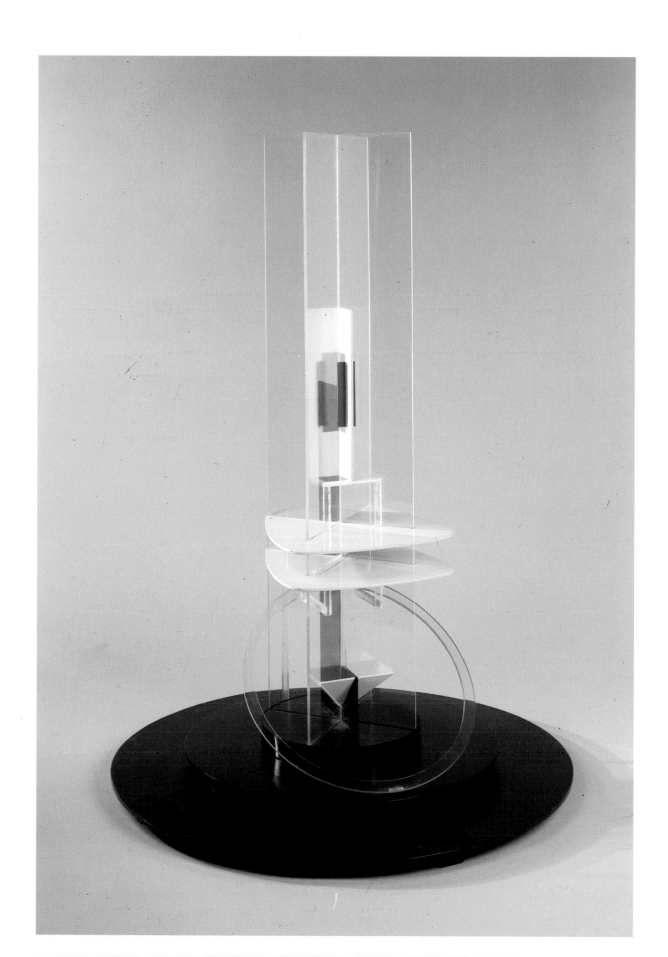

308
Gustav Klutsis
Study for poster, Electrification of the
Entire Country, *1920.*
Ink, gouache, and collage on paper,
46.3 x 27.5 cm.
Collection Merrill C. Berman.

309
Gustav Klutsis
Dynamic City, *1919.*
Gouache, foil, photomontage, collage, and
pencil on paper, 37.5 x 25.8 cm.
State Art Museum of Latvia, Riga.

310
Gustav Klutsis
Dynamic City, *1919.*
Oil with sand and concrete on board,
87 x 64.5 cm.
Collection George Costakis, Germany.

311
Gustav Klutsis
Construction, *1921.*
India ink, gouache, pencil, and sealing
wax on paper, 66.6 x 41.4 cm.
State Art Museum of Latvia, Riga.

312
Gustav Klutsis
Construction, *1921.*
Pencil and ink on paper, 52.1 x 43.5 cm.
State Art Museum of Latvia, Riga.

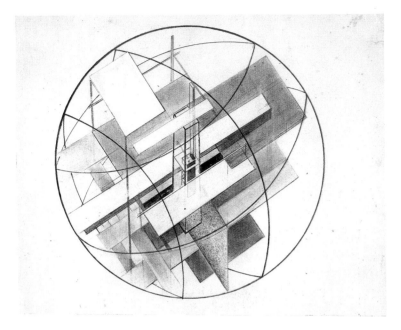

313
Gustav Klutsis
Construction, *1921.*
Gouache, ink, silverbronze, and sealing
wax on paper, 81.7 x 66.5 cm.
State Art Museum of Latvia, Riga.

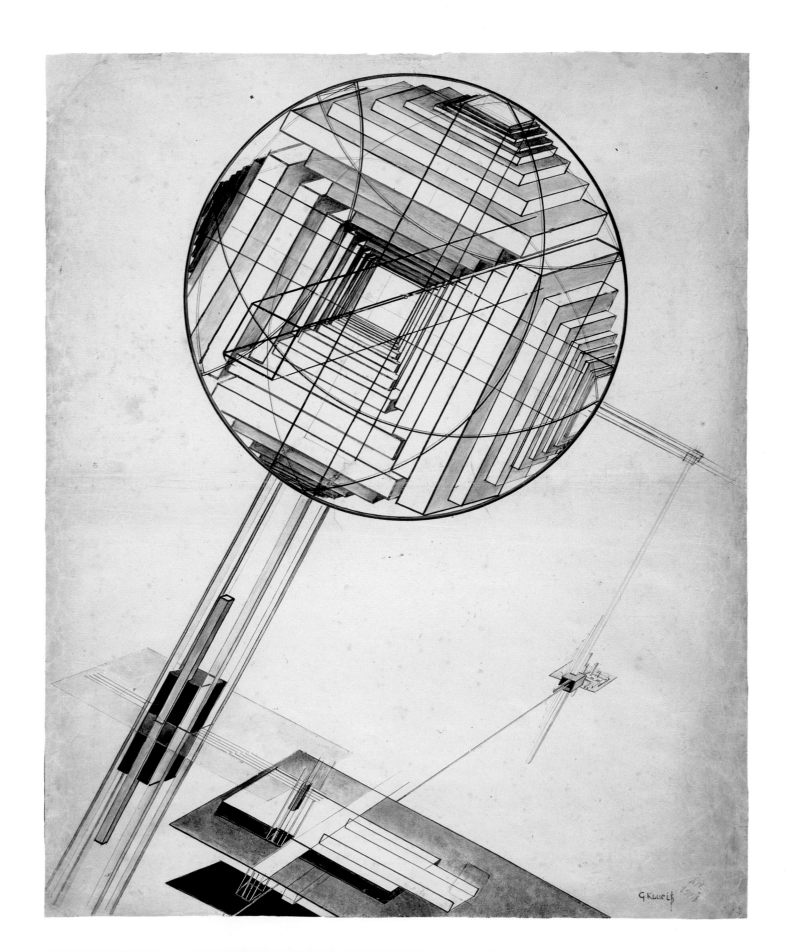

314
Elena Afanas'eva
Color and Space , *1924–25.*
Oil on canvas, 29. 2 x 39 cm.
Barry Friedman Ltd., New York.

315
Elena Afanas'eva
Color Composition, *1924–25.*
Oil on canvas, 33 x 33.3 cm.
Barry Friedman Ltd., New York.

316
Gustav Klutsis
Chromatic Table, *from* Color
Discipline Textbook for Vkhutemas
Students, *1924–30.*
Collage and india ink on paper,
30.8 x 20.8 cm.
State Tret'iakov Gallery, Moscow.

317
Mikhail Matiushin
Table from Guide to Color: Rules of
the Fluctuations of Color
Combinations, *1932.*
Gouache on cardboard, 12.5 x 143 cm.
Collection A. V. Povelikhina,
St. Petersburg.

318
Mikhail Matiushin
Table from Guide to Color: Rules of
the Fluctuations of Color
Combinations, *1932.*
Gouache on cardboard, 12.5 x 143.5 cm.
Collection A. V. Povelikhina,
St. Petersburg.

A Brief History of Obmokhu

Aleksandra Shatskikh

Studies of early Soviet art invariably devote a great deal of attention to the Society of Young Artists, or Obmokhu. The activity of its members proved an enabling factor in the emergence of Constructivism in the five years following the October Revolution, and the careers of many prominent artists traced their beginnings to Obmokhu. Yet, as scholars have noted, the history of Obmokhu has not been entirely clear; numerous questions have remained unanswered.

While researching the history of the First Free State Art Workshops, I have brought to light a number of circumstances and factual details which make it possible to strip away persistent inaccuracies in and distortions of the history of Obmokhu and to establish a more precise chronology and authentic account of the group's activity.

Both Soviet and Western scholars have relied above all on V. M. Lobanov's *Khudozhestvennye gruppirovki za poslednie 25 let* (*Artists' Groups over the Last Twenty-Five Years*), published by AKhR (the Association of Artists of the Revolution) in 1930, for their information on Obmokhu. For Soviet art historians, Lobanov's slender volume was for many decades nearly the only comprehensive work treating the multiple facets of artistic life in the immediate postrevolutionary years. Because Lobanov was a participant in and witness to the events he described, subsequent generations attributed to his book all the merits of a primary source; Lobanov's information, because it was firsthand, seemed authoritative and trustworthy. As a result, no critical judgment was brought to bear on the book: Lobanov's facts were neither doubted nor checked, and his mistakes and inaccuracies were reproduced in the work of one writer after another—as they are even today. Yet one needn't look far to determine that the book does, indeed, contain errors of fact. Thus, for example, Lobanov insists—and more than once—that the Twenty-First State Exhibition, which opened in March 1921, was the last exhibition organized by Izo Narkompros (the Department of Fine Arts of the People's Commissariat of Enlightenment).[1] The truth, however, is that both the Twenty-Second State Exhibition (on which more below) and the Twenty-Third (the hardly obscure exhibition of Marc Chagall's murals for the State Jewish Kamernyi Theater in Moscow) were also organized by Izo Narkompros.[2]

Lobanov was the official historian of and apologist for AKhR, and his book is a product of its times: it is undisguisedly tendentious, a polemic bent on repudiation of Izo Narkompros. It was Lobanov's aim to demonstrate, on the one hand, the bankruptcy of Izo Narkompros's pluralistic policy and, on the other, the weakness and unviability of various "Formalist" tendencies and movements in postrevolutionary art. Singling out Obmokhu—whose chief significance lay, according to Lobanov, "not in the formulation or realization of this or that artistic slogan so much as in its being a pioneer in the creation of new artists' groupings based, unlike the eclectic Narkompros exhibitions, on a selection of artists united by a shared principle"[3]—and juxtaposing it to other artists' associations served Lobanov's strategy. AKhR aspired to power, and its ideologues saw a concentrated "strike force" of artists as the chief means of attaining it. Lobanov chose Obmokhu, so it appears, in order to demonstrate the efficacy of such a ploy. The "postscripts," inaccuracies, and deliberate suppression of certain facts of Obmokhu's history in Lobanov's book were dictated by this biased purpose.

In the summer of 1919, at the moment of highest tension in the Civil War, a general mobilization into the Red Army was announced, and many students of the former Stroganov School in Moscow, who had just finished their first year at the new First Free State Art Workshops, were sent to the front. One of those called up was Georgii Shchetinin, who had been among the most active reformers of artistic education "from below"; he

had done immense organizational work at the school over a number of years.[4] At his departure, Shchetinin made a close friend pledge both to carry on his work at the First Free State Art Workshops and to write him regularly and in detail about everything that happened there. Shchetinin's friend was Georgii Echeistov, a student of Vladimir Favorskii's and later a well-known graphic artist, and he kept his promise to Shchetinin. Both young men were acutely aware that history was being made around them and through them, and they carefully preserved their notes, letters, and other papers. The 1919–21 correspondence between Echeistov and Shchetinin is invaluable, for it records events as they occurred and is marred by none of the distortions that afflict later reminiscences and memoirs.[5]

In a brief letter of September 15, 1919, Echeistov told Shchetinin, among other things: "A group 'without a supervisor' has formed out of Grigor'ev's workshop, and I'm in it. I'll work under G. Iakulov in a special workshop and learn about theater, and one can earn money with him." These lines require some elucidation: a reform introduced in the first months of the Soviet state had led to the creation of the experimental Svomas (Free Workshops), where a master-and-apprentice system, modeled on the utopian ideal of the Renaissance studio, was the basis of art education. The new professional schools in both Moscow and Petrograd were composed of individual workshops, in which classes were conducted by artists elected supervisors by the students. At the First Free State Art Workshops, created from the former Stroganov School, there were not only individual but special workshops, in which students of different classes could study; special workshops in stage and costume design were run by

fig. 1

The "workshop without a supervisor," First State Free Art Workshops, Moscow, 1920. From left, seated: Zharova, Kozlova, and Svetlov; standing: Prusakov, unidentified, Menshutin, Zhukov, Aleksandrov, I. Mistriuk, and Naumov.

fig. 2
Lentulov's workshop, First State Free Art Workshops, Moscow, 1920.
Standing, third from right, Komardenkov; center, Lentulov.

Aristarkh Lentulov, Fedor Fedorovskii, and Georgii Iakulov. Iakulov was highly regarded by the students, participated in many of their undertakings, and helped them to endure the hardships of those years. He put his workshop on an "economic" footing from its very first months: he paid wages for work, obtained commissions for his students, and so on.[6] A portion of the students at the First Free State Art Workshops, in particular those who at the time of the Revolution had been in the Stroganov School's senior classes, were entitled to study exclusively in the special workshops.[7]

According to a report written by Shchetinin, there were eighteen workshops in all at the First Free State Art Workshops (twelve in painting, three in sculpture, and three in architecture).[8] One of the painting workshops was headed by Boris Grigor'ev, who lived in Petrograd and made infrequent visits to Moscow (at the end of 1919, he and his family would leave Russia for good). At the beginning of the 1919–20 academic year, the students in Grigor'ev's workshop chose, for a number of reasons, to reject their teacher elected the year before and to form a group "without a supervisor," as was permitted under the provisional bylaws of the Free Workshops. In a draft autobiography, Echeistov later indicated: "At about this time my artistic credo begin to take shape under the influence of the Futurists (artists, painters, and poets). I didn't care for any of the Russian artists, I liked the French in Shchukin's gallery. So I joined up with Prusakov and Naumov, who had organized a workshop without a supervisor."

Aleksandr Naumov, a brilliantly gifted artist who died at an early age, and Nikolai Prusakov, who would become well known as a poster artist and designer, were among the school's most talented students, and had already received their basic professional training at the old Stroganov School. In 1919–20, Echeistov, Naumov, and Prusakov were joined in the "workshop without a supervisor" by Grigorii Aleksandrov, S. I. Egorov, Nikolai Glushkov, Klavdiia Kozlova, Nikolai Menshutin, Sergei Svetlov, Lidiia Zharova (who married Naumov in 1920), and Petr Zhukov (fig. no. 1). According to the testimony of Zharova-Naumova, Sergei Kostin and Mikhail Sapegin, among others, were frequent visitors to the workshop, where life drawing was well taught.[9] Like Echeistov, certain of the students in the "workshop without a supervisor"— Aleksandrov, Menshutin, Sapegin, Svetlov, and Zhukov— continued to study in Iakulov's stage-design workshop.

The "workshop without a supervisor" remained in existence until the spring of 1920. A number of the students, particularly those who were already clear about where their artistic futures lay and those who were employed filling commissions, considered their educations at an end and were given certificates attesting to their having completed a course of higher education. In the Free Workshops, and initially at Vkhutemas (the Higher Artistic-Technical Workshops), there were no strict prerequisites for graduation—a student presented his work to the Council of Professors, and if the Council judged the work to be mature, the young artist was given a certificate of completion. (It is for this reason that the graduation dates of the Free Workshops' and Vkhutemas's first graduates vary so widely.[10])

Over three days at the end of September 1919, Echeistov wrote a long letter (dated September 27–29) to Shchetinin, giving him the latest news:

What can I write "about art in Moscow"? It's tight. I'm counting on our workshops. As soon as I'm free {of his duties as secretary of the students' executive committee}, what a journal I'll start (unless I get lazy). Still, my being secretary pays off—I've been in the thick of things. A society of young artists, Obmolkhud, is being organized. I wrote the bylaws. (I emended them today, they need reworking and

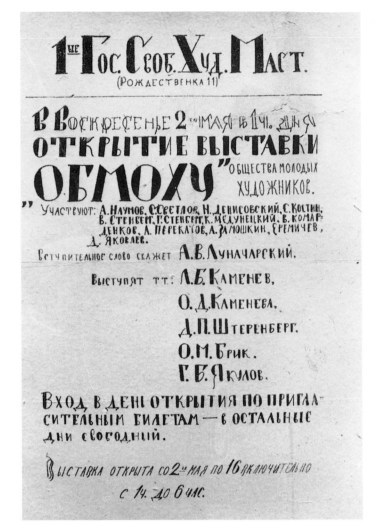

fig. 3
Poster for Obmokhu exhibition, Moscow, May 2-16, 1920. Collection N. D. Lobanov-Rostovsky.

polishing.) Sapegin, Naumov, Prusakov, Komardenkov, Kostin, and I—and, I can't remember, Stepanov and Denisovskii, too, I think— are the directors. We're organizing it to combat the artists in authority who exploit young talents (the Kostin–Grigor'ev incident and others).[11]

Echeistov's letter unambiguously attests that Obmolkhud, as Obmokhu was first called, began forming only in the autumn of 1919; the group could not, therefore, have held an exhibition in the spring of 1919, as Lobanov asserts. It should be noted that the young artists did not treat the organization of their society lightly but erected it on a carefully laid foundation; the group had bylaws,[12] elected directors (Nikolai Denisovskii, endowed with exceptional organizational skills, later became its president), and a seal.

All of the artists listed by Echeistov—with the exception of Sapegin, Aleksei Stepanov, and Echeistov himself—have been recognized by scholars as members of Obmokhu. The participation of both Sapegin—a student of Iakulov's and a future stage designer—and Stepanov—also a student of Iakulov's, who later worked at the State Jewish Kamernyi Theater—in the early stages of the organization of Obmokhu appears quite probable. As for Echeistov, a fire in the "workshop without a supervisor" in late 1919–early 1920 led him into a deep depression, and he stopped working. "The fire in our workshop," Echeistov wrote in his autobiography, "destroyed an enormous number of drawings completed over this time. It was a tremendous loss; I did almost nothing for the whole next year."[13]

With what exhibition of 1919 has the first Obmokhu exhibition been confused? At the end of the 1918–19 academic year at the First Free State Art Workshops, the new art school's first full year of operation, a showcase exhibition was held at the school's quarters at 11 Rozhdestvenka. At the exhibition, on view in June 1919, the works of students and teachers were displayed together, by workshop (the very organizing principle, that is, that Lobanov claims was Obmokhu's innovation). A large informative notice in the newspaper *Iskusstvo* (*Art*) is unambiguous on this point:

EXHIBITION OF WORKS OF THE STATE FREE ART WORKSHOPS

The first exhibition of more than one thousand works from the state industrial workshops closed on July 1st. The exhibition was divided up according to individual and decorative-and-production workshops. The workshops of the artists F. Fedorovskii, G. Iakulov, A. Lentulov, P. Konchalovskii, A. Morgunov, V. Tatlin, A. Grishchenko, B. Grigor'ev, Ul'ianov, the sculptor Vatagin, and others were represented.[14]

The author of the notice—in all likelihood Shchetinin, who published an extensive report on the First Free State Art Workshops' first year in the next issue of *Art*—emphasizes that "the exhibition itself was clearly organized as a decorative and production one. Still, the principle of revolutionizing everyday life is manifestly shared by the workshops of the artists G. B. Iakulov (very successful signboards for factories and public buildings), F. F. Fedorovskii (the maquettes for folk-dance performances were of interest), and, in part, A. V. Lentulov (stage-design maquettes) and by the students working out new types of posters, books, street and train decorations, and so forth." Lobanov's list of the kinds of work exhibited in what he calls the first Obmokhu exhibition, in the spring of 1919, matches the list in the notice.

The displaying of works by students and teachers as a single work of the entire workshop at the First State Free Art Workshops show, mistaken for the first Obmokhu exhibition, has caused Iakulov and Lentulov to be included among

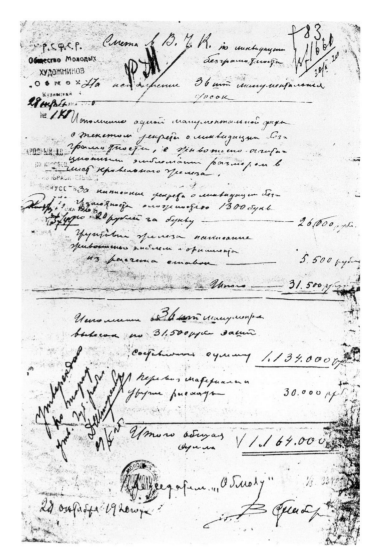

fig. 4
Invoice from Obmokhu to Narkompros, October 28, 1920. The document is stamped with two Obmokhu seals designed by Vladimir Stenberg.
Central State Archive of Russia, Moscow.

Obmokhu's members. Yet, as will become clear below, Iakulov and Lentulov never participated in Obmokhu's exhibitions and cannot be counted as members of the group (as they are in numerous descriptions of Obmokhu and in articles and monographs on their work).

The "decorative and production" principle singled out in the description of the exhibited works—a principle that was to enable the "revolutionizing of everyday life"—is especially noteworthy. The introduction of "art into life"—the chief slogan of the future Productivists and Constructivists—was naturally bound to play a defining role in the educational program of the First Free State Art Workshops. But the evolution and instilling of new forms followed a turbulent, contentious course; Echeistov wrote in the September 27–29, 1919, letter cited above: "Tatlin is leaving for Petrograd for good, with tears in his eyes because he wasn't understood at the Stroganov; and he won't have anything to do with the Second Workshops [the Second State Free Art Workshops, created from the Moscow School of Painting, Sculpture, and Architecture], doesn't acknowledge them. He got a commission and is going."[15] Open conflicts between the "purists" and Productivists would soon rattle artistic life, and the departure of the wounded Tatlin anticipates, as it were, the schism inside Inkhuk (the Institute of Artistic Culture)—though at Inkhuk, it would be the easel painters who would depart, leaving the field to the Productivists.

The principle of exhibiting by workshop adhered to at the 1919 showcase exhibition did shape the true first Obmokhu exhibition, which opened in May 1920 at the First Free State Art Workshops at 11 Rozhdestvenka. The poster announcing the exhibition (fig. no. 3) read:

First State Free Art Workshops
(11 Rozhdestvenka)

Sunday, May 2nd at 1 p.m. Opening of the Obmokhu (Society of Young Painters) exhibition.

Participants: A. Naumov, S. Svetlov, N. Denisovskii, S. Kostin, V. Stenberg, G. Stenberg, K. Medunetskii, V. Komardenkov, A. Perekatov, A. Zamoshkin, Eremichev, D. Iakovlev.

Opening remarks will be delivered by A. V. Lunacharskii.

Speakers: Comrades L. B. Kamenev,
O. D. Kameneva,
D. P. Shterenberg,
O. M. Brik,
G. B. Iakulov.

Admission on opening day is by invitation, and unrestricted on other days.

The exhibition will be open May 2–16, from 1–6 p.m.

The "workshop without a supervisor" and the "Iakulovists" and "Lentulovists" (not listed alphabetically but grouped by workshop on the poster) were represented at the exhibition. For a number of the students—including Georgii and Vladimir Stenberg, Vasilii Komardenkov, Aleksandr Zamoshkin, and Prusakov—the exhibition marked the occasion of their graduation. Sketches for festive decorations of streets and buildings and for the decoration of trains and ships, posters, designs for stage sets and costumes, and experimental works were on display.

The usefulness of such design work for various educational and propaganda undertakings of the Soviet state was obvious, and the leaders of Narkompros, headed by Anatolii Lunacharskii, decided to create an agit-production workshop from Obmokhu. Space for the workshop was found in the

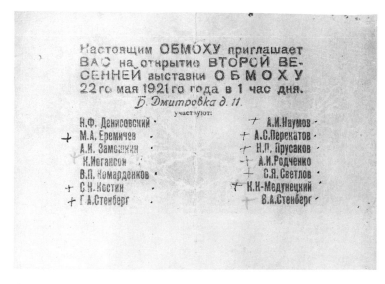

fig. 5
Invitation card to Obmokhu exhibition, Moscow, May–June 1921.

former Fabergé shop at 4 Kuznetskii most (on the corner of Neglinnaia Street), and funds for outfitting it were approved by Narkompros in September 1920.[16]

Obmokhu functioned not only as an association of like-minded artists but, above all, as a Productivist artel, filling commissions and serving the artistic needs of the new society and the new state. Surviving documents give some idea of Obmokhu's activities in 1920–21: Narkompros's Financial Department paid out specific sums "for the execution of a poster supporting the Decree on the Abolition of Illiteracy," "for the execution of four stamps for the All-Russian Special Commission to Abolish Illiteracy," for stencils, ornaments, slogan boards, and so on. A commission for "thirty-six monumental panels," to be made from sheets of iron roofing, was received and filled (fig. no. 4). The accounts and financial documents were signed by both Denisovskii, Obmokhu's president, and by Vladimir Stenberg, who signed himself as "chief of production" (and sometimes as president).[17]

This artel work provided the members of Obmokhu with their livelihood. Orders, which came chiefly from the departments and commissions of Narkompros, were filled collectively, hence the credit for them was also collective—the artel's "artistic production" was signed only "Obmokhu." Payment was likewise shared equally among all members who had helped fill a commission—and these included artists who never displayed their work at Obmokhu's exhibitions.[18]

It was the second Obmokhu exhibition, known in the scholarly literature as the third, that ensured the group's fame. That it was indeed the second rather than the third is reflected in the invitation card to the exhibition (fig. no. 5), whose announcement of Obmokhu's *Vtoraia vesenniaia vystavka* (*Second Spring Exhibition*) has been a source of bewilderment to scholars trusting Lobanov's enumeration.[19] The exhibition poster prepared by Komardenkov (fig. no. 6) states explicitly, moreover, that the exhibition was organized by Narkompros; it was officially the Twenty-Second Exhibition of the Central Section of Izo Narkompros. Lobanov skipped over this fact, which didn't jibe with his scheme of antithetical "eclectic Narkompros exhibitions" and exhibitions of "artists united by a shared principle." The exhibitors listed on the invitation card were, with the exception of Karl Ioganson and Aleksandr Rodchenko, mechanically transcribed by Lobanov onto his list of the "founders of Obmokhu."[20]

The second Obmokhu exhibition opened in Moscow on May 22, 1921, at 11 Bol'shaia Dmitrovka, the former Mikhailova Salon. Though Rodchenko and Ioganson participated in the exhibition, their works, along with those of Konstantin Medunetskii and Georgii and Vladimir Stenberg, were shown in a separate hall—constituting, as it were, an exhibition within the exhibition, as the famous installation photographs documenting the displays of only Rodchenko's "faction," confirm. Those months were a period of turmoil for the proponents of production art, and in that context the second Obmokhu exhibition was used as a forum for asserting the new forms championed by the First Working Group of Constructivists of Inkhuk, a group which had formed in the spring of 1921 and almost all of whose members (Aleksei Gan and Varvara Stepanova were the exceptions) participated in the second Obmokhu exhibition. So voluminous is the literature, generously sprinkled with documentary material, that has been devoted to the emergence and development of Constructivism in Russian art that there is no need to dwell here on the significance of the second Obmokhu exhibition. It ought rather to be emphasized that, thanks to this exhibition, the character of Obmokhu has forevermore been painted, so to speak, in Constructivist colors. For both contemporaries and succeeding generations, Obmokhu has been indissolubly

fig. 6
Poster for Obmokhu exhibition, Moscow, May–June 1921. Collection N. D. Lobanov-Rostovsky.

linked with the early stage of Constructivism, overshadowing and supplanting other aspects of Obmokhu's collective endeavor. The discussions which took place at Inkhuk in late 1921 solidified Obmokhu's status as a "society of Constructivists."

The "color constructions," "constructions of spatial structures," and "spatial constructions" shown at the second Obmokhu exhibition were the fruit of "laboratory Constructivism," of the theoretical and practical formulations worked out by the First Working Group of Constructivists, to which the five exhibitors with Obmokhu—Ioganson, Rodchenko, Medunetskii, and Georgii and Vladimir Stenberg—belonged from the first months of Inkhuk's existence. The "constructions of spatial structures" exhibited by the Stenbergs also had a direct connection with the program of study and student assignments in the special laboratory of Vkhutemas's Architecture Faculty which Vladimir Stenberg—senior assistant in the laboratory—had developed in close collaboration with the laboratory head, Anton Lavinskii.[21]

The conjunction of "laboratory" works of early Constructivism, on the one hand, and, on the other, distinctly utilitarian posters promoting the measures of the All-Russian Special Commission to Abolish Illiteracy made for the diversity and heterogeneity of both the second Obmokhu exhibition and the production of Obmokhu as a whole. Further self-definition by the participants in Obmokhu's exhibitions and crystallization of their artistic aspirations could lead only to splintering and the collapse of the society. The Stenbergs and Medunetskii formed a group of their own, forthrightly calling themselves Konstruktivisty (the Constructivists); their exhibition opened in January 1922.

In the autumn of 1922, the members of Obmokhu showed their work at the *Erste russische Kunstausstellung* (*First Russian Art Exhibition,* Berlin); Obmokhu's president, Denisovskii, had expended great effort on collecting and organizing work for the exhibition.[22] It is impossible, however, to label this Obmokhu's last collaborative venture, for each of Obmokhu's members showed his own individual works. In contrast to, say, the "Vitebsk school"—which was set off both at the exhibition and in the exhibition catalogue—Obmokhu did not exhibit as such in Berlin; by the time of the Berlin exhibition, Obmokhu no longer existed.

"The members of Obmokhu," Lobanov writes, "organized their fourth exhibition in conjunction with the Congress of the Comintern, showing their current Productivist works."[23] Nineteen twenty-three is the year assigned to this putative exhibition in the first volume of *Vystavki sovetskogo izobrazitel'nogo iskusstva* (*Exhibitions of Soviet Fine Art*), a reference work cited in all subsequent publications.[24] There was, however, no Congress of the Comintern in 1923; congresses were held in 1919, 1920, 1921, 1922, 1924, 1928, and 1935. An extensive program of cultural events did coincide with the Third Congress of the Comintern, held in Moscow in June–July 1921. The Hotel Kontinental', where the congress delegates were housed, was the site of an exhibition that included works by Kazimir Malevich, Tatlin, Il'ia Mashkov, and others; a fragment of this exhibition is visible in a photograph taken of a group of delegates.[25] Lobanov was surely describing this 1921 exhibition, inasmuch as in November 1922 all events in honor of the Fourth Congress of the Comintern were held in Petrograd; and in 1923, as has already been noted, there was no congress at all. It is highly unlikely that Obmokhu mounted two different exhibitions in June 1921; the second Obmokhu exhibition on Bol'shaia Dmitrovka, which opened at the end of May and was, consequently, on view in June, *was* Obmokhu's response to the Congress of the Comintern. A number of works by Obmokhu apparently were shown at the Hotel Kontinental' exhibition (information on this exhibition is extremely hard to come by), but one would be hard pressed to call it the fourth Obmokhu exhibition.

The catalogue of the *Vtoraia vystavka kinoplakata* (*Second Exhibition of Film Posters*), held in Moscow in February 1926, is the last place in which the name Obmokhu appears to denote the affiliation of one or another artist. It is true that only Naumov, Prusakov, and Grigorii Borisov (Prusakov's collaborator on many film posters) are listed here as members of Obmokhu. Neither the Stenbergs nor Medunetskii nor Rodchenko, all of whom also participated in the exhibition, are cited as such (which is only natural in the case of Rodchenko: like Ioganson, he was never identified anywhere as a "member of Obmokhu"). This forces one to assume that, for the former members of the First Working Group of Constructivists, the alliance with Obmokhu was a brief episode; they did not in the mid-1920s include themselves among its active members.

These facts about the history of Obmokhu, then, are clear. The association initially called Obmolkhud began forming in the autumn of 1919 at the First Free State Art Workshops, the former Stroganov School. Its initiators were students in the "workshop without a supervisor" (Aleksandrov, Echeistov, Egorov, Glushkov, Kozlova, Menshutin, Naumov, Prusakov, Svetlov, Zharova, and Zhukov), joined by the "Iakulovists" (Denisovskii, Kostin, Medunetskii, and Georgii and Vladimir Stenberg) and the "Lentulovists" (Mikhail Eremichev, Iakovlev, Komardenkov, Perekatov, and Zamoshkin). A portion of the first group (Aleksandrov, Echeistov, Egorov, Menshutin, Svetlov, and Zhukov) were also students of Iakulov's.

Obmokhu organized two exhibitions. The first Obmokhu exhibition was held May 2–16, 1920, at the First Free State Art Workshops at 11 Rozhdestvenka, the second (the Twenty-Second Exhibition of the Central Section of Izo Narkompros) in May–June 1921 at the former Mikhailova Salon at 11 Bol'shaia Dmitrovka. It is possible that Obmokhu participated in a June 1921 exhibition, at the Hotel Kontinental' on Teatral'naia Square, that coincided with the Third Congress of the Comintern. Those who participated in the two Obmokhu exhibitions were Denisovskii, Eremichev, Iakovlev, Ioganson, Komardenkov, Kostin, Medunetskii, Naumov, Perekatov, Prusakov, Rodchenko, Georgii and Vladimir Stenberg, Svetlov, and Zamoshkin. The activity of Obmokhu reached its peak in the 1920–21 season, after which it fell off; in 1922, Obmokhu ceased to function.

Following Obmokhu's dissolution, three of the participants in its exhibitions—Medunetskii and Georgii and Vladimir Stenberg—formed the Constructivists group in 1922, while in 1925 Denisovskii and Kostin joined Ost (the Society of Easel Painters). Denisovskii and Kostin, along with Svetlov, also participated in joint exhibitions with Iakulov, which were designated "exhibitions of Iakulov and his workshop."[26]

—Translated, from the Russian, by Jane Bobko

Notes

1. V. M. Lobanov, *Khudozhestvennye gruppirovki za poslednie 25 let* (Moscow: Obshchestvo AKhR, 1930), pp. 87, 90. Lobanov was taken "at his word" by the compilers of *Vystavki sovetskogo izobrazitel'nogo iskusstva,* where the Twenty-First State Exhibition is likewise labeled Izo Narkompros's "last." *Vystavki sovetskogo izobrazitel'nogo iskusstva. Spravochnik* (Moscow: Sovetskii khudozhnik, 1965), vol. 1, p. 74.

2. The invitation card reads: "June 1921. Twenty-Third Exhibition of the Central Section of Izo Narkompros. Murals by the artist Marc Chagall . . . In the hall of the State Jewish Kamernyi Theater (12 Bol'shoi Chernyshevskii)."

3. Lobanov, *Khudozhestvennye gruppirovki,* p. 105.

4. On Shchetinin's life and work, see A. S. Shatskikh, "'Prorubaia okno v chelovecheskoe miroponimanie . . .' Zhizn' G. B. Shchetinina (1891–1921)," in *Panorama iskusstv 8* (Moscow: Sovetskii khudozhnik, 1985), pp. 255–74.

5. Echeistov's letters and autobiography cited below are in a private archive, Moscow.

6. Nikolai Musatov, conversation with author, October 1985. Musatov, born in 1895, was a student of Iakulov's in the First Free State Art Workshops.

7. Thus Denisovskii and Musatov worked only in Iakulov's special workshop, Zamoshkin and Komardenkov only in Lentulov's, and so on.

8. G[eorgii] Shch[etinin], "I-yi god raboty gosudarstvennykh khudozhestvennykh masterskikh," *Iskusstvo* 7 (August 2, 1919), pp. 4–5.

9. Lidiia Zharova-Naumova, conversation with author, September 1983.

10. Thus Denisovskii gave 1919 as the year of his graduation, Komardenkov 1919 or 1920, and the Stenbergs 1920. As for the students in the "workshop without a supervisor," Aleksandrov, for example, graduated from Vkhutemas in 1924, Zhukov in 1920, Menshutin in 1922, Prusakov in 1920, and Svetlov in 1924. Manuscript Division, State Tret'iakov Gallery, Moscow, f. 91.

11. He was referring, according to Zharova-Naumova, to Grigor'ev's "appropriation" of the conception behind Kostin's stage-design work. A stage designer, painter, and graphic artist, Kostin—the nephew of N. N. Sapunov—later created many sets for the Bol'shoi Theater. Lidiia Zharova-Naumova, conversation with author, September 1983.

12. The bylaws Echeistov mentions evidently resembled to some degree those of Mastarchuv. Mastarchuv was created by Shchetinin and Echeistov in January 1919. See Shatskikh, "'Prorubaia okno v chelovecheskoe miroponimanie . . .,'" pp. 264–65.

13. A photograph of Zharova-Naumova taken in the burned-out workshop is reproduced in V. Dokuchaeva, *Lidiia Naumova* (Moscow: Sovetskii khudozhnik, 1984), p. 8.

14. "Vystavka rabot pervykh gosudarstvennykh svobodnykh khudozhestvennykh masterskikh," *Iskusstvo* 6 (July 8, 1919), p. 2.

15. Echeistov's letter makes it possible to be still more exact about the date of Tatlin's departure from the Moscow Svomas and indicates one reason for it. The work commissioned from Tatlin was a monument in honor of the anniversary of the October Revolution; as work on the monument progressed, it became the model for the *Pamiatnik III-emu Internatsionalu* (*Monument to the Third International*).

16. "Agitatsionno-proizvodstvennaia masterskaia Vysshikh gosudarstvennykh khudozhestvennykh masterskikh. Smeta," Central State Archive of Russia, Moscow, f. 2306, op. 31, d. 617, l. 53.

17. Quoted from documents in the Central State Archive of Russia, Moscow, f. 2306, op. 31, ed. khr. 614, l. 83, 84, 98.

18. Komardenkov's memoirs, published in abbreviated form as *Dni minuvshie* (Moscow: Sovetskii khudozhnik, 1972) are available in a fuller variant in the Central State Archive for Literature and Art, Moscow, f. 1337, op. 3, ed. khr. 49. Written late in Komardenkov's life, these memoirs contain many inaccuracies and distortions, making it impossible to rely on them to establish a consistent history of Obmokhu. Many particulars recalled by the artist, however, do allow one to reconstruct the day-to-day life of Obmokhu. Komardenkov describes in detail Obmokhu's functioning as an artistic-production artel.

19. Christina Lodder has paid particular attention to this apparent inconsistency, but advances an unlikely proposition: "The invitation to the 1921 show used the title *Second Spring Exhibition* rather than *Second Exhibition,* so it is possible that this was the group's second spring exhibition but its third show overall. (According to Lobanov, the 1919 exhibition also opened in the spring.) This seems the most probable explanation." Christina Lodder, "Constructivism and Productivism in the 1920s," in *Art Into Life: Russian Constructivism, 1914–1932,* catalogue for exhibition organized by the Henry Art Gallery, University of Washington, Seattle, the Walker Art Center, Minneapolis, and the State Tret'yakov Gallery, Moscow (New York: Rizzoli, 1990), p. 102.

20. Lobanov, *Kudozhestvennye gruppirovki,* p. 104.

21. Central State Archive for Literature and Art, Moscow, f. 681, op. 2, ed. khr. 411, l. 13.

22. V. P. Lapshin, "Pervaia vystavka russkogo iskusstva. Berlin. 1922 god. Materialy k istorii sovetsko-germanskikh khudozhestvennykh sviazei," *Sovetskoe iskusstvoznanie* 1 (1982), pp. 327–62.

23. Lobanov, *Khudozhestvennye gruppirovki,* p. 105.

24. "Chetvertaia vystavka Obmokhu," in *Vystavki sovetskogo izobrazitel'nogo iskusstva,* p. 114. The information about the exhibition given here relies on a single source—Lobanov.

25. *Kommunisticheskii internatsional* 18 (1921), p. 4708.

26. See, for example, the notice "Vystavka Iakulova," *Ermitazh* 12 (August 1–7, 1922), p. 14.

fig. 1
View of Obmokhu exhibition, Moscow, May-June 1921.

The Transition to Constructivism

Christina Lodder

Constructivism is advancing—the slender child of an industrial culture.

For a long time capitalism has let it rot underground.
It has been liberated by—the Proletarian Revolution.
—*Aleksei Gan (1922)*

From painting to sculpture, from sculpture to construction, from construction to technology and invention—this is my chosen path, and will surely be the ultimate goal of every revolutionary artist.
—*Karl Ioganson (1922)*

The rediscovery of Russian Constructivism has been a striking phenomenon of the past decade. The movement has acquired a heroic status for certain critics and artists of a Postmodernist persuasion. At the same time, original works and documents have begun to emerge from the former Soviet Union, permitting a more detailed and complex historical understanding of the period. This essay focuses on the initial emergence of a Constructivist position within the Russian avant-garde and, in particular, on the extraordinary exhibition that marked its first public manifestation, the Obmokhu (the Society of Young Artists) show of May 1921.

The idea of Constructivism has become a critical commonplace, variously understood, but at the moment of its invention it clearly carried specific implications and a real polemical edge. The First Working Group of Constructivists, also known as the Working Group of Constructivists, was formed in March 1921, within Inkhuk (the Institute of Artistic Culture) in Moscow.[1] The group comprised Aleksei Gan, Varvara Stepanova, Aleksandr Rodchenko, Karl Ioganson, Konstantin Medunetskii, and the brothers Georgii and Vladimir Stenberg.[2] They seem to have come together during the fascinating theoretical discussions conducted at Inkhuk during the previous three months, discussions which addressed the distinction that artists were starting to make between construction and composition as principles of artistic organization. The self-proclaimed Constructivists were united in their commitment to a viewpoint articulated by Rodchenko in January 1921: "All new approaches to art arise from technology and engineering and move toward organization and construction," and "real construction is utilitarian necessity."[3] Such a stance seemed indeed to crystallize their response to the pressing question of how artists could contribute to the new Communist order and celebrate the values inherent in the Bolshevik Revolution of 1917.

In their draft program of April 1, 1921, written by Gan, the group proclaimed a new synthesis of art and industry. They wanted to relegate their purely artistic explorations to the role of "laboratory work," and to extend their experiments with manipulating three-dimensional abstract forms into the real environment by participating in the industrial manufacture of useful objects. They called the new type of activity that they envisaged "intellectual production," proclaiming that their ideological foundation was "scientific communism, built on the theory of historical materialism" and that they intended to attain "the communistic expression of material structures" by organizing their material according to the three principles of *tektonika* (tectonics, or the socially and politically appropriate use of industrial material), construction (the organization of this material for a given purpose), and *faktura* (the conscious handling and manipulation of it).[4]

The strategies they proposed included investigating the Soviet building industry and establishing links with committees in charge of production. These measures were to be accompanied by a highly organized propaganda campaign of exhibitions and publications that would include a weekly journal, *Vestnik intellektual'nogo proizvodstva* (*The Herald of Intellectual Production*) and a bulletin. Gan explained:

In order to put our work on show, an exhibition of Constructivist spatial works should be staged, as testimony not only to what we are doing today but also to what we are aiming for and the tasks that we have set ourselves.[5]

Accordingly, about two months after the formation of the group, some of the Constructivists showed their current practical work at the *Vtoraia vesenniaia vystavka* (*Second Spring Exhibition*) of Obmokhu, more commonly known as the third

Obmokhu exhibition, which opened on May 22, 1921.[6] Altogether, fourteen artists participated: Nikolai Denisovskii, Mikhail Eremichev, Aleksandr Zamoshkin, Vasilii Komardenkov, Sergei Kostin, Aleksandr Naumov, Aleksandr Perekatov, Nikolai Prusakov, and Sergei Svetlov, as well as the Constructivists Medunetskii and the Stenberg brothers—who were members of Obmokhu—and Ioganson and Rodchenko, who were specially invited to contribute to this one show.[7]

The previous history of Obmokhu reveals a radical political commitment that would also underpin Constructivism. Although the precise chronology of the group is still somewhat unclear, Obmokhu seems to have been set up in the autumn of 1919 by students from the "workshop without a supervisor" at the State Free Art Workshops in Moscow.[8] The members had also come together through their work on various agitational projects during 1918, particularly the decorations of Moscow's streets for the revolutionary festivals. Medunetskii and the Stenberg brothers, who were living together by this time, had decorated the Post Office on Miasnitskaia (now Kirov Street) for May Day 1918 with the help of Denisovskii.[9] Subsequently, it appears, they had worked with the other future members of Obmokhu to decorate the Rogozhsko-Simonovskii district of Moscow for November 1918.[10] The artists later contributed numerous posters to the government's propaganda programs, such as the Campaign to Abolish Illiteracy, and, according to V. M. Lobanov, Obmokhu's first exhibition was devoted to such agitational work, which was displayed anonymously to emphasize the collective nature of the group's production.[11] He described the contents of their second exhibition as mainly posters, with a small number of abstract works and *tsvetokonstruktsii* (color constructions), presumably paintings. Lobanov's description corresponds to A. A. Sidorov's review of the May 1920 show, which suggests that some three-dimensional constructions were shown; Sidorov mentions "a statue . . . by comrade Stenberg made of sheet metal," alongside paintings by Naumov and others in the style of Boris Grigor'ev and Georgii Iakulov.[12] Lobanov's account identifies Obmokhu's *Second Spring Exhibition* as, in fact, their third exhibition overall, and this was confirmed by Vladimir Stenberg many years later.[13] He recalled that the third Obmokhu exhibition was held "in a kind of salon-café on Bolshaya Dmitrovka Street and Kuznetsky Bridge."[14]

There was no catalogue for the exhibition, although the invitation card survives. Fortunately, two installation photographs were reproduced soon after the event: one view in the spring of 1922 in the journal *Veshch'/Gegenstand/Objet* (*Object*), edited by El Lissitzky and Il'ia Erenburg in Berlin (fig. no. 1),[15] and the other the same year in the Hungarian avant-garde magazine *Egység* (*Unity*), published by Béla Uitz in Vienna (fig. no. 2).[16] The two images show adjacent corners of a large hall, in which constructions by Rodchenko, Ioganson, the Stenbergs, and Medunetskii are visible, as well as abstract paintings, some of which can now be identified as works by the Stenberg brothers and Medunetskii. The two photographs are devoted exclusively to the works by the First Working Group of Constructivists and give no indication of what the other nine artists showed. Indeed, *Egység* labeled its photograph of the exhibition "The Constructivists at the Obmokhu Exhibition" and included separate illustrations of work by Vladimir Stenberg and Ioganson (fig. no. 3).[17] The photograph of the Stenberg construction was almost certainly taken at the exhibition, as the molding on the ceiling conforms to that in the two views of the show. *Egység* also printed translations of the program of the Constructivist group ("A Konstruktivisták Csoportjának Programmja") together with "The Realistic Manifesto" ("Realista Kiáltvány") produced in August 1920 by Naum Gabo and Antoine Pevsner, albeit without mentioning

the authors of either statement.[18] It is possible that the Prusakov picture reproduced in *Egység* was another exhibit, since it is captioned "Gépkonstrukció. Pruszakov ('OBMOHU'). Moszkva. 1921."[19] If so, this is the only evidence concerning the work of other artists in the exhibition. Although entitled *Machine Construction* in the Hungarian label, this is a schematized figurative image, posterlike in style and apparently evoking the proletariat at work and leisure. It thus serves to underline the essential innovation of the Constructivists—their evocation of a contemporary industrial imagery through the language of materials and abstract form rather than through illustrative subject matter. The show was certainly acclaimed at the time for its highly original explorations of a new kind of constructed sculpture. For instance, Ulen (possibly Lissitzky writing under a pseudonym), in a survey of Russian exhibitions published in *Object* in 1922, emphasized:

The exhibitions of Obmokhu were new in form. There we saw art works not only hanging on the walls but also and most importantly filling the space of the hall.

These young artists have assimilated the experiences of the former generation, they work well, they have a subtle feeling for the specific qualities of materials and construct spatial works. Moving between the technology of the engineers and the aimless expediency of art, they are trying to progress further.[20]

The artistic innovations of the works exhibited are discussed in more detail below, but it should be noted that the attitudes and meanings they embodied were in fact firmly rooted in contemporary Russian culture. At a very general level, industry and the machine were seen in revolutionary Russia as the essential characteristics of the working class and hence of the new Communist order. More practically, industrialization was also regarded by the Party and Lenin as the key to political and social progress and to the consolidation of the Soviet state. Lenin stated in 1918, after the Treaty of Brest-Litovsk: "Those who have the best technology, organization, discipline and the best machines emerge on top . . . It is necessary to master the highest technology or be crushed."[21] This attitude was epitomized by his dictum "Communism equals Soviet power plus the Electrification of the Entire Country" and by his speech on December 22, 1920, to the Eighth Congress of Soviets (at which Vladimir Tatlin's Tower was displayed), in which he envisioned the future in the hands of the "engineers and agronomists" rather than of the "politicians."[22] With such official endorsement, the ideas of Henry Ford and Frederick Winslow Taylor concerning efficiency in industrial production attracted considerable interest.[23] In 1921 the first conference on Taylor's principles of time and motion (Taylorism) established NOT (the Scientific Organization of Work).[24] Aleksei Gastev, a poet committed to a utopian vision of the triumph of the machine and mechanization throughout Russian life, ran TsIT (the Central Institute of Labor), which was dedicated to studying the human machine and creating a new man through social engineering.[25] Platon Kerzhentsev, who had worked with Gan in Teo Narkompros (the Theatrical Department of the People's Commissariat of Enlightenment), wished to "introduce scientific principles not only into man's economic activity and production but into all organized activity and work."[26] These are merely instances of a prevalent discourse in which the machine was both metaphor for a new culture under construction and the practical means to rebuild the economy for the collective benefit of the people. Nevertheless, Gan—author of the Constructivists' program and Kerzhentsev's collaborator—links these ideas directly with the emergence of Constructivism.

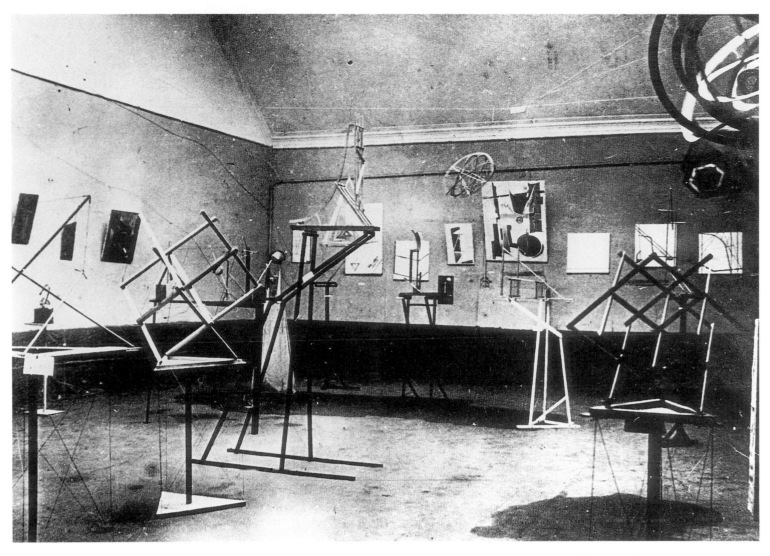

fig. 2
View of Obmokhu exhibition, Moscow, May–June 1921.

The same fusion of ideological and practical imperatives underlay the growing idealization of the machine and the worker by some factions within the artistic community. In November 1918 a debate was held in the Winter Palace over the question of whether art was "A Temple or a Factory."[27] Nikolai Punin, the principal speaker, argued that bourgeois art with its sacramental character was no longer relevant and that a proletarian culture would generate a completely new kind of art: "It is not a matter of decoration but of the creation of new artistic objects. Art for the proletariat is not a sacred temple for lazy contemplation but work, a factory, producing artistic objects for everyone."[28] Later, the newspaper *Iskusstvo kommuny* (*Art of the Commune*) argued that the existing division between art and industry was itself "a survival of bourgeois structures,"[29] and Osip Brik announced that "art is like any other means of production . . . not ideas but a real object is the aim of all true creativity."[30] Such attitudes were reinforced by official policy. Izo Narkompros (the Department of Fine Arts of the People's Commissariat of Enlightenment), committed to "art's penetration into industrial production,"[31] organized a conference in August 1919, where the Commissar of Enlightenment, Anatolii Lunacharskii, pronounced that "there is no doubt that production art is closer to human life than is pure art."[32] Subsequently, an Art and Industry Commission was set up under the Council of People's Commissars to examine how art could be harnessed to improve the quality of industrial products.[33]

Since the Revolution, the avant-garde had, with some success, sought to establish itself as the representative expression of the new order. Developments after 1919, however, increasingly involved the accommodation of the new values and expectations outlined above, prompting a radical reevaluation of attitudes toward abstraction and traditional artistic media. Already in February 1919 Punin had declared:

Suprematism has blossomed out in splendid colour all over Moscow. Posters, exhibitions, cafés—all is Suprematism. And this is extraordinarily significant. One can confidently assert that the day of Suprematism is nigh, and on that very day Suprematism must lose its significance in creative terms.

What was Suprematism? A creative invention without a doubt but an invention strictly confined to painting.[34]

Kazimir Malevich's departure from Moscow in the autumn of 1919 has indeed been attributed to his "creative isolation,"[35] and he later conceded that Suprematism had reached the climax of its influence that year.[36] Subsequent developments within Suprematism suggest the wider currency of the impulses manifest at the Obmokhu exhibition. Significantly, in Vitebsk Malevich began to adapt the Suprematist vocabulary to suit the creation of hypothetical architectural complexes.[37] Likewise, his follower Lissitzky evolved the proun as "an interchange station between painting and architecture";[38] and, lecturing in Berlin in 1922, he even declared:

Two groups claimed constructivism, the Obmokhu . . . and the Unovis {the Affirmers of the New Art} . . .

The former group worked in material and space, the latter in material and a plane. Both strove to attain the same result, namely the creation of the real object and of architecture. They are opposed to each other in their concepts of the practicality and utility of created things. Some members of the Obmokhu group . . . went as far as a complete disavowal of art and in their urge to be inventors, devoted their energies to pure technology. Unovis distinguished between the concept of functionality, meaning the necessity for the creation of new forms, and the question of direct serviceableness.[39]

Lissitzky's distinction was clearly valid by 1922, when positions had consolidated, although earlier there had perhaps been a broader consensus in the two groups' explorations of a machine-age aesthetic. On the one hand, as the Obmokhu exhibition demonstrates, the Constructivists did not immediately abandon the making of art objects. On the other, the Unovis group centered around Malevich also produced directly functional designs. In November 1920, the group's magazine published Il'ia Chashnik's project for a speaker's rostrum (later reworked by Lissitzky and known as the *Leninskaia tribuna* [*Lenin Tribune,* 1924, plate no. 142]), where the girder construction creates an emphatic aura of industrial utility.[40] Architectural and engineering projects were also apparently included in the 1920 and 1921 Unovis exhibitions in Moscow,[41] and by early 1921 Unovis had organized an architectural and technical faculty.[42]

In the gradual evolution toward a Constructivist stance within the Moscow avant-garde, particular attention should be paid to the role of Rodchenko as both artist and polemicist. In the spring of 1921 he was clearly the leading figure among the Constructivist contingent at the Obmokhu show. Whereas the others were still students, Rodchenko was one of the most progressive teachers at Vkhutemas (the Higher Artistic-Technical Workshops) set up in December 1920.[43]

In January 1919, Rodchenko, Stepanova, Aleksandr Vesnin, and other members of Askranov (the Association of Extreme Innovators) had demanded an exhibition space from Izo Narkompros because of "the sudden death of Suprbez [Suprematism and Non-Objectivity], its vitality pouring into the Association of Extreme Innovators."[44] Although a cogent chronology of Rodchenko's evolution is still needed, it is clear that in general terms he was seeking to move beyond Malevich's more "metaphysical" aesthetic. He came to regard the creative act less as an expression of personal inspiration and more as a quasi-scientific investigation into the inherent properties of painting, such as tone, color, line, texture, and organization. Far from being a Modernist assertion of the "autonomy" of art, such a standpoint represented an attempt, akin to that of the Russian literary Formalists at precisely this time, to reconceive art as a specialized, quasi-scientific activity and the artist himself as a species of worker.

An aspiration to establish a science of art also inspired the foundation of Inkhuk in early 1920.[45] Rodchenko was among the original members and was in fact commissioned by the Institute to write his statement entitled "Liniia" ("The Line," 1921). In this important text, while discussing new approaches to the application of paint, to color, and especially to line as the dominant element in pictorial organization, he declared:

The imprecise, broken line that the hand draws cannot compete with the straight, accurate ruled line, which gives precision to the structure.

The craft of painting is striving to become more industrial.

Drawing in the old sense is losing its value and giving way to the diagram or the engineering drawing.

Faktura in painting . . . is being forced out by mechanical techniques . . . which make it possible to analyze color, form, and material scientifically.[46]

The document is a precise evocation of the paintings Rodchenko was creating around 1919 and 1920, such as *Konstruktsiia No. 97* (*Construction No. 97,* 1919), in which a machine-like precision in the articulation of the surface and the linear construction emphasizes the impersonal and analytical quality of the painting process. The titles that Rodchenko was now giving his paintings are expressive of these concerns and also, of course, interesting in light of the subsequent coining of the term Constructivism.

It is important to be precise about the emergence of a new critical vocabulary. The noun *konstruktsiia* (construction), from the Latin *constructio,* was well established in Russian usage by the end of the nineteenth century. Like its English equivalent, it acquired clear connotations of engineering, referring to the construction of buildings, technological structures, or machines.[47] In 1912, the theorist Vladimir Markov had adopted the term *konstruktivnost'* (constructiveness) to denote the rational, logical aspect of art.[48] In early 1919, in the radical *Art of the Commune,* Ivan Puni used *konstruktsiia* in its strictly technical sense when he argued against the idea of production art and contrasted aesthetic criteria with the demands of *konstruktsiia:*

> *What are the principles of a contemporary industrial construction? Its principle is maximum utility . . . an artist does not have the right to interfere with the construction of an object, because an object simply will not be constructive {*konstruktivnyi*} if it is built according to the two principles of utility and aesthetics.*[49]

Indeed, it was precisely because *konstruktsiia* carried these connotations that the terms *konstruktor* (constructor) or *khudozhnik-konstruktor* (artist-constructor) first appeared in an artistic context to equate the maker of art with a worker in industry. Thus in December 1918 V. Dmitriev emphasized that the artist is "now only a constructor and technician."[50] Harnessing this technological emphasis to his own artistic techniques, Tatlin called his workshop at the State Free Art Workshops in Petrograd (where he started teaching in the spring of 1919) the Workshop of Material, Volume, and Construction.[51] Certainly, by early 1920, the idea of construction that underpinned the Constructivists' approach seems to have emerged sufficiently for Vasilii Kandinskii to issue a warning in his Inkhuk program:

> *Without any doubt, positive science can provide the Institute with extremely valuable material . . . Even though art workers right now may be working on problems of construction {*konstruktsiia*} (art still has virtually no precise rules), they might try to find a positive solution too easily and too ardently from the engineer. And they might accept the engineer's answer as the solution for art—quite erroneously. This is a very real danger.*[52]

The adoption of the term *konstruktsiia* to describe the works of art themselves may have been preceded, in fact, by the coining of *postroenie,* from the old Russian root *stroi* (a building, structure, or construct). This had a broad range of reference in general usage, embracing building structures, the construction of geometrical figures, structures of language and thought, and even the construction of a socialist society.[53] In the catalogue of the Tenth State Exhibition, *Bespredmetnoe tvorchestvo i suprematizm* (Non-Objective Creation and Suprematism), which opened in Moscow on April 27, 1919, Liubov' Popova referred to pictorial structure as *postroenie,* although she alluded to the strengths of the pictorial construction as "*sily konstruktsii.*"[54] At the same show, Rodchenko's titling of his 1918 paintings likewise employed *postroenie,* as in the groups of works under the headings of *Strogoe, nepodvizhnoe postroenie tsvetovykh ploskostei* (Severe, Static Structure of Colored Planes) and *Prostoe postroenie tsveta* (Simple Structure of Color).[55] The emerging artistic paradigm is epitomized by Gabo's statement in "The Realistic Manifesto" of August 1920, where he uses the verb *stroit'* (to construct) to emphasize the identification between art and scientific activities: "The plumb-line in our hand, eyes as precise as a ruler, in a spirit as taut as a compass—we construct our work as the universe constructs its own, as the engineer

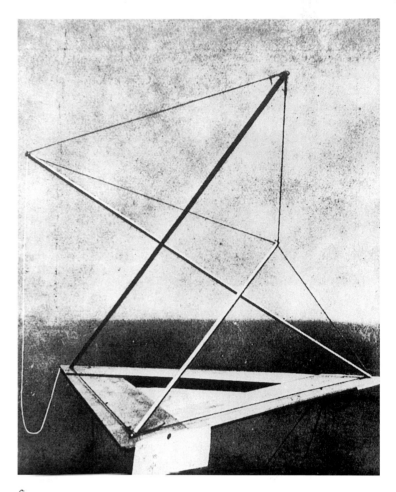

fig. 3
Karl Ioganson
Study in Balance, *ca. 1920.*
Whereabouts unknown.

constructs his bridges, as the mathematician his formula of the orbits."[56]

Within a few months, however, *konstruktsiia* was evidently replacing *postroenie* in avant-garde discourse and acquiring a more specific ideological context. At the Nineteenth State Exhibition in Moscow in the autumn of 1920, Rodchenko exhibited sixteen works with the title *Konstruktsiia,* all but five dated 1919, alongside other works, of 1918–20, that he called *Kompozitsiia (Composition).*[57] The former were clearly paintings; the catalogue entry for no. 102 reads *Konstruktsiia No. 97 (na kornichevom) (Construction No. 97 {On Brown}),* and for no. 117 *Konstruktsiia, Maslo, No. 11 (na chernom) (Construction, Oil, No. 11 {On Black},* 1920).[58] More research is needed to clarify the distinction and correlate the surviving works with the two categories. It appears that the constructions were more linear and flatly painted, as in *Construction No. 97,* whereas the compositions seem to have been more planar and spatial, and more modulated in texture and tone; an entry such as no. 90, *Kompozitsiia No. 78 (chernoe na chernom) (Composition No. 78 {Black on Black},* 1918), recalls such paintings as *Chernoe na chernom (Black on Black,* 1918, plate no. 240). At the exhibition Rodchenko also showed ten *proekty konstruktsii* (projects for constructions) of 1920.[59] These were probably his designs for Zhivskul'ptarkh (the Synthesis of Painting, Sculpture, and Architecture Commission), whose display apparently formed part of the exhibition.[60] Nikolai Khardzhiev later recalled seeing some of Rodchenko's "pseudo-architectural, dilettantish projects for buildings and a 'kiosk for the sale of literature.'"[61] In this instance, Rodchenko was using *konstruktsiia* in accordance with its established engineering usage. However, the polemical force of this new terminology, with its still more emphatic implications of a range of experience outside bourgeois categories of art, was most fully evident in Rodchenko's more metaphorical appropriation of *konstruktsiia* in the context of painting.

The immediate backdrop to the Obmokhu show was the artists' debates about the distinction between composition and construction that had been implicit in Rodchenko's contributions to the Nineteenth State Exhibition. These took place within the General Working Group of Objective Analysis at Inkhuk, which was opposed, as its name suggests, to the more subjective methods for analyzing works of art favored by Kandinskii, the founder and first director of the organization.[62] The oppositional faction included not only the future Constructivists but also painters such as Aleksandr Drevin, Popova, Stepanova, and Nadezhda Udal'tsova, the architects Vladimir Krinskii and Nikolai Ladovskii, and sculptors like Aleksei Babichev and Anton Lavinskii. After four months of discussion, between January and April 1921, the group gave rise to four distinct Working Groups, of which the first to be established was the Constructivists'.[63]

The participants discussed the issues both in general terms and in relation to analyses of specific works. They also produced pairs of drawings illustrating their personal understanding of what composition and construction entailed. In their statements, construction was generally conceived in terms of economy of materials, precision, clarity, and integration of overall organization, and conversely the absence of anything decorative, superfluous, or self-consciously aesthetic. The divergences revolved around certain fundamental problems. What were the relationships and the distinctions between construction in art and construction in the real world of structural design? How far was the concept of construction compatible with the medium of painting? In the evaluations of specific paintings, there was widespread agreement that Rodchenko's paintings alone authentically possessed the property of "construction."[64] Yet Rodchenko himself, like

Ioganson, Medunetskii, and the Stenberg brothers, was increasingly taking the view that construction and painting were incompatible:

In structures executed on a surface, the "construction" is only the projection of a potentially real structure, which in its surface form is merely a particular type of sketch or design, and not a construction as such.

A construction, which in the strict and pure meaning of the word is the organization of an actual object, can only be realized as material.[65]

The most powerful catalyst to the emergence of three-dimensional Constructivism was undoubtedly the exhibition in Moscow, in December 1920, of Tatlin's model for the *Pamiatnik III-emu Internatsionalu (Monument to the Third International,* 1919–20, fig. no. 4), greeted by Vladimir Maiakovskii as "the first object of October."[66] Tatlin declared that in this work he was restoring the essential unity of painting, sculpture, and architecture, "[combining] purely artistic forms with utilitarian intentions": "The results of this are models which stimulate us to inventions in our work of creating a new world and which call upon producers to exercise control over the forms encountered in our new everyday life."[67] His monument was intended, in its ultimate realization, to be a functioning building, a third higher than the Eiffel Tower, that would act as an administrative and propaganda center for the Communist Third International, an organization devoted to fostering world revolution. Within its open structure of iron beams, four glazed volumes, rotating at different speeds, were to house the various executive, legislative, and propaganda offices of the Comintern. The structural components of contemporary engineering, iron and glass—for Tatlin, the "materials of the new Classicism"—were clearly intended to express the new social order; as Lissitzky later wrote: "*Iron is strong, like the will of the proletariat, glass is clear, like its conscience.*"[68] Likewise the form Tatlin devised, the strong diagonal in conjunction with the two encircling spirals, expressed in symbolic terms the soaring utopian aspirations of Communism and the dynamic forces of historical progress.[69] The skeletal apparatus represented a distillation of new technology, evoking the girder construction of the Eiffel Tower itself, oil derricks, skeleton masts on ships, cranes, and mine shafts. The rotating transparent volumes within this structure summoned up the image of an enormous machine with gears and moving parts, a machine designed to generate world revolution. Appropriately, Tatlin's Tower was exhibited in the building where the delegates to the Eighth Congress of Soviets were meeting to discuss such issues as the electrification of Russia. The emphasis on utility, along with the scientific and industrial resonances of Tatlin's simple mathematical forms and contemporary materials, made the Tower a paradigm of new artistic possibilities for the avant-garde. The influence of the project is very apparent in the constructions shown at the third Obmokhu exhibition a few months later.

The Obmokhu exhibition included both spatial works and paintings conceived as "constructions." The installation photographs do not reveal whether Rodchenko exhibited any paintings. His most recent hanging constructions, however, clearly visible in fig. no. 2, show a marked change of emphasis in Rodchenko's three-dimensional work. In his *Belaia bespredmetnaia skul'ptura (White Non-Objective Sculptures),* which had been exhibited in 1919 (plate no. 290), the focus had been on building up flat geometric elements, probably made from card, to create quite complex configurations with overtones of urban architecture.[70] In contrast, the hanging spatial constructions examined the basic forms of Euclidean geometry in a more analytical way, investigating their internal spatial

fig. 4
Tatlin's model for the Monument to the Third International *on
exhibition in Petrograd, November 1920.*

structure and dynamic potential.

The series seems to have been begun in late 1920; the square construction was illustrated as *Prostranstvennaia veshch'* (*Spatial Object*) and dated 1920 in *Kino-fot* (*Cinema-Photo*) 2 (1922), while the hexagonal work (plate no. 296) was subsequently reproduced as *Prostranstvennaia konstruktsiia* (*Spatial Construction*) and dated 1921 (*Cinema-Photo* 4 [1922]). This dating suggests that Rodchenko explored the simpler geometrical forms (such as the square) before moving to more complex forms such as the hexagon and ellipse. At the exhibition, these hanging works were suspended from a series of wires attached to the cornices and apparently spanning three corners of the hall. Only the triangle, ellipse, hexagon, and a portion of the circle are visible in fig. no. 2, although it is possible that more were displayed than the photograph suggests. The existence of at least five of these constructions is documented: the four works at the Obmokhu exhibition and the square construction reproduced in *Cinema-Photo*. Of these, only one survives: the ellipse (fig. no. 5; compare plate no. 294). All of the works share a common method of construction. Concentric geometrical shapes were cut from a single flat piece of plywood. These essentially two-dimensional elements were then rotated within each other to form a three-dimensional construction, with each element held in place by the wire and the outer element acting as a framework for the whole. After exhibition, the wires could be removed and the sculptures collapsed back into a series of flat elements for storage. Indeed, the various components of the triangle, square, and circle constructions are visible in the background of the well-known photograph of Rodchenko in his specially designed work-suit.[71] The constructions explored the growth of a single geometric form from the plane into three dimensions. The mathematical emphasis clearly reflects the Constructivists' scientific orientation. At their inaugural meeting in March 1921 they had decided to invite a "mathematics expert" as well as an "engineer-technician" to work in the group, and they later produced slogans such as "Art is a branch of mathematics, like all sciences."[72] It is probably no coincidence that the closest visual parallels to Rodchenko's hanging constructions are found in modern scientific instruments such as gyroscopes.

The effect of Rodchenko's suspending the works was to further deny the sensations of mass and materiality. The dynamic potential was also intensified by the free movement of the construction on its wire. According to Vladimir Stenberg, Rodchenko shined lights onto the constructions at the exhibition to enhance the reflective qualities of the silver-painted surfaces.[73] This suggests that Rodchenko would have used metal had it been available, and it recalls Tatlin's model for the Tower, which was also made in wood and painted silver, although intended ultimately to be constructed in iron. The simple mathematical forms and the sense of rotation and movement may likewise have been responses to the rotating glazed elements within the Tower.

For the younger artists, the three-dimensional work of Tatlin and Rodchenko demonstrated how a work of art might embody rather than merely illustrate a machine-age sensibility. Previously, contemporary technological themes had, indeed, comprised the subject matter of paintings by the Stenberg brothers and Medunetskii. Some of these have come to light in recent years, permitting at least a schematic reconstruction of these artists' early development. As might be expected, their work at this time was fairly eclectic. Both Vladimir Stenberg's *Worker by the Car* (ca. 1920?)[74] and Georgii Stenberg's *Crane* (1920) celebrate an industrial imagery appropriate to the new proletarian society, and their treatment suggests a degree of fusion between men and machinery. Georgii's painting is less descriptive, the composition flatter and more dispersed, and

the use of color highly abstract. Such simplifications may have been a consequence of their concurrent work in poster design. The linear fluidity of *Crane* is developed further by Vladimir in his *Tsvetokonstruktsiia No. 4* (*Color Construction No. 4*, 1920, plate no. 286), where shapes and lines are disposed within a white ground, clearly indicating a new awareness of more abstract developments. In his *Tsvetokonstruktsiia No. 13* (*Color Construction No. 13*, 1919–20, plate no. 284), the central motif of four elongated red and black rectangles on a white ground is almost a direct quotation from Suprematism.[75]

Among the paintings in the Obmokhu exhibition were Vladimir's *Tsvetokonstruktsiia No. 10* (*Color Construction No. 10*, 1920–21, plate no. 285),[76] and *Tsvetokonstruktsiia No. 12* (*Color Construction No. 12*, 1920–21, plate no. 283), which are clearly discernible on the far wall in one view of the installation (fig. no. 1). The titles recall Rodchenko, as does the uncompromising austerity of the approach to color and design in these new works. It is interesting to compare Vladimir's *Color Construction No. 10* with his demonstration of "composition" (plate no. 244) from the pair of drawings he made for the Inkhuk debate. The painting is far more reductive, eliminating tonal modulation and artistic "touch" as well as rhythmical correspondences in the organization, while the elements are also less varied and autonomous. By taking certain lines right out to the frame and by running them parallel to the edges rather than at a tasteful diagonal, Stenberg ensured greater integration in the painting between the internal configuration and the painted object as a whole; whereas in the drawing, the design is a conventional "vignette" within a fictive aesthetic space. The painting evokes the impersonal graphic language of a diagram or some kind of mathematical illustration and as such it probably corresponds to Stenberg's idea of how a painting might be informed with the quality of "construction." Significantly, however, the drawing of a "construction" (plate no. 245) produced for the discussions is a study for a three-dimensional construction.[77] *Konstruktsiia prostranstvennogo sooruzheniia No. IV (zhelezo)* (*Construction of a Spatial Structure No. IV (Iron)*, 1921, plate no. 292 [*Spatial Construction KPS 42 N IV*]),[78] shown at the Obmokhu exhibition, is evidently an elaboration of the same conception; the curved diagonal is identical, while the vertical support in the sketch has been developed into a more complex diagonal and vertical component (each comprising three bars) and some of the crossbars have been omitted.

The artists' exploration of new materials encompassed works which occupied an intermediate position between pure painting and sculpture. Thus another exhibit was Georgii Stenberg's relief, *Tsvetokonstruktsiia iz materialov No. 7* (*Color Construction of Materials No. 7*, 1920, plate no. 289), just visible behind his constructions in fig. no. 2. This utilized a variety of materials including sand, paper, wire, circular and cylindrical metal elements, and a glass tube containing ground blue pigment—an exploration of the diversity of tone and texture recalling Tatlin's counter-reliefs of 1914–16. Vladimir later recalled:

They weren't simple color constructions like other artists made. We saw what other artists were doing and then tried to do it differently.
. . . we had color constructions of four types: one, simple color constructions; two, color constructions involving texture; three, color constructions that were like bas-reliefs; and four, color constructions that involved perspective, that is they were spatial. These were all lost in a fire.[79]

A very different approach is evident in Georgii Stenberg's freestanding works such as *Konstruktsiia prostranstvennogo sooruzheniia No. 11* (*Construction of a Spatial Structure No. 11*, 1921,

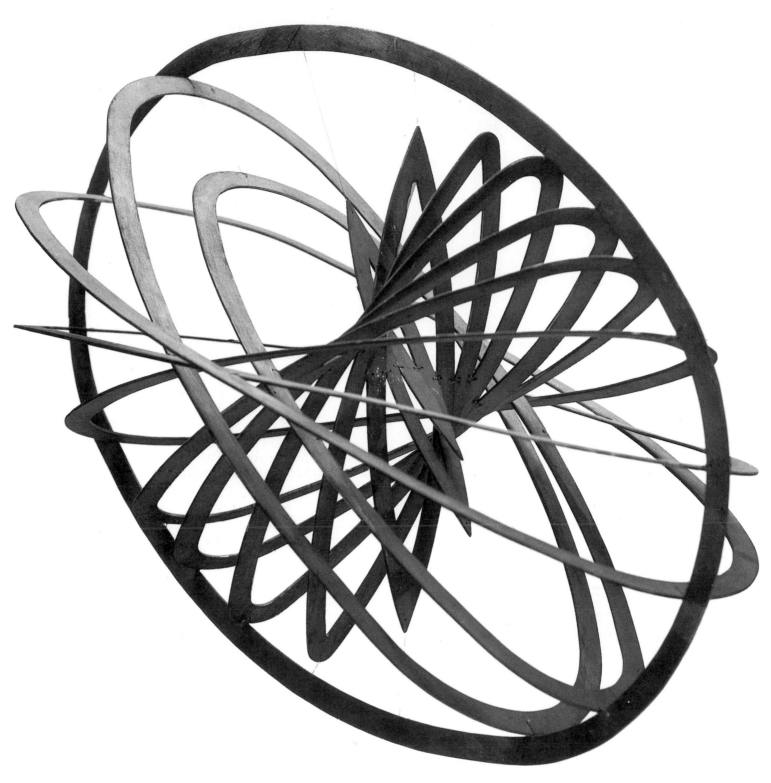

fig. 5
Aleksandr Rodchenko
Oval Hanging Construction Number 12, *ca. 1920.*
Plywood, open construction partially painted with aluminum paint,
and wire, 61 x 83.7 x 47 cm.
The Museum of Modern Art, New York. Acquisition made possible
through the extraordinary efforts of George and Zinaida Costakis,
and through the Nate B. and Frances Spingold, Matthew H. and
Erna Futter, and Enid A. Haupt Funds.

plate no. 293 [*Spatial Construction KPS 51 N XI*]), which is built up with a variety of small I-and T-beam metal elements enclosing a piece of glass. This work was probably executed in the spring of 1921 during the composition-versus-construction debates at Inkhuk and not long before the Obmokhu exhibition opened. A drawing entitled *Proekt konstruktsii* (*Project for a Construction,* signed and dated 1921) depicts a structure which is very close to this particular sculpture.[80] It demonstrates the same impulse to invest art with the materials and the impersonal finish of machine technology that is manifest in Vladimir Stenberg's *Construction of a Spatial Structure No. 4,* which is captioned *Hídrészlet-Konstrukció* (*Bridge Fragment Construction*) and dated 1921 in *Egység*.[81] The materials used, more uniform beam elements, evoke the prefabricated components of engineering construction and the entire conception here alludes, even more strongly, to a specific functional structure, or a fragment of one, such as a bridge or crane. The implied monumentality echoes Tatlin's Tower, as, of course, does the skeletal structure of standardized components and the general shift toward a machine aesthetic. Vladimir Stenberg later stressed that his constructions at this time were actually conceived as explorations that would eventually lead to projects for actual buildings.[82] Despite this assertion, the construction seems to have no direct technological application, but rather to exploit the language of technology to create an art work. It could even be argued, as Babichev did in 1922, that such works were "not rooted in any technical work" and were "in no way utilitarian" but represented "the confirmation of a new mechanical aestheticism."[83]

Not surprisingly, in view of their friendship, Medunetskii's artistic formation seems to closely parallel that of the Stenberg brothers. *Celebration* (ca. 1919), showing workers attending a revolutionary festival, recalls their work both formally and thematically.[84] His painted *Tsvetokonstruktsiia* (*Color Construction,* 1920, plate no. 278), has affinities with Georgii's *Crane* in its fluid handling and vivid color, and although Medunetskii's painting is ostensibly more abstract, it too evokes an imagery of metallic machine components. In *Tsvetokonstruktsiia No. 7* (*Color Construction No. 7,* 1921, plate no. 280), shown at the Obmokhu exhibition, the linear precision is analogous to that of Vladimir's *Color Construction No. 10,* and clearly the dominant influence on his work is Rodchenko. Likewise, Medunetskii's *Tsvetokonstruktsiia No. 9* (*Color Construction No. 9,* 1920–21, plate no. 279),[85] is reminiscent of Rodchenko's *Black on Black* paintings, which were exhibited at the Tenth State Exhibition, as well as his linear "constructions" of 1920. At the same time, it evokes an imagery of light projection.

Medunetskii's three-dimensional works (visible in fig. nos. 1–2) seem more purely abstract, less suggestive of functional forms than the Stenbergs' sculptures. They do, however, use industrially produced materials and elements. Thus in the one extant work, *Konstruktsiia prostranstvennogo sooruzheniia* (*Construction of a Spatial Structure,* usually known as *Spatial Construction,* 1920–21, plate no. 282), the metal circle has ridges on the inside and was evidently some type of coupling ring.[86] Yet the relationships between the components are far removed from those of any engineering structure. The shapes thread through each other with the minimum of contact, creating a very open, dematerialized form. Within this unifying configuration, the bent iron rod, painted red, is visually contrasted with the yellow sheen of the brass triangle, the more matte quality of the zinc ring, the S-shaped tin strip, and the painted marbling on the hollow cuboid, metal base. The construction is clearly an attempt to develop into three dimensions the type of linear spatial structure implied fictively in paintings such as *Color Construction No. 9.* This was equally true of the linear "drawing in space" of Medunetskii's lost iron

and tin *Spatial Construction* (1921, plate no. 281.1), known from a photograph and also visible, alongside a series of comparable works, in one view of the Obmokhu installation.

It is unclear whether Ioganson included any paintings, but his constructions, too, demonstrate a preoccupation with linear structure. In 1929, László Moholy-Nagy illustrated one of Ioganson's works from the exhibition (fig. no. 3) as a *Study in Balance,* explaining that if the string was pulled the composition would change to another position and configuration while maintaining its equilibrium.[87] The similarity between the manner of jointing in *Study in Balance* and that of the other constructions by Ioganson on display (for example, fig. no. 6) suggests that all the works could be adjusted and possibly collapsed and that he was exploring the movement of skeletal, geometric structures in a more pragmatically experimental and explicitly technical manner than was Rodchenko in his hanging constructions. Ioganson's works do not evoke any specific structure, yet the use of standardized elements and the emphasis on the transformation of form might appear to have more direct application to utilitarian structures such as portable, fold-up kiosks or collapsible items of furniture. These "laboratory" works seem to have been made from wood, which probably reflects the shortage of alternative materials at this time. Ioganson's particularly rigorous antiaestheticism expressed in these works was forcefully articulated the following year:

Artists who used to paint pictures are rejecting the picture and are going over to the construction or "into industry," as the customary expression has it. But this approach to the construction employs the devices, the method, and the tools of "the old art" without a practical objective or a definite goal, such as is required for mechanical construction.[88]

In early 1922, Medunetskii and the Stenberg brothers also presented a paper entitled "Konstruktivizm" ("Constructivism") at Inkhuk. They argued that the new approach was a response to the enfeebled state of contemporary "production culture," conditioned by "aesthetics," an inappropriate use of materials, and a wholly inadequate design methodology. In contrast, they defined the essential principles of Constructivism as spatial economy, functionalism, efficiency in the use of industrial materials, and rhythm resulting from the application of engineering technology. Finally, according to the surviving summary, they defined their own achievements and mission:

The first experimental works and their significance as propaganda.
The abstract solution of the basic problems of Constructivism.
The experimental design of the material spatial construction, and its interrelation with utility.
Achievements in space, form, and rhythm.
The communist expression of material spatial constructions.
Russian industry under the banner of Constructivism and its significance in the world market.[89]

This makes it clear that, from the start, the Constructivists were concerned not merely to promote a new aesthetic but to demonstrate their potential capabilities as designers of real objects and structures. "The first experimental works and their significance as propaganda" is presumably a reference to the 1921 Obmokhu exhibition, where they had sought to display their understanding of the essential principles of engineering construction, and their formal inventiveness within that framework, for the benefit of any manufacturers, administrators, or politicians who might care to observe and to give the artists a concrete role in building the new socialist environment. Theirs was an immensely ambitious and idealistic outlook, perhaps conceivable only at a time when, in practice, almost nothing was being made or built in Russia. However, 1921, which witnessed the birth of the Constructivist movement in art, also saw the implementation of the New Economic Policy and the first stirrings of a revival of industrial production. By the following year the Constructivist ethos was gaining increased currency among the avant-garde, and many Russian artists had, in a more wholesale fashion, renounced the making of paintings and sculptures in favor of immersing themselves in the design of buildings and propaganda stands, furniture and textiles, posters, advertisements, and books. The Obmokhu exhibition in the spring of 1921 marked a key moment in the transition toward an authentically Constructivist practice.

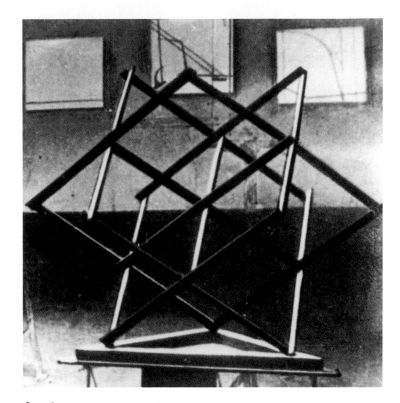

fig. 6
Karl Ioganson
Spatial Construction, *ca. 1921.*
Wood and metal wire.
Whereabouts unknown.

Notes

I should like to express my profound gratitude to my husband Martin Hammer for his invaluable contribution to both the content and form of this essay.

The epigraphs are from Aleksei Gan, *Konstruktivizm* (Tver': Tverskoe izdatel'stvo, 1922), p. 19, as translated in John E. Bowlt, ed., *Russian Art of the Avant-Garde: Theory and Criticism, 1902–1934* (London: Thames and Hudson, 1988), p. 222, and Karl Ioganson, "From Construction to Technology and Invention," trans. James West, in *Art Into Life: Russian Constructivism, 1914–1932*, catalogue for exhibition organized by the Henry Art Gallery, University of Washington, Seattle, the Walker Art Center, Minneapolis, and the State Tret'yakov Gallery, Moscow (New York: Rizzoli, 1990), p. 70.

1. See "Programma uchebnoi podgruppy konstruktivistov INKhUKa," 1921, private archive, Moscow, and "Report No. 1. The Assembly for the Organisation of the Working Group of Constructivists of Inkhuk" held on March 18, 1921, in S. O. Khan-Magomedov, *Rodchenko: The Complete Work*, ed. Vieri Quilici, trans. Huw Evans (London: Thames and Hudson, 1986), pp. 289–90.

For details concerning Inkhuk, see Christina Lodder, *Russian Constructivism* (New Haven and London: Yale University Press, 1983), pp. 78ff. and Khan-Magomedov, *Rodchenko*, pp. 55ff.

The name of the group has been given variously as the Working Group of Constructivists and the First Working Group of Constructivists. Archival material usually omits "First," but the group's first public pronouncement, published in August 1922 in the Moscow journal *Ermitazh* (Hermitage), used both names. See "Front khudozhestvennogo truda. Materialy k Vserossiiskoi konferentsii levykh v iskusstve. Konstruktivisty. Pervaia programma rabochei gruppy konstruktivistov," *Ermitazh* 13 (1922), pp. 3–4. The introduction in *Ermitazh* gave the group its full title, declaring that: "On December 13, 1920, the First Working Group of Constructivists was formed" (ibid., p. 3). It cited Rodchenko, Stepanova, and Gan as the founders and stated: "Directing their attention to the future culture of Communism and proceeding from present specific conditions, they worked out a program and production plan and started to enlist collaborators." These remarks were followed by "The First Program of the Working Group of Constructivists." The presence of both names in this publication suggests that they were used concurrently and interchangeably.

There is no archival evidence to support the assertion made in the *Ermitazh* announcement that the group was founded in December 1920. Gan repeated this elsewhere, notably in "Chto takoe konstruktivizm?" *Sovremennaia arkhitektura* 3 (1928), p. 79, and in *Konstruktivizm*, p. 3, where he also dates the group to 1920. Gan joined Inkhuk in 1920 (see Khan-Magomedov, *Rodchenko*, p. 57), and although his participation in the debates is not documented fully, it is possible that the crystallization of the group's ideas and membership may have begun informally toward the end of 1920. The archives, however, suggest that the group's inaugural meeting was held on March 18, 1921 (see "Report No. 1," in Khan-Magomedov, *Rodchenko*, p. 289). Although Gan was not present, he was chosen to be a member of the organizing group and it was decided to invite him to work in the group (ibid., items 2 and 7). Ten days later, he presented his report on the program and work plan ("Report No. 2. Meeting of the Plenum of the Working Group of Constructivists of Inkhuk," ibid., p. 290). It is clear from the transcription of the ensuing discussion that Gan was responsible for the terms *tektonika, faktura,* and

"construction," as well as for the attempt to create a coherent theory from the artists' rather vague ideas and aspirations (ibid., pp. 92–93 n. 14). It is also evident that although his program was ultimately accepted on April 1, 1921, there was a great deal of divergence among the members over precise meanings and specific details (ibid., p. 92).

2. All are listed in "Report No. 2," in Khan-Magomedov, *Rodchenko*, p. 290.

3. See "Protokol zasedaniia INKhUKa," January 1, 1921 and January 21, 1921, private archive, Moscow.

4. "Programma uchebnoi podgruppy" and Gan's draft program of the group that was approved on April 1, 1921 (reprinted as "Programme of the Working Group of Constructivists of Inkhuk," in Khan-Magomedov, *Rodchenko*, p. 290). The draft program, with few alterations, was published in August 1922 in *Ermitazh* under "Front khudozhestvennogo truda." These ideas were further elaborated in Gan's treatise *Konstruktivizm*, which had appeared by the summer of 1922, when it was reviewed. See V. Zhemchuzhnyi, "Aleksei Gan 'Konstruktivizm,'" *Ermitazh* 9 (1922), p. 8.

5. See "Programme of the Working Group of Constructivists of Inkhuk," in Khan-Magomedov, *Rodchenko*, p. 290, and the discussion of the March 28, 1921 meeting, ibid., p. 92 n. 14.

6. Date of opening from invitation card reproduced in Szymon Bojko, "Rodchenko's Early Spatial Constructions," in *Von der Fläche zum Raum/From Surface to Space: Russia, 1916–24*, catalogue for exhibition organized by the Galerie Gmurzynska, Cologne (Cologne: Galerie Gmurzynska, 1974), p. 18.

The invitation card referred to the show as the group's *Second Spring Exhibition*. According to V. M. Lobanov, the earliest chronicler of Obmokhu (writing in 1930), the 1921 show was the group's third exhibition. He listed four exhibitions organized by Obmokhu between its founding in 1919 and its dissolution in 1923. According to him, these shows took place in 1919, 1920, 1921, and 1922, the last in conjunction with the Fourth Congress of the Comintern in the summer of that year. (See V. M. Lobanov, *Khudozhestvennye gruppirovki za poslednie 25 let* [Moscow: Obshchestvo AKhR, 1930], pp. 104–5). Lobanov's account has formed the basis for work by other scholars (see *Vystavki sovetskogo izobrazitel'nogo iskusstva. Spravochnik* [Moscow: Sovetskii khudozhnik, 1965], vol. 1, pp. 37, 59, 74). Lobanov's labeling of the 1921 exhibition as the group's third show was also confirmed by Vladimir Stenberg (conversation with author, April 1974).

However, Aleksandra Shatskikh argues, on the basis of the correspondence between Georgii Echeistov and Georgii Shchetinin, that the group acquired its name only after September 1919, being initially called Obmolkhud, and that its first exhibition was held in May 1920, not in 1919 (see Aleksandra Shatskikh, "A Brief History of Obmokhu," in this volume). A contemporary review of the May 1920 exhibition, which explains the group's acronym, confirms this (A. A. Sidorov, "Khudozhestvennye vystavki," *Tvorchestvo* 2–4 [1920], p. 34). Although Lobanov gave the wrong year, the details of the show, as listed on the poster (reproduced by Shatskikh), correspond with Lobanov's account of the first exhibition, i.e., that it was held in the spring (opening on May 2nd) at the First State Free Art Workshops on Rozhdestvenka, and that Anatolii Lunacharskii and Lev Kamenev spoke at the opening. However, Lobanov's assertion that the first exhibition consisted entirely of agitational work does not accord with Sidorov's review, which described paintings and even a sculpture. Lobanov stated that the first exhibition (exclusively agitational work) was held on Rozhdestvenka, while the second (posters plus more formal investigations) was held in the group's studio in the former Fabergé shop on the corner of Neglinnaia Street and Kuznetskii most. Although this indeed was the location of their studio, his account is somewhat confused. Certainly there seems to be no reason for Lobanov to have exaggerated Obmokhu's importance by adding another exhibition; although Obmokhu was an agitational and collective organization, its interest in formal experimentation was far removed from the Realist cause Lobanov espoused. In view of this—and given Vladimir Stenberg's assertions—it is possible that there were four shows in all and that there was another exhibition devoted entirely to agitational work. It is possible, moreover, that such an exhibition took place prior to the May 1920 exhibition, and this would explain why the opening of the May 1920 show—a show, after all, by a new group of young artists—had such a lineup of eminent speakers (Lunacharskii, Kamenev, Ol'ga Kameneva, David Shterenberg, Osip Brik, and Georgii Iakulov). Likewise, it is possible that there was another exhibition, perhaps more informal, in Obmokhu's studio at some time after the May 1920 show and before the end of the year. As the first exhibition opened in the spring, the 1921 show could still have been the group's *Second Spring Exhibition* as well as its third show overall. Certainly the inclusion of "spring" in the title is puzzling, particularly since it is more reminiscent of the salons of czarist Russia than of the postrevolutionary avant-garde.

7. The contributors are listed on the invitation card, reproduced in Bojko, "Rodchenko's Early Spatial Constructions," p. 18.

8. Shatskikh, "Brief History of Obmokhu." It was registered within the Subsection for Artistic Work of Izo Narkompros before May 1920. "Iz deiatel'nosti IZO," *IZO. Vestnik Otdela izobrazitel'nykh iskusstv N.K.P.* 1 (March 10, 1921), p. 4.

9. See Alma Law, "A Conversation with Vladimir Stenberg," *Art Journal,* Fall 1981, p. 223 and E. A. Speranskaia, ed., *Agitatsionno-massovoe iskusstvo pervykh let Oktiabria. Materialy i issledovaniia* (Moscow: Iskusstvo, 1971), p. 70.

10. Speranskaia, *Agitatsionno-massovoe iskusstvo,* pp. 92, 125 n. 167.

11. Lobanov, *Khudozhestvennye gruppirovki,* pp. 104–5. It also contained "*levye iskaniia*" (left-wing or avant-garde explorations) which are not described. Clearly, for Lobanov the importance of Obmokhu lay in the fact that the "Productionist aspirations of the participants dominated over easel painting." Ibid., p. 106.

12. Sidorov, "Khudozhestvennye vystavki." He also suggests that this statue is well riveted.

13. Vladimir Stenberg, conversation with author, November 1974. See note 6 above.

14. Law, "Conversation with Vladimir Stenberg," p. 224. The invitation gave the address as 11 Bol'shaia Dmitrovka (reproduced in Bojko, "Rodchenko's Early Spatial Constructions," p. 18).

15. See Ulen, "Die Ausstellungen in Russland," *Veshch'/Gegenstand/Objet* 1–2 (1922), p. 19, reprinted in I. Matsa, ed., *Sovetskoe iskusstvo za 15 let. Materialy i dokumentatsiia* (Moscow and Leningrad: Ogiz-Izogiz, 1933), p. 138, where it is dated 1920.

16. See *Egység* 2 (1922), p. 9.

17. Ibid., p. 7. The issue also contained photographs of a Gabo relief (p. 8) and an Unovis composition exhibited in Moscow in 1921 (p. 10).

18. Ibid., pp. 5–6.

19. Ibid., p. 8.

20. Ulen, "Die Ausstellungen in Russland," p. 19.

21. Quoted in Richard Stites, *Revolutionary Dreams: Utopian Vision and Experimental Life in the Russian Revolution* (New York and Oxford: Oxford University Press, 1989), p. 147.

22. V. I. Lenin, "Iz doklada Vserossiiskogo tsentral'nogo ispolnitel'nogo komiteta i Soveta narodnykh komissarov o vneshnei i vnutrennei politike 22 dekabria," in his *Polnoe sobranie sochinenii* (1919), reprinted in Matsa, *Sovetskoe iskusstvo za 15 let,* pp. 63–64.

23. See Stites, *Revolutionary Dreams,* pp. 145–64. For contemporary enthusiasm about Ford's ideas, see I. M. Burdianskii, *Nauchnaia organizatsiia truda* (Leningrad: Priboi, 1925), pp. 23–25.

24. See L. Pamilla and V. Chukovich, *NOT—velenie vremeni* (Minsk: Belarus, 1973).

25. See E. H. Carr, *Socialism in One Country, 1924–1926* (London: Penguin, 1970), pp. 409–11.

26. P. M. Kerzhentsev, *Printsipy organizatsii. Izbrannye proizvedeniia* (Moscow: Ekonomika, 1968), p. 275, quoted in Stites, *Revolutionary Dreams,* p. 156.

27. M. L-in, "Miting ob iskusstve," *Iskusstvo kommuny* 1 (December 7, 1918), pp. 3–4, reprinted as "Miting ob iskusstve (24 XI 1918 g. v Petrograde)," in Matsa, *Sovetskoe iskusstvo za 15 let,* pp. 173–76.

28. Nikolai Punin, quoted in "Miting ob iskusstve," in Matsa, *Sovetskoe iskusstvo za 15 let,* pp. 175–76.

29. "Primechanie redaktsii," *Iskusstvo kommuny* 8 (January 26, 1919), p. 2.

30. Osip Brik "Drenazh iskusstvu," *Iskusstvo kommuny* 1 (December 7, 1918), p. 1.

31. David Shterenberg, "Pora poniat'," *Iskusstvo v proizvodstve* (Moscow: IZO Narkompros, 1921), p. 5.

32. "Rech' Narodnogo kommissara po prosveshcheniiu A. V. Lunarcharskogo," in *Pervaia vserossiiskaia konferentsiia po khudozhestvennoi promyshlennosti. Avgust 1919* (Moscow: Podotdel khudozhestvennoi promyshlennosti Otdela izobrazitel'nykh iskusstv NKP, 1920), pp. 63–64.

33. See N. Kol'tsova, "Programma-deklaratsiia khudozhestvenno-proizvodstvennoi komissi," *Tekhnicheskaia estetika* 10 (1967), pp. 14–15.

34. Nikolai Punin, "O novykh gruppirovkakh," *Iskusstvo kommuny* 10 (February 9, 1919), as translated in Larissa Zhadova, *Malevich: Suprematism and Revolution in Russian Art 1910–1930,* trans. Alexander Lieven (London: Thames and Hudson, 1982), p. 322.

35. Anatolii Strigalev, "The Art of the Constructivists: From Exhibition to Exhibition, 1914–1932," trans. James West, in *Art Into Life,* p. 29.

36. K. Malevich, "Sorok piat'. Vvedenie v teoriiu o pribavochnom elemente v zhivopise," 1925, private archive, Moscow, p. 81, quoted in Zhadova, *Malevich,* pp. 81, 130 n. 32.

37. See Zhadova, *Malevich,* pp. 96ff.

38. El Lissitzky and Hans Arp, *Die Kunstismen, 1914–1924* (Zurich–Munich–Leipzig: Eugen Rentsch Verlag, 1925), p. xi. Architectural titles for Lissitzky's prouns abound, e.g., *Proun*

1E. Gorod. Eskiz (Sketch for Proun 1E: Town, 1919–20, plate no. 206). See Peter Nisbet, "An Introduction to El Lissitzky," in *El Lissitzky, 1890–1941,* catalogue for exhibition organized by the Busch–Reisinger Museum, the Sprengel Museum Hanover, and the Staatliche Galerie Moritzburg Halle (Cambridge: Harvard University Art Museums, 1987), pp. 20–21.

39. El Lissitzky, "New Russian Art: A Lecture," in Sophie Lissitzky-Küppers, *El Lissitzky: Life, Letters, Texts,* trans. Helene Aldwinckle and Mary Whittall (London: Thames and Hudson, 1968), p. 340.

40. Chashnik's project was published in *UNOVIS. Listok* 1 (November 20, 1920).

41. Zhadova, *Malevich,* pp. 87ff.

42. Il. Chashnik, "Arkhitekturno-tekhnicheskii fakul'tet," *UNOVIS* 2 (January 1921), pp. 12–15.

43. See *Izvestiia VTsIK,* December 25, 1920.

44. Quoted in German Karginov, *Rodchenko,* trans. Elisabeth Hoch (London: Thames and Hudson, 1979), p. 60.

45. Of course, artists and writers such as David Burliuk and Vladimir Markov had begun the process of establishing a more scientific basis for artistic analysis before the Revolution. Indeed, it was Burliuk who had introduced the French term for the texture of the painted surface, *facture,* into Russian as *faktura* in 1912. (See his articles "Kubizm" and "Faktura" in *Poshchechina obshchestvennomu vkusu,* December 1912 or January 1913, pp. 95–101 and 102–10; the former is translated in Bowlt, *Russian Art of the Avant-Garde,* pp. 70–77). By 1914 Markov had explored in minute detail the practical and philosophical ramifications of the term *faktura* in relation to various arts and crafts (including sculpture, architecture, and icon painting), nature, and the machine. (See Vladimir Markov, *Printsipy tvorchestva v plasticheskikh iskusstvakh. Faktura* [St. Petersburg: Souiz molodezhi, 1914]). The importance of this process of analysis was endorsed by Izo Narkompros in February 1919 in its statement concerning "artistic culture," which emphasized the need to create precise definitions of "the elements of artistic activity" and to establish "objective criteria of artistic value." See "Polozhenie Otdela izobrazitel'nykh iskusstv i khudozhestvennoi promyshlennosti NKP po voprosu 'o khudozhestvennoi kul'tury,'" *Iskusstvo kommuny* 11 (February 16, 1919), reprinted in Matsa, *Sovetskoe iskusstvo za 15 let,* pp. 63–64.

46. A. M. Rodchenko, "The Line," trans. James West, in *Art Into Life,* p. 73.

47. See V. I. Dal', *Tolkovyi slovar' zhivogo velikorusskogo iazyka,* vol. 2 (Moscow and St. Petersburg, 1881), p. 152, where *konstruktsiia* is applied to buildings as well as to the structure of language; and the more detailed later definition in D. N. Ushakov, *Tolkovyi slovar' russkogo iazyka,* vol. 1 (Moscow: Sovetskaia entsiklopediia, 1935), p. 1443.

48. See Vladimir Markov, "Printsipy novogo iskusstva," *Soiuz molodezhi* 1 (April 1912), pp. 5–14, and *Soiuz molodezhi* 2 (June 1912), pp. 5–18, translated in Bowlt, *Russian Art of the Avant-Garde,* pp. 25–38.

49. Ivan Puni, "Tvorchestvo zhizni," *Iskusstvo kommuny* 5 (January 5, 1919), p. 1.

50. See V. Dmitriev, "Pervyi itog," *Iskusstvo kommuny* 15 (March 16, 1919), p. 3.

51. See Anatolii Strigalev, "From Painting to the Construction of Matter," in Zhadova, *Tatlin,* p. 24.

52. Vasily Kandinsky, "Program for the Institute of Artistic Culture," in Kenneth Lindsay and Peter Vergo, eds., *Kandinsky: Complete Writings on Art* (London: Faber and Faber, 1982), p. 471.

53. See D. N. Ushakov, *Tolkovyi slovar' russkogo iazyka,* vol. 3 (Moscow: Sovetskaia entsiklopediia, 1939), p. 648.

54. See "Liubov' Popova," in *Desiataia gosudarstvennaia vystavka. Bespredmetnoe tvorchestvo i suprematizm* (Moscow: Otdel IZO Narkomprosa, 1919), reprinted in Matsa, *Sovetskoe iskusstvo za 15 let,* p. 112. In the same statement, she also used the term *akonstruktivnost'* (nonconstructiveness) to denote the absence of construction and hence the antithesis of *arkhitektonika* (architectonics). The date of the opening of this show is given in Strigalev, "Art of the Constructivists," p. 28. *Zhivopisnoe postroenie* (painterly structure) or *zhivopisnoi stroi* (painterly construct) were also used by other artists to denote pictorial structure. See statements such as those by Aleksandr Shevchenko and Aleksei Grishchenko in the catalogue of the *Dvenadtsataia gosudarstvennaia vystavka. Tsvetodinamos i tektonicheskii primitivizm* (Moscow: Otdel IZO Narkomprosa, 1919), reprinted in Matsa, *Sovetskoe iskusstvo za 15 let,* pp. 117–20. Occasionally *struktura* (structure) was also used.

55. See *Desiataia gosudarstvennaia vystavka,* in Matsa, *Sovetskoe iskusstvo za 15 let,* p. 113.

56. Naum Gabo and Noton Pevzner [Antoine Pevsner], "Realisticheskii manifest," August 1920, original and translation reprinted in *Gabo: Constructions, Sculpture, Paintings, Drawings, Engravings* (London: Lund Humphries, 1957), p. 152.

57. *XIX vystavka VTsVB* (Moscow: Otdel IZO Narkomprosa, 1920), nos. 93–107 and 117. According to Rodchenko, this exhibition opened on October 2nd (see his recollections quoted in Karginov, *Rodchenko,* p. 86).

58. *XIX vystavka VTsVB,* pp. 8–9.

59. *XIX vystavka VTsVB,* nos. 125–34.

60. Strigalev, "Art of the Constructivists," p. 31.

61. Nikolai Khardzhiev, *K istorii russkogo avangarda* (Stockholm: Hylaea Prints, 1976), p. 124 n. 2.
    Khan-Magomedov stated that Rodchenko exhibited the kiosk and Sovdep (Soviet of Deputies building) designs along with twenty other sketches at this show (Khan-Magomedov, *Rodchenko,* p. 54).

62. For more details on the debates, see Khan-Magomedov, *Rodchenko,* pp. 83–89 and Lodder, *Russian Constructivism,* pp. 83–89.

63. See Khan-Magomedov, *Rodchenko,* pp. 83–89 and Lodder, *Russian Constructivism,* pp. 83–89.

64. See Khan-Magomedov, *Rodchenko,* p. 84 and the transcription of the discussion of Rodchenko's *Dva kruga* (*Two Circles,* ca. 1920), ibid., pp. 87–88 n. 5.

65. Rodchenko, "Line," p. 73.

66. Nikolai Khardzhiev, "Maiakovskii i Tatlin. K 90-letiiu so dnia rozhdeniia khudozhnika," reprinted in *Neue russische Literatur. Almanach* (Salzburg, 1978), p. 90.

67. See V. Tatlin, T. Shapiro, I. Meerzon, and P. Vinogradov, "Nasha predstoiashchaia rabota," *VIII s"ezd sovetov. Ezhednevnyi biulleten' s"ezda* 13 (January 1, 1921), p. 11. Translation adapted from "The Work Ahead of Us," in *Vladimir Tatlin* (Stockholm: Moderna Museet, 1968), p. 51.

68. See Tatlin et al., "Nasha predstoiashchaia rabota," p. 11, and Lissitzky, "New Russian Art," p. 337.

69. See Christina Lodder, "Tatlin's Monument to the Third International as a Symbol of Revolution," in Gabriel P. Weisberg and Laurinda S. Dixon, eds., *The Documented Image: Visions in Art History* (Syracuse: Syracuse University Press, 1987), pp. 275–88.

70. These works were dated 1918 when they were reproduced in 1922 in *Kino-fot* 5 (1922). They were, however, exhibited at the Tenth State Exhibition in 1919 under the title of *White Non-Objective Sculptures*.

71. See Lodder, *Russian Constructivism,* plate 1.33.

72. See "Report No. 1," March 18, 1921, and the list of slogans in "Programme of the Working Group of Constructivists of Inkhuk," in Khan-Magomedov, *Rodchenko,* pp. 289, 291.

73. Vladimir Stenberg, conversation with author, November 1974.

74. *Worker by the Car,* oil on canvas, 71 x 89 cm, State Architecture and Art Museum, Rostov-Iaroslavskii, reproduced in *Avantgarde, 1910–1930: Russian and Soviet Art* (Turku: Turku Art Museum, 1989), p. 54, details on p. 63.

75. The title is inscribed on the verso with the date 1918 (Giovanni Carandente, ed., *Arte russa e sovietica, 1870–1930* [Milan: Fabbri, 1989], p. 387). The date is more likely to be ca. 1920; the inscription is of questionable value since it could have been made any time before the work was acquired by the Tret'iakov in 1984.

76. Andrei Nakov, however, identifies *Color Construction No. 10* as a *Proekt prostranstvenno-konstruktivnogo sooruzheniia (Project for a Spatial-Constructive Structure)*. See A. B. Nakov, *2 Stenberg 2,* catalogue for exhibition organized by the Annely Juda Gallery, London (London: Annely Juda Gallery, 1975), p. 42. He asserts that works with such titles were "two-dimensional projects for three-dimensional works" (ibid., p. 71). Such a description could be applied to *Color Construction No. 10,* which has a stronger sculptural emphasis than the other paintings given this title (e.g., *Color Construction No. 12*). There is no *Project for a Spatial-Constructive Structure No. 10* listed in the January 1922 exhibition catalogue, the highest number in that series of works shown being no. 6 (see *Konstruktivisty. K. K. Medunetskii, V. A. Stenberg, G. A. Stenberg* [Moscow: Kafe poetov, 1922], no. 41). Nevertheless, it is possible that *Color Construction No. 10* has been mistitled and that Nakov's title is correct.

77. The drawing was probably executed in late 1920 or early 1921, while its *Composition* counterpart is dated 1920. Other drawings in the Inkhuk portfolio of the Costakis Collection are dated 1920 or April 1921, when the debate was concluded. For instance, Ioganson's pair of *Composition* and *Construction* drawings are dated April 7, 1921, Ladovskii's April 15, 1921, while Medunetskii's *Construction* is dated 1920. See Angelica Zander Rudenstine, ed., *Russian Avant-Garde Art: The George Costakis Collection* (New York: Abrams, 1981), pp. 110–27.

78. Title taken from *Konstruktivisty,* no. 42. It was identified by the artist in a conversation with the author, April 1974.

79. Law, "Conversation with Vladimir Stenberg," p. 225.

80. State Tret'iakov Gallery, Moscow, Soviet Graphics Inventory no. 13045, reproduced in *Art Into Life,* p. 95.

81. See *Egység* 2 (1922), p. 7. The title for these works employed by the Stenbergs in January 1922 in their exhibition catalogue *Konstruktivisty* was *Konstruktsiia prostranstvennogo sooruzheniia.* Andrei Nakov identified this particular work as *Konstruktsiia prostranstvennogo sooruzheniia IV,* catalogue no. 4 (see Nakov, *2 Stenberg 2,* p. 72).

82. Vladimir Stenberg, conversation with author, November 1974.

83. Aleksei Babichev, untitled notes, private archive, Moscow. The full quotation is cited in Lodder, *Russian Constructivism,* p. 97. Similar observations were made by Lissitzky in "New Russian Art," p. 337.

84. Konstantin Medunetskii, *Celebration,* undated, ca. 1919, oil on canvas, measurements unknown, Museum of Fine Arts, Syktyvkar. Reproduced in *Avantgarde, 1910–1930,* p. 45, details on p. 62.

85. The signature and date of 1921 on *Color Construction No. 7* suggest that *Color Construction No. 9* was also produced in 1921, although it is dated 1920 in *Art Into Life,* p. 46.

86. It was illustrated in the catalogue of the *Erste russische Kunstausstellung (First Russian Art Exhibition)* under the title *Raumkonstruktion (Spatial Construction)*. See *Erste russische Kunstausstellung* (Berlin: Galerie van Diemen, 1922).

87. L. Moholy-Nagy, *The New Vision: From Material to Architecture* (New York: Brener, Warren and Putnam, 1930), p. 109.

88. Karl Ioganson, "From Construction to Technology and Invention," p. 70.

89. K. Medunetskii, V. Stenberg, and G. Stenberg, "Outline of the Report on 'Constructivism,'" trans. James West, in *Art Into Life,* p. 82.

fig. 1
Display of student work from the color discipline, Basic Division, Vkhutemas, 1926.

The Place of Vkhutemas in the Russian Avant-Garde

Natal'ia Adaskina

The Moscow Vkhutemas (the Higher Artistic-Technical Workshops) has traditionally been regarded as one of the most significant centers of the Russian avant-garde. Its prominence was owing not solely to the natural confluence within its walls of many of the avant-garde's leading members but also—and with greater reason—to its having been there, in the workshops, that the principles of avant-garde artistic culture were forcefully revealed.

Even as Vkhutemas was being organized, in order to accommodate a number of changes demanded by the evolution of art, the need to derive teaching methods suited to the new artistic trends was one of the school's reasons for being. Analytical methods of investigating artistic form—methods born of the avant-garde's experimentation—were the cornerstone of Vkhutemas's pedagogical system. At Vkhutemas, the fundamental tendencies of the avant-garde movement were theorized and developed. Here, too, the contradictions that had accumulated within the avant-garde, the conflicts among its various strands, and the crises in its development were in dramatic evidence.

The creation and operation of Vkhutemas were not, of course, joined solely to considerations of the avant-garde; Vkhutemas was an institution with links to the artistic currents in Russian culture of the 1920s as a whole. The spirit of the avant-garde, however, and the tasks of the avant-garde movement shaped what was most essential in its character. The program of study and the teaching methods employed at Vkhutemas embodied in full the chief tenets and contradictions of the avant-garde: an orientation toward artistic experimentation; exploration of form; maximally individual, subjective creation uneasily allied with the search for collective, objective knowledge in the products of artistic experimentation; solution of the dilemma of analysis and synthesis in artistic practice and in the theorization of contemporary art; the variance between the avant-garde's programmatic orientation toward absolute innovation and the historicism that was characteristic of leading vanguard artists; and the search for ways to resolve the conflict between an orientation toward the irreplicably personal, the unique creation of genius, and an interest in industrial production, mechanical reproduction, and the organization of the life of the masses.

Before proceeding to the heart of this essay, a brief review of the history and structure of Vkhutemas is in order.[1] This summary is indispensable, inasmuch as where Vkhutemas has been described by scholars, it has often appeared to be a peculiar chimera, made up of elements which could not possibly have coexisted (but which did, in fact, characterize it at various times). It is essential that the reader have some notion of a structure that underwent continuous, and at times fundamental, change.

From the latter half of the nineteenth century, the system of art education in Russia, centered on the Imperial Academy of Arts, had been in a state of profound crisis. Piecemeal reforms were no solution: the system could not accommodate new artistic phenomena, which existed apart from and even in defiance of academic orientations; nor was it able to meet the demands which industrial development placed on art schools. The first problem was to a certain extent solved—other than by the flight of young people to art schools in Paris and Munich—through an expansion of the number of private schools and workshops in Russia (including "workshops without a supervisor"), where new methods of art education began to evolve. To the second problem there was for the time being no solution. Those artistic-and-industrial schools that existed in Russia were oriented entirely toward manual, artisanal methods in the fabrication of everyday objects, in

КОНЦЕНТР ФИЗКУЛЬТУРЫ
ОСНОВНОГО ОТДЕЛЕНИЯ

fig. 2
Foreground, display of student work from the space discipline,
Basic Division, Vkhutemas, 1926.

printing, and so forth, and failed to react at all to progress in industry.

The Moscow Vkhutemas came into being as a consequence of the reform of art education introduced in Russia immediately after the October Revolution. The reform was carried out in two stages. The first, in 1918, entailed the abolition of the academic system: the Academy of Arts and an array of art and artistic-and-industrial schools and academies in various Russian cities were put on an equal footing—all were converted into State Free Art Workshops.[2] It was thus that the First State Free Art Workshops (formerly the Stroganov Artistic and Industrial School) and the Second State Free Art Workshops (formerly the School of Painting, Sculpture, and Architecture) were created in Moscow.

The conversion of the Academy of Arts and other educational establishments into State Free Art Workshops was no mere formality; there were material changes. In the majority of the new institutions priority was given to "pure" art, to painting above all, and individual workshops were introduced, each workshop following one or another artist's own program and methods. The State Free Art Workshops thus endeavored to replicate the Renaissance studio, where the master worked amid apprentices and disciples and passed his experience and artistry on to them. Students were allowed, however, to elect workshop supervisors and to choose freely with whom to enroll. Izo Narkompros (the Department of Fine Arts of the People's Commissariat of Enlightenment) consistently adhered, moreover, to a policy of equal participation in artistic life for all movements, and set a quota for them in the workshops.

The State Free Art Workshops opened for classes in the autumn of 1918; for the first time in its history, art education in Russia was based on the principles of freedom and democracy. That the new institutions had as many definite shortcomings as incontestable virtues—both organizationally and pedagogically—gradually became apparent in the two years that followed.

It was in the State Free Art Workshops that a number of leading artists, primarily members of left movements, began to create a system of art education derived from the experience of the new art. As can be ascertained from archival materials, the programs of Kazimir Malevich, Georgii Iakulov, and Aleksei Babichev in the First Free State Art Workshops, and of Vasilii Kandinskii in the Second, were highly innovative. Through the efforts of these and other artists, new methods were originated which liberated students from the routine acquisition of professional skills; the new methods developed students' powers of perception and gave them the means to fix their perception in the wealth of artistic forms. Yet, insofar as the pursuit of primacy in formal discovery and invention (in general inherent in the avant-garde) continued inside school walls, there was no broad sharing of educational innovations among the workshops. There was a danger of creating closed circles, which would lead to students' merely duplicating the individual styles of their teachers.

A fair number of instructors, moreover, held to their old tested methods of teaching. And they were supported by a large proportion of students who during their previous years of study in the former schools had become accustomed to a certain logic in the stale programs and modes of instruction, and strove to preserve continuity.

As a whole, however, the State Free Art Workshops in Moscow were, during their two years of operation, a breeding ground for new initiatives. Avant-garde art continued to evolve, both within the educational framework and parallel to it; it assumed new forms. Thus at the exhibitions of Obmokhu (the Society of Young Artists), a group which had been formed in 1919 by students at the First State Free Art Workshops, there were already no Tatlinesque "selections of materials" but experimental constructions not seen heretofore. (The Obmokhu exhibition in May 1921 would be recalled as the crucible of Constructivism.) At the end of 1919, Sinskul'ptarkh (the Synthesis of Sculpture and Architecture Commission), which had been under the auspices of Izo Narkompros, was reorganized into Zhivskul'ptarkh (the Synthesis of Painting, Sculpture, and Architecture Commission) by young artists and architects, many of whom were at the time students in the State Free Art Workshops; it was the first group oriented toward forms that, consonant with a new phase of artistic evolution, synthesized the arts. These developments had their direct continuation inside a new educational institution on whose fate they exercised a substantial influence: Vkhutemas, which came into being when the First and Second State Free Art Workshops were merged in 1920.

The creation of Vkhutemas belongs to the second stage of the reform of art education, when educational institutions everywhere underwent consolidation. The reasons for this action were various;[3] two deserve mention. First, students had by this time become dissatisfied with the workshops' lack of clearly delineated programs and with a system that led to the mass production of "little Konchalovskiis" and "little Tatlins."[4] Second, among avant-garde artists, notions of the objectivity of formal laws were gaining more and more ground, leaving it clear that objective methods should be made the general basis of art education.

The Decree of the Council of People's Commissars on the Moscow Higher State Artistic-Technical Workshops was ratified on November 29, 1920, and signed by Lenin on December 18th. It is symptomatic that the decree was silent on the graduation of "pure" artists, traditionally the chief aim of art education; that is, unlike the State Free Art Workshops, Vkhutemas tilted from its inception in favor of an artistic-and-

fig. 3
Workshop in the Woodworking Faculty, Vkhutein, 1928. Photograph Aleksandr Rodchenko.

technical education. The decree also set out the structure of Vkhutemas. It would have eight faculties—Architecture, Painting, Sculpture, Graphics, Textiles, Ceramics, Woodworking, and Metalworking—for each of which a preparatory (or basic) division was envisioned.

The history of Vkhutemas/Vkhutein⁵ falls rather neatly into three basic periods, each corresponding to the tenure of one of its three rectors. The principal conflicts and many of the personnel changes at Vkhutemas were in one way or another, directly or more often indirectly, linked to the issue of Vkhutemas's orientation. The chief battles were fought over whether that orientation should be toward "pure" or production art.

Insofar as it is possible to characterize each of these periods succinctly and schematically, the sculptor Efim Ravdel''s term as rector (1920–23) can be labeled the period in which Vkhutemas's pedagogical methods (its so-called *distsipliny*, or disciplines) were formulated and its eight faculties, with a preparatory course (offered in the Basic Division) common to all, put in place. Ravdel''s term also witnessed the rise of Productivist tendencies (which, though they had been mentioned in the 1920 decree, had then yet to take root), culminating in the transfer of a number of left artists of a Constructivist orientation from the preparatory-course workshops to the production faculties.

Vladimir Favorskii, who served as rector during 1923–26, presided over the most fruitful and harmonious period in the history of Vkhutemas. In these years, its structure attained its final form. The preparatory Basic Course—where the formal-analytical disciplines had first been employed and which had originally been developed as an introduction to architecture and non-objective painting and later oriented toward production art—was rethought and adapted to encompass all varieties of artistic work, to the point of including the principles of Realist figurative art in its teaching. The Basic Course became, that is, the universal foundation of art education. An effort was likewise made to regulate and systematize the programs of Vkhutemas's faculties. During this period, moreover, "easel art" and production art attained, and maintained, an equal footing. It was not an artificial equilibrium, for Favorskii conceived the various fields of art as a single system, and he endeavored to make this belief the guiding principle of Vkhutemas.

Favorskii was succeeded in 1926 by Pavel Novitskii, and a technical preoccupation again came to the fore, accompanied this time by "sociologizing" tendencies in the fine-arts faculties. The notion of the formal oneness of all varieties of art, which had been so diligently nurtured in previous years, was discarded. The Basic Division, where students of all specializations were taught the same formal and artistic principles, was cut back sharply, the length of its course reduced from two years to six months. The links of each faculty to the others were considerably weakened. Vkhutein was splintered into self-contained faculties, each of whose fates was individually determined—and ceased to exist.

Let us return, however, to the matter of the avant-garde. Vkhutemas gathered together within its walls the most prominent representatives of avant-garde trends of the 1910s. A number of these artists—Aleksandr Shevchenko, Anna Golubkina, Aleksandr Drevin, Kandinskii, Petr Konchalovskii, Boris Korolev, Pavel Kuznetsov, Aristarkh Lentulov, Il'ia Mashkov, and Robert Fal'k, among others—were given their own workshops in the Painting and Sculpture faculties. Others—Vladimir Baranov-Rossine, Nadezhda Udal'tsova, Ivan Kliun, Aleksandr Vesnin, Liubov' Popova, Aleksandr Rodchenko, Aleksandra Ekster, and Aleksandr Os'merkin—received workshops in the Basic Division.

fig. 4
Baskov
Student work from the color discipline, Basic Division, Vkhutemas.

Throughout all the organizational changes and fluctuations in policy at Vkhutemas/Vkhutein, the workshops in the Painting Faculty preserved as best they could their character—acquired back in the days of the State Free Art Workshops—as self-sufficient studios centered about one master artist. They were an embodiment of the avant-garde cult of the artist as demiurge, of the absolute creative personality. The influence of these artist-teachers on their students can be discerned in the stylistic tendencies of later Soviet painting; distinct trends can be traced to students of Shevchenko, Fal'k, Kuznetsov, Konstantin Istomin, and others. There was, of course, no hard and fast correlation between such influence and a teacher's originality. David Shterenberg's students, for example, showed no discernible signs of his influence. (It is no coincidence that it was in Shterenberg's workshop that the student Aaron Rzheznikov organized, as was allowed under workshop rules, a "workshop without a supervisor" at the end of the 1920s.)

Not only the subjective and individual but the objective and universal—that is, both halves of the fundamental avant-garde antithesis—came into play at Vkhutemas. Even in its earliest stages, formal experimentation by the avant-garde took on the features of a scientific inquiry. Spontaneous self-expression, both in the work of a single avant-garde artist and in the self-reflexion of a group of artists, was constantly conjoined and intertwined with attempts to formulate objective laws of perception and form. The work of Kandinskii is without question the best example of this conjunction of the subjective and objective.

Kandinskii was at the forefront of the Russian avant-garde's artistic science, having organized Inkhuk (the Institute of Artistic Culture) in 1920 precisely for the conduct of objective investigations into the elements of art. Kandinskii drew up a research program for Inkhuk and initiated its implementation; shortly afterward, however, disagreements arose; Kandinskii departed, and Inkhuk followed a somewhat different course from that mapped by him. There is not space here to examine in detail the work and interaction of those affiliated with Inkhuk. Suffice it to emphasize Kandinskii's indisputable influence on an array of artists who would seem to have rejected his conceptions and methods. Certain of those artists were teachers at Vkhutemas. (The research at Inkhuk and the work of Vkhutemas were tightly interwoven.)

The work done at Vkhutemas testifies, above all, to the avant-garde's love of theorizing. The impulse to theorize—which at earlier stages (and in other social and cultural conditions) had found an outlet in manifestos and pamphlets and in oral, colloquial forms—now, at the beginning of the 1920s, was funneled into scientific papers (at Inkhuk) and academic programs (at Vkhutemas; at GVTM [the Higher State Theater Workshops], organized by Vsevolod Meierkhol'd; and elsewhere). Creative work—reflections on artists' individual and group evolution—continued to be the stuff of these new (to artists) genres of theorizing.

By this time, of course, theories had been advanced in some quantity by art critics and historians. Nikolai Tarabukin (also a member of Inkhuk) had already written his *Opyt teorii zhivopisi* (*Toward a Theory of Painting*, 1916), in which he defined the study of the history of art as the "analysis of the elements of artistic creations."[6] During the same period, Nikolai Punin's examination of contemporary tendencies in art had led him to a variant of the formal-analytical theory of art. Punin had also played a crucial role in defining the concept of "artistic culture," the theoretical underpinning of the measures enacted by the Petrograd Izo Narkompros in the immediate postrevolutionary period.[7] "Artistic culture" was a notion derived by theorists of the Russian avant-garde from the actual practice of new artistic trends. The values of "artistic culture"

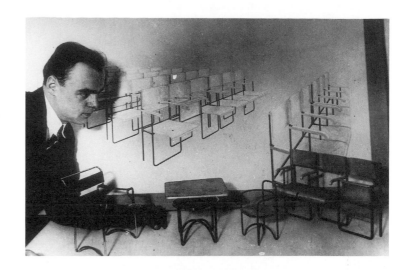

fig. 5
Petr Galaktionov with his diploma project: furnishings for a movie theater, Vkhutein, 1929.

fig. 6
Students in Lavinskii's workshop building a model of a rural reading room for display at the Exposition internationale des arts décoratifs et industriels modernes, *1925.*

were defined as purely professional ones, the product of the "sustained artistic labor" of various schools.

At the beginning of the 1920s, analysis—isolating among the wide range of professional artistic means and devices those of chief importance to a given movement, and making them absolutes in artistic work—became the chief method of the new art scholarship, as well as the organizing principle of artistic life—of exhibitions, museums, and art education.

Describing his plans for the Museum of Painterly Culture, Kandinskii wrote in 1920: "It will collect experiments in formal construction according to the principle of juxtaposition: color planes and linear planes; the alignment, collision, and resolution of planes; the relation of surface-plane and volume; treatment of surface-plane and volume as self-sufficient elements; the coincidence or disconnection of linear and painterly planes and volumes; experiments in the creation of purely volumetric forms, both unitary and combinational, and so forth."[8] It was certainly under the influence of these conceptions of Kandinskii's—though already in his absence—that Babichev and Popova evolved their research programs in the Monumental Art Section of the Working Group of Objective Analysis at Inkhuk. The same conceptions lay at the heart of the system of disciplines in the Basic Division of Vkhutemas—whose most active creator and coordinator was, again, Popova.

For Kandinskii, analytical work was merely an interim stage in the quest for synthesis, or, in his terminology, "monumental art." For members of the Objective Analysis Section at Inkhuk and for teachers in Vkhutemas's Basic Division in 1921–22, however, analytical work was no mere sideline or auxiliary stage but an artistic and theoretical value in its own right. For them, moreover, the synthesis of formal and analytical experimentation—when they spoke of synthesis—was not Kandinskii's "monumental art" but production art, a specifically Russian offspring of the analytical stage in the evolution of the avant-garde. This bears on the fate of the Basic Division in Vkhutemas's first period and of those production faculties which came under the influence of Rodchenko's group.

At Vkhutemas, it was Favorskii's policy, followed in 1923–26, which, in its conception of the unity of the arts and its support for the work of art as an integrated and finished expression of artistic reality, was kindred with the ideas of Kandinskii. There were, of course, critical discrepancies between Kandinskii's understanding of these matters and their interpretation by Favorskii's adherents. Thus, whereas Kandinskii sought to study the laws of artistry as a whole, embracing both the spatial and the temporal arts, Vkhutemas confined itself strictly to the spatial arts.

In the clash between the Constructivism of the Productivists and Favorskii's synthesizing, two principles of the Russian avant-garde—the mechanical and the organic, respectively—collided. (Although somewhat later, in the latter half of the 1920s, Petr Miturich, in the Printing Trades Faculty [as the Graphics Faculty had been renamed], rebelled against Favorskii's methods as mechanistic from the point of view of free artistic intuition.)[9]

The notion of the oneness of the formal laws of all the spatial

fig. 7
Aleksandr Rodchenko
Design for a signboard for Vkhutemas, 1924.

fig. 8
Cover for Vkhutein prospectus, 1929.

arts was the cornerstone of Vkhutemas's educational system and united proponents of diverse trends. Zhivskul'ptarkh had been the first to experiment in promoting this unity—prior to the establishment of Vkhutemas. Its exhibitions were noteworthy not merely for joining architects, painters, and sculptors in one show but for their astonishing blending of art forms. The painters Rodchenko and Shevchenko, the sculptor Korolev, the architects Nikolai Ladovskii and Vladimir Krinskii, and others exhibited works belonging to one and the same nontraditional genre: fantastic architectural projects for "houses of Soviets," kiosks, communal housing, and so on. These "paper projects," executed in the Cubo-Futurist painting style of the era, were presented more as "easel art" than traditional architectural production. They bore witness to the organic unity of formal conceptions held by representatives of different fields of art; to the significance, at that moment, of formal experimentation in painting for all types of art; and to the importance of space as the material and constructive principle of form—not just for architects and sculptors but also for painters, who had not turned merely by chance to creating architectural projects on paper.

Joining forces in Vkhutemas's Basic Course, Rodchenko, Popova, Anton Lavinskii, Vladimir Khrakovskii, Viktor Kiselev, Korolev, Ladovskii, and Krinskii—painters, sculptors, and architects—fashioned teaching methods based on their shared conceptions. In 1920, Ladovskii independently worked out "psychoanalytical" methods in the Obmas (the United Workshops of the Architecture Faculty). In 1920–21, an effort was made in the Basic Division to assign successive phases in the study of form in painting to separate workshops: "color" would be studied in certain of them, "volume in painting" in others, "construction" in yet others, and so on. At that time, Popova and Vesnin's workshop, for instance, was labeled "Discipline No. 1: Color." These first analytical endeavors were, however, still very imprecise.

During the next stage (1922–23), the artists worked at systematizing programs and student work, having added "volumetric" and "spatial" disciplines to the "painterly." The task of integrating the new disciplines into the training of students of all specializations was taken up by the architects Ladovskii and Krinskii.

As this effort proceeded, the aim of the Basic Course changed. Initially, when they created their introductory program—the analytical or, as they were also called, "objective" disciplines—the teachers of the Painting and Sculpture faculties had seen their goal as the training of "easel artists," of non-objective artists. During 1921–23, the notion of production art—whose forms were typically refutations of "pure" art—came to the fore and gathered momentum in vanguard circles. By late 1922–early 1923, a new preparatory course had been conceived; it was based on the analytical study of form according to a clear-cut logic—from surface-planarity through volume to space—and was intended to foster production artists.

A group composed of Rodchenko, Aleksandr Vesnin, Lavinskii, and Popova presented Vkhutemas's directors with a plan (of Popova's design) to convert the Basic Division into a design faculty with a two-year introductory program and a two-year course in production art—production art at that moment being conceived to include street and interior decoration, industrial graphics, clothing design, and so forth. It was a plan, that is, to prepare students for the very same work that the Constructivists-Productivists were turning to at the time. But the plan was rejected and never put into effect. Rodchenko, Lavinskii, and Kiselev—all now Productivists—moved to the Metalworking and Woodworking faculties and there began instituting changes, replacing old received notions

fig. 9
Students in Rodchenko's workshop, Vkhutemas, 1924.

of applied art with new Constructivist tenets. Popova had started teaching at GVTM under Meierkhol'd in 1921, and in 1923 left Vkhutemas.

Conflicts between the Productivists and the partisans of traditional artistic forms were a hallmark of the years 1923–24. While the Constructivists-Productivists—also known as the "Productivists from Lef [the Left Front of the Arts]"—resolved the "easel versus production" impasse unequivocally in favor of production art, Favorskii and his sympathizers—Nikolai Dokuchaev, Istomin, Pavel Pavlinov, and certain others—saw the matter differently.

Favorskii, whom the "Productivists from Lef" had trouble putting their finger on (was he an "easel painter," "applied artist," or "Productivist mystic"?),[10] by and large erased the distinction between the two areas of creation. According to Favorskii's theory, the evolution of form proceeded from surface-planarity through volume to space—in the same sequence, that is, as was followed in the courses of the Basic Division. Once he became Vkhutemas's rector in 1923, Favorskii aspired not only to shore up advances already made in the Basic Division and to make the preparatory course compulsory and profitable for students in all faculties but to extend the logic of the formal disciplines to Vkhutemas's structure and methods as a whole. Favorskii's theoretical views relied both on the traditions of European Formalism and on direct analysis of avant-garde art and the practices of Russian artists, his Vkhutemas colleagues included. The Productivists, nonetheless, did not view Favorskii as one of their own.

In the middle and late 1920s, Constructivist tendencies were strong in the Metalworking Faculty, where Rodchenko and Tatlin were teachers; in the Woodworking Faculty, where Lissitzky had been teaching since his return from Europe; and in the Textile Faculty—there the result of Varvara Stepanova's influence. In the Architecture Faculty, traditionalists, Formalists (Ladovskii and his colleagues), and Constructivists (the Vesnins and their followers) all battled for influence. The Formalists' theoretical and artistic orientation came closest to Favorskii's conceptions, though Favorskii was not reckoned, as were the Formalists, among the innovators.

More and more painters who had once belonged to the avant-garde—members of Bubnovyi valet (Jack of Diamonds), including Mashkov, Lentulov, and Konchalovskii; and artists of Orientalist and Primitivist allegiances—were flocking to traditionalism by this time. Their evolution led them further and further away from formal and artistic experimentation. As a result, they strove in their teaching practices as well to keep to the model of the turn-of-the-century Parisian studio—and one of a moderate bent at that.

In mid-decade, it was in the Basic Division and the Printing Trades Faculty that the formal and analytical methods created by non-objective artists in 1920–23 were adhered to most closely and consistently. They were employed by, among others, Istomin, Pavlinov, Khrakovskii, the sculptors Nina Niss-Gol'dman and Romual'd Iodko, and the architects (students of Ladovskii's) Viktor Balikhin, Mikhail Turkus, Mikhail Korzhev, and Ivan Lamtsov. Yet, while in the Basic Division attitudes toward these methods remained unchanged over the entire decade, members of the specialized faculties complained more than once that they amounted to an unnecessary academic exercise, a waste of students' time.

Toward the end of the 1920s, as mentioned earlier, Vkhutein witnessed a growing technical preoccupation, a tendency to, as Favorskii put it, "play engineer." The finely adjusted balance between artistic and technical disciplines in the education of designers (graphic artists, furniture designers, textile designers, ceramists, and so forth) and of architects was targeted for change, at the expense of the formal artistic disciplines. In the

fig. 10
Aleksandr Deineka
Vkhutemas, *illustration for* Revolutionary Moscow, *1921. The album was distributed among delegates to the Third Congress of the Comintern.*

training of "pure" artists (painters and sculptors), more and more attention was paid not to professional but to ideological requirements. It was Novitskii—a theorist and member of October, one of the last left groups in Soviet art—who presided over the adoption of technical and "sociologizing" approaches to art. His disposition toward sociologizing was shared by such "right" groups as OMAKhR (the Young People's Section of the Association of Artists of the Revolution), whose ranks included students at Vkhutein.

The pitched battle among artists' groups in the middle and late 1920s drew in a large number of Vkhutemas/Vkhutein's teachers and students. The most influential groups, apart from October and AKhRR (the Association of Artists of Revolutionary Russia; from 1928 the Association of Artists of the Revolution, or AKhR), were Ost (the Society of Easel Painters)—whose members included both Vkhutemas/Vkhutein teachers (Shterenberg and Nikolai Kupreianov) and graduates (such as Andrei Goncharov, Iurii Pimenov, Aleksandr Deineka, and Petr Vil'iams)—and Four Arts, an association that brought together diverse, chiefly middle-aged artists, many of whom taught at the school (Favorskii, Istomin, Miturich, Kuznetsov, Vera Mukhina, Ivan Zholtovskii, and others).

The October group stood for the avant-garde's movement into production. The members of AKhRR, among whom were many solidly left artists of the 1910s (such as Lentulov and Mashkov), were apostates who renounced the avant-garde entirely. The young artists of Ost adapted the avant-garde legacy to easel painting and figuration (it is here, perhaps, that the legacy of Vkhutemas is most pronounced). And Four Arts sought to preserve artistic culture in conditions of increasing ideological pressure. (Yet, while many artists of this group were at home with the latest innovations, they perceived them solely in the context of the centuries-long evolution of art.)

A tendency to fall back on tradition had existed at Vkhutemas alongside the enthusiasm for innovation inherited from the avant-garde of the 1910s. And although the study of traditions and history (of professional trades, art forms, and artistic trends and schools) was not put forward as the chief method of art education—as it had been, for example, at the former Stroganov School (everything there was based on a thorough study of styles) or in the architecture department of the Moscow School of Painting, Sculpture, and Architecture—it did, after a certain struggle, find a place in the programs of various faculties. That it did is not solely a measure of the influence of purely traditionalist tendencies having no relation whatsoever to the avant-garde; it is also an index of the avant-garde's own attention to history. For when they turned to the theorization of vanguard trends in art and to the creation of educational systems and teaching methods, Malevich, Moisei Ginzburg, Popova and her colleagues at Inkhuk, and other artists traced the historical evolution of art with great care, uncovering the "additional element" (Malevich's famous term) in each new movement. They sought to organize exhibitions in the new museums of painterly or artistic culture according to the same evolutionary outline.

It should be recalled that in 1923 Moscow's Museum of Painterly Culture moved to one of the Vkhutemas buildings at 11 Rozhdestvenka (previously the site of the Stroganov School). Rodchenko had been the museum's director in 1920–22; Vil'iams and Lazar' Vainer administered it, and Solomon Nikritin headed its Research Board, in later years (all were Vkhutemas graduates). There Nikritin applied the method of formal analysis to the study of masterpieces of the past and endeavored to find exact and reliable mathematical formulas for the older artists' work. In 1925, the museum was the site of the survey exhibition *Levye techeniia v russkoi zhivopisi za 15 let*

fig. 11
The former Vkhutemas building on Kirov Street, 1976. Photograph Aleksandr Lavrent'ev.

fig. 12
Sergei Sen'kin
Tablet for the former Vkhutemas building commemorating Lenin's
visit to the school on February 25, 1921; first version, 1960s.

(Left Trends in Russian Painting over the Past Fifteen Years).

But, of course, what linked Vkhutemas to the avant-garde above all and made it, for all the twists and turns in its orientation and history, a center of the avant-garde was the spirit of invention and experimentation which prevailed in the majority of its classrooms and workshops. The production faculties, under the guidance of such leading artist-constructors as Rodchenko, Tatlin, Lissitzky, and Stepanova, were a major site of innovation. Two vanguard movements—Constructivism and Rationalism—took shape in the Architecture Faculty. (Graduates of the Architecture Faculty included such major figures as Ivan Leonidov.)

But while unconcealed and programmatic innovation in architecture and design flourished at Vkhutemas, and was difficult to oppose, the situation in the Printing Trades Faculty was not so straightforward. Students in that faculty practiced Constructivist-style innovations, based on exploitation of the possibilities of typographical techniques, yet these innovations occurred outside rather than within the classroom, where formal mastery, achieved via the study of traditional techniques and devices, was wanted. Once students had acquired those skills, however, they incorporated in their work lessons learned from Rodchenko, Lissitzky, Gustav Klutsis, and other artists, who may not have been teachers in the Printing Trades Faculty but were continually at the center of students' attention. The vanguard artists' influence showed itself constantly, in both the students' assigned and their elective work.

By virtue of its concentrated atmosphere of exploration and innovation, Vkhutemas was for many years the site of diverse artistic undertakings. Among them were the Workshop of the Revolution—an attempt to translate the energy of the avant-garde into agitational forms—that Sergei Sen'kin, Klutsis, and others made plans to organize in 1924. A Projectionist Theater, an experiment by Nikolai Triaskin, Sergei Luchishkin, and Nikritin with Abstractionism in the theater, offered performances in 1923 and 1924. And the overwhelming majority of the participants in the *Pervaia diskussionnaia vystavka ob"edinenii aktivnogo revoliutsionnogo iskusstva* (*First Discussional Exhibition of Associations of Active Revolutionary Art,* Moscow, 1924), held in an exhibition space belonging to Vkhutemas, had connections to the school; they were teachers, students, or recent graduates.

What, then, was the role played by Vkhutemas in the history of the Russian avant-garde? Before attempting an answer, one should recall that Vkhutemas came into being when the avant-garde movement was already waning (its peak, of course, came in the mid- to late 1910s). Vkhutemas, by assembling vanguard artists to be its teachers, became a repository of the spirit of the avant-garde. And it met the avant-garde's quest for its own educational institution and teaching methods—methods which the avant-garde was obliged to create, because the values it championed were professional values.

With the adoption of the formal-analytical studies and synthesizing ideas of the avant-garde into art education, these values became an integral part of the artistic consciousness of Vkhutemas's graduates. And of succeeding generations. Because graduates of Vkhutemas became teachers in Moscow's institutions of higher education, the ideas and formal discoveries of the Russian avant-garde—which had become the ideas and practices of Vkhutemas—were part of the consciousness of young artists of the late 1950s and early 1960s. (Nor have these ideas lost their significance for art today.) Vkhutemas's introduction of the values of avant-garde art into artistic culture as a whole was, without question, its greatest achievement.

—Translated, from the Russian, by Jane Bobko

Notes

1. Thus far, research on Vkhutemas has been scattered throughout a large number of articles. The principal studies are those of R. Antonov, A. Lavrent'ev, S. O. Khan-Magomedov, and this author in the journal *Tekhnicheskaia estetika* and the *Tekhnicheskaia estetika* series of the Trudy VNIITE (nos. 28, 34, and 41 are the most pertinent). Khan-Magomedov's *VHUTEMAS. Moscou, 1920–1930*, trans. Joëlle Aubert-Yong, Nikita Krivocheine, and Jean-Claude Marcadé, 2 vols. (Paris: Editions du Regard, 1990) has recently appeared, and a volume entitled *Vkhutemas—Vkhutein. 1920–1930* is forthcoming from Sovetskii khudozhnik. There is reason to hope that the gaps in our knowledge of Vkhutemas will soon be filled.

2. The entire conversion was overseen by Narkompros, which at that time counted many leading artists among its members, most of them adherents of the left (Cubo-Futurists, non-objective artists, and Suprematists) or center (Cézannists, Orientalists, and Primitivists).

3. Narkompros's limited resources for the upkeep of educational institutions were one of the reasons. Nonetheless, the creation of Vkhutemas via the consolidation of the State Free Art Workshops is highly reminiscent of the measures adopted in a number of European countries in the 1900s and 1910s, when the demands of industrial development were met by merging academies of fine arts and schools of applied arts into a new type of art school.

4. The unhappy students once hung a placard in the First State Free Art Workshops' entryway, on which they had written: "Down with the titanic Picassos and Gauguins! It's enough to mass-produce Tatlins, Konchalovskiis, Fedorovskiis, Os'merkins, Lentulovs . . ." (the list continued through all the teachers' names).

5. Vkhutemas was renamed Vkhutein (the Higher Artistic-Technical Institute) in 1927.

6. N. Tarabukin, *Opyt teorii zhivopisi* (Moscow: Proletkul't, 1923), p. 6. The book was written in 1916.

7. The statute of the Department of Fine Arts and Artistic Industry on "artistic culture" was published in *Iskusstvo kommuny*, February 16, 1919. For a detailed discussion of this concept, see Svetlana Dzhafarova, "The Creation of the Museum of Painterly Culture," in this volume.

8. V. Kandinskii, "Muzei zhivopisnoi kul'tury," *Khudozhestvennaia zhizn'* 2 (1920), p. 20.

9. See N. Adaskina, "Iz istorii poligraffaka Vkhutemasa (Ob"ektivno-analiticheskie i tvorcheski-lichnostnye nachala khudozhestvennoi pedagogiki)," in *Sovremennyi dizain i nasledie Vkhutemasa,* Trudy VNIITE, vyp. 34 (Moscow: Vsesoiuznyi naucho-issledovatel'skii institut tekhnicheskoi estetiki, 1982).

10. *Lef* 2 (1923), p. 174.

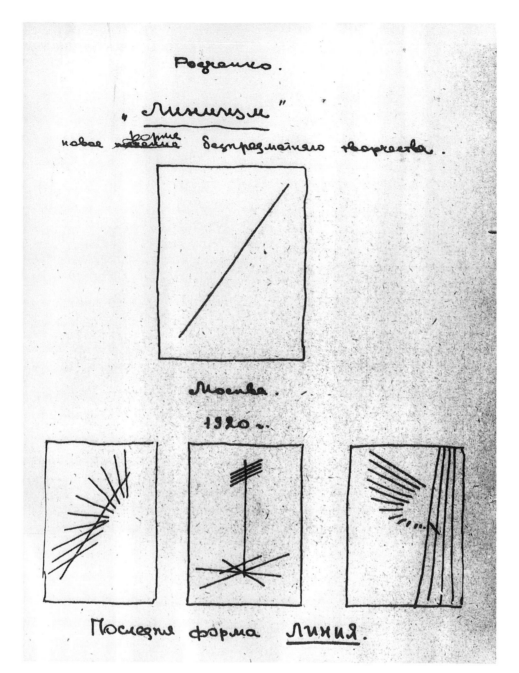

fig. 1
Page from Rodchenko's notebook with sketch
for cover for Linearism, *1920.*
A. M. Rodchenko and V. F. Stepanova
Archive, Moscow.

What Is Linearism?

Aleksandr Lavrent'ev

The term Linearism (*liniizm*) and the conception of painting it denoted were the invention of Aleksandr Rodchenko, who wrote at the end of 1919:

> LINEARISM *is a new tendency in non-objective creative work.*
> *The surface plane is, logically, being discarded, and so as to express greater constructedness, architecturalness in compositions—and there being no further need for it—that old favorite of painting's,* faktura *{density}, is being discarded, too.*[1]

It is legitimate to wonder to what purpose it behooved him to "discard," "discover," and issue declarations if the sole result was a handful of colored or white lines drawn with a brush over a black or colored ground. Rodchenko's own writings will provide the best answer.

The history of the Russian avant-garde in the 1910s and 1920s witnessed several fundamental discoveries about form in painting: the intersecting non-objective brush strokes, resembling the patterns of frost on glass, of Mikhail Larionov, promulgator of Rayism; the *Chernyi kvadrat* (*Black Square,* 1915) of Kazimir Malevich, inaugurator of Suprematism; the counter-reliefs of Vladimir Tatlin, fashioned from real rather than trompe l'oeil fragments of iron, wood, glass, and wire. One might say that the last links in this chain, in which Liubov' Popova's "painterly architectonics" also figured, were the inventive semi-engineered constructions of Georgii and Vladimir Stenberg and of Karl Ioganson—and two cycles by Rodchenko: the first, his paintings and graphic works composed of lines and points, and the second, three monochromatic canvases in which the surface of the painting had already crossed into the category of object. "Everything is finished. Primary colors. Each plane is a plane and there need be no representations."[2] A red, a yellow, and a blue canvas—these are no longer constructions, not compositions; they are the end stage of the experimentation of an extreme innovator.

> *Who saw a WALL . . .*
> *Who saw JUST A SURFACE PLANE—*
> *EVERYONE . . . AND NO ONE.*
> *One who had truly seen came and simply SHOWED*
> *the* square
> *This means opening eyes to the* surface plane.[3]

Thus is Malevich described in "Kto my?" ("Who Are We?"), the manifesto of the Constructivists written by Rodchenko and Varvara Stepanova in 1921–22. With his *Black Square,* Malevich showed the surface plane to be a reality in painting and a category of visual thinking.

> *And when in his laboratory one person set up*
> *the* square,
> *His radio reached all whom it behooved and whom it did not, then soon, on all the "ships of left art" sailing under white, black, and red flags . . . everything utterly, utterly everything was covered with squares.*[4]

Rodchenko's investigations into and analyses of non objective creation brought him to this necessity: the declaration of the line as the basis for modeling. "A new apprehension of the world," he noted, "has been elucidated in the line."[5]

> *Who saw an ANGLE,*
> *Who saw a FRAMEWORK, a PLAN?*
> *EVERYONE . . . AND NO ONE.*
> *One who had truly seen came and simply SHOWED*
> *the* line

And when yesterday in his laboratory one person set up the
        line, the grid, and the point,
His radio reached all whom it behooved and whom it did not, then
soon, and especially on all the "ships of left art" newly christened
"Constructivist," sailing under diverse flags . . . everything utterly . .
. utterly is being constructed of lines and grids.
        OF COURSE, *the square existed even previously, the line and the grid*
existed previously.
        Which is the crux.
Just this—THEY POINTED THEM OUT
                THEY PROCLAIMED THEM.
The square—1915, Malevich's laboratory.
The line, the grid, the point—1919, Rodchenko's laboratory.[6]

No one, it may be, wrote about experimentation and the laboratories of art with as much ardor as Rodchenko. And his attitude toward art always embraced a desire to affirm his pride of place, to "patent" the uniqueness and innovation of his every new series. In a draft "auto-monograph," Rodchenko enumerated the innovatory services he had rendered, among them that "I introduced and proclaimed the line as an element of construction and as an independent form in painting."[7]

As a painter, Rodchenko existed within the philosophical space of "left" painting and was connected to other artists by numerous personal and creative threads. His work is, in addition to all else, a reaction to what had happened and was happening in painting during 1917–21. Yet, as an extreme innovator and inventor, Rodchenko was sui generis, and his work should be appraised according to his own criteria of innovation, originality, technical mastery, and economy of expressive means. He himself was cognizant of the obstacles should his work be viewed from the vantage of different requirements, criteria, or positions. By the very existence of all those lines and circles painted on canvas, he laid down a new criterion of judgment.

It should be recalled that Rodchenko had announced two previous conceptions of painting—"dynamism of the plane" (constructed conjunctions of planes intersecting in space) and "concentration of color and form" (compositions of floating, gleaming colored spheres)—in works he displayed at his first solo exhibition (Moscow, 1918), the Fifth State Exhibition (Moscow, 1919), and the Tenth State Exhibition, *Bespredmetnoe tvorchestvo i suprematizm (Non-Objective Creation and Suprematism,* Moscow, 1919). Rodchenko conceived his new series, consisting solely of lines, in August 1919, in advance of the Tenth State Exhibition. Yet, though he had completed a number of the new works, Rodchenko did not exhibit them. In order to proclaim a new movement in non-objective painting, one or two works would not suffice; an entire cycle was needed, whose size and compositional variety would confirm the movement as a new artistic program.

"I revealed the composition and the tying-together of the canvas by means of it," Rodchenko wrote in his working notes.[8] By the "tying-together of the canvas" he meant the filling-up of the surface plane, of space. In each work, lines—on one or another colored ground; wide, with shaded edges, or crisp and narrow—form one or another configuration, representing, as it were, some event in the life of lines. Now they meet and intersect like two streaks of cloud; now, at the point of intersection, one line suddenly shoots upward and blossoms into filaments; now the lines turn on a central pivot and expand into space according to the principle of a hyperbolically contracted surface plane. Straight lines create a stable framework; concentric closed curves recall the trajectory of points. Ordinary lines, it turns out, can be animated just like any other form—and no less than the point.

I am thinking of painting several circles for Linearism and also of making a linear sculpture.
        I think I'll exhibit Linearism in June or July, when there'll be no fewer than 30 works in oil, and maybe even 50, for I've got 13. I must also write and print up 500 copies of a booklet on Linearism.[9]

Rodchenko indeed intended to construct a linear sculpture from wire, and had even accumulated a store of small steel rods. But he was forced to abandon the venture, inasmuch as it would have been a technically more demanding undertaking than was his work with cardboard, paper, or oils (which were always close at hand). Welding, or at the very least soldering, would have been entailed. At the time, not only the technical wherewithal but even space in which to work was hard to come by (Rodchenko and Stepanova were then living in the quarters of the Museum of Painterly Culture, where Rodchenko served as director).

A mountain of work, but I'm quite drained by my duties and the exertion it now takes to feed ourselves.
        I'm resting my hopes on summer and the warmth of the Sun.[10]

It was only at the Nineteenth State Exhibition (Moscow, 1920) that Rodchenko's "lines" were exhibited. The series included paintings (some twenty of them) and graphic works, as well as the text "Vse–opyty" ("Everything Is Experiment"), whose typewritten pages were mounted on a wall. The text explained why Rodchenko did not repeat his previous experiments, why each time he fashioned an ever newer series from new formal elements. His every cycle constituted a certain new possibility, a certain new world, albeit one consisting of planes, colored spheres, or lines. Rodchenko would later effect the same admixture of means, devices, and formal elements (circles, planes, and lines) in other areas—in architecture, design, graphics, and advertising.

It is useful to view Rodchenko in the company of other avant-garde artists, that is, in the same context in which his works were displayed at the celebrated Tenth State Exhibition, the Nineteenth State Exhibition, and $5 \times 5 = 25$ (Moscow, 1921), at which last Rodchenko's three monochromatic canvases were shown. When Rodchenko is thus positioned amid his colleagues, the principal elements of his system and his uniqueness are thrown into sharper relief. One can profit anew from the bit of advice offered by Rodchenko in "Everything Is Experiment":

In each work, I conduct a new experiment without the advantage of my past, and in each work I set a different task. If you survey my entire output over all this time, you will find one enormous and completely new work. If you want to tack the past on to it, get yourself to a museum and contemplate that.[11]

—Translated, from the Russian, by Jane Bobko

Notes

1. A. M. Rodchenko, notebook, 1917–20, A. M. Rodchenko and V. F. Stepanova Archive, Moscow.

2. A. M. Rodchenko, "Rabota s Maiakovskim," 1939, A. M. Rodchenko and V. F. Stepanova Archive, Moscow. Published in part in *A. M. Rodchenko. Stat'i, vospominaniia, avtobiograficheskie zapiski, pis'ma* (Moscow: Sovetskii khudozhnik, 1982), pp. 53–82.

3. A. M. Rodchenko and V. F. Stepanova, "Kto my?," 1921–22, A. M. Rodchenko and V. F. Stepanova Archive, Moscow. Published in *Aleksandr M. Rodchenko–Varvara F. Stepanova: The Future Is Our Only Goal,* ed. Peter Noever, trans. Mathew Frost, Paul Kremmel, and Michael Robinson, catalogue for exhibition organized by the Österreichisches Museum für angewandte Kunst, Vienna, and the A. S. Pushkin State Museum of Fine Arts, Moscow (Munich: Prestel, 1991), pp. 170–72.

4. Rodchenko and Stepanova, "Kto my?"

5. A. M. Rodchenko, "Liniia," 1921, A. M. Rodchenko and V. F. Stepanova Archive, Moscow.

6. Rodchenko and Stepanova, "Kto my?"

7. A. M. Rodchenko, "Laboratornoe prokhozhdenie cherez iskusstvo zhivopisi i konstruktivno-prostranstvennye formy k industrial'noi initsiative konstruktivizma," 1921–22, A. M. Rodchenko and V. F. Stepanova Archive, Moscow.

8. Rodchenko, notebook, 1917–20.

9. Ibid. The text of "Liniia" ("The Line") was completed in 1921 and reproduced by hectograph at Inkhuk (the Institute of Artistic Culture) in a small number of copies. Published in S. O. Khan-Magomedov, *Rodchenko: The Complete Work,* ed. Vieri Quilici, trans. Huw Evans (Cambridge, Mass.: MIT Press, 1987), pp. 292–94; in *Art Into Life: Russian Constructivism, 1914–1932,* catalogue for exhibition organized by the Henry Art Gallery, University of Washington, Seattle, the Walker Art Center, Minneapolis, and the State Tret'yakov Gallery, Moscow (New York: Rizzoli, 1990), pp. 71–73; and in *Aleksandr M. Rodchenko–Varvara F. Stepanova: The Future Is Our Only Goal,* pp. 133–35.

10. Rodchenko, notebook, 1917–20.

11. A. M. Rodchenko, "Vse–opyty," *1921,* A. M. Rodchenko and V. F. Stepanova Archive, Moscow. Published in *Aleksandr M. Rodchenko–Varvara F. Stepanova: The Future Is Our Only Goal,* pp. 130–32.

The Constructivists: Modernism on the Way to Modernization

Hubertus Gassner

"In life, mankind is an experiment for the future," Aleksandr Rodchenko wrote in his "Vse–opyty" ("Everything Is Experiment," 1921).[1] Now that this future is already past and we stand before the shambles of the greatest human experiment in history, we should take a close look at the utopianism of the Soviet-Russian avant-garde. In so doing, we may gain a deeper insight into the channels and links between formal experiments in art and social experiments with human life.

The avant-garde's utopianism began not with an enthusiastic vision of the future but with a rather skeptical question: How can one be an artist in the Soviet Union of the 1920s? This question—albeit in slightly modified form—is still relevant today, as is the answer Constructivism tried to provide. Today the question reads: How can one be an artist within a media culture?

The illusory (Western) world of mediated mass communication produced by the art and entertainment industry was, of course, unknown to the Soviet avant-garde artists of the 1920s. Yet some of the communication strategies devised by the Constructivists anticipated today's agony of reality under the impact of simulation technologies. And for good reason, since what was happening in Russia before their eyes and under their feet—or rather, *in* their eyes and *in* their stride—was no less than a preliminary stage of the ongoing third, mass-media, revolution: it was the second—the industrial—revolution.

It had been preceded by a two-stage political revolution: first the bourgeois, democratic revolution in February 1917, and then the proletarian, Communist revolution in October 1917. While it is widely believed, predominantly in the West, that the artistic revolution locked arms with the political revolution and even operated as its vanguard, this essay will argue—and, I hope, demonstrate—that even the avant-garde artists of the left were entirely unprepared when the second wave of the political revolution hit. Though they were not caught unawares by the quickened pace of history after the first salvo in February, the abrupt change of course in October took them by surprise.

Between the spring and autumn of 1917 there are more ruptures than there are continuities. It would be wrong to perceive the course of the political revolution, after its swerve in direction, as no more than an accelerated continuation of the initial phase. And during the 1920s there were further twists, sometimes in such rapid succession that artists occasionally stumbled in their race to stay abreast of social change. Struggling to keep pace, the initially united left front of art began to dissolve. Groups or individual artists split off and embarked on divergent courses. Others quit the race altogether. Those who stayed the course ran in clusters, often with one or another artist or theorist in the lead. Vladimir Tatlin was perhaps the only solo runner among them.

The following pages will discuss the evolution of both individuals and groups. Our focus will be on the breaks between historical stages and on the crises in art, since only a survey of the uneasy concurrence of developments within art and outside art can reveal, and offer a basis for evaluating, the context in which Constructivism emerged and grew.

The principal stages are:

•The quest for a new artistic identity in the wake of the February Revolution, and artists' attempts at alliance so as to assert their role in the new society

•The silence of artists after the October Revolution, their reluctance to cooperate with the revolutionary government, and their unenthusiastic alignment with the new rulers to secure artistic autonomy (1918–19)

- The gestation and birth of Constructivism at the juncture of political revolution and industrial revolution (1920–21)
- The crisis of Constructivism in 1925–26 and the transformation of the engineer of objects into the "engineer of the psyche"

To understand the profound shift in consciousness the avant-garde underwent in the early 1920s, one need only examine the discussion at Inkhuk (the Institute of Artistic Culture), of Varvara Stepanova's lecture "O konstruktivizme" ("On Constructivism"). Stepanova's extremely rationalist discourse on an instrumentalist concept of art survived the discussion uncontested: "Once purged of aesthetic, philosophical and religious excrescences, art leaves us its material foundations, which henceforth will be organized by intellectual production. The organizing principle is expedient Constructivism, in which technology and experimental thinking take the place of aesthetics."[2] What *was* openly and fiercely disputed was the crucial question of "how today's artists justify their existence" (Khrakovskii). Thus pressured, the artists responded with arguments ranging from the circumspect to the virulent: Boris Arvatov proposed the "propagandizing" of Russia's still "utopian" industrialization through Constructivism, in order to establish a basis for a Constructivist design of the living environment; Georgii and Vladimir Stenberg polemically executed artists in general: "They [artists] are good for nothing. They should be treated in the same way as the Cheka [secret police] treats counterrevolutionaries." Konstantin Medunetskii's false confidence ("Art ends with us") was present alongside an acknowledged sense of tragedy as art declared bankruptcy. For Arvatov, the "end of culture" had come because industrial techniques had supplanted cultural techniques. Inasmuch as artists were "useless to industry and unable to be engineers," their position was "tragic."

Given this dire situation, more than twenty artists and theorists within Inkhuk decided on November 24, 1921, to relinquish any self-sufficient pursuit of art and to apply themselves to the production of useful objects. The Constructivist theorist Nikolai Tarabukin celebrated this new development as a historic moment: "For the first time in the annals of art history, painters have become sensitive seismographs of future tendencies by, in a radical reorientation, deliberately rejecting their specific field of work."

This was the moment when Russian Modernism abandoned all opposition to the modernization of life effected by industrialization and mass production, and began to assume the functions of oil and engine in the machinery of progress. The stated goal was no longer just the reconciliation of consciousness and machine but the total alignment of human psychophysical being to machine mechanisms and motions. Yet if the Constructivists gave up the resistance to self-serving or profit-oriented technological progress that had until then characterized Modernism's critical distance from a merely market-driven modernity, the decision was not made with a light heart. Nor was the artists' dropping of their ambivalence about industrial modernization a logical result of developments within art, as some design historians claim. The evolutionary paths of Soviet Constructivism, marked by breaks and historical contingencies, hardly fit the streamlined phylogeny of industrial design.

Indeed, a closer analysis of Constructivist production art can show how its manufacturing methods and products contain a utopian surplus value that transforms even the individual utilitarian object into a *pars pro toto* of a cosmos harmonically structured by rhythmic movements. This utopian surplus lends these objects their aesthetic and ethical value and even bathes them in an aura of artistic autonomy—precisely the quality the Constructivists struggled to nullify on their flight into bare functionalism.

Paradoxes in Organizing Freedom
After the February Revolution

The artistic avant-garde began its limited performance in Russian history with the struggle for the independence of art from government interference. During 1917–18, the politics of "Futurism"—the period's generic term for all new trends from post-Cézannism to Suprematism to Tatlin's "culture of materials"—had been strictly anti-institutional. In the winter of 1918–19, however, more than a year after the October Revolution, the first attempts were made to establish the avant-garde, institutionally and ideologically, as the artistic spearhead of the Soviet state. This set the stage for the turbulent misalliance between "Futurists" and Communists— a story with several chapters that would come to an abrupt end with the government-ordained dissolution of all rival artists' groups in 1932

A preliminary chapter in this difficult marriage of autonomous art with government institutions opened, however, some time before October 1917. As early as February of that year, following the overthrow of the czar by the bourgeois-democratic revolution, the different artists' groups began to struggle for public influence.

The end of czarism not only gave artists the freedom from censorship and institutional tutelage they had long desired— the dictatorial Imperial Academy of Arts was closed, though not yet dissolved for good, on February 23, 1917—but offered them an unrestricted opportunity to form independent unions. The topic most passionately debated among the groups that began to emerge in ever increasing numbers, especially in Petrograd and Moscow, was the freedom of art and the threat posed to it by proposed new government institutions. In the course of artists' debates and meetings, the front separating the "left" avant-garde and the "right wing" was soon clearly delineated. The rightist spectrum ranged from members of the Academy, Realists, and Impressionists to the influential representatives of Mir iskusstva (World of Art). As these groups struggled for public influence, the area of contention gradually shifted from artistic rivalries to politics, and the fight for "true art" degenerated into a quarrel for power that would rage on throughout the 1920s, often spurring on the creativity of the artistic factions yet sometimes paralyzing it.

On the initiative of Maksim Gor'kii, fifty leading artists, writers, actors, and musicians met in his Petrograd apartment on March 4, 1917, to establish a commission for the "conservation and regulation of our art institutions and treasures left unattended after the abolition of the Imperial Ministry." The most active subsection of this self-proclaimed Commission for Artistic Affairs—the Department for the Preservation of Monuments—was headed by Aleksandr Benua (Alexandre Benois), the traditionalist painter and influential art critic from the World of Art circle. With Benua and several other members of his group occupying leading positions, the Commission was firmly in the hands of conservatives. Other commissions for the "future development of art in Russia" were also dominated by World of Art.

At the Commission's March 4th meeting, Benua proposed the establishment of a Ministry of Fine Arts as an independent affiliate of the existing Ministry of Education. With the creation of such an institution, the artistic intelligentsia would have vested themselves with governmental powers to carry out their arrogated function as Russia's cultural standard-bearers. Three days later, on March 7th, during a meeting at the Petrograd Institute of Art History, Count Zubov put Benua in charge of a commission for the organization of the proposed ministry. The same day, the press announced the Provisional Government's approval of the planned ministry. Benua, Nikolai Rerikh, and Sergei Diaghilev were named as prospective candidates for the ministerial post.

The "Futurists," who regarded the planned ministry and, specifically, the hegemonic claims of the World of Art camp as a threat to their newly gained freedom from government regimentation, focused their criticism on Benua, who for years had been feuding with the Cubo-Futurists and the Suprematists.[3] But it was not only the "Futurists" who fought the ministerial aspirations of their old adversary. To prevent both the establishment of a ministry of fine arts under Benua and the official appointment of Gor'kii's commission for the preservation of monuments, representatives of numerous artists' groups met on March 9 and 10, 1917, at the Academy of Arts in Petrograd to form a Union of Art Workers encompassing all fields of art (painting, sculpture, architecture, literature, theater, and music). The Union's mission was to preserve the independence of art from the state and to put the functions assigned to the ministry in artists' hands.

There were 1403 artists in attendance at the Union's assembly on March 12th in the Mikhailovskii Theater. According to newspaper reports, the entire artistic community of Petrograd was present.

Even though the Union's goal was to combine groups of all artistic directions in one organization so as not only to defend its members' professional interests but to embark on the broadly based cultural renewal of Russia, it immediately broke up into opposing factions. Thus prevented from performing any practical, efficient work, the Union was finally dissolved in the summer of 1918. Among its three factions—the "right bloc," under the informal direction of the poet Fedor Sologub; the nonpartisan center; and the "left bloc"—the last was in the minority. Yet the relatively small left group, representing an equally small vanguard minority in Russian art, managed, as the result of its vigorous commitment, to get four of its own on the twelve-member organizing committee in charge of setting up the Union: the poet Vladimir Maiakovskii (as representative of the Moscow artists), the painter Natan Al'tman (as representative of the groups Bubnovyi valet [Jack of Diamonds] and Soiuz molodezhi [Union of Youth]), the art critic Nikolai Punin, and the director Vsevolod Meierkhol'd.

To strengthen their influence on the assembly, members of the left bloc published a declaration—against the planned ministry and for the freedom of art brought by the February Revolution—in the Menshevik daily Den' (The Day) and the Bolshevik Pravda on the day before the meeting: "The revolution creates freedom. Without freedom there is no art. Democratic art is possible only in a free democratic republic." The proclamation was signed by the Freedom for Art Federation, whose twenty-eight members included Al'tman, Kseniia Boguslavskaia, Lev Bruni, Vera Ermolaeva, Aleksei Grishchenko, Aleksei Karev, Nikolai Lapshin, Ivan Puni, Rodchenko, Eduard Spandikov, Tatlin, Nikolai Tyrsa, Nadezhda Udal'tsova, the critics Sergei Isakov and Punin, the writers Bol'shakov and Il'ia Zdanevich, Meierkhol'd, and the composer Artur Lur'e. Al'tman, Punin, and Zdanevich were the Federation's secretaries.

On the day of the assembly, the Federation published another declaration in The Day, this time protesting the "undemocratic attempts by certain groups to seize control of cultural life through the establishment of a Ministry of Fine Arts." The Federation appealed to all artists participating in the Union's constituent assembly to vote for the Federation's own twelve candidates for the organizing committee. This appeal came in response to the proposed nomination of only two left artists, Al'tman and Marc Chagall, to the committee, alongside a majority made up of Realists and representatives of World of Art.

While most speakers at the assembly demanded a strict separation between art and politics, the "Futurists" did not equate that separation with art's complete abstinence from social commitment. Their call for freedom was directed against administrative encroachment on artistic creation and institutional control over artists and students.

With the meeting of the Union of Art Workers adjourned, the left, following Meierkhol'd's suggestion, held its own meeting at the Trotskii Theater in Petrograd on March 21st. After speeches by Maiakovskii, Zdanevich, and numerous others, the art critic Denisov from the left bloc presented fourteen theses "On the Activities of the Freedom for Art Federation." (Denisov's theses were separately published under the title "The Democratization of Art: Theses on the Program for the [Fundamental] Union of Left Artists.") In order to promote their cause, the artists also took to the streets. The meeting at the Trotskii Theater was accompanied by marches with posters and banners. Musicians and speakers appeared in the streets, there were performances in stalls, and from the platform of a truck a pamphlet was distributed that summarized the essential demands of the Federation: "Freedom for art—abolition of government tutelage. Complete decentralization of cultural life and autonomy for all institutions and associations that will be funded by the municipal authorities. Establishment of an All-Russian Artists Congress. Abolition of all academies, which shall be replaced by art schools responsible for the training of art teachers. Replacement of patronage by public support through subsidies and grants."

The demand for the decentralization of art institutions and for the autonomy of artistic creation was endorsed by numerous intellectuals in the Union of Art Workers, among them Sergei Makovskii, the editor in chief of the art magazine Apollon (Apollo) who was affiliated with World of Art, as well as the right-wingers around Sologub and numerous other left-of-center artists and intellectuals. Yet though they concurred with the left on many points, these latter groups, who felt an obligation to preserve and maintain cultural treasures from the past, considered it impossible to cooperate with the avant-garde "vandals" of the Freedom for Art Federation. The bourgeois-democratic revolution had only just begun, and already deep rifts had opened among the intellectuals. The different factions could not find a common denominator that would have enabled them to take even the first practical steps toward organizing themselves.

Infighting among rival artistic movements and personal animosity such as that between the "Futurists" and Benua were as much an obstacle to the self-organization of the artistic intelligentsia as was the fundamental conflict between the champions of art's unconditional freedom from government institutions and the "collaborators" who wanted to entrust the state with the protection of monuments and artistic treasures and with the organization of artistic education.

The struggle between the proponents of a new ministry of fine arts and the "autonomists" was only marginally about participation in governmental power or iconoclastic destruction of traditional values—these were merely the slogans the hostile camps flung at each other during the Union of Art Workers' tumultuous sessions. What was really at stake was the identity of the artistic intelligentsia and their role in the new society that had emerged out of the confusion and chaos of the February Revolution. The older generation of artists, including the members of World of Art, held especially fast to their traditional self-image as the nation's "upholders of culture." Accordingly, they considered it their mission to preserve cultural values and to disseminate and anchor them by educating the people. These tasks, they believed, could be accomplished only if the artistic and scientific elite worked closely with the government apparatus. For their opponents from the left, this cooperation of tradition-conscious art specialists and government officials portended the reestablishment of a cultural bureaucracy that would organize artistic culture according to its own conservative tastes and manipulate the people by force-feeding them the obsolete values of an outdated conception of art.

With their sights set firmly forward, the "Futurists" regarded the passing on of traditional values as secondary, if not an outright obstacle to the establishment of new values. This stance was directly opposed to the "upholder of culture" ideal shared by a majority of Russian intellectuals but shattered and buried—with the eager assistance of the left avant-garde—in the fierce quarrels of the Union.

Many intellectuals and artists had placed their high hopes for a "cultural renewal of Russia" in the Union of Art Workers, but with the majority of members maneuvering to maintain their status as "upholders of culture" and to use the organization for their own goals, the Union reached an intellectual and operational deadlock. At a session on May 11, 1917, Osip Brik, the theorist and organizer of Opoiaz (the Society for the Study of Poetic Language) and later founder of the Productivist movement, denounced the Union (which did, after all, have over eight hundred nominal members from almost all artistic groups) for its failure to achieve practical results. Many of those in attendance agreed with him.

After the October Revolution
In the tumultuous months following the February Revolution, the Union of Art Workers debacle revealed that artists and intellectuals were lost in their attempt to determine their position in the new society. While attitudes toward tradition and the new government were markers of an obvious divide, they were merely symptoms of the intelligentsia's quandary without czarism as a unifying counterforce and of their insecurity concerning their function in a rapidly changing society.

With the radicalization of the masses in the summer of 1917, the crisis among artists and intellectuals intensified. They had to learn that the "people" embraced them neither as cultural saviors nor as anything else. In the months between the anti-czarist February Revolution and the anti-bourgeois October Revolution, a growing number of people unceremoniously classified artists and other intellectuals, regardless of their personal property or political stance, as members of the hated bourgeoisie. "Intellectual" and "bourgeois" became synonymous in the minds of the radicalized masses. Artists—and all the members of the intelligentsia—suddenly saw themselves denounced as enemies of the working class and ranked among the "superfluous persons" of the detested past. The break between the insurgent masses and the intelligentsia culminated in the October Revolution. The ousting of the Provisional Government and the Bolshevik takeover gave most intellectuals outside the radical leftist parties such a shock that they remained silent for several months or passively boycotted the new rulers.

Attempts by the People's Commissar of Enlightenment, Anatolii Lunacharskii, to establish contacts with the artistic intelligentsia were summarily turned down in the first weeks and months following the October Revolution. Only days after the proclamation of the Soviet state on October 25th, the revolutionary government (the All-Russian Central Executive Committee) extended a widely publicized invitation to

Petrograd artists, writers, and actors to come to the Smolnyi Institute, the new seat of government, to discuss prospective cooperation. A mere six persons showed up: Aleksandr Blok, L. Reisner, and David Shterenberg, as well as the most active members of the Freedom for Art Federation, Al'tman, Maiakovskii, and Meierkhol'd. After this failure, Lunacharskii on November 12th asked Punin, Al'tman's co-secretary in Freedom for Art, to mediate between the government and the Union of Art Workers. Via Punin, he proposed the establishment of a Department of Artistic Affairs in which artists and government officials would be equally represented. The proposal was debated in the organizing committee and in the different factions. While the right and moderate groups rejected any cooperation with the Bolsheviks on political grounds, the representatives of the left wing feared for the freedom of art. In a third attempt Lunacharskii sent Brik, another active participant in Freedom for Art and the left bloc, to suggest the formation of a thirty-member Commission for the Preservation of Monuments, to be made up of fifteen delegates from the Union and fifteen representatives of "democratic" organizations. Once again, the membership as well as the organizing committee of the Union categorically refused, even though the committee members Al'tman, Punin, Maiakovskii, and Meierkhol'd had previously not shied away from contact with the Soviet government.

The majority of speakers at the Union meeting objected to the "Bolsheviks' seizing control over art," while the organizing committee blamed the Soviet government for having tolerated and even promoted the destruction of artistic treasures. Lunacharskii himself had offered his resignation to the Party in mid-November, because monuments and works of art had been damaged during the storming of the Winter Palace and the battles in Moscow. The Council of People's Commissars did not accept his resignation and on November 17th, the day of his third offer to the Union, Lunacharskii published his appeal "Protect the Property of the People!"

That all factions of the Union should have rejected even limited cooperation is all the more astonishing in view of Benua's collaboration with the Soviet commissars, only one day after the storming of the Winter Palace, on a plan to protect the Palace and the Hermitage. And as early as November, the Petrograd Council of Workers' and Soldiers' Deputies organized a Council on Museum Affairs and the Preservation of Artistic and Historic Monuments under the direction of Georgii Iatmanov. Benua and other members of World of Art were among the Council's members.

With the establishment of this Council by the revolutionary government, the Commission for Artistic Affairs Gor'kii had formed in March 1917 and dissolved after protests from the Union on April 27th was essentially reinstated. Benua was even appointed director of the Hermitage and, with the help of the authorities, gained considerable influence over the reorganization of artistic life during the first years after the October Revolution. The Union's left faction as well as some right-wing members opposed to the earlier Commission now saw what they had feared come to pass under completely different political circumstances. While the bourgeois Provisional Government had hesitated to undermine the Union's autonomy by forcing an alliance with Gor'kii's Commission, the Bolshevik government acted against many Union members' call for self-determination and subscribed to the preservationist approach by appointing the Council on Museum Affairs.

Anticipating such a move, the members of the left bloc took swift action. At the Union's meeting on November 17th, where Lunacharskii's offer to establish a Commission for the Preservation of Monuments was discussed, they submitted a resolution calling for the autonomy of artistic creation and sharply criticizing the commissar's plans as an attack on the freedom of art, particularly avant-garde art:

Commissar Lunacharskii's appeal touches only vaguely on the government's attitude toward the autonomy of art; it asks the present left movement to surrender meekly to stale academicism and to the bureaucrats of art. With this appeal to the Union of Art Workers, Lunacharskii openly undermines the beginnings of the only correct and viable attempt to build our future artistic culture, as that culture is propagated by left tendencies in art, and hands over power to the backward and irresponsible "custodians" of art.

When shortly after this resolution the Council on Museum Affairs was established, several members of the left bloc reconsidered the Soviet government's earlier proposal to establish a Department of Artistic Affairs—so that they might gain at least some administrative clout against the academicians and "custodians." When on December 2, 1917, the Petrograd daily *Nash vek* (*Our Age*) reported Lunacharskii's renewed plans for the formation of a Department of Proletarian Art within Narkompros (the People's Commissariat of Enlightenment), the Union of Art Workers responded with protests. Once more, the Union stressed that only an independent organization of artists was competent to decide cultural issues. Nonetheless, Izo Narkompros (the Department of Fine Arts of Narkompros) was officially formed on January 29, 1918, with Shterenberg as its head. Izo Narkompros's Art Board, which was not organized until March, was also chaired by Shterenberg and included two secretaries of the Freedom for Art Federation, Al'tman and Punin. The other members of the board—Karev, Sergei Chekhonin, Aleksandr Matveev, Petr Vaulin, and Iatmanov—represented more or less traditional artistic tendencies.

It was not only the conservatives from the Union of Art Workers who cried out that art had been "betrayed." The left bloc as well took "no responsibility for the actions of the persons in question"—meaning Al'tman, Punin, and the other members of the Art Board.[4]

Accusations and disclaimers were a predictable response. What sense would it have made to defend the freedom of art from government control only to desist unceremoniously once the new regime was in place? The months-long struggle of the Freedom for Art Federation and the left bloc would have been pointless—even if many of the left artists, writers, and critics sympathized politically with the Soviet government.

Reservations about collaborating with government institutions of any kind were not limited to the Petrograd avant-garde. Seeking to extend the reach and effectiveness of the Petrograd Izo Narkompros, Al'tman, Punin, and Lur'e went to Moscow in early April to form an Art Board there. In an appeal worded in typical "Futurist" diction and published in the newspaper *Anarkhiia* (*Anarchy*) on April 9, 1918, they specifically called on "comrades Maiakovskii and Tatlin," their fellow members in the Union's left bloc, to cooperate with Izo Narkompros.

The left bloc had sent Tatlin to Moscow on April 12, 1917, as a representative of the Union. His mission was "to get in touch with the left Moscow artists and establish contact with their organization or [if none existed] organize a left bloc." In Moscow, he was elected chairman of the left federation of the Professional Union of Artists and Painters, which was formed in the summer of 1917 (Rodchenko was appointed secretary). As in the Petrograd Union of Art Workers, three factions emerged in the Moscow Professional Union, though this time each faction or federation had its own chairman and secretary from the outset. The right federation consisted of older

painters from the Wanderers movement, the center of members of World of Art, and the left, or young, federation of Cubo-Futurists, Suprematists, and other non-objective artists. Establishment of the Professional Union was accompanied by the first public recognition, from more established quarters, of the avant-garde. In late 1917 the club of the left federation mounted an exhibition of Rodchenko's works; the first comprehensive exhibition of the Professional Union opened in May 1918.

Immediately after the October Revolution, Tatlin, like many other members of the left bloc, left the Union of Art Workers in Petrograd. On November 21st, the Moscow Professional Union elected him its delegate to the Art Department of the Moscow Council of Workers' and Soldiers' Deputies. By his own description in later years, Tatlin thus became one of the first artists to cooperate with the Soviet government, and it was only natural that he was appointed chairman of the newly-formed Moscow Art Board in April 1918. Tatlin remained in that position until June 1919 and managed to secure the cooperation of important members of the avant-garde, including Sof'ia Dymshits-Tolstaia, Vasilii Kandinskii, Aleksei Morgunov, Kazimir Malevich, Rodchenko, Władysław Strzemiński, and Udal'tsova. Yet none of these artists spontaneously decided to join Izo Narkompros. It took most of them a long time to examine and clarify their own attitudes toward the government. The anti-institutional stance had not yet disappeared.

The Supreme Ego of the Anarchists

Tatlin, like many other avant-garde artists, was politically closer to the anarchists than to the Communist Bolsheviks. On March 29, 1918, he published an appeal in *Anarchy* urging "all my confederates . . . to enter the breach I made in obsolete values" so that their minds could "embark on the path of anarchism."

The artist wrote this appeal in response to a "Letter to Our Comrades, the Futurists" published four days previously in the same paper by a certain Plamen and calling on the "Futurists" to put their work in the service of the revolution. The "Letter" criticized the nonpolitical wing of the "Futurists" who were supposedly preoccupied with decorating cafés and designing furniture for the bourgeoisie. The writer was referring to the Café Pittoresque, whose "Futurist" interior had been decorated in the winter of 1917–18 by numerous artists including Aleksandr Drevin, Rodchenko, Tatlin, and Udal'tsova under the guidance of the painter and stage designer Georgii Iakulov.

The Café Pittoresque was a milestone on the way to Constructivism. For the first time, the materials and formal vocabulary of the new non-objective art were applied to and synthetically integrated in a public space. Tatlin, in his response to the "Letter," agrees with the anarchist critics that "the 'Futurists' are overly concerned with café society and assorted embroideries for emperors and court ladies" (the latter probably an allusion to Ol'ga Rozanova's Suprematist embroidery designs shown in December 1917 at the *Vtoraia vystavka dekorativnogo iskusstva* [*Second Exhibition of Decorative Art*] in Moscow).

Tatlin conceded, nonetheless, that there were at the time no other public outlets for artists committed to social change: "I am waiting for well-equipped artistic workshops where the artist's psychic machinery can be accordingly overhauled." With the creation of the State Free Art Workshops in October 1918, his wish became a reality—at least in part, since well-equipped these workshops were certainly not.

In his open letter, Plamen differentiated between the bourgeois wing of the "Futurists" and the revolutionary forces in their ranks, namely, Maiakovskii. At the time the poet, conceptualist, and brilliant mouthpiece of the avant-garde still strongly sympathized with anarchist ideas and groups. His attitude was representative of that of most "Futurists" in the first months after the October Revolution, when the political anarchists were still tolerated by the Bolsheviks and even received limited support from the party's left wing under Nikolai Bukharin. After initial contacts with the Bolsheviks, and in particular with Lunacharskii, Maiakovskii grew disenchanted with their traditionalist cultural program and left Petrograd, soon after the Revolution. He went to Moscow, where he and two old friends from Cubo-Futurist days—the painter David Burliuk and the poet Vasilii Kamenskii—opened the Kafe poetov (Poets' Café) in Nastas'inskii Lane. "I remember the Kafe poetov in Moscow in 1918," Il'ia Erenburg wrote in his memoirs. "It was patronized by a crowd that did not exactly deal in poetry—speculators, women of doubtful reputation, young people who called themselves 'Futurists' . . . It was quite a peculiar place."

The ideology of the Kafe poetov was suffused by antiauthoritarian anarchism. In accordance with the anarchist tilt in the name of the Freedom for Art Federation, the three artists of the café called themselves the Federation of Futurists. With his two comrades, Maiakovskii published the *Gazeta futuristov* (*Futurists' Newspaper*), in whose first and only issue on March 15th he declared, in an "Open Letter to the Workers," that "Futurism" was the aesthetic counterpart of "socialism/anarchism" and that only a "revolution of the psyche" could liberate workers from the shackles of obsolete art. The collective declaration "Decree No. 1 on the Democratization of Art" pronounced spontaneous graffiti the only legitimate revolutionary art:

1. In keeping with the liquidation of the czarist regime, the existence of art *in the depots and sheds of human genius—the palaces, galleries, salons, libraries, and theaters—is* abolished *as of now.*

2. In the name of progress and the equality of all before culture, the Free Word *of the creative personality shall be written on the walls, fences, roofs, and streets of our towns and cities; on the backs of automobiles, coaches, and trams; and on the clothes of all citizens.*

The Russian Futurists' painting of their bodies before the war, the graffiti on the walls of the Kafe poetov, the Futurist *parole in libertà*—whatever broke out into the streets and announced the creative freedom of everyone everywhere was proclaimed the Revolution's true artistic form of expression. Art, in Maiakovskii and his friends' minds, was supposed to be politically effective without submitting to the state. According to their credo, only free and spontaneous art could set off the "revolution of the psyche" considered essential to the social and intellectual continuation of the political and economic revolution.

The manifestos in the *Futurists' Newspaper* breathed the old anarchic spirit of the Freedom for Art Federation. Only, the combative tone had become sharper after the October Revolution. The "Manifesto of the Flying Federation of Futurists," published in the same paper, called on the "proletarians" to join the "third, bloodless but nonetheless cruel, revolution, the revolution of the psyche."

The political anarchists accepted the *Futurists' Newspaper* as an organ of anarchism[5] and endorsed the House of Free Art briefly operated by Maiakovskii, Burliuk, and Kamenskii as one of the anarchist clubs in Moscow. The House, a restaurant requisitioned for the purpose by the trio, was dedicated to the "individual anarchism of creation," as their paper put it. But the House of Free Art existed for only a few days and was closed by the end of March. On April 14th, the Kafe poetov was shut down as well. Two days before, the newly-founded

Cheka had carried out its first raid in Moscow: in the anarchist clubs some six hundred people had been arrested and forced to hand over their arms. Feliks Dzerzhinskii, the head of the Cheka, announced that the majority of those rounded up were criminals and only one percent were "ideological anarchists."[6] It is not clear whether the closing of the Kafe poetov was a direct consequence of this police action. The coincidence of events, however, signals the end of a distinctly anarchistic phase in both the political revolution and the history of Russian "Futurism" (even though the political anarchists were not quite neutralized until 1920).

The fundamental opposition between the Bolsheviks and the anarchists, who had broad support among the Russian peasants and workers, lay in their attitudes toward the state. The anarchists categorically rejected the state as the ruling classes' instrument of oppression. The Bolsheviks, by contrast, considered it necessary to maintain the state throughout the transition from capitalism to Communism, even though the bourgeois form of the state had to be "broken up" during the revolution. "We need a revolutionary *government*," Lenin wrote in March 1919 in his "Letter from Afar." "For a certain transitional period we need the *state*. That is what distinguishes us from the anarchists. The difference between revolutionary Marxists and anarchists is not only that the former believe in centralized, Communist production on a large scale and the latter in industrial scatteration. No, the difference vis-à-vis government, vis-à-vis the state, is that we are *for* exploiting the revolutionary forms of the state in the fight for socialism whereas they are *against* it."

Given Maiakovskii's anarchistic stance, it seems logical that he first rejected Al'tman, Punin, and Lur'e's offer to cooperate with the Moscow Art Board of Izo Narkompros. The federalism and "individual anarchism of creation" promoted by him, Burliuk, and Kamenskii and the state socialists' principle of centralism and large-scale production ruled each other out. Only after a long period of hesitancy and under changed political circumstances would he finally decide, in the winter of 1918, to join Brik and collaborate with Izo Narkompros. For the moment, he continued to advocate the separation of state and art as proclaimed by the Freedom for Art Federation and the *Futurists' Newspaper.*

Being closer to anarchism than to Bolshevism or Communism, other members of the Federation also continued to cling to this principle after the October Revolution. Morgunov, Rodchenko, and Tatlin at one time or another all worked in the Activist Group of the Moscow Association of Anarchist Groups. On April 2, 1918, *Anarchy* published the following salute to Rodchenko and others among the future Constructivists: "With pride we look upon your creative rebellion. We congratulate the creator Rozanova on her impressive compositions of lively colors. We congratulate the creator Udal'tsova on her savage non-objective oil paintings. We congratulate the creator Rodchenko on his spirited three-dimensional constructions of colored forms . . ."

The fiercest of all the blasts of anarchist fervor gusted from the articles Malevich regularly wrote for *Anarchy* from March to July 1918. Inspired by revolutionary events, the artist for the first time used the medium of writing to develop and expand his Suprematist conception of art into a conception of the world. The artistic principle of non-objectivity served him as a starting point for a nihilistic ontology which negated material reality as well as any form of state. In a tone of acerbic sarcasm, Malevich tackled the official art policy of the new ruling powers. He rebuffed Al'tman, Punin, and Lur'e on their visit to Moscow with a taunting polemic entitled "On the Arrival of Voltairean Terrorists from Petersburg."[7] While he did not consider them capable of deposing Benua, his objections were of a more fundamental nature: "The appointment of kings, ministers, or soldiers of art is just as much an act of artistic counterrevolution as the opening of a café of any kind," Malevich wrote with a view to the anarchist criticism of the Café Pittoresque. "Whenever a state is being built, a prison will be erected once the state is there." Therefore the revolution must "destroy all foundations of the old so that states will not rise from the ashes."

In keeping with the anarchist principle of individualism, Malevich declared "our ego" to be "supreme." In his argument, the supremacy of the ego can only be realized by liberating it from the shackles of the state and material objects. The revolution of the psyche through "individual anarchic creation" proclaimed by the *Futurists' Newspaper* was also on Malevich's mind when he promoted anarchism: "The banner of anarchism is the banner of our ego and like a free wind our spirit will billow our creative work through the vast spaces of our soul."[8]

Speaking for the Suprematist group—which at the time included Morgunov, Liubov' Popova, Rodchenko, Rozanova, Udal'tsova, and Aleksandr Vesnin as well as the anarchist radical Aleksei Gan—Malevich used Lenin's dictum of the "breaking up" of the state as an analogy for the withering away of material reality: "Our creative work elevates neither palaces nor hovels, neither velvet gowns nor coarse clothes, neither songs nor words . . . Like a new planet in the blue dome over the sunken sun, we are the frontier to an absolutely new world, and we declare all things nonexistent."[9] Consequently Malevich at that point rejected any practical application of Suprematism for the poor or for the rich. Involvement in a government institution such as Izo Narkompros was anathema to him for the same reason. A year after Al'tman and Punin's appeal, in 1919, Malevich was finally willing to ease his stance toward the state. By that time, the more cooperative "Futurists" in Izo Narkompros had already attained many of their goals. The Freedom for Art Federation's old demand for the abolition of the Imperial Academy of Fine Arts had been fulfilled on April 12, 1918. In October of the same year it was replaced by the State Free Art Workshops, established first in Moscow and Petrograd and later throughout the country. The workshops were free not only in terms of free access for all students, regardless of their prior education, but also because the student body was free to elect its own teachers. Malevich taught at the State Free Art Workshops in Moscow until the autumn of 1919, when he joined the Popular Art School in Vitebsk and began to organize Unovis (the Affirmers of the New Art).

The organization of State Exhibitions also lay in the jurisdiction of Izo Narkompros. Al'tman and the other vanguard artists in Izo Narkompros took full advantage of this to introduce their comrades-in-art to the broad public in numerous solo and group exhibitions, thus promoting the notion of their leading role. In addition, Izo Narkompros organized extensive open exhibitions sponsored by the state but, in the absence of a selection committee, virtually beyond its artistic arbitration. Following these principles of funding and selection, the organizers achieved their own earlier demands that art be free but at the same time subsidized by the state.

As early as December 1918, the members of Izo Narkompros began establishing museums of a new type, the so-called museums of artistic culture. Created all over the country, they were endowed with important avant-garde works. Among their most active organizers after 1919 were Kandinskii, Malevich, Rodchenko, and Tatlin. Under its avant-garde leadership, the Museum Department of Izo Narkompros succeeded in establishing thirty-six museums of contemporary art; another twenty-six were in the planning stage when the department was dissolved in 1921. As Rodchenko, the head of the Moscow Museum Department, remarked with some satisfaction, "the department generously supplied the provinces with contemporary art, an achievement unprecedented in the world and an advance over the West the commune can rightly be proud of."[10]

With the formation of Izo Narkompros and the continuous expansion of its staff through the involvement of almost all important avant-garde artists, a rather contradictory situation emerged that would last for a brief two and a half years and prove extremely fruitful for the development of the artistic avant-garde. Artists who were largely hostile to the state, ideologically indebted to anarchism, and committed to the spiritual and organizational freedom of artistic creation had found an institutional vehicle to introduce their art to the masses in art schools, exhibitions, and museums funded by the state. And yet, despite this favorable position, the new tendencies in art were unable to gain broader acceptance either among the public or within the Party and the administration. They were tolerated, however, if only for a short time.

Immediately after the February Revolution, spontaneously formed artists' groups such as Join the Revolution!—with Brik, Bruni, Ermolaeva, Mikhail Le-Dantiu, Lur'e, Maiakovskii, Meierkhol'd, Tatlin, Dymshits-Tolstaia, and Viktor Shklovskii as members—had signaled their willingness to write and design catchy, expressive posters, banners, and manifestos for the "comrades." Publishing appeals and their telephone numbers, the artists' groups offered their services. It is unknown whether the revolutionary political forces took them up on their offer.

After the October Revolution, Malevich won the competition for decorations for the Congress of Committees on Rural Poverty. He created a Suprematist cover design for the delegates' document folder (plate nos. 123–125) and decorated the assembly hall of the Winter Palace with Suprematist shapes. With Mikhail Matiushin, he painted a huge, 900-foot-wide canvas within twenty-four hours. He designed speaker's rostrums (plate no. 130) and, with El Lissitzky, curtains (plate no. 136) for the 1919 meeting in Vitebsk of the Committee to Abolish Unemployment. Lissitzky gave an account of his and Malevich's joint activities in his 1922 lecture on "New Russian Art": "In Vitebsk we painted a 16,000-square-foot canvas for a factory celebration, decorated three buildings, and created the stage decorations for the festive meeting of the factory committee in the city theater." It is safe to assume that neither the representatives of the rural poor nor the delegates of the unemployed were fully aware or appreciative of Malevich's intended color symbolism: the black square stood for the economy, the red square for the Revolution, and the white square for pure action—and together they symbolized the anarchistic "revolution of the psyche." It was Malevich's intention that not only Suprematist painting but also the "new style of Suprematist decoration" would "expel the integrity of the object from consciousness," as he put it in the catalogue of the Tenth State Exhibition, *Bespredmetnoe tvorchestvo i suprematizm* (*Non-Objective Creation and Suprematism,* Moscow, 1919). Suprematist murals and interior decorations were meant to testify to the fall of objective reality and the dawning of purely spiritual action. The delegates, however, probably perceived them as stimulating and lively decorative patterns.

The fight against the material monuments of the past was also at the heart of what was probably the most spectacular decoration of a public space in the years immediately following the October Revolution—Al'tman's huge panels for the Classical and Baroque façades and passages onto Palace Square in Petrograd (plate nos. 103–106) and his cladding of the Aleksandr Column on the same square. The bright red, yellow, and orange flames licking at the column as a symbol of the overthrow of the czarist regime drove home their message of the destruction of the old world in a far more direct and convincing fashion than the symbolically overcharged Suprematist decorations. A contemporary reviewer pointed out the artistic merits of Al'tman's design:

A nearly exemplary solution of this task was demonstrated on the square with the designs of the artist Al'tman. The juxtaposition of old and new artistic elements is surprising, convincing, and perfectly unified. The artist does not try to outdo the old masters but, with unerring instinct, creates something entirely new and contrasting. The square in front of the Winter Palace is strictly architectonic and Al'tman complements it with purely painterly impressions; the square is symmetrical and harmoniously self-contained—Al'tman aims at mordancy, surprising effects, and peculiarities; the square is beautifully rounded in space—everything about Al'tman's design is planar, angular, and dynamic.[11]

The revolutionary message of Al'tman's Cubo-Futurist construction is not expressed in its formal vocabulary and color symbolism alone, nor is it a mere illustration of a given slogan or idea. The spiritual flame of the Revolution and the appeal for renewal are brought to life only in their visual contrast to the stone monuments to Imperial traditions.

Al'tman's contextually anchored, incendiary work remained an exception among the Suprematist and other non-objective contributions to the revolutionary celebrations. Unlike the more traditionalist and politically conservative artists, the representatives of these vanguard movements took part only sporadically in the extensive programs for the festive decoration of public spaces initiated by the state. In one instance, Gustav Klutsis along with other young artists executed a design by Kliun for the first anniversary of the October Revolution, painting the branches of the bushes on Moscow's Teatral'naia Square and in the Aleksandr Garden along the Kremlin wall a bright blue and wrapping the trees in silvery gauze. In 1920, Il'ia Chashnik, Nikolai Suetin, and Lissitzky helped Malevich paint Suprematist designs on building decorations and curtains in Vitebsk. The same year, posters with Suprematist designs appeared in the streets of Smolensk; and in Kiev, Aleksandr Tyshler, Kozineva-Erenburg, Isaak Rabinovich, and Shifrin—all of them students of Aleksandra Ekster's—covered the sides of agitprop boats with Suprematist compositions. Yet the majority of the Suprematists and future Constructivists probably agreed with Lissitzky when, immediately after his extensive decoration work for the 1920 celebration of May 1st in Vitebsk, he wrote that the artist did not have to earn "authorization to work creatively . . . by painting the prescribed posters and implementing all the other orders"—even though this kind of work numbered among "his duties as a member of the commune."

If avant-garde artists participated in the design of posters, banners, or whole buildings, squares, and bridges, they obviously did so out of a sense of duty rather than inner conviction or desire—and extra rations of food or clothes were certainly a further incentive. On the other hand, their contributions seldom met with much enthusiasm on the part of their patrons in the administration and the Party. In these quarters, figurative representations found much more willing takers, with allegorical figures favored even over realistic ones. As early as 1919, the Moscow Soviet publicly objected to the participation of the "Futurists" in the decoration of the revolutionary celebrations. At the beginning of the same year, Rodchenko and Stepanova wrote their defiant "Manifesto of the Suprematists and Non-Objectivists" against the philistines on the left and on the right:

Emphatically we praise the Revolution as the only motor of life . . . You small-minded materialists—be off with you! We salute all you comrades who are fighting for the new ideas in art . . . We painted our furious canvases amid the jeers and laughter of the bureaucrats and petit bourgeois who have fled. Now we repeat to the so-called proletariat of former servants of the monarchy and intellectuals who have taken their place: We will not give in to you. In twenty years, the Soviet Republic will be proud of these paintings.

It would take several more decades before this prophecy came true. But their dominating position in Izo Narkompros allowed the Suprematists and non-objectivists to circumvent the apparatchiks for a time and to use the financial and organizational means of the state to mount several large-scale exhibitions of their art, to purchase it for the collections of their newly established museums of artistic culture, and to disseminate it over the entire country.

The Work of Art as a "Thing"—A Way out of the Crisis?

During the planning phase of the museums of artistic culture, the concept of the work of art as a *predmet* (object) or *veshch'* (thing) appeared for the first time. The introduction of this concept into the discussion about the form and function of art within the new social framework initiated a radical re-evaluation of the set of ideas traditionally defining "art." Out of this reorientation, Constructivism was born.

On November 24, 1918, Izo Narkompros organized a conference at the Palace of the Arts (as the Winter Palace had been renamed) in Petrograd. The meeting was to debate whether art was "A Temple or a Factory" and its list of speakers included Lunacharskii, Punin, Brik, and Maiakovskii. *Iskusstvo kommuny (Art of the Commune)* covered the event in its premiere issue. In his speech, Punin distinguished between the activity of the bourgeois artist, who merely designed ornaments and decorations, and the activity of the worker, who treated "material" to create "things." Punin expected a "new era in art" if the artists followed the lead of the workers and began to produce "things." He strongly objected to the decoration of the streets for the revolutionary celebrations, since art thus employed regressed to bourgeois embellishment instead of rising to the level of industrial production.

According to Punin, the goal of "an autonomous proletarian art . . . is not a matter of decoration but of the creation of new artistic objects. Art for the proletariat is not a sacred temple for lazy contemplation but work, a factory, producing artistic objects for everyone."[12] He was aware that this conception of the artistic creation as a "thing" introduced a new paradigm, which has claimed validity to the present day.

In his speech, Punin did not yet differentiate between the terms "object" and "thing." Familiar with Tatlin's work for years and inspired by his counter-reliefs, Punin in his plea for the object implicitly criticized Malevich, Tatlin's great adversary, for his promotion of *bespredmetnost'* (non-objectivity). It should be noted that the Russian word *predmet* means material entities in general, while *veshch'* denotes a thing produced by human hands. "Thing" in conventional Russian usage hence connotes an artistically made object.

By 1919 the critic had come to regard the non-objectivity of Suprematism as obsolete: the future of modern art was in Tatlin's "culture of materials." Although Punin, reporting in 1919 on a visit to Moscow, could write that "Suprematism has blossomed out in splendid colour . . . Posters, exhibitions, cafés—all is Suprematism,"[13] he maintained that at the peak of its success Suprematism had already lost its creative value. As art it was merely decorative, perfectly suited for the bourgeois function of embellishment "in textile designs, in cafés, in fashion drawings" and hence hopelessly mired in the past. Seeing Suprematism in such "flagrant opposition to form as the principle of the new artistic era," Punin praised Tatlin's culture of materials as "the only creative force free enough to lead art out of the trenches of the old positions." The day would come when no one but art teachers would find interest in Suprematism, while Tatlin's works would emerge as the sole legitimate "new form."

Others shared Punin's views. Right from the outset, *Art of the Commune* endorsed the concept of the artistic "thing" in its theoretical essays on art and aesthetics. This concept launched a sweeping transformation of the traditional notion of art as an expression of feelings, emotions, moods, or ideas. The magazine's first issue, on December 7, 1918, published on its front page Brik's programmatic article "Drenazh iskusstvu" ("A Drain for Art"). Siding with Punin, Brik defined artistic works as "things" and, by using the word *veshch'*, switched the critical focus from the non-objective art of Suprematism to all artistic efforts that visualized emotions or ideas instead of shaping material "things."

Brik's slogan at the time—"Not idealistic fog but the material thing!"—reflects demands which were in fact prevalent among workers and insurgents after the February Revolution. They expressed the disdain the revolutionary proletarians and peasants felt for the Russian intellectuals and artists. Erenburg's memoirs record the writer Aleksei Tolstoi's summary of the conversations during the summer of 1917: "Will we go to the dogs or won't we? Will Russia be or will it not be? Will they slaughter the intellectuals or will they leave us alive?"

Devastated by war and food shortages, the hungry masses denounced intellectuals and artists as "parasites" who had no right to exist because they produced no material values but only ideas—and therefore did not work at all. As early as June 1917, the intellectual leader of the right bloc within the Union of Art Workers, Sologub, countered these attacks with the argument that the Russian intelligentsia belonged neither to the bourgeoisie nor the proletariat but constituted a third class of its own. Artists and intellectuals produced no material values as did the proletariat, yet unlike the bourgeoisie they did not create "merchandise [*tovar*] but ideas and forms."[14] The prevailing anti-intellectualism increased in the months following the October Revolution. As the situation worsened because of hunger and cold, the verbal attacks escalated into physical assaults. In the winter of 1917, the few liberal publications that still existed reported a regular "crusade" against the intelligentsia, a great majority of whom considered themselves on the side of the people in the fight against czarism. The standard question Russian artists and intellectuals had asked themselves since the nineteenth century—"What is the intelligentsia?"—underwent a dramatic revision as the intelligentsia's very right to exist was cast into doubt. The writers of *Art of the Commune* provided a pragmatic answer: they argued that in the new state artists had a right to exist only if they became specialists in the production of certain "things" and thereby voided the accusation of being parasitic fabricators of immaterial goods.

While Brik and Punin introduced the concept of the "thing" into the discussion of the future of art, the notion had figured first in the debates about the further existence or nonexistence of the intelligentsia. On March 31, 1918, Russian writers organized a large conference in Petrograd that focused on "The Tragedy of the Intelligentsia." Picking up Sologub's distinction between the proletarian "producers of things" and the intellectual "producers of ideas," the speakers agreed that the prerevolutionary intelligentsia had made a fatal mistake by concentrating on the social and educational sector and

neglecting the technological and industrial field. The idealization of the "people" and the desire to serve them had caused the intellectuals' uselessness in all practical matters and brought about their present "tragedy."[15] As in the Union of Art Workers after the February Revolution, so now there were demands for autonomous professional organizations and greater public recognition of the value of intellectual and artistic work. In return for their autonomy, the artists and intellectuals were called upon to show greater *professionalism* in dealing with their specific material. Instead of their genuine but often idealistic or romanticizing commitment to the people, an increased discipline in their actual professional work was required.

These arguments essentially reiterated the critique of the populist but often dilettantish intellectuals of the old type and the demand—put forth as early as 1909 in a volume of essays entitled *Vekhi (Guideposts)*—for a new, technically qualified intelligentsia. Fiercely debated when it was published, the book attacked the separate course the Russian intelligentsia had taken. Proceeding from an astute analysis and a polemical indictment of their hallowed principles, the authors demanded that Russians follow the example of the scientific, technological, and artistic intelligentsia of the West and adopt their "objective values," specialized knowledge, and professional institutions. "The average intellectual in Russia neither likes nor understands his job," Aleksandr Itsgoev wrote in *Guideposts*. "He considers his profession something accidental and insignificant that does not deserve great respect. If he loves his profession and invests all his energy in it, he can expect some contemptuous sarcasm from his comrades, be they genuine revolutionaries or just worthless phrasemongers. But real influence on the populace, a great specific weight in today's life, can only be reached with sound and solid expertise."

Ten years later, the situation of intellectuals and artists had not changed much. Significantly, it was the fledgling proletarian intelligentsia that provided the first catalyst for a reorientation. By 1918, Gor'kii would write in the journal *Novaia zhizn' (New Life)*:

> The cultural vanguard among the working class is beginning to see how important it is for workers to acquire scientific and technical knowledge . . . This appreciation of knowledge and work is new in Russia; it becomes apparent in the facts workers and union members cited in their memoranda urging the establishment of institutes for several industries including the ceramics, glass, and porcelain industries. It is quite characteristic that it was the workers who pointed out the necessity to quickly develop the handicrafts industry.[16]

The Constructivist theory of "production art" reacted to these stimuli from the proletarian intelligentsia by trying to synthesize artistic creation and crafts on a higher, i.e., industrial, level of productivity. For the implementation of this synthesis, artists and craftsmen alike had to rely on the scientific and technological advancement of their methods, tools, and materials.

To early Productivist theorists such as Brik, Boris Kushner, and Punin, this "reification" of works of art seemed to be the only rescue for art and artists. The strategies they developed to redefine the function of artists after the October Revolution undoubtedly laid the foundations for Constructivism. Yet it took another two years before the new concept of art sketched out in *Art of the Commune* and the developments within avant-garde art began to mesh. When in December 1921 the artists at Inkhuk approved Brik's proposal to end artistic experimentation and take up industrial production, it was the result of a long and complicated process of rapprochement between theoretical concepts and non-objective art. Even if neither side could claim leadership in this mutual process, the artists' permanent self-examination and the extreme intellectualization of their creative work between 1918 and 1921 point toward the dominance of theorizing in the formation of Constructivism.

"Professionalism," a word chosen no doubt in deference to the technical specialists of the West, became a key term in the budding Constructivists' efforts to redefine the role and function of artists and thereby to overcome their existential crisis. In texts written between 1918 and 1921, first Brik and Kushner and then Rodchenko, Stepanova, Gan, Arvatov, the Stenberg brothers, Medunetskii, and Karl Ioganson persistently stressed the necessity of abolishing artistic instinct in favor of a professional approach—based on appropriate methods of technical manufacture and construction—to the artistic materials of color and form. On the other hand, Tatlin as well as Malevich, Lissitzky, and the members of Unovis categorically rejected this rationalization of the creative process and defended the importance of intuition in the choice and treatment of materials. It was this disagreement about the role of intuition that accounted for the artists' differing attitudes toward technology. Neither Tatlin nor Unovis was generally opposed to the artistic use of technological tools and materials. But unlike the Constructivists at Inkhuk, they rejected the mechanization of creative methods and the reduction of the creative process to rational operations.

The rationalization of the creative process and its subjection to instrumentalist principles were the result of discussions held at Inkhuk between January and April 1921. The discussions dealt with the artistic relationship between composition and construction, the one being defined as unconscious intuition, the other as deliberate methodical calculation during the shaping of an aesthetic product. Before 1921, such methodological and technological terms and ideas had played a minor role, if any. Before the First Working Group of Constructivists of Inkhuk was formed in March 1921, and before the artists around Rodchenko began their close cooperation with the theorist Gan, artistic intuition was appreciated rather than denounced, and if technical issues were discussed, they were issues of painting technique. There is a difference between art historians like Punin or linguists like Brik or Shklovskii analyzing the materials and methods by which a given work of art is made, and artists and theorists translating this analytical approach of the Formalist school into practical instructions for the methodical construction of new works or "objects." For better or for worse, the scientific character and rationality of methods for analyzing art were transformed into rationalist, scientific methods of constructing art. Inkhuk, an association of Formalist academics, cultural theorists, and artists, was ideally suited for plotting this new course, which turned analytical methods into production methods and expanded them into a sociological theory of the artist's role in society.

While the theorists provided the language of Constructivism as early as 1918, Constructivism itself did not emerge until 1921, with artists tentatively probing what was for them uncharted ground. If Rodchenko in his programmatic essay "Liniia ("The Line," 1921) described the development from the figurative "picture" to the *faktura*-determined "objects" of color painting to the colorless, non-*faktura* line construction as a logical and conscious progression, it was due more to the artist's rationalizing hindsight than to the actual process of decision making during that dramatic period. His teleological reconstruction is, however, understandable when one recalls that the essay was commissioned by the Inkhuk director, Brik, and was meant to demonstrate the evolution that led to Constructivism and its creation of "objects."

In what was essentially an account of his own development over the previous three years, Rodchenko concluded that the treatment of paint as an autonomous expressive medium had led to a "painterliness":

The painterly approach was created, and the picture ceased to exist as such, becoming either a painting or an object . . .

Thus an element that appears arbitrary rose to lasting preeminence because it was the very essence of painting, it was professionalism in painting.[17]

Professional creation in this sense means the conscious, rationally calculated production of nonsymbolic objects, not the intuitive composition of paintings. By 1921, the time for "arbitrary" discoveries of new materials, methods, or techniques was apparently over. Intuition had been replaced by precise methods of construction and experimentally planned invention.

The *Art of the Commune* writers—particularly Brik, Punin, and Kushner—added a sociological element to these arguments for professionalizing artistic creation. Unlike the old intelligentsia, who had emphasized artists' political, moral, and pedagogical commitment to the uneducated and disenfranchised peasants and workers, the new theorists stressed artists' professional and technical skills, which were needed in the proletarian society—their practical expertise, which essentially put them on one level with the workers.

Brik coined the term "artist-proletarian" to express this new conception of the artist's role. It is interesting to compare Brik's texts with the notes Rodchenko made in April 1918, probably as an outline for an appeal of the left federation of the Professional Union of Artists and Painters. His manifesto "To the Artist-Proletarians" describes the avant-garde artist as a "proletarian of the paintbrush" and an oppressed "creator-martyr": "We, who are in a worse situation than the oppressed workers, are workers for our livelihood as well as creators of art. We, who live in holes, have neither paint nor light nor time for creating. Proletarians of the paintbrush, we must unite, must establish a Free Association of Oppressed Artists, must demand bread and studios and our existential rights."

In contrast to this view of the artist as a subproletarian who is joined with the revolutionary proletariat in poverty but not in his professional work, Brik's definition of the "artist-proletarian," formulated six months later, presents the artist in his positive future incarnation. In the interval between these two definitions, the anarchist phase of the Revolution ended, Lenin declared the dictatorship of the proletariat, and the Bolshevik Party took total control of the state.

These political changes were reflected in the shifting meaning of the term "artist-proletarian." Writing in 1918, Brik asks who will create the "art of the future" or "proletarian art."[18] He rejects the slogan "art for the proletariat" as well as the Proletkul't (Proletarian Culture) motto "art by the proletariat." The first slogan, Brik believes, is still mired in the old "consumerist thinking" since it simply replaces the bourgeois private patron with a proletarian "mass patron," without changing the role of the artist as merely a talented entertainer. Brik also denounces the Proletkul't idea that proletarian art can only be created by proletarians, illustrating his point with a reference to the Proletkul't studios where this approach has generated "not proletarian works but untalented parodies of outworn art forms of the past." He concludes: "proletarian art is neither 'art for the proletariat' nor 'art by the proletariat'. It is art by artist-proletarians. They and they alone will create the art of the future."

But what distinguishes the "artist-proletarian" from the bourgeois artist? Brik names two essential criteria. While the bourgeois artist considers creation "his own private affair" and produces works of art "to enhance his ego," the proletarian artist creates in order to fulfill "a socially important task" within the "collective." While the bourgeois artist seeks to please the masses, the proletarian artist "fights against their stubbornness and leads them in directions that will steadfastly advance art." Instead of repeating "stereotypes of the past," the artist-proletarian produces "ever new things" like an inventor in a field all his own.

In another article, Brik elaborates on several points of his concept of the proletarian artist.[19] First he gives an in-depth criticism of Proletkul't. The "confusion of the the terms 'workers' culture' and 'proletarian culture'" has led Proletkul't to adopt "long-outdated forms of petit-bourgeois Romanticism with its cheap heroism and vulgar folkishness." The "artist-proletarian," by contrast, will not express the will of the proletariat the way the bourgeois artist used to express his own ego but fulfill the tasks set by society with a high degree of professionalism, because: "You can't 'express' the will of other people, you can only 'execute' it." For all practical purposes that means expressive art, be it collective or subjective, has to give way to the functional execution of the "social task" in the appropriate medium. In addition, Brik stresses that "organization" is an "essential element of the proletarian movement" and must therefore also determine the work of the "artist-proletarian." (Brik's demand for artistic "organization" and his closing sentence—"We . . . demand the unconditional implementation of the dictatorship of the proletariat in all fields of cultural development"—read like an echo of Lenin's April 1918 article, "The Immediate Tasks of the Soviet Government," which called for "'harmonious organization' and dictatorship.") [20]

The term "artist-proletarian" underwent several metamorphoses over the next few years. During the formative phase of Constructivism, around 1921, it became "artist-constructor," and in 1922, when the Constructivists shifted from "pure" constructions to the production of utilitarian objects, they settled on "artist-engineer." Whatever the exact expression, the concept behind it is that originally defined by Brik. It can be summarized as follows:

• Professionalism instead of dilettantism
• Material and professional execution of socially important tasks instead of symbolic expression of the subjective ego or the collective will of the proletarian masses
• Production of ever new forms to fight against the taste stereotypes of the unenlightened masses
• Methodical organization of artistic creation

Elaborated during the first year after the October Revolution as a defense of artistic production, these criteria remained valid Constructivist guidelines throughout the 1920s. Yet although they proved fruitful in the beginning, they carried the seeds of their own destruction. The basic contradiction between artistic autonomy through professionalism, innovation, and the rejection of expressive art, on the one hand, and the employment of art as an instrument for implementing social tasks and organizing life, on the other, could be an open and productive one only as long as its dialectic balance was not upset by external political forces. By 1930 at the latest, the scale had tipped.

Brik's line of reasoning managed to combine the Formalist school's demand for the autonomy of artistic creation, the anti-intellectualism of the masses, and the Communist Party's demand for the dictatorship of the proletariat—albeit in a precarious and unstable synthesis.

Throughout the 1920s, the theoretical unity of the two

contradictory propositions had to be constantly restored by word and action. The numerous manifestos and programs formulated by the Constructivists during this period as well as the formation of groups such as Komfut (the Communists-Futurists), Lef (the Left Front of the Arts), Novyi Lef (New Lef), or October testify to the attempt to resolve or at least to bridge the intrinsic conflict.

Even if the balance among artistic autonomy, functional design, and Party discipline was frequently threatened in these years, it broke down only after 1930, when autonomy was subordinated to function and function was defined by the Party.

The Museum of Painterly Culture—A Museum of Objects

In the discussion about establishing new museums of artistic culture, the categories "object," "professionalism" of artistic creation, and "perfection" were developed and defined in the sense of an evolution of material treatment and introduced to a wider circle of artists. The original plan for the museums was formulated and proposed in July 1918 by Tatlin. His proposal still breathed the spirit of the Freedom for Art Federation, emphasizing the artists' autonomy in organizing the museums and selecting their collections. The museums were supposed to be institutions of "art and education for the masses." Tatlin described Izo Narkompros as "the only forum competent to . . . create a museum of contemporary, living art" and assigned it the task of independently compiling a list of artists who would be represented in the museums. The selected artists would then determine which of their works should go to the museums.

Malevich commented on the artistic policy for the planned museums in *Art of the Commune*.[21] In his usual anarchistic, "Futurist" tone, he sounded off against tradition and convention, demanding that only the most recent art be exhibited. Sharply attacking Benua and his Council on Museum Affairs, Malevich called on all the "living" to "break off their friendship" with the "conservatives" and be "as ruthless as life itself," since that was the only way "creative life" could grow.

Malevich envisioned the museum as a working research laboratory for artists rather than an exhibition space for passive viewing pleasure: "Instead of collecting all kinds of old trash, it is necessary to create laboratories for a global creative-development machine whose arbors will not turn out dead representations of objects but artists of living forms . . . We will produce I-beams, the electricity and light of colors."

Izo Narkompros's Declaration on Principles of Museum Administration was approved by the Art Board on February 7, 1919. It stressed the expertise of artists and the autonomy of the planned institution, stating: "Artists, as those solely competent in matters of contemporary art and as the forces who create artistic values, alone may oversee acquisitions of contemporary art and guide the artistic education of the country."[22] The declaration ended with an appeal to renew art by professionalizing it: "Artists! Unite in the fight for your professional culture of the future and against the oppressive fetishism of the past." And at the museum conference convened in Petrograd on February 11, 1919, the concept of artistic culture was endorsed. The conference speakers included Punin and Brik (who in "A Drain for Art" had already proclaimed the museum an exhibition and testing site of real "things.")

Punin and Brik's concept of art as "professional culture" for the creation of "real things" did not show its full impact until Rodchenko began endorsing it. As we learn from Stepanova's diary, on March 27, 1919, Brik met with Rodchenko, then the secretary of the left federation of the Professional Union of

Artists and Painters, to discuss the future cooperation of Izo Narkompros and the Professional Union in creating the museums of artistic culture. It was, apparently, the first encounter between the theorist of "production art" and the much younger artist, who one month later would make his spectacular debut at the Tenth State Exhibition and soon after that emerge as the ideological leader of the Moscow avant-garde artists. During their first meeting, Brik asked Rodchenko to present the left federation's ideas to Izo Narkompros in order to clarify the terms for a joint organization of the new museums.

Rodchenko, whose thoughts were written down by Stepanova after Brik's visit, posited a fundamental difference between Russian and Western painting and wanted the new museum to emphasize the independence and peculiarities of Russian painting. According to Rodchenko, Western painting is synthetic, whereas Russian painting, with its origin in the icon, is "decorative and analytical." In icons as well as signboards and the boldly colored *lubok* (illustrated broadside) and, finally, Suprematist and non-objective paintings, the surface plane is an autonomous expressive element: "This great decorative color-resplendent element is the prime mover of Russian painting, which we do not value, do not know."[23] Rodchenko suggested a selection and arrangement of works for the new museum that would present the autonomous evolution of Russian painting—culminating, of course, in the avant-garde.

Rodchenko was probably the first to propose an evolutionary display of art museum exhibits, an idea that was picked up in the 1920s in Western Europe and America and has since determined the way works are selected and arranged in museums of contemporary art all over the world. The notion of a logical development still informs our image of the history of modern art, even if it has long been recognized as an artificial, streamlined reconstruction of the true historical course of events—a myth created by the avant-garde to legitimize its own claim of being the ultimate destination of art history.

Yet the more radical aspects of Rodchenko's program never really caught on. In contrast to the principles of selection and arrangement that have since become common, his plan rejected the separation between "high" and "low" art and called for non-chronological juxtapositions. Quite contrary to the hierarchic classification of art that had been introduced in West European museums around 1900 and became standard policy in the 1920s, Rodchenko had no intention of banishing "inferior" art from the museum in order to elevate the tastes of the visitors. His plan put icons next to coarsely and brightly painted tin signboards, and mass-produced broadsides next to the Cubist or Suprematist works of professional painters. Rodchenko's selection criteria reflected not the stylistic standards of ostensibly objective art historians but a painter's professional interest in the employment and treatment of his material in the history of painting. In this context, considerations of genre or medium were as irrelevant as moral valuations of "high" and "low."

Faktura—The Tangible Things

The name chosen for the new museum in Moscow—the Museum of Painterly Culture—indicates its founders' conceptual position. They conceived of pictures as products of a cultural activity, painting, which in turn was considered a specialized method of treating paint. While outlining his views on the museum, Rodchenko was also preparing the Tenth State Exhibition, which opened on April 27, 1919—the first group exhibition in history dedicated exclusively to non-objective art. In this momentous exhibition, Malevich showed his metaphysical white-on-white paintings for the first time.

Rodchenko, on the other hand, exhibited a series of black-on-black paintings (for example, plate nos. 237, 240). Amazement and admiration among his fellow artists ran high. A few days before the opening of the show, Stepanova wrote in her diary:

His black paintings are actually the rage of the season. With these works, he has shown what faktura *is . . . No one else has achieved such variety and depth.*

The absorption of painting in itself as a professional element. A new, interesting faktura, *and exclusively painting, i.e., no 'coloring' but employment of the most unyielding color, black . . . In the 'black' works nothing besides painting exists. That is why their* faktura *is so immensely enhanced . . . Those shining, matte, muddy, uneven, and smooth parts of the surface result in an extraordinarily powerful composition. They are so effectively painted that they are in no way inferior to colors.*

In the black paintings, paint has ceased to figure as color or value; it is solely the treatment of its material substance that counts. Consequently, the finished work represents nothing and expresses nothing. Its artistic value springs solely from the variety of its surface effects and its very novelty. The concept of professionalism is precisely defined in these paintings: professional work means "absorption of painting in itself," i.e., in its specific material and methods—paint and the treatment of paint with the objective of making its physical qualities visible and palpable. The result is a richly diverse surface—a fascinating "object" without any depth of meaning or emotion.

The black *faktura* paintings were a smashing success with the Moscow artists. On April 29, 1919, two days after the exhibition opened, Stepanova wrote in her diary: "Anti [Rodchenko] has scored an amazing success . . . He has stunned everyone with his masterly skills, his *faktura,* and people see him in a completely different light now." In the wake of this success, Rodchenko became the leading figure among the Moscow avant-garde innovators, the chief Constructivist, and the quintessential production artist.

But not only painters embraced Rodchenko's black canvases as a seminal innovation. The works also stirred the interest of Brik. The opening of the Tenth State Exhibition initiated a close interaction between artistic practice and aesthetic theory which helped determine the further development from *faktura* painting to Constructivism and from the Constructivist laboratory experiments to Productivist art and factographic photomontage and photography. In Rodchenko, Brik apparently found the incarnation of his artist-proletarian who professionally produced objects instead of ideas. Stepanova, in any event, noted that at the exhibition Brik was "completely taken with Anti." Rather reserved during his visit with Rodchenko one month earlier, the magisterial Brik was now "quite jovial and said that because of Rodchenko, Malevich was finally passé . . . The black paintings simply astonished him."

What was it that astonished the theorist so much? Despite his limited oeuvre, Brik was valued as a crucial innovative force among the Formalist linguists as well as the Constructivists. The Russian concept of *faktura* had been introduced into aesthetic discourse as early as 1912 by David Burliuk and Vladimir Markov (Waldemars Matvejs) and had since become one of the most important categories in the "Futurist" theories of art and literature. From the beginning, *faktura* had denoted the visible and palpable result of the physical treatment of material. *Faktura,* as the critical element in the progress of art and the professionalization of the artist, was a recurring leitmotif in the manifestos and statements of Russian artists before 1920. In 1919, when Rodchenko was painting his black canvases, *faktura* once again became the center of attention, while Suprematism, with it temporarily predominant its anti-*faktura* agenda, had been losing some ground since 1915. "*Faktura* is the essence of the painterly surface," Popova wrote in her statement for the catalogue of the Tenth State Exhibition.

The linguists of the Formalist school, too, made *faktura* the dominant artistic standard. In his 1919 "Futurizm" ("Futurism"), Roman Jakobson defined works of art as objects that were autonomous through their *faktura*: "A clearly perceptible *faktura* needs no further justification; it becomes autonomous and requires new methods of design and new materials; the picture is pasted over with paper or sprinkled with sand. Finally, the use of cardboard, wood, sheet metal, etc., has become common."[24] Concurring with the artists and his fellow Opoiaz members, Shklovskii defined *faktura* as the essential characteristic of art in general in his article "O fakture i kontr-rel'efakh" ("On *Faktura* and Counter-Reliefs"): "*Faktura* is the main distinguishing feature of the particular world of specially constructed things which in their entirety we call art . . . The work of the artist-poet and the artist-painter ultimately aims at creating a permanent object that is tangible in all its details, a *faktura* object."[25] Shklovskii cites Tatlin's and Al'tman's material compositions as the most convincing examples of his definition of art. Suprematism, on the other hand, belongs to the "Symbolist school of painting" and is "essentially 'ideal' painting" since it strives to symbolize ideas through colors and abstract shapes instead of emphasizing the properties of the material and thereby differentiating and intensifying the tangible values of *faktura*.

The non-objective artists including Rodchenko and Stepanova shared this negative attitude toward the ideal, even metaphysical, symbolism of the Suprematists and especially of Malevich. After the opening of the Tenth State Exhibition, Stepanova wrote in her diary on April 29, 1919: "The only compromise admitted there is Suprematism. It would have been better to exclude it and exhibit only non-objective art." Rodchenko sang the same tune in his statement in the exhibition catalogue, where he compared his invention of colorless, black *faktura* with Columbus's discovery of the New World while belittling Malevich as the philosopher of an *ism:* "The death knell has sounded for color painting and now the last *ism* is being laid to eternal rest . . ."[26]

At that point, Shklovskii had not seen Rodchenko's black *faktura* paintings but his definition perfectly applies to their uncompromising gesture. In their radical concentration on *faktura,* their total exclusion of all other painterly values such as color, light, volume, and space, and their reduction of form to the edge of perceptibility, these paintings suddenly revealed the power of negation. The increasing concern with *faktura* as a design element in Russian avant-garde painting since 1912 assumed a completely new quality after Rodchenko's black paintings had demonstrated the practical and aesthetic consequences of the *faktura* concept: The picture lost its symbolic character; it became an object.

This sharp distinction between the artistic object and the symbolic picture led many contemporaries, as well as present-day scholars such as Rainer Grübel or Benjamin Buchloh, to the assumption that the *faktura* object was completely devoid of any outside references. Such interpretations see the reified work stripped of all meaning that transcends the self-referentiality of an index sign pointing to the qualities of its own material and making. It is true that some of Rodchenko's own statements suggest a reduction of his *faktura* paintings to the function of a self-referential sign. After all, he occasionally describes them as signs of his choice of materials, i.e., black paint, and as traces of his painting technique. But this disregard for all further references has a deliberate polemical edge to it. In the historical context of their creation, the meaning of the *faktura* objects was constituted by their very negation of all the emotional expressive qualities and ideal references that had bogged down the painting of the previous decades and distracted it from its essential nature.

This negation of tradition was, however, precisely defined. Traditional values were not simply rejected. They were replaced by new products which introduced new, not yet conventionalized codes of perception. In the catalogue of the Tenth State Exhibition, Rodchenko assembled—under the heading "Rodchenko's System"—quotations that expounded upon his black paintings. With statements like "That I destroy myself only shows that I exist" (Max Stirner) or "What invigorates life invigorates death" (Walt Whitman) he tried to prove that the rebirth of life relied on death as its necessary prerequisite. In this sense, the literary quotations are metaphors of the black *faktura* objects. Standing on the border between the old, dead art and a new, living art, the real things deal the pictorial illusions the deathblow.

Rodchenko's choice of anarchist writers like Max Stirner was not an accident. There are numerous indications that Rodchenko, nicknamed "Anti" by his friends, conceived of the black paintings as an explicitly anarchist answer to the ruling art. Since Courbet, artists have time and again used the color black to express anarchistic views, even if their works did not explicitly refer to the intended symbolic content. We have already mentioned Rodchenko's active involvement in the Moscow Association of Anarchist Groups. In the April 28, 1918, issue of *Anarchy,* he published his first theoretical text, a brief analysis of his experiments with shapes and colors entitled "The Dynamism of the Plane." In this article as well as in "Everything Is Experiment," he repeatedly used the term "expressive means," although without specifying what a painting "absorbed in itself" (in Stepanova's words) was supposed to express.

There is an astoundingly symbolic self-portrait of Rodchenko, painted in 1920 during the most radical phase of the liberation of his painting from all references. An egg-shaped, bald head rises from a turtleneck sweater. A hexagonal rhombus, overlaid by a large deep-black disc, covers half the wide-open eyes and the entire forehead. Is this strangely stigmatized face an affirmation of the color black as a symbol of anarchism or rather an affirmation of anarchistic individualism as propagated in "Rodchenko's System"? In this case the black paintings could be read as an "expression" of this affirmation. In a review of the Tenth State Exhibition, Lissitzky called Rodchenko an "individualist" who had started "the shift to the new materiality" with his black paintings.[27]

Such an interpretation of the *faktura* paintings leads one to wonder how Rodchenko and the future Constructivists could have abandoned this individualist, anarchistic attitude toward art and life in favor of the collectivist ideology of Constructivism, which negated not only the individual but also the role of intuition in the creative act, feeling, *faktura,* and material. In their stead, Constructivism postulated the system of forms, the nonmaterial line, the logically planned structure, the rational creative method, and the calculated effect.

In "The Line," Rodchenko described the artistic course he had taken after 1918 as a logical sequence of problems in the treatment of paint, and solutions through the invention of new painting techniques. The artist saw these "inventions of new discoveries" as an evolution taking place strictly within art, a kind of expedition into painting's uncharted territories which had previously been barred by tasks alien to art. What he did not mention was the possibility of art's evolutionary course being motivated, much less determined by, external societal tasks as Brik had outlined them in *Art of the Commune.*

It took a number of developmental factors, both within and outside art, to move the Moscow Constructivists grouped around Rodchenko along the way that led from individually composed *faktura* works to useful Constructivist "objects." It should be emphasized that I regard this development as only *one* possible way among "several theoretically conceivable evolutionary courses" pointed out by Iurii Tynianov and Jakobson in the journal *Lef* (*Left Front of the Arts*) in 1928.[28] The transition from the black *faktura* studies to functionally planned constructions cannot be sufficiently explained by certain "immanent laws" in the evolution of artistic materials and methods, even though the Constructivists liked to give their own genesis this stamp of finality. Nor can the historical circumstances provide a comprehensive answer. Only by "analyzing the correlation between the [artistic] sequence and other historical sequences" can the "question of the concrete choice of course" be clarified. This approach, propounded by Jakobson and Tynianov for art in general, should specifically be applied to the development of Russian Constructivism.

The Universe of the Line

Critical decisions on the road to Constructivism were made between the Tenth State Exhibition in April 1919, where Rodchenko first showed his black paintings, and the opening of the Nineteenth State Exhibition on October 2, 1920, to which he contributed fifty-seven works, most of them from his most recent, Linearist phase. With the introduction of the autonomous line as a new element in painting, Rodchenko took a crucial step toward Constructivism, replacing paint with the line as the essence of painting. Probably inspired by Kandinskii's article "O linii" ("On the Line," 1919),[29] Rodchenko began to explore the qualities of the line in several dozen non-objective pencil drawings (some made using a ruler, some not) in April and March 1919. In August, only a few months after the *faktura* paintings, he executed ten purely linear black-and-white paintings from the pencil sketches. The same month, he wrote in his notebook: "I have begun to paint canvases with linear themes . . . They will be unusual and new . . . Certainly I will draw a lot of criticism for my lines. People will say there is no painting without brushstrokes. But I see my task differently. Color has died in black and become irrelevant. Let the brushstroke die too."

In the exhibition, Rodchenko hung the pages of "Everything Is Experiment" alongside his linear paintings. The text presents the artist's non-objective work of previous years as a development that follows "immanent laws," with the painter solving "tasks" that result from formal experiments with the "line" and "paint." "The composition of the one (the line) and the *faktura* of the other (paint) constitute the value of painting and consequently amount to the discovery of painting itself." Despite the equality of line and paint suggested in this statement, the painter, in the course of his preoccupation with the line, is "confronted" with the question, "Is *faktura* a value in itself or does it only serve to intensify more fundamental tasks of the work? I believe the latter to be the case . . . Otherwise two works are created in one, one with its own intrinsic tasks and the other simply the pleasure of the surface. Together they become blurred in the distance and do not enhance the value of the whole."

Along with color and *faktura*, Rodchenko deliberately banishes the visual and haptic "pleasure" of surface attractions from painting. This amounts to a fundamental decision as to the intended reception of art. Hedonistic enjoyment and contemplative absorption in surface details are summarily rejected in favor of a rational perception of the line construction's economical form and functional implementation

of "intrinsic tasks." Straight lines are the most economical means to build constructions; anything that conceals the construction is superfluous, anticonstructive, dysfunctional.

With the drastic turn from *faktura* to the line, a necessary if not quite sufficient step toward merely functionalist painting had been taken. To transform the autonomous linear painting into a functional object, Linearism still had to pass through various stages:

- From the planar linear composition to the spatial line construction
- From the spatial line construction in the picture to the three-dimensional construction in the picture space
- From the economical structure and inner functionality of the plastic but autonomous spatial construction to the fulfillment of an external purpose by the constructed object

The shift from the flat line paintings of the first phase with their unstable picture space of intersecting straight lines and circles to the linear structures within the picture space beginning in late 1919 was certainly inspired by Rodchenko's cooperation with the architects of Zhivskul'ptarkh (the Synthesis of Painting, Sculpture, and Architecture Commission). He joined this association of painters, architects, and sculptors, who strove for a fusion of their fields, on November 18, 1919. The architectural tasks of the association soon prompted the painter to develop his flat linear compositions into tectonic constructions built solely of lines. Despite their architectonics, Rodchenko's linear structures— such as the 1919 sketches of kiosks (plate no. 115) or the sketches for the Soviet of Deputies building (plate no. 653)—as well as the projects of the architects Nikolai Ladovskii and Vladimir Krinskii, the sculptor Boris Korolev, and the painter Aleksandr Shevchenko, show the characteristics of an exploded order. The planned instability of the buildings with their hazardously projecting structural parts, leaning pillars, and precariously balanced girders; the dissolution of spatial blocks; the breaking up of the traditional rectangular framework; the displacement and penetration of irregularly shaped walls; and the confusing mixture of Constructivist ornament and tectonically functional form resulted in architectural collages rather than coherent complexes and in a discontinuously enclosed space. It is not without reason that these designs are frequently cited as precursors of Deconstructivist architecture.

Amid the revolutionary fervor of 1919–20, the parts were apparently still emancipated from the organizing structures and strictures of the whole. The designs of Rodchenko and other members of Zhivskul'ptarkh demonstrate an architecture of articulated conflicts and inner clashes that often goes to the limit of structural feasibility. Only at the end of the 1920s would functionalism introduce a new harmonizing unity into the architectural structure and subordinate the parts to a flexible architectonic framework.

Despite their Deconstructivist configuration, the architectural designs with their spatial, linear structures introduced a new phase in the defining of what constituted a work of art that ultimately led to Constructivism. Standing at the forefront of this development, Rodchenko was first as isolated as he had feared when he developed his Linearism. Looking back, in October 1920, at the exhibition of his line paintings, he wrote in his diary: "At the time none of the artists perceived them as paintings, but by the end of 1920 and the beginning of 1921 the first imitators of my art appeared on the scene. Many said the *line as a system* had opened their eyes to the *essence of construction.*"

It took several more external factors to prompt the

development from line constructions to the methodically structured "system" of Constructivism. The series of discussions among the artists at Inkhuk was one of those factors.

Inkhuk—The Factory of Objectivity

Rodchenko's discoveries in painting gained a broader audience when shortly after the exhibition of his line paintings, in early November 1920, he was appointed head of a "parallel" organizing committee of Inkhuk, which had been formed in opposition to the existing committee under Kandinskii.

After dramatic arguments between Kandinskii's and Rodchenko's followers about the tasks and programs of Inkhuk, Kandinskii and his supporters left the Institute for good on January 21, 1921. This also ended the two-year friendship between him and Rodchenko and Stepanova—the three artists had worked and lived together in Kandinskii's house from September 1919 until the autumn of 1920. But while they had collaborated to prepare the Nineteenth State Exhibition in October 1920, Kandinskii's expressive abstractionism and the objective outlook of Rodchenko's Constructivism had proved irreconcilable. Even peaceful coexistence seemed impossible in those days of struggle for a new art (although Brik had proposed cooperation). On February 4, 1921, the committee under Rodchenko was officially confirmed. The line represented by him and the committee members Brik, Briusova, Aleksei Babichev, Krinskii, Popova, and Stepanova had been victorious.

Not only the committee but also the General Working Group of Objective Analysis at Inkhuk was under Rodchenko's direction. The group counted among its members almost all the future Constructivists in Moscow. Even Malevich and Lissitzky made the long trip from Vitebsk to present Unovis's programs and work at Inkhuk. But the Working Group found little common ground with them or with Tatlin, who in 1919 had moved from Moscow to Petrograd (where he would work at the Museum of Artistic Culture/Ginkhuk [the State Institute of Artistic Culture]). No fruitful cooperation ever developed with either Vitebsk or Petrograd. The ideological differences were too glaring.

Between its formation on November 23, 1920, and May 1921, the General Working Group of Objective Analysis held twenty-eight sessions. In contrast to the analyses of the psychological and physiological effects of artworks of all types planned in Kandinskii's Inkhuk program, the group's program emphasized the "objective analysis of works of art" so as to clarify and define the primary and secondary elements of painting, sculpture, architecture, and so on, as well as their laws of organization, specifically the structural laws of "construction" and "rhythm." These laws were to be analytically "laid bare"—a term obviously borrowed from the Formalists. Characteristically, "emotion" and "representation" were ranked among the secondary elements of art to be analyzed, whereas Kandinskii's program had drawn upon the "analysis of artistic means of expression" and their "effects on the human psyche." In opposition to this subjective understanding of works of art as expressive signs, the group's program perceived them as objects devoid of individual artistic expression, hence not requiring any psychological empathy on the part of the viewer but rather an empirical, behavioristic analysis of his own physiological responses in order to apprehend the objects' effects. To implement their program, the Working Group held numerous sessions between January and April 1921, discussing the "analysis of the terms 'construction' and 'composition' and their respective definition." At the same time, works by Western painters such as Monet, Signac, and Matisse; by older Russian artists like Abram Arkhipov, Konstantin Korovin, Aleksandr Kuprin, Petr Konchalovskii, and Kandinskii; and by Suprematists and non-objectivists (Ekster, Klutsis, Malevich, Medunetskii, Rodchenko, Stepanova, and Tatlin) were analyzed to determine their Constructivist content.

The artists and theorists did not enter into these discussions with a clear, let alone a unanimous, definition of "composition" and "construction" and the difference between them. They began by analyzing individual works and tried to reduce the observations and evaluations of the group members, recorded in countless minutes, to a common denominator. By way of empirical induction, they hoped to find an objective definition of the term "construction."

Despite this effort at an inductive approach, the recorded results with their interim solutions, as well as the drawings made to illustrate the difference between composition and construction (plate nos. 244–253), show the outlines of a preconceived notion of "construction" which was clearly inspired by Rodchenko's line paintings. It is therefore not surprising that at the end of these sessions only Rodchenko's works were deemed "constructive" since they alone had completely replaced composition with construction. Rodchenko was more guarded, describing his black and line paintings as "striving for construction."

In the course of these "objective" analyses and terminological clarifications a general tendency to systematize and rationalize artistic creation became apparent. In Rodchenko's definition of "construction," its systemic character plays an important role: "Every system of construction requires the specific use of its own material, and every such system will be the invention or the perfecting of something, and not a reflection or portrayal."[30]

Constructions

In his hanging spatial constructions, Rodchenko for the first time consistently demonstrated the systemic character of construction in an aesthetically convincing manner. Each of the five—a square, a hexagon (plate no. 296), an oval (plate no. 294), a circle, and a triangle—was constructed of a single sheet of plywood. The artist cut the sheets in concentric bands of equal width and tilted them into space to create three-dimensional bodies that were not constituted of physical mass but of linear, uniform geometric figures. Like paintings, these constructions could not stand on their own and were therefore suspended from the ceiling—which emphasized their autonomy as monadic, nonutilitarian entities.

It would be an understatement of the facts to consider these constructions mere signs of Rodchenko's transition from painting to sculpture. Such an assessment would ignore the origins of construction in painting. Only the negation of painterliness explains the hanging construction's anti-individualist, universal geometric form, reproducibility, and independence from an individual creator or specific material that earlier on would have born the hallmark of the artist's *faktura*. The uniformly smooth silver paint emphasizes the absence of any surface *faktura* and evokes the impression of immateriality and weightlessness. The hanging spatial constructions hold no secrets. Their design is completely transparent and rational. The basic elements of painting—surface and color—have been transformed into movement and light. The metallic sheen of their surface underscores the disembodied effect of the hanging constructions (or "reflecting surfaces," as Rodchenko sometimes described them). Paint and the canvas or wooden surface of painting have been literally dissected and dissolved, and the destruction of matter gives birth to the pure construction as a reconstruction of the objective world according to the artist's plan.

Rodchenko created his series of hanging constructions between late 1920 and early 1921 while also working on a number of other wood constructions based on the principle of repetition of a single form. In these works, identical elements such as wooden rods or boards of equal measurements are assembled into three-dimensional constructions that are symmetrically arranged around a center. Like the hanging constructions, these smaller-scale constructions dispense with *faktura,* individual variations, and so forth. Rather, they are an exercise in combinatory rules to show that even uniform material elements can produce a variety of aesthetically satisfying constructions. The material plays only a minor role in the combinatory method. The construction follows the methods of building elementary structural systems and not the material. Rodchenko remarked: "I experimentally developed these most recent constructions to bind the constructor to the law of functionality of forms and their relationships and to demonstrate the universal principle that all sorts of constructions of different systems, types, and applications can be built from identical shapes."

Built on the principle of identical shapes and axially symmetrical shifts, these constructions are results of an *ars combinatoria* which experimentally explores and demonstrates the methods of the creation of forms. The construction method and the resulting system of forms are paramount while *faktura* and material play an inferior role. At this point, the functionality of the construction is still defined from within the system: a form is functional because it defines the other forms in the system and determines their function, not because it can be used to fulfill tasks outside the system. These constructions are hence functionally structured in themselves but their elements have no other function than to constitute this structure. The structure itself remains without any utilitarian function—while positively asserting its aesthetic function.

One conspicuous hallmark of the most advanced constructions of 1921 is their systemic character: a radically economic structure of uniform elements and homogeneous materials which can be arranged in various combinations that are consistently functional within the system. This systemic conception of construction differs considerably from the meaning given to the term in the discussions about construction versus composition where "construction" had primarily denoted architectural design and stability. This rather literal, easy-to-grasp notion of constructiveness is reflected in most constructions from the so-called "laboratory" phase of Constructivism, including the constructions of Tatlin, Vasilii Ermilov, Medunetskii, Georgii and Vladimir Stenberg, Naum Gabo, and Katarzyna Kobro, as well as some of Klutsis's and Rodchenko's constructions. None of these works display the systemic character defined by Rodchenko, for their formal elements are neither consistently uniform and homogeneous nor are they organized according to a rational combinatory method. Besides Rodchenko's hanging constructions and small wood constructions, only a few constructions and sketches by Klutsis and a number of Ioganson's constructions conform with the ideal of a systematic structure.

At the exhibition of Obmokhu (the Society of Young Artists) in May-June 1921, Ioganson presented some of the most individual and convincing constructions in the entire show. The six works, which have survived only in photographs, are constructed of pieces of squared timber arranged mostly at square but also at acute and obtuse angles. Three spatial constructions, exhibited side by side to emphasize the principle of variation, each consisted of identical wooden pieces which intersected in the center of the construction at varying angles. The skeletal structures were held together by wire or rope, which braced the ends of the wooden pieces for maximum countertension and overall stability. They were tilted to the side so that they rested on three vertices, which gave the structures a strong dynamic effect and made them appear much more complex than they actually were. Two other spatial constructions on triangular pedestals also had rectangular structures, with the formal elements symmetrically arranged around the center of each construction.

Ioganson's *Study in Balance* (ca. 1920), also shown at the Obmokhu exhibition, was organized according to the same method as the spatial constructions. Three movable rods, connected by rope, were mounted above a triangular base slab. By pulling the rope, the rods could be arranged in different configurations to change the entire structure.

These structures, made of standardized elements and homogeneous materials and rendered transformative through variable central connections or kinetic mounting, were exemplary models of Ioganson's concept of the "mechanical construction." Charts with two lines crossing at right or acute and obtuse angles served Ioganson to illustrate a thesis he presented at Inkhuk on March 9, 1922: "The design of every cold structure in space or any combination of hard material is a cross with right angles (or) with acute and obtuse angles."

With these drawings, Ioganson struck the balance of his previous work. At the end of his lecture, he summarized his own artistic development as a logical and necessary sequence: "From painting to sculpture, from sculpture to construction, from construction to technology and invention—that is the course I have chosen and I am sure it will also be the ultimate direction of every revolutionary artist."

In 1924, Ioganson gave up art in favor of technology and began to work in a rolling mill—not as an ordinary technician but as an "inventor" of design methods which he tried to translate from his sculptures to the construction of utilitarian objects. He contrasted the methods of "mechanical construction" and "invention" developed in his spatial constructions with the "unimaginative" and "stagnating" technology of the period—but also with "the procedures, methods, techniques, materials, and tools of art," which he considered "useless, flawed, primitive, and extremely insufficient" for the design of the future. Championing a rationally calculated design method, he polemically attacked Tatlin's selections of materials as well as the Suprematist compositions by Malevich and his Unovis followers for their intuitive treatment of material and unsystematic design. In their failure to progress beyond the methods of the "old art," these artists—in Ioganson's view—relapsed into a "wrong and noxious form of construction, i.e., into the 'good old art' or into mere playfulness."

In his lecture at Inkhuk, Ioganson stressed that the innovative, transformable "mechanical" construction was nothing but the "thing" itself, "organized according to Constructivist principles." Therefore it had "no existence above, below, or beyond the thing." Ioganson was thus the first to postulate the principle of concrete art and minimal art: that the work of art is a structured thing, i.e., the material implementation of a systematically designed structure that is transformable within the limits of its own system. Accordingly, the spatial construction is merely a self-explication of its methodically organized intrinsic structure.

Ioganson drew the necessary conclusions from this reification of art when he attempted to apply his originally artistic design method to the "invention" of industrial products. This created an entirely new situation as the structure now had to meet utilitarian requirements outside its own system—which basically amounted to a return to the "theme" or "content" of the old art in the new guise of utilitarian function. Only for one fleeting historic moment did the liberation of art from representational and expressive functions lead to its complete autonomy. The immanent functionality of systematically organized material was soon replaced by the external function of serving a "social task," as Brik put it. With the demand for the practical usefulness of artistic constructions, the spiritual effects of the newborn autonomous structural system were criticized as merely aesthetic. This was not a time for concrete or minimal art to flourish.

When the technological and industrial modernization of the Russian society set in with full force in 1920, the vanguard artists had to live up to their progressive self-image. The most radical ones renounced the principle of autonomy and plunged into the current of modernization, convinced that their "professional" artistic skills would enable them to influence its course. But once they had left the position of critical observers, they soon had to recognize that they were insufficiently equipped and trained to withstand the danger of drowning in the rough waves of progress. At best, the artists, like everyone else, became travelers in the inexorable stream of accumulation and utilization, unable to diagnose and demonstrate its motives and casualties.

The Obmokhu exhibition in 1921 had presented Ioganson's spatial constructions as well as Rodchenko's hanging constructions to the public for the first time. Both artists were members of the First Working Group of Constructivists at Inkhuk, which had been founded only a few weeks before. Ioganson and Rodchenko exhibited as guest artists since, unlike the Stenberg brothers and Medunetskii—who had also contributed works to the show—they did not belong to Obmokhu. In this fascinating, historically momentous exhibition, three types of constructions can be distinguished:

1. Ioganson's and Rodchenko's purely structural combinations or "cold" constructions, as Ioganson described them.

2. The "warm" constructions based on materials and not on a structural system. These include, to a certain extent, the Stenbergs' reliefs, but primarily Medunetskii's sculptures. His constructions focus on the aesthetic and constructive qualities of the material, which are heightened through contrasting forms and *faktura*. His *Spatial Construction* (plate no. 282), in particular, has pronounced "painterly" qualities with the red finish of the curved iron rod and the use of different colored metal parts. Medunetskii's other constructions, displayed on a table-like base at the exhibition, are also combinations of different materials with contrasting surfaces and textures. He predominantly used semifinished forged or industrially processed metal products but also found objects such as a plowshare, the metal handle of a pitcher, or a slat from a piece of furniture. During the reconstruction of these works it became apparent how much the curved or twisted forms were determined by the properties of the material, its strength, flexibility, and thickness. The form and *faktura* of the construction result from a synthesis of the artist's abstract formal and spatial vision, his intuitive, sometimes arbitrary, choice of materials according to "painterly" and "constructive" criteria, and the inherent properties of these materials. Symbolic references are, however, absent from these constructions—unless one is willing to read the parabolas and hyperbolas, which also recur in Medunetskii's paintings, as signs of the curvature of space-time (an interpretation that actually fits the same geometric forms in the works of Malevich, Klutsis, or Lissitzky).

3. The symbolic constructions by Georgii and Vladimir Stenberg. Constructed from the "materials of the new Classicism"—glass and iron—and set on rather unconventionally shaped pedestals, these "constructions of spatial structures" (plate nos. 291–293) represent "ideas" such as modernity, industrial revolution, and technological progress. These abstract structures were so close to their referents that critics gave them the label of "technological naturalism." The artists rejected this symbolic reading of their constructions, which they claimed were merely economically and functionally organized objects. Like Ioganson and Rodchenko, they tried to exclude the subjective effects of *faktura* from their constructions. All planes of their constructions were clear glass, a material that by its very smoothness, hardness, and transparency negates *faktura*.

What unites all these different constructions in the exhibition is the *rhythm of their structures.* In their programmatic and theoretical texts of 1920–22, all Soviet Constructivists unanimously declared rhythm the most important organizing principle and effect of their constructions. Given the three artistic positions toward structure, material, and symbolic function outlined above, it is not surprising that in the following years the Stenberg brothers made a successful career for themselves in the Soviet Union, first in the theater (plate nos. 642–645) and later as the country's most significant and sought-after designers of film posters (plate nos. 426–430). The synthesis of pictorial symbolization and decorative structure required in these media is clearly present in the brothers' constructions. Medunetskii, too, successfully progressed from his "painterly" material constructions to set designs for the avant-garde theater, while Ioganson and Rodchenko continued to experiment and develop their design methods and systems.

The 1921 Obmokhu exhibition was arguably the culmination of the short history of Constructivist object art. Soon after the opening of the show, the theorists of "production art" as well as the artists themselves came to regard the innovative but still autonomous constructions as studies in Productivist aesthetics rather than independent contributions to Constructivist art. The term "laboratory experiment" was coined as early as 1921; it downgraded the constructions in the Obmokhu exhibition and relegated Constructivist works to the status of basic research for future practical applications, thereby robbing them of any significance of their own which might have been worth pursuing.

After the materiological and methodological phases of Constructivism, and at the end of the search for "construction" in the artistic creations of the past and present, technological issues and functional demands increasingly determined the artistic discourse and the definition of Constructivism at Inkhuk. Rodchenko's own concluding definition, delivered in March 1921 toward the end of the discussions of the distinction between composition and construction, reads:

> *Construction is a thing or a task that is approached with a precise working schedule and in which all materials and all their specific components are organized and used according to their correct functions without adding anything superfluous. The correct approach to each space is construction.*
>
> *Construction is: goal—working plan—organization—material—economy.*
>
> *New things can be created only if there is Constructivist organization . . . Composition is always an expression of individualism and everything individualism implies.*

Constructivism arose from the criticism of the individualist compositional art of the past and immediate present and saw itself as its direct negation. Malevich and Tatlin were among those who had to face some heavy attacks. In Rodchenko's critical view, the Suprematist compositions were capable only of "filling empty spaces in an individualist manner," while

Tatlin in his counter-reliefs confined himself to selecting from available materials. "When [an artist] selects such materials as are at hand or fills an empty space with decorations, it is composition."

For Rodchenko, any kind of construction, whether on a surface or in space, in art or technology, requires a precise hierarchy and sequence of functions: after determining the "goal," i.e., the function of the construction, a working schedule is developed, which specifies the procedures and tools for reaching the goal; then the appropriate material is selected and processed and used as economically as possible.

From Individualist Anarchism to Technological Rationalism

This "evolutionary course" of artistic production toward anti-individualist systematization, rationalization, and mechanization was neither predictable before the Constructivist debates at Inkhuk began nor a natural result of these discussions. The decision in favor of collectivism had been preceded by the individualist anarchism of the black *faktura* paintings, which had convincingly embodied the concept of the work of art as an object and were closely connected with Rodchenko's belief in the principles of Stirner and Whitman. Moreover, his definition of construction was in glaring contrast to his affirmation of "abstract spiritual creativity" in January 1919 and his advocacy of Eastern over Western art during the planning of the Museum of Painterly Culture in March 1919: "Asiatic art is spiritual, was regarded with religious awe . . . The West treats art lightly, in material terms; the East worships art, elevates it above everything else, does not make it utilitarian."[31]

Similarly, Stepanova's statements of 1919–20 are diametrically opposed to the definitions and evaluations of composition and construction she gave but a short time later. In the catalogue of the Tenth State Exhibition she still praised "intuition" and "emotion" as positive values, explicitly calling the work of non-objective artists a "protest of the spirit against the materialism of the present."[32] As late as October 1920, in her manifesto "On the Possibilities of the Cognition of Art," written on the occasion of the Nineteenth State Exhibition, she defended the "miraculous"—in the sense of a transcendent quality—as an essential characteristic of art. At the same time, she strongly objected to the equation of mathematics and art: "The Formalist approach now being pursued in art is a tribute to the materialism of our time. But none of us will ever subordinate art to mathematics." The concept of the "artist-proletarian" as executor of objective "tasks" was still anathema to her. She considered the "starting point," "the creative impulse" to be as yet undiscovered and therefore to constitute something "incomprehensible," a "miracle" that could not be reduced to the calculated execution of a rationally formulated task.

A year later, on December 22, 1921, she delivered her talk "On Constructivism" at Inkhuk:

This revolutionary, destructive activity, which strips art down to its basic elements, has shocked the consciousness of those who work in art: it has confronted them with the problem of construction as an expedient necessity. Based on the further principle of the expedient implementation of work, a new Constructivist ideology has been formulated.

Being aware of this new activity is particularly important. Subconscious inspiration (a fortuitous phenomenon) is transformed into organized activity.

The intellect is our point of departure, taking the place of the "soul" of idealism.

From this it follows that, on the whole, Constructivism is also

intellectual production (and not thought alone), incompatible with the spirituality of artistic activity.[33]

How did this conversion from transcendentalism to intellectual rationalism come about? What prompted the abrupt turnabout from the rejection of functional tasks even within art to an organized implementation of practical purposes?

A sudden revelation cannot have been the only cause. So how can we explain this ideological and aesthetic about-face, which was soon followed by a change of paradigms in artistic practice: from the substance of paint to the immaterial structure, from the Deconstructivist jumble of lines to the planned, clear-cut organizing system? The discovery of the line as an independent constructive factor and the transition from *faktura* to Linearism do not suffice in themselves to elucidate the radical change of values from individualism to collectivism, from spiritualism to materialism, from non-utilitarian thinking to the principle of usefulness, from the incomprehensible "miracle" to the cogent intellectual system, and from imagination and intuition to logical calculation and mathematics.

There were a number of critical external developments, beginning in 1919, that contributed to the sharp swerve in the "evolutionary course" of art between 1920 and 1921. The enhanced institutional powers of the Soviet government after the end of the Civil War in the autumn of 1920 intensified the crisis in art which had been smoldering since the February Revolution.

Art of the Commune was forcibly closed in April 1919 and in September *Iskusstvo* (*Art*), the journal of Izo Narkompros, had to cease publication. The largely autonomous Professional Union of Artists and Painters was dissolved in December 1919. Several of its members—including Kandinskii, Rodchenko, and Stepanova—went on to found Inkhuk in order to protect the professional interests of artists. Under these circumstances, the formation of Inkhuk can hardly be considered a success of the avant-garde. On the contrary: after the dissolution and reorganization of Izo Narkompros in December 1920–early 1921, which cost the avant-garde most of its influence on the country's artistic life, Inkhuk became the vanguard artists' last refuge in Moscow.

The administrative autonomy of the artists was effectually stamped out. To make matters worse, on December 1, 1920, *Pravda* published a "Letter of the Central Committee of the Communist Party on the Proletkul't Organizations" that lumped the "Futurists" together with those "decadent elements" and "followers of an idealistic philosophy hostile to Marxism" who had exerted a "subversive influence" on Izo Narkompros as well as on the Proletkul't organizations. For this reason, both Izo Narkompros and Proletkul't had to be dissolved as autonomous organizations and put under the close control of the People's Commissariat of Enlightenment. In January 1921, Lunacharskii found it necessary to caution against a public "witch hunt" that would make the "Futurists" and non-objective artists "martyrs in the name of their ideas." Finally, in early 1921, the avant-garde lost its last institutional stronghold when the Museum Department led by Rodchenko, Kandinskii, and Tatlin was dissolved. Looking back at these hard times, Brik wrote: "The 'Futurists' were seriously committed to destroying the past and tried to use their positions within the administration for this purpose. They did not succeed. The guardians of philistinism proved to be stronger and threw the 'Futurists' out of all the commissariats."

By early 1921, with this chain of defeats, the influence that the anarchist avant-garde had on official art policy was at an end. Politically on the defensive and deprived of their organizational clout, avant-garde artists had to rethink their role and place in society for the third time, after the first crisis following the February Revolution and the second following October 1917.

A desperately defiant statement Maiakovskii made in the winter of 1920 reveals what this crisis meant for the individual artist: "We declare: to hell with individualism, to hell with words and emotions . . . so that we can even renounce our own personality . . . the poet can't be forced but he can force himself."

It was only now, three years after the Revolution, that the necessity of again redefining their role led the avant-garde to lock arms with technology and industrial production as the political-social revolution mutated into an industrial revolution. The most advanced artists kept up with this change. Artistic Modernism took the way of modernization—with the Constructivists in the lead. They marched along with the first "utopian" endeavors to industrialize the Soviet Union after the Revolution.

In December 1920, the Soviet government tackled the implementation of the Goelro (the State Commission for the Electrification of Russia) plan, which envisioned huge energy projects as the basis of the reconstruction and expansion of Russia's shattered economy and industry. Lenin, the moving force behind this plan, stressed its far-reaching implications for the future of Soviet society. His response to a question from the correspondent of the English *Daily Express* has often been quoted: "Electrification on the basis of the Soviet order will lead to the final victory of the foundations of Communism in our country, the foundations of a civilized life without exploiters, without capitalists, without landowners, without merchants." By the end of 1920, the electrification project was the talk of the day. The electrified utopia not only captured the minds and imaginations of economists and technicians but seduced artists as well, who gave free rein to visions of a fully mechanized and electrified life after the icy, dark winters of the war years. In 1920, for example, Klutsis created his first photomontage: a photograph of Lenin between the dark circle of the "old world" full of prisons, alcohol, and whips and the bright "new world" with the crystal cubes of Suprematist architecture. These buildings of the new world are inscribed with the word "electrification." (See also his study, from the same year, for the poster, *Elektrifikatsiia vsei strany* [*Electrification of the Entire Country*], plate no. 308.)

Two years later, in 1922, when "production art" began to venture out into real life, Klutsis was the first among the Constructivists to design his constructions for practical, everyday purposes. One of his large-scale projects for propaganda kiosks included a banner running around the construction proclaiming, "The development of industry brings salvation." These agitprop stands were successful models of the Constructivist concept of "utilitarian" objects. Their transparent, light framework construction fulfills the principle of economy. The utilization of all forms for set functions, the modular structure, and the multi-functional equipment with a picture screen, loudspeakers, a bookstall, poster holders, a speaker's rostrum, and so on make these structures convincing examples of how the Constructivist notion of aesthetics and function could be put into practice (plate nos. 109, 111–113).

In his summary of the Inkhuk members' joint effort to clarify the term "construction," Babichev wrote on September 5, 1921, that all the Inkhuk artists and theorists had unanimously concluded

that construction in artistic representation does not exist and that everything that was previously called construction or pretended to be construction belonged to an outwardly aesthetic order. Genuine construction appears only in perfect, utilitarian products. This conclusion coincided with a sudden, forceful awareness of the future of industry, which so far has managed without artists and threatened to fill everything with purely utilitarian buildings and objects that were completely unresolved as to their ability to orient perception.

The prospect of participating in the organization of life by organizing objects, buildings, and institutions was inspiring. In the discussion it was generally held that there was no acceptable reason to distinguish between the terms "artistic" and "utilitarian" if the object in question is constructed throughout.

This account neatly sums up the essential characteristics of the Constructivist object in its final utilitarian metamorphosis. The extremely high standards implied in the definition are striking: the object must be "perfect" both in appearance and substance. Mere surface treatment can result in no more than a *faktura* object. Consequently, a Constructivist object is not a designed surface but a three-dimensional, functional structure that is distinguished from common utilitarian objects by its perceptibility, i.e., it keeps stimulating the perception of its user. Furthermore, the Constructivist object must be "constructed throughout," meaning that its structure is systematically designed in all its details and that its body is identical with this structure.

The ideal Constructivist object in the final Inkhuk definition is hence a systematically constructed structure that fulfills a practical purpose and while being used is also consciously perceived by its consumer. The goal is, in short, a thing of perfection.

The Resurgence of the Subject

I would argue that the structure of this entirely constructed object is similar to the structure of human consciousness. If this is the case, the subject which was driven out of Constructivism by "objectification" reappeared in the congruence of object and subject. Its form had changed, of course, since subjectivity was present in the object not as the externalization of an empirical subject but in the form of a transcendental subject.

Ideally, the structure of the Constructivist object is the pure product of a conscious operation with formal elements, implemented according to a systematic design method. Consequently, the finished construction is the materialization of consciousness in a spatial structure that is unadulterated by the properties of the materials used.

Rodchenko's hanging spatial constructions as well as Ioganson's spatial constructions come very close to this Constructivist ideal. The definition proposed by Babichev declared absolute awareness in the production of structures to be the principal criterion of artistic value *and* usefulness, since the methodical design and implementation of a construction made it the product of real work.

This notion of artistic creation as a paradigm of conscious work is in direct opposition to the earlier view—shared by the Suprematists and non-objective artists before 1921—of artistic production as intuitive creation derived from the unconscious. The sudden turn had been prepared by the Formalist school with its conception of art as a method and of artists as professional masters in their field.

During the formative phase of Suprematism, Malevich described the relationship between rational thinking and intuition to Matiushin in a letter of July 3, 1913: "We have come to a point where we can dismiss the sense and logic of the old reason. But we must seek to recognize the sense and logic of a new, already emerging reason which, compared to the old, might even be a 'supra-reason.'" In his review of the *0.10* exhibition (Petrograd, 1915–16), Matiushin adopted this concept of a logic of the unconscious which becomes manifest in non-objective creation and reveals its logical structure to the viewer; "suprasense" denotes a "new, creative, intuitive reason that has superseded unenlightened intuition."[34]

The Formalist linguists then turned this logic of the unconscious into an operation, perceiving it not as the structure of the language of the unconscious but solely as the procedural logic of the treatment of material. This concept clearly reflects the analyst's, not the producer's, viewpoint.

For the Constructivist producer, on the other hand, there is a homologous relationship between the logical structure of his subconscious and the structure of the construction he creates. If the structure is completely systematic in its inner logic and entirely transparent in its making or functional modes, i.e., if the object is "constructed throughout," it appears as a homologous model of the producer's unconscious of which he has become fully aware. The artistic subject becomes as transparent as his creation. The previously impenetrable dark of his subconscious and body is illuminated and rendered transparent through the exposure of the logic of their functional modes.

When there is nothing remaining unenlightened in the subject and he has become completely aware of himself, he controls the language of his unconscious and the mechanisms of his bodily functions. He is able to organize his unconscious and his body rationally according to set goals, without having to heed and follow the demands of his inner voice. This thought must have struck the Constructivists in 1921 with sudden force, as Rodchenko's remarks in "The Line" show: "Until now, life, this simple thing, has not been properly seen; one did not know that it was so simple and clear, that one merely needed to organize it and free it from all excess. To work for life, not for palaces or temples, cemeteries or museums."[35]

Transparent to himself, the subject leaves all places of memory and fate behind; the light of reason has completely penetrated and exposed them for what they are—the museum as a place of unresolved desires and petrified experiences, as a depository of the collective unconscious and memory; the cemetery as a place of sorrow and surrender of the body and mind to death; the palace as a place of unenlightened and consequently false pleasures; the temple as a place of blind faith, obscure feelings, and nebulous hopes. The self-aware subject enters into life "to work among, for, and with all others," i.e., to organize his own, completely transparent life and the lives of the others through the "constructive technique."

The methodical, rational organization of formal elements in a systematically structured construction amounts to a preparatory model for the organization of life. Since it is nothing but the visualization of its own conscious creation, it is structurally akin to the self-reflection of a person's self-consciousness. Self-consciousness, in the sense of an ego that has become aware of itself, also knows the division into a producing subject and a produced object which in itself is a subject, i.e., the conscious ego. The self, as prior to the conscious ego, can only recognize itself by reflecting itself in the ego and thereby delimiting itself the way a frame delimits a mirror. Only in the delimited form of a conscious and therefore defined object (the conscious ego) can the self experience itself as an unlimited and determining subject. Only by observing itself in the creation of itself can an individual's self-consciousness recognize, and ultimately produce, itself.

By the same token, the entirely constructed and transparent construction observes its own production, or rather its own finished production, since the Constructivist thing is rendered conscious throughout but does not have a consciousness of its

own. It thus possesses the structure of self-consciousness without being conscious.

Only in the mediated identity with the conscious ego—the "differential indifference" of Post-Structuralism—does the unconscious or preconscious self produce itself and become aware of itself as producer. In Rodchenko's hanging spatial constructions and Ioganson's spatial constructions, this differential indifference is seen in one object. This object presents itself as a distinct, systematically constructed and unified structure, but at the same time it is clearly recognized as only *one* variant out of an infinite series of structural combinations. From this perspective, the unique construction appears as a contingent unity that would change its structure under altered conditions.

The absoluteness and monadic unity of the formal elements' reference system is vividly emphasized by the uniformity of the construction. Like the structure of pure self-consciousness freed from the gravity-bound body of the empirical ego, the hanging spatial constructions hover in space as allegories of the transcendental ego.

Differential indifference is also strikingly apparent in Lissitzky's and Klutsis's paintings of constructions. Hovering freely in the picture space, the axiometric structures have an effect of differential indifference because each time the viewer focuses on their identical elements they switch into a spatially inverse structure and thereby escape fixation. In the viewer's perception, the opposite spatial constellations thus merge into one indissoluble unity. The flat axiometric constructions integrate two or even more views of the same formal framework into one homogeneous but oscillating structure, provoking a continuous shift of the viewer's perceptual positions—which can be experienced as a perpetual alternation between the self's role as subject and the ego's role as object in the production of self-consciousness.

In works such as Klutsis's collage *Dinamicheskii gorod* (*Dynamic City,* 1919, plate no. 309) or Lissitzky's *Eight-Position Proun* (before 1924), the configuration of the formal elements remains the same while the optical structure changes substantially with each incremental turn. The same structural principle also distinguishes several of Klutsis's drawings of agitprop kiosks, which at first sight look like rationally organized construction plans. But a more detailed look reveals that the spatial relationships are deliberately contradictory: optical illusions result in "impossible figures" which could never be transferred from the drawing into real space.

The ambiguity of the two- and three-dimensional structures was carried over into the designs of multifunctional objects that became a trademark of Constructivist production art. The first issue of *Lef,* the Constructivist house organ from 1923 to 1928, presented works by students of Rodchenko's in the Metalworking Faculty of Vkhutemas (the Higher Artistic-Technical Workshops). One of those pieces was a "bed but also a chair and a desk," since "a thing must perform several different functions," as the accompanying commentary put it. The first exhibition of the Metalworking Faculty in 1923 included a number of such multi-functional objects invented by the students and their teacher. In her account of the exhibition, Stepanova distinguished three types of objects:

- An object that is fit for use in motion, i.e., organized like a means of production (for example, a mobile bookcase or movie theater that can be used anywhere)
- An object that can be dismantled and easily stored after use (such as a kiosk or bed)
- An object for private use that can fill functions in the communal apartment (for example, the bed-chair-desk mentioned above)

The concept of multifunctional furniture emerged from the transformative principle of the hanging spatial constructions and the constructions made of identical elements. Whether Ioganson further developed his spatial constructions in this direction while working in a factory is unknown. Klutsis employed the constructive principle of planes intersecting at right angles, which he had developed in his paintings of "construction," in numerous designs for information stands, shelf systems, and other functional constructions.

The design and production of multifunctional objects constituted a major part of the work done in Rodchenko's workshop in the Metalworking Faculty and to a lesser degree in the Woodworking Faculty at Vkhutemas throughout the 1920s. The furniture for the reading room of a workers' club, presented at the 1925 *Exposition internationale des arts décoratifs et industriels modernes* (*International Exhibition of Contemporary Decorative and Industrial Art*) in Paris is a typical example of this design concept. (In the mid-1920s, Rodchenko also worked in the Moscow Proletkul't workshop on transformable furniture for workers' clubs.) The reading room is equipped with movable bookcases, folding counter tops for multiple use, revolving drums for photo exhibitions, and a collapsible construction that includes a speaker's platform, a bulletin board, and a projection screen for slides and films. Nearly all the furnishings are "built on a principle that makes it possible to unfold the object on an ample space for work and to fold it down into compact proportions after work. Comrade Rodchenko considers this principle a typical quality of the modern object. For five years he has been conducting the work of the Metalworking Faculty at Vkhutemas according to this principle, and over the past few years the dynamically organized object has gained increasing acceptance and thus proved its viability and topical significance."

This enthusiastic commentary by Stepanova appeared in 1926 in *Sovremennaia arkhitektura* (*Contemporary Architecture*), the organ of OSA (the Union of Contemporary Architects).[36] As the magazine's editor in chief, Gan regularly published the most recent works of the Constructivist production artists, including Zakhar Bykov, Miller, Morozov, Shestakov, Stepanova, and Sokolov, most of them students of Rodchenko's at Vkhutemas. Their works followed the same principles of variability and multiple function Rodchenko had developed in the early 1920s.

In the combination furniture with complex functions, the Constructivist ideal of the object that is "constructed throughout" materialized in real life. As prototypes, they embody the idea of a new, objective reality that does not consist of massive objects and monumental buildings made to last and exist independent of people. The Constructivist conception of the object—and also of furniture and architecture—rests on the idea of the infinitely transformable structure made of minimal material elements. The transformation of each structure leads to constantly new functions. This structural metamorphosis enables the object to take a different shape with each reassigned function while its material elements remain the same.

In the Constructivist universe, objects exist solely as organs of human activity. They adjust to people's actions, expand and die with them, while constantly renewing their own shape and function. The Constructivist objects are congruent counterparts of the subject. Therein lies their utopian potential. Ideally, they would have transformed material reality into an unrestricted space in which free people could act. But in reality, they contributed to the total mobilization of the people, whose lives were sucked into the modernization process and restructured to the beat of machines.

The design theorist David Arkin remarked at the end of the 1920s that among the prototypes for workers' apartments developed at the Metalworking Faculty, the most frequent piece of furniture was the "multipurpose model, the divan-table or the chair-bed. But these outwardly efficient models solve in only a superficial manner the task of using the living space with maximum economy. Therefore, the enthusiasm for combination furniture apparent in the works of the young Constructivists is by no means a positive development."[37]

This critical comment by a Constructivist partisan shows that the designers of multifunctional furniture were not exclusively or even primarily concerned with the actual practical use of their creations. They held on to the principle of the "object constructed throughout" postulated by the Inkhuk Constructivists. A case can be made that they were only marginally interested in producing functional, inexpensive, or comfortable furniture for workers' apartments or clubs. For them, what was really at stake was the life or death of art in the painful rebirth of postrevolutionary society.

In a lecture at Inkhuk in March 1922, Kushner declared: "Not only the object is exhausted. Its functions too are dying off. It is thus being transformed into a useless thing while remaining materially intact." Under circumstances where art in its old, "individualist," bourgeois form had lost its function, the Constructivists' survival strategy was to focus on the dying object in order to revive it and thereby revive art. The rebirth of art after the Revolution could only happen as a rebirth of objects, since the individual and his artistic subjectivity were not granted that right. The translation of the object into the subjective form of the transcendental ego, which has neither flesh nor blood, mass nor *faktura* but exists only as the "cold structure" of self-consciousness, constitutes the greatness of this materialized utopia where the subject is identical with material work and the objects it produces. Yet at the same time, this utopian construction inevitably failed as a strategy for the rebirth of art, as it waived the critical distance from life, surrendering to its restraining forces and sometimes even strengthening them.

In 1913, years before the revolutionary changes in society, Shklovskii made an outline for his lecture on "The Resurrection of the Word," a kind of prelude to all Constructivist theories of art: "The word-image and its petrification . . . The death of objects . . . The theory of reversal. The task of 'Futurism'—the revival of objects, to return the experience of the world to the people . . . The resurrection of objects."[38] These preparatory notes read like a history of Constructivism in the 1920s—with the vital difference that Shklovskii referred to the death, revival, and resurrection of objects only in terms of art and perception and warned against mistaking art for life. Later, in an article in *Art of the Commune,* Shklovskii explicitly repeated this warning with regard to the theory of production art, but the Constructivists ignored him. They crossed the aesthetic boundary between art and life in order to resurrect the material and vital things. They gave them new forms. But art died in the process.

Could things have turned out differently in those perturbing times?

It may have been possible to hibernate in the "cold structures" of Constructivism but one couldn't live in them.

—Translated, from the German, by Jürgen Riehle

Notes

This essay is for Arthur Lehning.

1. A. M. Rodchenko, "Vse–opyty," 1921, A. M. Rodchenko and V. F. Stepanova Archive, Moscow.

2. Varvara Stepanova, "On Constructivism," in Alexander Lavrentiev, *Stepanova,* trans. Wendy Salmond (Cambridge, Mass.: MIT Press, 1988), p. 175.

3. See Jane A. Sharp, "The Critical Reception of the *0.10* Exhibition: Malevich and Benua," in this volume, for an account of their differences.

4. *Novaia zhizn',* March 27 and April 9, 1918.

5. *Revoliutsionnoe tvorchestvo* 1–2 (1918).

6. *Izvestiia,* April 16, 1918.

7. *Anarkhiia,* April 11, 1918.

8. *Anarkhiia,* March 30, 1918.

9. *Anarkhiia,* March 28, 1918.

10. *IZO. Vestnik Otdela izobrazitel'nykh iskusstv N.K.P.* 1 (March 10, 1921).

11. *Plamia* 35 (1919), p. 13.

12. Nikolai Punin, quoted in M. L-in, "Miting ob iskusstve," *Iskusstvo kommuny* 1 (December 7, 1918), reprinted as "Miting ob iskusstve (24 XI 1918 g. v Petrograde)," in I. Matsa, ed., *Sovetskoe iskusstvo za 15 let. Materialy i dokumentatsiia* (Moscow and Leningrad: Ogiz-Izogiz, 1933), pp. 175–76.

13. Nikolai Punin, "O novykh gruppirovkakh," *Iskusstvo kommuny* 10 (February 9, 1919) as translated in Larissa Zhadova, *Malevich: Suprematism and Revolution in Russian Art, 1910–1930,* trans. Alexander Lieven (London: Thames and Hudson, 1982), p. 322.

14. *Birzhevye vedomosti,* June 23, 1917.

15. *Vechernie ogni* 2 (April 1918).

16. *Novaia zhizn',* April 18 and May 1, 1918.

17. A. M. Rodchenko, "The Line," trans. James West, in *Art Into Life: Russian Constructivism, 1914–1932,* catalogue for exhibition organized by the Henry Art Gallery, University of Washington, Seattle, the Walker Art Center, Minneapolis, and the State Tret'yakov Gallery, Moscow (New York: Rizzoli, 1990), p. 71.

18. *Iskusstvo kommuny,* December 15, 1918.

19. *Iskusstvo kommuny,* January 12, 1919.

20. V. I. Lenin, "The Immediate Tasks of the Soviet Government," in *The Lenin Anthology,* ed. Robert C. Tucker (New York: W. W. Norton, 1975).

21. *Iskusstvo kommuny,* February 23, 1919. See also Svetlana Dzhafarova, "The Creation of the Museum of Painterly Culture," in this volume.

22. "Deklaratsiia Otdela izobrazitel'nykh iskusstv i khudozhestvennoi promyshlennosti po voprosu o printsipakh muzeevedeniia, priniataia Kollegiei otdela v zasedanii 7 fevralia 1919 g.," *Izobrazitel'noe iskusstvo* 1 (1919), p. 85.

23. Varvara Stepanova, diary, March 27, 1919, A. M. Rodchenko and V. F. Stepanova Archive, Moscow.

24. *Iskusstvo* 7 (August 2, 1919).

25. *Zhizn' iskusstva,* September 20, 1923. Shklovskii's essay was written in 1920.

26. *Desiataia gosudarstvennaia vystavka. Bespredmetnoe tvorchestvo i suprematizm* (Moscow: Otdel IZO Narkomprosa, 1919), pp. 29–30.

27. *Veshch'/Gegenstand/Objet* 3 (1922).

28. "Problemy izucheniia literatury i iazyka," *Novyi Lef* 12 (1928), pp. 36-37.

29. *Iskusstvo kommuny* 4 (February 22, 1919). On Rodchenko's Linearism, see Aleksandr Lavrent'ev, "What Is Linearism?" in this volume.

30. Rodchenko, "Line," p. 73.

31. Stepanova, diary, March 27, 1919.

32. *Desiataia gosudarstvennaia vystavka.*

33. Stepanova, "On Constructivism," p. 174.

34. M. Matiushin, "O vystavke 'poslednikh futuristov,'" *Ocharovannyi strannik. Al'manakh vesennii,* 1916.

35. A. M. Rodchenko, "Liniia," 1921, A. M. Rodchenko and V. F. Stepanova Archive, Moscow. This passage is not included in the published English translation cited above.

36. *Sovremennaia arkhitektura* 1 (1926), p. 36.

37. *Revoliutsiia i kul'tura* 11 (1929).

38. V. Shklovskii, *Zhili-byli* (Berlin, 1923), p. 306.

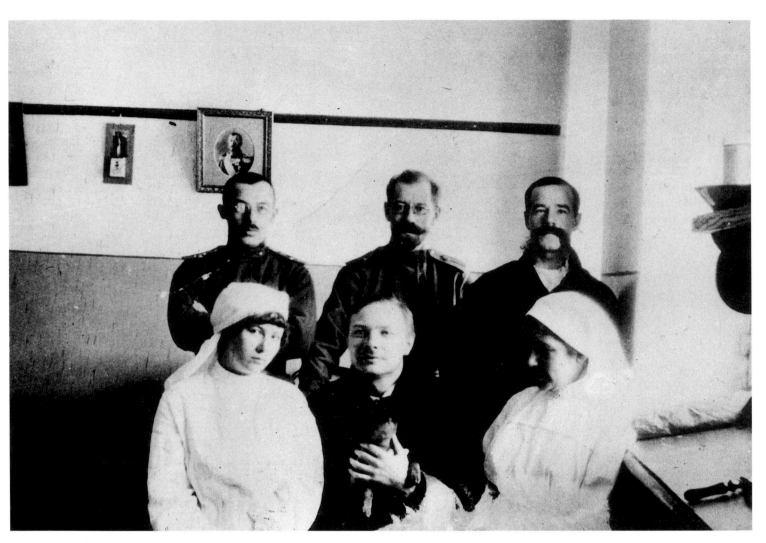

fig. 1
Larionov (center) in the hospital after being wounded in World War I,
1915.

The Third Path to Non-Objectivity

Evgenii Kovtun

Western scholars have sometimes failed to make a distinction between Abstractionism and non-objectivity, and use the terms interchangeably. Yet Vasilii Kandinskii and Kazimir Malevich are linked only by non-figuration—at which they arrive by disparate, quite unshared paths. The nonrepresentational element in their work grows out of different roots; Kandinskii and Malevich stand in as sharp an opposition as Hume and Hegel do in philosophy.

The abstract artist proceeds from the particular to the general, turning away from the tangibility of objects. In Kandinskii one may often observe a "semi-figurative" sketch gradually being translated into a pure abstraction. This is the path "from the bottom up."

Non-objectivity comes about by an opposite process. The artist starts from general structural regularities that are universal in character and makes them tangible in non-objective forms. This is the path "from the top down," from the general to the particular. Hence there are no natural or earthly realia, not even any that are "cleansed" of figuration, concealed behind Malevich's non-objective forms. Non-objectivity "populates" space with a new reality which comes into being according to laws analogous to those of nature.

Contemporary scholars rightly distinguish two currents within the movement toward non-figuration: that of Kandinskii, i.e., what could be called expressive abstraction, and that of Malevich, i.e., geometric abstraction. Artists of the one persuasion—in the words of Lev Iudin, a pupil of Malevich's—prefer to "experience" (thus Kandinskii), the others, to "construct" (thus Malevich and Mondrian). Yet even at the time, a third, middle, path to non-objectivity could be discerned in Russian art; its adherents attempted to reconcile opposing trends, wanting simultaneously to experience and to construct. This was the path first taken by Mikhail Larionov with his Rayism.

Art historians have caused quite a muddle in pinpointing the origin of Rayism, dating it as far back as 1909—a time when Larionov was producing Primitivist works. Iurii Annenkov, writing in 1966, was the first to set out a spurious chronology of Larionov's work: "Nineteen nine was the decisive year in the artistic biography of Larionov and Goncharova, and in the destinies of art in general: in that year both exhibited paintings which laid the foundation of the first abstract movement, dubbed 'Rayism' (Larionov's term) . . . Numbers of 'Rayist' paintings by Larionov and Goncharova appeared, between 1909 and 1912, at the avant-garde exhibitions of Jack of Diamonds, Free Aesthetics, and Donkey's Tail."[1] As it happened, Annenkov listed precisely those exhibitions which did not show Rayist works and managed to keep silent about those which had them in abundance.

Following Annenkov, other writers added their voices to the confusion. Waldemar George, author of a 1966 monograph on Larionov, moved the Rayist work *Steklo* (*Glass*) from the 1912 Mir iskusstva (World of Art) exhibition to 1909. We note the same antedating in the catalogue of the 1969 Larionov show in New York. The author of the catalogue essay, François Daulte, headlined one of its sections "The Rayonniste Period (1909–1912)" and advanced the fiction that Larionov had made his first declaration on Rayism in 1910 in A. Kraft's studio.[2] Camilla Gray, who had access to Russian sources, did not make such gross misstatements, but even she assigned *Glass* to 1909 and had it exhibited in a one-day Larionov show which took place in 1911 at the Society of Free Aesthetics in Moscow. Yet among the 124 canvases listed in the catalogue of that exhibition neither *Glass* nor any other Rayist painting appears.

What was Larionov's reaction to the misdating of his works? As indulgent as could be; he even abetted it. As early as in the catalogue of the *Exposition Natalia Gontcharova et Michel*

Larionov held in June 1914 at the Galerie Paul Guillaume in Paris, he changed the dates of many works, assigning them to earlier times. Larionov was inarguably among the pioneers of non-figurative painting (in the 1940s, which saw a wave of enthusiasm for Abstractionism, researchers sought out "precursors" of the movement; Michel Seuphor's 1949 book about the origins of abstract art recalled the by-then-forgotten Rayism)[3] and was not averse to being ranked as the very first. In Larionov's solo shows in New York (1969) and Brussels (1976), his *Abstraktnaia kartina* (*Abstract Painting*) was assigned to 1907 (!)—to a time, that is, when the artist was interested in signboards and was painting his *Parikmakhery* (*Barbers*). *Abstract Painting*, executed in the spirit of "painterly Purism," is clearly a work of the early 1920s, and entirely out of place with Larionov's Primitivist works.

The earliest "trace" of Rayism can be observed in Larionov's illustrations to a small book by Aleksei Kruchenykh, *Starinnaia liubov'* (*Old-Time Love*), which was published in mid-October 1912. Larionov thereafter showed Rayist canvases simultaneously at two exhibitions: *Glass* and *Etiud luchistyi* (*Rayist Study*) at the World of Art exhibition in November 1912, and *Luchistaia kolbasa i skumbriia* (*Rayist Sausage and Mackerel*) at the Soiuz molodezhi (Union of Youth) exhibition which opened on December 4th. Prior to this there had been no mention of Rayism either in the press or in exhibition catalogues.

The most representative showings of Rayism were at the *Mishen'* (*Target*, Moscow, 1913), *No. 4. Futuristy, luchisty, primitiv* (*No. 4: Futurists, Rayists, Primitives*, Moscow, 1914), and *Moskva. 1915 god* (*Moscow: The Year 1915*, Moscow, 1915) exhibitions. By this time, Natal'ia Goncharova, Aleksandr Shevchenko, and Sergei Romanovich were already working by the canons of Rayism. A special role in the rise of Rayism was played by a remarkable painter of Larionov's group, Mikhail Le-Dantiu. Il'ia Zdanevich implies in an unpublished article of 1918 that Le-Dantiu was the force behind Larionov's Rayism. He writes: "Rayism is taking shape—the unsuccessful realization of a colleague's brilliant discoveries."[4] And indeed, in Le-Dantiu's paintings of 1912 and 1913 one may make out the appearance of Rayist structures.

In 1913 Larionov published a brochure, *Luchizm* (*Rayism*), and an article, "Luchistaia zhivopis'" ("Rayist Painting"), in the *Oslinyi khvost i mishen'* (*Donkey's Tail and Target*) miscellany. The artist laid down the main tenets of his theory most succinctly in a pamphlet entitled *Luchizm Larionova* (*The Rayism of Larionov*), which was distributed to the public at a debate at the *Target* exhibition and from which the following is excerpted:

Doctrine of irradiability. Radiation of reflected light (color dust). Reflectivity. Realist Rayism, depicting existing forms. Rejection of forms in painting as existing apart from their imaging in the eye. Provisional representation of the ray by the line. Erasure of the barriers between nature and what is referred to as the surface of the painting. The rudiments of Rayism in antecedent arts. The doctrine of the creation of new forms. Spatial form. Form—which arises from the intersection of rays from various objects—isolated by the volition of the artist. Conveyance of sensations of the non-finite and the transtemporal. The structuring of paint according to the laws of painting (i.e., of faktura {density} and color). The natural downfall of all preceding art, which, thanks to Rayist forms, has become, like life, merely an object for the artist's observation.[5]

Rayism, according to Larionov's thinking, would sever painting from objectivity and turn it into an autonomous and self-sufficient art of color. The painting would cease to be a reflection of the world of objects—it would become itself an object, a part of reality aesthetically organized by the artist.

We do not see objects themselves—they are a kind of Kantian "thing in itself"—but we perceive aggregates of rays emanating from objects, which are depicted in the painting as lines of color. Larionov divides Rayism into a Realist species, which retains traces of objectivity, and a wholly nonrepresentational species, in which external links with the visible world have been sundered.

Larionov's tenet on light and color is of particular interest. Light refracted through particles of matter causes coloration, or "color dust," as the artist calls it. Here he anticipates the view expressed by the philosopher Pavel Florenskii in 1919:

Thus light is continuous. Not so optical media, which become saturated with light and pass it on to us: they are not continuous, they are granular; they constitute a kind of finest dust and themselves contain other dust, so fine as to defy any microscope, yet consisting of separate granules, distinct bits of matter. Those glorious hues which adorn the heavenly sphere are nothing but a means of relating indivisible light and fractured matter: we may assert that the coloration of sunlight is that aftertaste, that change of aspect, which is imparted to the sunlight by the dust of the earth, and possibly by the even finer dust of the sky.[6]

The critics looked upon Rayism as one of the varieties of abstract art; but the matter was more complex. Impressionism, preoccupied with color values, relegated plastic construction to the background. Cubism, by contrast, developed the structural element at the expense of the painterly. Velimir Khlebnikov, speaking of the Russian avant-garde, observed quite cogently: "As the chemist splits water into oxygen and hydrogen, so these artists have broken down the art of painting into its constituent forces, now isolating the element of color, now that of line."[7]

Larionov had no wish to sacrifice either. His Rayism was an astonishing attempt to combine the apparently incompatible: the vibrating color of Impressionism and the clarity of construction peculiar to Cubism. Their outward non-objectivity notwithstanding, the Rayist works of Larionov—with their movement toward nature, their luminous and intricately vibrating painting—call up natural sensations and associations. His *Luchistyi peizazh* (*Rayist Landscape*, 1912–13, fig. no. 3) is a case in point. The painterly-spiritual visionariness of Kandinskii and the stark non-objectivity of Malevich's Suprematism alike were alien to Larionov. Always receiving creative impulses from the visible world, he was unable to sever all links with nature. This singularity—Rayism's opposition to both Abstractionism and Suprematism—was noted at the time by Nikolai Punin, who held that the theory of Rayism had been advanced by Larionov "as a barrier against certain rationalistic tendencies of Cubism" and in practice was "the fruit of very subtle realistic juxtapositions."[8]

The Rayist canvases, especially those labeled "Realist Rayism," revealed the nature of Larionov's painterly gift and laid bare the wealth of *faktura* which was vehicle for the "color dust." Without a subject and virtually or entirely without an object, these works left the viewer one-on-one with painterly values. Larionov remarked on this himself: "What is precious to the lover of painting finds its maximum expression in the Rayist painting. The objects we see in life play no role there, while what constitutes the very essence of painting can be shown best of all: the interplay of color, its saturation, the interrelations of color masses, depth, *faktura*—by this persons interested in painting may become totally absorbed."[9] Non-objectivity may instantly expose the poverty of an artist's painterly gift, but it is also capable of announcing the wealth of another's.

Larionov's Rayism did not appear ex nihilo; the artist himself pointed to the "rudiments of Rayism" in the art preceding it. In the late paintings and drawings of Mikhail Vrubel' (such as *Shestikrylyi serafim* [*Six-Winged Seraph*, 1904] and the *Proroki* [*Prophets*, 1903–4] cycle) one discovers plastic structures which, as it were, presage the Rayist structures of Larionov. Nikolai Tarabukin reports that "in N. A. Prakhov's possession there was a pencil drawing of a male nude done as if in a 'Rayist' manner. Thus even this shortlived movement in painting, 'invented' by M. Larionov, was to a certain extent anticipated by Vrubel'."[10] A fair number of such "Rayist" drawings by Vrubel' are to be found in the collection of the State Russian Museum in St. Petersburg.

The artist Pavel Mansurov linked the emergence of Rayism even more specifically with Vrubel' in his account of an episode in Larionov's (and in Vrubel''s) career which had been unknown to scholars. In 1899, Vrubel', working on his ceramic panel for the main façade of the Hotel Metropol' in Moscow, invited a number of students from the School of Painting, Sculpture, and Architecture to be his assistants. Among these was Larionov, who spent some two weeks working under Vrubel'. We shall not find any direct results of this contact in Larionov's work; but at the end of his account, Mansurov makes a canny observation about the backgrounds in Vrubel''s paintings, which resemble "frost-covered windows."[11] This might seem a superficial hallmark, a chance resemblance, yet latent tendencies in the development of Vrubel''s plastic form, astutely detected by Larionov, are discernible in it.

The art historians without reservation assigned the Russian artist a place among the pioneers of Abstractionism, and Larionov readily accepted this role. But they failed to notice in Larionov's Rayism—outwardly non-objective—values and qualities unknown to abstract art: the readjustment toward "naturalness" and a painterly response to visible reality that was non-objective yet permeated by a vital sense of the values of nature. Rayism is neither lyrical nor expressive abstraction. As for Larionov, he was indeed a "precursor"—but of other painterly-plastic undertakings, which still await detailed investigation.

In 1912, the same year in which Rayism originated, Pavel Filonov, presenting the first fruits of his creative work, wrote an article entitled "Kanon i zakon" ("Canon and Law")—an early outline of the principles of analytical art. This marked a new understanding of the world and a new creative direction taken in opposition to Western Cubism and Russian Cubo-Futurism. Filonov wrote:

I am given to understand that Cubo-Futurism and Picasso could not have failed to influence my theory in one way or another. I am perfectly aware of what Picasso is doing although I haven't seen his paintings; but I must say that he personally hasn't influenced me any more than I have him, and he hasn't ever laid eyes on me, even in his dreams. On the other hand, there's not a thing that is done in our or whatever other line that wouldn't have had an influence on me, positive or negative. His influence was one of the negative ones. What in our thinking could we have borrowed from Cubo-Futurism, whose mechanical and geometrical foundations have led into a blind alley? Here is what Cubo-Futurism comes down to: purely geometrical representation of the volume and movement of things in time, hence also in space; of mechanical tokens of objects in motion, i.e., mechanical tokens of life, rather than of an organically movement-creating life, pervasive, transfiguring, and manifesting itself as such at any given moment of rest or motion.[12]

Cubism, as Filonov understood it, was the logical and willed construction of form abetted by the geometrizing of the

fig. 2
Mikhail Larionov
Portrait of a Man (Rayist Construction), *1913.*
Lithograph with painted additions, 11.2 x 9.2 cm.
State Russian Museum, St. Petersburg.

fig. 3
Mikhail Larionov
Rayist Landscape, *1912-13.*
Oil on canvas, 71 x 94.5 cm.
State Russian Museum, St. Petersburg.

depicted object. This is the way of the canon, the way of a framework and rules of construction prepared in advance. The logical, rational element dominated in Cubism, and this did not suit Filonov any more than such an approach to creative work suited Khlebnikov, who wrote:

> If the world were caught in a net
> Of numbers a hundred score,
> Would minds be nobler than before?
> No—more pitiful yet.[13]

Filonov set his analytical method in contrast to Cubism. He distinguished two approaches to the creation of a painting—the "preconceived" (by canon) and the "organic" (by law):

> In revealing the structure of a form or a painting, I have the option to proceed according to how I envisage the structure of the form, i.e., in a preconceived way; or to proceed after observing and laying bare the law of its organic development. Consequently, my revelation of the structure of the form will be either preconceived, i.e., canonical, or organic, i.e., according to law.[14]

This is Filonov's first use of "organic," a term that occupies an important place in his conception of art.

The primacy of nature, to be sure, was proclaimed by all movements, even the most non-objective ones. But Cubism evolved in a different direction, where the secondary products of the material culture of man determined the forms of art. The geometrizing of Cubism and its mechanization of forms, particularly acute in the work of Fernand Léger, reflect this growing orientation toward the secondary, a process that the French Purists carried to its logical conclusion, likening the painting and its forms to the machine.

In analytical art, the relationship between artist and nature is entirely different. Filonov is consciously oriented toward the primary, that is, toward nature. For him, the evolution of life is the pattern or model which, when followed by the artist, yields a work of art. He strives to imitate not the forms which nature creates but the methods by which it "operates." This is the organic path in artistic creation.

A painting by Filonov grows like a living organism. From the points of contact of a brush or pen—called *edinitsy deistviia* (units of action) by the artist—there emerge complex varieties of *faktura* of differing "timbre." "Draw each atom persistently and accurately," Filonov wrote, "persistently and accurately work the color into each atom, so that it perfuses it as heat does the body or becomes organically joined to the form, as in nature the cell tissue of a flower is fused with its color."[15] Filonov's "units of action" are the indivisible particles, the color-imbued "atoms" which make up the infrastructure of his paintings.

The cardinal difference between Filonov and the artists of the avant-garde surrounding him lies in his aspiration to make visible what is in principle invisible. He wanted to expand the possibilities of representational art by adding the invisible (yet supremely important) elements of nature, society, and man's spiritual world to the ranks of images.

Filonov considered that the artists of his time—both Cubists and Realists—maintained too narrow and one-sided a relationship with nature, capturing only two of its properties—color and form—in their work, whereas any phenomenon has an innumerable quantity of no less valuable properties. He wrote: "Since I know, see, intuit that there are in any object not just two attributes—form and color—but a whole world of visible or invisible phenomena, their emanations, reactions, waxings and wanings, genesis, being, known or secret properties, which in their turn have sometimes incalculable attributes, I unequivocally reject the 'two attributes' dogma of contemporary Realism and all its sects on the right and the left as unscientific and moribund."[16]

This is why Picasso's "reformation" appears to Filonov "scholastically formalistic and bereft of revolutionary significance." Picasso, like Il'ia Repin, paints merely the form and color of the "periphery of objects," plus or minus the "orthography of a school, a nation, a tribe, or a master."[17] From such a vantage point, "even Picasso with his violin is a Realist": "the violin is whole, the pitcher is whole; the violin and pitcher are broken into pieces and artificially placed on the canvas."[18]

"I see, know, intuit"—these are the three modes of creation Filonov describes as at the artists's disposal.

The Realist paints by sight. He operates with color and form. His paintings also render the invisible—a psychological state or the features of man's inner world—but through the visible.

The Cubist paints not only by sight but also by knowledge: Picasso's pitcher is painted simultaneously from various sides and from within. He also paints what is invisible (from a fixed perspective) but in principle visible.

Filonov reproduces *what is in principle invisible* (in such works as *Formula petrogradskogo proletariata* [*Formula of the Petrograd Proletariat*, 1920–21, plate no. 342] and *Pobeda nad vechnost'iu* [*Victory over Eternity*, 1920–21]). He renders the invisible not through the visible, as the Realists and Cubists do, but through novel plastic solutions. This constitutes Filonov's qualitative breakthrough, and this is what makes him unique; no wonder that Kruchenykh called him the "eyewitness of the invisible."

Filonov theorized about the difference between the *glaz vidiashchii* (seeing eye) and the *glaz znaiushchii* (knowing eye). The first comes to know by the transmission of form and color; with the aid of the second, the "knowing eye," the artist, supported by intuition, reproduces processes that are invisible or hidden. Filonov described the process thus:

> From a certain angle of vision, from one side, or, to a certain degree, from either the back or the front of an object, everyone always sees only a part of what he is looking at. Further than that even the acutest seeing eye does not reach; but the knowing eye of the investigator and inventor, the master of analytical art, strives for exhaustive seeing, insofar as that is possible for man. He gazes with his analytical faculty and with his brain, and with these he sees into places which the eye of the artist does not begin to reach. Thus, for example, one may, seeing only the trunk, branches, foliage, and blossoms of, let us say, an apple tree, at the same time know, or by analysis strive to know, how the slender fibers of the roots take up and absorb the fluids of the soil, how these fluids ascend by way of the cells of the living wood, how they are disbursed in a continual reaction to light and warmth, made over and transformed into the molecular structure of the trunk and branches, into green leaves, into white and red blossoms, into green and then yellow and then pink apples, and into the coarse bark of the trunk. This is what should interest the master, not the appearance of the apple tree. The trousers, shoes, coat, or face of a man are not so interesting as the emergence of thought and its processes in the man's head.[19]

In depicting these processes, Filonov renders them by invented form, that is, non-objectively. In most of the artist's paintings one may observe a combination of two principles, the figurative and the non-objective, wherein lies the uniqueness of Filonov's structures. When Malevich or Mondrian paint a non-objective canvas, there is nothing figurative in it, whereas a Filonov painting may "begin" as a figurative one and "continue" as a pure abstraction. Or a lengthy non-objective "overture" may usher in a figurative image, as in Filonov's large canvas *Tsvety mirovogo rastsveta* (*Flowers of Universal Blossoming*, 1915).

Filonov's *Formula kosmosa* (*Formula of the Cosmos*, 1918–19) evidently was his first pure abstraction, whereupon followed the non-objective *Belaia kartina* (*White Painting*, 1919, plate no. 340), *Victory over Eternity, Oktiabr'* (*October*, 1921), and, finally, the brilliant *Formula vesny* (*Formula of Spring*, 1928–29, fig. no. 4). The last is an entirely non-objective painting, but one replete with the life of nature. No flowering trees here or landscape background; instead, the artist produces a powerful sensation of the vernal exultation of nature, of its living "organics," via pure color, breaches of deep blue, an unceasing movement of microstructures, and the capricious rhythm of large forms. This painting is not a state but a process comparable to a biological one. Filonov's *Formula of Spring*, the crowning achievement of his painting, marks, as does Larionov's Rayism, the third path to non-objectivity.

On this path we also encounter the school of Mikhail Matiushin, a broad movement in painting which is only beginning to be studied. It developed from the 1910s to the 1930s in parallel with Suprematism, but was overshadowed by Malevich's school; it is only in our day that the shadow is thinning. Exhibitions of Matiushin's work in Leningrad (1990) and Karlsruhe (1991), held thanks to the initiative of Alla Povelikhina, were the first to document the range and genuine significance of this movement. It reached its culmination in the 1920s, in the Workshop of Spatial Realism at the Petrograd Academy of Arts and in the Section on Organic Culture at Ginkhuk (the State Institute of Artistic Culture) in Leningrad. But it traced its beginnings to the work, ideas, and person of the poet and artist Elena Guro, who died in 1913.

In the annals of the Russian avant-garde one encounters the formula "Larionov–Goncharova"; "Matiushin–Guro" became another such formula, but with a difference: if in the first pair, Larionov played the leading role, in the second the creative initiative and the spirit of experimentation were Guro's. This state of affairs was acknowledged by Matiushin more than once in his diary—for example, in 1934: "Lena sensed the link between color and sound, wanted to express landscape by sound. M[isha] did not grasp this yet."[20]

With the urban focus in poetry and Cubism's geometrizing in painting at their height, Guro's work turns, ahead of the times, to nature. She appeals to the "redeeming earth" and strives to match the creative process to the rhythms of nature. "Try to breathe as firs rustle in the distance, as the wind sweeps and surges, as creation breathes; to emulate the breathing of the earth and the strands of the clouds."[21]

The movement toward nature produced in Guro's work a spirituality of rare elevation and purity. Yet this spirituality is free from any schematic abstraction or Symbolist freight of meaning. The most capacious, cosmically grandiose images of her prose and poetry are always warmed by a sympathetic and spontaneous feeling for nature: "And they tipped the cup of heaven for all; all drank and heaven was not lessened."[22]

Guro's painting no less than her writing gives evidence of a movement toward nature. Guro's palette, unlike that of Cubism, contains no ochre, umber, heavy earth tones, or areas painted in a local color of red, blue, or yellow. If in their contacts with nature the Cubists gravitated toward inorganic forms, to the world of crystal and rock, Guro orients her painting toward the forms and hues of animate nature, toward the organic world. Multiple gradations and shadings of green—the color shunned by the Cubists because of its too "earthy" associations—create a translucent glow in her canvases. Guro's aspirations in painting may also be ascertained from the lines of her diary: "I will build a palace from the

fig. 4
Pavel Filonov
Formula of Spring, *1928-29.*
Oil on canvas, 250 x 285 cm.
State Russian Museum, St. Petersburg.

apertures of heaven. All who arrive there will receive bright greenish-with-a-touch-of-pink or watery-blue crystals of sky. And more—there will be fluffy silvery raiments, delicate ones."[23]

Guro achieves a high degree of generalization of color and form, without losing the immediacy of impressions from nature. The objects in her canvases seem to have lost their weight and to exist in an airy state of suspension, while the material substance of her pigments has been transformed without remnant into luminously vibrating, softly shimmering smoke wreaths of color, as if endowed with a spiritual property.

There is yet another singularity to the organization of color in Guro's paintings: the simultaneous deployment, as of voices in a Bach fugue, of several colors which, as they develop and change interdependently, set off and enrich one another. In the 1920s, Matiushin and his pupils theorized about this device of color-interweaving, grounding it in the dynamics of three-color relationships: "primary color," "environment," and the "color coupling" which occurs between them. "Hitherto," Matiushin wrote, "artists have had difficulty placing two interrelated colors, and would lean more heavily on one of them. Rarely did any of them suspect *how* from the joining of two colors a third emerges. This enigmatic 'third color' was what we kept encountering in our work from life."[24]

Guro's ideas on art, as developed by Matiushin, gave rise to a new movement in Russian painting—as contemporaries, too, realized.[25]

Matiushin's creative orientation was the same as Guro's: "Nature tells us: 'do not imitate me while depicting me. Yourselves create as I do. Study My Creation.'"[26] To this axiom—"Yourselves create as I do"—all of Matiushin's school adhered, exploring the "means" and "methods" by which nature "operates." It is only in this sense, and not as a return to figuration, that one must understand Matiushin's words: "I was the first to give the signal for a return to nature."[27]

On April 14, 1923, he wrote in his diary: "At the society yesterday I revealed our motto: Zor-Ved [*Zrenie i Vedanie* (Seeing and Knowing)]."[28] And on May 22nd, the journal *Zhizn' iskusstva* (*The Life of Art*) published his manifesto "Ne iskusstvo, a zhizn'" ("Not Art but Life"), which shed light on both halves of this formula. "Knowing" is not "knowledge." "Knowing" means penetration into an inaccessible realm by means of intuition—the faculty upon which the work of Matiushin and his followers, and their investigations into space and color, were broadly based. As early as 1916, appraising what innovation Suprematism had wrought, Matiushin observed: "Objectivity has properties unknown to human reason, whose essence may be grasped not in objects' tangible form but as transformed by a higher intuitive intelligence."[29] Now, seeing interacting with knowing, that is, intuitive reason, formed the basis of *rasshirennoe smotrenie* (expanded viewing), whose theory and practice Matiushin was working out with his colleagues. His students from the Workshop of Spatial Realism—Boris, Georgii, Mariia, and Kseniia Ender, as well as Nikolai Grinberg—joined him at the Section on Organic Culture at Ginkhuk. Gifted artists and musicians, they made up the original core of Matiushin's group. Within their professional spheres, all of them possessed the indispensable faculty of intuition. Matiushin commented of Boris Ender: "Boris is very talented, and much in painting is revealed to him."[30] Not "known" but "revealed"—precisely the point.

Matiushin's school attained its peak in the 1920s. Non-objective principles and properties, distinct from those of Suprematism and even contrary to them, appeared in the works of Matiushin and of the Enders. The curved line rather than the straight was the basis of their plastic structures; color evolved according to the organic laws of nature. This is why we witness

fig. 5
Mikhail Matiushin
On the Death of Elena Guro, *1918.*
Watercolor on paper, 38.1 x 27 cm.
State Russian Museum, St. Petersburg.

fig. 6
Matiushin and Ol'ga Gromozova at Guro's grave, Uusikirkko, 1913.

in the work of Boris and Mariia Ender an astonishing regular phenomenon: while distancing itself from the object, entirely forswearing it, their painting nonetheless approaches nature, provides, as it were, a purified concentrate of natural sensations. This quality emerges with particular intensity in Mariia Ender's *Opyt novoi prostranstvennoi mery* (*Experiment in a New Spatial Dimension,* 1920, plate no. 329) and in numerous works of Matiushin's disciples.

"Organic" was the key word in the theories of Filonov and Matiushin. Though Larionov did not use it, the essence of Rayism is kindred with that concept. The movements these artists inaugurated in painting marked the third path to non-objectivity—a path that revealed in non-objectivity new qualities and values.

—Translated, from the Russian, by Walter Arndt

fig. 7
From left, Mariia, Boris, Kseniia, and Georgii Ender, ca. 1905.

fig. 8
Boris Ender, 1914.

Notes

1. Iurii Annenkov, "Mikhail Larionov i Nataliia Goncharova," in his *Dnevnik moikh vstrech* (New York: Inter-Language Literary Associates, 1966), vol. 2, pp. 213–14.

2. François Daulte, "Michel Larionov," in *Michel Larionov*, catalogue for exhibition organized by Acquavella Galleries, New York (New York: Acquavella Galleries, 1969), n. pag.

3. Michel Seuphor, *L'Art abstrait, ses origines et ses premiers maîtres* (Paris: Maeght, 1949).

4. I. M. Zdanevich, "Okrest iskusstva M. Le-Dantiu," 1918, Manuscript Division, State Russian Museum, St. Petersburg, f. 177, d. 37, l. 5.

5. *Luchizm Larionova*, pamphlet distributed at the debate on "The East, National Character, and the West," March 23, 1913.

6. Sviashch. Pavel Florenskii, "Nebesnye znameniia. (Razmyshleniia o simvolike tsvetov)," in his *Stat'i po iskusstvu*, vol. 1 of his *Sobranie sochinenii* (Paris: YMCA-Press, 1985), pp. 57–58.

7. Velimir Khlebnikov, "Otkrytie khudozhestvennoi galerei," in his *Tvoreniia* (Moscow: Sovetskii pisatel', 1987), p. 619.

8. N. Punin, "Impressionisticheskii period v tvorchestve M. F. Larionova," in *Materialy po russkomu iskusstvu* (Leningrad: Gosudarstvennyi russkii muzei, 1928), vol. 1, p. 297.

9. Timofei Bogomazov et al., "Luchisty i budushchniki. Manifest," in *Oslinyi khvost i mishen'*, July 1913, pp. 9–48.

10. N. M. Tarabukin, *Vrubel'* (Moscow: Iskusstvo, 1974), p. 111.

11. Pavel Mansurov, letter to Evgenii Kovtun, May 28, 1971, private archive of Evgenii Kovtun, St. Petersburg.

12. P. N. Filonov, "Kanon i zakon," 1912, Manuscript Division, Pushkin House, St. Petersburg, f. 656.

13. V. Khlebnikov, *Zangezi* (Moscow, 1922), p. 27.

14. Filonov, "Kanon i zakon."

15. P. N. Filonov, "Ideologiia analiticheskogo iskusstva," in *P. Filonov*, catalogue for exhibition organized by the State Russian Museum, Leningrad (Leningrad: Gosudarstvennyi russkii muzei, 1930), p. 42.

16. See P. N. Filonov, "Deklaratsiia 'Mirovogo rastsveta,'" *Zhizn' iskusstva* 20 (1923), pp. 13–15.

17. Ibid., p. 13.

18. Pavel Filonov, letter to Vera Sholpo, June 1928, in E. F. Kovtun, "Iz istorii russkogo avangarda (P. N. Filonov)," *Ezhegodnik Rukopisnogo otdela Pushkinskogo doma na 1977 god* (Leningrad: Nauka, 1979), pp. 229–30.

19. P. N. Filonov, "Kratkoe poiasnenie k vystavlennym rabotam," in *Pavel Nikolaevich Filonov. Zhivopis'. Grafika. Iz sobraniia Gosudarstvennogo russkogo muzeia*, catalogue for exhibition organized by the State Russian Museum, Leningrad (Leningrad: Aurora, 1988), p. 108.

20. M. V. Matiushin, diary, February 9, 1934, Manuscript Division, Pushkin House, St. Petersburg, f. 656, tetrad' no. 15. The entry was made by Mariia Ender, who recorded Matiushin's words.

21. E. Guro, "Bednyi rytsar'," Manuscript Division, State Saltykov-Shchedrin Public Library, St. Petersburg, f. 1116, ed. khr. 3, l. 48.

22. Elena Guro, "Bednyj rycar' (The Poor Knight)," in *Elena Guro: Selected Prose and Poetry*, ed. Anna Ljunggren and Nils Åke Nilsson (Stockholm: Almqvist and Wiksell, 1988), p. 192.

23. Elena Guro, "Elena Guro's Diary," in *Elena Guro*, p. 63. Entry for June 5, 1911.

24. M. V. Matiushin, "Tvorcheskii put' khudozhnika," 1934, Manuscript Division, Pushkin House, St. Petersburg, f. 656.

25. After the breakup of the Union of Youth, Matiushin endeavored to organize a new artists' group. In a letter to Matiushin, Filonov noted: "You want to link your group's idea with the ideas of Elena Guro." Pavel Filonov, letter to Mikhail Matiushin, 1914, Manuscript Division, State Tret'iakov Gallery, Moscow, f. 25, ed. khr. 11, l. 1 oborot.

26. M. V. Matiushin, diary, April 16, 1923, Manuscript Division, Pushkin House, St. Petersburg, f. 656, tetrad' no. 2.

27. M. V. Matiushin, diary, December 1922, Manuscript Division, Pushkin House, St. Petersburg, f. 656, tetrad' no. 2.

28. Ibid.

29. M. Matiushin, "O vystavke 'poslednikh futuristov,'" *Ocharovannyi strannik. Al'manakh vesennii*, 1916, p. 18.

30. M. V. Matiushin, diary, April 14, 1923, Manuscript Division, Pushkin House, St. Petersburg, f. 656, tetrad' no. 2.

319
Mikhail Matiushin
Movement in Space, *1918.*
Oil on canvas, 124 x 168 cm.
State Russian Museum, St. Petersburg.

Mikhail Matiushin
Self-Portrait "Crystal," *1917.*
Oil on canvas, 70 x 37.3 cm.
Private collection, St. Petersburg.

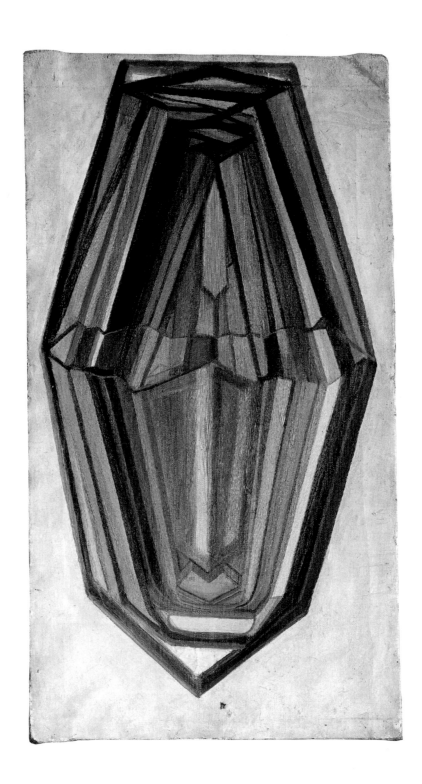

321
Mikhail Matiushin
Untitled (Abstract Composition),
1919.
Oil on canvas, 32 x 42 cm.
Courtesy Martin Muller Inc. and
Modernism Inc., San Francisco.

322
Boris Ender
Portrait of Karl Liebknecht, *1919.*
Oil on cardboard, 100 x 69 cm.
State Museum of Fine Arts,
Nizhnii Tagil.

323
Boris Ender
Untitled (Pulsating Color), *1921.*
Watercolor on paper, 22 x 27.3 cm.
State Museum of the History of the City
of St. Petersburg.

324
Boris Ender
Colors of Nature, *1925.*
Watercolor on paper, 22 x 24.5 cm.
Private collection, Moscow.

325
Boris Ender
Extended Space, *1922–23.*
Oil on canvas, 69.1 x 97.8 cm.
Collection George Costakis, Germany.

326
Boris Ender
Colors of Nature, *1924.*
Watercolor on paper, 22.5 x 27.5 cm.
Collection Zoia Ender-Masetti, Rome.

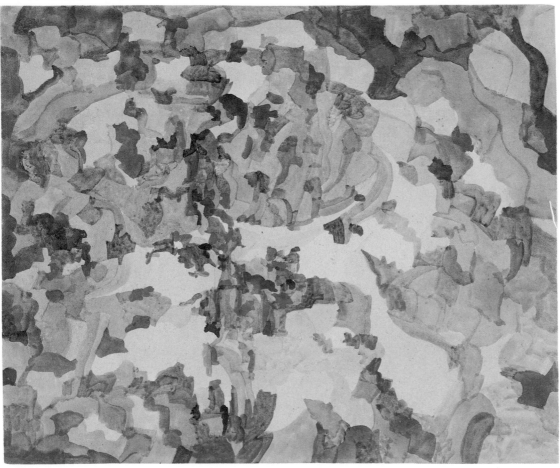

327
Boris Ender
Cosmos, *1923.*
Watercolor on paper, 18 x 16.6 cm.
Collection Zoia Ender-Masetti, Rome.

328
Boris Ender
In Peace, *1927.*
Oil on canvas, 90.2 x 80 cm.
Collection Zoia Ender-Masetti, Rome.

329
Mariia Ender
Experiment in a New Spatial
Dimension, *1920.*
Oil on canvas, 65.6 x 65.6 cm.
State Russian Museum, St. Petersburg.

330
Mariia Ender
Non-Objective, *1920s.*
Oil on canvas, 95 x 58 cm.
State Lunacharskii Museum of
Fine Arts, Krasnodar.

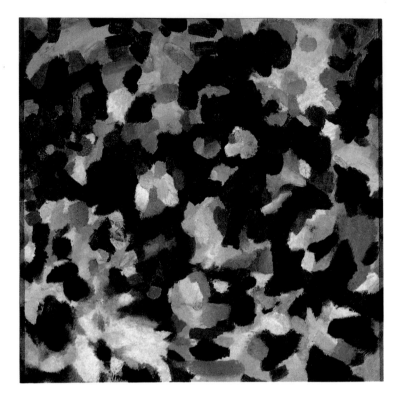

331
Kseniia Ender
Untitled, *1924–26.*
Collage on paper, 32 x 27.9 cm.
Collection George Costakis, Germany.

332
Kseniia Ender
Untitled, *1924–26.*
Collage on paper, 31.3 x 27.6 cm.
Collection George Costakis, Germany.

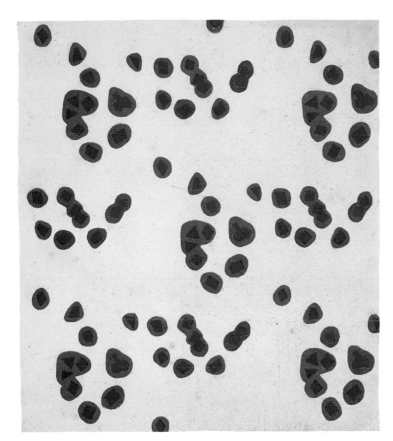

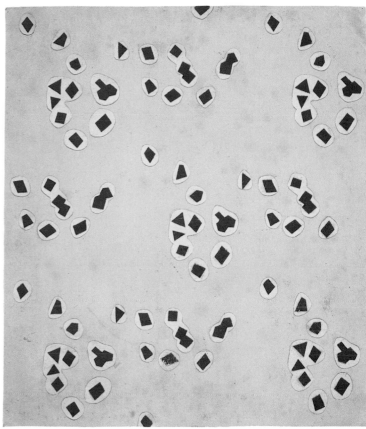

333
Kseniia Ender
Untitled, *1924–26.*
Collage on paper, 26.5 x 18.7 cm.
Collection George Costakis, Germany.

334
Kseniia Ender
Untitled, *1924–26.*
Collage on paper, 17.4 x 28.7 cm.
Collection George Costakis, Germany.

335
Mariia Ender
*Decorative design on a dark-red
background, 1924–26.
Colored paper, gouache, and collage on
cardboard, 35.2 x 41.4 cm.
State Tret'iakov Gallery, Moscow.*

336
Kseniia Ender
*Untitled, 1924–26.
Collage on paper, 31.8 x 27.2 cm.
Collection George Costakis, Germany.*

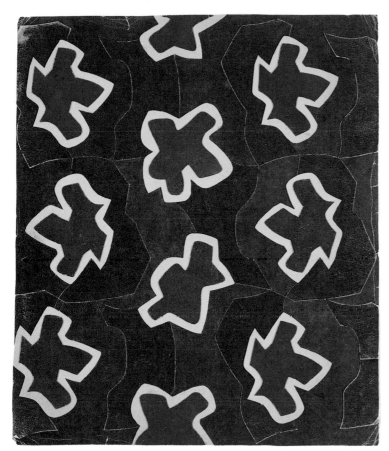

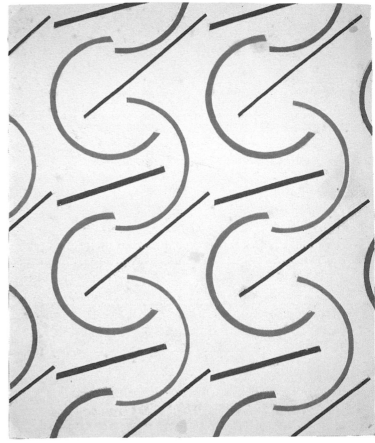

337
Pavel Mansurov
Non-Objective Composition, *1918.*
Oil on canvas, 49.5 x 39 cm.
State Art Museum, Omsk.

338
Pavel Mansurov
Painterly Formula No. 88, *1924.*
Oil on board, 85.5 x 21.5 cm.
Staatliche Museen Preussischer
Kulturbesitz, Nationalgalerie, Berlin.

339
Pavel Mansurov
Painterly Formula, *1927.*
Oil on board, 132.5 x 36 cm.
Galerie Gmurzynska, Cologne.

342
Pavel Filonov
Formula of the Petrograd Proletariat,
1920–21.
Oil on canvas, 154 x 117 cm.
State Russian Museum, St. Petersburg.

343
Pavel Filonov
Man in the World, *1925.*
Oil on paper mounted on canvas,
107 x 71.5 cm.
State Russian Museum, St. Petersburg.

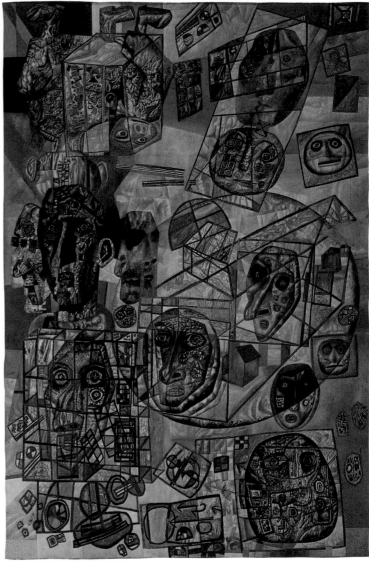

344
Mikhail Plaksin
Gas Spectrum, *1920.*
Oil on canvas, 81.2 x 81 cm.
State Tret'iakov Gallery, Moscow.
Gift George Costakis.

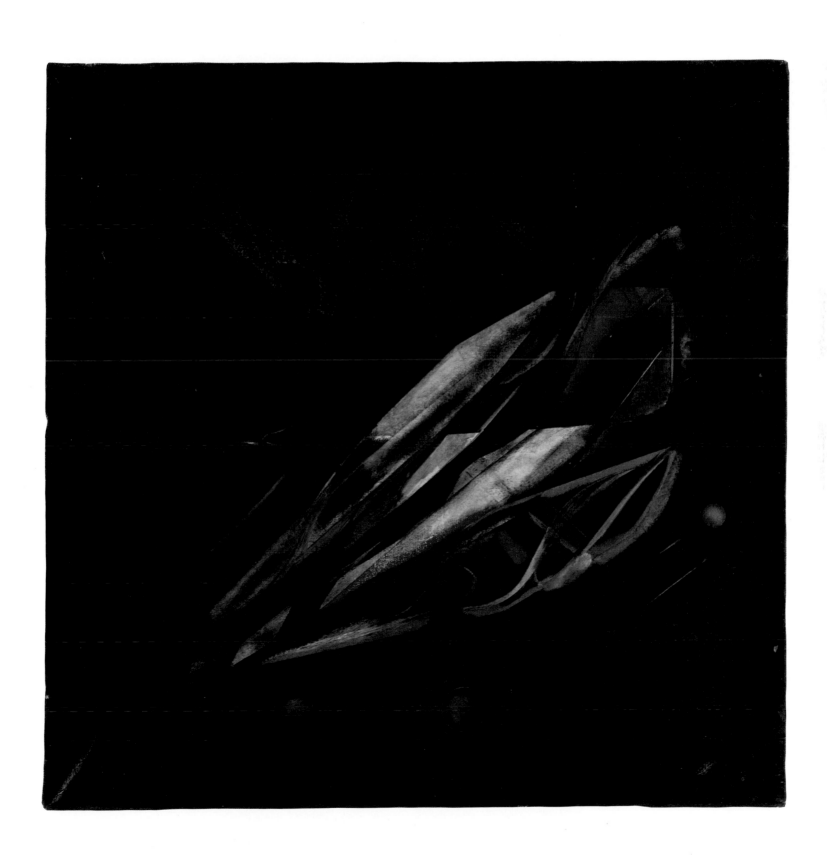

345
Mikhail Plaksin
Planetary, *1922.*
Oil on canvas, 71.9 x 61 cm.
Collection George Costakis, Germany.

Aleksandr Labas
Abstract Composition: Oval, *1921.*
Oil on canvas, 79 x 71 cm.
Collection L. B. Labas, Moscow.

347
Kliment Red'ko
Suprematism, *1921*.
Oil on canvas, 74.5 x 52 cm.
State Tret'iakov Gallery, Moscow.
Gift George Costakis.

348
Kliment Red'ko
Husband and Wife, *1922.*
Oil on canvas, 67.5 x 32.6 cm.
State Tret'iakov Gallery, Moscow.

349
Kliment Red'ko
Dynamite, *1922.*
Oil on canvas, 62.8 x 47.5 cm.
Collection George Costakis, Germany.

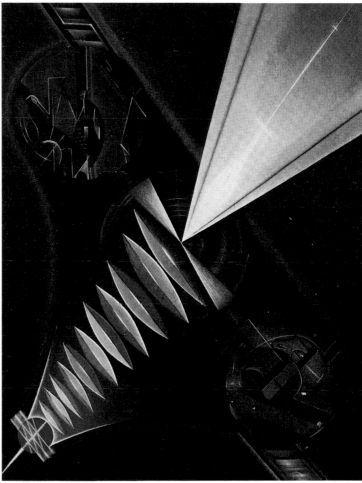

350
Kliment Red'ko
Composition I, *1924.*
Oil on canvas, 175 x 70 cm.
Muzeum Okręgove, Chełm.

351
Kliment Red'ko
Composition II, *1924.*
Oil on canvas, 175 x 70 cm.
Muzeum Okręgove, Chełm.

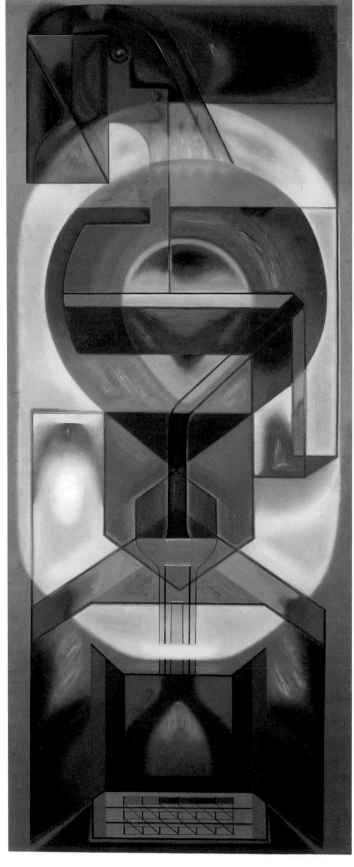

352
Kliment Red'ko
Uprising, *1924–25.*
Oil on canvas, 170.5 x 212 cm.
State Tret'iakov Gallery, Moscow.
Gift George Costakis.

354
Ivan Kliun
Red Light: Spherical Composition,
1923.
Oil on canvas, 69.1 x 68.9 cm.
Collection George Costakis, Germany.

355
Ivan Kliun
Spherical Composition, *1923.*
Oil on canvas, 64.5 x 64.5 cm.
Museum Ludwig (Collection Ludwig,
Cologne).

356
Ivan Kliun
Spherical Space, *1922.*
Oil on cardboard, 61 x 55 cm.
State Tret'iakov Gallery, Moscow.
Gift George Costakis.

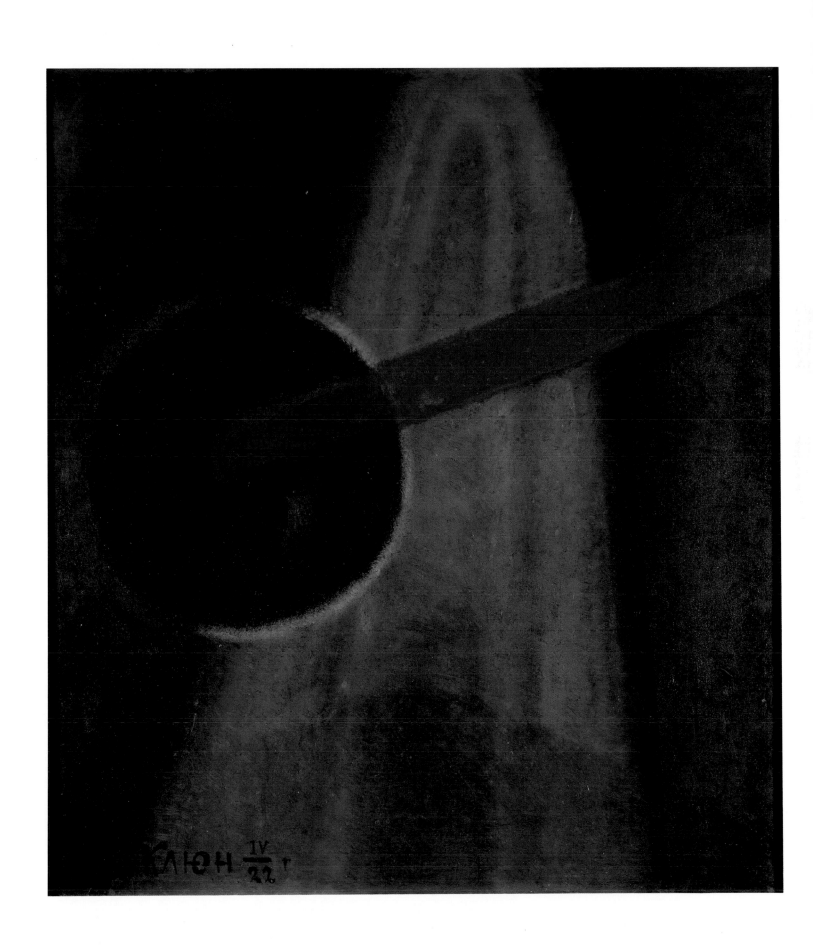

357
Ivan Kudriashev
Trajectory of the Earth's Orbit
Around the Sun, *1926.*
Oil on canvas, 68.5 x 75.5 cm.
State Tret'iakov Gallery, Moscow.

358
Sergei Luchishkin
Abstract Composition, *1924.*
Oil on canvas, 76.5 x 71.2 cm.
Museum Ludwig (Collection Ludwig,
Cologne).

359
Sergei Luchishkin
Coordinates of a Painterly Plane,
1924.
Oil on plywood, 95 x 95 cm.
State Tret'iakov Gallery, Moscow.

360
Sergei Luchishkin
Coordinates of the Relationship of
Painterly Masses: Abnormal, *1924.*
Oil on plywood, 44 x 26.5 cm.
State Tret'iakov Gallery, Moscow.

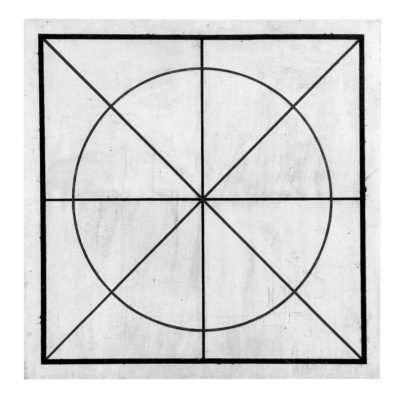

359
Sergei Luchishkin
Coordinates of a Painterly Plane,
1924.
Oil on plywood, 95 x 95 cm.
State Tret'iakov Gallery, Moscow.

360
Sergei Luchishkin
Coordinates of the Relationship of
Painterly Masses: Abnormal, *1924.*
Oil on plywood, 44 x 26.5 cm.
State Tret'iakov Gallery, Moscow.

361
Aleksandr Tyshler
Color-Dynamic Tension in Space,
1924.
Oil on canvas, 133 x 89 cm.
Collection Il'ia Sel'vinskii Family,
Moscow.

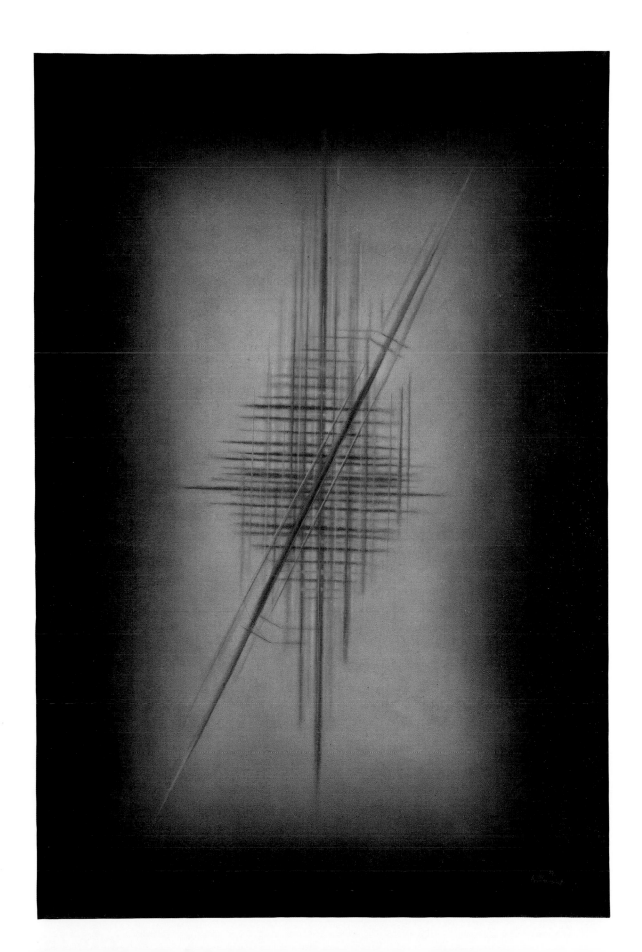

Aleksandr Tyshler
Color-Dynamic Tension in Space:
Front and Profile, *1924.*
Oil on canvas, 102 x 102 cm.
Collection F. Syrkina, Moscow.

Aleksandr Tyshler
Color-Form Construction in Red,
1922.
Oil on canvas, 101 x 65.5 cm.
State Tret'iakov Gallery, Moscow.

364
Konstantin Vialov
Untitled (Design for a Spatial
Construction), *1922–23.*
Gouache and watercolor on paper,
27.7 x 19.3 cm.
Galerie Stolz, Cologne.

365
Konstantin Vialov
Untitled (Design for a Construction),
1922.
Watercolor, ink, and pencil on paper
mounted on cardboard, 23 x 18.2 cm.
Galerie Stolz, Cologne.

366
Konstantin Vialov
Two Designs for Constructions or
Radio Towers, *1922.*
Pencil on paper mounted on paper,
23.3 x 11.2 cm.
Collection George Costakis, Germany.

367
Konstantin Vialov
Study for Construction of Theater
Set, *1923.*
Gouache and pencil on paper,
25.5 x 16.2 cm.
Collection George Costakis, Germany.

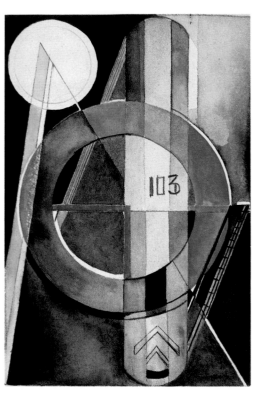

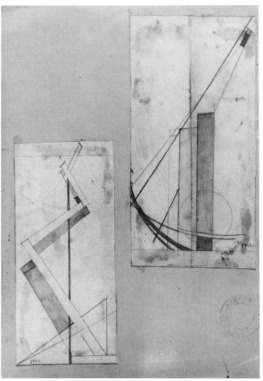

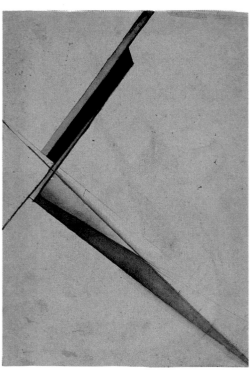

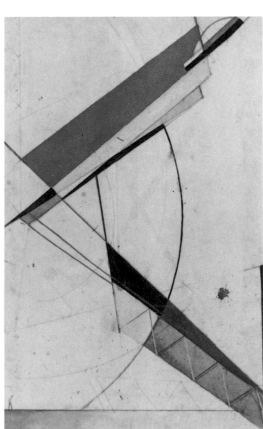

368
Konstantin Vialov
Traffic Cop, *1923.*
Oil on canvas, 106 x 86 cm.
State Tret'iakov Gallery, Moscow.

369
Solomon Nikritin
Man and Cloud, *1930.*
Oil on canvas, 142.3 x 142.3 cm.
Collection George Costakis, Germany.

370
Aleksandr Labas
Dirigible and Children from an
Orphanage, *1930.*
Oil on canvas, 160 x 80 cm.
State Russian Museum, St. Petersburg.

371
Aleksandr Labas
In the Airplane Cabin, *1928.*
Oil on canvas, 78 x 92 cm.
State Tret'iakov Gallery, Moscow.

372
Aleksandr Labas
Night in October, *1929.*
Oil on canvas, 103 x 72 cm.
State Russian Museum, St. Petersburg.

373
Aleksandr Labas
The Approaching Train, *1928.*
Oil on canvas, 99 x 79 cm.
Collection John Githens, New York.

374
Aleksandr Tyshler
Guliai-Pole (Makhno's Gang), *1927.*
Oil on canvas, 187 x 200 cm.
State Museum of Russian Art, Kiev.

375
Aleksandr Tyshler
Inundation, *1926.*
Oil on canvas, 142 x 72.5 cm.
Collection F. Syrkina, Moscow.

376
Aleksandr Tyshler
The Director of the Weather, *1926.*
Oil on canvas, 142.4 x 81.4 cm.
Collection F. Syrkina, Moscow.

377
Aleksandr Deineka
In the Donbass Region, *drawing for*
At the Factory Bench, *1925.*
India ink and gouache on paper,
29.7 x 28.8 cm.
State Tret'iakov Gallery, Moscow.

378
Aleksandr Deineka
Before the Descent into the Mines,
1925.
Oil on canvas, 246 x 209.8 cm.
State Tret'iakov Gallery, Moscow.

379
Aleksandr Deineka
Relaxation, *1928.*
Brown india ink on paper, 26 x 43.2 cm.
State Russian Museum, St. Petersburg.

380
Vladimir Liushin
A Delegation of American Workers
Arrives in the Village, *1928.*
India ink on paper, 35.4 x 44.4 cm.
State Tret'iakov Gallery, Moscow.

Aleksandr Deineka
Demonstration, *1928.*
India ink on paper, 38.9 x 29.9 cm.
State Tret'iakov Gallery, Moscow.

383
Aleksandr Deineka
Poster, Let's Mechanize the Donbass!,
1930.
Lithograph, 101 x 82 cm.
Lenin Library, Moscow.

385
Aleksandr Deineka
Poster, Proletarian Cadres to the
Ural-Kuzbass!, *1931.*
Lithograph, 70 x 103 cm.
Lenin Library, Moscow.

386
Iurii Pimenov
Hamburg, *1928.*
Watercolor and india ink on paper,
60.5 x 49.5 cm.
State Tret'iakov Gallery, Moscow.

387
Iurii Pimenov
Races, *1928.*
Watercolor, india ink, and graphite
pencil on paper, 49 x 39.1 cm.
State Russian Museum, St. Petersburg.

388
Iurii Pimenov
Painters in the Studio (A. D.
Goncharov and Iu. I. Pimenov), *1928.*
Gouache and india ink on paper,
49.6 x 39.6 cm.
State Tret'iakov Gallery, Moscow.

389
Iurii Pimenov
Study for poster, New Workers'
Settlements; Slogan: We Are
Building, *1929.*
Watercolor and india ink on paper,
96 x 68.8 cm.
State Tret'iakov Gallery, Moscow.

Poster, Everyone Must Be at the
Review!, *1928.*
Lithograph, 107 x 73 cm.
Lenin Library, Moscow.

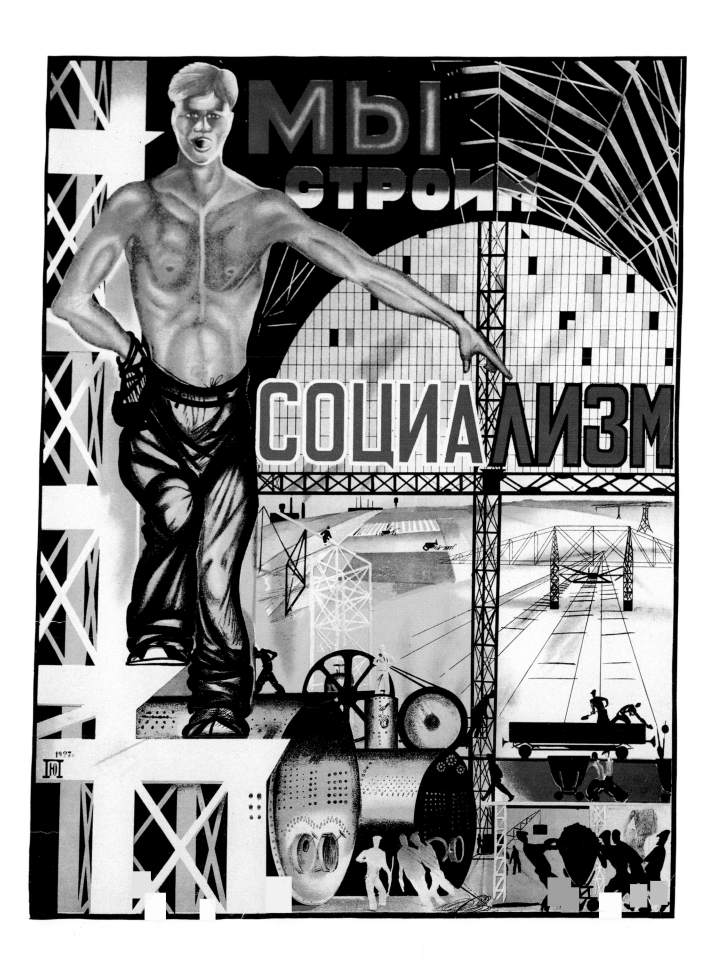

392
Konstantin Vialov
Poster, Kuznetskstroi, *1931.*
Lithograph, 108.5 x 75.5 cm.
Collection Merrill C. Berman.

394
Iurii Pimenov
On the Balcony, *1930.*
Oil on canvas, 139.7 x 73.7 cm.
Museum Ludwig (Collection Ludwig,
Cologne).

395
Iurii Pimenov
Girls Holding Balls, *1929.*
Oil on canvas, 159 x 102 cm.
State Tret'iakov Gallery, Moscow.

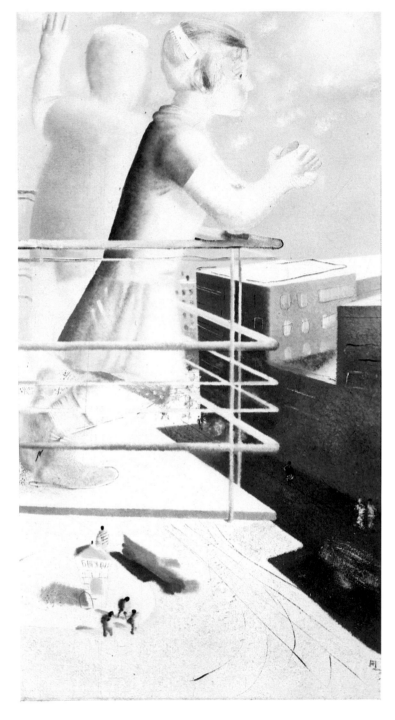

Iurii Pimenov
Milk Factory, *1930.*
Oil on canvas, 177.5 x 142 cm.
Private collection.

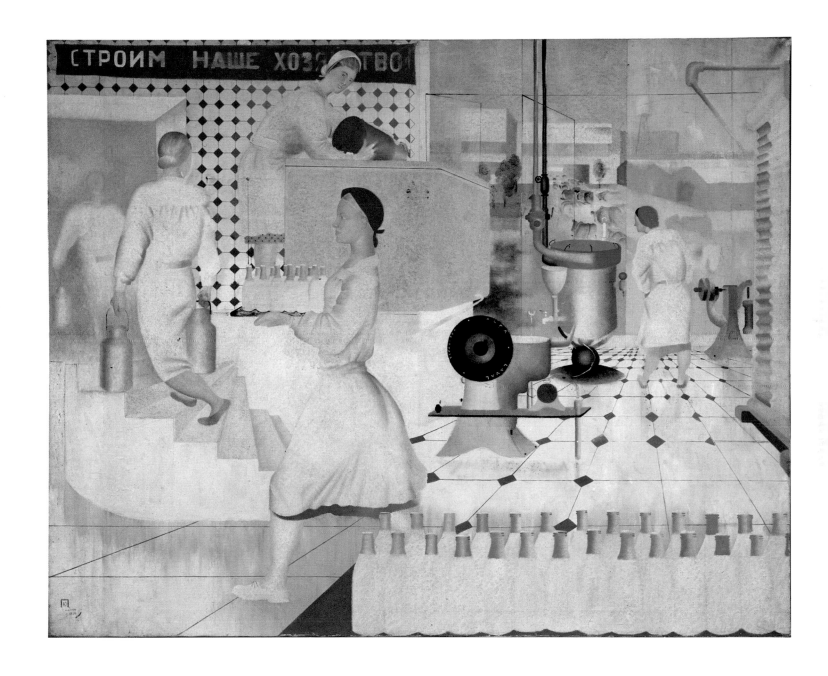

397
Kazimir Malevich
Red Cavalry, *1928–32.*
Oil on canvas, 91 x 140 cm.
State Russian Museum, St. Petersburg.

398
Kazimir Malevich
Sportsmen (Suprematism in
Sportsmen's Contours), *1928–30.*
Oil on canvas, 142 × 164 cm.
State Russian Museum, St. Petersburg.

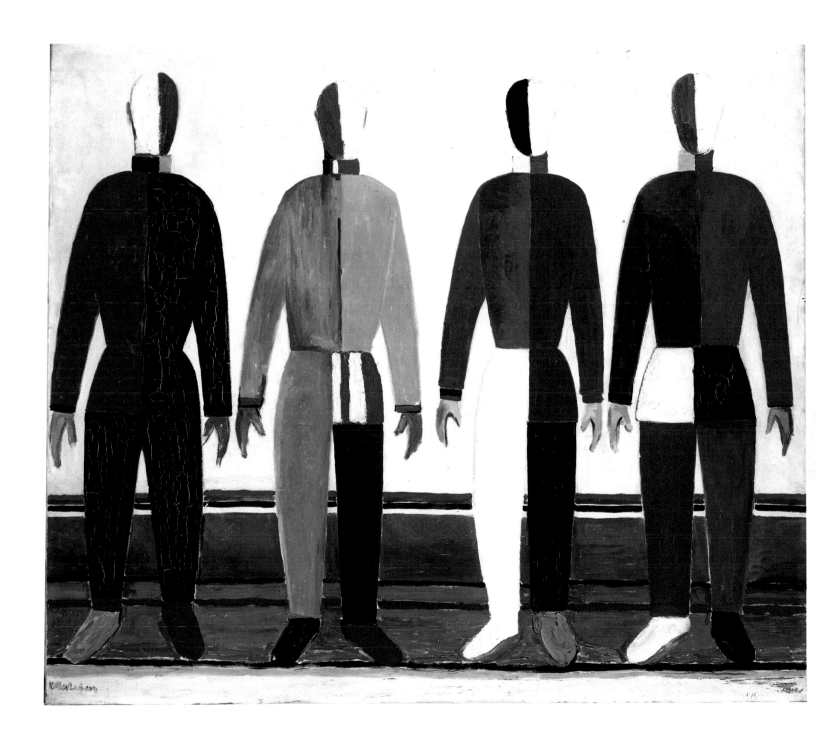

399
Kazimir Malevich
Girls in a Field, *1928–30.*
Oil on canvas, 106 x 125 cm.
State Russian Museum, St. Petersburg.

400
Kazimir Malevich
Three Female Figures, *1928–32.*
Oil on canvas, 47 x 63.5 cm.
State Russian Museum, St. Petersburg.

401
Vladimir Sterligov
Balance, *1928.*
Oil on canvas mounted on board,
23 x 17.5 cm.
Private collection, St. Petersburg.

401.1
Konstantin Rozhdestvenskii
The Field, *early 1930s.*
Oil on canvas, 50 x 62.7 cm.
Collection of the artist, Moscow.

402·
Kazimir Malevich
Torso in a Yellow Shirt, *1928–30.*
Oil on canvas, 98.5 x 78.5 cm.
State Russian Museum, St. Petersburg.

403
Anna Leporskaia
Woman with a Vase, *1932–34.*
Oil on canvas, 100 x 63 cm.
State Tret'iakov Gallery, Moscow.

404
Anna Leporskaia
Figure at a Colored Column, *1932–34.*
Oil on canvas, 59.5 x 48 cm.
State Tret'iakov Gallery, Moscow.

405
Vera Ermolaeva
Woman with Rake and Child, *1933.*
Gouache and whiting on paper,
29.5 x 22 cm.
State Russian Museum, St. Petersburg.

406
Vera Ermolaeva
Woman with Child, *1933.*
Gouache, tempera, and whiting on paper,
29.4 x 22.1 cm.
State Russian Museum, St. Petersburg.

407
Kazimir Malevich
Female Figure on a White
Background, *1928–30.*
Oil on plywood, 84.5 x 48 cm.
State Russian Museum, St. Petersburg.

408
Kazimir Malevich
Suprematism: Female Figure,
1928–30.
Oil on canvas, 126 x 106 cm.
State Russian Museum, St. Petersburg.

409
Nikolai Suetin
Suprematist Icon, *1929.*
Pencil, watercolor, and gouache on paper,
19.7 x 14.8 cm.
Collection Lew Nussberg, United States.

410
Nikolai Suetin
Composition, *from the series*
Suprematist Icons, *1927.*
Pencil and gouache on paper,
23.4 x 15.1 cm.
Collection Lew Nussberg, United States.

411
Nikolai Suetin
Sketch for Suprematist Icon, *1927.*
Pencil on paper, 15.7 x 14.5 cm.
Collection Lew Nussberg, United States.

Nikolai Suetin
Woman with a Saw, *1927–28.*
Oil on board, 55 x 33.3 cm.
State Russian Museum, St. Petersburg.

413
Kazimir Malevich
Self-Portrait, *1933.*
Oil on canvas, 73 x 66 cm.
State Russian Museum, St. Petersburg.

Kazimir Malevich
Portrait of N. N. Punin, *1933*.
Oil on canvas, 69.5 x 57 cm.
State Russian Museum, St. Petersburg.

415
Mikhail Veksler
Film poster for Fridrikh Ermler,
Children of the Storm, *1926.*
Lithograph, *106 x 70 cm.*
Museum für Gestaltung Zurich,
Plakatsammlung.

416
Aleksandr Rodchenko
Film poster for Dziga Vertov, Cine-Eye,
1924.
Lithograph, 92.7 x 69.8 cm.
The Museum of Modern Art, New York.
Gift of Jay Leyda.

417
Nikolai Prusakov
Poster, Second Exhibition of Film
Posters, *1926.*
Lithograph, 108 x 71.6 cm.
Collection Merrill C. Berman.

418
Aleksei Gan
Poster, First Exhibition of
Contemporary Architecture, *1927.*
Letterpress, 107.3 x 70.5 cm.
Collection Merrill C. Berman.

419
Aleksandr Rodchenko
Trade-union poster, Machinery That
Maims? Behind a Union-Erected
Grille It's Tamed, *1924.*
Intaglio, 25 x 35.5 cm.
A. M. Rodchenko and V. F. Stepanova
Archive, Moscow.

423
Anton Lavinskii
Film poster for Sergei Eizenshtein,
Battleship Potemkin, *1926.*
Lithograph and autotype, 72 x 104 cm.
Lenin Library, Moscow.

424
Anton Lavinskii
Study for poster, Dobrolet, *1923.*
Gouache on paper, 80 x 110 cm.
Galerie Natan Fedorowskij, Berlin.

429
**Georgii and Vladimir
Stenberg**
Film poster for High-Society Wager,
1927.
Lithograph, 108 x 73 cm.
Lenin Library, Moscow.

430
**Georgii and Vladimir
Stenberg**
Film poster for Dziga Vertov,
The Man with the Movie Camera,
1929.
Lithograph, 110 x 70 cm.
Lenin Library, Moscow.

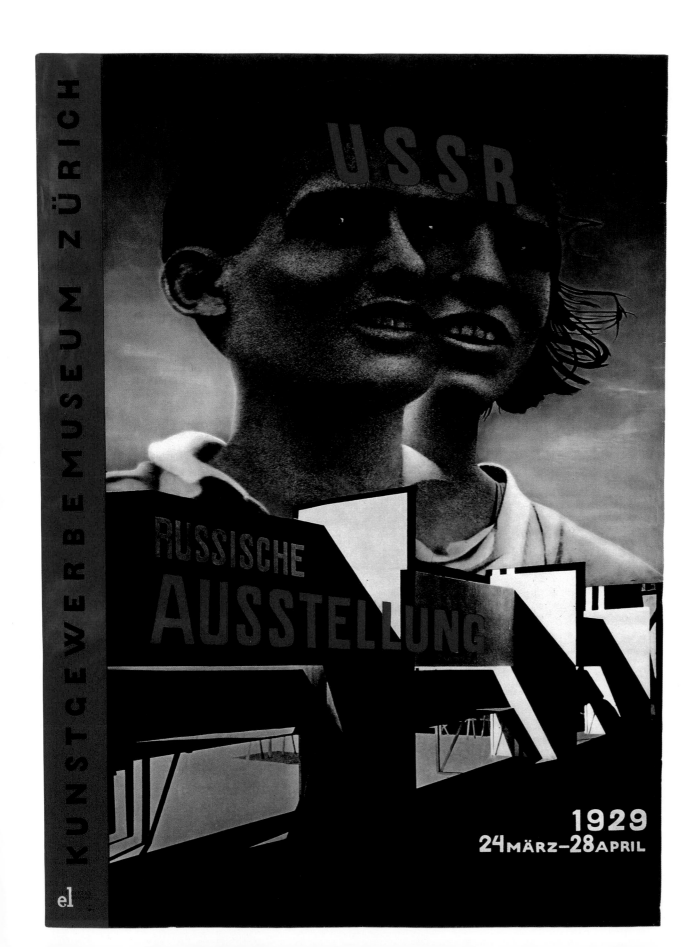

432
Gustav Klutsis
Poster, For the Building of Socialism
under Lenin's Banner, *1930.*
Mixed media, 97 x 71 cm.
Collection Merrill C. Berman.

433
Gustav Klutsis
Poster, Development of
Transportation Is One of the Most
Important Tasks in the Fulfillment of
the Five-Year Plan, *1929.*
Lithograph, 73.5 x 55.9 cm.
Collection Merrill C. Berman.

434
Gustav Klutsis
Poster, Communism Equals Soviet
Power plus Electrification, *1930.*
Lithograph, 73 x 52 cm, 101 x 71 cm
framed.
Museum für Gestaltung Basel,
Plakatsammlung (Museum of Applied
Arts, Basel, Poster Collection).

435
Gustav Klutsis
Poster, Without Heavy Industry We
Cannot Build Any Industry, *1930.*
Lithograph, 104. 5 x 73. 8 cm.
Collection Merrill C. Berman.

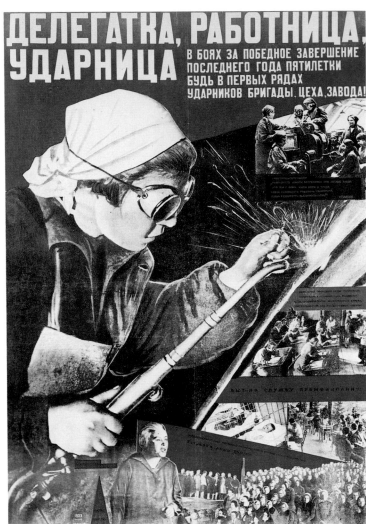

Valentina Kulagina
Study for poster, We Are Building,
1929.
Collage and gouache on paper,
57.5 x 36.2 cm.
Collection Merrill C. Berman.

Brigade KGK-3
Workers of the Kolkhozes, *1931*.
Lithograph, 100 x 70 cm.
Museum für Gestaltung Zurich,
Plakatsammlung.

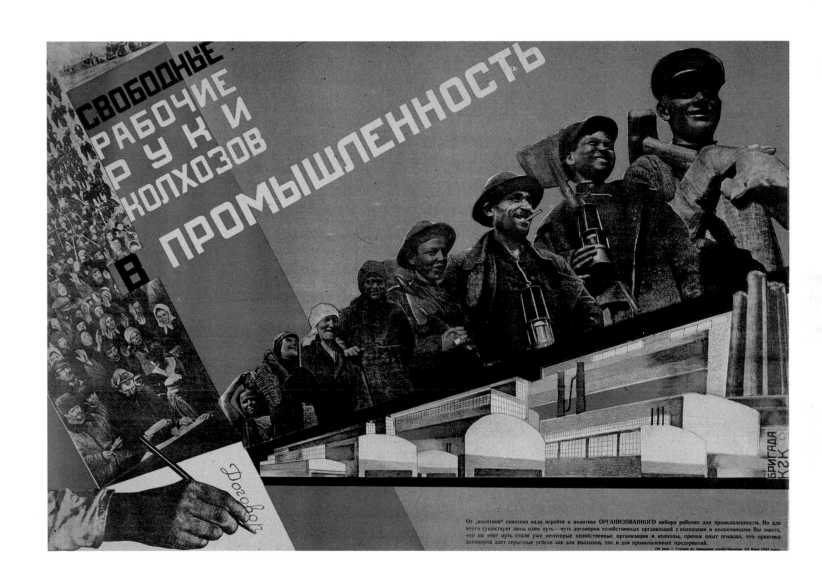

442
Nikolai Dolgorukov
Poster, Let's Create a Powerful Base
for Industrialization in the East!,
1931.
Lithograph, 105 x 74 cm.
Collection Merrill C. Berman.

443
Nikolai Dolgorukov
Poster, Let's Harness the Volga's
Powerful Energy to the Cause of
Socialist Reconstruction!, *1931.*
Lithograph and intaglio, 102 x 71 cm.
Lenin Library, Moscow.

444
Nikolai Dolgorukov
Poster, Transport Worker! Armed
with a Knowledge of Technology,
Fight for the Reconstruction of Our
Transport System!, *1931.*
Lithograph, 104.4 x 72.8 cm.
Collection Merrill C. Berman.

445
Gustav Klutsis
Study for poster, Lenin and Socialist
Reconstruction, *1927.*
Collage and photomontage on paper,
58.5 x 37.5 cm.
State Art Museum of Latvia, Riga.

446
Gustav Klutsis
Study for poster, More Steel, *1928.*
Collage, photomontage, gouache, and foil
on paper, 53.5 x 35.5 cm.
State Art Museum of Latvia, Riga.

447
Gustav Klutsis
Study for poster, Workers, Everyone
Must Vote in the Election of Soviets!,
1930.
Pencil, collage, and photomontage on
cardboard, 54.1 x 35.7 cm.
State Art Museum of Latvia, Riga.

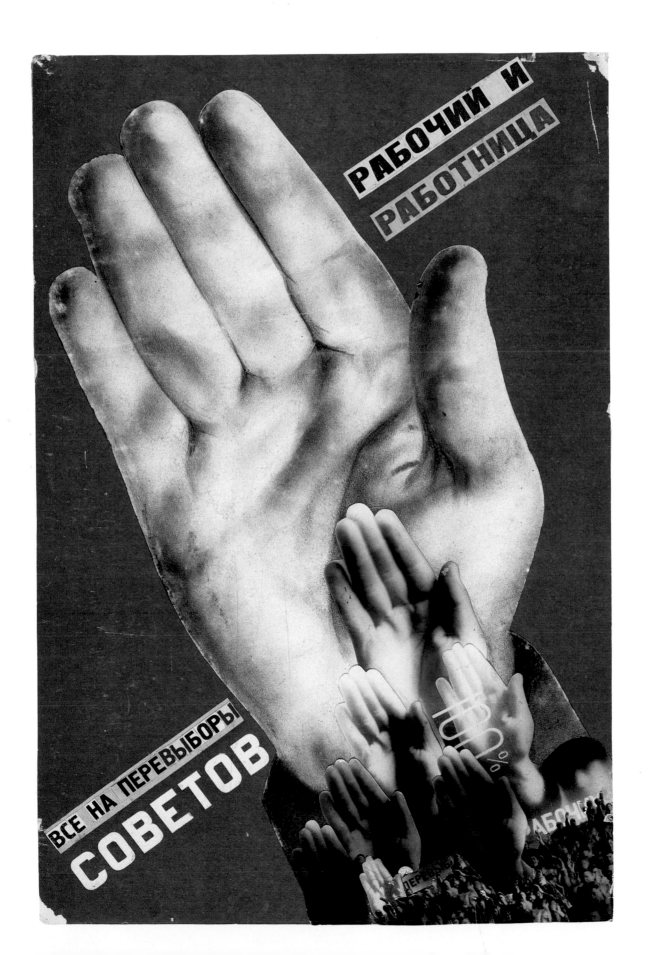

448
Gustav Klutsis
Study for poster, To the Fight for Fuel
and Metal, *1932.*
Photomontage, gouache, india ink, and
pencil on cardboard, 44.5 x 32.5 cm.
State Art Museum of Latvia, Riga.

449
Gustav Klutsis
Poster, To the Fight for Fuel and
Metal, *1932.*
Mixed media, 141 x 100 cm.
Lenin Library, Moscow.

450.1
Gustav Klutsis
Poster, Let's Return the Coal Debt
to the Country!, *1930.*
Lithograph, 101.6 x 71.2 cm.
Collection Merrill C. Berman.

450.2
Gustav Klutsis
Poster, Let's Return the Coal Debt
to the Country!, *1930.*
Lithograph, 101.6 x 71.2 cm.
Lenin Library, Moscow.

451
Gustav Klutsis
Poster, The Victory of Socialism in
Our Country Is Guaranteed, *1932.*
Lithograph in four parts, each
104 x 73 cm.
Collection Merrill C. Berman.

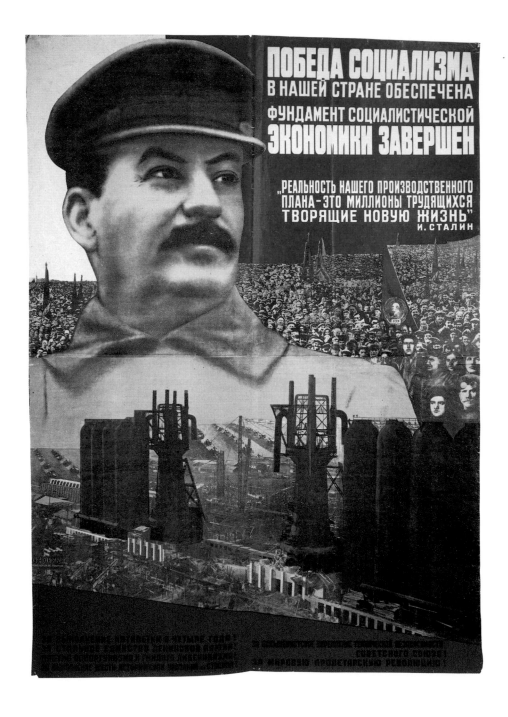

452
Aleksandr Rodchenko
The Photographer Georgii Petrusov,
1929.
Photograph, vintage print,
17. 5 x 23. 5 cm.
Galerie Alex Lachmann, Cologne.

452
Aleksandr Rodchenko
The Photographer Georgii Petrusov,
1929.
Photograph, vintage print,
17. 5 x 23. 5 cm.
Galerie Alex Lachmann, Cologne.

453
Aleksandr Rodchenko
Portrait of Lili Brik, *from the series*
Renault, *1929.*
Photograph, vintage print, 28 x 16.5 cm.
Galerie Natan Fedorowskij, Berlin.

453
Aleksandr Rodchenko
Portrait of Lili Brik, *from the series*
Renault, *1929.*
Photograph, vintage print, 28 x 16.5 cm.
Galerie Natan Fedorowskij, Berlin.

454
Aleksandr Rodchenko
Woman on the Telephone, *1928.*
Photograph, vintage print, 17 x 12 cm.
Museum Ludwig (Collection Ludwig,
Cologne).

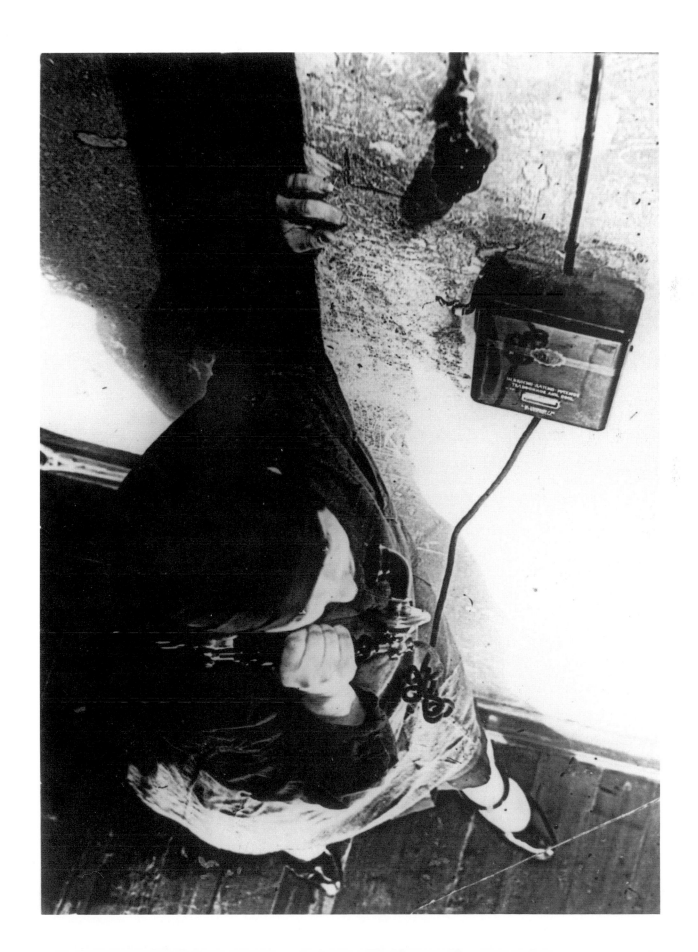

455
Aleksandr Rodchenko
Sawmill in Vakhtan, *1930.*
Photograph, vintage print, 17 x 22.9 cm.
Galerie Alex Lachmann, Cologne.

456
Aleksandr Rodchenko
Planks, *1931.*
Photograph, vintage print,
22.8 x 29.2 cm.
The Museum of Modern Art, New York.
Gift of the photographer.

457
Aleksandr Rodchenko
Man Pulling Boards, *1924.*
Photograph, vintage print, 29 x 23 cm.
Museum Ludwig, Cologne.

458
Aleksandr Rodchenko
Untitled (Worker in White Jacket),
1928.
Photograph, vintage print,
29.2 x 23.2 cm.
The Museum of Modern Art, New York.
Provenance unknown.

461
Boris Ignatovich
The Hermitage, Leningrad, *1929.*
Photograph, vintage print, 38 x 50 cm.
Galerie Alex Lachmann, Cologne.

462
Aleksandr Rodchenko
Park of Culture, *1927–28.*
Photograph, vintage print, 30 x 24.3 cm.
Museum Ludwig (Collection Ludwig, Cologne).

463
Boris Ignatovich
In the Harbor of Leningrad, *1929.*
Photograph, vintage print, 24 x 18 cm.
Galerie Alex Lachmann, Cologne.

464
Georgii Petrusov
The Dam of the Dneproges
Hydroelectric Station, *1934.*
Photograph, vintage print, 56.5 x 41 cm.
Galerie Alex Lachmann, Cologne.

465
Boris Ignatovich
Mechanical Piling of Wood in the
Harbor of Leningrad, *1929.*
Photograph, vintage print, 24 x 18 cm.
Galerie Alex Lachmann, Cologne.

466
Boris Ignatovich
Factory, *1931.*
Photograph, vintage print, 18 x 24 cm.
Galerie Alex Lachmann, Cologne.

467
Boris Ignatovich
Smokestacks and Factories of an
Industrial Plant in Leningrad, *1931.*
Photograph, vintage print, 13 x 18 cm.
Galerie Alex Lachmann, Cologne.

468
Georgii Zimin
Figure, *1928–30.*
Photogram, vintage print, 22.5 x 16.6 cm.
Galerie Alex Lachmann, Cologne.

469
Georgii Zimin
Balance, *1929–30.*
Photogram, vintage print, 23.1 x 16.8 cm.
Galerie Alex Lachmann, Cologne.

470
Georgii Zimin
Utensils, *1928–30.*
Photogram, vintage print,
18.2 x 24.2 cm.
Galerie Alex Lachmann, Cologne.

471
Georgii Zimin
Still Life with Screws, *1928–30.*
Photogram, vintage print, 23 x 29.5 cm.
Galerie Alex Lachmann, Cologne.

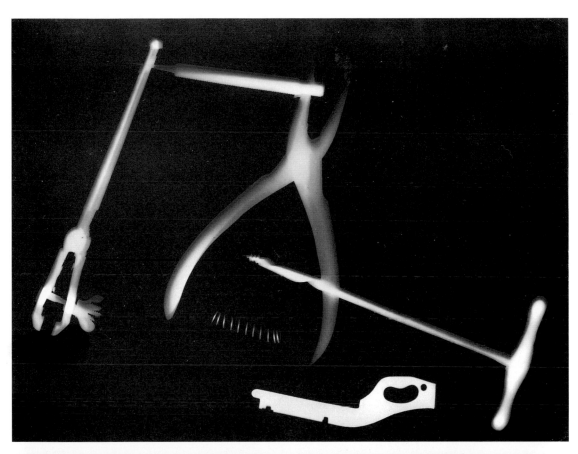

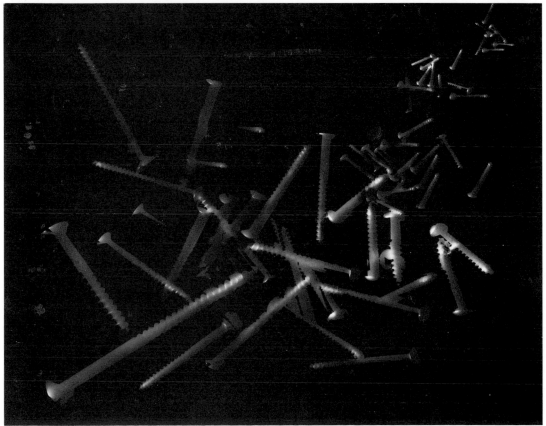

473
Georgii Petrusov
Caricature of Aleksandr Rodchenko,
1933–34.
Photograph, vintage print, 29.3 x 40 cm.
Galerie Alex Lachmann, Cologne.

474
El Lissitzky
Study for cover for Frankreich,
ca. 1929–30.
Photomontage, vintage gelatin silver
print, 28 x 21.1 cm.
Houk Friedman, New York.

475
El Lissitzky
Study for cover for SSSR na stroike,
ca. 1930.
Photomontage, vintage gelatin silver
print, 26.8 x 18 cm.
Houk Friedman, New York.

476
El Lissitzky
Runner in the City, *ca. 1926.*
Photomontage, vintage gelatin silver
print, 12.5 x 10.5 cm.
Courtesy Houk Friedman, New York.
Thea Berggren Collection.

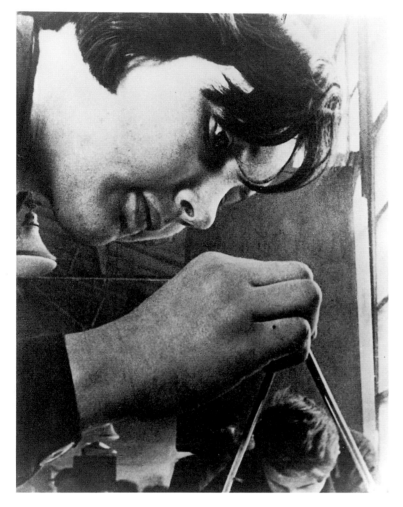

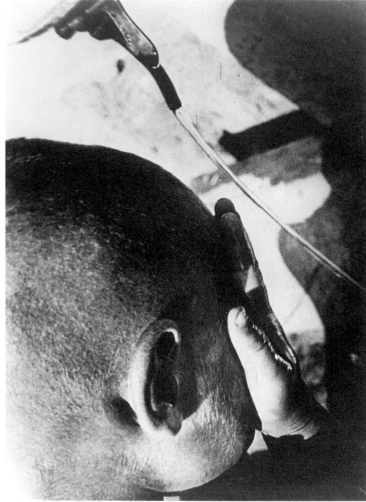

479
Elizar Langman
Young Man Brushing His Teeth,
early 1930s.
Photograph, vintage print, 17.3 x 24 cm.
Galerie Alex Lachmann, Cologne.

480
Elizar Langman
Grain, *1930.*
Photograph, printed from original
negative, 24.3 x 34.6 cm.
Solomon R. Guggenheim Museum,
New York.

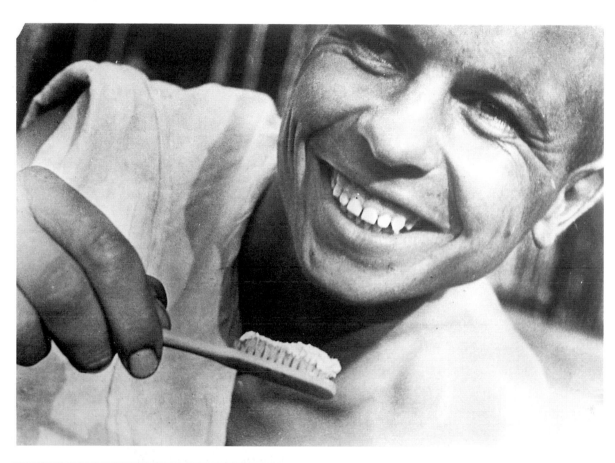

481
Georgii Zel'ma
Airplanes, *1931–32.*
Photograph, vintage print,
29.9 x 20.5 cm.
Galerie Alex Lachmann, Cologne.

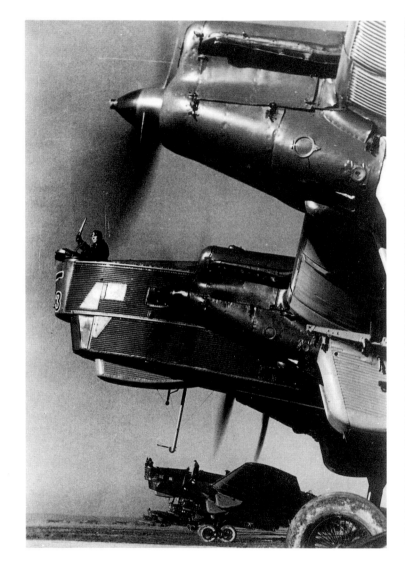

The Poetry of Science: Projectionism and Electroorganism

Irina Lebedeva

By the 1920s, notions of the tasks confronting art were undergoing revision and young artists rejected many of the aesthetic and philosophical ideas of the older Russian avant-garde. The younger generation used the artistic idiom of non-objectivity to offer new interpretations of scientific and technological achievements, which were now stripped of their earlier, almost mystical aura. Despite their seemingly irreconcilable differences, the Productivists—who sought to enlist scientific advances in the remaking of everyday life and who rejected the easel painting—and the members of Ost (the Society of Easel Painters, 1925–32)—who took a romantic view of scientific and technological progress and who argued for the renewed viability of the easel painting—were united in their view of industry as the most significant sphere of human endeavor, worthy of the closest attention.

At the beginning of the decade, new ideas of this sort were being formulated at the Moscow Vkhutemas (the Higher Artistic-Technical Workshops), which had become not merely a place for acquiring professional skills but the scene of fierce quarrels among various student groups. In 1924, their wrangles were put on public view at the *Pervaia diskussionnaia vystavka ob"edinenii aktivnogo revoliutsionnogo iskusstva* (*First Discussional Exhibition of Associations of Active Revolutionary Art*), a show of work by faculty, students, and recent graduates of Vkhutemas that opened on May 11th at 54 Tverskaia Street. "This exhibition is truly a 'discussional' one," wrote the critic Iakov Tugendkhol'd. "It includes seven different groups of young artists, each of them at odds with its neighbor, and all of them with the public, and each claiming the label 'left' for itself alone."[1] Nikolai Triaskin later recalled: "This was an exhibition where people walked about waiting for a fight to break out, for we defended our convictions very hotly, while remaining comrades among ourselves."[2]

Triaskin exhibited with the Proektsionisty (Projectionists), whose other members were Sergei Luchishkin, Solomon Nikritin, Mikhail Plaksin, Kliment Red'ko, and Aleksandr Tyshler (several of whom, a year later, were members of Ost). Their works, whose number exceeded that of any other exhibiting group, betrayed an interest in formal and analytical questions. In paintings such as Luchishkin's *Koordinaty zhivopisnoi ploskosti* (*Coordinates of a Painterly Plane*, 1924, plate no. 359), Nikritin's *Tektonicheskoe issledovanie* (*Tectonic Research*, 1921–24), Plaksin's *Planetarnoe* (*Planetary*, 1922, plate no. 345), Red'ko's *Arkhitektonika prostranstva* (*Architectonics of Space*, 1923), and Tyshler's *Organizatsionnye koordinaty napriazheniia tsveta* (*Organizational Coordinates of Color Tension*, 1923), the group endeavored to render such complex physical phenomena as radio and electricity and to convey the mechanics of motion and the expansiveness of space.

The critics, however, took a negative view of these canvases. Aleksei Fedorov-Davydov, for instance, wrote: "The hunger for knowledge, for Positivism, has never, it seems, been as strong as it is now. This materialistic way of thinking expresses itself in the urge to rationalize everything. This urge is sometimes carried to extremes, as it is by the 'Projectionists' . . . whose paintings are more reminiscent of geometrical drawings."[3] Tugendkhol'd's reaction was similar: "The exhibition is something of a landmark, all the more welcome since the paintings shown evince a definite turning away from the non-objective abstraction recently in vogue and toward figuration—a contemporary genre. To be sure, not all of the participants in the exhibition have moved beyond the stage of quasi-scientific schematization. The schematic works of Tyshler, Nikritin, Red'ko (in part), and others fall into this category, though they are not without merit in their handling of line and color."[4]

The members of the Projectionist group, linked by personal

friendships[5] as well as by artistic affinities, first came together in 1922.[6] During that year, they organized an experimental Projectionist Theater at Vkhutemas and participated in an exhibition at Moscow's Museum of Painterly Culture.[7] That exhibition, held at 52 Povarskaia Street from December 25th to 27th, combined permanent exhibits from the museum with works that were to be added to the *Erste russische Kunstausstellung* (*First Russian Art Exhibition*, Berlin, 1922), in which 180 artists were already represented, when it traveled to its next scheduled stop in Paris.[8]

Tugendkhol'd wrote of the exhibition at the museum:

One must welcome the effort to return to the investigation of color, to work on canvas, to work on paintings—such attempts at a deeper study of the qualities of paint and its application as are evident in the work of Nikritin, Red'ko, Tyshler, and Labas. There is still, of course, excessive sophistry, yet the unexpected sonority of saturated color and the loving attention to the surface of the painting itself are pleasing. Nikritin has a fine feeling for depth and its connection with this or that color, form, and density {faktura}. Red'ko studies the interdependence of painting and the sensation of movement . . . Labas treats the surface of his work with the loving care of an icon painter.

I repeat: all this as yet amounts to little more than "laboratory experiments." Yet even so, it represents a small step forward, out of the four walls of the laboratory and into the flesh-and-blood reality of the living world. A step forward from the one-sidedness of Malevich's purely color Suprematism and Tatlin's colorless Constructivism.[9]

Tugendkhol'd's juxtaposition of Malevich and Tatlin, the recognized leaders of the older Russian avant-garde, with the younger generation of left artists is highly symptomatic. Creation of their own artistic language was an essential element of the Projectionists' program. The group's organizer and chief theorist, Nikritin, wrote:

In 1922 two signal events occurred in Moscow, which—as always happens with profound *manifestations of an era—met with too little attention from the local critical press: just a few unrevealing articles in* Pravda, Izvestiia, Working Moscow {Rabochaia Moskva}, *and* Spectacles {Zrelishcha}. *These two events were a series of performances by the Projectionist Theater and an exhibition of works—to be sent abroad—by the "united group of young artists," the Projectionists. Both the performances and the paintings were a counterweight to the Suprematism of Malevich and the Constructivism of Tatlin and Rodchenko.*

{The Projectionists} appeared without any fanfare or earth-shattering manifestos; they were fed up with the endless, unproductive barrage of public declarations (an old tradition with the Italian Futurists). They came forth with a clearly defined philosophy of their art and a cycle of finished works.[10]

From the start, the Projectionists also positioned themselves in opposition to production art. "This latest fad," Nikritin wrote, "is all the more ridiculous for claiming to construct everyday life (!!!). Whereas any sensible person understands that daily life is determined not by artfully constructed beds, kiosks, clothing, or theater sets but by the *technical level of the instruments of production and the clarity of the ensuing worldview.*"[11] The Projectionists' slogans, as formulated by Nikritin, proclaimed the following:

1. The surface plane of the painting possesses meaning insofar as efficiently organizing lines of projection lead from it to an optimal culture of everyday life.

2. Painters must stay in their places, that is, not enter production.

3. Their works should be exclusively planned *and* methodical; *on their basis a thousand schools and laboratories should arise,*

cultivating a new ability and consciousness among the masses—in relation to an optimal social-technical function of materials.[12]

The works by the Projectionists exhibited at the Museum of Painterly Culture in 1922 and chosen to accompany the *Erste russische Kunstausstellung* to Paris were not shown in that city, after all (nor had they been shown in Berlin or listed in the catalogue). Instead, the show reopened in Amsterdam in May 1923. There, judging by documents retained by the family of David Shterenberg—the head of Izo Narkompros (the Department of Fine Arts of the People's Commissariat of Enlightenment) and the organizer of the exhibition—sales of works out of the show were brisk.[13] Red'ko later wrote: "As for last year's works, which had been on exhibit in Moscow—where are they now? In Berlin? Amsterdam? Paris? Venice? Who knows!"[14]

Red'ko published his "Deklaratsiia elektroorganizma" ("Declaration on Electroorganism") at the time of the 1922 exhibition, and it is evidently this conjunction that has caused scholars to refer to the Projectionists as the "Electroorganism group." In a draft of the declaration, dated December 23, 1922, Red'ko describes the tenets of his movement:

THE ART OF TODAY *is the worldview of the substance of radio, from which "potentiality"—energy in a variety of forms—arises. Light is the highest manifestation of matter . . . The art of "today" explains anew the concept of the "abstract," as well as how time exists in and of itself and how cognition is directed toward perception.*

Inasmuch as today's known value of the speed of light has outstripped all velocities previously known to exist, artists study the elements that constitute new periodic states of electromatter, constructing their works according to the spatial mechanics of two reciprocal forces—compression and expansion, distancing and approach . . .

The art of "today" explains: I build out of water, out of air, out of wind, out of dynamite, and these are the elements of the architectonics of the electroorganism. On the basis of the "electroorganisms" that we have created (works painted on a two-dimensional surface), we can say that our art, welcoming the unmediated worldview of the savage, bases its unmediated worldview on the culture of the periodic state of the elements of modern physics, on the ideas of medicine, on the ideas of the struggle for a common world and for control of the process of (a) creative and (b) mechanical work . . .

The artist of "today" . . . observing a periodicity in the "nature" of chaotic phenomena, systematizes that periodicity's objective factor by (a) measuring it (i.e., the factor) by mental apprehension, (b) advancing it to an electroorganism, and (c) establishing its movement in time—in the guise of "timbre" (the rising and falling function), in the guise of the space of the visible and audible, space encompassable by memory, and astronomical space.

That which is perceived is "realized" by the technical devices of "cinema"—by an economical, mobile utilization of electro-energy. "Cinema" is the problem of form in painting; cinematic technique is the means of realization. The light and color of cinema are crowding out "paint," which yields to the strength of "light-matter." The two-dimensional cinematic plane "electrokinetically" reveals the method of mastering the essence of the electroorganism in painting . . .

To study the forms of "electroorganism" is to draw nearer the forms of nature (to approach—from the first image formed by the primitive—a higher technological culture). "Electroorganism" as an entity (a) reveals in art new methods of studying the forms of the earth in relation to the forms found in the astronomical "absolute"; (b) discovers new elements in nature, explaining them in art; and (c) psychically cultivates "influence" over the spectator . . . "Electroorganism" is neither "Naturalism" nor "Realism" nor "Futurism" nor "Constructivism," for it originates in the properties of "universal demand" and "consumption."

"Electroorganism in art" is first a system of the psycho-philosophy

of "intersocial life" and of "astronomical being" and, second, an architectonics that raises the concept of the abstract to the essence of the maximum unit of velocity, replacing various philosophical systems such as Naturalism, Realism, Futurism, and Constructivism, and clarifying physical-psychic relationships in the "electroorganism."[15]

During 1922–23, Red'ko produced a large series of paintings and drawings under the general rubric of *Electroorganism*: *Dinamit* (*Dynamite*, 1922, plate no. 349), *Skorost'* (*Speed*), *Dinamika form i tsveta* (*Dynamics of Forms and Color*), *Dinamika fokusa* (*Dynamics of Focus*), and others. These experimental compositions were a reflection of Red'ko's enthusiastic embrace of the results of the scientific and technological revolution. "We are moving into the realm of science," he had written in 1921, "This is the first unmistakable sign of . . . the rebirth of art . . . We are great prophets. We train our reason, sharpen our powers of observation by means of analysis, and gather what is dispersed in dynamic forms . . . In art a pregnant silence reigns. What an extraordinary time lies before our young generation! Everyone is moving into the exact sciences."[16]

Such utopian ideas about the all-embracing possibilities of scientific and technological progress were a characteristic feature of the time. In his effort to represent complex physical phenomena or technically equipped factories and laboratories, Red'ko created, above all, fantasies on scientific and industrial themes in which the human figure was merely an element of stylized structures and mechanisms (some of these canvases were shown at the *First Discussional Exhibition*).[17] "*There is nothing picturesque!*" he wrote. "One has to penetrate to the innermost heart of things and calculate the physical world . . . *Space and gravity—these are the fundamental problems* to which to apply the power of the artist."[18]

The declaration of the Projectionists published in the catalogue of the *First Discussional Exhibition* was entitled "Nashi ocherednye lozungi" ("Our Slogans on This Occasion") and asserted:

The artist is the inventor of new SYSTEMS which objectively signify objects and works of art . . .

Paintings and three-dimensional structures are the most convincing means of expressing the PROJECTIONS (the METHOD) of the organization of materials . . .

The artist is a producer not of consumer goods (cupboards and pictures) but of PROJECTIONS (the METHOD) of the organization of materials . . .

MILLIONS OF PRODUCERS WILL MAKE THE NORMALIZED OBJECTS OF DAILY LIFE . . .

Art is the science of an objective system of the organization of materials . . .

Every organization comes into being through the METHOD.[19]

Nikritin, author of the catalogue declaration, had been at work on the theory of Projectionism during 1923–24.[20] "Projectionism," he had written in 1923,

is a doctrine postulating the evolutionary character of the "laws" of the world, a doctrine that teaches that nature is "today" evolving toward the tangible realization of universal organization . . . I call Projectionism the sole and final doctrine in the sense that it presents in its basic traits the only objective way to a genuine realization of the world's energy, hence also of the life of each separate human being.

I call this doctrine the final one in the sense that the interrelation between man and the world outlined in it cannot fail to be objectively regarded as the final form of interrelation, given the magnitude of its embrace of the whole . . .

I call this doctrine Projectionist because the Projectionist, universally planned intellectual comprehensibility of every human

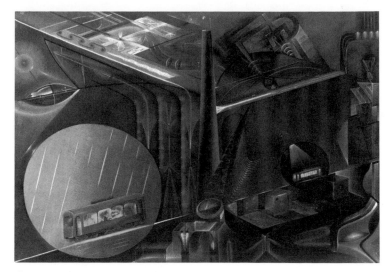

fig. 1
Kliment Red'ko
Composition (Factory), *1922.*
Oil on canvas, 69.5 x 101 cm.
State Kasteev Kazakhstan Museum of Arts, Alma-Ata.

action and word in relation to the realization of the world's energy and hence also the energy of each separate human being, his actual (not political, but social) well-being, is the cardinal, most urgent task of our age, the single goal to struggle for.[21]

The artist, according to this theory, should produce not works of art but only their "projections," on whose basis any person in any number of schools or laboratories could create an object. Theater, for its part, was regarded as a projection of theater in general, of a theater that, disconnected from any text, could function in any country. Unity of actor and spectator could be achieved by means of mobile abstract sets and evocative, "self-sufficient" sound. One of the historians of Ost, Vladimir Kostin, has written that "for all the theoretical weakness of the basic tenets of Projectionism, it must be said that it, along with certain other movements of the twenties, anticipated one of the fashionable trends in contemporary West European art—so-called Conceptual Art."[22]

Surviving archival documents include a text composed by Red'ko for the *First Discussional Exhibition* in which he outlined the goals of the Projectionists—or Method—group:

The work of the Method group flows from the evolutionary development of the bases of formal achievements in art.

For us, easel painting is the most expansive school of philosophy.

Monumental painting and architecture are one of the bases of a fundamental understanding of the laws of the plane.

All this defines the essence, indicative of our fundamental link with the science of the past. In the present . . . investigation of the color environment and its influence on the work located in it. In the future . . . the Method group applies its achievements in laboratory analysis and synthesis to economic production . . . The Method group extends its hand to its comrades in other left groups working alongside it, developing the tasks of contemporary art by means of collective thought . . .

The ideology of the Method group: "Struggle."

First, as a movement Forward—{toward a} historical goal.

Second, with those who are against us.

The naming of this group "Method" will explain to our spectator what is to come and enable him to think ahead to our subsequent results in 1925, 1926, 1927, and the years following.[23]

For all Nikritin's and Red'ko's desire to provide a theoretical underpinning for the group, which they represented as united in its artistic aims and practice, the works shown by the Projectionists at the *First Discussional Exhibition* revealed a variety of interests among the young painters. Such works as Plaksin's *Planetary* and *Pervobytnoe* (*Primordial*) or Red'ko's *Periodicheskaia osnova sinteticheskogo obraza (glubina)* (*The Periodic Basis of a Synthetic Image {Depth}*, 1924) and *Monumental'noe postroenie fizicheskogo razvitiia (soprikosnovenie)* (*Monumental Construction of Physical Development {Continuity}*, 1924) were quests for a harmonious conjoining of abstract ideas from the exact sciences with sense perception of the surrounding world. Red'ko did not write by accident apropos these paintings: "All these works are *labor over feeling.*"[24]

Non-objective canvases in which emotion played a significant part may also be found among the early works of Labas. And during the same years, Tyshler constructed "fantastic decorative compositions, made up of details of machines and other apparatuses. Executed in reddish-orange and light and dark blue on a black ground, they were all but phosphorescent, radiating now a cold, now a hot light, which gently suffused the dark surface of the canvas."[25]

In his introduction to the catalogue for Red'ko's solo exhibition in Moscow in 1926, Fedorov-Davidov offered this description of Red'ko's works in that vein: "The attempt to represent in visual form abstract formulae and phenomena of electro-technology has led to abstract-utopian compositions whose subject, in the end, is emotional feeling. They are the purest expression of analytical and rationalizing painting, which aspired to find a painterly-emotional formula for scientific and technological phenomena."[26] The element of mythologizing inherent in these paintings carried the subject depicted beyond the confines of purely formal experiment.

The works of Nikritin and Luchishkin were of a different, more concrete, nature. At the *First Discussional Exhibition*, Nikritin showed his *Tectonic Research*—comprised of texts, photographs, sketches, reliefs, and a three-dimensional construction—and Luchishkin fifteen analytical works, including *Coordinates of a Painterly Plane* and *Koordinaty sootnosheniia zhivopisnykh mass. Anormal'* (*Coordinates of the Relationship of Painterly Masses: Abnormal*, 1924, plate no. 360). Luchishkin later recalled:

When I graduated, it turned out that the chief factor in my being awarded the title of an artist of the first rank was not my diploma painting but the analytical works I showed at the Discussional Exhibition. *They were the crowning stage of my formal experiments. I was looking for the foundations of our creative work and reasoned thus: if there are coordinates for measurement of the plane, there must be coordinates of compositional structure and coordinates of the relationship of masses. And I found them by means of analysis and juxtaposition of a large quantity of masterpieces of world art. I demonstrated everything graphically: I showed not only all types of the coordinates of the normal but also deviations; I supplied a chart of the basic types of compositional structures, with examples. After the exhibition, these analytical works became part of the collection of the Museum of Painterly Culture, and many years later I discovered them at the Tret'iakov Gallery.*[27]

Triaskin contributed to the *First Discussional Exhibition* models, sketches, and photographs of an *Universal'nyi teatral'nyi stanok* (*Universal Theatrical Set*). Of the "constructive system" embodied in these exhibits Triaskin wrote many years later: "I did not belong to the group of those [at the exhibition] who called themselves Constructivists—the Stenberg brothers, Gan, and, I believe, Denisovskii. I felt that constructions should be functional in a goal-oriented way . . . I exhibited sets for clubs and theaters which could be raised, lowered, or moved apart."[28]

These works did have a utilitarian cast, since they were earmarked for the performances of the Projectionist Theater,[29] in which Nikritin and Luchishkin participated with Triaskin. Triaskin's mobile sets were also employed in an experimental production of Anatolii Mariengof's tragedy, *Zagovor durakov* (*A Conspiracy of Fools*), in the Hall of Columns of the House of Unions in Moscow on May 16, 1923. A small exhibition—of Luchishkin's color charts and of Triaskin's sketches and movable constructions, made from laths, of a cube, a sphere, and a cone—was held in the lobby of the hall. "I had set things up," Triaskin subsequently recalled, "so that if you pulled one or another cord, everything changed shape—these planes moved over here, and those over there. The laths also changed position, depending on the angle from which you viewed them, and you had only to tug at them to get a new work of art."[30]

Petr Vil'iams, Iurii Pimenov, Luchishkin, and A. Akhmanitskaia were among the performers. "[Sergei] Esenin came, and [Vadim] Shershenevich, of course. There was a pretty big crowd," Triaskin recalled.

All the chairs had been removed, there was room to stand only along the sides, and in the middle was my ladder. And since we couldn't pay for the ladder, nobody had done any rehearsing on it. The

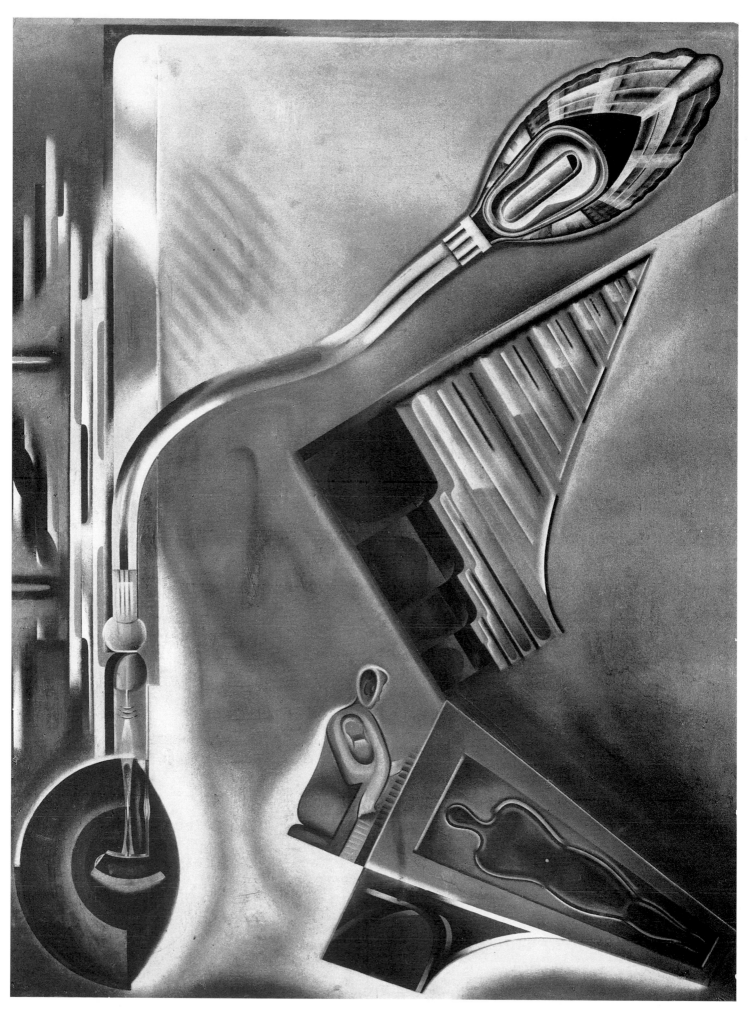

fig. 2
Kliment Red'ko
Composition, *1923.*
Oil on canvas, 105 x 81 cm.
Muzeum Okręgove, Chełm.

audience had already gathered and the ladder had been brought in, but the actors didn't know what to do with it: they would press it in one place, and all of a sudden the rungs would fly upward; they would pull elsewhere, and suddenly the whole thing would come apart. They did all they could; they struggled with that ladder throughout the performance, and at last left it for dead, just some kind of triangle standing there. I was, naturally, quite upset.[31]

Triaskin had also provided the actors playing fools at the funeral of Anna Ioannovna a kind of hoop into which to climb. Yet the hoop, like the ladder, did not work as intended. Pimenov, Luchiskin, and Vil'iams, inside the hoop, "were bumped by someone (and this while they were delivering their lines) . . . And until the hoop collided with something else, they were unable to get out. The upshot was that a remarkable review appeared . . . [under the title] 'A Conspiracy of Fools against the Public.'"[32]

A review by a certain Müller, published in a newspaper abroad, rendered a somewhat unexpected judgment on this production. He discerned a danger in the tilt toward technological development and the worship of the machine that had become symptomatic of the age. "I was struck even more forcefully," he wrote, "by the new liturgical music in the House of Unions. The ceremony I am talking about was held in honor of the official liturgy of the so-called Engineerists (Projectionists) . . . A Stations of the Cross of sorts, an enactment of the sacrifice of the lesser species of the individual to the higher order of a mechanized, almost soulless, collective man."[33] He took particular note of artists' universal absorption in industry and technology:

Lately in Russia, the machine has become a new idol that greedily devours ever new victims. Many efforts have already been made to reveal the machine's mysterious essence; now they are about to subject their own lives and the entire productivity of the globe to its laws.

The worship of the machine in the new Russia has all the hallmarks of an ardently espoused cult. This was very evident to me on my visits to the studios and workshops of the new artists.[34]

"Worship of the machine" was not, however, a uniform phenomenon. Thus the works of Aleksandr Deineka, Pimenov, and Vil'iams—the leaders of Ost—embodied a romantic faith that the problems and tasks presented by the new era could be solved with the help of scientific and technological advances. Among the Productivists, by contrast, interest in engineering assumed a utilitarian cast and the human being was, in many ways, considered subordinate. Whereas for the Projectionists, man was the affirmation of the self-sufficient value of the future fruits of civilization. The period during which the achievements of science and technology served as the Projectionists' fundamental subject was, moreover, a brief one. Those who became members of Ost changed their orientation.[35] (This is not to say, however, that the activity of the Projectionists was merely a stage in the formation of the aesthetics of Ost.)

Any innovative idea, once it has attained the peak of development in the work of great artists, inevitably leads, if blindly pursued, to a dead end. The search for new spheres in which to apply the discoveries made earlier is one means of escape. By joining the formal achievements of the previous generation of vanguard artists to new themes and subject matter—wherein lay their originality—the Projectionists marked one route out of impasse.

—Translated, from the Russian, by Walter Arndt

Notes

1. Ia. T[ugendkhol'd], "Diskussionnaia vystavka," *Izvestiia*, May 31, 1924.

2. N. A. Triaskin, "Vospominaniia," 1988, private archive, p. 12.

3. A. Fedorov-Davydov, "Khudozhestvennaia zhizn' Moskvy," quoted in *Russkoe i sovetskoe iskusstvo* (Moscow, 1975), p. 16.

4. Tugendkhol'd, "Diskussionnaia vystavka."

5. Labas was friendlier with Tyshler and Nikritin, Triaskin with Luchishkin, and Red'ko with Nikritin than each was with the others, according to Triaskin's memoirs. Red'ko and Nikritin, the chief theorists of the group, had met in Kiev in 1920; they came to Moscow together to enroll at Vkhutemas, and for a long time lived and studied in the same workshop. Yet as early as November 1920, Red'ko noted in his diary: "We shall never understand one another. He because of his desire to enlist comrades-in-arms in his cause and disciples of his theory, which does not exist for me; and me because I also see before me possibilities of following certain principles which in the course of my life I shall endeavor to establish with all the strength of my talent." Central State Archive for Literature and Art, Moscow, f. 2359, op. 1, ed. khr. 118, l. 16.

6. In a text written by Nikritin, evidently in 1925, he describes the circumstances leading to the formation of the Projectionist group:

On December 31, 1920, Nikritin gave a talk at Vkhutemas on the subject of "Problems of Contemporary Art (Theater and Painting)." His basic argument was that no existing group in art (theater and painting) was responsive to the conditions of the era; that young artists must create their own artistic organization; and that this organization must be, on the one hand, a group of painters and, on the other, a group of theater artists—the two groups united in a single federation capable of expanding and attracting to its ranks workers in other arts who adopt the viewpoint of the new association.

The talk was followed a discussion, as a result of which it was decided to create such an association. To this end, an organizing committee was elected . . . The association was founded, and it carried on its work (in painting, architecture, and theater) until the spring of 1922. That spring the association was disbanded, but a (theater) group of four remained, resolved not to give up but to continue the association's work—for the time being, only in theater. These four—Bogatyrev, Luchishkin, Nikritin, and Svobodin—were also the founders and organizers (the core leaders) of the Projectionist Theater. So as to advance this movement, steps were taken to strengthen theatrical work, to develop and expand it; as a result, a theater workshop, in full operation and giving performances, was organized" (Central State Archive for Literature and Art, Moscow, f. 2717, op. 1, ed. khr. 76, l. 1).

7. The Museum of Painterly Culture continued thereafter to play an important role in the lives of these artists. Nikritin, Labas, and Tyshler were members of its Research Board, and Triaskin and Nikritin conducted tours.

Different sources provide different lists of the group members who participated in the exhibition: Nikritin, Red'ko, Tyshler, Labas, and Komissarenko (Ia. Tugendkhol'd, "Vystavka v Muzee zhivopisnoi kul'tury," *Izvestiia*, January 10, 1923); Vil'iams, Komissarenko, Labas, Luchishkin, Nikritin, Red'ko, Triaskin, and Tyshler (V. P. Lapshin, "Pervaia vystavka russkogo iskusstva. Berlin. 1922 god. Materialy k istorii sovetsko-germanskikh khudozhestvennykh sviazei," *Sovetskoe iskusstvoznanie* 1 [1982], pp. 327–62); Borisov, Labas, Tyshler, Nikritin, Luchishkin, Triaskin, and others (Central State Archive for Literature and Art, Moscow, f. 2717, op. 1, ed. khr.

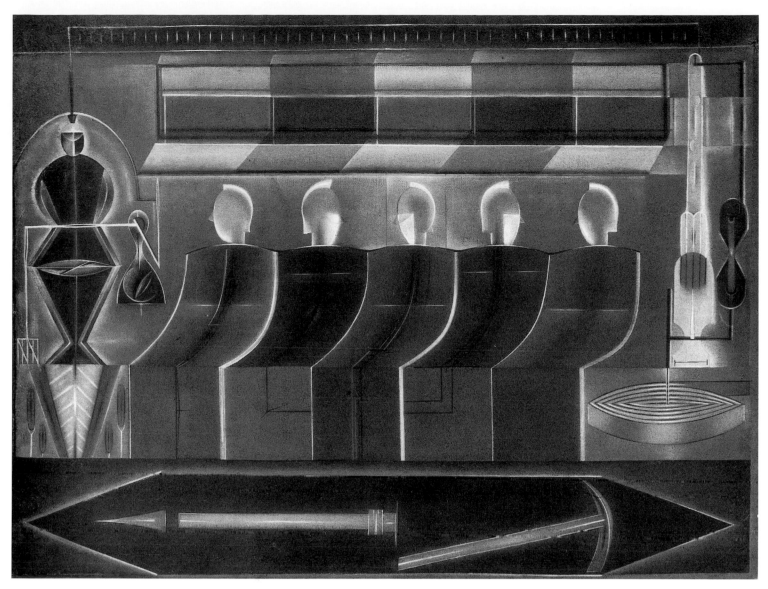

fig. 3
Kliment Red'ko
Compositional Study, *1922.*
Oil on canvas, 49 x 64 cm.
Muzeum Okregove, Chelm.

15, l. 16); Nikritin, Luchishkin, Labas, Komissarenko, Plaksin, Red'ko, Triaskin, and Tyshler (V. Kostin, *OST* [Leningrad: Khudozhnik RSFSR, 1976], p. 20).

8. All information in this essay on the *Erste russische Kunstausstellung* is taken from Lapshin, "Pervaia vystavka russkogo iskusstva."

9. Tugendkhol'd, "Vystavka v Muzee zhivopisnoi kul'tury." Luchishkin, noting that the exhibition consisted largely of abstract works, later wrote apropos his own paintings:

The works by Labas, Tyshler, and Red'ko, as well as two works of mine executed in {Nadezhda} Udal'tsova's workshop, which were selected {for the Erste russische Kunstausstellung} *were initially shown in the Museum of Painterly Culture . . . In them I wanted to go beyond those devices that Udal'tsova sanctioned—to liberate spatiality from the conventions of planarity, to express the fluidity of space, its infinite changeability—and I began to destroy planar composition and to endow it with a free fluidity, which led to a particular complexity of composition and coloring" (S. A. Luchishkin,* Ia ochen' liubliu zhizn'. Stranitsy vospominanii *{Moscow: Sovetskii khudozhnik, 1988},* p. 60).

10. Central State Archive for Literature and Art, Moscow, f. 2717, op. 1, ed. khr. 15, l. 15, l. 7.

11. Ibid., l. 10.

12. Ibid., l. 25.

13. See Lapshin, "Pervaia vystavka russkogo iskusstva."

14. Central State Archive for Literature and Art, Moscow, f. 2359, op. 1, ed. khr. 92, l. 13.

15. Ibid., l. 41–42.

16. Central State Archive for Literature and Art, Moscow, f. 2359, op. 1, ed. khr. 118, l. 24–25.

17. *Formula "Ia"* (*Formula of the Ego,* 1923), now in the Muzeum Okręgove, Chełm, Poland, was one of them. The drawing *Formula "Ia". Sidiashchii za roalem* (*Formula of the Ego: At the Piano,* 1923) in the Central State Archive for Literature and Art, Moscow, bears this inscription by the artist: "*Formula of the Ego* refers to questions of psychiatry and is a letter to those perplexed by the *Electroorganism* paintings."

18. Central State Archive for Literature and Art, Moscow, f. 2359, op. 1, ed. khr. 118, l. 24–25.

19. *Katalog. I-aia diskussionnaia vystavka ob"edinenii aktivnogo revoliutsionnogo iskusstva* (Moscow, 1924), p. 9.

20. In 1924 he had written, in particular:

BASICS
1. All intellectual work of the masses concentrated on one discipline—on the Projectionist expression of an organizational classification and methodology—is the realization of Projectionism.
2. The contemporary art of Projectionism is tectonics (it is the algebra of organizational science).
3. Its spectator is a well-prepared master of the guild.
4. Its task is to train cadres of instructors from all branches of industry in the laws of tectonics and their proper application.
5. Its goal is: (a) the masses (every person) knowing the laws of tectonics and how to apply them in the arrangement of materials, at work, in their biological-social life; (b) a way of life in which the business and work-connected part of each day includes, by its very structure, all the abundance of economic blessings . . .

7. Every worker who realizes point no. 1 in his work is a Projectionist. (Central State Archive for Literature and Art, Moscow, f. 2717, op. 1, ed. khr. 17, l. 24).

21. S. Nikritin, "Edinstvennoe i poslednee. Materialisticheskaia sistema konstruktivnogo idealizma," 1923, Central State Archive for Literature and Art, Moscow, f. 2717, op. 1, ed. khr. 16, l. 51–52.

22. Kostin, *OST,* p. 19.

23. Central State Archive for Literature and Art, Moscow, f. 2359, op. 1, ed. khr. 92, l. 16–17. Red'ko made this diary entry on May 29, 1924: "I'm deliberating on the theoretical grounding of my 1923–24 works, which I'm thinking of entitling *Luminism,* since this is the logical outgrowth of my work on periodicity" (Manuscript Division, State Tret'iakov Gallery, Moscow, f. 137, ed. khr. 44, l. 11). He defined Svechenizm (Luminism) thus:

1. Painting is the organizer of atmospheric phenomena.
2. Astronomy and meteorology are an analytic means of painting.
3. Light in painting is not light but luminosity.
4. Synthesis of color-forms in painting in the passage of currents of matter through luminosity.
5. The Northern Lights are an index of the new scientific foundation of luminosity in the energy of light.
6. The consciousness of painting: the movement of gaseous currents in the atmosphere—measured by luminosity (*Central State Archive for Literature and Art, Moscow, f. 2359, op. 1, ed. khr. 92, l. 32*).

24. Ibid., l. 47.

25. F. Syrkina, *Aleksandr Grigor'evich Tyshler* (Moscow, 1966), p. 13.

26. *Vystavka kartin i risunkov K. N. Red'ko. 1914–1926* (Moscow, 1926), p. 8.

27. Luchishkin, *Ia ochen' liubliu zhizn',* p. 67.

28. Triaskin, "Vospominaniia." He considered the works of the Constructivists to be of an aesthetic cast. Nikolai Triaskin, conversation with author, March 20, 1991.

29. Nikritin wrote a brief history of the Projectionist Theater workshop—which combined the features of a "laboratory, school, and experimental theater studio"—from its founding on January 10, 1922 to its demise in February 1925. He described the course of the workshop's formal investigations into "general laws of the spatial and temporal organization of motion" and the "architectonics of a common mobile culture," as well as the charting in analytical tables of these and other laws—of acoustic value, stage construction, and an actor's mastery of his role. The workshop gave two demonstrations in 1922, the first—on August 29th—a closed one at a private high school, and the second—on October 16th—an open one at the House of Publishing. The first was a particular success, Nikritin noted: "One of the leaders of what was then the Meierkhol'd Theater, [Ivan] Aksenov, as well as the poet [Aleksei] Kruchenykh, the drama critic L'vov, and many others, talked of the beginning of a new theater." Following the "failure" of its first true performance—the production of *A Conspiracy of Fools* in May 1923—the workshop moved to the Central Institute of Labor, headed by Aleksei Gastev. In the spring of 1924, the workshop offered a partial performance of a script of its own devising, *1924-yi god* (*The Year 1924*). S. Nikritin, "Masterskaia Proektsionnogo teatra," 1925?, Central State Archive for Literature and Art, Moscow, f. 2717, op. 1, ed. khr. 21, l. 48–56.

30. Triaskin, "Vospominaniia," p. 43.

31. Ibid., p. 40.

32. Ibid., p. 41. Another newspaper review described the event thus:

> *Another pretentious extravaganza . . . no, sorry, one more*
> *"production feat" . . . which featured drums being beaten in the*
> *galleries, while below, six young people in skullcaps said, "A E I O*
> *U," shuffled their feet, dragged a staircase, parallel bars, and other*
> *movable supports from place to place, and in between declaimed verses*
> *by Mariengof . . . The theater is called Projectionist. People in the*
> *know explain that this means the "projection" or a prophecy of the*
> *ideal theater of the future.*
>
> *This "theater of the future" is a great thing.* (A. Lezhnev,
> "'Zagovor durakov.' Masterskaia Proektsionnogo teatra," Rabochaia
> gazeta *113 {1923}, Central State Archive for Literature and Art,
> Moscow, f. 2717, op. 1, ed. khr. 95, l. 6).*

33. Miuller, "Mashinopoklonniki," translation of review of October 13, 1923, Central State Archive for Literature and Art, Moscow, f. 2717, op. 1, ed. khr. 95, l. 9–10.

34. Ibid., l. 8.

35. Red'ko did not join Ost, and in 1927—after a trip to northern Russia, where he completed a number of figurative works in illustration of Luminism—went to France. Triaskin left Moscow for a teaching position in Kiev in 1926.

fig. 1
Nadezhda Udal'tsova
Self-Portrait, 1923.
Oil on canvas.
State Tret'iakov Gallery, Moscow.

Terms of Transition: The *First Discussional Exhibition* and the Society of Easel Painters

Charlotte Douglas

The decline of abstract styles during the 1920s and the emergence of an innovative figurative art had manifold attendant causes and motivations. Russian artists shared in the widespread European rejection of idealism after the Great War and, like artists further West, heard a "call to order." The unique revolutionary conditions in the country also made them eager to maneuver for their own place in the evolving social system, and many sought to redefine their art in Marxist, or at least materialist, terms. "Once purged of aesthetic, philosophical and religious excrescences," the avant-garde artist Varvara Stepanova wrote, "art leaves us its material foundations, which henceforth will be organized by intellectual production."[1] Pressed to define the usefulness of easel painting at a time of extreme physical and social hardship, the avant-garde, while still committed to abstraction in the years after the Revolution, rejected the idealist roots of non-objective art, and could think of no better use for it than the design of objects and theater sets. "There can be no question of painting in Suprematism; painting was done long ago, and the artist himself is a prejudice of the past," Kazimir Malevich wrote in 1920, and Liubov' Popova echoed: "The role of the 'representational arts'—painting, sculpture, and even architecture . . . has ended, as it is no longer necessary for the consciousness of our age, and everything art has to offer can simply be classified as a throwback."[2]

Under these circumstances it is not surprising that those who argued for the cultural viability of painting as a form of art turned to the image. Some made the change relatively early. By 1923 Aleksandr Drevin and Nadezhda Udal'tsova had already abandoned abstraction. Udal'tsova's *Avtoportret (Self-Portrait,* fig. no. 1) of that year perfectly expresses the precarious situation of the avant-garde. It shows the artist anxiously clasping her hands before her, a hesitant expression on her face. The painting's surface shimmers with short, stabbing brush strokes that produce a reflecting surface through which the uncertain artist appears an insubstantial and shifting apparition. The young Kliment Red'ko, after listening to Malevich lecture at Vkhutemas (the Higher Artistic-Technical Workshops), noted in his diary: "He reduces painting to the level of a secondary means. Malevich and the others seek out extremes because they are not genuine painters."[3]

Red'ko belonged to a group of students at Vkhutemas who refused either to abandon painting or to indulge in a retrospective Naturalism that made its appeal to the masses. All were at some time under the tutelage of the avant-garde, and many were themselves talented abstract artists. In the mid-1920s these young artists turned to figuration in the attempt to go beyond the utilitarian precepts of their mentors and to develop a viable and socially relevant Modernism. For models they turned to contemporaneous trends further West, to late Expressionism and *Neue Sachlichkeit* (New Objectivity) in Germany and to *Valori Plastici* (Plastic Values) and metaphysical artists in Italy. Nourished for years on their professors' tales of Western Europe and isolated by the course of political events from the Western nations of the world, these artists of the younger generation were eager to communicate with their colleagues abroad and to make their mark in the international world of art.

In the spring of 1924, in the wake of Lenin's death, the class warfare waged in the name of the proletariat had begun to heat up. Official and spontaneous committees scoured the cities, hunting down "Nepmen" profiteers and evicting leftover members of the "bourgeoisie" from their apartments, assigning their rooms instead to more deserving "workers." The writer Mikhail Bulgakov noted in his diary, "In Moscow there are numerous arrests of people with 'good last names.' Again people are being sent away."[4]

It was in this unstable atmosphere in Moscow that on May 11th the *Pervaia diskussionnaia vystavka ob"edinenii aktivnogo revoliutsionnogo iskusstva* (*First Discussional Exhibition of Associations of Active Revolutionary Art*) opened in an exhibition space that belonged to Vkhutemas out on the further reaches of Tsverskaia Street, some two miles from the Kremlin. The show presented paintings, sculpture, constructions, theater maquettes, books, typographical designs, analytical charts and schemes—more than two hundred works by thirty-eight artists, most either faculty, students, or recent graduates of Vkhutemas. Indeed, the exhibition was labeled "discussional" because it did not advance a unified point of view, either as to style or in its approach to the problem—still unresolved—of the social mandate of contemporary art. Rather, it was a public extension of those intense debates that took place continuously wherever artists congregated, but most particularly in the workshops and dormitories of Vkhutemas.

The exhibition gave a rather perfunctory nod to the Constructivists. By 1924 these members of the old avant-garde had backed themselves into an artistic and political corner. Having for four years loudly and insistently rejected the value of easel painting and traditional aesthetic concerns, they now found themselves unwanted by the very "means of production" they had hoped to transform. Geometrical designs were conceived as "classless" at a time when Soviet society was increasingly perceived to be class based. But perhaps more importantly, to be economically viable for the new state, industrial design had to appeal to the taste of the consumer, and Constructivist applied designs had failed utterly to attract the masses.

In the exhibition, two competing groups of Constructivists engaged in a late wrangle over precedence and orthodoxy. Calling themselves Konstruktivisty (Constructivists), Vladimir and Georgii Stenberg and Konstantin Medunetskii condescendingly hung only photographs and plans of previous work. They made no statement of principles; their program had been clearly defined already, they wrote rather grandly in the catalogue, by their exhibitions in Paris, Berlin, Munich, Leipzig, Dresden, Frankfurt, and Amsterdam. The First Working Group of Constructivists, still led by Aleksei Gan, but by this time made up of a new group of younger artists that no longer included Aleksandr Rodchenko and Stepanova, exhibited children's books, work clothes, and designs for tables and kiosks.

The First Working Organization of Artists, recent graduates of Vkhutemas, displayed architectural constructions and theater maquettes. Their catalogue manifesto stressed "organization" and the importance of directing one's consciousness toward the development of new forms in art and society. A group of two—Ivan Papkov and Konstantin Parkhomenko—that called itself Byt (Ordinary Life) showed landscapes and views of interiors. A Union of Three—Andrei Goncharov, Aleksandr Deineka, and Iurii Pimenov—who had all been graphics students under Vladimir Favorskii, showed satirical illustrations and stylized figural canvases. Only the sculptor Iosif Chaikov, who had been educated in Paris and was on the faculty at Vkhutemas, appeared without benefit of any collective. At thirty-six the oldest artist in the exhibit, he showed a collection of Cubist studies and a vaguely Constructivist project for a memorial to Iakov Sverdlov.

Almost half of the exhibition consisted of work by the Proektsionisty (Projectionists)—Sergei Luchishkin, Solomon Nikritin, Mikhail Plaksin, Red'ko, Nikolai Triaskin, and Aleksandr Tyshler. In a striking anticipation of the Conceptual Art of the early 1970s, the Projectionists maintained that artists should produce not objects of art or the things of daily life but their projects or "projections," that is, the ideas, conceptions, plans, and experiments associated with such objects. The inheritors of the analytical studies pursued at Inkhuk (the Institute of Artistic Culture), they presented the results of their research and analysis as their art. They saw themselves as creators of a "Method," whereby things might be produced by almost anyone.[5] Nikritin was the guiding inspiration of this group. He took a special interest in theoretical and analytical questions of composition, and in the search for general laws. After his graduation from Vkhutemas he became chairman of the Research Board at the Museum of Painterly Culture, and led his colleagues in its "analytical cabinet" in the exploration of conceptual and formal problems.

At the *First Discussional Exhibition,* Nikritin's work occupied a whole wall; the "tectonic research" that he had done over the last three years—texts, photographs, sketches, reliefs, and a three-dimensional construction—filled a large map case. Nikritin advised his viewers that this display required some two hours of study, and he thoughtfully provided a stepladder for their convenience. In a bravado gesture he also exhibited a naturalistically rendered portrait with the notation: "I am exhibiting this as a demonstration of my professional skill. I reject it because I consider it reactionary."[6]

Red'ko, who for a time had shared a studio with Nikritin, had already been working for two years on a theory of *elektroorganizm* (electroorganism) and searching for ways to depict light as a "unit of electroorganisms' structure" and "the highest expression of matter." The new art would necessarily be based in science, he believed, and he was inclined to depict people and nature in forms drawn from mechanical engineering. At the *First Discussional Exhibition* his works bore such titles as *Periodicheskaia osnova sveto-sinteticheskogo razvitiia (peremeshcheniia)* (*The Periodic Basis of Light-Synthetic Development {Displacement}*, 1923) and *Metamorfozy optiki* (*The Metamorphoses of Optics,* 1923), and some displayed slick machinelike forms suggesting psychophysical relationships.

Like Nikritin, Luchishkin had examined dozens of recognized masterpieces in the course of a search for formal regularities. At the *First Discussional Exhibition* he presented large graphic charts illustrating the results of his research on compositional structure, and his statistical conclusions concerning the usual proportions of figure to ground. He classified various standard types of compositional arrangements and their visual forces, and showed that for vertically oriented rectilinear paintings, the proportion of the area of figure to background is normally 1:1.[7]

Plaksin showed brightly colored abstract works, and Triaskin models and sketches of his Constructivist "universal" theatrical sets.[8] Under the general heading "A Methodology of Normalized Perception," Tyshler, who had recently produced some refined and colorful abstract works, contributed to this exhibition black-humored paintings of armless and legless invalids.

Among the Konkretivisty (Concretists) were Petr Vil'iams and Konstantin Vialov. Vialov's *Militsioner* (*Traffic Cop,* 1923, plate no. 368) drew an analogy between the regulation of the speed and course of an automobile and social progress. A single full-length figure of the traffic cop in a long coat raises his baton to direct traffic. At the lower left, a tiny open roadster with a driver and two passengers in touring caps has come to a halt. A schematic clock in the upper right imitates the traffic signals. Vialov's red-and-black color scheme and his flat, decorative style suggests a graphic rather than a painterly resolution of current problems.

The exhibition was the first public demonstration of the new generation's break with their elders. It makes clear two primary interests on the part of these students: continuing the analyses learned from the Inkhuk studies of the old avant-garde, with the aim of establishing *systems* within which the formal elements of a work of art might be understood, and the search for a contemporary way to continue painting—one that avoided both the dilettantish and reactionary Impressionism of the members of AKhRR (the Association of Artists of Revolutionary Russia) and the overworked restatements of Cézanne and Matisse favored by Bubnovyi valet (Jack of Diamonds). The former interest resulted in a kind of schematic abstraction, illustrations of the results of analytical studies that had few bases for further development. The latter was the beginning of a road that in just half a dozen years would lead to the new generation's artistic and political downfall.

These young artists had had an exceptionally fine education in art. In many cases they had started their training before the Revolution, and even as teenagers had become familiar with the best of Western contemporary work, particularly through Sergei Shchukin's collection in Moscow.[9] At the State Free Art Workshops and at Vkhutemas they studied Cézanne with the Jack of Diamonds artists (Il'ia Mashkov, Petr Konchalovskii, Robert Fal'k, Aristarkh Lentulov), as well as color and design with Stepanova, Popova, Aleksandr Vesnin, and other Inkhuk artists. But the attraction they felt to painting was then completely at odds with what they were being taught by the avant-garde. It was fostered not only by the Jack of Diamonds contingent of the faculty at Vkhutemas but also by their own involvement with the Museum of Painterly Culture.

The Museum had begun in 1919 as a government-sponsored collection of paintings bought from a list of approved artists—predominantly the avant-garde. Until June 1921 the works of art had been acquired by a purchasing commission of Narkompros (the People's Commissariat of Enlightenment) and came under the supervision of Inkhuk. They were regarded as a treasure of the new nation and, secondarily, as a teaching collection. As part of a program to cultivate the arts in all sections of the country, many of the works assembled were distributed to provincial museums. By the autumn of 1922, however, the artists of Inkhuk, already ambivalent about their own former work and consequently unclear about the function of the museum, found themselves unable to cope with administering the collection, and its day-to-day supervision was temporarily transferred to the energetic Vil'iams, then only twenty years old.[10] With the appointment of Vil'iams, the museum became the center of activity for the new generation of painting students at Vkhutemas, including the Projectionists Nikritin, Luchishkin, Aleksandr Labas, Plaksin, Red'ko, and Tyshler.

The international awareness and the eager ambitions of this group of aspiring artists were clear even while they were still in school. When the decision was made to travel the very successful exhibition of Russian art that had opened in Berlin at the Galerie van Diemen in October 1922 (the *Erste russische Kunstausstellung* [*First Russian Art Exhibition*]), David Shterenberg, the head of Izo Narkompros (the Department of Fine Arts of the People's Commissariat of Enlightenment) and the organizer of the exhibition, returned from Berlin to Moscow in search of additional work.[11] For his benefit the students quickly arranged a show of their work at the museum. The exhibition was held from December 25th to 27th, and to their delight Shterenberg took most of the work back to Berlin.[12] The young artists expected their work to go on to Paris, the next scheduled stop for the van Diemen show, but just at that time international politics intervened. In January 1923, alleging Germany's default on reparation payments, French and Belgian troops occupied Germany's industrial Ruhr District. In the ensuing controversy, Russia sided with

Germany, with whom she was allied, and France thereupon rejected the exhibition's visa applications. For several months Shterenberg sought alternative venues, but Russia's steadily cooling relations with other Western countries made his task difficult. Finally, although Holland had not yet officially recognized the Soviet Union, arrangements were made through preexisting connections to move the show to Amsterdam. There, for the month of May 1923, the Projectionists had their first exposure abroad.

The Museum of Painterly Culture moved again in 1923—this time to one of the buildings at 11 Rozhdestvenka, the former Stroganov School and First Free State Art Workshops, where the Vkhutemas faculty was teaching its Basic Course.[13] Lazar' Vainer, a genteel thirty-eight-year-old sculptor who in the years before World War I had attended the Ecole des Beaux-Arts in Paris, was made director of the museum, and Vil'iams became his deputy. The Vkhutemas students, delighted with the collection's new proximity, took up jobs there, and continued to regard it as their own. The museum's extensive collection of foreign art journals afforded them a window to the contemporary West, and the sympathetic administration made room for their lectures, reports, and a series of small solo exhibitions of their research work. Guest lecturers provided a sense of working in an already established avant-garde tradition. The abstract and analytical work done between 1922 and 1924 by these young people may be regarded as one of the extreme reaches of the Russian avant-garde. These talented and irrepressibly energetic artists for a short time seemed to inherit the legendary creative momentum of the first generation, which was then in the process of self-destructing.

A new artistic organization devoted exclusively to painting was formed in 1925. Most of the members were friends from the Museum of Painterly Culture and their recent student days at Vkhutemas. Many, including Pimenov, Labas, Deineka, Goncharov, Luchishkin, Vil'iams, Tyshler, and Konstantin Vialov had exhibited together just eleven months previously at the *First Discussional Exhibition.* The first exhibition of the new group, Ost (the Society of Easel Painters), opened on April 26, 1925, in the Museum of Painterly Culture. But even a cursory look around would tell a visitor to the show that this was a different kind of exhibition. The Constructivists were nowhere to be seen; Ordinary Life was also absent; and Luchishkin's analytical studies had been replaced by a long horizontal view of striding members of the Young Communists League, led by a brass band.[14] Deineka—a graduate at seventeen from the Khar'kov Art School and then, at age twenty-six, on the verge of finishing Vkhutemas—showed a major work, one of his first in a series of industrial themes. In the dramatic, almost monochromatic *Pered spuskom v shakhtu* (*Before the Descent into the Mines,* 1925, plate no. 378), groups of miners wait before the gridlike structure of a mine-shaft elevator. The figures are squat, the rhythmic undulations of their dark clothing edged precisely. The symbolic, monumental nature of the figures is amplified by an environment given only in fragments—an inclined rectangle indicates the horizontal plane of the floor, an area of open wire mesh frames a pair in profile on the right, a figure on the left stands isolated on empty ground. Deineka, an admirer of Ferdinand Hodler's symbolic figures, here adapts to painting graphic devices used in woodcuts and engraving by his professor at Vkhutemas, Favorskii. The diagonally textured area behind the two figures in the upper right, for example, is remarkably similar to the hatched areas that define the spaces for figures in many of Favorskii's prints.

A new addition to the group was the painter Shterenberg, the former head of Izo Narkompros, who two and a half years earlier had taken the group's first efforts to Berlin and

Amsterdam. Shterenberg's authoritative position, and his ability to cope with the paperwork involved in registering the organization and guiding it through the bureaucratic mazes, made him the logical choice for president of the new organization. The young artists particularly appreciated Shterenberg's international connections, and hoped that his leadership would ensure their exposure in the West.

Shterenberg's early Soviet work focused on the physical qualities of painted texture and collage. His *Prostokvasha* (*Clabber*, 1919), for example, is a daring and idiosyncratic work. The skewed asymmetric composition is simplified to the point of abstraction, but enriched by color and texture. An ascetic small white container of farmer's cheese perches on the edge of a green marbleized table top, its intense orange label punctuating the flat blue background. Typically for Shterenberg, the carton is seen from the side, the scribbled expanse of the table in an elongated view from above; together they form a kind of floating abstraction momentarily snatched from the everyday world. In the second half of the 1920s, Shterenberg's techniques become more restrained, and the optimistic emphasis on texture and sensation disappears.

Ost was to last six years in remarkably stable form. The group held four yearly exhibitions in Moscow from 1925 through 1928. Their initial political stance was simple: they were children of the Revolution. In spite of the fact that many of them came from the middle class, there was never any question about their view of themselves as the promise of a new socialist art, about the responsibility they felt as the artistic strength of the new regime, or about their complete allegiance to it. Their view of art, however, was broad and flexible enough to encompass a variety of approaches. Some emphasized graphic techniques combined with a completely finished surface, as opposed to the sketchiness advocated in by others. Some were emphatically painterly. Ost's treatment of industrial themes tended to be romantic and lyrical or decorative, and not overly tendentious.

The variety of Ost's approaches to the new art was supported by Anatolii Lunacharskii's principle of aesthetic neutrality for Narkompros. Although sympathetic to the notion of a proletarian art, Lunacharskii foresaw a very gradual evolution in this direction, one in which the artistic intelligentsia would participate fully. He attempted to distinguish the government's duty to encourage various artistic approaches from the Party's function in giving preference to a particular artistic direction among its members. Until the mid-1920s the Party resisted the insistent demand from literary and art groups to endorse a genuine official style. In a decree of June 1925, however, it finally capitulated, supporting the goal of a culture that was specifically proletarian. The Party rejected, nonetheless, the growing militancy of the cultural radicals, calling instead for tact and tolerance toward "fellow travelers," and for free competition among the various groups and movements.[15]

In the early years Ost artists avoided the sort of blatant didacticism common among the AKhRR artists. They cautioned Ekaterina Zernova, for example, when her work strayed too far from the usual poetic treatment that she had applied equally to portraits of children and depictions of tanks. She writes in her memoirs, "I was surprised and distressed when once Andrei [Goncharov] came to me with someone else from Ost and they both tried to convince me not to do works such as *Rybokonservnyi zavod* [*The Fish-Canning Factory*, 1927, fig. no. 2] and *Tomat-piure* [*Tomato Puree*]. Goncharov said, 'We took you into Ost, but we can exclude you. Think about it.' But having thought about it, I decided not to change my orientation."[16]

Of particular importance for Ost members, as well as other

fig. 2
Ekaterina Zernova
The Fish-Canning Factory, *1927*.
Oil on canvas, 85 x 63 cm.
State Tret'iakov Gallery, Moscow.

fig. 3
Petr Vil'iams
Autorace, *1930*.
Oil on canvas, 151 x 213 cm.
State Tret'iakov Gallery, Moscow.

young Soviet artists, were the exhibitions of contemporary German art held in Russia in the mid-1920s. In October 1924, the *Pervaia vseobshchaia germanskaia khudozhestvennaia vystavka* (*First German Survey Exhibition*), the return show of the 1922 Russian exhibition in Berlin, opened in Moscow at the Historical Museum.[17] A year later Moscow's Museum of New Western Art organized *Nemetskoe iskusstvo poslednego piatidesiatiletiia* (*The Last Fifty Years of German Art*), composed of works from their own collection, and in the spring of 1926, it devoted a section of the exhibition *Revoliutsionnoe iskusstvo zapada* (*Revolutionary Art of the West*) to postwar German art. These three exhibitions made available to Russian artists a wide variety of German artistic alliances, including the Red Group and the November Group, and in particular, work by Käthe Kollwitz, Otto Nagel, Max Pechstein, Otto Dix, Max Beckmann, and George Grosz, among others. They also engendered an almost unanimous condemnation of Expressionism by the critics; in spite of the progressive political stance of the Germans and the oppositional nature of their images, reviewers found little to like. Opinions in the press varied from a reserved understanding to outright rejection and disgust. Most reviewers argued that Expressionism's emotional distortions, its display of neuroses and cynicism, together with its lack of an alternative positive vision, offered little to Russian artists searching for a new art. Lunacharskii, who was very familiar with Western art currents, took one of the most positive views. He approved of the German work that had socially propagandistic aims more than of the domestic "gallicizing Formalists" (Lef, or the Left Front of the Arts) and the "simplifying Naturalists" (AKhRR), but nevertheless concluded that the 1924 exhibition gave "very few models" to the Russians. By 1926 he was less restrained: "The German intelligentsia working under the flag of Expressionism has intensified those already extreme illnesses that traumatize us with the poisonous compositions expounded by half-Realists, half-Expressionists like Dix and Grosz. Beyond a certain line there simply begins incomprehensibility and mannerism." Lunacharskii advises Western artists to learn a "high form of expressiveness."[18]

While the critic Nikolai Tarabukin also approved of the fact that German artists did not simply illustrate events as did the AKhRR artists, he maintained that the "anarchic ideology, the purely individualistic protest against bourgeois society, leads to naked nihilism, to 'protest for the sake of protest.'"[19] The most vigorous in his condemnation of Expressionism was the influential twenty-four-year-old Marxist critic Aleksei Fedorov-Davydov. The Soviet viewer is *"stunned,"* he exclaimed, "by the hopelessness and the 'general negation,' even in the canvases of Communist artists from the Red Group and the November Group. Two-thirds of the artists 'consider their task the destruction of the bourgeois layer of society by the means available to art.' [But this revolutionary] destruction [has to] take place 'in the name of something,' that is, from a definite positive ideal . . . There is no general fighting position. From here the unavoidable path is to mysticism . . . The workers are . . . depicted as 'dumb, faceless monsters' . . . Instead of faces you see only ciphers or question marks."[20] Fedorov-Davydov repeated these observations in 1926, characterizing Western socialist art as "an art of a proletarianizing intelligentsia crushed by the horrors of war and poverty, an intelligentsia that is oriented now toward the proletariat and world revolution because of their economic and social position."[21]

Many *artists*, however, felt quite differently from the critics, and found significant inspiration in the German work. Even in AKhRR, artists such as Fedor Bogorodskii responded to the 1924 exhibition with a greater expressiveness. Luchishkin

fig. 4
Iurii Pimenov
The Seizing of an English Blockhouse (The Northern Front), *1928 (detail).*
Oil on canvas, 199 x 289.5 cm.
L'vov Picture Gallery.

fig. 5
Iurii Pimenov
Disabled Veterans, *1926.*
Oil on canvas, 104 x 70 cm.
State Russian Museum,
St. Petersburg.

emphasized the importance of the 1924 exhibition for the members of Ost: "We took Expressionism—clearly visible in the artworks exhibited, especially in the works of G. Grosz and O. Dix—as a set of devices that emphasized the social essence of the works. It seemed to us that expressiveness helped to accent the revolutionary direction."[22] And Pimenov wrote, "I was attracted by Expressionism, by George Grosz and Dix; their corrosive and bizarre precision interested me."[23]

Russian artists were particularly attracted by the graphic qualities of German art. Pimenov's works such as *Tennis* (1927) and *Beg* (*Race,* 1928) adopt the mannered stylization characteristic of 1920s advertising graphics throughout Europe and the United States. The elegant elongated figures engaging in vigorous exercise against backgrounds composed of Bauhaus architecture and steel girders produce a kind of sanitized Art Deco. In Vil'iams's *Avtoprobeg* (*Autorace,* 1930, fig. no. 3), sleek-lined touring cars race down a dirt road carved out of newly industrialized land. The race is observed by groups of tiny figures, presumably employees who manufacture the cars in the low Bauhaus-design factories in the background. The dust, the wide sky, and expanse of horizon give a sense of raw land and the endless possibilities of the new country. On a building in the distance a red sign proclaims RIGHT OF WAY TO THE AUTOMOBILE! in an unsubtle reference to the newly constructed society.

But in such works as Pimenov's *Invalidy voiny* (*Disabled Veterans,* 1926, fig. no. 5) and *Vziatie angliiskogo blokgauza (Severnyi front)* (*The Seizing of an English Blockhouse {The Northern Front},* 1928, fig. no. 4) the distortions learned from Expressionism are more evident. In *Disabled Veterans* two blind and bandaged men confront the viewer full-length against a poisonous green sky and the charred rubble of burned-out buildings. The face of the right-hand figure, his white eyes open but unseeing, is contorted into a scream, and has been directly modeled on Edvard Munch's famous image. In *The Seizing of an English Blockhouse,* a subject drawn from the English, French, and American invasion of northern Russia in 1918–19, a group of irregulars advance on a fort at the very moment that one of their group is struck and falls backward, his blue hand raised high, clutching the empty air. Fedorov-Davydov could approve of such works because of their abstraction, the stylized distance from the subject, and the artist's intention to convey his horror and repudiation of war.[24]

As the 1920s progressed, several of the Ost artists took advantage of Expressionism's capacity for more caustic social and political commentary. This potential was most brilliantly exploited by Nikritin in his series of menacing occluded figures and screaming women (fig. nos. 6–7). But by the time these works were painted the anguish they expressed was looked upon as disloyal and so kept them from being exhibited. By the end of the decade Nikritin was reduced to composing inspirational panels for public spaces, such as *Kapitalisticheskii rai* (*Capitalist Heaven,* ca. 1929) for the Central Museum of Labor and *Prosveshchenie u iakutov* (*Education among the Yakuts,* ca. 1929) for the Museum of Public Education.[25]

The increasingly inflexible insistence of the authorities on artistic optimism in the face of any calamity was made clear to the artists by the time of the *Vystavka khudozhestvennykh proizvedenii k desiatiletnemu iubileiu Oktiabr'skoi revoliutsii* (*Art Exhibition on the Tenth Anniversary of the October Revolution*), which opened in January 1928. The grisly 1921 famine in southern Russia had troubled Luchishkin and he chose it as a subject worthy of Expressionism's emotional power. When he presented his initial sketch of a grieving mother and her starving family for approval for the exhibition, however, Lunacharskii refused to allow it. "Famine in the Volga region was a difficult experience," he told the young artist, "but we

fig. 6
Solomon Nikritin
Screaming Woman, *1928.*
Oil on canvas, 60.7 x 51.8 cm.
Collection George Costakis,
Germany.

fig. 7
Solomon Nikritin
Man with a Top Hat, *1927.*
Oil on canvas, 68.4 x 28.2 cm.
Collection George Costakis,
Germany.

are celebrating our grand holiday, why cloud it with these memories?" Luchishkin painted another subject for the anniversary exhibition, but stubbornly completed the offending work and hung it at the next (and last) Ost exhibition. Reaction was so severe that he subsequently destroyed the work (fig. no. 8).[26] In *Starik (The Old Man, 1925–26)*[27] Shterenberg addresses a similar theme, but with his typical restraint. A single full-length figure of an elderly peasant faces the viewer from a monochromatic, snowy field. The undulating outlines of the figure are reminiscent of Deineka's stolid miners, but the unrelieved isolation of the peasant, his setting completely barren save for the wisps of dry grass at his feet, conveys the terrible quandary of the peasantry. Destitute, in a community that had turned chaotic and sinister, the peasants found themselves cut off from the soil and hungry for its comforting spirit as well as for the food it might have produced.

Many of the Ost artists cultivated an estranged and melancholic Surrealism. In their work, themes ostensibly concerned with revolutionary social reality often are suffused with ambiguities of meaning that reflect the moral dilemmas of the time. Red'ko, Luchishkin, Labas, and Tyshler, while pursuing subjects that exalted technology, communality, and Party leadership, developed highly personal styles that conveyed a fantastic and dehumanized threat within these hypnotic ideas. The inclination to Surrealism derived not from its French exponents, whose associations in Russia were with the Lef group, but from the *Neue Sachlichkeit* artists, well known through the German exhibitions and cultural associations, and from the Italian *Novecento* (Twentieth Century) and the artists associated with *Valori Plastici*.

Beginning with Russian participation in the 1924 Venice Biennale, artistic connections between Russia and Italy were extensive. The most important role in this association was played by the Museum of New Western Art. Here in the late 1920s, thanks to its director's special interest in contemporary Italian art, Ost artists could see recent work by Carlo Carrà, Giorgio de Chirico, Filippo de Pisis, Felice Casorati, Massimo Campigli, Mario Tozzi, Giorgio Morandi, Gino Severini, Piero Marussig, and many others.[28] These artists' approaches to painting, which tended to submerge individual emotions, were especially suited to the Russian inclination to visual archetypes and hesitancy before obvious demonstrations of personal feelings. Surrealism's mixed messages and double entendre precisely reflected the odd social juxtapositions and alienations that characterized Russia in the 1920s.

Red'ko and Nikritin, leading participants in the *First Discussional Exhibition,* had refused to join Ost or to send any work to the first Ost exhibition. Nikritin considered the organization "inferior" (*nepolnotsennyi*) from the point of view of theory, and Red'ko traveled instead and worked on organizing his own exhibition, which opened just before the second Ost exhibition in the spring of 1926.[29] In his diary he noted, "They [Shterenberg, Labas, Vil'iams, Deineka, Pimenov, and Vialov] came around from Ost. They looked at my work stiffly. [But] I didn't agree to pull out my best canvases for the Ost exhibition."[30]

Yet although he did not participate directly in Ost, Red'ko abandoned his electroorganisms in the name of a similar socially tendentious art. Just before the *First Discussional Exhibition* closed he wrote in his diary, "I am thinking about a plan for future work. In painting we have arrived at the creation of a social theme. This is the demand of our worldwide contemporaneity, and the requirement of our class as the Communist builder. We will make new works of art in which there will be an epic severity of construction and a strict reckoning. In direct connection with this I want to do a picture

fig. 8
Sergei Luchishkin
Hunger in the Volga Region, *ca. 1927.*
Destroyed.

called *RKP* [*The Russian Communist Party*]."[31] But even this straightforward subject ended in a picture that is far from unambiguous. Retitled *Revoliutsiia* (*Revolution*) and then *Vosstanie* (*Uprising*, 1924–25) in the course of two years, the painting is a large geometric cityscape that depicts the leaders of the Revolution arranged inside a tilted square and surrounded by ranks of workers parading like so many small tin soldiers. Lenin occupies the geometric center of the canvas, waving his arms as if conducting the assembly in a mass performance or as if directing traffic, and the whole scene is bathed in a Surrealistic red glow (plate no. 352). In time this unnatural wash of color became dominant in Red'ko's work, producing, in works such as *Portret I. V. Stalina* (*Portrait of Iosif Stalin*, 1940), an eerie and haunting double message.

There is nothing ambiguous about Nikritin's *Sud naroda* (*People's Court*, 1933–34, fig. no. 9). The dark faceless figures around the table covered in official red, the room empty of objects and people, the ominous step spotlit at the lower left, and the carafe and glass at the nearest edge of the table all give evidence of extinguished life, of an event too dreadful to depict. The invisible threat in Nikritin's work can be made clear by comparing it with a similar scene as rendered by the AKhR (the Association of Artists of the Revolution) artist Boris Ioganson. *Sovetskii sud* (*A Soviet Court*, 1928, fig. no. 10) also depicts judges seated behind a table draped in red, the carafe and water glass are there, but Ioganson is still concerned with social justice—here between a former landowner and a peasant woman with a baby. In Nikritin's picture all such ritual would be pointless.

Labas's art combines a genuine appreciation of transportation technology with a clear realization of the consequent subordinate position of simple two-legged human beings. In his work from about 1927, people are reduced to ephemera by the technological power of engines and aircraft. Later his trains, escalators, and rockets become even more dominant and people disappear. Labas's aviation themes coincided with one of the main goals of the First Five-Year Plan: the development of a self-reliant Soviet aviation industry. The defense effort was led by Kliment Voroshilov, then Commissar for Military and Naval Affairs, and the population was bombarded with the slogan "Proletariat! To the Airplane!" *V kabine* (*In the Airplane Cabin*, 1928, plate no. 371), however, gives quite a different image of air travel, imparting an existential complex of emotions by the most economical means. The viewer looks down the aisle from the front of the plane as passengers sit bolt upright, their arms drawn close to their bodies. Beneath and around them is empty space; they sit suspended in an airy nothing. There is no sense of motion, no motor or any other indication of modern technology. The presence of the winged plane is given by the barest suggestion of a few gray lines in the white expanse. The passengers' hanging weight and tension are emphasized by a mindless frolicking dog, who is unaware of the complexities of this strange and fearful experience.

In *Pervyi sovetskii dirizhabl'* (*The First Soviet Dirigible*, 1931), three-quarters of the width of the canvas is dominated by an enormous dirigible, a red star scratched across its upper surface, emerging from a hangar that seems much too small to contain it. Below and to either side groups of people grasp frail tether lines. Labas's figures are bodiless, and dwarfed by the giant airship that they hold but in no way control. They themselves are identifiable only in the aggregate, and by the occasional tiny red flags rising from their midst. The dirigible, a flurry of soft grays, is the only real flesh-and-blood subject of the work.

Luchishkin's *Shar uletel* (*The Balloon Has Flown*, 1926, fig. no. 11), shown at the third Ost exhibition, is unambiguously pessimistic. The diminutive figure of a child dressed in blue stares straight ahead from between two apartment buildings that are so tall that the space between them narrows as they ascend to the top of the canvas. The viewer is led into the depth of the picture by a line of six leafless trees planted behind the buildings in uniform round holes, but is then abruptly halted by a blank wooden fence. High in the sky at the top center of the canvas is a small bright-red balloon, its short string dangling as it is carried aloft into a bleak sky by an unseen wind. Small scenes of daily life are discernible through the windows of the buildings: a woman looking out, a man with his arms raised, and the body of a suicide hanging from the ceiling. In Luchishkin's *Vytianuv sheiu, storozhit kolkhoznuiu noch'* (*With Neck Held High It Guards the Kolkhoz Night*, 1930, fig. no. 12), the unmoving presence of a towering anthropomorphic piece of machinery threatens, while purporting to protect, people so tiny and fragile that they are scarcely distinguishable from the hay in which they sleep.

Tyshler could be straightforwardly horrific, as in his *Boinia* (*Slaughterhouse*, 1925), or charmingly funny as we see him in *Direktor pogody* (*The Director of the Weather*, 1926, plate no. 376). But in the late 1920s in works such as *Liricheskii tsikl, No. 4* (*Lyrical Cycle, No. 4*, 1928, fig. no. 13), he typically employs an eccentric, seriocomic imagery that finds refuge from reality in absurdity. In Tyshler, Ost's anti-Realist tendencies reach their culmination.

The Ost artists were followed in Vkhutemas/Vkhutein by a group of militant young believers in a purely proletarian art. Their graduation in the years 1927 to 1930 coincided with Stalin's encouragement of the class war, and with the forced industrialization and collectivization of the First Five-Year Plan. Even before graduation, these neophyte artists preached strict sociopolitical tests for content and style in the arts, and with fundamentalist fervor threw themselves into political and organizational maneuvering for power in the art world. Within a remarkably short time they had taken over the leadership of AKhR and OMAKhR (the Young People's Section of AKhR),[32] conducted a purge of some of the older members of these organizations, and proceeded to attack other art groups, prominent critics, and government-run museums for their lack of proletarian orthodoxy.

Not content with OMAKhR and AKhR as platforms, militant proletarians were the driving force in organizing a centralized umbrella organization—FOSKh (the Federation of Associations of Soviet Artists)—and in 1931 they established their own Russian Association of Proletarian Artists (RAPKh). RAPKh artists lectured their colleagues on the dangers posed by ideologically dubious "fellow travelers" in the arts and on the evils of "bourgeois" artistic styles. In a campaign for "differentiation," they identified and publicized "nonproletarian" class elements in other artistic groups in an attempt to create "pure" class-based organizations. By the end of the decade they had become the de facto instrument of political oversight in the arts.

The proletarianization of art was put into practice most efficiently through an artists' cooperative, Vsekokhudozhnik (the All-Russian Cooperative Association "Artist"), organized in 1929. It bought and sold members' paintings, arranged local and traveling exhibitions, and distributed monthly salaries based on potential sales. Vsekokhudozhnik was an outgrowth of Vserabis (the All-Russian Union of Workers in the Arts), and was headed by its former president, Iuvenalii Slavinskii.[33] Vsekokhudozhnik acquired political power through its close connections to the Party and vast economic power as it came to represent increasing numbers of artists.

In the late 1920s the Ost artists, so recently the vanguard of revolutionary art, found themselves open to the dangerous charge of opposing the Revolution and the dictatorship of the proletariat, and were increasingly on the defensive. At a general conference called in 1928 to discuss yet again the validity of easel painting, Shterenberg defended the "great cultural value" of painting and reminded the audience of the Party resolution three years previously which affirmed that aesthetic questions were not yet at the stage where an official proletarian art could be defined.[34] But among themselves the Ost artists, too, argued about the role of studio painting under such extreme social conditions and differed heatedly as to the extent and manner of their involvement with collectivization and industrialization.

The question of the membership of Ost itself became a public topic of debate. The fundamentalists of AKhRR and RAPKh harped on the "bourgeois tendencies" of Labas, Shterenberg, Tyshler, and others, and demanded that if artists such as Vil'iams, Luchishkin, and Pimenov aspired to the status of "fellow travelers"—they had no hope of being transformed into proletarians—they separate themselves from the others in the group. Lev Viaz'menskii, a founder of RAPKh, in print accused Ost work of being "reactionary," "anti-Semitic," and "Fascist."[35]

At the end of January 1931, Ost split in two, a victim of the "process of differentiation." Vil'iams, Pimenov, Luchishkin, Zernova, and a group of younger members left to form the Brigade of Artists, while Shterenberg, Labas, Tyshler, Goncharov, and twenty-three others remained in Ost. The Brigade of Artists lost no time in rejecting its past and aligning itself with the most rabid elements of the art world. Their first official meeting on February 3, 1931, was a model of their new political expediency and an effort to make up for lost time:

> In the name of those gathered, greetings were sent to the Central Committee of the Communist Party, to Comrades Voroshilov and Maksim Gor'kii, and to foreign revolutionary artists. The meeting recognized the necessity of publishing a special album entitled The Five-Year Plan in Four Years, dedicated to Gor'kii.
>
> It was resolved to confer upon Comrade Voroshilov the title Honored Worker in the Visual Arts. In order to raise the defense capabilities of the country it was resolved to work a day for the fund to build the dirigible Klim Voroshilov.[36]

The aesthetic platform of the new organization was no less zealous:

> We are for a collective and planned purposefulness in the creative process . . .
>
> We are for publicistic art as a means of intensifying art's language of images in the struggle for the urgent tasks of the working class.
>
> Our former practice under the conditions of the old Ost contained elements of petit-bourgeois and bourgeois influences. This was expressed in the closed cliquishness of the group, in aesthetic Formalism, and in its distance from the tasks of socialist construction. Now that we have recognized our mistakes and have broken off from the other part of Ost, the task of eliminating our own shortcomings stands before us.
>
> As to creative discipline, we are against exhibitions spontaneously presenting the uncoordinated production of individual artists . . .
>
> We are for exhibitions with a single creative and production plan that is obligatory for each member of the brigade, for the collective working out and fulfilling of this plan, for involving the public at large in the process of affirmation and verification of the work being done.[37]

The Brigade of Artists did not hesitate to accuse their former friends of "Formalism," a charge that carried with it

fig. 9
Solomon Nikritin
The People's Court, 1933–34.
Oil on canvas.
State Tret'iakov Gallery, Moscow. Gift George Costakis.

fig. 10
Karl Ioganson
A Soviet Court, 1928.
Oil on canvas, 80 x 108 cm.
State Tret'iakov Gallery, Moscow.

dangerous counterrevolutionary overtones. Labas's *Soviet Dirigible,* they wrote, is a "typical Formalist work. The artist was interested not in the real depiction of a dirigible and the relationship of the people in the picture to it but in a self-sufficient play of colors."[38]

In their anxiety to prove their zeal and rectify past mistakes, the Brigade also subjected their own previous work to public criticism. Vil'iams's *Autorace* was berated for its departure from the realistic depiction of a contemporary manufacturing plant: "Neither the strict geometricity of the architectural outlines nor the autos rented from foreign advertising posters nor the presence of the 'masses' eliminates the unfortunate impression that before us is a virgin provincial landscape bearing no resemblance to the panorama of the Nizhne-Novgorod automobile plant."[39] Pimenov's *Seizing of an English Blockhouse* was criticized for its elongation of the figures and their high cheekbones, but most crucially for "THE SYMBOLIZED DISPLAY OF PERSONAL EXPERIENCES (the partisans with their fingers torn off)."[40] Nor was even Deineka's *Oborona Petrograda* (*Defense of Petrograd,* 1928), the most popularly successful work in the Ost genre and a work destined to become an icon of the Revolution, immune from attack: "The graphic quality and the linear precision that are its distinguishing features . . . cross over into SCHEMATIZATION AND RATIONALISM."[41]

To the relief of many people who hoped it would put an end to the ominous threats implicit in such denunciations, on April 23, 1932, the Central Committee of the Communist Party abolished all artists' and writers' groups. Citing the narrowness of existing organizations in the country, it ordered single national unions for artists, writers, and those in other creative disciplines.[42] Two months later the Moscow section of the Union of Soviet Artists held its first meeting.[43] Yet the new organization did not eliminate the Vsekokhudozhnik cooperative but, rather, attached itself to it, especially in the selection of the board that passed on works of art. Not only did Vsekokhudozhnik now control, through the sale and exhibition of works, much of the art seen in the country, but its committees of artists exercised the power to enforce the lowest-common-denominator interpretation of Socialist Realism through public slander and intimidation of their fellow artists.

The first major exhibition in Moscow under the new administrative arrangements was the local showing of the jubilee exhibition, *Khudozhniki RSFSR za 15 let* (*Artists of the RSFSR over the Past Fifteen Years*), organized in 1932 in Leningrad to commemorate fifteen years of Soviet rule. A massive exhibition of over two thousand works of art, including 950 paintings done since 1917, it opened at its Moscow venue in June 1933. But here the works were hung not with their respective artistic organizations, as they had been in Leningrad, but rather according to their assessed contribution to a proletarian aesthetic. The paintings were divided into three general groups: those that were regarded as clear contributions to proletarian art, works by "fellow travelers," and works by artists who had been "'infected with all kinds of Formalist diseases and influenced by their bourgeois experiences.'"[44] These contaminated works—by Malevich, Vladimir Tatlin, Natan Al'tman, Ivan Kliun, Popova, Rodchenko, Pavel Filonov, and Nikolai Suetin—were crowded into one small room, in numbers greatly reduced from the Leningrad show.[45] Shterenberg, Udal'tsova, and Drevin, figurative but still suspect, were isolated in another small room of their own. The Ost artists were relegated to the section of "fellow travelers"; through a concerted effort by his colleagues, Tyshler, who had been excluded from the Leningrad show, was permitted to exhibit with them. The Brigade artists generally made it into the first division of genuinely Soviet art.[46]

fig. 11
Sergei Luchishkin
The Balloon Has Flown, *1926.*
Oil on canvas, 106 x 69 cm.
State Tret'iakov Gallery, Moscow.

fig. 12
Sergei Luchishkin
With Neck Held High, It Guards the Kolkhoz Night, *1930.*
Oil on canvas, 77 x 117 cm.
State Tret'iakov Gallery, Moscow.

Nikritin was, of course, absent. The star of the show was clearly Deineka's *Mat' (Mother)*, an unsentimental portrait of a woman in robust health with an overly sweet child in her arms. The Ost artists fared badly when compared to this model: "The personages of the young 'Westerners'—the Ost artists—often looked too schematic and seemed a soulless appendage to an urbanized civilization. Contrasting the 'machine-ized' person in the works of Vialov at the end of the twenties or Zernova's *Peredachi tankov [Transfer of Tanks]* (1931) with Deineka's *Mother,* [one reviewer] wrote, 'Instead of dry thematic structures, here before us is a lyrical image of a mother with baby in her arms . . . but what a mother! This is no pathetic bourgeois female . . . not a mother married to a tyrant husband . . . this is a strong image of an energetic, independent, free woman . . .'"[47] Deineka's one-time colleague in Ost, Luchishkin, did not fare as well. The current head of Narkompros, Andrei Bubnov, spied the small hanging figure of the suicide in one of the windows of *The Balloon Has Flown* and had the painting summarily removed from the exhibition.[48]

By now the complete collapse of any hope for a new figurative art was at hand. As the 1930s progressed, Vsekokhudozhnik, in the form of its Art Board, wielded almost unlimited power over the lives of the artists. Discussions of works of art submitted to it took on the aspect of criminal trials. When Nikritin submitted his canvas *Staroe i novoe (The Old and the New,* ca. 1930–35, fig. no. 14) for consideration, he faced a panel chaired by Slavinskii and composed of the artists Bogorodskii, Aleksandr Gerasimov, Pavel Sokolov-Skalia, Nikolai Mashkovtsev, Deineka, Fridrikh Lekht, Aleksandr Grigor'ev, and the critics Osip Beskin and Ol'ga Bubnova.[49] As was typically the case, the work was used as a pretext for destroying the painting career of this independent-minded artist.

The "old and the new" was a popular subject in the 1920s as artists tried to define the change in society and to work out an image of the future. Nikritin's painting is a monumental and symbolic work; he probably hoped it would prove a suitable composition for another of his murals. It consists of a group of just four figures. The "old" is represented by the two outside figures, a nude and a beggar: the "Venus" on the left, rendered in a neoacademic style, covers herself with her hands and shyly draws her knees together, while the legless beggar on the right, the figure of a contemporary Buddha, displays a round tin, empty except for a mysterious tiny sphere. The two central figures, a young man and woman, are set counter to these images of false bourgeois idealization and cruel economic reality. The woman, in a worker's coverall, stands boldly with legs apart, one hand on her hip and the other pointing off to the right in a gesture of command. The young man lunges across the left foreground, staring fixedly at an unmarked globe in his hands. The sphere of the globe covers the pubic area of the female worker and rhymes visually with the empty tin and small sphere of the invalid. The entire work is bathed in a golden patina which distances it still further from reality and emphasizes its mytho-symbolic nature. We may guess that, on the most obvious level of the work, the artist is opposing the contemporary position of women to that of the past, and the bleak life of a veteran of imperialist wars to the global interests and peaceful intentions of contemporary youth. The enigmatic spheres point to the possibility of a more metaphysical interpretation.

At the outset of Vsekokhudozhnik's inquisition into this painting, Nikritin defended his work by describing the preparatory sketches he made for it, emphasizing that they were done from life; he named the place where he had seen the worker and vouched for the existence of the friend whom he

fig. 13
Aleksandr Tyshler
Lyrical Cycle, No. 4, *1928.*
Oil on canvas, 73.4 x 55.6 cm.
Museum Ludwig (Collection Ludwig, Cologne).

had noted in the act of looking for a town on a globe. But the initial hostility of the committee was not to be assuaged. Lekht objected to the unrealistic posture of the young man, Deineka to the "odd" position of the ball; Grigor'ev called the picture a "defamation"; Gerasimov said it did not merit their attention. But instead of simply dismissing the work as unacceptable, the committee proceeded to a vicious attack on Nikritin himself. Gerasimov called him "undesirable" and said, "This type of artist was once very common. He is one of those people who want to talk at all costs about themselves." Sokolov-Skalia insidiously linked him to the enemy abroad: "Such a peculiar man! And so terribly individualistic! Comrades, we sometimes read catalogues of foreign exhibitions, especially from Italy; there are things such as this . . . I regard it as an eclectic work derived from other sources, namely, it is adopted from the eclectic Italian Fascists." Mashkovtsev posed the rhetorical question of whether a Communist could have created such a picture, and piously answered it himself: "I cannot recollect that a single shadow of this tendency would ever have occurred in the case of comrades of the Party." And Lekht delivered the coup de grace: "What we see here is a calumny . . . It is a class attack, inimical to the Soviet power." In response to this assault, Nikritin abandoned any attempt to appease his accusers and, with an eye on history, characterized the type of paintings that had, in fact, met with Vsekokhudozhnik's approval: "[They stand] in no relation whatever to Soviet painting. These works follow the line of least intellectual resistance. (I am confessing what I think—perhaps to-day I am speaking for the last time.) What I am looking for is a great socialist style, versatile, philosophical. I am convinced that I am on the right track. Time will be our judge."

Slavinskii, in the last word of the meeting, disavowed the panel's personal responsibility for the opinions expressed: "The description which has been given here by all the members of the commission is to be regarded as the opinion of our artistic public. I should like to express the deepest regret that these views have not penetrated the consciousness of a stubborn painter."[50]

Tyshler and many other Ost painters suffered the same sort of humiliation and intimidation at the hands of Vsekokhudozhnik and the Moscow section of the Union of Soviet Artists. Labas and Shterenberg were suppressed as Formalists; as late as 1947, Red'ko was expelled from the Union for the same disease. Other members of the original group were led by their fundamental belief in the Revolution step by step into an aesthetic position from which there was no escape. With each increase in artistic limitations, with each quantum jump into personal vilification and conformity, some dropped out. But many never found a place to draw the line, and although this allowed them to continue working and even to become part of the artistic administration, they ended mired in the aesthetic bog to which they had contributed.

The first generation of the Moscow avant-garde had similarly failed to respond to the spiritual needs of its time. When abstract artists abandoned painting and their interest in the nature of humanity and the universe in favor of publicistic propaganda and objects of daily use, they renounced the role of artists as prophets and seekers of a high truth. At a crucial time in history they remained silent about the complexities of the human situation, about people's hopes, doubts, fears, and ambiguities. They failed to offer guidance, insight, or understanding to a public caught in events that were destroying the old certainties. For a time it seemed possible that the resulting artistic vacuum might indeed be filled by a new generation, possessed of a new artistic vision. But they, too, were overtaken by a militant fundamentalism, partly of their own making, that through increasing intimidation reduced most of Russian art to a shadow of its former self.

fig. 14
Solomon Nikritin
The Old and the New, *ca. 1930–35 (detail).*
Oil on canvas, 100 x 120 cm.
State Savitskii Museum of Art, Nukus.

Notes

1. Varvara Stepanova, "On Constructivism," in Alexander Lavrentiev, *Stepanova*, trans. Wendy Salmond (Cambridge, Mass.: MIT Press, 1988), p. 175.

2. K. Malevich, *Suprematizm. 34 risunka* (Vitebsk: Unovis), p. 3, as translated in K. S. Malevich, "Suprematism. 34 Drawings," in his *Essays on Art*, ed. Troels Andersen, trans. Xenia Glowacki-Prus and Arnold McMillin (London: Rapp & Whiting, 1969), vol. 1, p. 127; Lyubov' Popova, "Commentary on Drawings," trans. James West, in *Art Into Life: Russian Constructivism, 1914–1932*, catalogue for exhibition organized by the Henry Art Gallery, University of Washington, Seattle, the Walker Art Center, Minneapolis, and the State Tret'yakov Gallery, Moscow (New York: Rizzoli, 1990), p. 69. Popova's original text is in the Manuscript Division, State Tret'iakov Gallery, Moscow, f. 148, ed. khr. 17, l. 4.

3. V. I. Kostin, comp., *Kliment Red'ko: Dnevniki, vospominaniia, stat'i* (Moscow: Sovetskii khudozhnik, 1974), p. 63. Entry for November 18, 1920.

4. M. A. Bulgakov, "Pod piatoi. Moi dnevnik," *Ogonek* 51 (December 1989), p. 17. Entry for April 15, 1924.

5. V. Kostin, *OST* (Leningrad: Khudozhnik RSFSR, 1976), p. 19.

6. The painting was his *Portret L. Ia. Reznikova* (Portrait of L. Ia. Reznikov). *Katalog. 1-aia diskussionnaia vystavka ob"edinenii aktivnogo revoliutsionnogo iskusstva* (Moscow, 1924), p. 11.

7. In addition to their kinship with the widespread efforts at classification taking place at this time in many fields, Luchishkin's analytical work and formal studies generally associated with the Museum of Painterly Culture overlap considerably with early-twentieth-century perceptual studies and with Gestalt psychology.

8. Nikritin, Luchishkin, and Triaskin invented a Projectionist Theater, which utilized mobile abstract sets and "pure" speech sounds similar to *zaum'* (transrational language). Performances were given in 1923 and 1924.

9. Luchishkin and Zernova both mention the importance to them of Shchukin's collection, to which they had been given access even as secondary-school students.

10. At that time the paintings which had been in storage were reassembled as a museum at 52 Povarskaia Street.

11. At the time of the Revolution, Lenin appointed Anatolii Lunacharskii, a writer and critic and an old friend from his years of exile, Commissar of Enlightenment. David Shterenberg, an artist whom Lunacharskii had known and reviewed when both lived in Paris, became head of Izo Narkompros.

12. The Projectionists were not the only additions to the Berlin exhibition. At the beginning of 1923, Shterenberg took to Berlin more work by Popova, Udal'tsova, Kudriashev, and others, as well as a quantity of porcelain and other decorative art. According to Shterenberg's records, 19 artists and 193 works of art were added to the show at this time. V. P. Lapshin, "Pervaia vystavka russkogo iskusstva. Berlin. 1922 god. Materialy k istorii sovetsko-germanskikh khudozhestvennykh sviazei," *Sovetskoe iskusstvoznanie* 1 (1982), pp. 349, 360.

13. The Museum of Painterly Culture was opened to the public at this venue on October 15, 1924. Its holdings eventually went to the State Tret'iakov Gallery.

14. *Truby (Komsomol'skoe shestvie)* (*Horns {Young Communists League Parade}*, 1925), State Tret'iakov Gallery, Moscow.

15. *Kul'turnaia zhizn' v SSSR. Khronika 1917–1927* (Moscow: Nauka, 1975), p. 571.

16. E. S. Zernova, *Vospominaniia monumentalista* (Moscow: Sovetskii khudozhnik, 1985), p. 61. *The Fish-Canning Factory* is now in the State Tret'iakov Gallery, Moscow, and *Tomato Puree* in the Astrakhan Kustodiev Picture Gallery.

17. The exhibition was in Moscow from October 18th to November 30, 1924. From there it traveled to Saratov and Leningrad.

18. G. Zumpf, "Vystavki nemetskogo iskusstva v Sovetskom soiuze v seredine 20–kh godov i ikh otsenka sovetskoi kritiki," in *Vzaimosviazi russkogo i sovetskogo iskusstva i nemetskoi khudozhestvennoi kul'tury* (Moscow: Nauka, 1980), p. 191. The author is quoting from A. V. Lunacharskii, "Vystavka revoliutsionnogo iskusstva zapada," in *A. V. Lunacharskii ob izobrazitel'nom iskusstve* (Moscow: Sovetskii khudozhnik, 1967), vol. 1, pp. 319–20.

19. Zumpf, "Vystavki nemetskogo iskusstva," p. 186.

20. Ibid., pp. 186–87. Zumpf is summarizing Fedorov-Davydov's article, "O nekotorykh kharakternykh chertakh nemetskoi vystavki," *Pechat' i revoliutsiia* 6 (1924).

21. A. A. Fedorov-Davydov, "Po vystavkam," *Russkaia sovetskaia khudozhestvennaia kritika. 1917–1941* (Moscow: Izobrazitel'noe iskusstvo/Sovetskii khudozhnik, 1982), p. 262.

22. S. A. Luchishkin, *Ia ochen' liubliu zhizn'. Stranitsy vospominanii* (Moscow: Sovetskii khudozhnik, 1988), p. 103.

23. *N. N. Kupreianov. Literaturno-khudozhestvennoe nasledie* (Moscow: Iskusstvo, 1973), p. 27.

24. Fedorov-Davydov, "Po vystavkam," p. 258.

25. V. I. Kostin, "Poiski i eksperimenty Solomona Nikritina," in *Sredi khudozhnikov* (Moscow: Sovetskii khudozhnik, 1986), p. 63.

26. Luchishkin, *Ia ochen' liubliu zhizn'*, pp. 116–17.

27. This picture is also called *Edinolichnik* (Loner).

28. Boris Ternovets, the director of the Museum of New Western Art, was particularly close to the Italians. He wrote one of the first books on de Chirico, and made extensive trades of Russian work—including that of Ost—for contemporary Italian art.

29. Kostin, *Kliment Red'ko*, p. 16. Red'ko showed some two hundred works at this solo exhibition. His relations with Ost became strained to some extent because the Museum of Painterly Culture had refused him space for his exhibition.

30. Ibid., p. 73. Entry for March 21, 1926.

31. Ibid., p. 67. Entry for June 10, 1924.

32. AKhRR was forced to reorganize early in 1928, and at that time it changed its name to AKhR.

33. Slavinskii was a former orchestra conductor at the Bol'shoi Theater, a Party activist, and had been a union organizer since 1916.

34. "Vystuplenie khud. D. Shterenberg," in *Iskusstvo v SSSR i zadachi khudozhnikov* (Moscow: Izd. kommunisticheskoi akademii, 1928), pp. 93–94.

35. I. Matsa, ed., *Sovetskoe iskusstvo za 15 let. Materialy i dokumentatsiia* (Moscow and Leningrad: Ogiz-Izogiz, 1933), p. 576.

36. *Izogazeta brigada khudozhnikov* 1 (1931), p. 1.

37. The signatories included Vil'iams, Vialov, Zernova, Luchishkin, Pimenov, and, oddly, Nikritin, who at this late hour seems to have made an attempt to rehabilitate himself. Matsa, *Sovetskoe iskusstvo za 15 let,* p. 579.

38. *Izogazeta brigada khudozhnikov* 5–6 (1931), p. 41.

39. *Izogazeta brigada khudozhnikov* 1 (1931), p. 5.

40. *Izogazeta brigada khudozhnikov* 2–3 (1931), p. 8.

41. Ibid., p. 9.

42. The Decree on the Restructuring of Literary and Artistic Organizations said in part: "At the present time, when cadres of proletarian literature and art have managed to develop and new writers and artists have come forward in factories, plants, and collective farms, the frameworks of the existing proletarian literary and art organizations . . . are already too narrow and are impeding a serious range of artistic work. This situation creates a danger of transforming these organizations from the means of the greatest mobilization of Soviet writers and artists for the tasks of socialist construction into a means of cultivating closed groups isolated from the political tasks of contemporaneity and from significant groups of writers and artists sympathetic to socialist construction." "O perestroike literaturno-khudozhestvennykh organizatsii," in *Vo glave kul'turnogo stroitel'stva* (Moscow: Moskovskii rabochii, 1983), vol. 1, pp. 350-51.

43. A national Union of Artists of the USSR was not established until 1957.

44. Luchishkin, *Ia ochen' liubliu zhizn',* p. 134. Luchishkin is here quoting from an unattributed source.

45. A. I. Morozov, "K istorii vystavki 'Khudozhniki RSFSR za 15 let' (Leningrad-Moskva, 1932–35)," *Sovetskoe iskusstvoznanie* 1 (1982), p. 132.

46. Vil'iams, a member of the Brigade of Artists, was initially included in the first division, but his works were ignominiously removed to the Ost room the day after he joined Goncharov, Labas, and Nisson Shifrin in their request that Tyshler be allowed to exhibit. Luchishkin, *Ia ochen' liubliu zhizn',* p. 134.

47. Morozov, "K istorii vystavki 'Khudozhniki RSFSR za 15 let,'" p. 154.

48. Luchishkin, *Ia ochen' liubliu zhizn',* p. 134.

49. Kurt London, *The Seven Soviet Arts* (London: Faber, 1937; Westport, Conn.: Greenwood Press, 1970). Artists formerly associated with a wide variety of groups participated in the work of Vsekokhudozhnik. Many, but far from all, were previously members of AKhRR and RAPKh. Beskin, who wrote catalogues for the Soviet export exhibitions, is best known for a fiendish book on "Formalism."

50. Transcript of the Art Board of Vsekokhudozhnik from April 10, 1935, as translated in London, *The Seven Soviet Arts,* pp. 223–29.

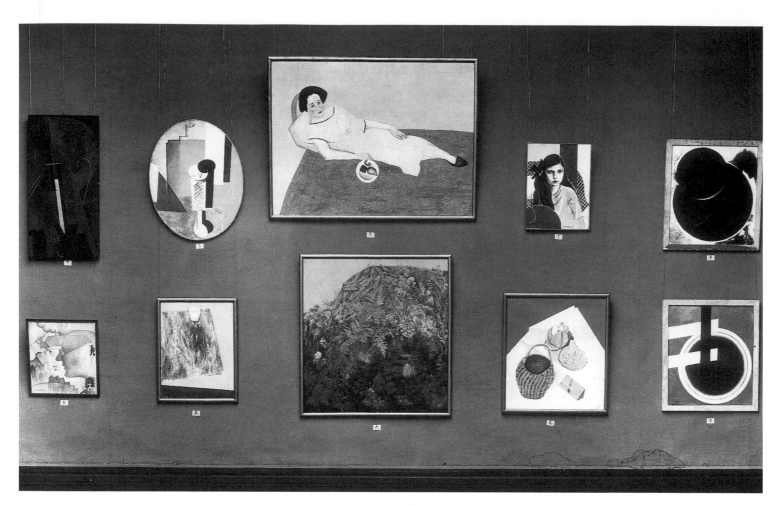

fig. 1
View of exhibition in the Russian pavilion, Venice Biennale, 1924.
Fondo artistico e fototeca, Archivio storico delle arti contemporanee
della Biennale di Venezia.

The Russian Presence in the 1924 Venice Biennale

Vivian Endicott Barnett

In the 1920s, contemporary Soviet art was exhibited in numerous cities in the West. The well-known *Erste russische Kunstausstellung* (*First Russian Art Exhibition*) took place in Berlin in the autumn of 1922 and then traveled to Amsterdam the following year.[1] There was an *Exhibition of Russian Painting and Sculpture* at the Brooklyn Museum in New York in 1923, and the next year a *Russian Art Exhibition* was held at the Grand Central Palace in New York. The *XIV Esposizione internazionale d'arte della città di Venezia* (*Fourteenth Venice International Art Exhibition*), which featured the Padiglione del U.R.S.S. (the Russian pavilion), also took place in 1924.[2] The *Exposition internationale des arts décoratifs et industriels modernes* (*International Exhibition of Contemporary Decorative and Industrial Art*) was presented in Paris in 1925, the *Mostra internazionale delle arti decorative* (*International Exhibition of Decorative Art*) in Monza near Milano in 1927, and the *Exposition d'art russe ancien et moderne* (*Exhibition of Russian Art Past and Present*) in Brussels in 1928; there was an exhibition of Soviet art in England in 1929. In 1930–31 several exhibitions were held in Berlin, Vienna, Paris, Stockholm, and Zurich. Moreover, the work of Russian artists living in the West was presented often in France and Germany during the twenties.[3]

Unlike the other exhibitions, the *Esposizione internazionale d'arte della città di Venezia,* better known as the Venice Biennale, was a regular event in which Russian art had been included since the first Biennale in 1895. The organizers of the 1924 Biennale were particularly eager to show recent works by artists in the Soviet Union because a decade had passed, and the Revolution had taken place, since works had last come from Russia to Italy for display at the Russian pavilion. In both 1907 and 1914, the Venice Biennale had featured works by Russian artists. Thus, official as well as personal channels between organizers and participants had already been established.

This essay will focus on the organization of the 1924 exhibition, the works of art that finally arrived for the Russian pavilion, how the Russians presented them, and how they were received critically in Italy. Based on the records and photographs preserved in the Archivio storico delle arti contemporanee della Biennale di Venezia, the identity of specific objects and their installation can be determined. It is also known which works were purchased for Italian collections and which were kept in the West at the artists' behest.

By the summer of 1923, efforts were initiated by the Italians through the trade delegations of both countries to encourage Soviet participation in the *XIV Esposizione internazionale,* which was scheduled to open in April 1924.[4] Giovanni Bordiga and Ilario Neri, the principal Italian organizers, invited the Russians to submit a list of "representative and notable artists," who would each be represented by one or more works. Although in earlier years they had been in direct contact with the commissioner of the Russian section of the Biennale, F. Barenshtam, in 1923 the organizers turned to the Delegazione commerciale italiana in Moscow for assistance. On June 11, 1923, Bordiga, who was president of the *Esposizione internazionale,* wrote to the Italian foreign minister, noting that, following the end of World War I, the shows of foreign art at the Biennale had all been resumed with the exception of the Russian pavilion—because there were still no diplomatic relations between Russia and Italy. "For this reason," he requested, "I beg Your Excellency to indicate whether I may initiate the necessary steps through the Russian trade delegation in Rome and also with the possible assistance of the Italian mission in Moscow." As a director of the *Esposizione internazionale,* Neri sent repeated letters and telegrams from Venice to the Ministry of Foreign Affairs in Rome and to the Delegazione commerciale italiana in Moscow. On September

29, 1923, he wired the Italian trade delegation: "We beg you to reply promptly to our letters regarding the Russian artistic participation in the next show."

The first indication of any progress in the negotiations came in the postscript to Neri's letter of November 27th to the same delegation: "From news received indirectly, it appears that a committee for the Russian-art competition in Venice has already been selected. Please be so kind as to be precise also in this respect." The next day, Neri received a telegram from Signor Paterno, the spokesman for the Italian trade delegation in Moscow, stating: "As wired Foreign Ministry, confirm Russian participation." Likewise, the Ministry of Foreign Affairs confirmed that the Delegazione economica italiana in Moscow had indicated the acceptance in principle by the government of the USSR of the invitation to participate in the Biennale.

In December 1923, Neri contacted Iordanskii, the Soviet representative in Rome, and, in a letter dated December 26th, inquired who had been selected commissioner, for he wished to approach him directly. Upon learning that the commissioner was Petr Kogan, president of the Russian Academy of Artistic Sciences, professor at Moscow University, and director of the Institute of Art and Archeology, Neri wrote to him in Moscow. In his letter to Kogan dated January 9th, Neri emphasized that all the works exhibited in the Biennale must reach Venice by late March and that he needed a list of objects as soon as possible. The response, however, was not sent until late February.

During this time the Italian trade delegation in Moscow continued to play a crucial role in the negotiations, since formal diplomatic relations between the two countries were resumed only on February 7, 1924. On January 19th, Paterno sent a telegram to Neri: "Please wire immediately if the Russian government may show applied art such as etchings, engravings, lace, wood carving, porcelain, architecture. For paintings wish to know how many pictures will be permitted each participant." Three days later, Neri indicated the organizers' preference for "*arte pura*" and added that "for each artist two works will be enough while solo shows of two prominent artists would be desirable." In a letter also dated January 22nd, Neri explained to Paterno that "as an exception, and especially from the point of view of ornamenting the rooms, it is agreed that some objects of decorative and applied art may be included but always in a very discreet and limited manner . . . However, regarding the number of works, we are of the opinion that, as a general rule, no artist may exhibit more than two."

When Kogan responded to Neri's letter, he apologized for the delay and explained: "I was not able to answer your letter right away because the great loss suffered in Russia with the death of V. I. Lenin has delayed our work in recent days."[5] He stated that "we will take into consideration your wish that our section represent products most characteristic of Russian art." Kogan also inquired about the possibility of finding additional space to augment the Russian pavilion in case there should not be enough room to display the works and about the possibility of including decorative arts and porcelain in the exhibition.

By March, a tone of urgency can be detected in the telegrams sent to Kogan requesting information and repeating that the Biennale would open on April 24th. Italy's new ambassador to the USSR, Manzoni, transmitted the reply to Neri on April 5th: "Kogan informs Russian works [in] exhibition will reach Venice beginning of May. Paintings section includes about sixty works [by] principal artists. Other three sections [are] sculpture, theater design, decorative arts and porcelain. If administration will provide space in main pavilion Russian presence could be greater."

In a letter to Bordiga dated April 4th, Ambassador Manzoni wrote that "since the beginning of my stay in Moscow, I have been occupied with securing and speeding up the Russian involvement in the Venetian exhibition. I have found the best cooperation in this matter from the commissar of enlightenment, Lunacharskii, who lived in Italy for five years and knows and understands our language. Thanks to his good offices, the commissar of finance has approved the sum of 11,000 gold rubles (equal to 137,500 Italian lire) for construction on the Russian pavilion and for the costs of the Russian participation. Thanks to his good offices, the principal Russian artists have been persuaded to be represented in Venice with their best works. In this endeavor, Commissar Lunacharskii has been actively assisted by Professor Kogan."[6] An enclosed article from *Izvestiia,* dated March 26th, stated that one hundred prominent artists had been invited to participate in the Venice Biennale, which the People's Commissar of Enlightenment considered to be "of the utmost importance." Ambassador Manzoni also sent Neri a translation of an article in the April 18th issue of *Izvestiia*: "The exhibition committee has more than 300 examples of paintings, works on paper, and sculpture, which come from different regions of the USSR but are presently in Moscow together with the items from the capital. The objects from Leningrad will arrive in a few days. In all, more than 500 works will be represented, among which many have as their theme contemporaneity. For example, *V. Lenin in the Mausoleum* (Shadr), the portrait of Trotskii (Annenkov), and other pictures from the Museum of the Red Army will be sent to Venice. Besides the major cities, there will be representative art from different places in Russia such as Armenia, Ukraine, etc."

In mid-May there was another flurry of telegrams. Bordiga cabled the representative of the Soviet trade delegation in Rome, inquiring when the works of art would reach Venice: "Commission together with works supposed to arrive May 5. Delay worries us more since exhibition now crowded is great success." Finally, on May 16th, Ambassador Manzoni could wire Venice: "1398 works sent yesterday [via] Brenner [Pass]." And a telegram from Kogan read: "Paintings sent we leave Friday 16 via Berlin." The Soviet organizers arrived in Venice in early June. In addition to the commissioner, Kogan, and the secretary general, Boris Ternovets, the organizing committee included A. Bakushinskii, Boris Shaposhnikov, V. Domogadskii, Abram Efros, A. Kondrat'ev, M. Kristi, A. Sidorov, Iakov Tugendkhol'd, and B. Vipper. According to an article in *Il Popolo d'Italia* from June 6th, Kogan explained in an interview that "our delay was due to the great distance between the two countries and to the infinite formalities which we had to overcome." Although the works of art had still not arrived, he was glad to participate in the Biennale. Kogan was quoted as saying that "As for the artistic movements, there is none of any representative value today in Russia which we have not collected . . . The decorative arts on which we place great importance—which is a direct manifestation of the artistic sense of our people—are widely represented." Kogan concluded: "We believe that we have done something worthy of the Biennale."

According to the official catalogue of the *XIV Esposizione internazionale,* there were 176 paintings, 19 sculptures, and 300 watercolors, as well as 80 examples of decorative art, in the Russian pavilion.[7] Newspaper accounts also confirmed a total of approximately 600 works of art. The catalogue separated the works by medium, listed the artists alphabetically, and provided titles—without dates—in Italian. It stated, however, that all the objects had been executed during the preceding decade.

From the catalogue, it is immediately apparent that works

from a wide spectrum of styles and regions were presented in the Russian pavilion. Portraits by Natan Al'tman and Iurii Annenkov, landscapes by Anatolii Arapov and Igor' Grabar', Suprematist works by Kazimir Malevich and Liubov' Popova, and political-historical canvases by Boris Kustodiev and N. D. Nikonov were included. The Museum of the Red Army in Moscow lent eleven works: Annenkov's *Portret L'va Trotskogo* (*Portrait of Lev Trotskii*, 1923, no. 7), Sergei Chekhonin's *Portret Sidiakina* (*Portrait of Sidiakin*, no. 21), Vasilii Iakovlev's *Gazeta na fronte* (*Newspaper at the Front*, 1923, no. 55), Konstantin Iuon's *Parad na Krasnoi ploshchadi v Moskve* (*Parad Krasnoi armii*) (*Parade in Red Square in Moscow {Parade of the Red Army}*, 1923, no. 57), S. M. Karpov's *Agitpunkt* (*Agitation Committee*, no. 59), Kustodiev's *Bol'shevik* (*The Bolshevik*, 1920, no. 89) and *Portret N. Kuz'mina* (*Portrait of N. Kuz'min*, 1923, no. 90), Pavel Kuznetsov's *Na Krasnoi ploshchadi* (*On Red Square*, 1923, no. 99), Kuz'ma Petrov-Vodkin's *Posle boia* (*After the Battle*, 1923, no. 130), Petr Shukhmin's *Provodnik* (*Guide at the Front*, 1923, no. 165), and Sergei Konenkov's sculpture of the *Krasnyi kazak* (*Red Cossack*, no. 182). All of the works by Malevich, Aleksandr Rodchenko, Varvara Stepanova, Aleksandr Vesnin, and Popova listed in the catalogue were entitled *Suprematizm* (*Suprematism*) and stood in stark contrast to the works from the Museum of the Red Army. Since the pictures are reproduced neither in the official catalogue of the Biennale nor in photographs taken in Venice, identification of the works by the last four artists remains difficult.

Six photographs of the installation in the Russian pavilion were, however, published in an article by Ternovets.[8] Two Suprematist paintings by Rodchenko (nos. 137, 138) are clearly visible at the far right in one of the installation shots (fig. no. 1). Adjacent to Al'tman's *Portrait of a Girl* (1923, no. 1),[9] above, and David Shterenberg's *Natiurmort s korzinkoi* (*Still Life with Basket*, 1922–23, no. 164), below, the two Rodchenkos are presented with other paintings by Al'tman, Annenkov, and Shterenberg: on the same wall, at the top (from left to right), are Al'tman's *Rossiia. Trud* (*Russia: Work*, 1921, no. 3; plate no. 107), *Natiurmort* (*Still Life*, 1920, no. 2),[10] and Shterenberg's *Zhenshchina na divane* (*Woman on a Couch*, no. 161); below are Annenkov's *Vesna* (*Spring*, no. 10) and Shterenberg's *Natiurmort na mramornom stole* (*Still Life on Marble Table*, 1920s, no. 163) and *Peisazh* (*Landscape*, no. 162). Also listed in the Biennale catalogue, as no. 6, is Al'tman's *Petrokommuna* (*Petrocommune*, 1921, plate no. 108). According to lists of objects not exhibited but kept in storage, *Petrocommune* as well as two still lifes by Al'tman were (probably) among the hundreds of works stored in Venice.

In the center of another view of the installation (fig. no. 2), Annenkov's *Portrait of Lev Trotskii* is immediately flanked, on the left, by his portraits of Polonskii (1922, no. 9) and Aleksandr Tikhonov (1922, no. 8)[11] and, on the right, by Abram Arkhipov's *Molodaia khoziaika* (*Young Proprietress*, 1924, no. 15) and Iuon's *Parade in Red Square in Moscow.*[12] Farther to the right, Nikonov's *V"ezd Krasnoi armii v Krasnoiarsk* (*Entrance of the Red Army into Krasnoiarsk*, no. 123) hangs below Shukhmin's *Guide at the Front*. Petrov-Vodkin's *After the Battle*[13] can be seen at the upper left. A photograph of the entrance to the main gallery shows works by Kustodiev—including *Zimnii peisazh* (*Winter Landscape*, no. 85), *Portret Tat'iany Chizhovoi* (*Portrait of Tat'iana Chizhova*, 1924, no. 86),[14] *Kupchikha* (*The Merchant's Wife*, 1918, no. 88),[15] and *The Bolshevik.*[16] There were also a landscape and the *Portret Adol'fa Mil'mana* (*Portrait of Adol'f Mil'man*, no. 114) by Il'ia Mashkov, and *Natiurmort* (*Still Life*, 1922, no. 153) by Martiros Sar'ian. Robert Fal'k's *Krasnaia mebel'* (*Red Furniture*, 1920–23, no. 35) and *Zhenshchina v belom* (*Woman in White*, 1922–23, no. 42)[17]; Petr Konchalovskii's *Avtoportret s zhenoi* (*The Artist and His Wife*, 1923, no. 60), *Semeinyi portret* (*Family*

Portrait, 1923–24, no. 61), *Agava* (*Agave*, 1916, no. 65),[18] and *Lezhashchaia naturshchitsa* (*Reclining Nude*, 1923, no. 67); and numerous landscapes by Sar'ian are also easily identifiable from photographs.[19] Another wall was devoted to pictures by Kuznetsov, including *Devushka s verbliudom* (*Girl with Camel*, late 1910s–early 1920s), *Mirazh v stepi* (*Fata Morgana on the Steppe*, 1910s), several still lifes, and *Red Square in Moscow* (nos. 91–99).

Although there are no photographs of the works by Malevich, they can be identified as *Chernyi kvadrat* (*Black Square*), *Chernyi krest* (*Black Cross*), and *Chernyi krug* (*Black Circle*), all circa 1923, and six planit drawings.[20] Whether the works were actually exhibited remains doubtful. Likewise, Boris Ender's canvas (*Extended Space*, 1922–23, no. 27; plate no. 325), which was acquired later by George Costakis, traveled to Venice but may not have been on view.[21] Several paintings and works on paper by Aleksandra Ekster were photographed at the time of the Biennale in Venice and are also known from publications: for example, studies for sets and costumes for Iakov Protazanov's film *Aelita* (released in 1924) and stage designs for Calderón's *La Dama duende* (produced at the Moscow Art Theater in 1921), Innokentii Annenskii's *Famira Kifared* (*Thamyris the Cithara-Player,* produced at the Kamernyi Theater in Moscow in 1916), and Shakespeare's *Romeo and Juliet* (produced at the Kamernyi Theater in 1921; compare plate nos. 610–611).[22]

The Biennale catalogue contains a four-page introductory text by Ternovets summarizing the diverse artistic tendencies presented in the Russian pavilion. He begins by defining and contrasting the two schools of art which had developed in Moscow and St. Petersburg/Petrograd at the end of the nineteenth and beginning of the twentieth centuries. He cites the exhibitions of Bubnovyi valet (Jack of Diamonds) as evidence for Moscow's artistic supremacy and also mentions the Moscow collectors Sergei Shchukin and Ivan Morozov. Ternovets refers to the influence of Cézanne, especially on the art of Konchalovskii and Mashkov. He goes on to say that "beside this main current run other, less plentiful streams. It is easy to imagine that the spirit of the Orient must have its interpreters in the half-Asian city of Moscow. The personality of Pavel Kuznetsov took shape during his trips across the steppes of eastern Russia." Ternovets states that Cubism was dominant in Moscow, however, as it was in other centers of artistic activity. Not only Annenkov but also Malevich, Popova, Ekster, and Al'tman developed their work out of Cubism. He mentions the "transitory action of non-objective art, which refutes the representation of the visual world and which is currently known in Russia by the name 'Suprematism' . . . The majority of extremist painters, gathered under the common denominator of 'constructors,' have expressed their profound aversion to the traditional forms of easel painting and are attempting to find through direct participation in the procedures of the textile, metallurgical, and printing industries the solution to their problems." He singles out Shterenberg as an artist who is sympathetic to extremist tendencies but who has tried to express the pictorial aspect of the visual world but, at the same time, using the discoveries of the new technology.

Ternovets emphasizes that the Soviet festivals of recent years, the new monumental ornamentation, may have been marked by an extremist orientation but that, in his view, the sympathies of the Russian proletariat do not lie in this artistic direction. The people prefer a solid and vigorous Naturalism. A tendency toward an art based on the observation and study of nature and a particular interest in subjects of contemporary life are evident in the work of the young but already influential AKhRR (the Association of Artists of Revolutionary Russia).

Iakovlev, Shukhmin, Pavel Radimov, and Evgenii Katsman represent this movement in the present exhibition. He concludes by stating that "the artistic life of the USSR presents a picture of passionate searching, sometimes questionable and sometimes gainsaid by the struggle and competition between diverse tendencies, but a stirring picture which gives us the image of a people in quest of new forms for a new life."

The critical response to the exhibits in the Russian pavilion focused on the opening, which took place at 10 A.M. on Thursday, June 19th, with the Soviet ambassador, Iur'enev, present. According to the *Gazzetta* of June 20th, "the ceremony took place with simple and decorous solemnity." In addition to Kogan, several members of the Soviet committee, including Ternovets, Shaposhnikov, and Kondrat'ev, were present, as was Sar'ian. Kogan led a tour of the galleries but without giving a speech, "which was not necessary. The public could thus appreciate even better the interesting and varied body of works assembled in the pavilion. The only drawback was the lack of space for a suitable presentation of the extremely large number of objects on display." According to *Emporium*, Kogan delivered a few remarks in French, expressing his satisfaction that the USSR had resumed diplomatic relations with Italy "after the period of the Revolution and the suspension of Russia's relations with other countries."

Even before the pavilion opened, an unsigned article in the *Corriere italiano* of June 12th stated that the Russian delegation was larger and more imposing than any of the others. "The Russian pavilion will be distinguished from the others in that the commission concerns itself not only with choosing the works but also with showing the entire present situation of Russian art with all its disparate tendencies . . . Many say that the exhibition is the most beautiful opportunity for Bolshevik propaganda: no, it is rather the first and well-deserved affirmation of the art of a people who for a decade were not in contact with our Western world. And Italy—who should not fear Communist infiltration—is most happy, especially in Venice, to host such a worthy collection."

Writing in the August 7th issue of *Epoca*, Alberto Francini said of the exhibit that "there seemed to be no real correspondence between [Soviet] life and an art that today appears not merely traditional but behind the times. Yet, if one thinks about it, this situation is quite logical, since the consequence of the Revolution could only be to give value to the taste of the people who, not having had time to become the elite, had to be satisfied with the obvious and old-fashioned displays." He discussed the paintings of Konchalovskii and expressed his preference for the work of Fal'k and Aleksandr Kuprin. At the end of his article, Francini singled out "the few interesting ceramics on which revolutionary decorations appear."

Francesco Sapori also mentioned the ceramics—especially those from Mezhigorsk in Ukraine—and focused on the pictures by the Armenian artist Sar'ian.[23] He gave particular emphasis, however, to the work of Annenkov, "who accepts with open eyes some of the postulates of Cubism in order to confront realistically and alone the radical problem of form." When one considers his monumental *Portrait of Lev Trotskii*, one sees that "this painter of revolutionary Russia knows how to unite the expressive force of the past with the anguished achievements of today."

Sar'ian was well represented, with ten paintings listed in the catalogue (as had Fal'k and Kuznetsov), and surpassed only by Konchalovskii with thirteen works. According to a detailed list in the Biennale archives, however, there were sixty pictures by Konchalovskii shipped in two crates to Venice, where they were stored by the administration of the Biennale. According to another official document, 193 works sent from the Soviet Union and twenty pictures shipped from Berlin to Venice were placed on deposit with the managing director of the Biennale due to lack of space in the Russian pavilion. Three works by Fal'k, for example, as well as four by Popova, nine by Ekster, and nine by Malevich were stored rather than exhibited in Venice. The Biennale catalogue includes only nine works by Malevich, and for this reason the question arises whether his works were actually on view. There is one work by Vladimir Tatlin on the list of objects sent from Berlin, although the artist is not mentioned in the Biennale catalogue.

The detailed list of works shipped from Berlin to Venice requires further attention. Evidently, three of the four Suprematist paintings and the works on paper by Popova (nos. 132–134, 388) were not exhibited. Likewise, Stepanova's Suprematist picture (no. 167), one of Rodchenko's Suprematist paintings (no. 141), and three works by Al'tman mentioned above (*Petrocommune* and two still lifes {nos. 4–5}) were apparently not on view, although they were listed in the catalogue. In addition, four works by Aleksandr Vesnin and six by Ekster, which do not appear to have Biennale catalogue numbers, were shipped from Berlin and stored in Venice. From a comparison of this list with the checklist in the catalogue for the *Erste russische Kunstausstellung,* it appears likely that works by Al'tman, Ekster, Popova, Rodchenko, Stepanova, and Tatlin first exhibited in Berlin in 1922 may have been sent in 1924 to Venice. Two works by Al'tman—*Russia: Work* and *Petrocommune*—along with Ekster's painting *Venetsiia* (*Venice,* no. 34), and, it may be, the same four pictures by Popova were listed in the catalogues for both the *Erste russische Kunstausstellung* and the Venice Biennale.[24]

There can be no doubt that the Russians sent more works to Venice than could possibly be accommodated in the Russian pavilion in the Giardini pubblici. It is unclear what happened to the sixty pictures by Konchalovskii after the conclusion of the Biennale. The artist visited Italy later that year, however, and probably reclaimed the works when he was in Venice. On September 3, 1924, Ekster contacted the organizers of the Biennale, requesting that the paintings not exhibited but stored in the British pavilion be returned to her in Italy. In 1925, after the close of the Biennale, Kogan wrote on behalf of Ekster to say that her three paintings shipped in November had still not arrived in Paris, where she was then living. Nevertheless, the fact remains that numerous non-objective works listed in the Biennale catalogue were not exhibited in the Russian pavilion and that the impact of Suprematist art was really less significant than implied by the Biennale publications.

At least thirty-five works were purchased out of the Biennale and remained in Italy. In November 1924, Konchalovskii's *Family Portrait* was purchased by the Galleria d'arte moderna in Venice for 3,530 lire and Arkhipov's painting *Leto* (*Summer,* no. 16) was acquired by the Civica galleria d'arte moderna in Genoa for 2,500 lire. Giorgio Georgiadis of Trieste bought Arkhipov's *Young Proprietress* and Giovanni Dallavilla purchased Kuznetsov's *Girl with Camel* and Sar'ian's canvas *Erevan* (1924, no. 154). Vittorio Lodigiani of Milan bought numerous objects, including Grabar''s *Na lazorevom nebe* (*Blue Sky,* 1923, no. 51), Konchalovskii's *Derev'ia* (*Trees,* no. 72), Kuprin's *Kreml'* (*Kremlin,* no. 84), and Mashkov's *Iuzhnyi peisazh. Zakat solntsa* (*Southern Landscape: Sunset,* no. 121). The well-known Florentine collector Charles Loeser acquired Vasilii Rozhdestvenskii's *Krymskii peisazh* (*Landscape in the Crimea,* no. 145) for 6,000 lire. Not only paintings and works on paper but also the decorative arts were purchased by private collectors as well as by the Museo delle arti decorativi in Monza. Ceramics, lacquer boxes, plates, water jugs, and statuettes were sold from the Russian pavilion during the

fig. 2
View of exhibition in the Russian pavilion, Venice Biennale, 1924.
Fondo artistico e fototeca, Archivio storico delle arti contemporanee
della Biennale di Venezia.

summer and autumn of 1924.

The Russian organizers apparently stayed in Italy past the close of the exhibition. Ternovets, who traveled to Florence and Rome, remained in contact with Domenico Varagnolo of the Biennale secretariat. On October 31st, from Florence, he wrote a postcard in Italian saying that "today I want to meet Mr. Pozzi and visit Mr. Loeser, who acquired the landscape by Rozhdestvenskii." On January 1, 1925, Ternovets was again in Venice before traveling to Milan and Monza with Kogan on their way to Paris. A few days later, in an undated letter from Milan to Varagnolo and Bazzini, Ternovets mentioned that he had visited Lodigiani and seen his "interesting collection." Since the Biennale offices were closed on New Year's Day, he was "very sorry not to have been able to say goodbye personally. Please accept my warmest thanks for all the support and expression of friendship and kindness which I found in Venice. It is with feelings of deepest and most sincere gratitude that I will think of my stay in this beautiful city . . . In fifteen months I hope to see all of you and to renew our friendly relations."

On January 7, 1925, Kogan wrote from Milan to thank the Biennale committee and to say that he was sorry not to have been able to do so in person: "Unfortunately, due to various formalities, I was obliged to stay in Rome longer than I had planned and since then I have come to Milan to clarify the possibility of our participation in the exhibition of decorative arts in Monza. I consider it to be my most pleasant duty to tell you that I will never forget the thoroughly friendly welcome which we received from the administration of the Venice Biennale, the perfect order and superior culture which we found in Italy and in beautiful Venice. I hope to have the pleasure of seeing the entire committee again at the next Biennale in 1926."[25]

Notes

1. See Andrei B. Nakov, "This Last Exhibition which was the 'First,'" in *The First Russian Show,* catalogue for exhibition organized by Annely Juda Fine Art, London (London: Annely Juda Fine Art, 1983), pp. 6–47; Peter Nisbet, "Some Facts on the Organizational History of the Van Diemen Exhibition," in *The First Russian Show,* pp. 67–72; and Helen Adkins, "*Erste russische Kunstausstellung,*" in *Stationen der Moderne* (Berlin: Berlinische Galerie, 1988), pp. 184–96.

2. I am grateful to Charlotte Douglas and Vasilii Rakitin, who encouraged me to pursue the subject, and especially to Dr. Sergio Pozzati, director of the Fondo artistico e fototeca of the Archivio storico delle arti contemporanee della Biennale di Venezia, who permitted me to study the archival material and was extraordinarily helpful during my trips to Venice in August 1989 and June 1990.

3. See Christina Lodder, "Exhibitions of Russian Art after 1922," in *The First Russian Show,* pp. 80–83.

4. All correspondence and other documents are located in the archives for the *XIV Esposizione internazionale* in the Archivio storico delle arti contemporanee della Biennale di Venezia, Palazzo Corner della Regina, Venice. All documents have been transcribed as written; the translations are mine.

5. Lenin died on January 21, 1924.

6. Anatolii Lunacharskii lived in Bologna and also in Paris before World War I. He was familiar with Western culture and was influential in arranging for the *Erste russische Kunstausstellung* and for the *Pervaia vseobshchaia germanskaia khudozhestvennaia vystavka* (*First German Survey Exhibition*), the German Expressionist exhibition in Moscow in 1924. See Jane Kristof, *Critic and Commissar: A. V. Lunacharskii on Art* (Ann Arbor, Mich.: University Microfilms, 1972).

7. XIV Esposizione internazionale d'arte della città di Venezia, *Catalogo,* 3d ed. (Venice: Carlo Ferrari, 1924), pp. 222–46.

8. Boris Ternovetz, "La Section russe à l'Exposition internationale de Venise," *La Renaissance de l'art français* 7, no. 10 (October 1924), pp. 535–47. The same text that appeared in the Biennale catalogue is translated into French and accompanied by illustrations. For additional information on Ternovets, see L. S. Aleshina and N. V. Iavorskaia, comp., *B. N. Ternovets. Pis'ma. Dnevniki. Stat'i* (Moscow: Sovetskii khudozhnik, 1977).

9. Also known as *Portret Sil'vii Grinberg* (*Portrait of Sil'viia Grinberg*). Reproduced in Mark Etkind, *Nathan Altman,* trans. Manfred Denecke (Dresden: VEB Verlag der Kunst, 1984), p. 78.

10. Reproduced ibid., p. 58.

11. See *A Selection of Russian Works,* sale catalogue for Christie's, London, October 5, 1989, no. 424.

12. Reproduced in Mikhail Guerman, *Art of the October Revolution,* trans. W. Freeman, D. Saunders, and C. Binns (New York: Abrams, 1979), no. 185.

13. Reproduced ibid., no. 164.

14. Mark Etkind, *Boris Kustodiev,* trans. Ashken Mikoyan and Vladimir Vezey (New York: Abrams, 1983), p. 267.

15. Ibid., p. 274.

16. Ibid., p. 276.

17. Reproduced in Giovanni Carandente, ed., *Arte russa e sovietica, 1870–1930* (Milan: Fabbri, 1989), pp. 258–59.

18. Reproduced in Vladimir Kemenov, *Konchalovsky,* trans. N. Lukoshkova (Leningrad: Aurora, 1973).

19. See Alexander Kemensky, *Martiros Sarian,* trans. Ashken Mikoyan (Leningrad: Aurora, 1975).

20. See *Kazimir Malevich, 1878–1935,* catalogue for exhibition organized by the National Gallery of Art, Washington, D.C., the Armand Hammer Museum of Art and Cultural Center, Los Angeles, and the Metropolitan Museum of Art, New York (Los Angeles: Armand Hammer Museum of Art, 1990), pp. 16, 211, 221.

21. Reproduced in Angelica Zander Rudenstine, ed., *Russian Avant-Garde Art: The George Costakis Collection* (New York: Abrams, 1981), no. 540.

22. Ternovetz, "La Section russe," p. 545 and Ugo Nebbia, *La Quattordicesima Esposizione d'arte a Venezia—1924* (Bergamo: Istituto italiano d'arti grafiche, 1924), pp. 160, 162–63.

23. Francesco Sapori, "La XIV Esposizione d'arte internazionale a Venezia," *Nuova antologia,* October 1924, pp. 22–24. See also Nebbia, *La Quattordicesima Esposizione,* pp. 167, 169 and Ternovetz, "La Section russe," p. 543.

24. Kustodiev's *The Merchant's Wife* or *Kupchikha za chaem* (*Merchant's Wife at Tea*) was reproduced in the catalogue of the *Erste russische Kunstausstellung* (no. 105) and also shown in the Biennale (no. 88).

25. Although the Soviet Union did not participate in the 1926 Biennale, Kogan was again commissioner in 1928 and Ternovets was a member of the committee.

fig. 1
*Paintings by Goncharova, Larionov, Lentulov, Malevich, Rodchenko,
Rozanova, and Shterenberg among works awaiting shipment to the art
museum in Penza, January 1920.*
A. M. Rodchenko and V. F. Stepanova Archive, Moscow.

The Creation of the Museum of Painterly Culture

Svetlana Dzhafarova

Among the new museums that proliferated in Moscow in the first years of the Soviet state, the Museum of Painterly Culture was clearly the most distinctive; it was without precedent anywhere in the world. The museum was exceptional, above all, because it had been created and was administered directly by artists themselves—by the most notable representatives of the left art of the 1920s: Vladimir Tatlin, Sof'ia Dymshits-Tolstaia, Kazimir Malevich, Aleksandr Drevin, Aleksandr Rodchenko, Varvara Stepanova, and Vasilii Kandinskii. Early in the 1920s, stewardship of the museum passed into the hands of a younger generation of artists—Petr Vil'iams, Nina Kogan, Aleksandr Labas, Aleksandr Tyshler, and Solomon Nikritin—who had come to prominence after the October Revolution. It was the artists who were in charge of acquisitions, registry and storage, and the assembling of a central collection in Moscow and of collections to be sent to the provinces, and the artists who organized representative exhibits, engaged in analytical and scholarly work, amassed a library, and arranged the most timely exhibitions, as well as tours and lectures on issues in contemporary art.

Like all the new museums which it had been resolved to create from "examples of living art," the Museum of Painterly Culture was initially called the Museum of Artistic Culture. "Artistic culture" became so entrenched a concept that the museum was often called by its old name even after assuming the new one. The later name signaled a turning away from "plastic culture" (three-dimensional works, at any rate, proved a burden in the peregrinations, arduous enough as they were, of the museum's collection from one Moscow address to another in search of more or less temporary haven) and had the added advantage of serving to distinguish the Moscow museum from Petrograd's Museum of Artistic Culture.

In a 1925 guide to Moscow museums, the Museum of Painterly Culture was fourth in a group of eight,[1] and was briefly described as a collection of Futurist and Cubist paintings. It stood out, however, for the way in which its collection was presented: "The Museum has set itself not only the usual goal for a collection of paintings but also, in part, an educative and cultural one, seeking to bring the spectator inside contemporary artistic-and-technical investigations and to illuminate for him the complicated and, at times, still poorly elucidated paths by which they proceed." The guide also noted that apprehension of the museum's works entailed a certain difficulty and demanded from the spectator "suitable preparation and knowledge of the history of the new art."[2]

It is not possible at this time to reconstruct step by step the brief but eventful life, from 1919 to 1929, of the Museum of Painterly Culture. Yet from memoirs, archival documents, and contemporary periodicals, one can trace the origins of a truly new type of artistic institution, one that was avant-garde in its aspirations.

I

The idea of establishing a museum of contemporary art crystallized amidst a museum renaissance and flurry of museum creation.

An enormous quantity of works of art "of all times and peoples," appropriated from their previous owners by the state after the Revolution and stored to prevent theft and removal abroad, had accumulated in Moscow. A desire to classify them, determine their value, and group them together led to the creation of specialized museums—the Furniture Museum, the Porcelain Museum, the Museum of Eastern Art (Ars Asiatica), and the First and Second Museum of New Western Painting (as Sergei Shchukin's and Ivan Morozov's galleries of Impressionist and Postimpressionist works were renamed).

In the outlying districts of Moscow, fourteen proletarian

museums were created, distinguished by the heterogeneous contents of their temporary exhibits. It should be emphasized that only one of them—the A. V. Lunacharskii Seventh Proletarian Museum at 26 Staro-Basmannaia Street, which opened on the first anniversary of the Revolution—had a significant number of works by contemporary artists (Aristarkh Lentulov, Il'ia Mashkov, Petr Konchalovskii, Pavel Kuznetsov, and David Burliuk) in its collection; the museum had been installed in the former home of the collector Isadzhan (Isak) Isadzhanov.[3]

Such small district museums stood in contrast to "supermuseums" with holdings numbering in the thousands, and were intended for workers from nearby factories, who would not need to expend any extra effort traveling about the city from their place of work in order to visit the realm of the beautiful and to be exposed, very often for the first time, to the storehouse of culture—which was henceforth the property of every proletarian.

The idea of making artistic treasures accessible to the masses, together with the belief in their educative value, constituted the cornerstone of all museum creation.

In the summer of 1919, Narkompros (the People's Commissariat of Enlightenment) ratified the Statute on a Unified National Museum Fund, which provided for an orderly, integrated system of registering art works and for strict adherence to scholarly criteria and government policy in allotting works to the Republic's museums, whether they served the capital or other cities, districts, and provinces. This statute made into law a plan for the creation of museums drawn up by the artist and art historian Igor' Grabar', which had been announced at the end of 1918 and had already begun to be implemented. Full implementation of the plan required tremendous energy and faith on the part of scholars and museum professionals, for their exertions on behalf of the national heritage took place during years of deprivation brought on by civil war and foreign intervention.

II

Perceiving themselves as "proletarians of the paintbrush" (a formulation of both Kandinskii's and Rodchenko's), left artists were quick to join in the public life of the new workers' and peasants' state. Abram Efros, an observant and incisive art critic and an eyewitness to events, described the interrelation of artists and the state thus:

Futurism became the official art of the new Russia. Its life in the Republic of the Soviets proved a paradox. It came to power from another quarter. The dispute over power was settled not by a preference in art but by a preference in people. "Futurism" wasn't needed, but the "Futurists" were; Realism, on the contrary, was needed, but Realists weren't. The former were embraced, and the latter spurned, not as artists but as public individuals of art, as citizens of aesthetics . . . The left artists made friendly overtures to left politicians as people of a kindred temperament: radical, logical, and destructive. The left artists said to the left authorities: "A left art befits a left state. The right artists aren't on your side, because their art is the fruit of a reactionary social order. Futurism is the artistic form of Communism. A Communist in art can't not be a Futurist."[4]

Malevich—another example—joined the Presidium of the Commission on the Preservation of Monuments, as well as the Museum Commission of the Moscow Soviet (along with representatives of museums and archives, collectors, and art historians such as Nikolai Romanov, Grabar', Nikolai Mashkovtsev, and Shchukin), which decided the fate of private estates and collections and granted charters of immunity. It was as the result of this collaboration with art professionals,

apparently, that Malevich distanced himself from old notions of what a museum should be as his vision of a new museum of contemporary art took shape.

Left artists were involved in the work of Izo Narkompros (the Department of Fine Arts of the People's Commissariat of Enlightenment) from the moment of its creation on January 29, 1918. Malevich, Antoine Pevsner, Tatlin, Dymshits-Tolstaia, Władysław Strzemiński, and Drevin attended the May–November 1918 sessions of the Artistic and Building Subsection[5] of the Moscow Izo Narkompros at which a network of museums of contemporary art, with a central all-Russian museum in Moscow, was planned and where the guiding principles of state exhibitions, tours, and lectures sufficient to satisfy an enormous audience were discussed. Malevich's insistence on the necessity of left artists' training "their own" lecturers[6] gives some indication of the direction these discussions took. Many of the debates centered on the need to affirm the new revolutionary art via exhibitions. Pevsner noted that the idea of disseminating such exhibitions the length and breadth of Russia was a particularly significant one, and never before entertained.

An active group of artists of the "left camp" regarded the arranging of exhibitions and the creation of museums of artistic culture as part and parcel of the new organizational effort to which many had dedicated themselves unreservedly. Their position was inflexible enough: "Our object," said Pevsner, "is to educate the popular masses in a new direction . . ."[7]

The influence of left artists on the evolution of ideas about the preservation of artistic monuments and the creation of museums was not long in making itself felt. Artists' relations with the old organizational structures, moreover, quickly became contentious. In mid-January 1918, one of the chief proposals for restructuring entailed replacing the former administrations of the city's museums with artistic councils and curators chosen from among artists and the museums' junior staff, all to be nominated and confirmed by the Department of Plastic Arts of the Museum Commission. The Tret'iakov Gallery was the primary target of the proposal, since its acquisitions profile and collection of contemporary art made it more attractive than the scholarship-oriented Historical Museum, Rumiantsev Museum, or Museum of Fine Arts as a field for the artists' innovations.

Such innovations, however, were what Grabar' and the Tret'iakov Gallery's professional staff desired least of all, and they adopted a strongly protective stance. They were concerned that the museum not be transformed into "one more Moscow exhibition hall, where the exhibits will determine the tastes and allegiances of the artist-curators [rather than the reverse]."[8]

The Tret'iakov's defense held, and the artists focused their energy on the creation of "their own" museum of contemporary art. Yet the artists' activity continued to be resisted from within the gallery, as became evident when, in the late 1920s, the Museum of Painterly Culture became first a branch of the Tret'iakov Gallery and then a mere department, and ultimately was abolished entirely.

III

The idea of creating a museum of "living art" heralded a specific stage of maturity in the self-awareness of artists of the new tendencies, a stage at which the need to take stock of the existing multiplicity of forces, methods, and discoveries was finally acknowledged. This occurred at precisely that juncture in the evolution of the Russian avant-garde when the first stage—with its typically Russian acceptance of Western influences, absorption of them into itself, and filtering them through its own "ego"—was far behind, and the second stage—the peak of original discoveries and a period marked by the emergence of new trends—had been succeeded by a third, characterized by recognition of the need to attract a new audience and not just a narrow circle of admirers, and by a desire to effect the "return" to the world (the West included) of accumulated experience and invention. By 1917–18, the chief discoveries had already been made and the pioneering *maîtres* already had followers and disciples; formulations were being honed and individual solutions derived from the generative systems of Cézannism, Cubism, Suprematism, Constructivism, and expressive abstraction. There were meetings of the minds and partings of the ways; Constructivism was soon triumphant at Inkhuk (the Institute of Artistic Culture) and Vkhutemas (the Higher Artistic-Technical Workshops); while in its own way Suprematism maintained a quality of universality. In such a context, the possibility of viewing the entire spectrum of ideas, already endowed with their own tradition and evolution within the broad phenomenon of the avant-garde, and of artists' making classifications and rendering judgments according to their own standards—as the initiators of the new museum had in mind—might have seemed illusory. For the first time, a museum devoted to a specific phenomenon was being created while that phenomenon was still in full swing, before it had become history.

Artists' dissatisfaction with the critics who, from the beginning of the 1910s, had attempted to interpret the new art impelled them to offer their own analysis of their and their colleagues' art. Thus Ol'ga Rozanova accused the critics and their brethren of bad faith, citing as a prime example Aleksandr Benua's "Kubizm ili Kukishizm" ("Cubism or *Je-m'en-foutisme*"), a scathing 1912 review that discounted the significance of "vanguard trends." "Opponents of the New Art," wrote Rozanova, "fall back on this calculation, rejecting its self-sufficient meaning and, having declared it 'Transitional,' being unable even to understand properly the conception of this Art, lumping together Cubism, Futurism, and other phenomena of artistic life, not ascertaining for themselves either their essential differences or the shared tenets that link them."[9] After offering her own estimation of all previous art, she defined the essence of the new art:

Only contemporary Art advanced in all fullness the seriousness of such principles as those of dynamism, volume, and equilibrium in a painting, the principle of gravity and weightlessness, of linear and planar dislocation {sdvig}, of rhythm, as well as the regular division of space, layout, the planar and surface dimension, density {faktura}, color relations, and many more. These principles, which set the New Art apart from the Old, have only to be enumerated for one to be convinced that they are in fact that Qualitative—and not merely quantitative—New Basis which proves the "Self-sufficient" meaning of the New Art. Principles heretofore unknown, signifying the emergence of a new era in creative work—an era of purely artistic achievements.

An era of the final emancipation of the Great Art of Painting from Literary, Social, and crudely everyday attributes uncharacteristic of it at its core. The elaboration of this valuable world outlook is the service of our times, irrespective of idle speculation about how quickly the individual trends created by it will flash by.[10]

Rozanova's precise conception of the evolution of contemporary art and faith in the correctness of her chosen path were evidently what prompted her to join the Moscow Art Board of Izo Narkompros and, with Rodchenko, the Artistic and Industrial Subsection, as well as to perform truly missionary work organizing art schools, free artistic-and-trade workshops, and museums of artistic culture throughout the country.

As at the beginning of the 1910s, so at the end of the decade there was virtually no critic who brought to contemporary art the discrimination evident in Varvara Stepanova's review of the posthumous Rozanova exhibition (the First State Exhibition) held in Moscow in the winter of 1918–19. "Closely examining Rozanova's Suprematist period," wrote Stepanova, "we see that Rozanova's Suprematism is contrary to that of Malevich, who constructs his works from a composition of quadrate forms, while Rozanova constructs hers from color. For Malevich, color exists solely to distinguish one plane from another; for Rozanova, the composition serves to reveal all the possibilities of color on a plane. In Suprematism, she offered a Suprematism of painting, not of the square."[11]

Scholars have attributed to Rozanova authorship of an appeal "to the St. Petersburgers"[12] issued by the Council of the left federation of the Moscow Professional Union of Artists and Painters in response to the arrival in Moscow in April 1918 of leaders of the Petrograd Izo Narkompros—Nikolai Punin, Natan Al'tman, and Artur Lur'e—for the organization of the Art Board:[13] "Comrades, we welcome the creation of a commission on artistic matters from among vanguard artists and believe that the new art will not lie in basements but will assume its proper place in new creative work."[14]

Rozanova knew well from her own experience how works of the new art were purchased out of exhibitions in the years before the Revolution, when the largesse of the factory-owner Levkii Zheverzheev hardly covered the cost of paints and canvas and low-paying technical work on the side was necessary for subsistence. After the Revolution, the private collector disappeared, although certain individuals—Shchukin, Morozov, Isadzhanov, Valentina Labinskaia, Nadezhda Dobychina, and some more incidental figures—kept up this role for left artists. Yet it was left artists who had the least cause for dismay: their names were at the top of the list the moment the state became the new buyer of art. "Legalizing" sales of art, making them systematic and thereby providing a rather wide circle of artists with a means of earning a living was of greatest expediency and most fully warranted in the case of the creation of the Museum of Artistic Culture in the capital and—the next step—of a network of similar museums throughout the country. For many artists, the purchases made by the Museum Bureau and Izo Narkompros at exhibitions and in artists' studios during 1918–22 constituted, on one hand, their sole means of support and, on the other, moral compensation for the neglect of the new art before the Revolution and a vindication of its unwavering orientation toward the future.

IV

Rozanova's writings are one index of the self-awareness of the artists of her circle, and her organizational work one example of the social engagement of left artists. Under the heading "Nashi zadachi" ("Our Tasks"), Malevich offered his list of activities in which artists might invest their energies in the new society:

1. A war on academicism
2. An administration of innovators
3. The creation of a worldwide collective on artistic affairs
4. The establishment of embassies of the arts in other countries
5. The creation of stationary museums of contemporary art throughout the country
6. The creation across the entire Russian Republic of a traffic artery for living exhibitions of creative art
7. The establishment of a Central Museum of Contemporary Creative Work in Moscow
8. The appointment of commissars of artistic affairs in the provincial cities of Russia

    10. *The publication of a newspaper on artistic matters for the broad masses*[15]

Malevich's description of the attitude of museum professionals toward the new trends in art in preceding years matched Rozanova's assessment of the critics' stance: "The work of the innovators was driven, by conditions created by these refined connoisseurs, into cold attics, into squalid studios and there awaited its lot, pinning its hopes on fate . . . All the old museums were built on chance, and the emergence of new museums on a chance amateur, who robbed, who pawnbrokered the work of a starving artist for a few pennies and made a name for himself."[16] He gave this account of the evolution of the idea of creating a new museum:

The Art Board discussed the creation of a museum of contemporary art, then the creation of a museum of painterly culture, and ended with a museum to be created primarily on the basis of painterly culture.

This is an enormous concession, an enormous step backward, an enormous covenant with yesterday . . .

Now they're laying the foundations of a museum primarily of painterly culture. Under this banner they'll gather everything that is more painterly than not. Consequently, all trends of the school will end up here.[17]

Malevich had jealously watched over the makeup of the new museum's collection, concerned with the ratio of exhibits "from the past" to those representing specific tendencies of the new art—and favoring the latter. He had accused the members of the Art Board of being soft and of maneuvering, locating the reason for their behavior in the composition of the board: the members were all left artists, but of a varying leftism. Majority opinion had yielded a list of 143 artists representing a rather wide range of artistic achievement. Among them were members of Mir iskusstva (World of Art)—Benua, Aleksandr Gaush, Evgenii Lansere, Sergei Chekhonin, Nikolai Krymov, and Nikolai Rerikh; the Realists Abram Arkhipov, Aleksandr Moravov, and Sergei Maliutin; members of Golubaia roza (Blue Rose)—Kuznetsov, Matiros Sar'ian, Pavel Utkin, and Elena Bebutova; members of Bubnovyi valet (Jack of Diamonds)—Robert Fal'k, Lentulov, Vasilii Rozhdestvenskii, Aleksandr Kuprin, Mashkov, Petr Konchalovskii, and Aleksandr Os'merkin; former members of the Soiuz russkikh khudozhnikov (Union of Russian Artists)—Leonard Turzhanskii, Konstantin Iuon, Sergei Gerasimov, Konstantin Korovin, and Vasilii Baksheev; members of Oslinyi khvost (Donkey's Tail)—Mikhail Larionov, Natal'ia Goncharova, Mikhail Le-Dantiu, Aleksandr Shevchenko, and David and Vladimir Burliuk; and vanguard artists of various allegiances: Malevich, Tatlin, Pevsner, Kandinskii, Rozanova, Dymshits-Tolstaia, Rodchenko, Ivan Kliunkov, Nadezhda Udal'tsova, David Shterenberg, Aleksei Morgunov, Drevin, Aleksei Grishchenko, Vera Pestel', Liubov' Popova, Boris Shaposhnikov, Strzemiński, Mikhail Men'kov, Aleksandr Vesnin, Pavel Mansurov, Aleksandra Ekster, Mikhail Matiushin, Iakov Pain, Ender, Pavel Filonov, Petr Miturich, Vladimir Baranov-Rossine, Iosif Shkol'nik, Vera Ermolaeva, Al'tman, and others.[18] Malevich labeled this selection the consequence of traditional professional criteria, whereas he conceived the museum as "a place where men are all gathered together . . . To create, furthermore, an image of man only in his contemporary form resulting from his latest transfiguration and not to drape over his shoulders the mantles and togas of the past."[19]

In Malevich's eyes, the museum's novelty lay in the devotion to painting which guided it (it should be noted that sculptors, too—Sergei Konenkov, Anna Golubkina, Aleksandr Matveev, Petr Bromirskii, and others—had originally been included in the list of recommended artists), and he regarded the dissemination of the works of the country's artistic forces to every far corner as the central museum's chief function. This was a universal function and had enormous transformative implications:

In this way, the living cause of exemplars of creation penetrates throughout the country and will be a stimulus to the transformation of forms in life and of artistic representations in industry.

Since the museum will be comprised of the most diverse forms of representation, installation will be a matter of extraordinary importance, for installation plays a large role in its construction and conception, and in order to reveal the museum's true face, it is necessary to alter the old principle of arranging works by by schools and trends, by eras and events.

I suggest, therefore, that the walls of the museum are surfaces on which works should be placed in the same sequence as a composition of forms is placed on the surface of a painting, that is, if on the surface of a painting there emerge rows of identical forms, then the work itself loses intensity, and vice versa.

If we arrange a row of identical works on a surface, we get an ornamental line, which cancels out the power which might have been revealed with heterogeneous juxtapositions.

The most advantageous installation, therefore, is the sequence: icons, Cubism, Suprematism, the classics, Futurism—painterly perception.[20]

Rodchenko and Stepanova were also involved in deliberations on the future shape of the museum, and Stepanova recorded Rodchenko's views on the matter in a March 27, 1919, diary entry:

Brik, the current head of the Department of Fine Arts, got the idea of enlisting the support of the Professional Union of the New Art; he was at the Union today—a whole series of issues in this connection were discussed, one of them—of great importance—the organizing of the Museum of Painterly Culture. The end result is that the Union will hold a closed debate for its members on the subject and then submit a report to the Board {the Museum Board of Izo Narkompros}. Anti {Rodchenko's nickname} and I talked it over. His thoughts boiled down to approximately the following.

French painting should not be lumped together with Russian, inasmuch as Russian painting follows its own path, only we stubbornly refuse to see it, don't value it, and idolize Westerners. To combine the pictures of Russian painters with the museums of Shchukin and Morozov means to subscribe to our own bankruptcy, to close off our past, which is just as rich as that of the French. Above all, this boundary must be drawn: Russian painting does not exist in a line of succession from the West, and if the West finds some reflection in it, that is only a minus for the essence of Russian painting.

We follow our own path, and our painting is so different from the West that it is inept and sinful to jumble them together. Western painting's element, its significance, is the easel painting, a painting of set dimensions, made to measure for a room—for an office or museum; therein lies its sense and purpose, that is the outward hallmark of Western painting. Western painting is an investigation into light and volume—into form. Western painting can never be compared with Russian, for Russian painting is diametrically opposed to it: outwardly—there are no set dimensions but rather inordinately large canvases and microscopic ones—and inwardly—an investigation into space and surface plane, a desire to conquer space of any dimensions whatsoever. Ergo it is clear that Western painting is in essence easel painting and synthetic. Russian painting is decorative and analytical. Ergo the tasks pursued in painting by West and East are entirely different, and one is not comparable with the other. Russian painting's source is the icon—decorative adornment, that is, a value unto itself, unlike applied ornament, which has no life of its own but exists only as an adjunct to an object. This great decorative, color-resplendent element is the prime mover of Russian painting, which we do not value, do not know.

We have to take our painting out into the streets, onto the fences and roofs . . . Because that's how we cultivated the icon, the signboard, and the lubok *{illustrated broadside}. And it's clear in my mind that we must create and display our Russian culture of painting, which, unfortunately, we consider worthless—and we try to follow strictly in the leading strings, and at the bidding, of the West.*

I envision the arrangement of the Museum of Painterly Culture thus:

Icons
Signboards
The lubok *(for its connection with graphic art)*
Impressionism
Futurism
Cubism
Orphism
Suprematism
Non-objective creation

This arrangement is by trend, with one immediate caveat: checking off Impressionism, Futurism, Cubism, and so on, we are confronted right away with a whole series of artists whom it is impossible to assign to one or another of these rubrics, for extreme individuality is one of Russian painting's peculiar characteristics, and therefore I think the stages in the culture of painting ought to be set out not according to particular movements in painting but according to exhibiting organizations and groups—this subdivision into groups is likewise a characteristic trait.

Thus, concretely, the museum should be divided into these sections:
Icons
Signboards
The lubok
World of Art (Sar'ian, Sapunov, Kuznetsov, Iakulov, Lentulov)
Donkey's Tail and Target (Larionov, Goncharova, Zdanevich, Le-Dantiu, Bart)
Primitivism (Shevchenko)
Color Dynamics (Grishchenko)
Expressionism (Kandinskii)
Jack of Diamonds (Mashkov, Konchalovskii, Rozhdestvenskii, Kuprin, Fal'k)
Suprematism (Popova, Malevich, Kliun, Men'kov, Udal'tsova, Drevin)
Non-objective creation (Rozanova, Rodchenko, Tatlin)

Asiatic art is spiritual, was regarded with religious awe, with faith, the creation of the artist not endowed with charming effect but considered something grand and spiritual. The West treats art lightly, in material terms; the East worships art and elevates it above everything else, does not make it utilitarian.[21]

Dymshits-Tolstaia and Tatlin had put forward their ideas on how the museum should be organized at a meeting of the Moscow Art Board in the autumn of 1918. They rejected the selection of objects based on individual taste that had ruled museums and private collections and which, in their opinion, was a feature of the "life of the past." The new museums ought to acquire works of art "based on the principle that [museums] truly represent in full the best examples of the artists produced by the nation."[22]

V

In December 1918, Anatolii Lunacharskii, the People's Commissar of Enlightenment, had approved the list of 143 artists whose paintings and sculptures were to be bought for the State Museum Fund. The Moscow Purchasing Commission and the Artistic and Industrial Subsection of Izo Narkompros had quickly begun acquiring works from which a separate collection for the Museum of Artistic Culture would be drawn.

At this juncture, the proposals concerning the character and organization of the museum were refined and elaborated, first at a meeting of a special commission on the museum's creation in Petrograd and later at a series of meetings of Izo Narkompros. The resulting special statute on the Museum of Painterly Culture and definition of the concept of artistic culture were presented to the museum conference convened on February 11, 1919, at the Palace of the Arts (as the Winter Palace had been renamed).

The conference approved the statute on the museum unanimously and endorsed the concept of artistic culture, which was declared the criterion by which works would be selected for the museum's collection and which was outlined thus:

1. The concept of artistic culture is one of the positive achievements of contemporary creative work, which in the course of recent decades has amplified, in the main, questions of the professional quality of artistic works and thereby of their universal significance.

2. The concept of artistic culture is thus linked to the strivings of new artistic schools and may be revealed only by them.

3. The concept of artistic culture is at the same time an objective criterion of artistic value, insofar as that is defined as a professional value.

4. The concept of artistic culture contains, in accordance with the very meaning of the word "culture" as a dynamic activity, a creative element; creative work presupposes creation of the new, invention; artistic culture is nothing other than the culture of artistic invention.

5. By sustained artistic labor, contemporary schools of art have been able to reveal many elements of artistic activity and thereby to establish the objective criterion of artistic value as a professional value.

6. These elements are: (1) material: surface, elasticity, density, weight, and other qualities of material; (2) color: saturation, intensity, relation to light, purity, transparency, independence, and other qualities of color; (3) space: volume, depth, dimension, and other properties of space; (4) time (movement): in its spatial expression and in connection with color, material, composition, and so forth; (5) form, as a result of the interaction of material, color, and space and in its pure guise, composition; (6) technique: painting, mosaics, reliefs of various sorts, sculpture, stonework, and other types of artistic technique.

7. While there are no grounds for thinking that mankind has arrived at the sum total of artistic elements, further discoveries in this area cannot alter the direction of artistic activity as professional activity.

8. The evolution of and alteration in artists' treatment of the aforementioned elements is the evolution of art itself, and changes of every kind in this area can be objectively and precisely established for every given artistic phenomenon individually.

9. Artistic culture, as the culture of invention, can be revealed only insofar as artists either radically altered their treatment of the aforementioned elements or discovered these elements.

10. Inasmuch as artistic culture is the achievement of contemporary schools of art, it can be utilized as a principle of contemporary artistic activity, and artists thereby have every basis for aspiring to reveal via this culture an image of man, primarily in his latest transfiguration. Works of the past—even those inventions that broke new ground in their time but have no connection with contemporary formations—need not be utilized, since they have lost much of their active force and thus their cultural significance.[23]

The general mood may also be gauged from excerpts from Izo Narkompros's Declaration on Principles of Museum

Administration and reports prepared for the museum conference. The declaration, approved by the Art Board at a February 7, 1919, session, stated that

(1) artists, as those solely competent in matters of contemporary art and as the forces who create artistic values, alone may oversee acquisitions of contemporary art and guide the artistic education of the country; (2) as professionals organizing their world outlook on the basis of universal artistic culture, artists must be allowed access to art works of the past—so as to select from the mass of artistic monuments that which is characteristic of artistic culture and, having made their selections, to create a museum, for themselves as professionals and for the growth of the nation's artistic life—a museum of creative artistic culture.[24]

Punin's theses on the relation between artists and museums drew attention to the divide separating them and to the psychological peculiarities of the professions of artist and museum administrator:

The aspiration of museum professionals in the West and in Russia in recent times to expand their influence. The special reasons for Russian museum administrators' enthusiasm for aesthetic pretensions in connection with artists' unsuccessful aspiration to museum work . . .
The professional qualities of the museum administrator as principles of his negative attitude toward artistic creation. Museum administrators' battle with artists . . .
The claim of contemporary artistic schools on the museum and the special bases of this claim. The organized state of contemporary artistic creation. The activism of artists in connection with their role as artistic educators and with the activism of the workers' movement . . .
The ideological foundations of the contradictory professional interests of the museum administrator and the artist. The museum professional as a scholarly machine, curator, and researcher. The artist as a creative and educative force . . .
The basis of the Museum of Artistic Culture as a museum of the creative and educative. Artistic culture as an objective criterion in the appraisal of artistic monuments . . .
Selection as the method of building the Museum of Artistic Culture . . .[25]

In his report, Grishchenko enumerated the distinctions of the new museum:

The Museum of Painterly Culture should reveal the essential element of painting, of its creative inventiveness in the realm of color, architectonics, composition, and faktura . . .
The Museum of Painterly Culture is not for the education but for the illumination of the spirit and the creative work of the masses, for the nurturing and building of the artist's trade . . .
The Museum of Painterly Culture must embrace the painterly art of the individual artist and of a collective of artists in the interests of an exchange of energy and vital powers . . .
The Museum of Painterly Culture is always adding new holdings, now from this quarter, now from that, in accordance with the spirit and movement of the living creative basis of painterly art . . .
The Museum of Painterly Culture serves as a guarantee of and a solid foundation for the renewal of art in the country.[26]

By 1920, the idea of artists working in museums had gained a foothold in certain circles, and it raised artists to a position in the cultural and social hierarchy higher than the one they had previously occupied. In his report to the museum conference, Sergei Ol'denberg concluded: "It is absolutely essential that the artist join in museum work alongside the scholar, and not only in those activities of museums touching on the arts but in their activities in general; not only when it comes to displays, where there can be no substitute for the creative and experienced eye of the artist, but in approaching every object, whether a monument of nature or of culture, from the vantage of the arts, from the vantage of a certain artistic intuition."[27]

—Translated, from the Russian, by Jane Bobko

Notes

1. The other museums were the Tret'iakov Gallery, the Tsvetkov Gallery, the Museum of Icon-Painting and Painting (the former Ostroukhov Gallery), the Museum of Eastern Art, the Museum of Fine Arts (the former Museum of Aleksandr III), the First Museum of New Western Painting (the former Shchukin Gallery), and the Second Museum of New Western Painting (the former Morozov Gallery). P. Pertsev, *Khudozhestvennye muzei Moskvy. Putevoditel'* (Moscow: Gosudarstvennoe izdatel'stvo, 1925).

2. Ibid., pp. 81–82.

3. The holdings of this museum were later absorbed into the State Museum Fund; some went to the State Tret'iakov Gallery, others to the State Mustafaev Azerbaijan Museum of Art in Baku.

4. A. Efros, "Kontsy bez nachal," in F. Stepun, ed., *Shipovnik. Sbornik literatury i iskusstva,* vol. 1, pp. 109–25, as quoted in *Tvorchestvo* 3 (1990), p. 15.

5. The Artistic and Industrial Subsection was created largely at the initiative of Ol'ga Rozanova, who had been elected to the Moscow Art Board, and was briefly headed by her.

6. T. V. Vlasova, "Iz istorii khudozhestvennoi zhizni Moskvy. Deiatel'nost' Vserossiiskogo tsentral'nogo vystavochnogo biuro (1918–1921)," *Sovetskoe iskusstvoznanie 23. Sbornik statei* (Moscow, 1988), p. 320.

7. Ibid.

8. Iu. N. Zhukov, *Sokhranennye revoliutsiei* (Moscow, 1985), pp. 73–74.

9. Ol'ga Rozanova, "Osnovy Novogo Tvorchestva i printsipy ego neponimaniia," *Soiuz molodezhi* 3 (March 1913), p. 18.

10. Ibid., pp. 20–21.

11. Varst [Varvara Stepanova], "Vystavka Ol'gi Rozanovoi," *Iskusstvo* 4 (February 22, 1919), pp. 2–3.

12. See Vera Terekhina, "Life–Work of Olga Rozanova," in *Olga Rozanova, 1886–1918,* catalogue for exhibition organized by the Helsingin kaupungin taidemuseo (Helsinki: Helsingin kaupungin taidemuseo, 1992), pp. 9–17.

13. The Petrograd Narkompros had immediately organized two departments, the Department of Fine Arts (Izo) and the Department of Museums and Protection of Antiquities. The initial members of the former's Art Board were David Shterenberg (chairman, and also head of Izo), Natan Al'tman, Aleksei Karev, Aleksandr Matveev, Nikolai Punin, Sergei Chekhonin, Petr Vaulin, and Georgii Iatmanov. They were later joined by Vladimir Baranov-Rossine, Iosif Shkol'nik, Vladimir Maiakovskii, and Osip Brik. On April 11, 1918, a similar Art Board was created in Moscow; it had the same rights as the Petrograd board and was considered part of the All-Russian Board on Fine Arts Affairs. The members of the Moscow board were Pavel Kuznetsov, Il'ia Mashkov, Aleksei Morgunov, Kazimir Malevich, Ivan Zheltovskii, Sof'ia Dymshits-Tolstaia, Nadezhda Udal'tsova, Stanislav Noakovskii, Robert Fal'k, Ol'ga Rozanova, Aleksandr Shevchenko, Boris Korolev, Sergei Konenkov, and Vasilii Kandinskii; Vladimir Tatlin was its chairman, as well as assistant director of Izo. The makeup of the board later changed.

14. "Obrashchenie Soveta levoi federatsii peterburzhtsam," *Anarkhiia* 4 (1918).

15. K. Malevich, "Os' tsveta," *Izobrazitel'noe iskusstvo* 1 (1919), p. 27.

16. Ibid., p. 28.

17. Ibid., p. 27.

18. Artists are given in the order in which they appeared in the list published in "Otchet o deiatel'nosti Otdela izobrazitel'nykh iskusstv Narkomprosa," *Izobrazitel'noe iskusstvo* 1 (1919), p. 74.

19. Ibid., p. 29.

20. Malevich, "Os' tsveta," p. 30.

21. Varvara Stepanova, diary, March 27, 1919, A. M. Rodchenko and V. F. Stepanova Archive, Moscow.

22. Central State Archive for Literature and Art, Moscow, f. 665, op. 1, ed. khr. 31, l. 1.

23. "Otchet o deiatel'nosti Otdela izobrazitel'nykh iskusstv Narkomprosa," pp. 73–74.

24. "Deklaratsiia Otdela izobrazitel'nykh iskusstv i khudozhestvennoi promyshlennosti po voprosu o printsipakh muzeevedeniia, priniataia Kollegiei otdela v zasedanii 7 fevralia 1919 g.," *Izobrazitel'noe iskusstvo* 1 (1919), p. 85.

25. "Tezisy po dokladu N. Punina po voprosu ob otnoshenii khudozhnika k muzeinoi deiatel'nosti," *Izobrazitel'noe iskusstvo* 1 (1919), p. 86.

26. "Tezisy po dokladu khud. Grishchenko 'Muzei zhivopisnoi kul'tury,' priniatye Otdelom izobrazitel'nykh iskusstv Moskvy i Petrograda," *Izobrazitel'noe iskusstvo* 1 (1919), pp. 86–87.

27. *Khudozhestvennaia zhizn'* 1 (1920), p. 11.

Fragmentation versus Totality: The Politics of (De)framing

Margarita Tupitsyn

Il y a du cadre, mais le cadre n'existe pas.

—Jacques Derrida

Let us start by comparing two photographs which were produced in the era of the First Five-Year Plan for publication in a periodical and which deal with the identical theme of paving a street. Arkadii Shaikhet's *Katki* (*Steamrollers,* 1931, fig. no. 3) functions through its insistence on an intelligible presentation of labor captured in expanded space and from a conventional viewpoint. Aleksandr Rodchenko's photograph of the same subject, a fragment from the series *Stroitel'stvo mostovykh. Leningradskoe shosse* (*Paving Streets: Leningradskoe Highway,* 1929, fig. no. 2), opposes Shaikhet's image with its suppressed horizon and its severe reduction of the machine's body. Unlike Shaikhet, whose interpretation of the paving process grasps its totality in one snapshot, Rodchenko reveals this productive operation through a set of fragments, each of which can be recognized, in compliance with the spirit of the time, as an "interior monologue" of the productive forces regarding the means of production.

Shaikhet's criticism of Rodchenko's type of press photography is voiced in his article "Sorevnovanie foto-reporterov razvertyvaetsia" ("The Competition of the Photojournalists Unfolds"), published in *Sovetskoe foto* (*Soviet Photo*) in 1929. There he writes: "Many photojournalists who submit vivid snapshots [to magazines] experience complete disappointment when the editors do not grasp their 'points of view.' Often they [editors] simply do not understand how a photograph can be tilted or, simply said, 'fall,' or how one can publish a photograph with a close-up, for example, of the details of machines, the movements of hands, etc. . . . Above all, editors approve of photographs in which all the events are fitted into absolutely concrete and intelligible forms for the reader."[1]

Expressing his opposition to just such a viewpoint on press photography, Rodchenko states in a lecture presented at the October group's meeting in 1930 that his goal is "to photograph not a factory but the work itself from the most effective point of view" and that "in order to show the grandness of a machine, one should photograph not all of it but give a series of snapshots."[2] In the same lecture Rodchenko divides all press photography into what he himself defends and terms *foto-kadry* (photo stills) and what he criticizes and labels as *foto-kartiny* (photo pictures). The latter, according to him, are based on an "organic" representation of various everyday scenes and on an attempt "to photograph the scene in its entirety." He concludes that "the issue now is not to take 'photo pictures' but [to produce] 'photo stills.'"[3] Rodchenko expresses no interest in photography separated from a functional framework such as a periodical, and points out that it is in the periodicals that one finds the best examples of his and his colleagues' photography. This last statement is especially important to bear in mind when one encounters photographs from the era of the First Five-Year Plan as isolated images, that is, apart from their original framework comprised by the mass-media function of a periodical. This problem of decontextualization is especially apparent when one deals with images which were produced as elements in a series and which aimed not only to have a significant political impact on the magazines' readers but also to defend specific formal strategies—such as, for example, Rodchenko's adherence to the device of seriality. But before turning to Rodchenko's and other photographers' series published in such magazines as *Daesh'* (*Let's Produce!*), I would like to reconstruct the sources for Rodchenko's views on photography as they are articulated in his 1930 lecture.

In the early 1930s, the schism between the concepts of "photo picture" and "photo still" constituted the basis for various debates between the members of the photographic section of the October group, led by Rodchenko, and those

fig. 1
Boris Ignatovich
Dynamo, 1929.
Photograph, printed from original negative, 24.2 x 16 cm.
Courtesy Margarita Tupitsyn.

fig. 2
Aleksandr Rodchenko
From the series Paving Streets: Leningradskoe Highway, *1929.*
Photograph, printed from original negative, 19.1 x 28.6 cm.
Courtesy Margarita Tupitsyn.

fig. 3
Arkadii Shaikhet
Steamrollers, *1931.*
Photograph.
Courtesy Margarita Tupitsyn.

photographers, Shaikhet among them, who belonged to ROPF (the Revolutionary Society of Proletarian Photographers). Because ROPF's "photo pictures" so closely embodied the structural principle defended in the late 1920s and early 1930s by Realist painters, the nature of the October–ROPF controversy is rooted in the discussions on photography initiated by the Productivist critics in *Novyi Lef* (*New Lef*). Among other issues, these critical exchanges involved questioning of the painting as an object able to perform adequately in a culture requiring a constant turnout of multipliable images, and the promotion of the photographic image as the only valid substitute for the painting. Specifically, the arguments were against a transferral of various structural techniques from painting to photography. Believing that photography and photomontage provided the only viable language to record the process of industrialization, the Productivist critics and artists concentrated on formulating a new photographic discourse.

In 1928, the first year of the First Five-Year Plan, clarification of the position of photography in a socialist society was especially urgent, since at that moment the activities of various Realist painters—including the most conservative group, AKhRR (the Association of Artists of Revolutionary Russia)—were on the rise. In the same year, AKhRR's production received the ultimate stamp of official approval when the entire Politburo made a visit to one of the group's exhibitions. AKhRR's artists traveled to factories and collective farms and painted what they saw with the "'bad immediacy' of a photographic naturalism" (to use Fredric Jameson's phrase). By duplicating a process which photography performed faster and more effectively, AKhRR's production mounted a "Thermidor" against not only experimental photography but also photography as a medium in general. Recognizing this ongoing competition for the title of a true revolutionary art, *New Lef*'s critic Osip Brik quickly assessed that AKhRR painters were trying "to regain lost positions and [to turn to a] reproduction of reality in line with photography."[4]

Brik's essay "Foto-kadr protiv kartiny" ("The Photo Still versus the Picture"), from which this last quotation comes, was one of the first discussions of the issue of photography versus painting. In 1926, when the article was published in *Soviet Photo,* Brik already represented a new phase of the Russian Formalist school, which, unlike the earlier one with its emphasis on a "set of techniques," demonstrated a growing interest in "sociologism," a tendency to "reach beyond 'pure' Formalism toward a position more inclusive and more congruent with the 'social demands' of the time."[5] In "The Photo Still versus the Picture," Brik still avoids criticizing painting as a technique (that would mean a rejection of abstract production as well) and instead attacks painting for the "idea of reproducing nature." This explains why in the title he chose the word *kartina* rather than *zhivopis'*: the latter specifically implies painting as a technique, whereas the former suggests painting as an iconic sign, besides carrying an additional meaning conveying a sense of the "picturesque." By relying on this subtle play of meanings, Brik conveys his disillusionment with the artificial quality of Realist painting. Similarly, the conventional translation of *foto-kadr* in Brik's title as simply "photograph" is inaccurate,[6] because *kadr* (still) was no doubt borrowed by Brik from the language of cinema in order to suggest that the kind of photography he promotes has more to do with the filming process than with that of painting. From this more careful reading of the title of Brik's article, it becomes apparent that the critic is urging everyone to stop judging photography from the viewpoint of aesthetics and to begin seeing it not as a supplement to the fine arts but as a "child of technical . . . traditions." Brik asserts that "The photographer must show that it is not just life ordered according to aesthetic laws which is impressive, but also vivid, everyday life itself as it is transfixed in a technically perfect [photo still]."[7]

In 1928, Brik published another essay on the same subject, in which he specifically criticized Rodchenko's photography for its detachment from the "social demands" of the time and for attempting to resolve purely painterly goals by means of photo language.[8] Alluding most likely to Rodchenko's series *Dom na Miasnitskoi* (*House on Miasnitskaia Street*, 1925) and *Sosny. Pushkino* (*Pine Trees in Pushkino*, 1927), Brik wrote that "one should not depict an isolated building or a tree which may be very beautiful but which will be . . . painting, will be aesthetics."[9] In other words, the critic suggests that Rodchenko, at least in these specific photographs, continues to keep photography within the domain of "easel art." Rodchenko's own articles published in *New Lef* in 1928 indicate that, for him at that time, the issue of "how" to photograph was turning from a mere continuation of his Formalist interests developed in painting and his early photographs into a means of finding a "new (have no fear) aesthetics, impulse, and pathos for expressing our new socialist facts through photography."[10] Rodchenko understood that in order to reveal the "everyday life of modern man" it would not be enough simply to record its facts by "using the same photographic approach that was employed under the old regime or under the influence of Western art."[11] Instead, he saw the formal devices of photographing objects from above or below as the "points of contemporaneity" whose practice, together with the "what" to be represented, would result in the victory of true Realism. The arguments which Rodchenko had with Brik and other critics, such as Boris Kushner, were based on the latter's assumption that for Rodchenko the "how" of photography was still a longing for Formalism, which by that time they automatically associated with similar trends in Western art. In reality, Rodchenko's notion of the "how" was shifting away from Viktor Shklovskii's concept of *ostranenie* (making strange) or Roman Jakobson's idea of the "laying bare of the device." Instead, the "how" was becoming a way for the artist to separate himself from visions of reality based on a perception of the world as a continuous organic entity and practiced by Realist painters and photographers like Shaikhet. Unlike this model of reality, which is associated with Lukácsian Realism, Rodchenko's model echoed Brechtian aesthetics, which claimed that "The spirit of realism designates an active, curious, experimental, subversive . . . attitude toward . . . the material world; and the 'realistic' work of art is therefore one that encourages and disseminates this attitude, yet not merely in a flat or mimetic way or along the lines of imitation alone."[12]

Another essay, written by Sergei Tret'iakov in response to Rodchenko and Kushner and published in *New Lef* in 1928, should be mentioned because it seems that Rodchenko's production in 1929 for mass-circulation periodicals such as *Let's Produce!* and the arguments stressed in his 1930 lecture specifically reflect the influence of Tret'iakov's position on photo discourse. In fact, it seems that Tret'iakov helped Rodchenko to assure himself that his "how" acquired a functional rather than a formal base. In his response to Rodchenko and Kushner, Tret'iakov begins by saying, "the question cannot be resolved by cheap recourse to the 'primacy of content,' by asserting that the 'what' is more important than the 'how,'" and then explains how formal elements may satisfy the practical need to expose certain important fragments (contents) in each given subject. One of Tret'iakov's comments is especially relevant to Rodchenko's photograph from *Paving Streets: Leningradskoe Highway* discussed above. He writes:

"When a machine is photographed its essential detail is singled out, while its other less important parts are obscured and made lighter."[13] Thus, for Tret'iakov, formal devices could no longer be judged apart from the nature of their appropriation.

As mentioned earlier, the impact on Rodchenko of Brik's and Tret'iakov's positions on photography surfaces in his lecture on the social meaning of photography given in 1930 at the October group's conference in Moscow. The influence of Brik's terminology in "The Photo Still versus the Picture" is detectable in Rodchenko's division of press photography into "photo pictures" and "photo stills," and like Brik, Rodchenko criticizes painting for its lack of documentary qualities. In his lecture Rodchenko addresses this issue: "Eighty to ninety percent of any magazine is built on factual material, and neither painting nor drawing can give the sensation of today, the actuality of events and their documentary nature; and thus we put our trust in photography, since it shows what happened at a place and factually convinces us of it."[14]

As Rodchenko tells us in his lecture, the best examples of his and his colleagues' photography were those published in popular magazines. To trace that production one must turn to periodicals like *Let's Produce!*, which throughout 1929 systematically printed the "photo stills" of Rodchenko, Boris Ignatovich, Roman Karmen, Dmitrii Debabov, and others. This production was directly inspired by the themes of the First Five-Year Plan, during which, according to Ignatovich, "the dynamism of public life became one of the biggest influences on Soviet photography."[15] As a rule, the subject matter of these photographs was not chosen by the photographers; it was selected for them by the various factories and plants who commissioned their work. Sometimes the photographers would receive a whole list of industrial sights which they would then have to photograph. Both Rodchenko and Ignatovich chose not to record specific sights or scenes in a single photograph (photo picture) but rather to cover a page or two of a magazine with a series of photo stills, capturing fragments of an industrial sight, a place of everyday activities, or simply the process of work itself. The resulting series of photo stills, based on a severe fragmentation of imagery and condensation of space, presented the spectator with a multileveled vision of the work area and treated labor itself not as a routine but as a truly dynamic and unpredictable process. Each photo still in such a series is centered on the device which Ignatovich calls "packing," that is, "maximum condensation of a photo still."[16] This, in turn, served as one of the strongest ways of resisting the expanded space promoted by ROPF photographers and eventually adopted by Socialist Realists.

A recent attempt to characterize these two treatments of postrevolutionary themes was made by Yve-Alain Bois, who, in a discussion of the two periods in El Lissitzky's work, uses the labels "'Brechtian' Lissitzky" and "'Stalinist' Lissitzky." The first refers to the artist's production reflecting the Brechtian belief that "one must present the spectator with a riddle, give him or her the theoretical means with which to solve it, and leave it at that. It is up to the audience to find the solution, to wake to a political consciousness."[17] The second refers to Lissitzky's late production, which, according to Bois, conveys "a revolutionary content by means of the cathartic illusionism upon which the traditional [art] was based."[18] As is evident from the October–ROPF controversy, the schism between these two positions, historically known as the "Brecht–Lukács debate," vastly transcends Lissitzky's case and touches a much wider community of artists who relied on the photographic image during the period of the First Five-Year Plan.[19]

In his comparison of Lissitzky's two periods (Brechtian [Suprematist] and Stalinist), Bois turns to Jean-François Lyotard's discussion of Lissitzky's Suprematist poster *Klinom*

fig. 4
Boris Ignatovich
Still Life, *1928.*
Photograph, printed from original negative, 16. 8 x 23. 2 cm.
Courtesy Margarita Tupitsyn.

krasnym bei belykh (*Beat the Whites with the Red Wedge*, 1920, plate no. 138), saying that unlike this work, which "physically disorients the spectator, and forces him or her into a relationship with the image that is no longer passive, the proto-socialist-realist image . . . drawn in perspective, depicts [imagery of workers and labor] with which the spectator is supposed to identify."[20] In the case of October versus ROPF, this difference between the two models of "social" spaces can be observed not on the level of a non-objective work vis-à-vis a Realist one, but rather on the level of two different modes of representational art. As far as Rodchenko's and Shaikhet's versions of steamrollers are concerned, for example, one can see that in Shaikhet's photograph the spectator is offered the space of labor as the model "for the investment of desire"; the photograph "is used to incite [the spectator] to a behavior that reproduces this experience."[21] This representation of social reality leaves no space for reflectivity; nothing in it can any longer be "surprising," that is, distance-creating and leaving room for doubts or critique. These images are supposed to be endlessly repeated, subjected to mimetic acts, to identification with the space of desire which such a representation proposes. By contrast, Rodchenko's decision to represent a steamroller is based on the Brechtian alienation effect, which is focused on the agenda of revolutionary art where both the artist and the spectator are assumed to be active participants in the shift of reality. In Rodchenko's words, "a photographer employs fragmentation for a sharper and conflictual perception of content."[22] Brecht's model also relies on shock, which brings us back to Tret'iakov, who "saw shock as a key to changing the mode of reception of art and to disrupting the dismal and catastrophic continuity of everyday life."[23] For him, "this disruption [was] a prerequisite for any revolutionary reorganization of everyday life."[24]

In this sense, the series by Rodchenko, Ignatovich, and others published in *Let's Produce!* functioned to disrupt the continuity of everyday life and to concentrate on and expose the elements (contents) which certified the presence of a new reality. Contrary to that, the highly publicized photo story by Maks Al'pert and Shaikhet called *24 chasa iz zhizni rabochei sem'i Filippovykh* (*Twenty-Four Hours in the Life of the Working-Class Filippov Family*, 1931, fig. nos. 7–9) insists (as the title itself suggests) on continuity and the presence of a narrative foundation underlying this representation. Each snapshot in this photo story presents a clear and complete "photo picture" of a certain event in the life of the family, and in every case, the snapshot is explained by an unambiguous descriptive caption telling the viewer exactly what is going on and thus leaving him without what Brecht calls a "riddle." *Twenty-Four Hours,* along with most of ROPF's production, may be placed in the context of Lukácsian Realism, which "implies the ultimate possibility of some full and nonproblematical 'representation of reality.'"[25]

The aforementioned debates on photography in *New Lef* and the photographic practices of Rodchenko and Ignatovich in periodicals such as *Let's Produce!* provided a theoretical base for the October group's photography section, which was formed in 1930, two years after October issued its first general declaration of purpose. The photography section included Viktor Gruntal', Boris Ignatovich, B. Zhemchuzhnii, Karmen, Abram Shterenberg, Ol'ga Ignatovich, Elizaveta Ignatovich, Moriakin, Elizar Langman, and Dmitrii Debabov.[26] In addition, the heads of various *fotokruzhki* (photo workshops) were accepted into the October group (many photojournalists of the 1930s came out of such *fotokruzhki*). What connected the members of the October photography section was their interest not in art photography but in photojournalism, which was supposed to agitate the masses in favor of the *novyi byt* (new way of life). It was also an

fig. 5
Elizar Langman
Old and New Semenovka, *1931.*
Photograph, 28.6 x 17.4 cm.
Courtesy Margarita Tupitsyn.

obligation on the part of all responsible photojournalists to be affiliated with newspapers and magazines in addition to the *fotokruzhki* at the factories and collective farms. In the photography section's program, a special emphasis was given to distinguishing the October members' methods from those practiced in "left photography like Man Ray's, Moholy-Nagy's, etc."[27] This indicates once again that Rodchenko and his colleagues no longer defended the use of formal devices apart from the necessity of emphasizing crucial aspects of a productive process. All the ideas endorsed on the pages of *New Lef* in 1928 are summarized in one of the passages of the October photography program:

> *We are for a revolutionary photography aesthetically unconnected with either the traditions of autonomous painting or the non-objectivity of "left photography." We are for a revolutionary photography, materialist, socially grounded, and technically well equipped, one that sets itself the aim of promulgating and agitating for a socialist way of life and a Communist culture. We are against "Akhrovshchina" {"AKhRRism"} . . . flag-waving patriotism in the form of spewing smokestacks and identical workers with hammers and sickles . . . We are against picturesque {emphasis added} photography and pathos of an old, bourgeois type.*[28]

There were two major public showings of photography produced by the October group members. The first, in 1930, was part of a general October group exhibition at Gor'kii Park. The photography section included the periodical *Radioslushatel'* (*Radio Listener*), with photographic illustrations by Rodchenko, Ignatovich, and Gruntal', as well as Rodchenko's photographs of the poet Vladimir Maiakovskii, Moscow buildings, and a series of an automobile factory entitled *AMO*. The second exhibition opened at the House of Publishing in May of 1931 and was entirely dedicated to photography, presenting the photography section not as a subdivision of the October association but as a separate entity. It was during this second event that a conflict between the October photography section and ROPF, whose members also participated in the exhibition, began. A declaration by ROPF was published in *Proletarskoe foto* (*Proletarian Photo*) in 1931 and signed by the photographers Semen Fridliand, Shaikhet, Al'pert, Iakov Khalip, and others. Although in that text they assert that they "are not against unusual angles of observation and shifted positions of the camera during photographing,"[29] they nonetheless accuse Rodchenko and other "left" photographers of following the path of Western photo-practitioners such as Moholy-Nagy, and thus confine the problematics of the October photographers within the context of Formalist issues, rather than realizing that the true argument concerned a conflict between two different visions of "social being."

Thus, although Rodchenko and other October members insisted on their notion of the "how" as a functional rather than aesthetic element, their critics continued to associate their goals with Formalist photographic discourse as it presented itself in the West. As a result, ROPF's members and a number of critics refused to accept the October production as press photography. In response to the October–ROPF exhibition, the critic L. Mezhericher, for one, claimed that the photographs exhibited by October were not press photography but an aestheticized production, and that since Rodchenko negated the importance of content, he negated photojournalism to its core. In a specific discussion of works such as Langman's *Kruzhevnitsa* (*Lacemaker*, 1931, fig. no. 6), which Mezhericher calls the "apogee of Formalism," he expresses his appreciation of its technical mastery yet labels it a "typical aesthetic snapshot, an example of a senseless adoration of a fragment of reality plucked from its surroundings without reason."[30] Both

fig. 6
Elizar Langman
Lacemaker, *1931.*
Photograph, 22.2 x 29.2 cm.
Courtesy Margarita Tupitsyn.

figs. 7, 8, 9
Maks Al'pert and Arkadii Shaikhet
From the series, Twenty-Four Hours in the Life of the
Working-Class Filippov Family, *1931.*
Photographs, printed from original negatives, 22.1 x 28.5 cm each (left),
29 x 22.3 cm (above).
Courtesy Margarita Tupitsyn.

Mezhericher and the authors of the ROPF declaration, in their criticism of October's production, adopt a stance of "confidence in the possibility of deducing political and ideological positions from a protocol of purely formal properties of a work of art."[31] In the 1930s this "criterion," which Jameson, among other authors, attributes to Lukács, was rapidly becoming a vital weapon against anyone who continued to diverge from conventional methods of representation.

By raising a question about the "substance of form" in regard to the press photograph, Mezhericher brings us to Roland Barthes's later analysis of the same issue, and specifically to Barthes's assessment that the press photograph embodies the "co-existence of two messages, the one without a code (the photographic analogue), the other with a code (the 'art,' or the treatment, or the 'writing,' or the rhetoric, of the photograph)."[32] It was precisely the presence of the second "message" that set October's photography apart from ROPF's.

Mezhericher's critique of Langman's *Lacemaker* as a "fragment of reality plucked from its surroundings" brings us to the larger context of the Marxist crusade against fragmentation. Mezhericher, like all other critics, photographers, and painters who fit into the Lukácsian model of Realism, believed that they were realizing Marx's project of emancipation, whose most fundamental characteristic was "to make the world whole, to connect the disconnected." By trying to organize the world into a single "photo picture," the ROPF photographers mistook this artificial unity for Marx's holistic drive to overcome fragmentation and alienation. As far as the "whole" is concerned, its "reunification" in ROPF's oeuvre is chiefly iconic, whereas October's choice is usually an indexical representation of a supposedly similar (but detached) referent via its fragment, a part which in turn premises a context-establishing totality. October's photography, as fragmented as it looked, pointed to the life beyond the frame and thus aimed at a much more global model of "reunification."[33]

In a strict sense, fragmentation is not a purely artistic device; it was initially hypothesized as the state of reality caused by the "nonorganic" phenomena of capitalism. From Marx's utopian standpoint, the course of reality is characterized by its departure from fragmentation toward unity. Such a paradigm of dialectical change was (in Marx's opinion) identifiable with progress, for as Hegel had said, "the truth is the whole." In the early 1930s, the Soviet mythmaking apparatus claimed that the limits of progress had been reached, such that reality ceased to be fragmented. The State required that artists implement this ideological claim via closing up (i.e., framing) the representational system. As a result, photographers were forced more and more to include images which would identify referents for the masses' aspirations other than those based solely on the desire for production. If before photographers aimed at avoiding identifying political personalities and instead concentrated on the representation of the anonymous masses and the process of voting, coal mining, or constructing itself, now they were required to include the portraits of Stalin and/or Lenin as those people in whose name all the activities were performed. To see this difference, one may compare Gustav Klutsis's poster *Vypolnim plan velikikh rabot* (*Let Us Fulfill the Plan of Great Projects*, 1930), in which the artist reduces representation to just voting hands, with Arkadii Shishkin's photograph *My za kolkhoz!* (*Voting Unanimously for the Kolkhoz*, 1929). In the latter, not only are the workers and peasants themselves shown but a portrait of Stalin, cropped yet ever present, is included. This photograph aims at not allowing the viewer to equate Stalin, the authority, with what Kant (following Plato) called *parergon* (supplement).

In addition to Langman's *Lacemaker*, a number of other

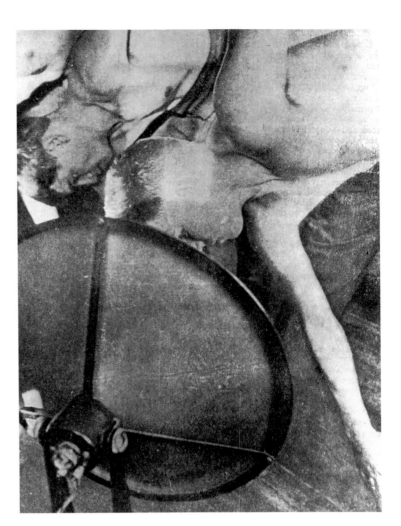

fig. 10
Elizar Langman
Gymnastics on Radio, *1931.*
Photograph, 29.2 x 21.9 cm.
Courtesy Margarita Tupitsyn.

photographs exhibited at the House of Publishing met harsh criticism in the press precisely because they continued to refrain from the politics of framing. Rodchenko's *Pioner-trubach* (*Young Pioneer with a Horn,* 1930, fig. no. 12), Langman's *Gimnastika po radio* (*Gymnastics on Radio,* 1931, fig. no. 10), and Ignatovich's *Novaia Moskva* (*New Moscow,* 1931, fig. no. 11) were all cited as bad examples of press photography. *Young Pioneer with a Horn* is photographed from a worm's-eye view; both horn and Young Pioneer are severely fragmented. Langman's gymnasts are photographed in extreme close-up and are set within very complex spatial relationships, allowing the photographer to blur the distinction between the top and the bottom of the image. Similarly, Ignatovich's representation of Moscow is focused on the clash of old values, symbolized by the image of a cathedral, and the new revolutionary aspirations, expressed through political banners whose messages are broken up into syllables.

All three photographs are based on the structural concept of "deframing" (*décadrage*), which, according to Gilles Deleuze, is not "programmatically justified" and which designates abnormal points of view but is not the same as an oblique perspective or a paradoxical angle (precisely what was meant earlier as a change in the function of the "how").[34] These points of view refer to another dimension of an image which resides beyond all narrative or, more generally, pragmatic justification, perhaps tending to confirm that the visual image has a legible function beyond its visible function. Deframing refers to an "absolute aspect by which the closed system opens onto a duration which is imminent to the whole universe, which is no longer a set, and does not belong to the order of the visible."[35] In this sense, the comment made by the critic I. Bokhonov about Rodchenko's photograph *Pionerka* (*Young Pioneer Girl,* 1930, fig. no. 13)—"Why is [she] looking upward? [The Young Pioneer Girl has no right to look upward,] that has no ideological content. Pioneer Girls and Komsomol Girls should look forward"—is not, as John Bowlt believes, an "absurd criticism."[36] Rather, it exposes the conflict between the politics of "framing," identified here as "forward," and the politics of "deframing," which is "upward." For Soviet ideologues, "forward"—that is, the horizontal or diachronic (read Lukácsian)—fitted into the domain of the visible future; whereas "upward"—that is, the vertical or synchronic (read Brechtian)—was synonymous with the unknown, unseen, and unpredictable.

The increasing criticism of the October group's photography, the exclusion of Rodchenko from the association in 1932, and the disbanding of the photographic section itself coincide with a general persecution of avant-garde art in the early 1930s. In his discussion of the Brecht–Lukács debate, Peter Burger identifies nonorganic works of art with the avant-garde and positions organic work as a defender of the illusion of a world that is whole.[37] Such an analysis explains why the Soviet establishment was becoming increasingly supportive of the organic work of art and suppressing the nonorganic. Political pressures demanded the reign of illusion and a simulation of collective unity rather than the reflection of what even Lukács calls the "alienated inner lives of individuals" unable "to transcend the atomistic and fragmented worlds."[38] Beginning in 1932, the politics of deframing employed by the avant-garde photographers was being suppressed by the ideological enterprise of incarnating the "whole," which soon after crystallized into the huge metalinguistic system known as Socialist Realism.[39]

fig. 11
Boris Ignatovich
New Moscow, *1931.*
Photograph, printed from original negative, 28.6 x 19.6 cm.
Courtesy Margarita Tupitsyn.

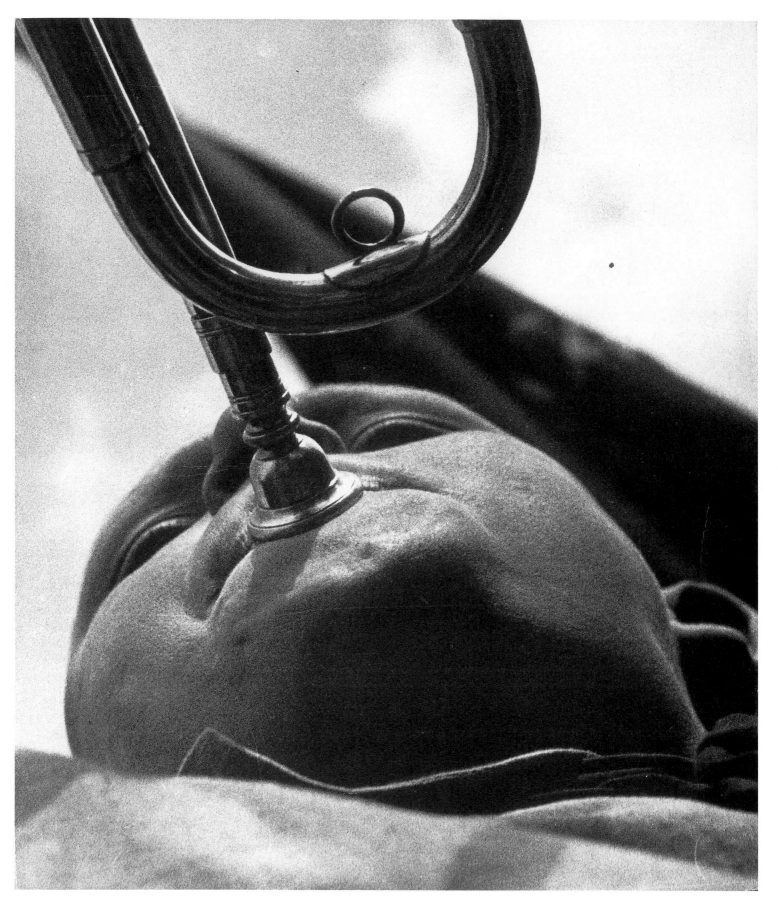

fig. 12
Aleksandr Rodchenko
Young Pioneer with a Horn, *1930.*
Photograph, printed from original negative, 27 x 23.1 cm.
Courtesy Margarita Tupitsyn.

fig. 13
Aleksandr Rodchenko
Young Pioneer Girl, *1930.*
Photograph, printed from original negative, 29.3 x 20.6 cm.
Courtesy Margarita Tupitsyn.

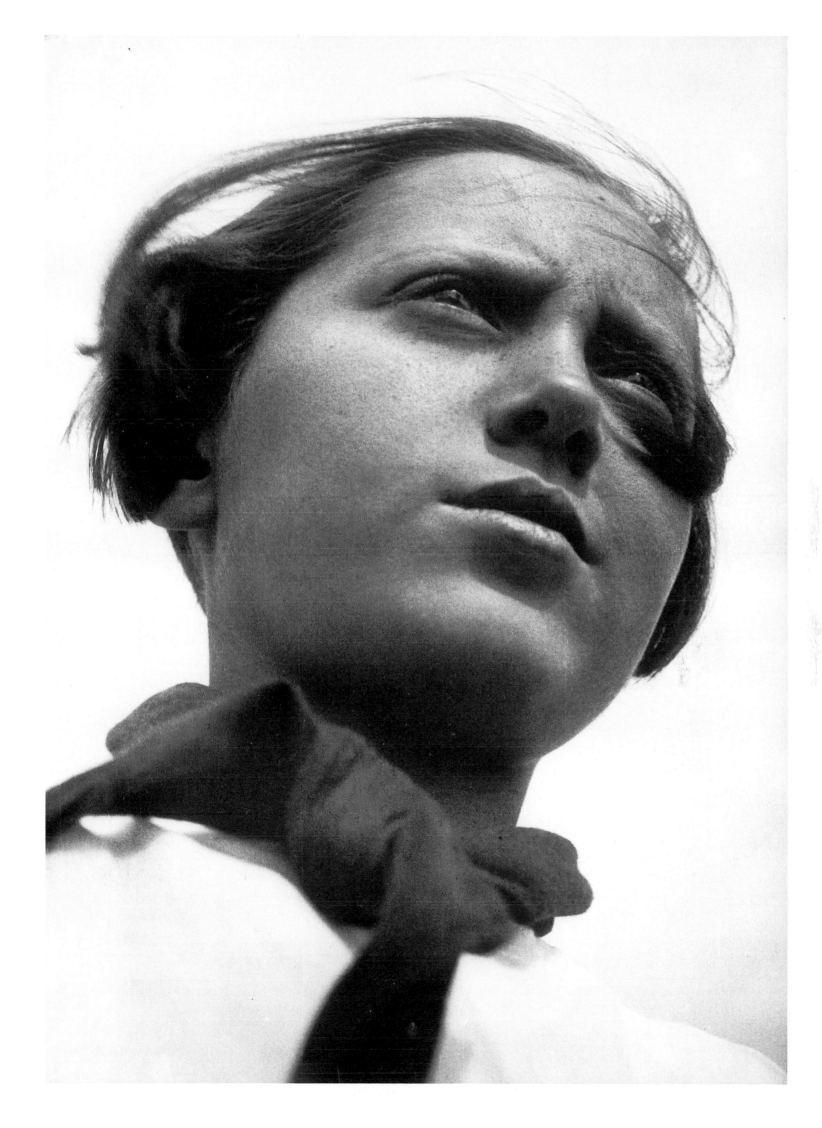

Notes

I am very grateful to Liliia Issakovna Ukhtomskaia of *Soviet Photo* for her support and guidance during my research in Moscow in 1988–89. I would also like to thank the Social Science Research Council for a grant to study Soviet photography of the First Five-Year Plan.

1. A. Shaikhet, "Sorevnovanie foto-reporterov razvertyvaetsia," *Sovetskoe foto* 23 (December 1929), p. 713.

2. Aleksandr Rodchenko, "Doklad Rodchenko o sotsial'nom znachenii fotografii," 1930, A. Rodchenko and V. Stepanova Archive, Moscow.

3. Ibid.

4. Osip Brik, "Foto-kadr protiv kartiny," *Sovetskoe foto* 2 (1926), p. 41, as translated in David Elliott, ed., *Alexander Rodchenko,* catalogue for exhibition organized by the Museum of Modern Art, Oxford (Oxford: Museum of Modern Art, 1979), p. 90.

5. Victor Ehrlich, *Russian Formalism: History–Doctrine,* 2d rev. ed. (The Hague: Mouton and Co., 1965), p. 120.

6. See, for example, Ossip Brik, "The Photograph versus the Painting," trans. John E. Bowlt, in Christopher Phillips, ed., *Photography in the Modern Era: European Documents and Critical Writings, 1913–1940* (New York: Metropolitan Museum of Art and Aperture, 1989), pp. 213–18.

7. Brik, "Foto-kadr protiv kartiny," p. 42, as translated in Elliott, *Alexander Rodchenko,* p. 91.

8. Osip Brik, "Ot kartiny k foto," *Novyi Lef* 3 (1928), pp. 29–33.

9. Ibid., p. 33.

10. Aleksandr Rodchenko, "Predosterezhenie," *Novyi Lef* 11 (1928), p. 37.

11. Alexander Rodchenko, "A Caution," trans. John E. Bowlt, in Phillips, *Photography in the Modern Era,* p. 265.

12. Fredric Jameson, *The Ideologies of Theory* (Minneapolis: University of Minnesota Press, 1988), vol. 2, p. 141.

13. Sergei Tretyakov, "From the Editor," trans. John E. Bowlt, in Phillips, *Photography in the Modern Era,* p. 272.

14. Rodchenko, "Doklad Rodchenko o sotsial'nom znachenii fotografii," 1930. Rodchenko is most likely referring here to the drawings by Aleksandr Deineka which were published in *Let's Produce!* along with his and Ignatovich's photographs.

15. Boris Ignatovich, notebook, Collection of the Ignatovich Family, Moscow.

16. Ibid.

17. Yve-Alain Bois, "El Lissitzky: Radical Reversibility," *Art in America,* April 1988, p. 167.

18. Ibid.

19. The legacy of the Lukács–Brecht debate is crucial for understanding how revolutionary art of the 1920s and early 1930s degenerated into Stalinist mythos. Neither name was unfamiliar to Soviet contemporaries—artists, critics, and photographers—since both Georg Lukács and Bertolt Brecht actively discussed their cultural views in such Moscow publications as the journal *Das Wort* (*The Word*). Lukács lived in Moscow and together with the philosopher Mikhail Livshits was instrumental in shaping the basic principles of Socialist Realism. Contrary to Lukácsian "messianic Marxism" with its philosophy of the "totality," Brecht's cultural strategy was in some ways akin to Mikhail Bakunin's "critical Marxism"— which adds one more link between Russia and Brecht.

20. Bois, "El Lissitzky," p. 169.

21. Ibid.

22. Aleksandr Lavrent'ev, "Kadriruet Aleksandr Rodchenko," *Sovetskoe foto* 1 (1978), p. 34.

23. Andreas Huyssen, *After the Great Divide: Modernism, Mass Culture, Postmodernism* (Bloomington: Indiana University Press, 1986), p. 14.

24. Ibid.

25. Jameson, *Ideologies of Theory,* vol. 2, p. 139.

26. The October group was the first to admit women as photojournalists.

27. *Izofront. Klassovaia bor'ba na fronte prostranstvennykh iskusstv. Sbornik statei ob"edineniia Oktiabr'* (Leningrad and Moscow: Izofront, 1931), p. 150.

28. Ibid., pp. 149–50.

29. Semen Fridliand et al., "Prodolzhaem tvorcheskuiu diskussiiu," *Proletarskoe foto* 2 (1931), p. 14.

30. L. Mezhericher, "Segodniashnii den' sovetskogo reportazha," *Proletarskoe foto* 1 (1931), p. 10.

31. Jameson, *Ideologies of Theory,* vol. 2, pp. 136–37.

32. Roland Barthes, "The Photographic Image," in *Image–Music–Text,* trans. Stephen Heath (New York: Hill and Wang, 1977), p. 19. "Substance of form" is an ironic term coined by Barthes to ridicule Zhdanovism. See Roland Barthes, "Myth Today," in his *Mythologies,* trans. Annette Lavers (New York: Hill and Wang, 1972), p. 112.

33. See Alvin W. Gouldner, *Against Fragmentation: The Origins of Marxism and the Sociology of Intellectuals* (New York and Oxford: Oxford University Press, 1985).

34. See Gilles Deleuze, *Cinema 1: The Movement Image,* trans. Hugh Tomlinson and Barbara Habberjam (Minneapolis: University of Minnesota Press, 1986).

35. Ibid., p. 17.

36. See John Bowlt, "Alexandr Rodchenko as Photographer," in *The Avant-Garde in Russia, 1910–30: New Perspectives,* catalogue for exhibition organized by the Los Angeles County Museum of Art and the Hirshhorn Museum and Sculpture Garden, Smithsonian Institution, Washington, D.C. (Los Angeles: Los Angeles County Museum of Art, 1980), p. 57. Bokhonov made this comment at a meeting of the selection committee for the *Moskovskie mastera fotoiskusstva* (*Moscow Masters of Photo Art*) exhibition in March 1935.

37. Peter Burger, *Theory of the Avant-Garde* (Minneapolis: University of Minnesota Press, 1984), p. 86.

38. Raman Selden, *Contemporary Literary Theory* (Lexington: University Press of Kentucky, 1985), p. 34.

39. Ironically, the story of the October–ROPF controversy, interpreted here within the framework of the Lukács–Brecht debate, came to a close in 1936, after a series of articles connected with another debate between Formalism and Naturalism were reported in the press under the rubric "Perestroika [Restructuring] of an Artist." These debates and discussions continued to echo in the postwar period. See Margarita Tupitsyn, "Veil on Photo: Metamorphoses of Supplementarity in Soviet Art," *Arts Magazine,* November 1989, pp. 79–84.

483
Aleksandr Vesnin
Sketch for Vkhutemas emblem, 1921–22.
Gouache and pencil on paper, 10 x 10 cm.
State Shchusev Museum, Moscow.

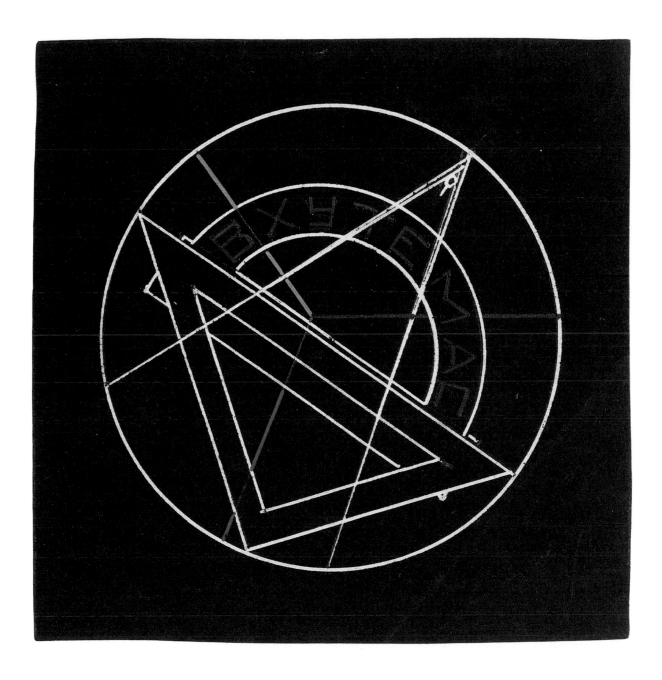

486
Galina and Ol'ga
Chichagova
Book illustration, Airplane, *1922–23.*
India ink and gouache on paper,
24 x 19.9 cm.
Private collection, Moscow.

487
Galina and Ol'ga
Chichagova
Cover for N. G. Smirnov and
Galina and Ol'ga Chichagova,
A Book for Children about the
Newspaper, *1926.*
Lithograph, 26 x 22 cm.
Private collection, Moscow.

488
Galina and Ol'ga
Chichagova
Study for cover for How Chocolate Is
Made, *1920s.*
India ink, collage, and colored paper on
paper, 26.8 x 23.6 cm.
Private collection, Moscow.

489
Galina and Ol'ga
Chichagova
Book illustration, On This Island
There Lives an Elephant, *1922–23.*
India ink and collage on paper,
26.7 x 23.7 cm.
Private collection, Moscow.

490
Nikolai Suetin
Cover for G. Genkel', Henry Ford,
1925.
Lithograph, 23 x 15.6 cm.
Collection Helix Art Center, San Diego.

491
Liubov' Popova
Cover for Musical Novelties *5 (1924).*
Lithograph, 30.9 x 23 cm.
Collection Helix Art Center, San Diego.

492
Artist Unknown
Cover for Theater Artistry *1 (1922).*
Lithograph, 21.6 x 17.8 cm.
Collection Helix Art Center, San Diego.

493
Gustav Klutsis
Cover for Furnace *9 (1923).*
Lithograph, 25.5 x 17.8 cm.
Collection Helix Art Center, San Diego.

494
Gustav Klutsis
Cover for M. Lazarev (music) and
Anatolii Bezymenskii (lyrics), Party ID
No. 224332, 1925.
Lithograph, 35.1 x 24.8 cm.
Collection Helix Art Center, San Diego.

495
Gustav Klutsis
Cover for Proletarian Students *5*
(1923).
Lithograph, 25.5 x 17.8 cm.
Collection Helix Art Center, San Diego.

496
Valentina Kulagina
Cover for Aleksei Kruchenykh,
Lenin's Language, *1925.*
Lithograph, 19 x 14.2 cm.
From the Resource Collections,
The Getty Center for the History of Art
and the Humanities.

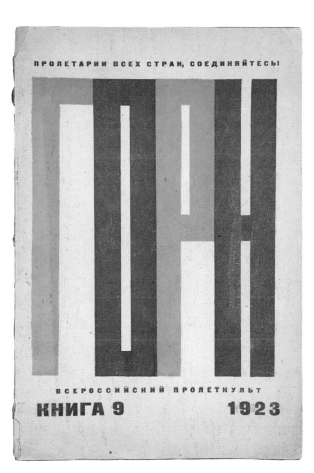

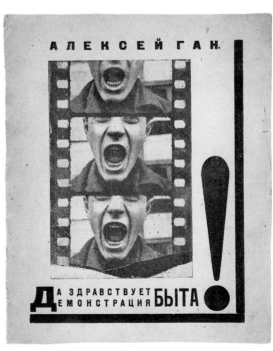

501
Aleksandr Rodchenko
Advertising poster, Shouldn't We
Produce Pencils We Can Use?, *1923.*
Gouache on paper, 29.5 x 19 cm.
A. M. Rodchenko and V. F. Stepanova
Archive, Moscow.

502
Aleksandr Rodchenko
Advertising bookmark for Gosizdat,
News, *1924.*
Gouache on paper, 17 x 8 cm.
A. M. Rodchenko and V. F. Stepanova
Archive, Moscow.

503
Aleksandr Rodchenko
Advertising bookmark, News of the
Day, *1924.*
Gouache on paper, 13 x 10 cm.
A. M. Rodchenko and V. F. Stepanova
Archive, Moscow.

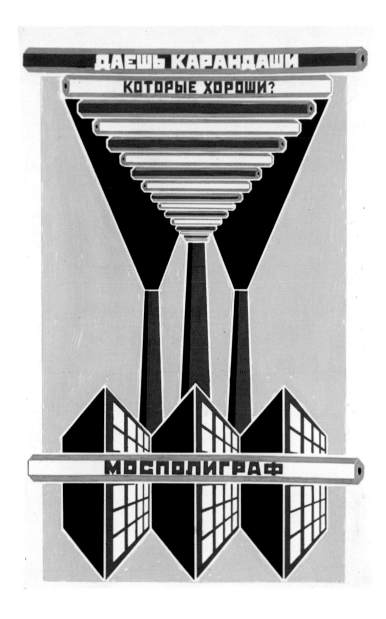

504
Aleksandr Rodchenko
Cover for New Lef *1 (1927).*
Lithograph, 22.7 x 15.5 cm.
Maiakovskii Museum, Moscow.

505
Varvara Stepanova
Cover for Red Students *10 (1929).*
Intaglio, 30.5 x 23 cm.
A. M. Rodchenko and V. F. Stepanova
Archive, Moscow.

506
Varvara Stepanova
Cover for Soviet Cinema *1 (1927).*
Intaglio, 28.5 x 37.5 cm.
A. M. Rodchenko and V. F. Stepanova
Archive, Moscow.

507
Varvara Stepanova
Cover for Vladimir Maiakovskii,
Menacing Laughter, *1932.*
Lithograph, 24. 2 x 51. 6 cm.
Collection of Prints and Drawings,
The Federal Institute of Technology,
Zurich.

508
Nikolai Sedel'nikov
Cover for Artists' Brigade 2–3 (1931).
Lithograph, 30. 1 x 21. 9 cm.
Collection Helix Art Center, San Diego.

509
Gustav Klutsis
Window design, This Is the Standard,
for the All-Union Printing Trades
Exhibition, *Moscow, 1927.*
Gouache, india ink, colored paper, and
sandpaper on cardboard mounted on
cardboard, 25.9 x 89.4 cm.
State Art Museum of Latvia, Riga.

510
Gustav Klutsis
Study for cover for Cultural
Construction, *1928.*
Collage, gouache, india ink,
photomontage, varnish, and colored paper
on cardboard, 50.2 x 34.5 cm.
State Art Museum of Latvia, Riga.

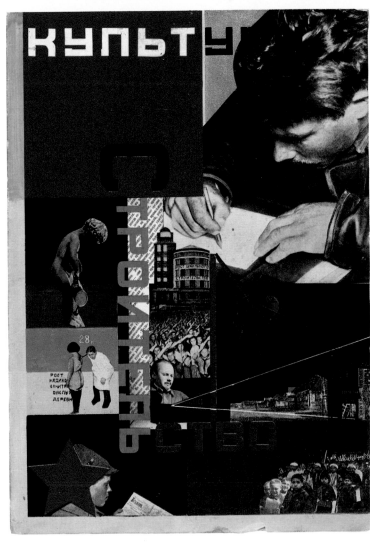

513
El Lissitzky
Cover for Artists' Brigade *4 (1931).*
Lithograph, 31.5 x 22.2 cm.
Collection Helix Art Center, San Diego.

514
Solomon Telingater (design)
and Boris Ignatovich
(photograph)
Cover for Artists' Brigade *1 (1931).*
Lithograph, 28.7 x 21.6 cm.
From the Resource Collections,
The Getty Center for the History of Art
and the Humanities.

515
Aleksandr Rodchenko
Cover for Let's Produce! *6 (1929).*
Lithograph, 30 x 23 cm.
Collection Helix Art Center, San Diego.

516
**Georgii and Vladimir
Stenberg**
Cover for Artists' Brigade *7 (1931).*
Lithograph, 30.5 x 22.9 cm.
Collection Helix Art Center, San Diego.

517
Mechislav Dobrokovskii
Cover for Artists' Brigade *5–6 (1931).*
Lithograph, 29.8 x 21.9 cm.
Collection Helix Art Center, San Diego.

518
El Lissitzky
Cover for Construction of Moscow 5
(1929).
Lithograph, 30.5 x 46.4 cm.
Collection Helix Art Center, San Diego.

519
Gustav Klutsis and
Vasilii Elkin
Cover for Construction of Moscow 8
(1928).
Lithograph, 30.3 x 45.8 cm.
Collection Helix Art Center, San Diego.

520
Georgii and Vladimir
Stenberg
Cover for Construction of Moscow *7*
(1929).
Lithograph, 30.5 x 45.8 cm.
Collection Helix Art Center, San Diego.

521
Georgii and Vladimir
Stenberg
Cover for Construction of Moscow *11*
(1930).
Lithograph, 30.2 x 42 cm.
Collection Helix Art Center, San Diego.

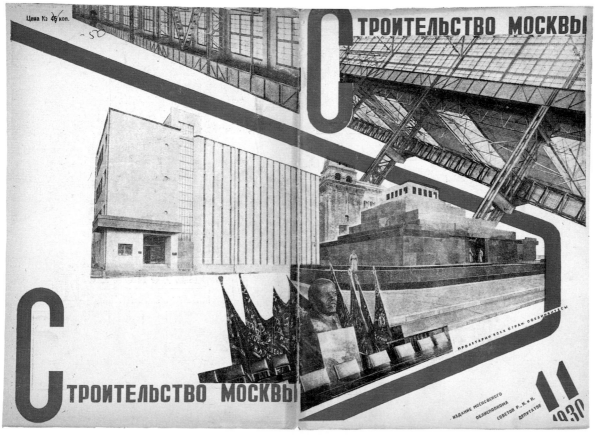

522
Solomon Telingater
Typographical layout for E. Edman and
Solomon Telingater, Immer bereit!,
1930.
Lithograph, 22.3 x 36.6 cm.
Private collection, Moscow.

523
Solomon Telingater
Cover for Anatolii Bezymenskii,
Young Communists League, *1928.*
Lithograph, 34.3 x 26.3 cm.
From the Resource Collections,
The Getty Center for the History of Art
and the Humanities.

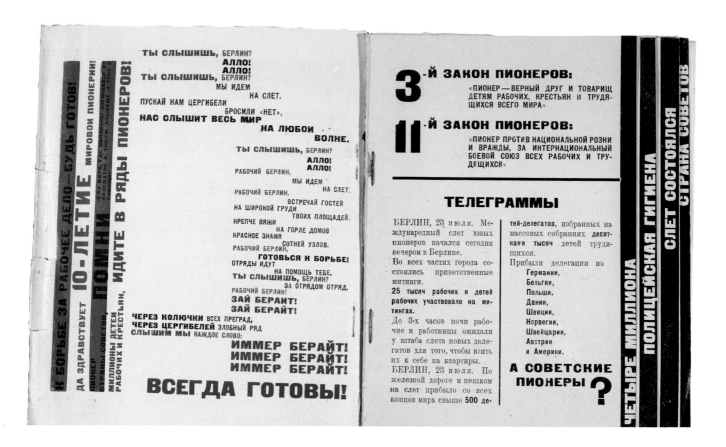

526
El Lissitzky
Cover for URSS en construction
6 (1934).
Lithograph and intaglio, 42 x 30 cm.
Lenin Library, Moscow.

527
**Aleksandr Rodchenko
(and Varvara Stepanova?)**
Cover for SSSR na stroike *12 (1935).*
Lithograph and intaglio, 42 x 30 cm.
Lenin Library, Moscow.

528
Aleksandr Rodchenko
Cover for SSSR na stroike *12 (1933).*
Intaglio, 41.5 x 30 cm.
*A. M. Rodchenko and V. F. Stepanova
Archive, Moscow.*

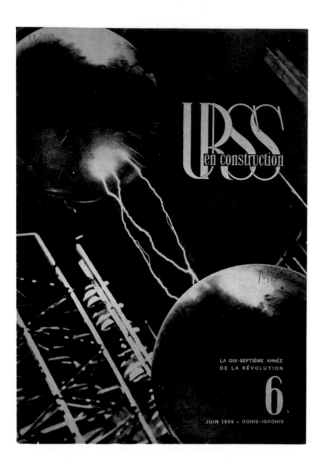

529
Aleksei Sotnikov
Baby bottles and tray, 1930.
Porcelain, set 35 x 15 cm.
All-Russian Museum of Decorative and
Folk Art, Moscow.

530
Vladimir Tatlin
Sketch for a creamer, 1923.
Pencil on paper, 19.8 x 17.8 cm.
State Bakhrushin Museum, Moscow.

531
Vladimir Tatlin
Sketch for a creamer, 1923.
Pencil on paper, 21 x 26.6 cm.
State Bakhrushin Museum, Moscow.

532
Vladimir Tatlin
Sketch for a teapot, 1923.
Pencil on paper, 19.1 x 22.3 cm.
State Bakhrushin Museum, Moscow.

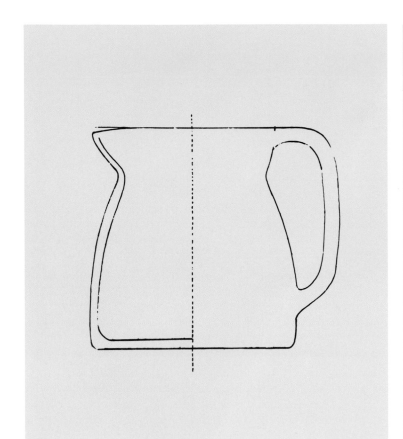

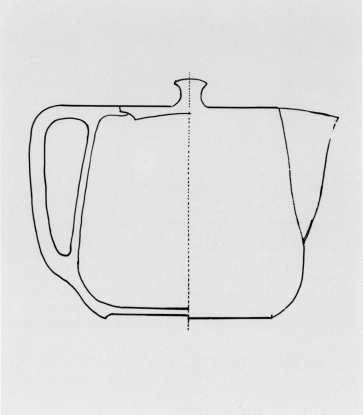

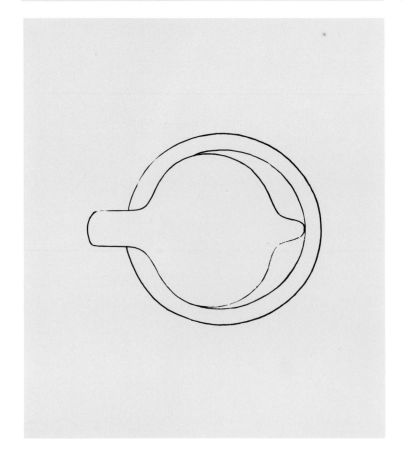

535
Artist Unknown
Pitcher/measuring glass, made in the Ceramics Faculty of Vkhutemas, after 1922.
Painting and overglaze on porcelain, 17.3 cm high.
Collection V. A. Dudakov and M. K. Kashuro, Moscow.

536
Pavel Kozhin
The New Way of Life, 1930.
Overglaze and stenciling on porcelain, Dulevo Porcelain Factory, teapot, 14 cm high, 9.5 x 8 cm base; mustard pot, 6.5 cm high, 7 x 5.5 cm base.
Kuskovo State Porcelain Museum.

537
Nikolai Lapshin
Cup and saucer, 1923.
Porcelain, cup 5.6 cm high, 9.5 cm diameter, saucer 14.7 cm diameter.
Collection V. A. Dudakov and M. K. Kashuro, Moscow.

538
Nadezhda Pashchinskaia-Maksimova
Cup, Everyone to the Educational Trip, and saucer, Study, Study, Study, early 1930s.
Porcelain, cup 5.7 cm high, 8.4 cm diameter, saucer 14.9 cm diameter.
Collection V. A. Dudakov and M. K. Kashuro, Moscow.

539
Trifon Podriabinnikov
Physical Culture and Relaxation
service, 1934.
Overglaze, airbrush, and gilding on
porcelain, Dmitrov Porcelain Factory,
sugar bowl 9.9 cm high, 8.6 cm base;
teapot 12.5 cm high, 10 cm base;
cup and saucer.
Kuskovo State Porcelain Museum.

540
Trifon Podriabinnikov
Cup and saucer, Cogwheels, 1934.
Overglaze, stenciling, and gilding on
porcelain, Dmitrov Porcelain Factory,
cup 6 cm high, saucer 15 cm diameter.
Kuskovo State Porcelain Museum.

544
Artist Unknown
Scarf, Industrialization Is Lenin's
Path to Communism, 1917–1927,
1927.
Cotton, 76 x 76 cm.
Trekhgornaia Textile Mill, Moscow.

545
Ol'ga Rozanova
Sketch for an embroidered handbag, 1916.
Graphite pencil on paper, 28.5 x 25.5 cm.
State Russian Museum, St. Petersburg.

546
Ol'ga Rozanova
Sketch for an embroidered handbag, 1916.
Graphite pencil on paper, 21.3 x 21.8 cm.
State Russian Museum, St. Petersburg.

547
Ol'ga Rozanova
Sketch for a handbag, 1916–17.
Watercolor and india ink on paper,
35 x 23.2 cm.
State Russian Museum, St. Petersburg.

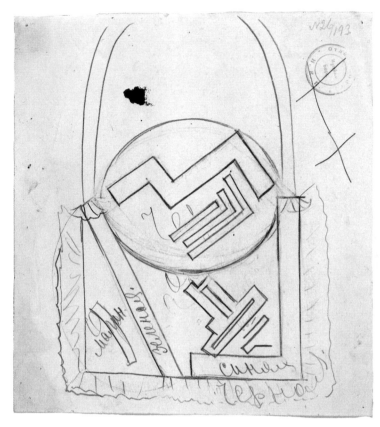

548
Nadezhda Udal'tsova
Composition, *1916.*
Gouache on paper, 18.5 x 19.5 cm.
Collection A. A. and E. D. Drevin,
Moscow.

549
Nadezhda Udal'tsova
Design for a decorative panel, 1916–17.
Gouache on paper, 47 x 40 cm.
Collection A. A. and E. D. Drevin,
Moscow.

550
Nadezhda Udal'tsova
Design for a rug, 1916.
Gouache on paper, 44 x 65 cm.
Collection A. A. and E. D. Drevin,
Moscow.

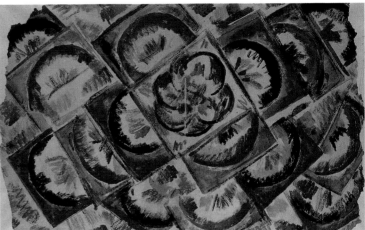

551
Liubov' Popova
Textile design, 1923–24.
Gouache and india ink on paper,
35.5 x 24.8 cm.
Tsaritsyno Museum of Applied Arts,
Moscow.

552
Liubov' Popova
Textile design, 1923–24.
India ink and watercolor on paper,
30.5 x 20.8 cm.
Tsaritsyno Museum of Applied Arts,
Moscow.

553
Varvara Stepanova
Textile design, 1924.
Gouache on paper, 44.5 x 53 cm.
A. M. Rodchenko and V. F. Stepanova
Archive, Moscow.

554
Varvara Stepanova
Textile sample, 1924.
Flannel, 44 x 62.5 cm.
A. M. Rodchenko and V. F. Stepanova
Archive, Moscow.

555
Aleksandr Rodchenko
Textile design, 1924.
India ink on paper, 13 x 30.5 cm.
A. M. Rodchenko and V. F. Stepanova
Archive, Moscow.

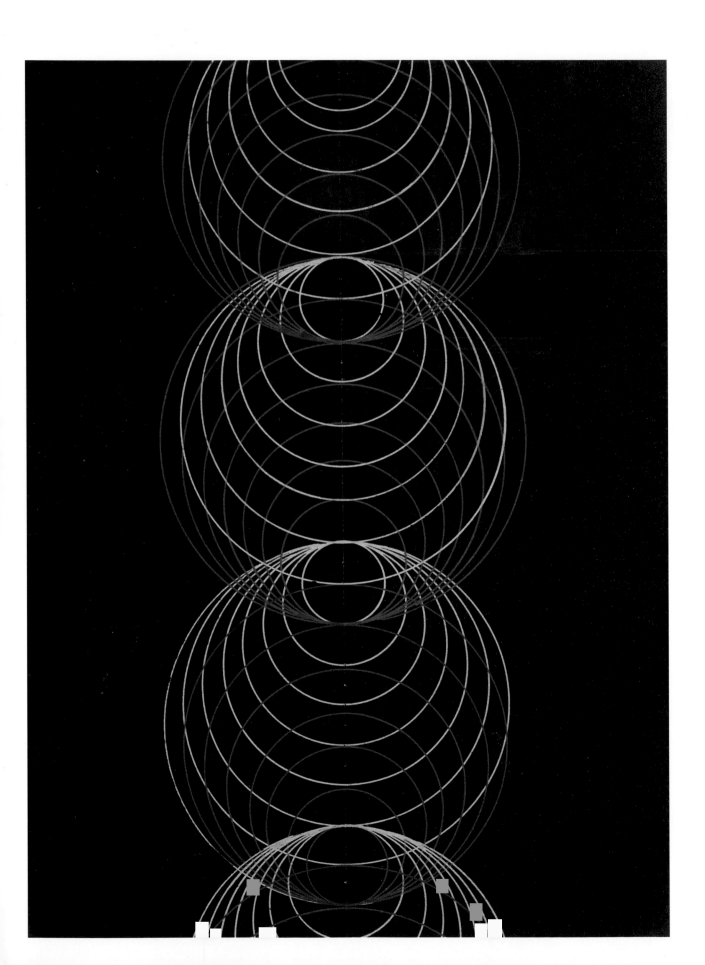

556
Varvara Stepanova
Textile design, 1924.
Gouache on paper, 31.8 x 27.7 cm.
A. M. Rodchenko and V. F. Stepanova
Archive, Moscow.

557
Varvara Stepanova
Textile design, 1924.
Gouache on paper, 38.5 x 30.5 cm.
A. M. Rodchenko and V. F. Stepanova
Archive, Moscow.

558
Liudmila Maiakovskaia
Rosebuds, *before 1927.*
Airbrush on velvet, 34.4 x 28.6 cm.
Maiakovskii Museum, Moscow.

559
Liudmila Maiakovskaia
Fragments of a Cogwheel, *1927.*
Airbrush on velvet, 6.5 x 18 cm.
Maiakovskii Museum, Moscow.

560
Liudmila Maiakovskaia
Colored Planets, *1927*.
Airbrush on silk, 27.5 x 32.5 cm.
Maiakovskii Museum, Moscow.

561
Liudmila Maiakovskaia
Needle Pattern, *1927*.
Airbrush on velvet, 21.6 x 38.4 cm.
Maiakovskii Museum, Moscow.

562
Liudmila Maiakovskaia
Red Autumn, *1927*.
Airbrush on velvet, 49.5 x 54.7 cm.
Maiakovskii Museum, Moscow.

563
Artist Unknown
Tunnel, *late 1920s or early 1930s.*
Dress cotton, 26 x 46 cm.
Mukhina College Museum,
St. Petersburg.

564
Artist Unknown
Propellers, *late 1920s or early 1930s.*
Cotton, 31 x 42 cm.
Ivanovo State Museum of History and
the Revolution.

565
Artist Unknown
Electrification, *late 1920s or early*
1930s.
Sateen, 68.5 x 62.5 cm.
Ivanovo State Museum of History and
the Revolution.

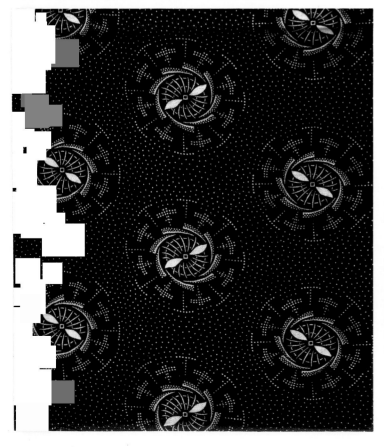

566
Artist Unknown
Airplanes, *1931.*
Dress cotton, 31.5 x 70.6 cm.
Mukhina College Museum,
St. Petersburg.

567
Artist Unknown
All-Union Communist Party,
late 1920s or early 1930s.
Asta dress fabric, 35 x 25 cm.
Mukhina College Museum,
St. Petersburg.

568
Artist Unknown
Motorcycle Riders, *late 1920s or*
early 1930s.
Sateen, 75 x 62 cm.
Ivanovo State Museum of History and
the Revolution.

569
Artist Unknown
Transmission, *late 1920s or early 1930s.*
Cotton, 22 x 25 cm.
Collection T. K. Strizhenova, Moscow.

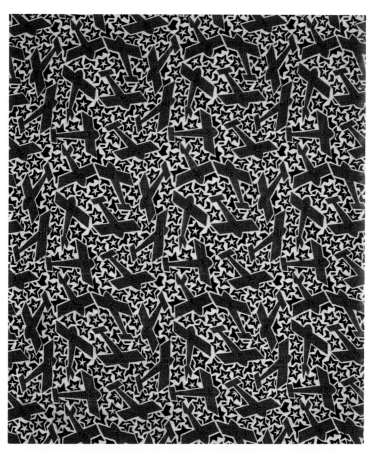

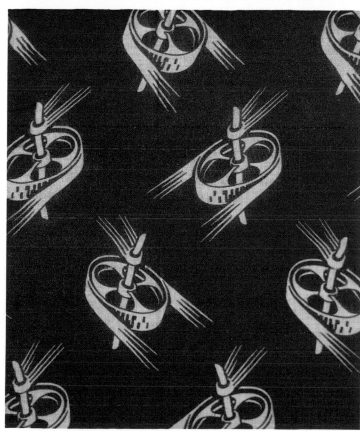

570
Sergei Burylin
Airplanes, *1930.*
Cotton, Great Ivanovo-Voznesensk Textile
Mill, 19 x 25 cm.
Ivanovo State Museum of History and the
Revolution.

571
Sergei Burylin
Airplanes, *late 1920s or early 1930s.*
Cotton, Great Ivanovo-Voznesensk Textile
Mill, 100.5 x 72.5 cm.
Ivanovo State Museum of History and
the Revolution.

572
Sergei Burylin
Factories, *late 1920s or early 1930s.*
Cotton, Great Ivanovo-Voznesensk Textile
Mill, 15.5 x 17 cm.
Ivanovo State Museum of History and
the Revolution.

573
Sergei Burylin
Tractor Driver at Work, *late 1920s*
or early 1930s.
Muslin, Kokhma Textile Mill,
23 x 25 cm.
Ivanovo State Museum of History and
the Revolution.

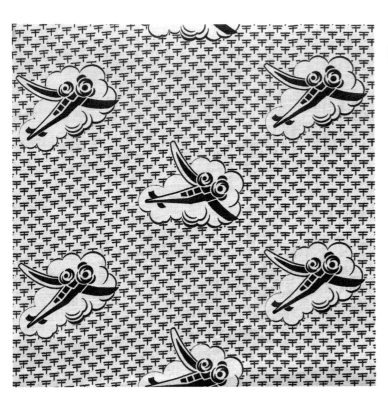

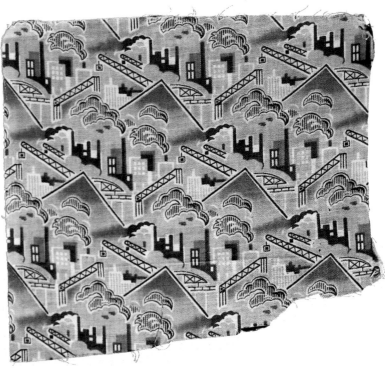

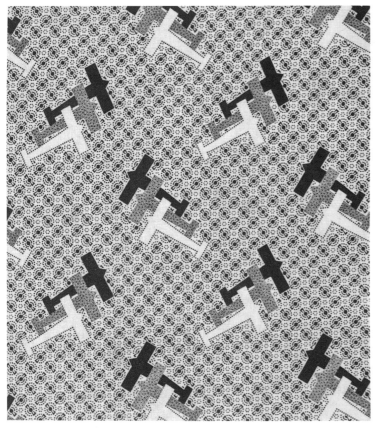

574
Sergei Burylin
Sketch for Fragments of a Cogwheel
textile design, 1929.
Gouache on paper, 14 x 14 cm.
Ivanovo State Museum of History and
the Revolution.

575
Sergei Burylin
Sketch for Coal Recycling *textile design,*
late 1920s or early 1930s.
Gouache, ink, and whiting on paper,
14 x 14.6 cm.
Ivanovo State Museum of History and
the Revolution.

576
Sergei Burylin
Industry, 1930.
Wool, Great Ivanovo-Voznesensk Textile
Mill, 98 x 70 cm.
Ivanovo State Museum of History and
the Revolution.

577
Artist Unknown
Textile sample, late 1920s or early 1930s.
Dress sateen, 35 x 78.5 cm.
Mukhina College Museum,
St. Petersburg.

578
Artist Unknown
Textile sample, late 1920s or early 1930s.
Dress voile, 31 x 86 cm.
Mukhina College Museum,
St. Petersburg.

579
Artist Unknown
Textile sample, late 1920s or early 1930s.
Dress sateen, 23.5 x 69.5 cm.
Mukhina College Museum,
St. Petersburg.

580
Artist Unknown
The Five-Year Plan in Four Years!,
late 1920s or early 1930s.
Fustian, 17.5 x 27 cm.
Ivanovo State Museum of History and
the Revolution.

581
Sergei Burylin
Factories, *1930.*
Muslin, Kokhma Textile Mill,
85 x 61 cm.
Ivanovo State Museum of History and
the Revolution.

581

582
**Dina Lekhtman-
Zaslavskaia**
Weavers at Looms, *1930.*
Dress sateen, First Cotton-Printing
Factory, Moscow, 33 x 80 cm.
Mukhina College Museum,
St. Petersburg.

583
Sergei Burylin
Tractors, *1930.*
Cotton, Great Ivanovo-Voznesensk Textile
Mill, 24 x 25 cm.
Ivanovo State Museum of History and
the Revolution.

584
Sergei Burylin
Industrial Motif, *late 1920s or*
early 1930s.
Cotton, Great Ivanovo-Voznesensk Textile
Mill, 21 x 19 cm.
Ivanovo State Museum of History and
the Revolution.

585
Artist Unknown
Abolition of Illiteracy, *1930*.
Asta dress fabric, 37 x 59 cm.
Mukhina College Museum,
St. Petersburg.

586
Vera Loseva
Miner, *1930*.
Asta dress fabric, V. Slutskaia Factory,
Leningrad, 101 x 75 cm.
Mukhina College Museum,
St. Petersburg.

587
Zinaida Belevich
Children's Demonstration, *1930*.
Asta dress fabric, V. Slutskaia Factory,
Leningrad, 25 x 34 cm.
Mukhina College Museum,
St. Petersburg.

588
Sarra Buntsis
The Forge, *1931.*
Dress fabric, V. Slutskaia Factory,
Leningrad, 26 x 35 cm.
Mukhina College Museum,
St. Petersburg.

589
Sarra Buntsis
Sketch for The Forge *textile design,*
1930.
Tempera, gouache, and whiting on paper,
18.7 x 25 cm.
Mukhina College Museum,
St. Petersburg.

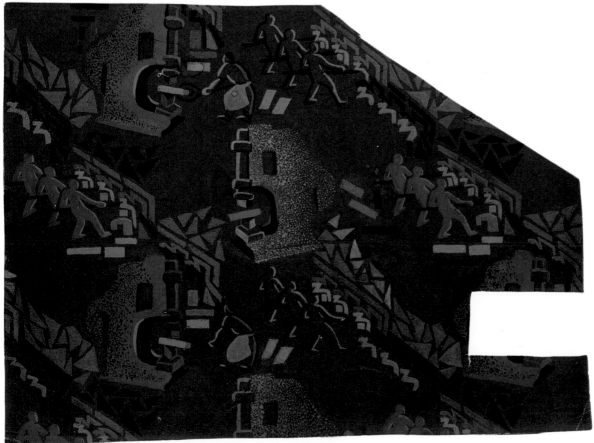

590
Sarra Buntsis
Tractors, *1931.*
Asta dress fabric, V. Slutskaia Factory,
Leningrad, 99 x 74 cm.
Mukhina College Museum,
St. Petersburg.

591
Sarra Buntsis
Spinning: Old and New, *1931.*
Bankabroshi dress fabric, V. Slutskaia
Factory, Leningrad, 26 x 35 cm.
Mukhina College Museum,
St. Petersburg.

592
Raisa Matveeva
Water Sport, *1930.*
Dress cotton, Zinov'ev Factory, Ivanovo,
40 x 60 cm.
Mukhina College Museum,
St. Petersburg.

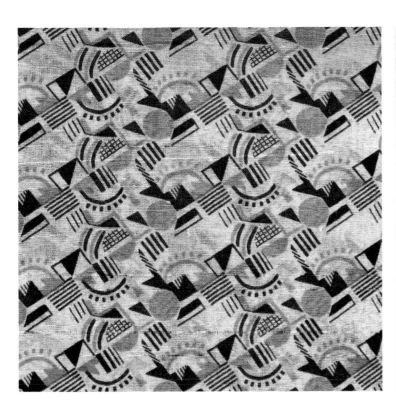

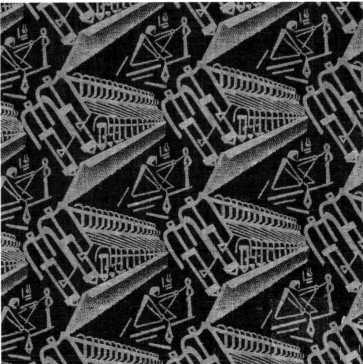

593
Mariia Vasil'eva
New Village, *1930.*
Cotton, Zinov'ev Factory, Ivanovo,
50 x 73 cm.
Mukhina College Museum,
St. Petersburg.

594
Mariia Nazarevskaia
Red Army Soldiers Help with the
Cotton Harvest, *1932.*
Sateen, First Cotton-Printing Factory,
Moscow, 53 x 72 cm.
Mukhina College Museum,
St. Petersburg.

595
Petr Vil'iams
Portrait of V. E. Meierkhol'd, *1925.*
Oil on canvas, 210 x 138.5 cm.
State Tret'iakov Gallery, Moscow.

596
Vladimir Tatlin
Costume design for Richard Wagner,
Der fliegende Holländer, 1915–18.
Pencil on paper, 65 x 50 cm.
State Bakhrushin Museum, Moscow.

597
Vladimir Tatlin
Costume design for Richard Wagner,
Der fliegende Holländer, 1915–18.
Charcoal on paper, 72.2 x 51 cm.
State Russian Museum, St. Petersburg.

598
Vladimir Tatlin
Set design: a mast, for Richard Wagner,
Der fliegende Holländer, 1915–18.
Pencil on tracing paper, 74 x 51 cm.
State Bakhrushin Museum, Moscow.

599
Vladimir Tatlin
Prototype of women's clothing, 1923.
Pencil on paper, 77 x 56.8 cm.
State Bakhrushin Museum, Moscow.

600
Vladimir Tatlin
Everyday Clothes, 1923.
Pencil on paper, 107.7 x 71.5 cm.
State Bakhrushin Museum, Moscow.

601
Vladimir Tatlin
Prototype of men's clothing, 1923.
Pencil on paper, 62 x 39.5 cm.
State Bakhrushin Museum, Moscow.

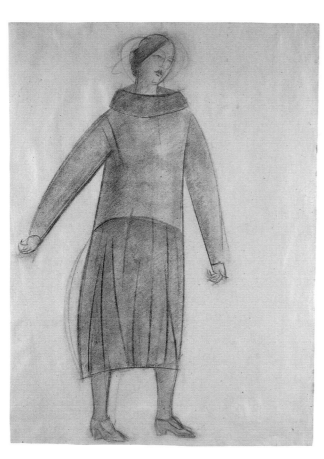

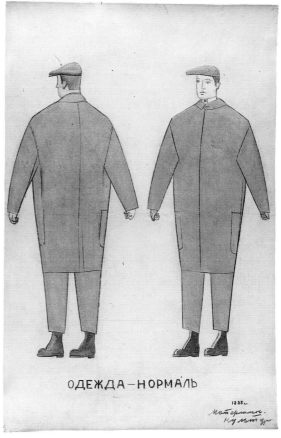

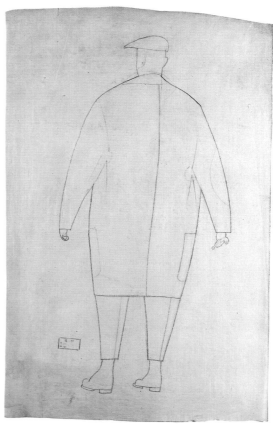

602
Vladimir Tatlin
Set design for Velimir Khlebnikov,
Zangezi, Experimental Amateur Theater
of the Museum of Artistic Culture,
Petrograd, 1923.
Pencil on paper, 34.9 x 50.9 cm.
State Bakhrushin Museum, Moscow.

603
Vladimir Tatlin
Set design for Velimir Khlebnikov,
Zangezi, Experimental Amateur Theater
of the Museum of Artistic Culture,
Petrograd, 1923.
Charcoal on paper, 72.2 x 107.8 cm.
State Bakhrushin Museum, Moscow.

604
Vladimir Tatlin
*Costume design: Anguish, for Velimir
Khlebnikov, Zangezi, Experimental
Amateur Theater of the Museum of
Artistic Culture, Petrograd, 1923.
Charcoal on paper, 54.6 x 38.2 cm.
State Bakhrushin Museum, Moscow.*

605
Vladimir Tatlin
*Costume design: Laughter, for Velimir
Khlebnikov, Zangezi, Experimental
Amateur Theater of the Museum of
Artistic Culture, Petrograd, 1923.
Charcoal on paper, 55.2 x 37.6 cm.
State Bakhrushin Museum, Moscow.*

606
Aleksandra Ekster
Set design: Act II, for Oscar Wilde,
Salomé, Kamernyi Theater, Moscow,
1917.
Watercolor on paper, 18 x 28 cm.
State Bakhrushin Museum, Moscow.

607
Aleksandra Ekster
Costume design (variant): Sadducees, for
Oscar Wilde, Salomé, Kamernyi Theater,
Moscow, 1917.
Gouache on cardboard, 67.2 x 52 cm.
State Bakhrushin Museum, Moscow.

608
Aleksandra Ekster
Costume design: Salomé, for Oscar Wilde,
Salomé, Kamernyi Theater, Moscow,
1917.
Gouache, bronze, and silver on
cardboard, 68.9 x 44.2 cm.
State Bakhrushin Museum, Moscow.

609
Aleksandra Ekster
Costume design: a slave in green, for
Oscar Wilde, Salomé, Kamernyi Theater,
Moscow, 1917.
Gouache, india ink, and whiting on
cardboard, 70.2 x 34 cm.
State Bakhrushin Museum, Moscow.

609
Aleksandra Ekster

610
Aleksandra Ekster
Costume design: Benvolio, for William
Shakespeare, Romeo and Juliet,
Kamernyi Theater, Moscow, 1919–21.
Gouache and silver on cardboard,
54 x 37.4 cm.
State Bakhrushin Museum, Moscow.

611
Aleksandra Ekster
Costume design for a woman, for William
Shakespeare, Romeo and Juliet,
Kamernyi Theater, Moscow, 1919–21.
Gouache on cardboard, 54.7 x 35 cm.
State Bakhrushin Museum, Moscow.

612
Vadim Meller
*Costume design: a monk, for Juliusz
Slowacki,* Mazeppa, *First State
Ukrainian Dramatic Theater, Kiev,
1920.
India ink and gouache on paper,
50.5 x 32.5 cm.
Collection G. Iu. Ivakin, Kiev.*

613
Vadim Meller
*Costume design for the Assyrian Dances
in* Masks, *1920.
Gouache on cardboard, 60 x 28 cm.
Collection G. Iu. Ivakin, Kiev.*

614
Aleksandr Vesnin
Costume design: a guard, for Jean Racine, Phèdre, *Kamernyi Theater, Moscow, 1921–22.*
Gouache and bronze powder on paper, 51.9 x 36.5 cm.
State Bakhrushin Museum, Moscow.

615
Aleksandr Vesnin
Costume design: Aricia, for Jean Racine, Phèdre, *Kamernyi Theater, Moscow, 1921–22.*
Gouache, whiting, and bronze powder on paper, 52.3 x 34.8 cm.
State Bakhrushin Museum, Moscow.

616
Vadim Meller
*Costume design: a worker, for Georg
Kaiser, Gas, Berezil' Theater, Kiev, 1923.
Watercolor, india ink, and pencil on
paper, 48 x 32 cm.
Private collection, Germany.*

617
Vadim Meller
*Costume design: an officer, for Georg
Kaiser, Gas, Berezil' Theater, Kiev, 1923.
Watercolor and india ink on paper,
45 x 21 cm.
Private collection, Germany.*

618
**Galina and
Ol'ga Chichagova**
Costume Design No. 7, *1921–22.*
Gouache on paper, 32 x 24.5 cm.
Private collection, Venice.

619
Ivan Puni
*Costume design: T, for theatricalized
opening of his solo show at Galerie
Der Sturm, Berlin, 1921.*
*Gouache, india ink, and graphite on
paper, 34.5 x 22 cm.*
Private collection, Zurich.

620
**Galina and
Ol'ga Chichagova**
Costume Design No. 6, *1921–22.*
Gouache on paper, 29.5 x 20.5 cm.
Private collection, Venice.

621
Ivan Puni
*Costume design: You, for theatricalized
opening of his solo show at Galerie
Der Sturm, Berlin, 1921.*
*Gouache, india ink, and graphite on
paper, 36 x 22 cm.*
Private collection, Zurich.

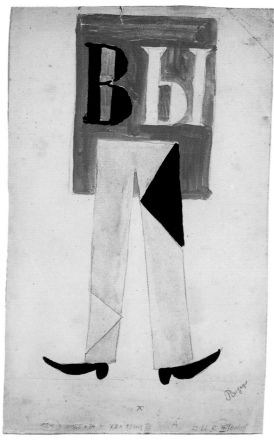

622
Georgii Iakulov
Set design for Charles Lecocq, Giroflé-
Girofla, Kamernyi Theater, Moscow,
1922.
Whiting, gouache, and pencil on paper,
37.5 x 44.6 cm.
State Bakhrushin Museum, Moscow.

623
Ivan Puni
Costume design: K (Red Dancer), for
theatricalized opening of his solo show at
Galerie Der Sturm, Berlin, 1921.
Gouache, india ink, and graphite on
paper, 24 x 16.5 cm.
Private collection, Zurich.

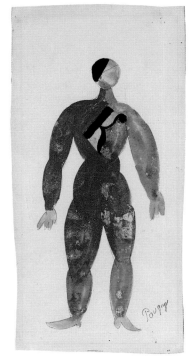

624
Aleksandr Rodchenko
Costume design: a bourgeois, for Aleksei
Gan (after Evgenii Zamiatin), We,
1919–21.
Pencil, gouache, and india ink on paper,
53.1 x 36.7 cm.
State Bakhrushin Museum, Moscow.

625
Aleksandr Rodchenko
Costume design: a policeman, for Aleksei
Gan (after Evgenii Zamiatin), We,
1919–21.
Pencil, gouache, and india ink on paper,
52.9 x 36.6 cm.
State Bakhrushin Museum, Moscow.

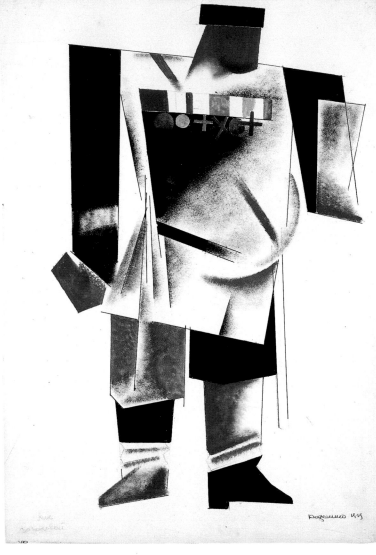

626
Varvara Stepanova
Costume design for Aleksandr Sukhovo-
Kobylin, The Death of Tarelkin,
State Institute of Theatrical Art,
Moscow, 1922.
India ink on paper, 35.5 x 34.5 cm.
State Bakhrushin Museum, Moscow.

627
Aleksandr Rodchenko
Costume design: a singer, for Aleksei Gan
(after Evgenii Zamiatin), We, *1919–21.*
Pencil, tempera, and india ink on paper,
53 x 36.7 cm.
State Bakhrushin Museum, Moscow.

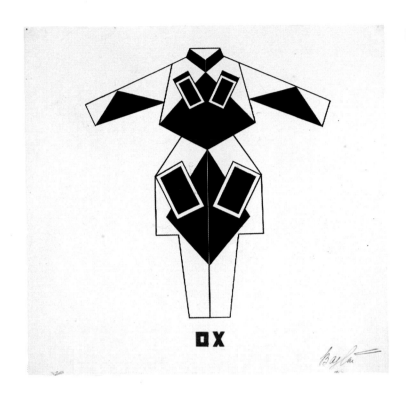

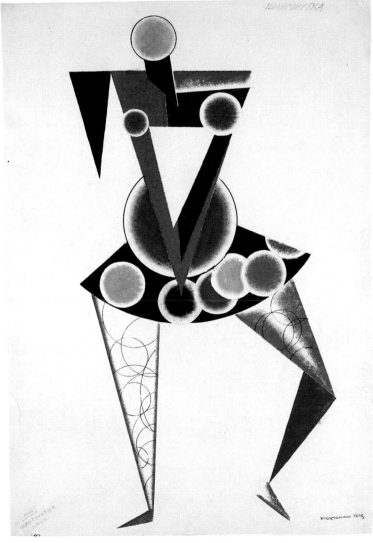

628
Liubov' Popova
Set design for Fernand Crommelynck,
Le Cocu magnifique, *State Institute of*
Theatrical Art, Moscow, 1922.
Gouache on paper, 50 x 69 cm.
State Tret'iakov Gallery, Moscow.
Gift George Costakis.

629
Liubov' Popova
Production Clothing for Actor No. 7,
for Fernand Crommelynck, Le Cocu
magnifique, *State Institute of*
Theatrical Art, Moscow, 1922.
Ink, gouache, varnish, and collage on
paper, 32.8 x 23.3 cm.
Collection Merrill C. Berman.

630
Liubov' Popova
Set design for Sergei Tret'iakov,
The Earth in Turmoil, *Meierkhol'd*
Theater, Moscow, 1923–24.
Photomontage, gouache, newspaper, and
photographic paper collage on plywood,
49 x 82.7 cm.
Collection George Costakis, Germany.

631
Liubov' Popova
Costume design for Sergei Tret'iakov,
The Earth in Turmoil, *Meierkhol'd*
Theater, Moscow, 1923–24.
Watercolor, india ink, and pencil on
paper, 34.5 x 25.5 cm.
Private collection, Germany.

632
Liubov' Popova
Costume design for Sergei Tret'iakov,
The Earth in Turmoil, *Meierkhol'd*
Theater, Moscow, 1923–24.
Watercolor, india ink, and pencil on
paper, 25.5 x 17.4 cm.
Private collection, Germany.

633
Aleksandr Vesnin
*Sketch for an Electron robot for G. K.
Chesterton,* The Man Who Was
Thursday, *Kamernyi Theater, Moscow,
1922–23.
*Gouache on paper, 20 x 13.5 cm.
State Bakhrushin Museum, Moscow.*

634
Aleksandr Vesnin
*Costume design for a man, for G. K.
Chesterton,* The Man Who Was
Thursday, *Kamernyi Theater, Moscow,
1922–23.
*Gouache, india ink, and pencil on paper,
39.7 x 27.5 cm.
State Bakhrushin Museum, Moscow.*

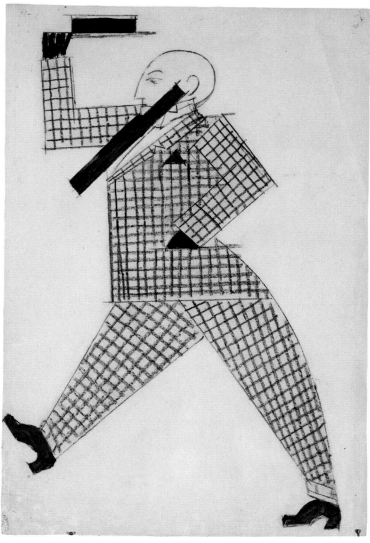

635
Aleksandr Vesnin
*Costume design for a woman, for G. K.
Chesterton,* The Man Who Was
Thursday, *Kamernyi Theater, Moscow,
1922–23.
Gouache, india ink, collage, and pencil
on paper, 39.5 x 27.3 cm.
State Bakhrushin Museum, Moscow.*

636
Aleksandr Vesnin
*Drawing of the transformation of the
stage set during the performance, for
G. K. Chesterton,* The Man Who Was
Thursday, *Kamernyi Theater, Moscow,
1922–23.
Pencil on paper, 27 x 18 cm.
State Shchusev Museum, Moscow.*

637
Aleksandr Vesnin
*Sketch for furniture and props for G. K.
Chesterton,* The Man Who Was
Thursday, *Kamernyi Theater, Moscow,
1922–23.
Gouache and pencil on paper, 19 x 13 cm.
State Bakhrushin Museum, Moscow.*

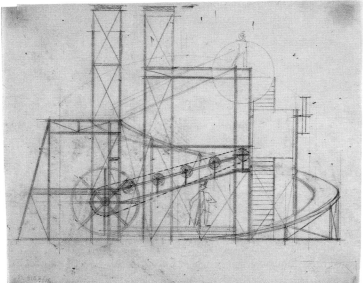

638
Konstantin Vialov
Costume design for a man, for Vasilii
Kamenskii, Sten'ka Razin, *Theater of*
the Revolution, Moscow, 1923–24.
Watercolor and india ink on paper,
25 x 21 cm.
Private collection, Germany.

639
Konstantin Vialov
Costume design: ironworkers, for Vasilii
Kamenskii, Sten'ka Razin, *Theater of*
the Revolution, Moscow, 1923–24.
Watercolor, gouache, india ink, and
pencil on paper, 35.5 x 26.5 cm.
Private collection, Germany.

640
Anatolii Petritskii
Costume design for Giacomo Puccini,
Turandot, *State Opera, Khar'kov, 1928.*
India ink, whiting, collage, and pencil on
paper, 72 x 52 cm.
Private collection, Germany.

641
Anatolii Petritskii
Costume design for Reingol'd Glière,
The Red Poppy, *State Opera, Khar'kov,*
1927.
Watercolor, gold, silver, and pencil on
paper, 72 x 52 cm.
Private collection, Germany.

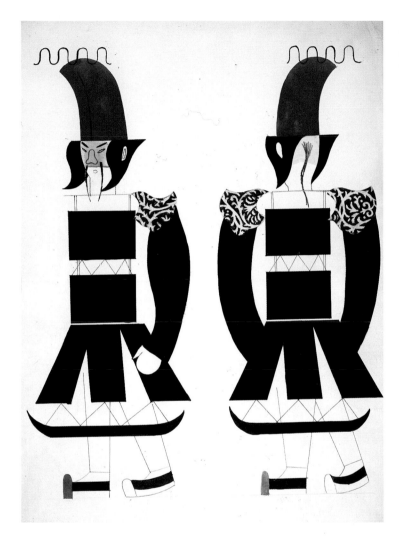

642
Georgii and Vladimir Stenberg
Costume design for Charles Lecocq,
Le Jour et la nuit, *Kamernyi Theater, Moscow, 1926.*
Gouache and whiting on plywood,
60.8 x 33.8 cm.
State Bakhrushin Museum, Moscow.

643
Georgii and Vladimir Stenberg
Costume design for Charles Lecocq,
Le Jour et la nuit, *Kamernyi Theater, Moscow, 1926.*
Gouache on plywood, 61 x 34 cm.
State Bakhrushin Museum, Moscow.

644
Georgii and Vladimir Stenberg
Costume design for Charles Lecocq,
Le Jour et la nuit, *Kamernyi Theater, Moscow,*
1926.
Pencil and gouache on paper,
36.2 x 16 cm.
State Bakhrushin Museum, Moscow.

645
Georgii and Vladimir Stenberg
Costume design for Charles Lecocq,
Le Jour et la nuit, *Kamernyi Theater, Moscow,*
1926.
Pencil, india ink, and gouache on paper,
36.2 x 16.1 cm.
State Bakhrushin Museum, Moscow.

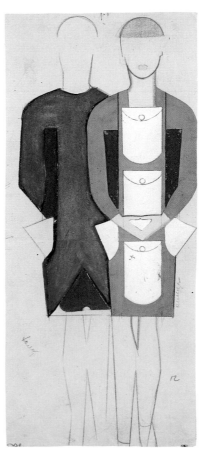

646
Anatolii Petritskii
Costume design: rowers, for Viktor Oranskii, The Soccer Player, *State Opera, Khar'kov, 1929.*
Gouache, pencil, india ink, and watercolor on paper, 72. 8 x 55 cm.
State Bakhrushin Museum, Moscow.

647
Anatolii Petritskii
Costume design: soccer players, for Viktor Oranskii, The Soccer Player, *State Opera, Khar'kov, 1929.*
Gouache, india ink, and watercolor on paper, 72. 5 x 55 cm.
State Bakhrushin Museum, Moscow.

648
Valentina Khodasevich
*Costume design: captain of the Soviet
soccer team, for Dmitrii Shostakovich,*
The Golden Age, *Theater of Opera
and Ballet, Leningrad, 1930.
Watercolor and pencil on paper,
28 x 18 cm.
Private collection, Germany.*

649
**Tat'iana Bruni and Georgii
Korshikov**
*Design for a sports costume for Dmitrii
Shostakovich,* Bolt, *Theater of Opera
and Ballet, Leningrad, 1930–31.
Gouache and india ink on paper,
37.4 x 27.4 cm.
Private collection, Germany.*

650
Aleksandr Sashin
Costume design for Nikolai Gogol', The Inspector General, House of Publishing, Leningrad, 1927.
Watercolor on paper, 48.7 x 35.1 cm.
State Russian Museum, St. Petersburg.

651
Aleksandr Sashin
Costume design: Bobchinskii, for Nikolai Gogol', The Inspector General, House of Publishing, Leningrad, 1927.
Watercolor on paper, 51.2 x 34.3 cm.
State Russian Museum, St. Petersburg.

652
Aleksandr Rodchenko
Architectural Fantasy; *section, 1920.*
Colored india ink on paper, 26 x 21 cm.
State Tret'iakov Gallery, Moscow.

653
Aleksandr Rodchenko
Architectural Fantasy; *plan of the*
Soviet of Deputies building, 1920.
Colored india ink on paper, 26.2 x 21 cm.
State Tret'iakov Gallery, Moscow.

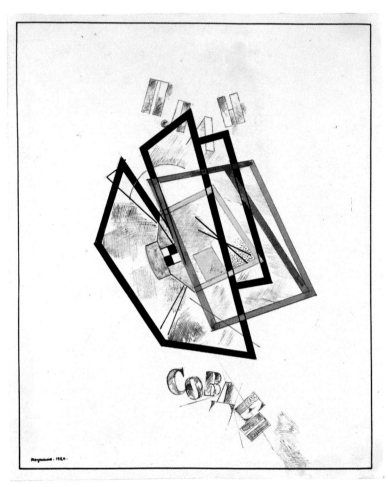

654
Nikolai Ladovskii
Experimental project, Zhivskul'ptarkh:
communal house; elevation, 1920.
Pencil, colored pencil, and colored india
ink on tracing paper mounted on paper,
31 x 40 cm.
State Shchusev Museum, Moscow.

655
Nikolai Ladovskii
Experimental project, Zhivskul'ptarkh:
communal house; section, 1920.
India ink and pencil on paper,
39 x 31.3 cm.
State Shchusev Museum, Moscow.

656
Nikolai Ladovskii
Architectural Fantasy No. 5, 1919.
Graphite pencil on paper, 35 x 22 cm.
State Tret'iakov Gallery, Moscow.

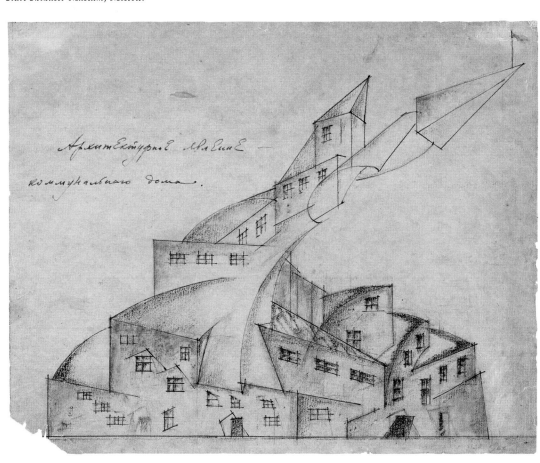

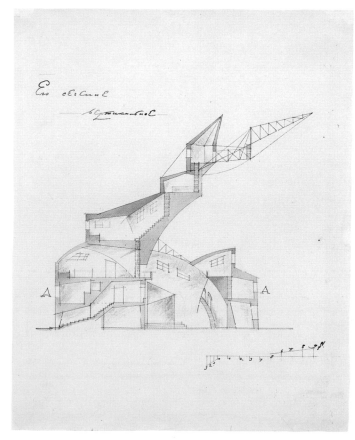

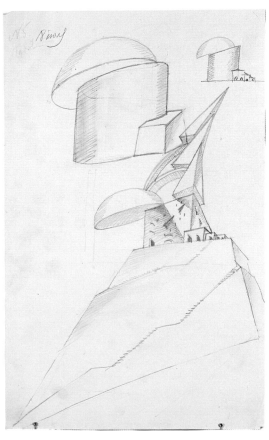

657
Vladimir Krinskii
Experimental project, Zhivskul'ptarkh:
Temple of Communion among Nations;
plan, section, and elevation, 1919.
India ink and watercolor on cardboard,
33 x 41 cm.
State Shchusev Museum, Moscow.

658
Vladimir Krinskii
Experimental project, Zhivskul'ptarkh:
communal house; perspective, 1920.
India ink, watercolor, and pencil on
tracing paper, 11 x 14 cm.
State Shchusev Museum, Moscow.

659
Vladimir Krinskii
Experimental project, Zhivskul'ptarkh:
Temple of Communion among Nations
(variant); perspective and plan, 1919.
India ink and watercolor on paper,
16.5 x 11.5 cm.
State Shchusev Museum, Moscow.

660
Vladimir Fidman
Architectural Fantasy No. 6;
plan and perspective sketches, 1919.
Pencil and sepia on paper, 36.5 x 22.8 cm.
State Tret'iakov Gallery, Moscow.

661
Nikolai Istselenov
Architectural Fantasy No. 2;
general plan and elevation, 1919.
Graphite pencil on paper, 36.5 x 23 cm.
State Tret'iakov Gallery, Moscow.

662
Vladimir Fidman
Architectural Fantasy No. 9;
elevations, 1919.
Colored pencil on paper, 35 x 22 cm.
State Tret'iakov Gallery, Moscow.

663
Nikolai Istselenov
Architectural Fantasy No. 2;
elevation and perspective, 1919.
Graphite pencil on tracing paper,
35 x 22 cm.
State Tret'iakov Gallery, Moscow.

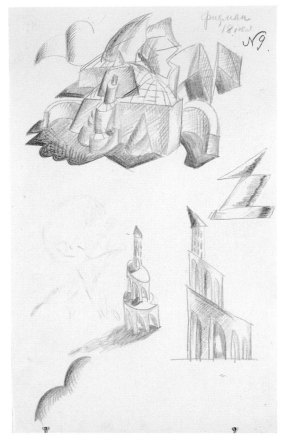

664
Boris Korolev
Architectural Fantasy, *1919.*
India ink and colored pencil on paper,
35.3 x 22 cm.
State Tret'iakov Gallery, Moscow.

665
Boris Korolev
Architectural Fantasy No. 13; *sketches*
of the plan and perspective, 1919.
Graphite pencil on cardboard,
37 x 23 cm.
State Tret'iakov Gallery, Moscow.

666
Boris Korolev
Architectural Fantasy, *1919.*
India ink and colored pencil on paper,
35.3 x 22 cm.
State Tret'iakov Gallery, Moscow.

667
Boris Korolev
Architectural Fantasy No. 1;
plan and elevation, 1919.
Graphite pencil on cardboard,
37 x 23 cm.
State Tret'iakov Gallery, Moscow.

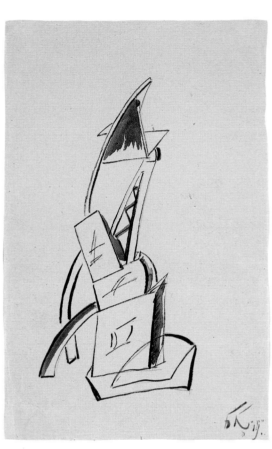

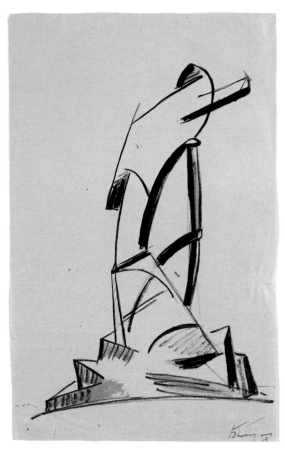

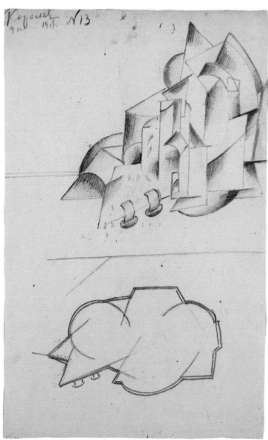

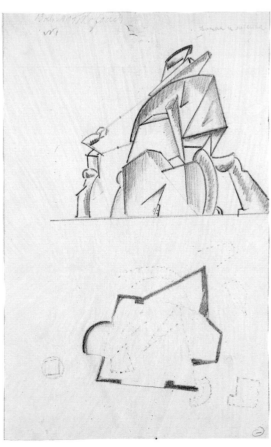

668
Iakov Chernikhov
Architectural Fantasy, *from the series*
Architectural Fantasies: 101
Compositions, *1920–30.*
Gouache on paper, 30 x 24 cm.
International Iakov Chernikhov
Foundation.

669
Iakov Chernikhov
Composition, *1920s.*
Gouache on paper, 29.8 x 24.5 cm.
International Iakov Chernikhov
Foundation.

670
Iakov Chernikhov
Experimental Composition, *from the*
series The Foundations of
Contemporary Architecture, *1920–28.*
Watercolor and india ink on paper,
29.9 x 23.8 cm.
International Iakov Chernikhov
Foundation.

671
Iakov Chernikhov
Composition, *1920s.*
Gouache on paper, 30 x 23.8 cm.
International Iakov Chernikhov
Foundation.

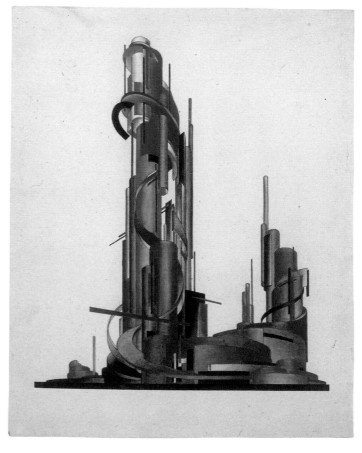

672
Iosif Chaikov
Project for an Arch, *drawing for*
Tractor Factory, *1922.*
India ink and graphite pencil on paper,
33.4 x 23.4 cm.
State Tret'iakov Gallery, Moscow.

673
Iosif Chaikov
Electrifier, *study for a sculpture*
(variant), 1921.
Watercolor, india ink, and graphite
pencil on paper, 34.6 x 25.2 cm.
State Tret'iakov Gallery, Moscow.

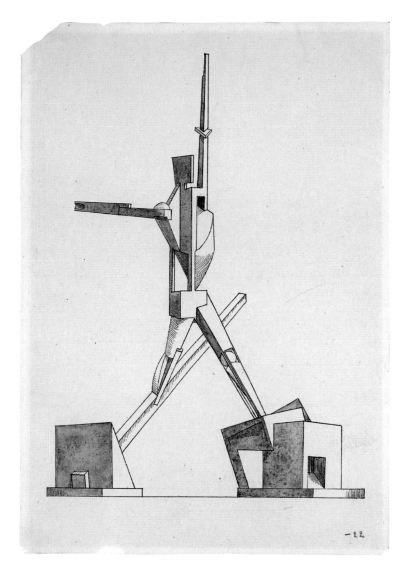

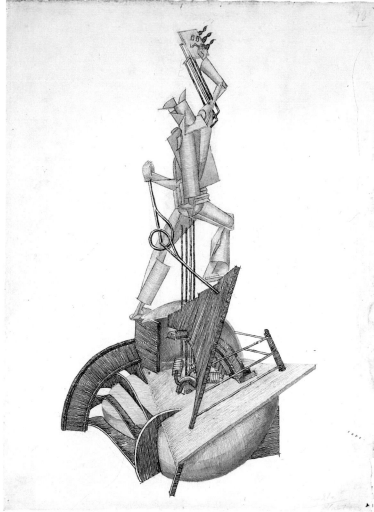

674
Ivan Lamtsov
*Student assignment, Vkhutemas
(workshop of Nikolai Ladovskii): project
for a grain elevator; perspective, 1922.
Pencil on paper, 21 x 33 cm.
State Shchusev Museum, Moscow.*

675
Lidiia Komarova
*Student assignment, Vkhutemas, on the
demonstration of mass and weight, early
1920s.
India ink on paper, 71 x 53 cm.
State Shchusev Museum, Moscow.*

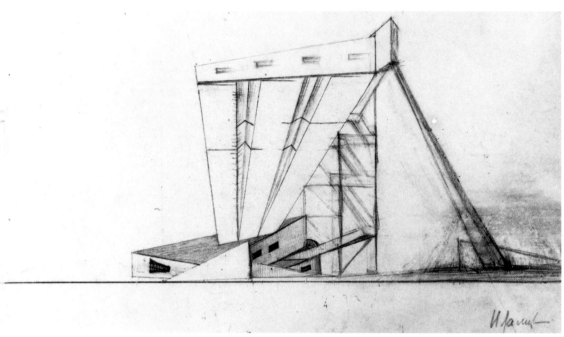

676
Ivan Lamtsov
*Student assignment, Vkhutemas
(workshop of Nikolai Ladovskii):* Beam
on Two Points of Support; *elevation,
1922.*
*India ink, charcoal, and pencil on paper
mounted on cardboard, 30 x 64 cm.
State Shchusev Museum, Moscow.*

677
Lidiia Komarova
Student assignment, Vkhutemas:
Trackwalker's House; *plan, section, and
elevation, 1923.*
*Pencil on paper, 45 x 49 cm.
State Shchusev Museum, Moscow.*

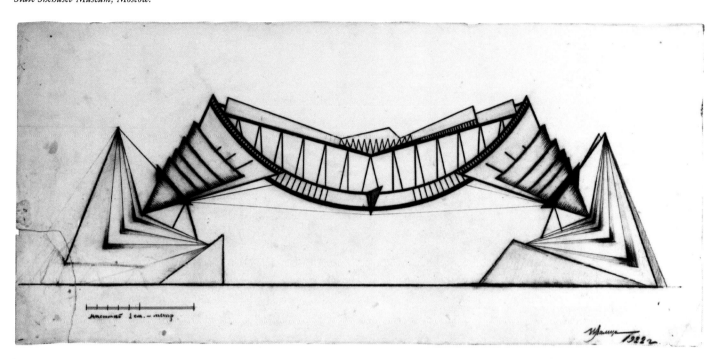

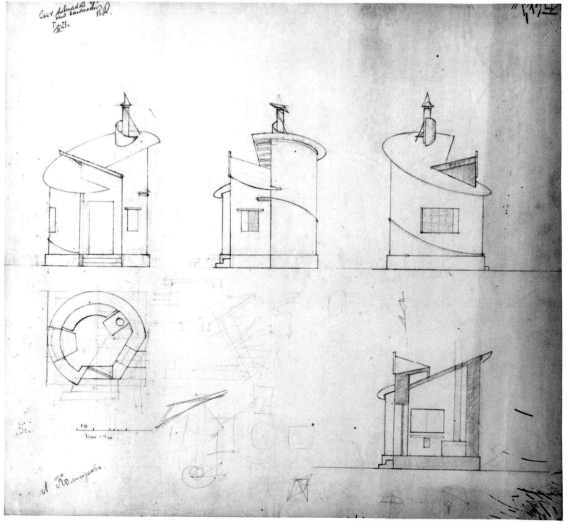

678
Vladimir Krinskii
Experimental project for Vesenkha, the
Council of the National Economy,
Moscow; elevation, 1922–23.
Pencil and colored pencil on tracing paper,
30.5 x 13 cm.
State Shchusev Museum, Moscow.

679
Aleksandr, Leonid, and
Viktor Vesnin
Model of competition project for the Palace
of Labor, Moscow, 1922–23,
reconstruction 1980.
Strathmore board, basswood core, and
plywood base, approx. 61 x 76.2 x
45.7 cm.
Los Angeles County Museum of Art.

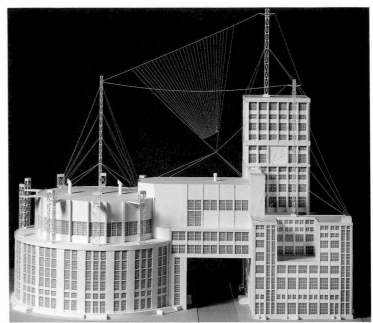

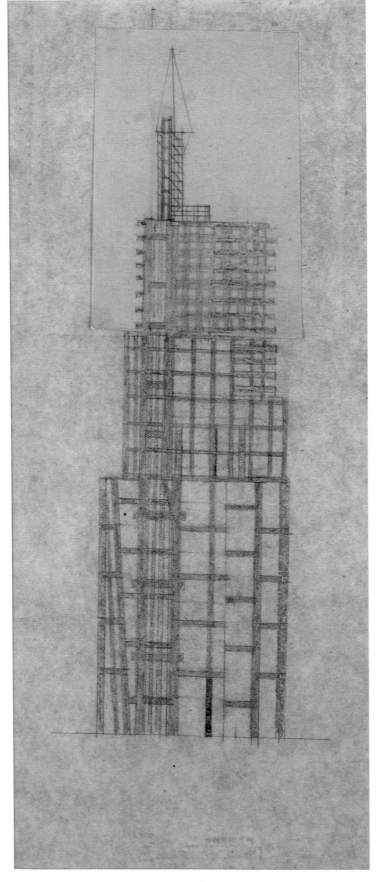

680
Vladimir Krinskii
Emblem of Asnova, 1923.
India ink on paper mounted on
cardboard, 35 x 48 cm.
State Shchusev Museum, Moscow.

681
Aleksandr, Leonid, and
Viktor Vesnin
Competition project for the Palace of
Labor, Moscow; elevation, 1922–23.
Pencil on tracing paper, 53 x 60 cm.
State Shchusev Museum, Moscow.

682
Aleksandr, Leonid, and
Viktor Vesnin
Competition project for the Palace of
Labor, Moscow; perspective, 1922–23.
Pencil on tracing paper, 16.8 x 21 cm.
State Shchusev Museum, Moscow.

683
Konstantin Mel'nikov
Competition project for the Moscow
bureau of Leningrad Pravda; *elevation*
showing each floor opened up to its
maximum extension, 1924.
India ink on paper, 67.5 × 51 cm.
State Shchusev Museum, Moscow.

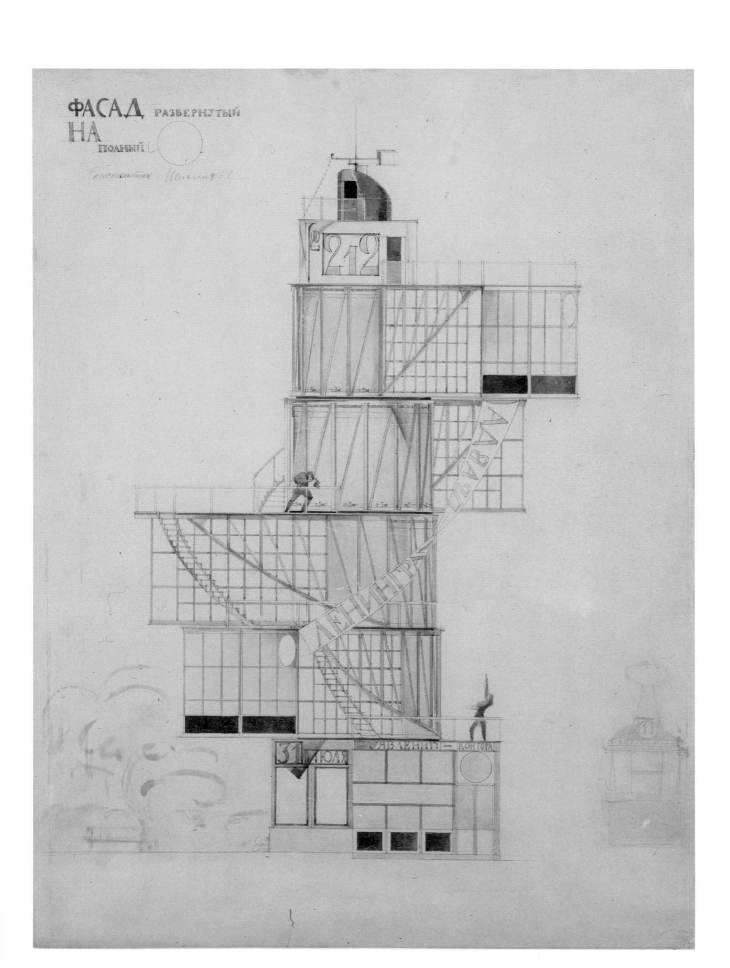

684
Aleksandr and Viktor Vesnin
Competition project for the Moscow bureau of Leningrad Pravda; *perspective, 1924.*
Pencil on paper, 70.5 x 36 cm.
State Shchusev Museum, Moscow.

685
Il'ia Golosov
Competition project for the Moscow bureau of Leningrad Pravda; *axonometric section, 1924.*
India ink and watercolor on paper, 67 x 51.5 cm.
State Shchusev Museum, Moscow.

686
Viktor and Aleksandr Vesnin
Project for an airplane hangar; elevation, 1924.
Pencil on tracing paper, 13.5 x 50 cm.
State Shchusev Museum, Moscow.

687
Aleksandr Vesnin
Design for decorations for the construction site of a monument to Karl Marx; plan of the square, plan, and opening up of the decorations, 1919–20.
Colored pencil, whiting, gouache, and pencil on tracing paper, 69 x 101 cm.
State Shchusev Museum, Moscow.

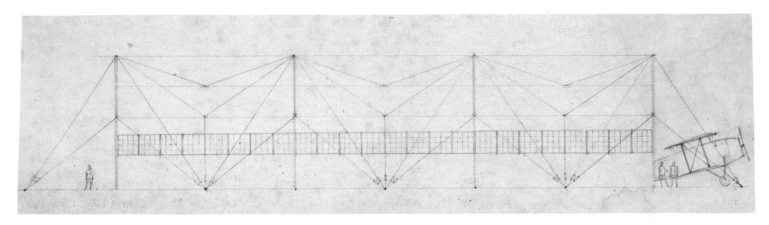

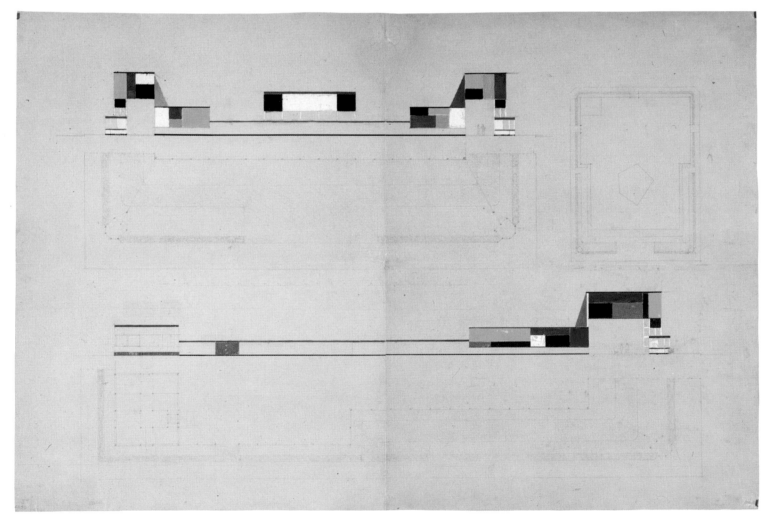

688
Georgii Krutikov
*Diploma project, Vkhutemas (workshop of
Nikolai Ladovskii),* A City on Aerial
Paths of Communication: *communal
house; perspective, 1928.
India ink and pencil on photographic
paper, 114.5 x 88 cm.
State Shchusev Museum, Moscow.*

689-690
Georgii Krutikov
*Diploma project, Vkhutemas (workshop of
Nikolai Ladovskii)*, A City on Aerial
Paths of Communication; *table no. 1:*
A Mobile Living Unit; *table no. 2:*
Organization of the Dwellings:
Variant No. 1; *table no. 3:*
Organization of the Dwellings:
Variant No. 2; *table no. 4:*
Organization of the City, *1928.*
*Collage, paper, india ink, and
photographs on cardboard, 47.8 x 143 cm.
State Shchusev Museum, Moscow.*

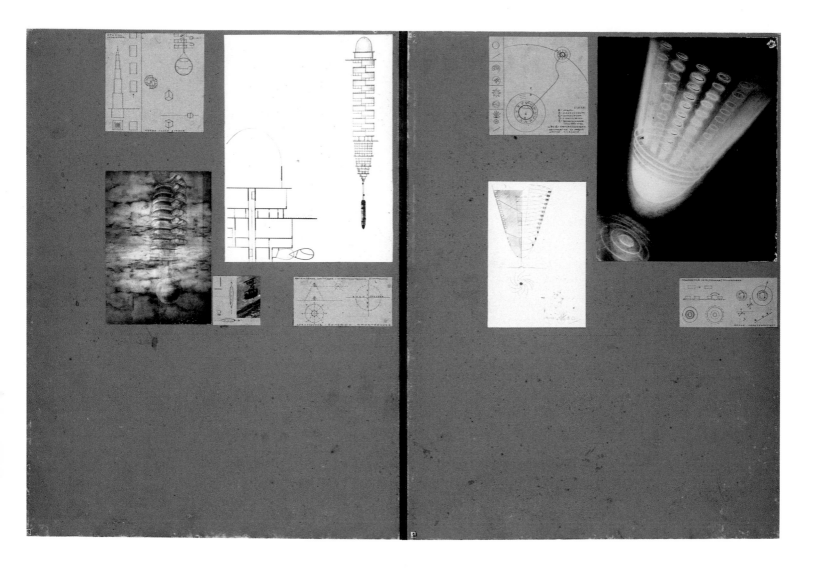

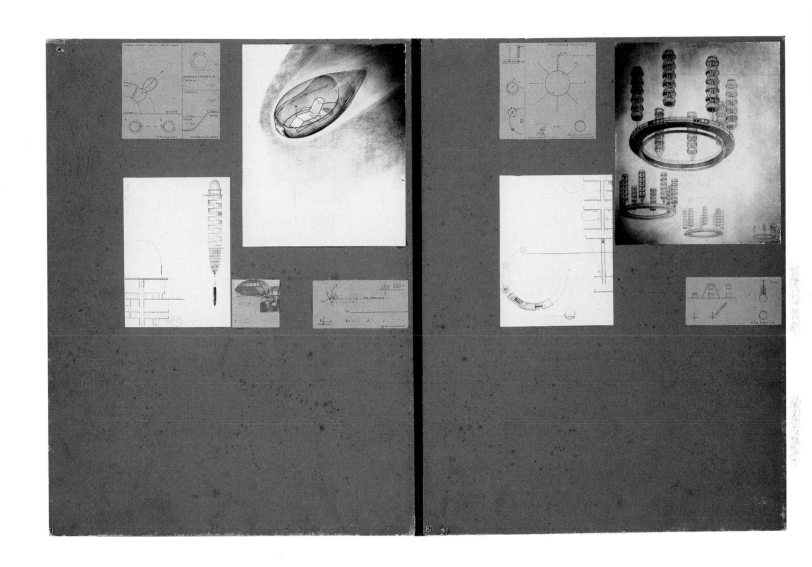

691-692
Georgii Krutikov
Diploma project, Vkhutemas (workshop of Nikolai Ladovskii), A City on Aerial Paths of Communication; *table no. 1:* Visual Distortion of a Moving Form; *table no. 2:* Composition of Moving Constructions; *table no. 3:* Form Generation of a Dynamic Element; *table no. 4:* Evolution of the Form of the Automobile and the Railroad Train, *1928.*
Collage, paper, india ink, and photographs on cardboard, 47.8 x 143 cm.
State Shchusev Museum, Moscow.

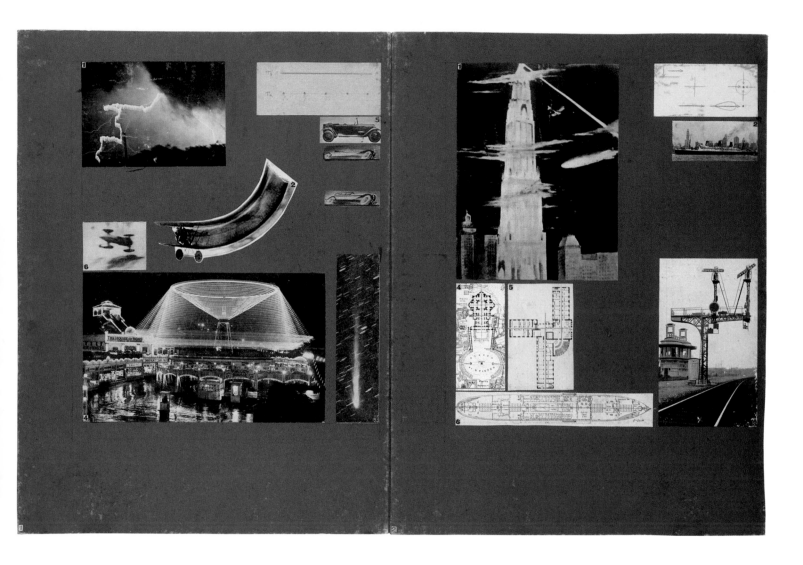

693
Aleksandr Nikol'skii with his students, N. Miturich, A. Petelin, and D. Savitskii
Project for Cornerstone, *a monument to Lenin in a square at the Finland Station, Leningrad; elevation, 1924. Ink, pencil, and watercolor on cardboard, 63.5 x 90.5 cm.*
State Saltykov-Shchedrin Public Library, St. Petersburg.

694
Aleksandr Nikol'skii, Ivan Bel'dovskii, Vladimir Gal'perin, and Aleksandr Krestin
Project for the 500-seat Labor Meeting Hall; elevation, plans, and section, 1926–27. Watercolor and india ink on cardboard, 51.7 x 74.4 cm.
Manuscript Division, State Saltykov-Shchedrin Public Library, St. Petersburg.

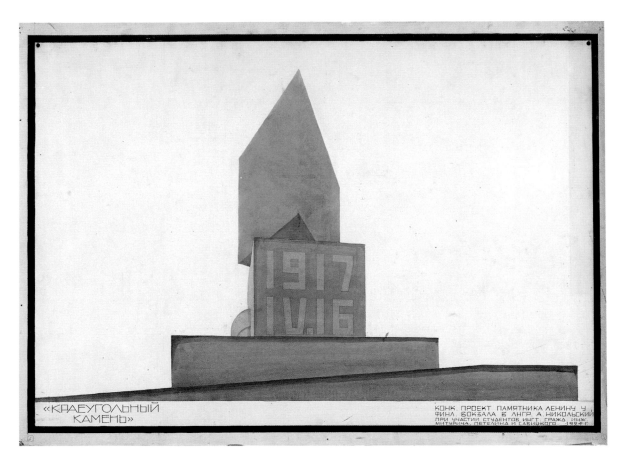

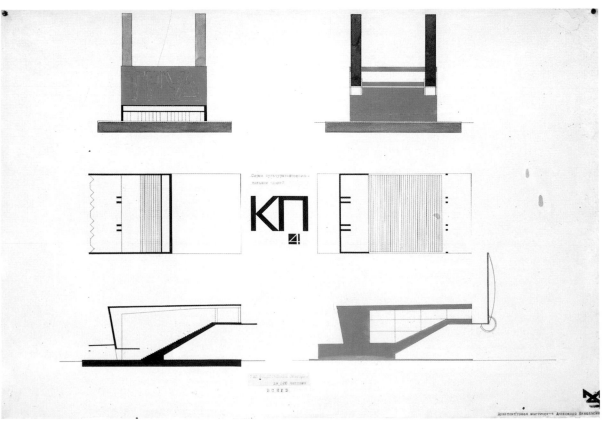

695
Aleksandr Nikol'skii
Project for a tram stop with a barbershop and restrooms on a square in Leningrad; perspective, elevation, section, and plan of the square, 1927.
Pencil and ink on cardboard, 47.8 x 69.9 cm.
State Saltykov-Shchedrin Public Library, St. Petersburg.

696
Aleksandr Nikol'skii
Project for a movie theater and a restaurant; plans, elevations, sections, and perspectives, 1926–27.
India ink on cardboard, 49.3 x 72 cm.
State Saltykov-Shchedrin Public Library, St. Petersburg.

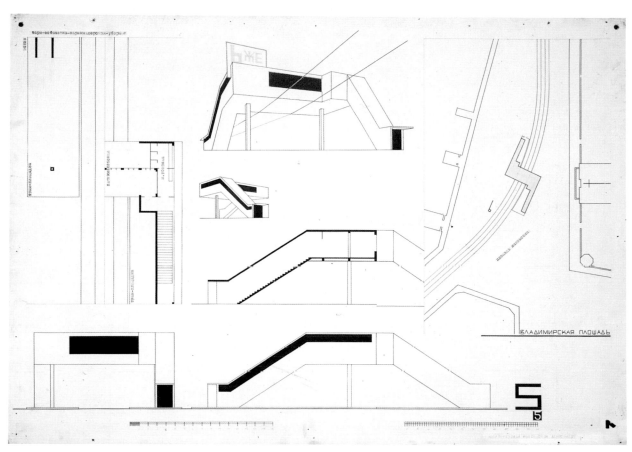

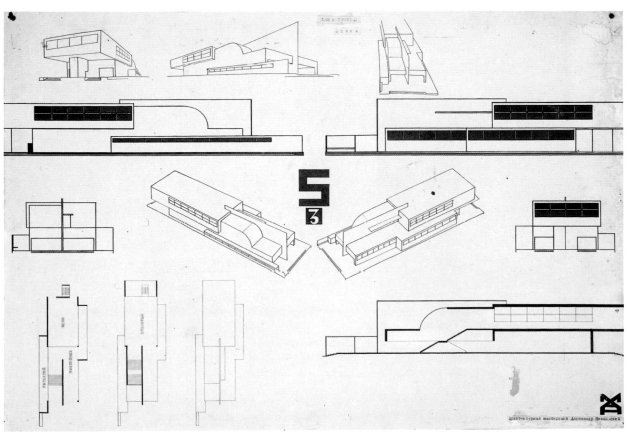

699
Il'ia Golosov
*Competition project for the Lenin House of
the People, Ivanovo-Voznesensk;
elevation, 1924.
India ink, gouache, and colored india ink
on paper mounted on cardboard,
31.2 x 72.9 cm.
State Shchusev Museum, Moscow.*

700
Il'ia Golosov
*Competition project for the Elektrobank
building, Moscow; perspective, 1926.
India ink and gouache on paper,
68 x 98.5 cm.
State Shchusev Museum, Moscow.*

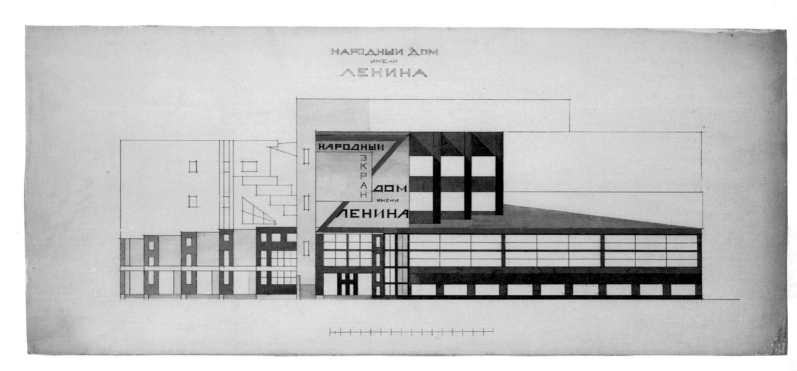

701
Nikolai Sokolov
*Vkhutemas project (workshop of
Aleksandr Vesnin): resort hotel; plans,
elevation, sections, and axonometric, 1928.
India ink, colored india ink, whiting,
and collage on paper, 55.5 x 88 cm.
State Shchusev Museum, Moscow.*

702
Petr Sokolov
*Project for an advertisement booth;
elevations, 1926.
India ink on paper, 51.5 x 36.5 cm.
State Museum of the History of the City
of St. Petersburg.*

703
Petr Sokolov
*Project for an advertisement booth;
elevation and plan, 1926.
Watercolor and india ink on paper,
51.5 x 36.5 cm.
State Museum of the History of the City
of St. Petersburg.*

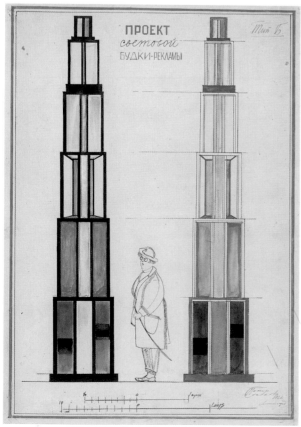

704
Nikolai Sokolov
Vkhutemas project (workshop of
Aleksandr Vesnin): resort hotel;
perspective, 1928.
India ink, watercolor, gouache, and
whiting on paper, 109 x 36 cm.
State Shchusev Museum, Moscow.

705
Nikolai Sokolov
Vkhutemas project (workshop of
Aleksandr Vesnin): resort hotel;
axonometric, 1928.
India ink, watercolor, gouache, and
whiting on paper, 109 x 36 cm.
State Shchusev Museum, Moscow.

706
Konstantin Mel'nikov
Mel'nikov's house; plans of the cellar, first and second floors, and mezzanine; section, elevation, and site plan, 1927.
Gouache on blueprint,
29.7 x 90.7 cm.
Historical-Architectural Archive, Moscow.

707
Konstantin Mel'nikov
Mel'nikov's house; explanatory note on the project, 1927.
Red and violet ink and pencil on paper, 34.5 x 20.3 cm.
Historical-Architectural Archive, Moscow.

708
Konstantin Mel'nikov
Mel'nikov's house; site plan, plans of the floors and mezzanine, section, and elevation, 1927.
Gouache, red and black ink, pencil, india ink, and watercolor on Whatman paper, 33 x 61 cm.
Historical-Architectural Archive, Moscow.

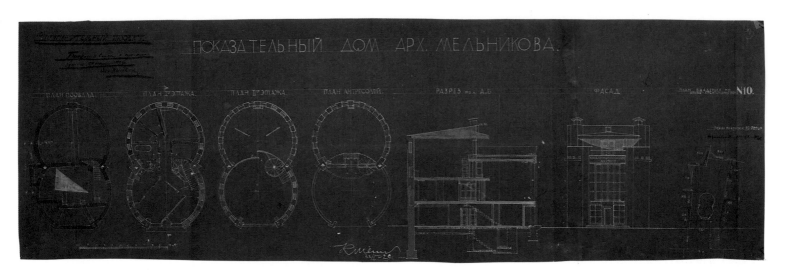

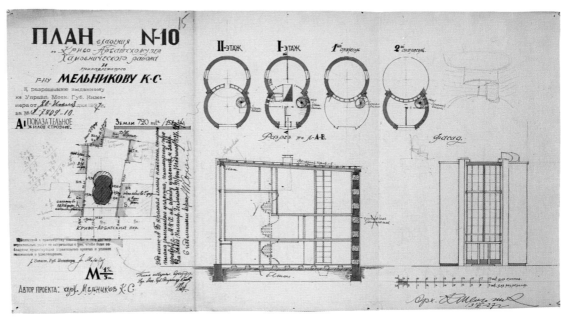

709
Konstantin Mel'nikov
Club of the Rubber Factory, Moscow; site plan and plan of the first floor, 1927.
Gouache and india ink on Whatman paper, 32.8 x 89.8 cm.
Historical-Architectural Archive, Moscow.

710
Konstantin Mel'nikov
Club of the Rubber Factory, Moscow; elevation, 1927.
India ink on Whatman paper, 32.9 x 76.5 cm.
Historical-Architectural Archive, Moscow.

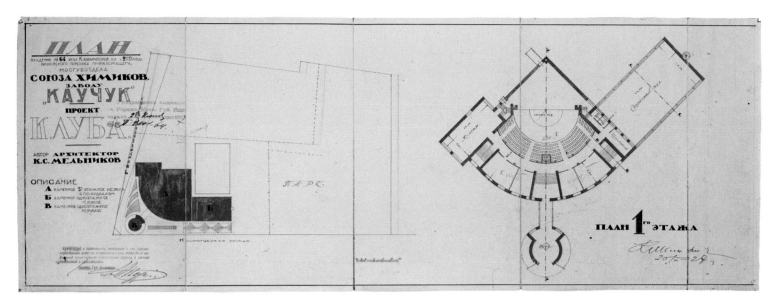

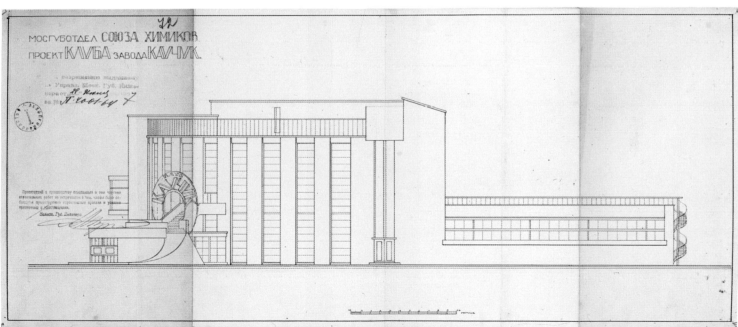

711
Aleksandr, Leonid, and
Viktor Vesnin
First version of competition project for the
Lenin Library, Moscow; perspective, 1928.
India ink on paper, 67 x 99 cm.
State Shchusev Museum, Moscow.

712
Konstantin Mel'nikov
Club of the Freedom Factory, Moscow;
elevation, 1927.
India ink on tracing paper,
32.7 x 80.7 cm.
Historical-Architectural Archive,
Moscow.

713
Panteleimon Golosov
Competition project for the Pravda
printing plant and publishing center,
Moscow (variant); perspective, 1930–35.
Pencil on waxed paper, 30.5 x 51.4 cm.
State Shchusev Museum, Moscow.

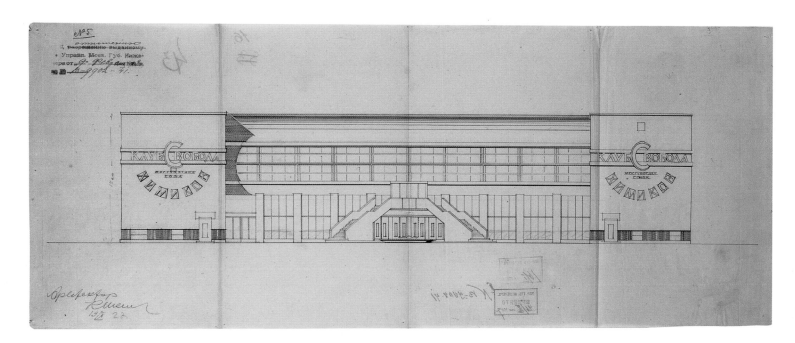

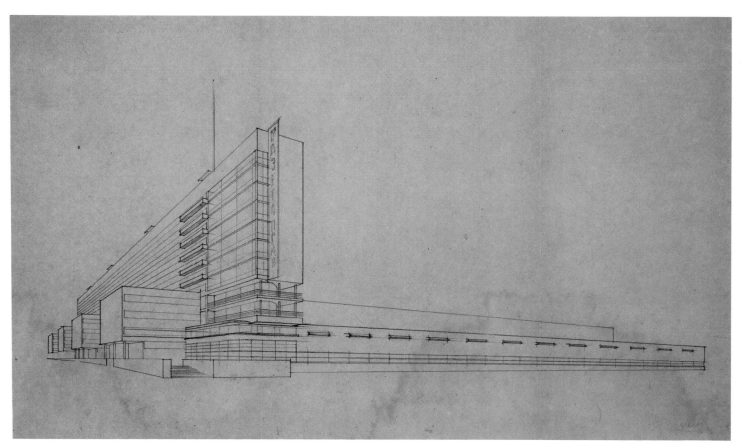

714
Ivan Leonidov
*Competition project for the Proletarskii
district Palace of Culture, Moscow;
general plan of the gymnasium, 1930.
Whiting and collage on paper mounted
on cardboard, 35 x 33 cm.
State Shchusev Museum, Moscow.*

715
Ivan Leonidov
*Competition project for the Proletarskii
district Palace of Culture, Moscow;
auditorium, elevation, 1930.
Whiting and collage on paper mounted
on cardboard, 35 x 33 cm.
State Shchusev Museum, Moscow.*

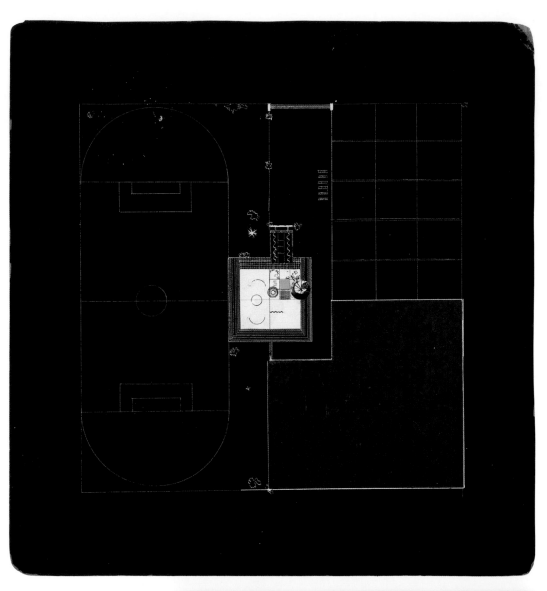

716
Ivan Leonidov
Competition project for the Proletarskii
district Palace of Culture, Moscow;
gymnasium, elevation, 1930.
Whiting and collage on paper mounted
on cardboard, 33 x 35 cm.
State Shchusev Museum, Moscow.

716
Ivan Leonidov
Competition project for the Proletarskii
district Palace of Culture, Moscow;
gymnasium, elevation, 1930.
Whiting and collage on paper mounted
on cardboard, 33 x 35 cm.
State Shchusev Museum, Moscow.

717
Aleksandr Deineka
Poster, Let's Turn Moscow into a
Model Socialist City of the
Proletariat!, *1931.*
Lithograph in two parts,
each 103 x 72 cm.
Lenin Library, Moscow.

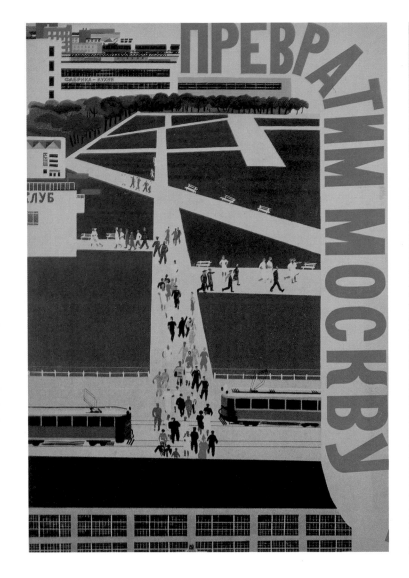

Aru team: Nikolai Beseda, Georgii Krutikov, Vitalii Lavrov, and Valentin Popov with Aleksandr Deineka (artist)

Competition project for the Palace of Soviets, Moscow; perspective, February–May 1931.
India ink, gouache, whiting, and pencil on paper, 118 x 118 cm.
State Shchusev Museum, Moscow.

719
Naum Gabo and
Antoine Pevsner
Competition project for the Palace of
Soviets, Moscow; section and main
elevation, July–December 1931.
India ink and pencil on paper,
96.5 x 147.2 cm.
State Shchusev Museum, Moscow.

720
Naum Gabo and
Antoine Pevsner
Competition project for the Palace of
Soviets, Moscow; plan and section,
July–December 1931.
India ink on paper, 98.3 x 85.5 cm.
State Shchusev Museum, Moscow.

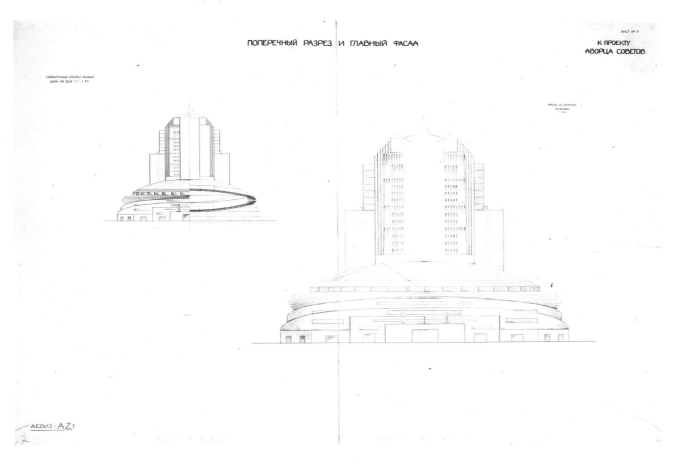

ПОПЕРЕЧНЫЙ РАЗРЕЗ И ГЛАВНЫЙ ФАСАД

К ПРОЕКТУ
АВОРЦА СОВЕТОВ

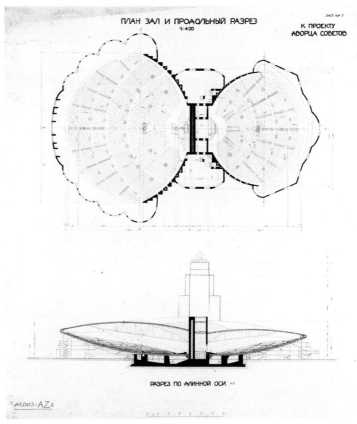

ПЛАН ЗАЛ И ПРОДОЛЬНЫЙ РАЗРЕЗ
1:400

К ПРОЕКТУ
АВОРЦА СОВЕТОВ

РАЗРЕЗ ПО ДЛИННОЙ ОСИ

721
Aleksandr Nikol'skii
Competition project for the Palace of Soviets, Moscow; section and elevation, February–May 1931.
India ink, gouache, and collage on paper, 71.6 x 95.8 cm.
State Shchusev Museum, Moscow.

722
Aleksandr Nikol'skii
Competition project for the Palace of Soviets, Moscow; sections and elevation, February–May 1931.
India ink, pencil, and collage on paper, 70.7 x 94.7 cm.
State Shchusev Museum, Moscow.

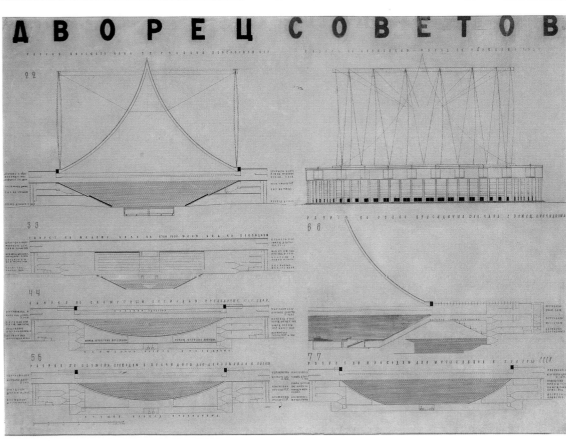

Moisei Ginzburg, Gustav Hassenpflug, and Solomon Lisagor

Competition project for the Palace of Soviets, Moscow; axonometric and perspective, March–July 1932. India ink and hand-colored photographs on paper, 97.2 x 96.5 cm. State Shchusev Museum, Moscow.

Moisei Ginzburg, Gustav Hassenpflug, and Solomon Lisagor
Competition project for the Palace of Soviets, Moscow; situational plan, axonometric, March–July 1932. India ink, watercolor, gouache, and collage on paper, 97.2 x 97.2 cm. State Shchusev Museum, Moscow.

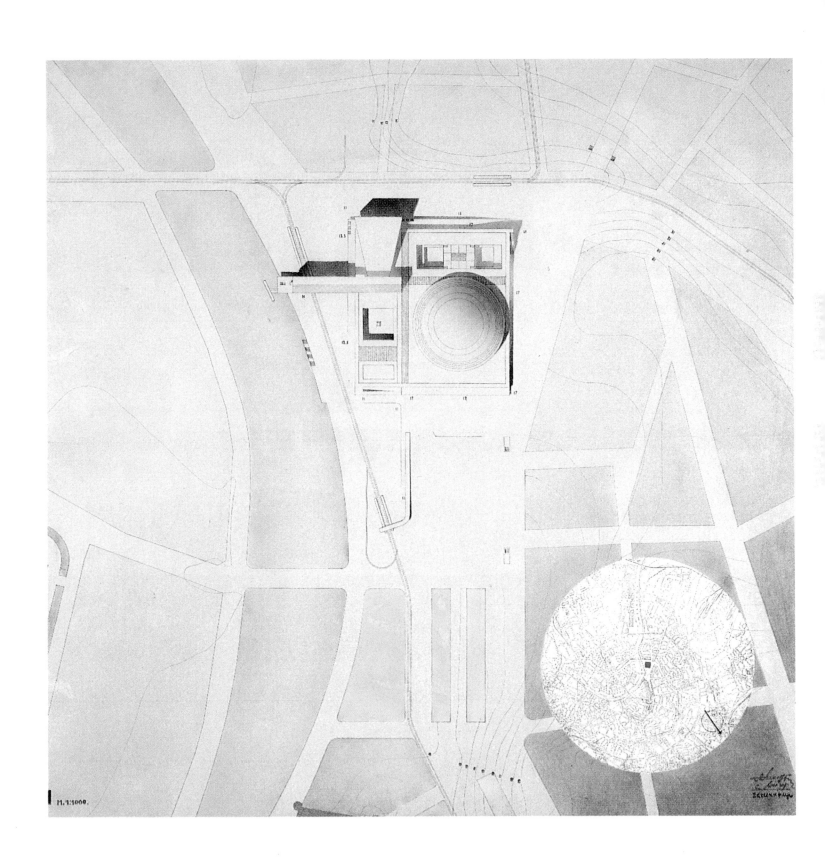

M.1:1000.

725
Nikolai Ladovskii
Competition project for the Palace of
Soviets, Moscow; elevation,
February–May 1931.
India ink on paper, 62.5 x 93 cm.
State Shchusev Museum, Moscow.

726
Artist Unknown
Slogan, Red Building of the Soviets,
Palace of Soviets, Moscow; plan, section,
and axonometric, 1931.
India ink, whiting, and collage on paper,
72.5 x 104 cm.
State Shchusev Museum, Moscow.

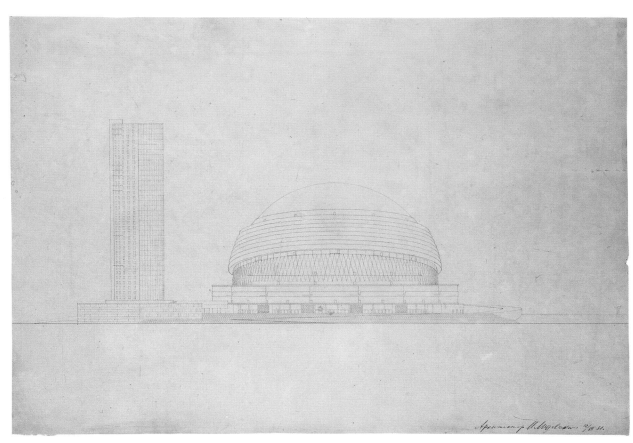

727
Konstantin Mel'nikov
*Competition project for
Narkomtiazhprom, the People's
Commissariat of Heavy Industry,
Moscow; elevation, 1934.
Watercolor and india ink on paper,
78 x 115 cm.
State Shchusev Museum, Moscow.*

728
Konstantin Mel'nikov
*Competition project for
Narkomtiazhprom, the People's
Commissariat of Heavy Industry,
Moscow; plan, 1934.
India ink, watercolor, and pencil on
paper, 73 x 115 cm.
State Shchusev Museum, Moscow.*

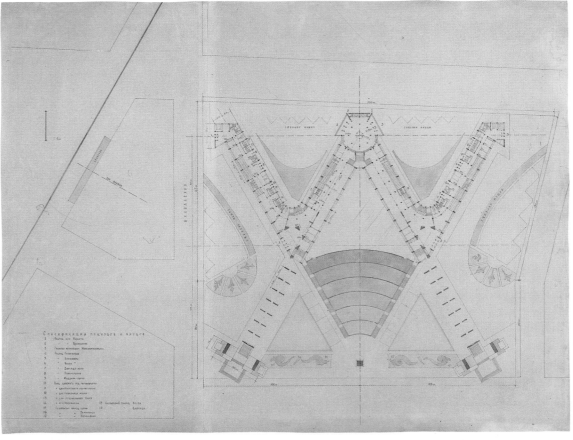

729
Ivan Leonidov
Competition project for
Narkomtiazhprom, the People's
Commissariat of Heavy Industry,
Moscow; elevation, 1934.
India ink, watercolor, whiting, and
bronze powder on paper, 82 x 141 cm.
State Shchusev Museum, Moscow.

730
Ivan Leonidov
Competition project for
Narkomtiazhprom, the People's
Commissariat of Heavy Industry,
Moscow; general plan, 1934.
India ink, gouache, and whiting on
double tracing paper, 45 x 102 cm.
State Shchusev Museum, Moscow.

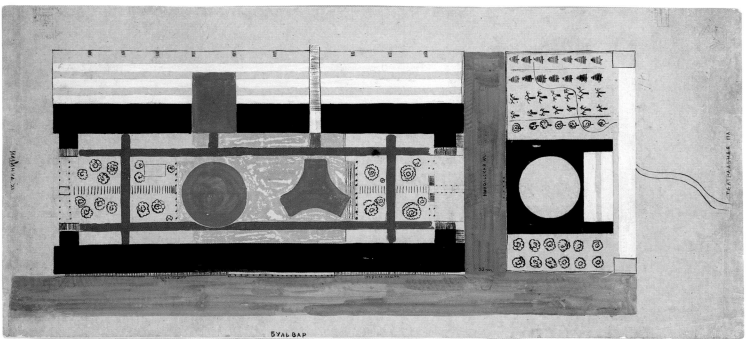

731
Ivan Leonidov
*Competition project for
Narkomtiazhprom, the People's
Commissariat of Heavy Industry,
Moscow; perspective with cupolas of St.
Basil's Cathedral, 1934.
India ink on paper mounted on plywood,
50 x 50 cm.
State Shchusev Museum, Moscow.*

732
Ivan Leonidov
*Competition project for
Narkomtiazhprom, the People's
Commissariat of Heavy Industry,
Moscow; perspective, 1934.
India ink, gouache, and whiting on
paper, 162 x 45 cm.
State Shchusev Museum, Moscow.*

733
Aleksandr and Viktor Vesnin
Competition project for Narkomtiazhprom, the People's Commissariat of Heavy Industry, Moscow (variant); perspective, 1934. India ink, watercolor, pencil, and whiting on paper, 44 × 110.5 cm. State Shchusev Museum, Moscow.

The Art of the Soviet Book, 1922–32

Susan Compton

The year 1923, when Aleksandr Rodchenko designed *Pro eto* (*About This*) and El Lissitzky *Dlia golosa* (*For the Voice*, fig. no. 1), has often been regarded as the watershed in Soviet book design.[1] These two books of Vladimir Maiakovskii's poetry, printed in large editions with distinctive covers and inventive illustrations, marked a high point in an area in which Soviet artists excelled. Such designs did not, of course, leap fully formed like Athena from the head of Zeus; outstanding designs had been produced before the political revolutions of 1917. The years 1912–16 had seen unparalleled invention in books made by Futurist artists and writers.[2] Most of these had been produced, however, in editions of a few hundred copies, and by lithographic processes with minimal work by printers; some copies were further personalized by hand coloring, such as Ol'ga Rozanova's decorations to Aleksei Kruchenykh's *Utinoe gnezdyshko . . . durnykh slov* (*A Duck's Nest . . . of Bad Words*, 1913).[3] *Tango s korovami* (*Tango with Cows*, 1914)[4] was exceptional in relying on the work of professional printers for the setting of Vasilii Kamenskii's typographic poems. Furthermore, although remarkable publications like these were known to the art world, they reached only a very small public consisting mainly of people interested in avant-garde art.

After the political revolutions of 1917, avant-garde artists and writers—who were among the first to embrace the October Revolution—were able to reach a wider public with a few expensively produced publications such as *Izobrazitel'noe iskusstvo* (*Fine Art*), an official periodical of Izo Narkompros (the Department of Fine Arts of the People's Commissariat of Enlightenment), whose head, the artist David Shterenberg, designed the journal's Cubistic cover. The contents of its single issue reflect the brief power of artists such as Kazimir Malevich and Vasilii Kandinskii, though, whether for technical or ideological reasons, its publication was delayed: the editorial is dated May 1918, the imprint date is 1919, but the journal did not come out until early in 1920.[5] Its printing, particularly of photographs of art works, was exemplary and *Fine Art* was later recognized as an equal to European art journals.

Between 1918 and 1920, a number of high-quality monographs on established avant-garde artists—for instance, on Kandinskii and Marc Chagall[6]—were also published, but writers and artists continued their experiments with books produced largely by hand.[7] This was an attractive proposition because of the scarcity of paper in those years of civil war and because the books could be made in the studio, without the complication of publishing and printing houses. An album of colored linocuts was prepared by Liubov' Popova and another, in black and white, by Rodchenko;[8] Varvara Stepanova experimented with words as well as imagery in her poem *Gaust chaba* (1919), which, although she was a competent typist, she wrote by hand over newsprint.[9] The culmination of these projects was the hand-decorated catalogues, typed by Stepanova, which Rodchenko and Popova—with Aleksandra Ekster and Aleksandr Vesnin—made for their exhibition *5 x 5 = 25*, held in Moscow in September 1921 (plate nos. 264, 269). They used the occasion to announce their move away from experimental easel painting into design and their Moscow show—held at the All-Russian Union of Poets—was mounted in two parts, the second dedicated to applied arts: stage design and graphics.

Characteristic of the graphics were hand-lettered posters with surprisingly Expressionist script, such as one advertising a debate during the show.[10] Among the participants in the debate were the writers Ivan Aksenov and Kruchenykh, who both had direct experience of the exhibitors' graphic work: two etchings by Ekster had been published in Aksenov's 1916 book of poetry, *Neuvazhitel'nye osnovaniia* (*Weak Foundations*), and she had also designed the cover for his book on Picasso;[11] Stepanova had made montages for *Gly-gly*, a Dadaist text by Kruchenykh (plate no. 97).[12] After *5 x 5 = 25*, Rodchenko went on working with Kruchenykh, making covers for his small books with made-up words for titles, *Tsotsa* (plate no. 89) and *Zaum'*.[13] For these he used handwriting, inscribing author's name and book title with colored crayons; for a third, larger-format printed book, *Zaumniki (Transrationals*, fig. no. 2), he made two linocuts, one with the three authors' names, the title, and a geometric design for the front cover, and the other with the publisher's imprint and his own name for the back. He cut narrow block capitals for the letters and thin lines for the design, so that the paper color (pink or green) showed through when the linocut was printed in black.[14]

Rodchenko's innovation for *Transrationals* has a parallel in his collaboration with the filmmaker Dziga Vertov on Vertov's newsreels, which were released from May 1922 onward.[15] Silent film required lettering which could be read very quickly by the cinemagoer and Rodchenko wrote white letters on a black background—especially appropriate for film—or black letters on a specially created white ground, which more closely resembled a book page.[16] He conceived the intertitles as an intrinsic part of the film itself, not just intervals between shots,[17] and incorporated one of his own three-dimensional constructions in the film titles. A photograph of this was reproduced on the title-page of *Kino-fot (Cinema-Photo)* 2.[18]

This journal was launched at the end of August 1922 with a cover designed by Rodchenko, who worked closely with Aleksei Gan, the author of *Konstruktivizm (Constructivism)*, printed in Tver' the same year.[19] Gan apparently worked directly with the printers: the text is composed, like a manifesto, of a series of slogans, to which he gave emphasis by varying the typography—using larger and smaller letters, capitals and lowercase, and differently weighted underlining.[20] Suitable typefaces did not, however, exist for display letters for cover design, and hand lettering continued to be used for Soviet book covers in the early 1920s. For his preliminary cover design Rodchenko drew ingenious "stretched" letters, writing KONSTRUKTIVIZM tall and thin on top of the author's name; the final version shows Gan's preference for simplicity: the title appears below his name, drawn in white lettering—a device borrowed from film titles; the design is sometimes credited to Gan himself, but was by Rodchenko.[21]

The collaboration of Gan and Rodchenko on *Cinema-Photo* marked a turning point in the design and content of Soviet periodicals. The covers of all six issues were dominated by Rodchenko's boldly lettered title. As befits a film and photography magazine, the covers included photographs and photomontages; indeed, Rodchenko developed montage technique while working on *Cinema-Photo*. For the first issue he arranged a page of printed material from 1921, overlapping the elements as he had done in his earlier collage works of art; he used a similar method for his montage on the cover of the second issue, this time overlapping discrete photographs. The third issue includes his *Psikhologiia (Psychology)* and *Detektiv (Detective)*, which are described as "montages from a book on cinematography by [Lev] Kuleshov."[22] *Detective* demonstrates how Rodchenko approached photomontage from his work on film: he links photographs of people and objects into a story by means of slogans that function like film titles. The cover of *Cinema-Photo* 4 carries one of his first mature photomontages, made by transforming a still photograph from Maiakovskii's 1918 film *Ne dlia deneg rodivshiisia (Not for Money Born)* through the superimposition of an unlikely photographic element: he clad the shrouded corpse in an airplane-coffin.[23]

As well as charting Rodchenko's progress with photomontage, the pages of *Cinema-Photo* reveal a new awareness in Moscow of contemporary publications from

fig. 1
El Lissitzky
Cover for Vladimir Maiakovskii, For the Voice, *1923.*
Zincograph, 19 x 13.5 cm.
Lenin Library, Moscow.

Western Europe. The first issue included an article on dynamic painting by Ludwig Hilberseimer, illustrated with an example by Viking Eggeling; there was also a drawing of Charlie Chaplin by Fernand Léger. The latter came not from a Dada journal, as stated in *Cinema-Photo,* but from the book *A vse-taki ona vertitsia (And Yet the World Goes Round),* published in Berlin in January 1922.[24] The author of this Russian text—written in Brussels in 1921—was the widely traveled Il'ia Erenburg, whose theme was the internationalism of the new art. He gave a list of essential journals including the Parisian *L'Esprit nouveau,* the Dutch *De Stijl,* and the Russian *Fine Art. And Yet the World Goes Round,* with its striking cover designed by Léger, was the first book to unite new Soviet and European art; it included reproductions of work by Léger, Lissitzky, Theo van Doesburg, Picasso, Vladimir Tatlin, and Rodchenko. The book was soon known in Moscow—before July, Rodchenko had received a copy from Berlin.[25]

Links with European publications were strengthened by Lissitzky, who left Moscow late in 1921 for Berlin, where he teamed up with Erenburg to found and edit *Veshch'/Gegenstand/Objet (Object),* an "international review of modern art" with title and opening manifesto in Russian, German, and French.[26] The first issue—a double one—came out in April 1922 with a dramatic typographic cover, where a black bar slanted diagonally across the colored page anchors the lettering. An earlier publication date had been envisioned, as the date line "February" is included in two unused variant cover designs, where the title, instead of being set against the diagonal bar, is enclosed in a circle, drawn over a vertical element.[27] Lissitzky may have rejected the circle for his final design for *Object* because it was such a dominant feature of Suprematist art, but he did not abandon Suprematism: on the title page of *Object* 3, he paired reproductions of Malevich's "Suprematist objects"—a black square and circle—with a photograph of "technical objects"—a locomotive pushing a snowplow—previously published in Erenburg's book. The unlikely combination assisted the declared purpose of the magazine—to introduce Russian art to Europeans and European art to Russians—because, at the time, the Parisian Purists attached particular significance to the word "object." A text on Purism by Amadée Ozenfant and Claude Jeanneret (Le Corbusier) must have been received with interest when published in Russian translation in *Object,* especially by Russians who had espoused *veshchizm* (the culture of things) the year before.[28] Lissitzky kept in touch with Moscow artists: in March he had written to Rodchenko, inviting him to reply to a survey of artists on art conducted by *Object* and to send photographs of his work for publication in the journal;[29] regular two-way traffic also resulted in the new international character of *Cinema-Photo,* since Hilberseimer's essay on dynamic painting was taken directly from *Object* 3.

In Berlin, Lissitzky soon established his presence in avant-garde publications: an issue of *De Stijl* was devoted to a Dutch version of his picture book *Suprematicheskii skaz pro dva kvadrata (A Suprematist Tale about Two Squares),* and he was invited to provide cover designs for the leading journals *Wendingen (The Turn), Broom, G, MA (Today), Merz,* and *Zenit (Zenith).*[30] Lissitzky thus found common ground with left-leaning activists across the European art world. He contributed and borrowed ideas, and the special quality of his design can be seen in Maiakovskii's *For the Voice.* For the book's cover, he linked horizontal and vertical typography, using a device from acrostics and crossword puzzles, where the same letter is shared between words.[31] Inside the book, he helped the reader find the poems by creating an index system using Suprematist symbols as well as words; he reproduced a drawing as frontispiece but invented a new style of illustration from

fig. 2
*Aleksandr Rodchenko
Cover for Aleksei Kruchenykh, Grigorii Petnikov, and Velimir Khlebnikov,* Transrationals, *1922.
Lithograph, 21.2 x 14.8 cm.
The British Library Board.*

typographic elements for the poems. Some of his motifs can be
connected with contemporary European design: the question
marks and capitals for "A vy mogli by?" ("And could you?")
resemble those on the cover of van Doesburg's manifesto,
Wat is Dada?;[32] the printed hands for "Prikaz No. 2 armii
iskusstv" ("Command No. 2 to the Army of the Arts") are like
the ones Kurt Schwitters had used on the covers of his journal
Merz since January 1923.[33] The similarities can hardly be by
chance, for Lissitzky was close to both artists; Schwitters had
printed Lissitzky's thoughts on typography in *Merz* 4.
Lissitzky's dictum: "The words on the printed sheet are learnt
by sight, not by hearing"[34] aptly describes his design of
For the Voice.

During 1923, artists in Moscow continued to be aware of
international publications. Gustav Klutsis ran the letters
GORN together when he modernized the cover of the journal
Gorn (*Furnace,* plate no. 493),[35] as had been done with the letters
BLEU on the three issues of the Dada magazine published in
Mantua in 1920–21.[36] This resemblance may, however, be
fortuitous, because the enlargement of a four-letter word to the
width of a magazine cover could lead to a common result.
Klutsis designed simple, sans serif letters, printing them
alternately in black and brown; this contrasts with *Bleu,* where
the single-colored sans serif letters include an unusual diagonal
to avoid the roundness of B and U. Klutsis varied the formula
for another journal, *Proletarskoe studenchestvo* (*Proletarian
Students,* plate no. 495), where he used alternately colored
letters in another strong yet simple cover design. Effective sans
serif lettering had already been designed by Anatolii Lavinskii,
in 1922 at the Moscow Vkhutemas (the Higher Artistic-
Technical Workshops), for the covers of Maiakovskii's poems,
13 let raboty (*Thirteen Years of Work,* fig. no. 3).[37] Here the poor
typeface inside the two volumes stands in strange contrast to
the sensitive design and printing on the covers, but this is a
feature—or weakness—of Soviet books from the 1920s.

It was Rodchenko rather than Lavinskii who designed the
journal *Lef* (*Left Front of the Arts*)—a substantial publication
launched, with Maiakovskii as editor, in March 1923.[38] As he
had done for *Cinema-Photo,* Rodchenko invented for *Lef*'s cover
a formula capable of variation; in the second issue, he
substituted a photomontage for the words that appeared above
the title in the first (fig. no. 4). Cover and montage are credited
to "konstruktivist Rodchenko" ("the Constructivist
Rodchenko"), making the allegiance of the magazine clear—
though an illustrated article on George Grosz gives an
unexpected Expressionist character to this issue, and this is
increased by Rodchenko's cover photomontage of figures in
close-up combined with newspaper headlines and text to
suggest a factual story. A different kind of story is conveyed by
his montage on the cover of *Lef* 3 (fig. no. 5), where the spirit of
Dada seems momentarily to have conquered Constructivist
design. A biplane, bearing the letters LEF, drops a fountain
pen, which nearly hits an ape; the ape, in turn, directs a barbed
arrow at the plane. Each motif is separate, as on the cover of
Le Coeur à barbe, a single number of a "transparent journal"
edited by Tristan Tzara, issued in Paris in April 1922 with a
cover-design "story" composed of disconnected images cut
from nineteenth-century prints.[39]

In contrast, Rodchenko's covers for the four issues of *Lef*
published in 1924 are more typical of Russian Constructivist
design and bear little relation to the design of contemporary
European periodicals. The difference may have been
intentional, so as to highlight the distinctive quality of Soviet
design. For instance, in *Lef* 4, *Gorod* (*Metropolis*)—a
photomontage by a Bauhaus student, Paul Citroën—was
reproduced opposite a montage by Popova representing her set
for Vsevolod Meierkhol'd's multimedia production of

fig. 3
Anatolii Lavinskii
Cover for Vladimir Maiakovskii, Thirteen Years of Work, *vol. 1,*
1923.
Lithograph, 17.9 x 11.9 cm.
The British Library Board.

fig. 4
Aleksandr Rodchenko
Cover for Lef 2 (1923).
Lithograph, 23 x 15.5 cm.
From the Resource Collections,
The Getty Center for the History of Art
and the Humanities.

fig. 5
Aleksandr Rodchenko
Study for cover for Lef 3 (1923).
Photomontage, 16.5 x 14.5 cm.
Museum Ludwig (Collection Ludwig, Cologne).

Zemlia dybom (The Earth in Turmoil).[40] The juxtaposition points up the contrast between the European approach, based on densely arranged cut-up photographs, and the looser Russian montage style, with its more direct relationship to film. No doubt in 1924 Rodchenko and Maiakovskii aimed at giving *Lef* a Soviet style in anticipation of the forthcoming *Exposition internationale des arts décoratifs et industriels modernes* (*International Exhibition of Contemporary Decorative and Industrial Art*) in Paris, for which Rodchenko was chosen to design the catalogue.[41] Textile designs by Popova, sports clothes by Stepanova, and book covers by Rodchenko—like the ones which had been illustrated in two colors in *Lef* [42]—were shown in Paris in 1925. The exhibition also included Rodchenko's fittings for a workers' club with sloped reading desks and shelves which served admirably to display the front covers of Soviet books and journals: photographs taken at the time show how effective they were.[43] During 1925, Rodchenko and Stepanova also designed covers for Soviet technical manuals;[44] compared with the unremarkable typographic covers of standard publications, theirs often create an immediate visual awareness of the subject (automotive engineering, for instance) and must have served as an inducement for workers to read. Rodchenko and Stepanova recognized that covers of books and journals could serve as "posters" for their contents.

In the USSR, books and journals for sale were displayed in kiosks, and architectural drawings for outdoor structures were sometimes reproduced on book covers. Valentina Kulagina's *Radio-orator* formed a striking counterpart to the lettering on Kruchenykh's book, *Iazyk Lenina* (*Lenin's Language*, plate no. 496),[45] but, by the time Klutsis used one of his elaborate architectural motifs on the cover of Kruchenykh's *Chetyre foneticheskikh romana* (*Four Phonetic Novels*, fig. no. 6)[46] in 1927, such imaginative designs had generally been superseded by photographs of real buildings.

This move toward more direct representation in books and journals reflected a changing political climate with a desire for greater realism; Rodchenko used his own photographs for nearly all the covers of *Novyi Lef* (*New Lef*) when *Lef* resumed publication under this title in 1927.[47] He did not always use an unaltered photograph: for the third issue of 1928, he displayed the title over his own photograph of a street book-advertisement poster. He substituted the magazine title for the books on the poster and obliterated the slogan "Vse novye izdaniia" ("All New Publications"), and he touched out an obtrusive overhanging wire.[48] In photography, as earlier in photomontage, Rodchenko was indebted to cinematography, and the bizarre angles of many of his photographs reproduced in *New Lef* create an effect not unlike stills from Soviet films. In 1927, he continued to be engaged in work for the cinema: a photograph of the reporters' room he had designed for Kuleshov's film, *Zhurnalistka* (*The Presswoman*), was published in *New Lef* 5.[49]

Familiarity with film technique as well as with photography is reflected in Rodchenko's design for the cover of Erenburg's *Materializatsiia fantastiki* (*The Materialization of Fantasy*, fig. no. 7).[50] For this he combined lettering with a photograph of a face in close-up and, instead of printing the whole head in positive or negative, printed the outer sections positively and left the central section in negative. He thus achieved strange three-dimensional effects, very appropriate for a flat book cover: the black-and-white image has an element of mystery which suits the book's title and contents. Equally effective, but in a different tradition, is the photographic cover which Lissitzky made the same year for *Arkhitektura. Raboty arkhitekturnogo fakul'teta Vkhutemasa 1920–1927* (*Architecture: Works from the Architecture Faculty of Vkhutemas, 1920–1927*, fig. no. 10).[51] He added red and black lettering to a photograph

fig. 6
Gustav Klutsis
Cover for Aleksei Kruchenykh, Four Phonetic Novels, *1927.*
Lithograph, 25 x 16.8 cm.
The British Library Board.

of his own hand holding a compass, printed on graph paper, which he had used in 1924 as a component of a self-portrait, *The Constructor*.[52] There he had combined drawing and stenciling with direct exposure and superimposed photographic negatives—one of them of his hand, which he had printed on top of his face. He had developed such techniques while living in the West and seeing examples of superimposition of negatives and photograms (yielded by placing an object on light-sensitive paper) by Man Ray.[53] In 1928, he used another photograph from 1924 as a cover for Il'ia Sel'vinskii's *Zapiski poeta* (*Notes of a Poet*).[54] Lissitzky's double-exposure of Jean Arp neatly reflects the two parts of Sel'vinskii's tale, which consists of the autobiography of the fictitious "Evgenii Nei" (whose name Lissitzky inscribed on Arp's collar) and "his" poems. Behind the Swiss artist's head is the Dada periodical *391*, which may seem a curious choice for a book by the Constructivist writer Sel'vinskii.[55] However, when Lissitzky had made his photograph of Arp in 1924, differences between Dada and Constructivism had seemed blurred because artists of both movements were working for related political aims—the building of a new society. But by 1928, the First Five-Year Plan in the Soviet Union and the rise of Fascism in Germany made Lissitzky's choice strangely inappropriate, even though the design is striking and "talks" to Rodchenko's cover for *The Materialization of Fantasy*.

The Five-Year Plan, put forward in 1927 by Stalin and ratified in 1928, resulted in a punishing drive to modernize the USSR. Canceling NEP (the New Economic Policy), the First, and then Second, Five-Year Plan placed the Soviet economy on a warlike footing which was accepted as a necessary stage in the rapid achievement of industrialization and the furtherance of Socialism. Many artists and writers spent time at the "front"— the construction sites of huge dams for hydroelectric power, new steelworks, and so forth. The almost revolutionary excitement of the time can be seen in a book of verses— *Komsomoliia* (*Young Communists League*, plate no. 523), by Anatolii Bezymenskii[56]—designed by Solomon Telingater, a younger colleague of Lissitzky's. Inside a dull hard cover— anticipating the standardization of the late 1930s—Telingater brought the poems alive by varying the length of lines and by filling the spaces to left and right with stylized drawings or unlikely textures; he also included realistic photographs in lively layouts that impelled the reader onward through the book. The following year Telingater helped Lissitzky design an unusual catalogue for the *Vsesoiuznaia poligraficheskaia vystavka* (*All-Union Printing Trades Exhibition*) in Moscow.[57] The two designers made an easy-to-use index to the sections of this comprehensive exhibition by graduating the height of the pages and using a different color for the top of each section. The cover was remarkably restrained, with bands of red and silver unevenly overlapped as though applied with an airbrush. Telingater's personal style was often more brash: he made an amusing cover for Semen Kirsanov's *Slovo predostavliaetsia Kirsanovu* (*Kirsanov Is to Speak*, fig. no. 9)[58] in a tall, thin format; his eccentric layout on the cover and inside the book seems more appropriate to Dada than to the Five-Year Plan.

The fervor generated by the Plan—in some cases spontaneous—lasted into the 1930s: a successor to Telingater's *Young Communists League* is Stepanova's design for *Groznyi smekh* (*Menacing Laughter*, plate no. 507), a republication of Maiakovskii's Rosta (the Russian Telegraph Agency) posters two years after the poet's death.[59] Here she varied the size of the pages, alternating full-width pages, carrying text, with half-width pages, carrying reduced reprints of Maiakovskii's cartoonlike posters. Stepanova gave the book an up-to-date appearance with dramatic photographic endpapers of marching Red Army soldiers; over them she printed a line from

fig. 7
Aleksandr Rodchenko
Cover for Il'ia Erenburg, The Materialization of Fantasy, *1927.*
Lithograph, 17.2 x 13.2 cm.
The British Library Board.

日本活動寫真

B
O
K
C

fig. 8
El Lissitzky
Cover for Japanese Cinema Exhibition, *1929.*
Lithograph, 14. 8 x 42 cm.
From the Resource Collections,
The Getty Center for the History of Art
and the Humanities.

Maiakovskii's poster verses: "Everyone to arms, Comrades!" In what must have seemed, in 1932, a timely preface (reprinted from the earlier publication), Maiakovskii explained: "These are not just verses. The illustrations are not intended as graphic ornamentation. This is a continuous record of the most difficult three-year period in the revolutionary struggle . . ."[60]

The early 1930s were difficult years for artists, who had to come to terms with increasing loss of freedom of design. Both Stepanova and Rodchenko, however, seem to have been able to adjust to restrictions placed on artistic invention by decrees of 1932 and 1934.[61] One of the main projects on which they worked with other avant-garde artists gave slightly more scope to designers, because *SSSR na stroike* (*USSR in Construction*, plate nos. 527–528) was a propaganda journal, intended for foreign consumption.[62] In the issues which he designed, Rodchenko continued to exercise his skill at page layout, even though his inventive photomontages of 1933 gave way in 1935 to discrete photographs artfully arranged, and in 1936 to even more mundane images.[63] By this time, Rodchenko had abandoned the unusual viewpoints which had made his earlier photographs so original. In the last years of the 1920s, his photographs in *Daesh'* (*Let's Produce!*)[64] and *30 dnei* (*Thirty Days*)[65] had given those journals a quality of realism close to that of cinema; by 1936, this was discredited as Formalism.

Like Rodchenko before him, Lissitzky had absorbed influences from cinema by the time he made his masterly photomontage cover for the journal *Brigada khudozhnikov* (*Artists' Brigade,* plate no. 513) in 1931.[66] The connection dated to 1929, when he designed a catalogue for a Moscow exhibition of Japanese cinema (fig. no. 8),[67] though his design reflected an interest in film rather than an influence from it. He used strips of film as edging for some of the pages and arranged stills inventively, with the actors seeming to look at each other across the page. But that same year he met Sergei Eizenshtein and Vertov and became close friends with the latter, who, according to Lissitzky's widow, learned the technique of multiple exposure from Lissitzky. In turn, when he worked on *USSR in Construction,* Lissitzky laid out photographic material "like Vertov's running of a documentary film."[68]

In 1931, *Artists' Brigade* published a report of a Moscow lecture in which Lissitzky summed up the current state of book design in the Soviet Union.[69] He wanted the book to be the unified work of author and designer, otherwise "splendid exteriors will constantly be produced for unimportant contents and vice-versa," yet he was against too much individuality, because "at our book exhibitions, the question of what, whither, why and for whom is not clear. Every book attempts to shout down its neighbour." He thus advocated the standardization of dimensions and types of books which increasingly came about in 1934–35. He deplored the lack of experimentation in typeface design in the Soviet Union compared with pre-Depression Germany, and no further experimentation took place in the USSR because of the hardening political situation. There was, nonetheless, a fundamental difference between Russian book designers and their West European counterparts in the ten years under discussion: the constant aim of the best Soviet designers was to reach a mass market rather than an elite; the fulfillment of this aim is amply demonstrated by the Soviet books and periodicals illustrated here.

fig. 9
Solomon Telingater
Cover for Semen Kirsanov, Kirsanov Is to Speak, *1930.*
Zincograph, 21.5 x 19.6 cm.
Lenin Library, Moscow.

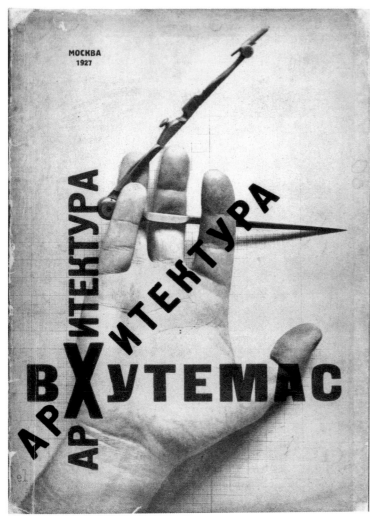

fig. 10
El Lissitzky
Cover for Architecture: Works from the Architecture Faculty of Vkhutemas, 1920–1927, *1927.*
Lithograph, 24.2 x 17 cm.
The British Library Board.

Notes

1. V. V. Maiakovskii, *Pro eto* (Moscow and Leningrad: Gosizdat, 1923), cover and photomontages reproduced in A. N. Lavrent'ev, ed., *A. M. Rodchenko, V. F. Stepanova. Mastera sovetskogo knizhnogo iskusstva* (Moscow: Kniga, 1989), plates 69–79; V. V. Maiakovskii, *Dlia golosa* (Berlin: Gosudarstvennoe izdatel'stvo RSFSR, 1923). A facsimile of the latter was published by Verlag Gebr. Koenig, Cologne, and Jaap Reitman Inc. Art Books, New York, in 1973.

2. For detailed discussions of these books, see Susan P. Compton, *The World Backwards: Russian Futurist Books, 1912–1916* (London: The British Library, 1978); Gerald Janecek, *The Look of Russian Literature: Avant-Garde Visual Experiments, 1900–1930* (Princeton: Princeton University Press, 1984); and Evgenii F. Kovtun, *Russkaia futuristicheskaia kniga* (Moscow: Kniga, 1988).

3. A. Kruchenykh, *Utinoe gnezdyshko . . . durnykh slov* (St. Petersburg: EUY, 1913).

4. V. Kamenskii, *Tango s korovami. Zheleznobetonnye poemy* (Moscow: Izd. pervogo zhurnala russkikh futuristov, 1914).

5. For dating, see Bengt Jangfeld, *Majakovskij and Futurism, 1917–1921* (Stockholm: Hylaea Prints, Almqvist and Wiksell, 1977), p. 34.

6. V. V. Kandinskii, *Tekst khudozhnika* (Moscow: Otdel Izobrazitel'nykh iskusstv Narodnogo komissariata po prosveshcheniiu, 1918); A. Efros and Ia. Tugendkhol'd, *Iskusstvo Marka Shagala* (Moscow: Gelikon, 1918).

7. An account of books produced by Kamenskii and Kruchenykh in independent Georgia from 1917–21 is given in Luigi Magarotto, Marzio Marzaduri, and Giovanna Pagani Cesa, eds., *L'Avanguardia a Tiflis: Studi, ricerche, cronache, testimonianze, documenti* (Venice: Università degli studi di Venezia, 1982).

8. *6 graviur L. Popovoi,* cover reproduced in Angelica Zander Rudenstine, ed., *Russian Avant-Garde Art: The George Costakis Collection* (London: Thames and Hudson, 1981), plate 834; other linocuts, ibid., plates 833, 836, 838, 840, 843, 845, 847. *Graviury Rodchenko 1919,* title page and three linocuts reproduced in Selim O. Khan-Magomedov, *Rodchenko: The Complete Work,* ed. Vieri Quilici, trans. Huw Evans (London: Thames and Hudson, 1986), p. 38.

9. Fifty-four copies, four of them numbered, were issued in 1919. See E. F. Kovtun, "Varvara Stepanova's Anti-Book," trans. John E. Bowlt, in *Von der Fläche zum Raum/From Surface to Space: Russia, 1916–24,* catalogue for exhibition organized by the Galerie Gmurzynska, Cologne (Cologne: Galerie Gmurzynska, 1974), p. 57.

10. The debate was advertised for September 25, 1921; the poster is reproduced in Alexander Lavrentiev, *Varvara Stepanova: A Constructivist Life,* ed. John E. Bowlt, trans. Wendy Salmond (London: Thames and Hudson, 1988), p. 57, where information that the exhibition was held in two parts is also given.

11. I. Aksenov, *Neuvazhitel'nye osnovaniia* (Moscow: Tsentrifuga, 1916) and *Pikasso i okrestnosti* (Moscow: Tsentrifuga, 1917).

12. Stepanova's illustrations for *Gly-gly* are reproduced in Lavrentiev, *Varvara Stepanova,* pp. 18–29; part of Kruchenykh's play was published in his *Ozhirenie roz. O stikhakh Terent'eva i drugikh* ([Tiflis?, 1918]). *Gly-gly* does not appear as a separate book in any of the extensive listings of Kruchenykh's works. Rodchenko included a quotation from it in his statement in

the catalogue of the Tenth State Exhibition, *Bespredmetnoe tvorchestvo i suprematizm* (*Non-Objective Creation and Suprematism,* Moscow, 1919), translated in John E. Bowlt, ed., *Russian Art of the Avant-Garde: Theory and Criticism, 1902–34* (New York: Viking, 1976), p. 149.

13. Kruchenykh's books *Tsotsa* and *Zaum'* were, like *Zaumniki,* published in 1922, according to the listing on the back of his anthology *Zudesnik. Zudutnie zudesa* (Moscow, 1922). The cover of a copy of *Tsotsa* with collaged photograph is reproduced in *Von der Malerei zum Design: Russische konstruktivistische Kunst der zwanziger Jahre/From Painting to Design: Russian Constructivist Art of the Twenties,* catalogue for exhibition organized by the Galerie Gmurzynska, Cologne (Cologne: Galerie Gmurzynska, 1981), p. 219; the British Library's copy has tissue collage only. The cover of *Zaum'* is reproduced in Khan-Magomedov, *Rodchenko,* p. 117.

14. A. Kruchenykh, G. Petnikov, and V. Khlebnikov, *Zaumniki* ([Petrograd]: EUY, 1922).

15. The first of Vertov's *Kino-pravda* (*Cinema-Truth*) newsreels was released in May 1922. See Jay Leyda, *Kino: A History of the Russian and Soviet Film* (London: George Allen & Unwin, 1960), p. 427.

16. Several of Rodchenko's film titles are reproduced in *Von der Malerei zum Design/From Painting to Design,* pp. 75, 77–81.

17. See "Konstruktivisty," *Lef* 1 (1923), p. 251, translated and discussed in Vlada Petrić, *Constructivism in Film: "The Man with a Movie Camera"; A Cinematic Analysis* (Cambridge: Cambridge University Press, 1987), pp. 11–12.

18. Six issues of *Kino-fot* were published between August 1922 and January 1923; it was intended as a weekly or possibly fortnightly publication but appeared intermittently between these dates. The page from *Kino-fot* with a photograph of Rodchenko's construction is reproduced in *Von der Malerei zum Design/From Painting to Design,* p. 78.

19. Aleksei Gan, *Konstruktivizm* (Tver': Tverskoe izdatel'stvo, 1922).

20. El Lissitzky recorded that Gan was one of the first Soviet designers to work in the printing house along with the compositors. See his "Our Book," in Sophie Lissitzky-Küppers, *El Lissitzky: Life, Letters, Texts,* trans. Helene Aldwinckle and Mary Whittall (London: Thames and Hudson, 1968), p. 363. Lissitzky may not have known that Il'ia Zdanevich had trained as a compositor in Tiflis in 1917 in order to be able to do his own typography; see *Iliazd,* catalogue for exhibition organized by the Musée national d'art moderne, Centre Georges Pompidou (Paris: Centre Georges Pompidou, 1978), p. 14.

21. Rodchenko's first design for the cover of Gan's book is reproduced in Khan-Magomedov, *Rodchenko,* p. 133. Khan-Magomedov gives the information that Rodchenko designed the cover as printed. Ibid., p. 131.

22. *Detective* is reproduced in Lavrent'ev, *A. M. Rodchenko, V. F. Stepanova,* plate 62.

23. Both are reproduced in Susan Compton, "Art + Photography," *The Print Collectors' Newsletter* 7, no. 1 (March–April 1976), p. 13.

24. *Kino-fot* 1 (August 25–31, 1922), p. 10. It has not been possible to find a 1921 Dada journal which includes this drawing by Léger for Ivan Goll's *Chaplinade*; three of these drawings had been published earlier in 1922 in I. G. Erenburg, *A vse-taki ona vertitsia* (Berlin: Gelikon, 1922).

25. L. M. Kozintseva, letter to Aleksandr Rodchenko, July 10, 1922: "Rada ochen', chto vam ponravilas' 'A vse-taki . . . ,'" in *A. M. Rodchenko. Stat'i, vospominaniia, avtobiograficheskie zapiski, pis'ma* (Moscow: Sovetskii khudozhnik, 1982), pp. 116–17.

26. *Veshch'/Gegenstand/Objet* 1–2 (March–April 1922), 3 (May 1922). It was announced in the third issue that the fourth would be devoted to recent Russian art, and the fifth to American; neither was published, but *Zenit* 18–19 (October 1922) carried an article by Erenburg and Lissitzky on recent Russian art which may have been intended for the fourth issue.

27. The two designs in pencil and india ink belonging to the Stedelijk van Abbemuseum, Eindhoven, are reproduced in Claude Leclanche-Boulé, *Typographies et photomontages constructivistes en U.r.s.s.* (Paris: Papyras, 1984), figs. 42, 47.

28. In the autumn of 1921, before Lissitzky left Moscow, Osip Brik had identified Constructivism and *veshchizm* as the current modes of thinking at Inkhuk (the Institute of Artistic Culture). See Selim O. Khan-Magomedov, *Pioneers of Soviet Architecture,* ed. Catherine Cooke, trans. Alexander Lieven (London: Thames and Hudson, 1987), pp. 146–47.

29. El Lissitzky, letter to Aleksandr Rodchenko, March 3, 1922, in *A. M. Rodchenko. Stat'i . . . ,* p. 115.

30. Lissitzky made covers for *Wendingen* 4, no. 11 (November 1921), published in the late summer or early autumn of 1922; *MA: Aktivista folyóirat* 7, no. 8 (August 1922); *Zenit: Revue internationale pour le Zenitisme et l'art nouveau* 2, no. 17–18 (October 1922); *Broom* 4, no. 3 (February 1923) and 5, no. 3 (November 1923); and *Merz* 2, no. 8–9 (April–July 1924), as well as the typographical arrangement of an article in *G: Zeitschrift für Gestaltung* 2 (September 1923), p. 2. Lissitzky may have been responsible for the title and layout of early numbers of *G*. See *El Lissitzky, 1890–1941,* catalogue for exhibition organized by the Busch-Reisinger Museum, the Sprengel Museum Hanover, and the Staatliche Galerie Moritzburg Halle (Cambridge, Mass.: Harvard University Art Museums, 1987), p. 187.

31. He had used the formula for the cover of R. V. Ivanov-Razumnik, *Maiakovskii. Misteriia ili buff* (Berlin: Skify, 1922), reproduced in *El Lissitzky, 1890–1941,* plate 89.

32. Theo van Doesburg's manifesto, *Wat is Dada?,* was on sale at a "Kleine Dada soirée" held at the Haagsche Kunstkring on January 10, 1923. See Arturo Schwarz, ed., *Almanacco Dada: Antologia letteraria-artistica; Cronologia repertorio delle riviste* (Milan: Feltrinelli, 1976), p. 637. A copy of *Dlia golosa* belonging to the Dutch architect J. J. P. Oud is inscribed by Lissitzky, May 14, 1923; see *El Lissitzky, 1890–1941,* p. 187.

33. Covers of *Merz* 1 (January 1923), 2 (April 1923), 4 (July 1923), and 6 (October 1923) are reproduced in Schwarz, *Almanacco Dada,* p. 689.

34. El Lissitzky, "Topography of typography," in Lissitzky-Küppers, *El Lissitzky,* p. 359.

35. *Gorn. Literaturno-khudozhestvennyi i obshchestvenno-nauchnyi zhurnal Vserossiiskogo i Moskovskogo proletkul'tov* 8 (1923).

36. *Bleu* 1 (July 1920), 2 (August–September 1920), 3 (January 1921); cover reproduced in Schwarz, *Almanacco Dada,* p. 656.

37. V. V. Maiakovskii, *13 let raboty,* 2 vols. (Moscow: MAF, 1922–23).

38. *Lef. Zhurnal levogo fronta iskusstv* 1 (March 1923). Seven issues appeared before August 1924, when the State Publishing House ceased its publication because of continued criticism that the journal was incomprehensible to the masses.

39. *Le Coeur à barbe. Journal transparent,* April 1922. Paul Eluard, Georges Ribemont-Dessaignes, Erik Satie, Marcel Duchamp, and Tristan Tzara were among the contributors. The cover is reproduced in M. Giroud, *Cabaret Voltaire; Der Zeltweg; Dada; "Le Coeur à barbe," 1916–22* (Paris: Jean Michel Place, 1981), p. 223.

40. The two montages are reproduced in Dawn Ades, *Photomontage,* rev. ed. (London: Thames and Hudson, 1986), figs. 85, 117. Ades (p. 72) also gives a translation by Michael Skinner of the text on photomontage which accompanied these examples in *Lef* 4 (1924), p. 41.

41. *Exposition internationale des arts décoratifs et industriels modernes. Comité de la Section de l'URSS: l'art décoratif et industriel de l'URSS* (Moscow, 1925).

42. Book cover designs by Rodchenko were included in *Lef* 1 (1923); Lavinskii's project for a book kiosk and Stepanova's project for sports clothing in *Lef* 2 (1923); and fabric designs by Popova, Stepanova, and Rodchenko in *Lef* 2 (1924).

43. See photographs in German Karginov, *Rodchenko,* trans. Elisabeth Hoch (London: Thames and Hudson, 1979), pp. 174–75.

44. For example, Rodchenko's cover for I. V. Gribov, *Zazhiganie, osveshchenie i pusk avtomobilii* (Moscow: Transpechat', 1925) and Stepanova's for S. R. Dadyko and N. D. Martynov, *Vagonnoe delo po programme shkol uchenichestva Zh. d. transporta* (Moscow: Transpechat', 1925), reproduced in Lavrent'ev, *A. M. Rodchenko, V. F. Stepanova,* plates 40–41.

45. A. E. Kruchenykh, with Aliagrov [Roman Jakobson], *Iazyk Lenina. Odinadtsat' priemov leninskoi rechi* (Moscow: Izdanie Vserossiiskogo soiuza poetov, 1925).

46. A. E. Kruchenykh, *Chetyre foneticheskikh romana* (Moscow: Izdanie avtora, 1927).

47. *Novyi Lef* 1–12 (1927–28). All covers were by Rodchenko.

48. The photograph of the advertisement is reproduced in Karginov, *Rodchenko,* plate 80, where it is dated 1924.

49. *Vasha znakomaia, Novyi Lef* 5 (1927), opposite p. 33. *Vasha znakomaia* was the working title for the film, changed to *Zhurnalistka* after the photograph was published. An illustrated account of Rodchenko's work on the film is given in Khan-Magomedov, *Rodchenko,* pp. 189–95.

50. I. Erenburg, *Materializatsiia fantastiki* (Moscow: Kinopechat', 1927).

51. *Arkhitektura. Raboty arkhitekturnogo fakul'teta Vkhutemasa 1920–1927* (Moscow: Izdanie Vkhutemasa, 1927).

52. *The Constructor* is reproduced in Lissitzky-Küppers, *El Lissitzky,* fig. 118; the hand is reproduced ibid., fig. 122. The hand was also used for an English advertisement for Pelikan ink. See *El Lissitzky, 1890–1941,* p. 191.

53. There is an example of a photogram by Man Ray with a description of the technique in *Merz* 2, no. 8–9 (April–July 1924), p. 88. The issue was edited by Lissitzky and Schwitters.

54. I. L. Sel'vinskii, *Zapiski poeta. Povest'* (Moscow and Leningrad: Gosudarstvennoe izdatel'stvo, 1928). For the cover Lissitzky used his double profile of Arp against the journal *391* (12 [March 1920]), taken in the summer of 1924. See Lissitzky-Küppers, *El Lissitzky,* p. 52.

55. See Gail Weber, "Constructivism and Soviet Literature," *Soviet Union* 3, pt. 2 (1976), pp. 294–310.

56. A. I. Bezymenskii, *Komsomoliia. Stranitsy epopei* (Moscow: Kommunisticheskii soiuz molodezhi, 1928).

57. *Vsesoiuznaia poligraficheskaia vystavka. Putevoditel',* proekt i detalirovka El' Lisitskogo, tipograficheskoe oformlenie S. B. Telingatera (Moscow: Izdanie K-ta Vsesoiuznoi poligraficheskoi vystavki, 1927).

58. S. I. Kirsanov, *Slovo predostavliaetsia Kirsanovu* (Moscow: Gosizdat, 1930).

59. V. V. Maiakovskii, *Groznyi smekh. Okna Rosta,* ed. K. Soliadzhin (Moscow and Leningrad: Gosudarstvennoe izdatel'stvo khudozhestvennoi literatury, 1932).

60. Translated in Edward J. Brown, *Mayakovsky: A Poet in the Revolution* (Princeton: Princeton University Press, 1973), p. 209.

61. By a decree of June 6, 1931, the Council of People's Commissars of the RSFSR empowered Glavlit (the Chief Administration for Literary Affairs and Publishing) to exercise control over manuscripts and drawings; a decree of August 11, 1934, declared that the technical makeup of all books was to be decided by the censors. See Maurice Friedberg, "Soviet Books, Censors and Readers," in M. Hayward and L. Labedz, eds., *Literature and Revolution in Soviet Russia, 1917–62* (London: Oxford University Press, 1963), pp. 199–200.

62. Lissitzky's role as occasional designer for the propaganda journal *SSSR na stroike/USSR in Construction/USSR im Bau/URSS en construction* is discussed in Peter Nisbet, "An Introduction to El Lissiztky," in *El Lissitzky, 1890–1941,* pp. 44–45.

63. Compare the cover by Rodchenko for *SSSR na stroike* 12 (1933); pages with photomontages from 12 (1935) and cover of 5 (1937) reproduced in Khan-Magomedov, *Rodchenko,* p. 261.

64. For example, *Daesh'* 14 (1929). See Khan-Magomedov, *Rodchenko,* p. 246.

65. For example, *30 dnei* 12 (1928), pp. 62–63. Three photographs are reproduced in Khan-Magomedov, *Rodchenko,* p. 245.

66. *Brigada khudozhnikov. Organ federatsii rabotnikov prostranstvennykh iskusstv* 4 (1931).

67. El' Lisitskii, *Vystavka Iaponskoe kino* (Moscow: Gosnak, 1929).

68. See Lissitzky-Küppers, *El Lissitzky,* p. 88.

69. *Brigada khudozhnikov* 4 (1931), p. 23. Translated as "Do Not Separate Form from Content!" in *El Lissitzky, 1890–1941,* pp. 61–62.

fig. 1
Natan Al'tman
Plate, Land to the Workers, *1919.*
Porcelain, 24.3 cm diameter.
State Russian Museum, St. Petersburg.

Soviet Porcelain of the 1920s: Propaganda Tool

Nina Lobanov-Rostovsky

Soviet porcelain of the 1920s owes much to the young Soviet government's need for propaganda. It can be divided into several categories: straightforward propaganda pieces; symbolic and commemorative pieces; figurines representing characters of the new Soviet epoch; the traditional, with themes representing eternal Russia and rural life as well as Russian fairy tales; and the avant-garde, including Cubist, Suprematist, and abstract pieces. However, all porcelain decorated at the State—later renamed the Lomonosov—Porcelain Factory[1] during the first ten years after the October Revolution (1917–27) was in one way or another meant to be used for propaganda purposes even when free of slogans or abstract in form and design. This porcelain represented a new state, a new era, a new people, and the Soviet government, avid for foreign currency, sent hundreds of pieces abroad to exhibitions and to trade fairs. Thanks to this, certain propaganda pieces, which were later destroyed or simply disappeared in the USSR during the Stalinist era, have survived in foreign collections. Some of these pieces are contemporary testimony to the activities of the American Relief Administration and to the importance and activities of men such as Lev Trotskii and Grigorii Zinov'ev during the first years after the Revolution—whereas Stalin, who destroyed both men, does not appear on any early propaganda porcelain. Soviet porcelain of the 1920s has become an art document of the epoch.

Revolution and Propaganda

During the Civil War the White leaders were military men with only a narrow understanding of politics. Although they believed in the justice of their cause just as firmly as the revolutionaries believed in theirs, they never thought it necessary to explain their political and social views to their subordinates or to the masses. To them, politicking and propaganda smacked of the subversive and were to be avoided.

The Bolshevik leaders were revolutionaries. In their underground work their chief task had been to persuade others of the correctness of their views in order to acquire followers. The teaching of Marxism, i.e., propaganda, was therefore considered necessary, indeed crucial. Lenin's ideas strongly influenced Soviet attitudes toward propaganda.[2] Lenin argued in his writings that one should not seek to fight ideas with ideas but should instead suppress the opposition's ideas and its organs—that is, one should censor the press. He also wrote that organization and propaganda were two sides of the same coin; a well-organized network could facilitate the work of propaganda, and the very process of carrying out agitation would help the work of organization.

From October 1917 to the spring of 1921, the Bolsheviks were in a desperate struggle to maintain power as the Civil War raged throughout Russia. Their survival depended in good part upon the Red Army created by Trotskii and upon the success of agitation and propaganda (agitprop) campaigns directed toward reconciling the populace, literate and illiterate, to the new government and the socialist way of life.

Anatolii Lunacharskii, the brilliant head of Narkompros (the People's Commissariat of Enlightenment), enlisted artists and writers to help in the battle for hearts and minds. Artists were urged to leave their studios and to design street pageants praising the Revolution, as well as decorations for the celebrations on May 1st and the anniversary of the October Revolution. They also painted the exteriors of agitprop trains, boats, and trucks with colorful revolutionary messages. Filled with trained agitators and representatives from various commissariats, these agitprop trains, boats, and trucks were sent systematically around the country. Each train was equipped with a small library, a bookstore, a printing press for producing pamphlets, a gramophone for broadcasting Lenin's speeches, and a coach fitted out for meetings and for showing short agitational films. Some of the films were aimed specifically at the peasants, telling them about more efficient agricultural methods and urging them to learn how to read and write and to be inoculated against diseases.

Other successful forms of agitational art were political posters and Rosta (the Russian Telegraph Agency) windows. Political posters and wall newspapers had become substitutes for ordinary newspapers throughout war-torn Russia. In 1919, Mikhail Cheremnykh devised a new type of wall newspaper for Rosta, which consisted of the usual bulletin conveying the latest news in telegraphic style and was illustrated with satirical sketches that were either handpainted or stenciled. These bulletins were mounted onto a board that would fit into the ordinary store window, where, unlike the wall newspapers, they were safe from wind, rain, and graffiti. Vladimir Maiakovskii, Dmitrii Moor, and many other fine artists and writers produced Rosta windows, which were usually changed weekly.

Never before had artists and writers been so closely linked with the politics of their country. They took themselves very seriously and, like the political authorities, issued orders and decrees. The new republic became a vast canvas and stage for artists of various tendencies.

The State Porcelain Factory

The Soviet leaders, immediately after the October Revolution, had the idea of using porcelain as a means of propaganda both within Russia and abroad. It was this decision which made the State Porcelain Factory a fertile field as well as a haven for artists who wanted to aid in the task of social and cultural reconstruction.[3]

The former Imperial Porcelain Factory, located on what is now Obukhovskaia oborona Avenue in the southern outskirts of St. Petersburg, was founded in the first half of the eighteenth century and worked exclusively for the Imperial court, to which it supplied dinner services, articles for the adornment of palaces and yachts, replacement pieces for the existing services, and presentation pieces (including services, vases, figurines, and other works of art) to be given away by the Imperial household. During World War I, it outfitted the Imperial army and army hospitals. Many of its workers went to war, leaving behind only a skeleton labor force.

After the February and October Revolutions, the artistic administration of the country presented a picture of extreme confusion and, at times, anarchy, as did just about everything else. The Bolsheviks had given relatively little thought to the way in which they would administer the country after assuming power. Many pragmatic decisions had to be made in education, art, and industry. There were no set procedures and in many cases specialists were able to keep the jobs they had had before the Revolution. This was the case at the Imperial Porcelain Factory, where the reorganization took place fairly swiftly and smoothly. After the February Revolution it came under the aegis of the Ministry of Trade and Industry of the new regime, which took absolutely no notice of the factory. Everyone at the factory stayed on and it was supposed to be ruled by a workers' control commission. Artists and sculptors ranked as workers, so there was no "class" problem. The sculpture workshop headed by Vasilii Kuznetsov and the painting workshop headed by Rudol'f Vil'de continued working on prerevolutionary models. The artistic side of the factory, however, was threatened with closure because there was no outlet for its wares. Meetings were held and a petition presented to the ministry with no concrete result. After the October Revolution, the factory came briefly under the jurisdiction of the People's Commissariat of Agriculture and, a

few months later, by a decision of the Council of People's Commissars of March 23, 1918,[4] it was placed under the authority of Izo Narkompros (the Department of Fine Arts of the People's Commissariat of Enlightenment). This was a fortunate choice, for Lunacharskii at Narkompros was both a member of the Bolshevik inner circle and a highly cultivated man who had traveled widely. He had access to Lenin and was able to defend artistic projects and artists of various persuasions when necessary.

One of the problems the Bolshevik government had was finding paper and other materials for its propaganda campaign. This was an obstacle they did not encounter, initially, at the State Porcelain Factory, which they found full of unpainted plates, ready to be covered with slogans and revolutionary themes. This stock of blank porcelain was available at the factory because the practice had been, year in and year out, to produce a certain quantity of articles in advance: dinner services, platters, plates, jugs, teapots, cups and saucers, up to the "biscuit" stage. These were stamped with the monogram of the reigning czar and the current year, then stored away until an order came through from the Imperial household for a service or for gifts for distinguished visitors. The required items would then be painted, glazed, and fired.

Most of the blank porcelain found in the factory at the time of the Revolution dated from the reign of the last czar, Nikolai II (1894–1917). There was also a stock of blanks bearing the monogram of his father, Aleksandr III (1881–94), and of his grandfather, Aleksandr II (1855–81), and a few pieces which went back to Nikolai I (1825–55), though these were very rare. As each czar died, the leftover blanks, stamped with his monogram, were probably pushed to the back of the storage shelves where they gathered dust until the Revolution.

During the first two months after the overthrow of the Romanovs, artists at the porcelain factory painted on pieces which had been marked simply with the date 1917. (These pieces are today extremely rare.) Between April and December 1917, they painted on pieces marked with a crownless eagle in a hyphenated circle and the date 1917—the monogram of the Provisional Government, which had been designed by Ivan Bilibin. Between January and May 1918, the crownless eagle in a hyphenated circle continued to be used but without a date. Then, the factory artists became more pragmatic and used earlier monogrammed plates, but covered the Imperial monogram with an oval or a diamond-shaped patch of dark-green or black paint and added the State Porcelain Factory mark of hammer, sickle, and cog, and the year. This mark was designed by Aleksei Karev. From 1921 onward, they usually left the Imperial monogram uncovered and simply added the State Porcelain Factory mark and the year. Thus one usually finds both Soviet and Imperial marks on propaganda porcelain of the immediate postrevolutionary years.

Despite the unsettled conditions there was no break in production. At the very first meeting of the new management it was decided to abandon the difficult prerevolutionary methods of underglaze painting, and Sergei Chekhonin was elected to the post of artistic director, a post he held during 1918–23 and 1925–27. Superbly trained and experienced in the fields of architectural ceramics, enamel, graphic design, miniatures, and gilding, he experienced no difficulty in bridging the two worlds of painting and ceramics. On the contrary, suddenly his worlds came together. Though some people accused Chekhonin of having sold out to the Revolution,[5] anyone who knows his work realizes that this was not so. Chekhonin's firm commitment to artistic innovation was neither increased nor decreased by the consequences of the Revolution. He was inspired not by revolutionary ideology but by purely artistic interest in the possibilities of new designs that might integrate and transform economic and social reality. Chekhonin's excellence as an artist and his resolutely undogmatic approach made other artists happy to work with him and allowed several styles to coexist at the State Porcelain Factory. Natal'ia Dan'ko, for example, the gifted sculptor who had been Kuznetsov's assistant in his workshop since 1914, stayed on as head of the workshop after Kuznetsov's departure in 1919.

A triumvirate consisting of Petr Vaulin, Chekhonin, and David Shterenberg—all of them on the Art Board of the Petrograd Izo Narkompros—was in charge of the general direction of the factory: Vaulin took care of administrative and economic matters, Chekhonin supervised all artistic matters, and Shterenberg was the Izo Narkompros representative. The directors of the porcelain factory worked in close collaboration with the workers' commission. At first, there were twelve workers in the painting section and one hundred workers in all at the factory.[6] The lack of technical ability among most of these workers and their low output forced the artistic director to start off with the production of very simply decorated porcelain. The factory artists were obliged to familiarize themselves with artisanal-type work so as to acquire the habit of using a brush and bright colors with ease. Chekhonin's reputation attracted many additional artists, well-known and unknown, to the art department of the factory, including Mikhail Adamovich, Vasilii Timorev, Varvara Freze, Elizaveta Rozendorf, Elena Dan'ko (Natal'ia's sister), Mariia Ivashintsova, Elizaveta Potapova, Aleksandra Shchekotikhina-Pototskaia, and Ekaterina Iakimovskaia in 1918; Ekaterina Bol'sheva, Liubov' Gaush, Alisa Golenkina, Mariia Kirillova, Mariia Lebedeva, and Varvara Rukavishnikova in 1919; Nadezhda Kulikova and Bazilka Radonich in 1920; and Rene O'Konnel' in 1922. (Zinaida Kobyletskaia, who had worked at the Imperial Porcelain Factory from 1912–14, rejoined in 1918.) Established artists such as Natan Al'tman, Ivan Alekseev, Veniamin Belkin, Mstislav Dobuzhinskii, Vasilii Kandinskii, Boris Kustodiev, Nikolai Lapshin, Vladimir Lebedev, Aleksandr Matveev, Ivan Puni, and Valentin Sherbakov created designs for the State Porcelain Factory. None of these established artists except Dobuzhinskii knew how to paint on porcelain, and Dobuzhinskii never painted on porcelain for the factory. In 1923 the Suprematists Kazimir Malevich, Nikolai Suetin, and Il'ia Chashnik worked for the State Porcelain Factory. In the late 1920s there was a new influx of artists, including Mikhail Mokh, Aleksandr Samokhvalov, Ivan Riznich, and Aleksei Vorobevskii. The last two are still alive, and Vorobevskii is still painting porcelain for the Lomonosov Porcelain Factory.

For many artists, working at the factory was their first professional experience. As long as they had been well trained their inexperience did not worry the directors of the factory, who were attempting to create a porcelain "nursery" for the new state. They banked on the ideals and the excitement of the Revolution to inspire the artists' creative powers. Under Chekhonin's guidance, many of the now characteristic designs of elegantly calligraphed slogans and inscriptions, monograms and dates, emblems, garlands, and flowery borders were developed. He adapted his mastery of graphic art to porcelain and transferred the vignettes he so loved to plates and to cups and saucers. (His style of calligraphy is still used on commemorative porcelain being produced at the Lomonosov Porcelain Factory today.)

Traditional and Contemporary Sources

Propaganda porcelain was the child of the October Revolution but it had several grandparents: first, the *lubok* (illustrated broadside), which existed in Russia from the seventeenth

fig. 2
Sergei Chekhonin
Plate, Science Must Serve People, *1918.*
Porcelain, 24 cm diameter.
Private collection, London.

century onward; second, icons, which are not only objects of worship in the Orthodox Church but are painted to be "read" by the onlooker as pictorial commentaries on the Scriptures; and third, the Russian tradition of graphic design in newspapers and journals. The hundreds of satirical journals published during the two years following Nikolai II's October Manifesto of 1905, establishing a limited freedom of the press, were very open and mordant in their criticisms of the government and of established institutions. This period was like an open university course for many artists, during which they acquired a civic consciousness and learned the importance and social significance of artistic endeavor. Chekhonin, Dobuzhinskii, and Kustodiev were all designing for satirical journals in the years 1905–7.

The contemporary sources of inspiration for propaganda porcelain were the Revolution and its heroes, past and present, and their ideas; Lenin's Plan for Monumental Propaganda[7] as well as the agitprop campaigns; revolutionary posters and Rosta windows; and designs for the decoration of streets and squares for revolutionary festivities.

The same slogans and aphorisms that were appearing in wall newspapers and on posters and on some of the newly erected monuments could also be read on propaganda porcelain. Class struggle and the new revolutionary morality were important themes. Slogans often expressed an opposition of old and new. Extracts from speeches by or about Lenin provided a common source of inspiration, as did quotations from European utopian-socialist writers, revolutionary activists of many nationalities, and the *Communist Manifesto*. Texts were also taken from classical authors such as Ovid and Cicero, from Fedor Dostoevskii and Lev Tolstoi, even from the Gospels. Some artists placed their hope in "Labor, Science, and Art" as a means of reeducating the social consciousness of the masses, and this is reflected in their designs and maxims. The range of source material was paralleled by an equally wide range of treatment; each artist had favorite motifs and a characteristic manner of execution.

Propaganda, Symbolic, and Commemorative Pieces

In 1918 a sculpture of Karl Marx in porcelain—possibly the first sculpture of Marx—was commissioned by the Soviet government and executed at the State Porcelain Factory by Kuznetsov. The same year Chekhonin decorated a series of plates with brief slogans: "He Who Is Not with Us Is against Us," "Struggle Gives Birth to Heroes," "The Mind Cannot Tolerate Slavery," and "What Has Been Produced by Working Hands Cannot Be Swallowed by a Lazy Belly." Chekhonin, who was a consummate graphic artist, managed to make every inscription look elegant: on the plate decorated with the slogan *Delo nauki sluzhit' liudiam* (*Science Must Serve People*, 1918, fig. no. 2), the stylized black letters circling the edge of the plate, interspersed with small, colorful flowers and leaves, are both powerful and appealing. His work, as already mentioned, was characterized by an attachment to the past as well as enthusiasm for the present and the future, and for different trends in art. Thus, we have Chekhonin's depiction of the hammer and sickle plus part of a cog representing industry (the mark of the State Porcelain Factory) surrounded by very naïve field flowers and leaves (fig. no. 3), showing his attachment to folk art, followed by a plate known as *Kubisticheskii dizain s serpom i molotom* (*Cubist Design with Hammer and Sickle*, 1919, fig. no. 4). Chekhonin also designed various plates and platters with a red ribbon winding along the edges intended to convey the atmosphere of festively decorated streets with fluttering banners and streamers.

The banner that hung from the General Staff Arch in

fig. 3
Sergei Chekhonin
Plate, Blue Emblem with Flowers, *1918.*
Porcelain, 24.5 cm diameter.
Private collection, London.

fig. 4
Sergei Chekhonin
Plate, Cubist Design with Hammer and Sickle, *1919.*
Porcelain, 25.8 cm diameter.
Private collection, London.

Petrograd on the first anniversary of the October Revolution was reproduced in a green-and-red plate, *Zemlia trudiashchimsia* (*Land to the Workers,* 1919, fig. no. 1), designed by Al'tman. The green field incorporates a red rhombus containing a factory with tall stacks, a sickle, and an ear of wheat all painted in red, with the inscription, also in red, circling the edge. According to Al'tman's widow, the two colors were specifically chosen to represent the land and the workers. Everything was carefully thought out—the clear, strong lettering and the equal space and value accorded to the two colors.[8] The monumental style of the design emphasizes the importance and the essence of the theme. Several identical plates and a few watercolors and studies by Al'tman, supplemented by descriptions from contemporary witnesses, are all that remains as evidence of Al'tman's extraordinary transformation of Palace Square, the Winter Palace, and the General Staff Arch and Building on the first anniversary of the October Revolution (plate nos. 103–106). Russia was on the verge of collapse, yet Al'tman was allotted fifty thousand feet of canvas to mount Futurist constructions and designs on the Winter Palace walls and on the General Staff Arch. The Aleksandr Column was turned into a Futurist sculpture.

Al'tman also produced a famous portrait of Lenin drawn from life (he was one of the few artists allowed this privilege), which was included as one of the elements in the composition of the plate *Kto ne rabotaet, tot ne est* (*He Who Does Not Work Does Not Eat,* 1921, fig. no. 5) designed by Adamovich. In addition to Lenin's portrait it depicts ration cards, half an Imperial eagle, and a red star, accompanied by LENIN and RSFSR. Dancing around the border in multicolored letters is the slogan. This slogan is an adaptation of II Thessalonians 3:10—"if any would not work, neither should he eat"—and was incorporated into the Constitution of the RSFSR in 1918. It is interesting to note that in the prototype of this plate created in 1921, the red star of the Revolution is on top of the eagle, obliterating and crushing it. When copies of the plate were ordered, however, the factory artists obviously thought it a pity to cover up the eagle, so they painted the star underneath. One often finds such anomalies in agitprop porcelain.

Soviet heraldry acquired great importance in the decoration of art porcelain. An elegantly executed hammer and sickle on their own, or a hammer and sickle entwined with flowers and foliage, or RSFSR elegantly calligraphed and frequently adorned with flowers and gold, are often the only designs on plates by Chekhonin and other artists. The vast RSFSR, which stretched from Finland to the Bering Strait, was founded in November 1917, and was for five years the one and only republic; the USSR was established only at the end of December 1922. (An error frequently made by fakers of propaganda porcelain is to decorate a plate or a vase with USSR and the date 1919, 1920, or 1921.)

Adamovich made sketches for several colorful propaganda plates containing the emblems of the new republic complemented by revolutionary symbols and slogans. His best plates, however, are those depicting life in the Red Army, where he served during 1919–21 between two stints at the porcelain factory. He created several plates glorifying the Red Army on its fifth anniversary, and one plate (fig. no. 6) honoring Trotskii, the creator of the Red Army. Trotskii, second in importance only to Lenin as a leader of the Bolshevik Revolution, was defeated by Stalin in the power struggle that followed Lenin's death in 1924, exiled in 1929, and assassinated by a Stalinist agent in Mexico City in 1940. This plate survived in a collection in Paris.

In Western collections one often sees plates, figurines, or large dishes with the full-face portrait or profile of Zinov'ev—another subject that one never encounters in public or private

fig. 5
Mikhail Adamovich
Plate, He Who Does Not Work Does Not Eat, *1921.*
Porcelain, 25 cm diameter.
Private collection, London.

fig. 6
Mikhail Adamovich
Plate, Fifth Anniversary of the Red Army, *1922.*
Porcelain, 24 cm diameter.
Private collection, London.

collections in Russia.

Zinov'ev was one of Lenin's chief collaborators before and after the October Revolution. He returned with him to Russia in the famous sealed train in April 1917. A member of the Central Committee of the Communist Party and of the Politburo, he was also elected chairman of the Executive Committee of the Comintern in 1919. During the summer of 1920 he presided at the First Congress of the Peoples of the East, held in Baku. This meeting was convened to organize the Moslem world against colonial imperialism, with 1,891 delegates—two-thirds of them already Communists and forty-four of them women—representing thirty-two nations ranging from Morocco to Manchuria. Several pieces of porcelain were designed to commemorate it (fig. no 7).

Zinov'ev reached the pinnacle of his power in 1923–24 as one of the triumvirate, with Stalin and Lev Kamenev, which prepared to take over after Lenin's death. But Stalin turned on the other two and had Zinov'ev stripped of power and expelled from the Party in November 1927. In 1936 Zinov'ev appeared as a defendant at the first show trial, was sentenced to death for treason, and was executed.

The celebration of the second anniversary of the October Revolution is the subject for several plates executed by Vil'de, an artist of the older generation who worked from 1906 until the mid-1930s in the Imperial/State/Lomonosov Porcelain Factory, eventually becoming head of the painting workshop. Vil'de's anniversary plates were always highly decorative. One of the best known has a cobalt-blue border decorated with leaves, flowers, and tools, beautifully executed in etched gold and oxidized silver. The cavetto is decorated with a red banner inscribed, in gold letters, "Victory to the Workers" and "25th Oct." Above the banner, also in gold, are the dates 1917–1919. When the oxidized silver blade of the sickle is rubbed clean the letters RSFSR appear.

Numerous plates were designed to celebrate May 1st, the workers' holiday banned under the czars. One such plate, oval in shape (fig. no. 8), has a design by Vil'de that consists of a bouquet incorporating pliers and a hammer entwined with a red ribbon. At the top of the plate are the words "We Celebrate while Working." At the bottom is the date May 1, 1920.

Fascinating from a historical and documentary point of view is the large *Podpisnoe bliudo (Signature Platter, 1918–23?*, fig. no. 9).[9] It is based on a design by Chekhonin that incorporates most of his artistic concepts. The center is painted with a magenta sunburst background emanating from a stylized sun enclosing the date 1917 and illuminating the part of the globe depicting Russia; it is framed by a hammer and sickle. Multicolored letters in the middle of the cavetto read "Autographs of the Architects of the Great Russian October Revolution." A twirling red ribbon and oak leaves circle the cavetto. (Oak and laurel leaves are traditionally reserved for heroes. The red riband derives from the design of the service for the Knights of the Order of St. Aleksandr Nevskii, from the Gardner Factory, commissioned by Ekaterina II in 1777 and completed in 1780.) The border is decorated with leaves and seventeen facsimile signatures. Clockwise from the bottom, they are the signatures of: Abel Enukidze, V. Iakovleva, V. Volodarskii, Zinov'ev, Trotskii, Moisei Uritskii, K. Eremeev, A. Riazanov, Nikolai Krestinskii, Lunacharskii, Vladimir Ulianov (Lenin), Georgii Chicherin, Aleksandra Kollontai, Vladimir Bonch-Bruevich, S. Gusev, and S. Zorin. Between Uritskii and Eremeev there is an indecipherable signature (which some have read as Podbelskii). It is noteworthy that neither Nikolai Bukharin's nor Stalin's signature is included.

One of the signatories, Kollontai, was a member of the Central Committee of the Communist Party and became People's Commissar for Social Welfare after the Revolution.

fig. 7
Vasilii Timorev
Plate, Congress of the Peoples of the East under the Presidency of Zinov'ev, *1920.*
Porcelain, 36 cm diameter.
Christie's, London.

fig. 8
Rudol'f Vil'de
Plate, We Celebrate while Working, May 1, 1920, *1920.*
Porcelain, 28 x 19 cm.
Private collection, London.

628

She also became the first Soviet woman ambassador—indeed the world's first woman ambassador in modern times—and, after brief postings to Norway and Mexico, was sent to Sweden (1930–45), where she was very popular. Kollontai liked propaganda porcelain and took several fine pieces with her to Sweden as gifts for government officials and personal friends. One of the items was a platter dated 1925, with a beautiful painting on it of Léon Bakst's famous costume design for Vaslav Nijinsky as Iskander in the ballet *La Péri*. (The original costume design is in the collection of the Metropolitan Museum, New York.) This platter was probably painted as a tribute to Bakst, who had died in Paris in 1924. There are several other platters at the Lomonosov Porcelain Factory Museum painted after Bakst costume designs.

A plate designed by Golenkina (fig. no. 10) is a good example of how Soviet artists drew upon themes from Russia's past. The plate is decorated with a torch-bearing red rider on a winged horse, also red (the Revolution), flying over collapsing monuments (the past) which are in flames. Clouds of smoke billow upward. The winged horse and its rider are backed by golden rays. The border is circled with black letters proclaiming, in German, "We Shall Set the World Ablaze with the Fire of the Third International." (A similar plate with the slogan in Russian can be seen at the State Historical Museum in Moscow.) The winged horse and its rider are Soviet adaptations of Il'ia Muromets, the peasant's son on his flying horse. Though the old pagan religion was finally vanquished by Christianity in the Slavic countries, vestiges of it remained in Russian epic poems. Among the most popular of these is the series devoted to Il'ia Muromets, who, though a good Christian, is portrayed with a number of features apparently derived from the pagan god of lightning, Perun.[10] Golenkina also seems to have been influenced by Bilibin's famous woodcut of this subject.

Other plates, drawing their inspiration from icons of St. George slaying the dragon (the triumph of Christianity over paganism), show a Red Army soldier, on horseback or on foot, slaying a dragon (the Revolution suppressing the counterrevolution).

Many Soviet propaganda plates have German inscriptions. There were various reasons for this. German was the language of Marx and was spoken by most international revolutionaries. In addition, German inscriptions may have been aimed at the Baltic states where German was the lingua franca. Lenin had hoped, moreover, for a German and European revolution. These hopes died after the failure of the November 1918 uprisings in Germany and the murders of the revolutionary heroes Karl Liebknecht and Rosa Luxemburg, both of whom appear on propaganda plates by Chekhonin. However, German continued to be used in propaganda for a few more years, perhaps because the unstable situation in Germany led the Soviet government to believe that Germans would be susceptible to Communism.

Numerous colorful plates and cups and saucers were painted by Shchekotikhina-Pototskaia, who also contributed many designs for plates that were executed by other artists at the porcelain factory. Shchekotikhina's trademarks are exuberant colors and subjects from eternal Russia: peasants feasting, bell ringers, betrothal scenes, the sun and the moon, motherhood, Snegurochka the Snowmaiden, fishermen, and accordion players.

Shchekotikhina came from a family of Old Believers whose traditional crafts were icon painting, illumination of old books, and embroidery. Her studies and her trip through northern Russia in 1910, sponsored by her art school, deepened her love and knowledge of naïve, native Russian art forms. A trip to Paris in 1913, at a time when Sergei Diaghilev's "Russian Seasons" were dazzling Parisians, further increased her

fig. 9
Sergei Chekhonin
Signature Platter, *1918–23?*
Porcelain, 54 x 38.5 cm.
Christie's, London.

fig. 10
Alisa Golenkina
Plate, We Shall Set the World Ablaze with the Fire of the
Third International, *1920.*
Porcelain, 23.8 cm diameter.
Private collection, London.

awareness that there was much to be proud of in her Russian heritage. Her familiarity with icons encouraged her to disregard perspective in her many fantastic compositions for porcelain. Her designs are full of energy and impetuous rhythm with exaggerated frontal figures and objects.

Occasionally she portrayed people of the new regime. *Progulka matrosa v Petrograde. 1 maia 1921 goda* (*The Sailor's Stroll in Petrograd, May 1, 1921,* 1921, fig. no. 11) shows a patriotically tattooed sailor of the Baltic Fleet strolling along a quay in Petrograd, arm-in-arm with his appropriately tattooed sweetheart.[11] The background includes colorful sailboats on the Neva River and the former Stock Exchange Building (now the Central Naval Museum), flanked by the Rostral Columns—all well-known Petrograd landmarks. The columns were designed to act as lighthouses, and the gas-fired torches are still lit on special occasions. They are lit on this dish to mark the fact that the Civil War was over at long last, and Russia was at peace. This made the First of May, 1921, a very special celebration.

Figurines

After the October Revolution, the State Porcelain Factory began producing sculptures reflecting the new reality. There was first a bust of Marx, in two sizes, by Kuznetsov (1918) and then *Krasnogvardeets* (*The Red Guard,* 1918), also by Kuznetsov. This defender of the people's state is the first Soviet sculpture in porcelain representing a man of the new epoch. It was Natal'ia Dan'ko, however, who became the acknowledged chronicler of the characters of the new Soviet era. She trained in the studios and workshops of four fine sculptors including Leonid Shervud, who had studied under Rodin. In 1910–11, Kuznetsov took her and another assistant with him when he went to Rome and Turin to oversee the final stages of the execution of reliefs and figures for the Russian pavilions at the *Esposizione internazionale di Roma* (*Rome International Exhibition,* Rome, 1911) and the *Esposizione internazionale d'industria e de lavoro* (*International Exhibition of Industry and Labor,* Turin, 1911). Thus, Dan'ko saw the monuments and statues of Rome, Florence, Venice, and Milan. In 1914, when Kuznetsov was appointed head of the sculpture workshop at the Imperial Porcelain Factory, Dan'ko went along as his assistant. From 1919, when Kuznetsov decided to leave Petrograd, until the factory was evacuated during World War II, she remained as head of the sculpture workshop.

Basing her work on the old folk traditions of Russian genre figurines, she set about creating figurines with contemporary relevance. Dan'ko's basic theme was the people in the street and in everyday life: men, women, and children, soldiers and sailors of the Revolution, bureaucrats, gypsy fortune tellers, and, later, cooperative farmers—a chronicle in porcelain of the first ten years of the citizens of the Soviet state. Dan'ko worked 313 months at the porcelain factory and created 311 works of art.[12] A dozen of the best-known and best-loved are: *Partizan v pokhode* (*Partisan on a Campaign*), *Matros* (*The Sailor*), *Matros so znamenem* (*Sailor with a Banner*), *Vyshivaiushchaia znamia* (*Woman Sewing a Banner*), *Militsionerka* (*The Militia Woman*), *Gadalka* (*The Fortune Teller*), *Rabotnitsa govoriashchaia rech'* (*Factory Woman Making a Speech*), *Mal'chik s krasnoi gazetoi* (*Newspaper Boy*), *Anna Akhmatova, Piatiletie Krasnoi armii* (*Fifth Anniversary of the Red Army* group statue), *Prodavshchitsa tsvetov* (*Flower Girl*), and *Khuligan s balalaikoi* (*Street Hooligan with Balalaika*). Then there is her amazing chess set, *Krasnye i belye* (*The Reds and the Whites*). This set was designed and produced in 1922–23 for exhibitions abroad. The Red king is a worker holding a sledgehammer, the Red queen a peasant woman holding a sheaf of wheat; the White king is a skeleton wearing a black cloak, the White queen a woman with a horn of plenty out of which gold pieces spill. The Red pawns represent busts

fig. 11
Aleksandra Shchekotikhina-Pototskaia
Plate, The Sailor's Stroll in Petrograd, May 1, 1921, *1921.*
Porcelain, 35.9 cm diameter.
Gilman Paper Company Collection.

of peasants, each holding a sheaf of wheat and a sickle; the White pawns represent busts of slaves, wrapped thrice in black chains. The subject matter and the modeling are remarkable. Ideally, the pieces should be laid out on a red-and-white board. The chess set was shown and sold in Paris in 1925, and orders for it came in from as far away as Australia.

Another Dan'ko creation is a statuette consisting of two Soviet stevedores unloading sacks stamped AMERICAN MEAL USA and GOSTORG PETROGRAD RSFSR (Gostorg being the acronym for the State Trading Agency). The prototype of the figurine was created in 1922 and quite a few were produced. It is proof in porcelain and a surviving Soviet reminder of the generosity of the United States and the work of the American Relief Administration (ARA), which saved millions of lives in the RSFSR during the great famine of 1920–21 in the Volga region. A member of the Soviet government later wrote: "The people of the Soviet Union will never forget the generous help of the American people." The same government was to order the arrest of all Soviet citizens who had worked for the ARA on the grounds that they were potential spies.[13]

The famine, which claimed millions of lives, provided tragic subject matter for the porcelain artists. Plates and dishes were painted for a charity sale to raise money for the starving population. These items carried on the reverse a special mark designed by Chekhonin and painted by hand. It consisted of the State Porcelain Factory mark and the notations "1921" and "To benefit the starving," all in gold. There are apparently twenty-three pieces with this mark. The auction never took place and the pieces remained at the factory. Some were eventually sold. Three pieces with this mark can be seen at the Kuskovo State Porcelain Museum, near Moscow, and one at the British Museum, London.

Constructivist, Cubist, Suprematist, and Other Abstract Porcelain

Most of the avant-garde artists in the RSFSR in the early 1920s created one or more designs for either the State Porcelain Factory or the Ceramics Faculty at Vkhutemas (the Higher Artistic-Technical Workshops) in Moscow. Many of these designs were never executed, as was the case with Liubov' Popova's Cubist composition for a cup and saucer. Aleksandr Vesnin created several designs for porcelain in Constructivist style, of which only one was executed—probably by a Vkhutemas student—on Dulevo ceramic. It is based on a design by Vesnin commemorating the Third International, and the sharp linear elements and gold-silver-and-black color scheme are characteristic of his work. Lebedev made Cubist designs for plates that were executed. Lapshin's tea service and plates decorated with an abstract pink-white-and-black design are well known abroad; examples of this service can be seen at both the Ludwig Museum in Cologne and the Badisches Landesmuseum, Karlsruhe. A single example exists at the Lomonosov Porcelain Factory Museum of a plate decorated with a design by Vladimir Tatlin, painted by Chekhonin. However, as it is based on a costume sketch for a protagonist in *Tsar' Maksimilian i ego nepokornyi syn Adol'f (The Emperor Maksimilian and His Disobedient Son Adol'f)*, a folk drama produced in Moscow in 1911 and in St. Petersburg in 1912, it is arguable that it was not designed specifically to decorate porcelain. From 1927 to 1930, Tatlin was a teacher at Vkhutein (the Higher Artistic-Technical Institute) in Moscow; he taught in the Metalworking and Woodworking faculties and, in due course, in the Ceramics Faculty as well. Tatlin designed a milk jug meant to be used as a milk bottle for babies in the many collective nurseries that had sprung up. One of his students, Aleksei Sotnikov, later made a series of baby bottles and a tray in which they could be carried, ten at a time (plate no. 529).

Sotnikov joined the Dulevo Porcelain Factory, near Moscow, as a sculptor in 1934, and his sculpture *Sokola (The Falcon)* became the factory mark. Aleksandr Rodchenko created spherical black, red, and white designs for an eight-piece tea service in 1922. It was not executed during his lifetime.

Kandinskii made a few sketches for the decoration of porcelain in 1921 before leaving Russia for Germany. Three of these sketches are at the library of the Lomonosov Porcelain Factory. Others are in private collections in Moscow and in museum collections in France (at the Centre Georges Pompidou, Paris) and Germany.

Although Kandinskii designed for porcelain, he had a decorative as opposed to utilitarian conception of applied art. The cups and saucers with Kandinskii designs simply show characteristic, colorful elements from the pictorial imagery of his pre-Bauhaus period. They are not created with the curved surface of the cup in mind. Moreover, the designs for the saucers are for the center of the cavetto, rather than circling it, which means that the decoration is partly concealed when the cup is resting on the saucer. (Of course, in Russia many people drank from the saucer, and Kandinskii may have designed with this habit in mind).

(As Kandinskii did not paint on porcelain himself and, having left Russia, could not supervise the cups and saucers painted according to his designs, one wonders whether it is right to attribute them to Kandinskii. When the original artist has no involvement in the reproduction process, is the work still his?)

Early Kandinskii cups and saucers are extremely rare. There are none at the Lomonosov Porcelain Factory Museum. Contemporary exhibition catalogues show that a cup and saucer with a Kandinskii design were exhibited at the *Erste russische Kunstausstellung (First Russian Art Exhibition,* Berlin, 1922), and three cups and saucers with a Kandinskii design were exhibited at Stockholm in 1923.[14]

In the 1960s, a student of Rodchenko's, Zakhar Bykov, became director of the Stroganov School of Applied Art in Moscow and suggested that students in the ceramics section paint cups and saucers based on the designs of Kandinskii and of Rodchenko. Most Kandinskii cups and saucers in museums and in private collections date from this period, though they frequently bear an earlier date.

Malevich, founder and leader of the Suprematist movement, and two of his followers, Suetin and Chashnik, arrived in Leningrad from Vitebsk in 1922.

At the end of 1922, Al'tman and Shterenberg returned from the *Erste russische Kunstausstellung,* having learned that there was a tremendous interest abroad in Russian avant-garde designs and painting. They must have reported this to their colleagues at Izo Narkompros, which was in charge of exhibitions within the country and abroad and under whose aegis the State Porcelain Factory found itself. The result was that Malevich, Suetin, and Chashnik were asked, either by Nikolai Punin or by Chekhonin, to create some decorative designs for the State Porcelain Factory.

There were two kinds of ceramic design undertaken by these three artists. In the first, the complete object was rethought along Suprematist lines; in the second, Suprematist decoration was painted onto existing plates and cups and saucers of standard design.

Malevich designed a teapot that looks like a locomotive and some demitasse cups that are, literally, cups cut in half (plate nos. 185–186). The teapot is modeled in an ordered scale of cylinder and sphere to curve and of square to rectangle. Balancing the masses and thus achieving dynamic tension was one of the objectives of Suprematism. Though Malevich did not intend the teapot to be a functional object, but rather a study of the interaction of forms, it is agreeable to handle and pours well.

Suetin designed another curious teapot, a milk jug, and a series of inkstands which look like a horizontal arkhitekton or spatial composition. The inkstands are cuboid in form and stand on a base made up of square and rectangular slabs laid on a quarter-circle. Sometimes they have a large standing disc at the back.

All these ideas were original and thought-provoking, but only a few such experimental pieces were produced.

Suprematists considered the color white—and therefore white porcelain—an ideal medium since it expressed weightlessness. To Malevich it also symbolized infinity. Onto this white background they painted their designs made up of red, yellow, black, and white triangles, rectangles, squares, and circles, which seem to interact and to float, defying the laws of gravity and generating a remarkable energy.

In 1920, in Vitebsk, Malevich wrote the text and made the lithographs for *Suprematizm. 34 risunka* (*Suprematism: 34 Drawings*), published in 1921. The album provided a survey and graphic paraphrase of his major Suprematist paintings of 1915 onward. Malevich never painted plates himself, but designs from the album were used by factory artists to decorate plates. The design on one such plate (plate no. 187) is the same as that of the lithograph entitled *Aeroplan letit* (*Airplane Flying*) in *Suprematism: 34 Drawings*. The oil painting of *Airplane Flying* (1915) is in the collection of the Museum of Modern Art, New York.

Suetin and Chashnik made designs for the decoration of teapots, coffee pots, plates, cups and saucers and also painted on all these items themselves. Chashnik's 1923 design for a cup and saucer consisting of a black circle bisected by a red axial stripe was one of his most successful designs for porcelain. In the Central Lenin Museum, Moscow, there is another bold design by Chashnik for a platter with LENIN and a red square in its black cavetto (plate no. 146). It was designed to honor Lenin after his death in 1924 and ensuing deification, and reminds one of the sacred monogram IHS on church plates.

Most early Suprematist pieces were intended for export. Chashnik or Suetin would paint a prototype item which they signed or initialed, adding the word "Suprematism" and the number 474, as well as a black square within a square, the symbol of the followers of Unovis (the Affirmers of the New Art) and of Suprematism. These prototypes usually remained at the factory, or inside Russia. The factory artists would make copies to be sent to exhibitions and trade fairs abroad. The backs of the authorized factory copies are usually marked *po ris Chashnika* ("based on design by Chashnik") or *po ris Suetina* ("based on design by Suetin"). The entire 1922–24 Suprematist output probably consisted of less than one thousand items. It is what one might call first-edition Suprematism. Subsequent authorized repeats are in the same category as other later editions and should be considered as such. (The demand for Suprematist ceramics in recent years has caused many signed, posthumous pieces to appear on the market.)

Suprematism and its basic motifs were taken up by many artists working in ceramics in the late 1920s and early 1930s at the Lomonosov Porcelain Factory and at the Dulevo Porcelain Factory. Indeed, thanks to the fact that Suetin was art director at the Lomonosov Factory from 1932 to 1954, Suprematism gained a new lease on life there, when artists elsewhere had turned to Socialist Realism.

Design Training

Experimental work and training was carried out at Vkhutemas, which had replaced the State Free Art Workshops in 1920. In 1927, the Moscow Vkhutemas became Vkhutein.

(Vkhutemas/Vkhutein workshops existed in both Petrograd and Moscow.) Experimental work also went on at the Central Artistic Ceramic Laboratory (1922–23), the Artistic Bureau of the State Experimental Institute of Silicates (1924–28), and the Commission for the Study of Ceramics at the State Academy of Artistic Sciences (1926–29).[15]

Exhibitions Abroad

In 1921, the New Economic Policy (NEP) was launched. Diplomatic relations began to be normalized and foreign trade was encouraged. The Lomonosov Porcelain Factory was placed under the aegis of the Academic Center of Scientific and Artistic Institutions of the RSFSR. At the same time, the People's Commissariat of Foreign Affairs reserved for itself the factory's entire output of artistic wares for five years. Services were ordered for the new Soviet embassies and hundreds of pieces were sent abroad to advertise the new regime and bring back desperately needed hard currency. The first exhibition of Russian porcelain abroad was, as mentioned above, at the *Erste russische Kunstausstellung*. The ceramics section included 125 plates, cups and saucers, and teapots. This exhibition went on to Amsterdam in 1923. Other exhibitions took place in Tallinn, Estonia (1923); Lyons (1923); Stockholm (1923); Paris (the *Exposition internationale des arts décoratifs et industriels modernes* [*International Exhibition of Decorative and Industrial Art,* 1925]); Lyons (1926); Monza, Italy (1927); Paris (1928); New York, Philadelphia, Boston, and Detroit (1929); Monza (1930); Leipzig (1930); Winterthur, Zurich, St. Gallen, and Basel, Switzerland (1931); and Vienna (1931). The pieces that did not sell in Paris in 1925 were sent to England, where they were sold at a shop in Hampstead called Fortunate Finds.

Propaganda porcelain was also sold in special state stores in Petrograd and Moscow. At first, the State Porcelain Factory had no store, but eventually it was decided to turn the former Kornilov Bros. porcelain store on Nevskii Avenue in Petrograd into a showcase for the factory. (The store is still selling Lomonosov Porcelain Factory wares today, at 63 Nevskii Avenue.) Despite their relatively high prices, all the items sold rapidly, fully recovering production costs. This caused Izo Narkompros to worry that propaganda porcelain was being bought by collectors and foreigners rather than by the workers for whom it was intended. A lively eyewitness account—by Elena Dan'ko—has survived of the store on what was then known as October 25th Avenue:

Anyone who remembers the Petrograd of those years—the jagged wildernesses of its avenues and its deserted houses plunged into darkness and cold, their windows starred with the traces of recent bullets—will remember too the window-display of china on October 25th Avenue. There, on dazzling white plates, red stars glittered, the hammer and sickle shone with the dull gleam of gold on porcelain, and fabulous flowers were plaited into the initials of the RSFSR. There stood tiny porcelain Red Guards, sailors, and partisans, and new Reds and Whites chess sets sparkled. A large plate bore the legend, encircled by a garland of flowers: "We Will Turn the Whole World into a Blossoming Garden." Passersby would stop at the window and gaze long at the china. This china was a message from a beautiful future . . . This china went the rounds of the capital cities of Europe.[16]

Today Soviet porcelain of the 1920s is being exhibited and collected not only in Russia and Europe but also in Japan and the United States. Whether featuring revolutionary slogans or Suprematist designs, these plates cause the viewer to notice and remember them, thus fulfilling the intentions of their creators.

Russian Fabric Design, 1928–32

Charlotte Douglas

After the devastation of the Civil War and Lenin's consequent economic reforms that emphasized individual initiative and allowed limited free enterprise, there was widespread reaction on the part of Bolshevik activists against such apparent ideological "backsliding." Among young Marxist artists there was a drive to develop a pragmatic critical theory and to apply simple tests for political content in art, as well as a concerted effort to enlist the Party's approval and support. By the late 1920s, all artistic media in the country were being subjected to strong pressures to bear a clear and persuasive ideological message. The primary organ of these pressures was not the government directly or Communist Party ideologues but the artists themselves, many of whom had formed influential organizations that moved the class warfare that was engaging other sectors of society into the arts. These young people saw themselves as upholding the Party line, and they carried on their agitation through organizations and exhibitions, social education and political maneuvering, and publications, especially the journals *Iskusstvo v massy* (*Art to the Masses,* 1929–32), the organ of AKhR (the Association of Artists of the Revolution); *Za proletarskoe iskusstvo* (*For Proletarian Art,* 1931–32), the publication of RAPKh (the Russian Association of Proletarian Artists); and *Brigada khudozhnikov* (*Artists' Brigade,* 1931–32), the journal of FOSKh (the Federation of Associations of Soviet Artists).

The older generation of avant-garde fabric artists such as Ol'ga Rozanova, Varvara Stepanova, and Liubov' Popova had rejected figuration in textile patterns in favor of geometric designs, which offered a distinct break from former styles and appeared devoid of all references to particular social classes. Abstract or non-objective textiles were seen as a means of establishing a new life, international in scope and classless in structure.

The younger textile artists and critics, to a large extent the students of the abstract designers, in the late 1920s abandoned the geometric principles that had been the foundation of their training. They argued instead that fabric, as a basic visual element in the everyday environment, was a major weapon in the struggle for current social ideals—collective farm life, sports, industrialization, engineering, and electrification. These young designers were militant in their search for a proletarian rather than a classless art, and they led the charge against both the old floral designs, which they considered patently bourgeois, and the recent Constructivist geometries, which they associated with leftist political deviations. They themselves became the inventors of a brilliant new Soviet figurative ornament, and they attempted to force its production throughout the textile industry.

A major display of the work of both generations of textile artists took place between October 1928 and February 1929 at the exhibition *Bytovoi sovetskii tekstil'* (*Soviet Textiles for Daily Life*), held at Vkhutein, Moscow's famous Higher Artistic-Technical Institute. Timed to coincide with the official beginning of the First Five-Year Plan—Stalin's forced march of the Soviet Union into industrialization—the exhibition was a broad survey of all elements of the textile industry: there were displays by various factories and their in-house designers; by sales agents, who exhibited samples of cloth along with the corresponding sales records; by schools, including various regional technical schools and Vkhutein; and by individual faculty members and designers who were selling their work either directly to factories or to the All-Union Textile Syndicate—an association of factories and trusts and an administrative body for the industry (fig. nos. 1, 4). The purpose of the exhibition was to consider the Soviet textile industry as a whole and to establish a starting line for its coming five-year sprint to rectify severe fabric shortages. The exhibition had been suggested by the Society of Textile Artists, the artists' professional organization, and eagerly supported by the active and politically conscious students at Vkhutein, many of whom were women and all of whom were close to graduation. The official sponsors were the Chief Art Administration and the All-Union Textile Syndicate. Over fifty Vkhutein students took part, about a third of whom were students of weaving and the rest designers of printed fabric (fig. nos. 2–3).[1] The work of established artists and faculty such as Liudmila Maiakovskaia, Evgeniia Pribyl'skaia, and Varvara Stepanova was prominently shown. The designs attributed to individual artists—as opposed to one or another of the factory collectives—were predominantly geometric. Some of the Vkhutein students, however, exhibited their latest "theme" designs.

A jury composed of representatives of the Art Administration, the Textile Syndicate, the Academy of Artistic Sciences, and various arts organizations under the aegis of the Central Committee of the Communist Party awarded prizes for designs. Unable to agree on an "ideal solution to the problem of decorating fabric under contemporary conditions," the jury failed to award a first prize, but second and third prizes were given both to working artists and to students. Among the sixteen second-prize winners were Maiakovskaia, Oskar Griun, and K. A. Shchuko, and the students Mariia Anufrieva and Tat'iana Chachkhiani (fig. nos. 5–6, plate nos. 558, 561). The thirteen third-prize winners included Stepanova and Pribyl'skaia (fig. no. 7, plate no. 554).[2] The majority of the prizewinning designs were abstract. In a review of the section of student weaving, the work was unfavorably compared to the weaving by Bauhaus students that had been shown at Vkhutein the previous spring; the poor results were attributed to some extent to the school's lack of adequate equipment.[3] The exhibition had yet another purpose, one which was less overt but nevertheless present in the minds of many of the organizers. They hoped that the exhibit would give an impetus to the establishment of a central design studio that would serve all the textile factories and trusts. Such a studio would obviate the need for design studios associated with individual factories and make it possible to respond efficiently to market demands.[4] A central studio would also limit the need for French pattern books.

Prior to World War I, Russian factories subscribed to albums of French fabric designs that were issued at intervals in Paris. These provided the main source of clothing and upholstery designs manufactured for the urban middle class. In addition to the French designs, which were sometimes modified slightly by the factory artists, traditional cotton floral patterns were produced for rural and provincial use, and special designs aimed at local tastes were made for export eastward— to Central Asia, Persia, western China, Mongolia, and Afghanistan.

World War I, the two revolutions, and the Civil War effectively destroyed the Russian textile industry. Of the almost nine hundred factories operating in Russia in 1913, fewer than a third had reopened by 1921, and these were capable of producing only the most basic types of cloth— sometimes completely unprinted. The next several years were spent in reorganization and in the gradual recovery of the industry. By 1927 the industry had just about regained its 1913 level of production, but many of the former managers and workers had been lost and the industry was contending with inadequate administration and inexperienced workers recently arrived from the countryside. By late in the decade, therefore, with industrial output gradually improving, the question of again subscribing to the Parisian pattern books was being considered throughout the industry. Such a suggestion met

fig. 2
Vkhutein display at the Soviet Textiles for Daily Life *exhibition, Moscow, 1928 (detail).*

fig. 3
Vkhutein display at the Soviet Textiles for Daily Life *exhibition, Moscow, 1928.*

fig. 4
Factory displays at the Soviet Textiles for Daily Life *exhibition, Moscow, 1928.*

fig. 5
Displays by Shchuko (left) and Maiakovskaia (right) at the Soviet
Textiles for Daily Life *exhibition, Moscow, 1928.*

fig. 6
Liudmila Maiakovskaia
Geometric, *ca. 1927.*
Airbrush on silk, 54 x 40 cm.
Maiakovskii Museum, Moscow.

fig. 7
Third- and fourth-prize winners at the Soviet Textiles for Daily
Life *exhibition, Moscow, 1928.*

with opposition for a number of reasons. Hard-currency resources were extremely scarce, and the subscriptions cost three thousand to four thousand gold rubles apiece.[5] Relatively little fabric other than fabric for clothing was being produced, yet the subscription patterns were not suitable even for all types of this fabric; they offered nothing for workers' or peasants' dress fabric, for example, or for the export market.

A central design studio under the aegis of the Textile Syndicate would be more efficient, it was argued, and serve as a focus for the best of the country's designers. The studios attached to factories were considered both politically retrograde and of questionable skill, especially by the young designers who argued that people with an old, prerevolutionary mentality could not be trusted to create the bulk of the new designs for production. Removing the factory studios promised to eliminate the politically "backward" and troublesome artists of the factory studios, as well as to reduce the number of politically less desirable designs on the market. In early 1928, some saw a centralized studio as an opportunity to stop reproducing foreign designs altogether and to create more ideologically appropriate new designs.[6] And in the event that Parisian designs were considered necessary after all, only one subscription would be needed.[7]

Members of the Textile Syndicate hesitated, arguing that the factory designers were also capable of creating original and appropriate designs. They spoke of making sure that *existing* designs were suitable for the type of cloth and were interesting, that the various regions were supplied with the proper types of fabric, and that any new designs be responsive primarily to the taste of consumers.[8] Even so, it could be argued that, organized into a central studio with advice from industry representatives, factory artists might do even better.[9]

By 1928 the Vkhutein students had created a textile division within OMAKhR (the Young People's Section of the Association of Artists of the Revolution). The parent organization, AKhR, was a well-established, aggressively proselytizing group of middle-aged men, whose advocacy of popular and quasiproletarian themes in painting received solid financial and political support from the army and from labor organizations. It had been founded in 1922 in defense of easel painting in a naturalistic mode, and in bitter opposition to the notion of replacing painting with the industrial arts, as advocated by avant-garde groups. The idea of admitting fabric designers into the main organization can hardly have been received by older members with enthusiasm. But the young people's section was dominated by the energetic Vkhutein students, both men and women, who were committed to social proselytizing by means of mass-produced objects and who were adroit at political infighting.

Lacking an appropriate art-political organization to join after graduation, the OMAKhR students threatened and cajoled AKhR into accommodating their concerns in a major reorganization. Nor did they hesitate to lecture their older colleagues on their rigid approach to style, lest "the struggle against naked Formalism . . . turn into a struggle against formal investigations of a new content" and "content [be] understood as passively naturalistic, the purely contemplative perception of our epoch."[10] In the fall of 1928, thirty-five members of OMAKhR joined AKhR, several assuming administrative positions. In the June 1929 OMAKhR exhibition, dedicated to the tenth anniversary of the Young Communists League, the textile artists exhibited thematic or agitational designs (fig. nos. 8–12).[11]

The *Soviet Textiles for Daily Life* exhibition in the winter of 1928–29 and the OMAKhR exhibition in the spring of 1929 inaugurated a heated debate throughout many organizations and the press that would last for the next three and a half years.

fig. 8
Anufrieva, Balloons, *fabric design in OMAKhR exhibition, Moscow, 1929.*

The young designers had, in some sense, taken up where the old avant-garde left off. From their teachers they had learned that the new Marxist country required an entirely new art, one invented and enforced by the artists, with support from above. But whereas the old avant-garde, under the influence of Lenin's early internationalist aspirations, had argued in favor of abstraction because of its classlessness, its lack of a specifically bourgeois history, the new designers, adopting the contemporary political viewpoint that looked to "revolution in one country," argued for a precisely *proletarian* art, an art that would strengthen the grip of the "dictatorship of the proletariat." Neither group questioned the role of the artist or the necessity of enforcing an "official" art that was specific to the new economic organization of the country. Both generations of artists saw the design of everyday objects as a means of raising the political consciousness of the masses. In the new Soviet state, the "masses" meant, for the most part, an illiterate and superstitious peasantry and undisciplined workers of recent peasant extraction.

At the time of the June 1929 exhibition, Frida Roginskaia, an historian of textiles and an influential writer, urged the industry to accept the new agitational designs for more extensive production,[12] but, in fact, the few thematic designs that already had been produced had elicited very little enthusiasm on the part of consumers. There were those who would try to surmount this difficulty by broadening the artistic base of design work, attracting as many artists to it as possible, because "the attempt of textile artists to monopolize the right to design fabric is an unhealthy phenomenon."[13] As time went on and consumers continued to avoid the new designs, the debates grew angry. Petr Rusin (Rusinov), artist, Party candidate, and head of the studio at the leading First Cotton-Printing Factory, declared unequivocally, "The market doesn't need your ideological art even for free!"[14] The Textile Syndicate and the sales agents—who were considered the "market experts"[15]—were also hostile to the agitational designs. They saw their primary task as selling cloth, regardless of Marxist analyses of the content of its printed pattern, so as to supply a product badly needed by society and to strengthen the recovering textile industry.

The young designers, however, branded this outlook pure "market capitalism." The resistance on the part of consumers, they said—most notably, the deep desire for floral patterns—was precisely *proof* of the social necessity for the uplifting effect of the new themes. "Of all the objects of daily use, textiles most clearly reflect the ideology of the ruling class of the epoch in which they were created," and so "every textile design has a social origin," the AKhR group asserted, and plant forms clearly derived from the feudal epoch.[16] Roginskaia agreed, but with somewhat less assurance. "The problem of plant ornament," she wrote, "is actually very complex—its solution is ahead of us." She disputed the opinion that "flowers always and for everyone are beautiful in the same way": "Actually, of course, this is not so . . . Naturally, plant ornament should have a large place in Soviet textile design, since a good part of the textiles goes to the peasantry. But it is also completely obvious that in an epoch of transition to collective agriculture, to methods of working the land using tractors and cultivators, to an era of building colossal collective farms, a design with plant elements must acquire a completely different character."[17]

Aleksei Fedorov-Davydov, a prominent Marxist art historian and a representative of the Chief Art Administration, was chairman of the *Soviet Textiles for Daily Life* exhibition committee. Writing in the introduction to the catalogue, he characterized fabric as "ideological goods" with great potential, because "the millions of yards of fabric distributed yearly penetrate to the smallest corners and the furthest peoples of the

fig. 9
Daria Preobrazhenskaia
Transportation, *late 1920s–early 1930s.*
State Russian Museum, St. Petersburg.

country."[18] The thought that *everyone* had to wear clothes, and that they wore them for a great *length of time,* was particularly appealing to Fedorov-Davydov: "The pictures produced even by such mechanically reproduced figurative popular art as posters or postcards cannot be compared with the extent of distribution or the length and constancy of a dress's or dish's or piece of furniture's action on the psychology of a person . . . An object's design appeals directly to our emotions, often bypassing logical associations. It is perceived purely reflectively, and it is stamped on a person's most fundamental psychological life and social behavior."[19]

The new generation of textile artists, like many of the young activists who led the class war on other fronts, were both militant in their beliefs and consummate political organizers. Frustrated by the All-Union Textile Association's reluctance to mandate the new designs and by the slow progress of the proposed central design studio, they had by the middle of 1929 succeeded in attaching to the Association an Art Council dominated by the AKhR artists and eventually headed by I. S. Perepelitsyn. Through this organ the AKhR textile artists gained ideological control of most of the designs that went into production throughout the country. New patterns produced by factory studios and other organizations were supposed to receive prior approval from the Council, which enforced rigid Marxist social and class criteria.[20] The Council saw its primary task as the removal of all designs that were "alien to the [proletarian] class, harmful, or neutral."[21] This powerful position occupied by the younger generation was further consolidated by the closing of Vkhutein in 1930 and the transfer of the Textiles Faculty to the Art Department of the Moscow Textile Institute, a department headed by one of their own, Mariia Nazarevskaia. The moderate opposition found itself open to the dangerous charge of opposing the Revolution and was increasingly on the defensive. The artist-activist Nadezhda Poluektova wrote in late 1930, "And if now it is not possible for those estranged elements to engage us in an open fight about principles, if one must not openly refuse to recognize the proletarian dictatorship, then there are other methods of fighting: lies, slander, double-dealing, deceit, sabotage—the classical methods of enemies and beloved methods of right and left opportunists."[22]

While debates about the efficacy and appropriateness of the new agitational designs raged on, the Art Council *acted,* conducting a thorough purge of the old designs. The Council swarmed through factory archives and studios, inspecting thousands of the old designs for ideological purity. Between late 1929 and the spring of 1931, Perepelitsyn's organization destroyed some 24,000 textile drawings and designs—most of them floral—and ground the flowers off thousands of the metal rollers used for printing fabric.[23]

Only about one out of three design proposals submitted to the Council passed the ideological test; there was no test for artistic quality. But even approved designs might be long kept from production, for they were apt to run into trouble with the workers in the factory studios who prepared the drawings for transfer to the rollers. Feeling injured by the raids made on their studio archives and libraries, their work supplanted by new "unpretty" drawings whose aesthetic quality they questioned, factory artists were likely to refuse to have anything to do with the new patterns. Thus the ideological screening by the Art Council acted as a persistent roadblock to the production of any fabric at all by the beleaguered industry. Yet any attempt by the factories to modify or circumvent the Council's policies brought on vociferous public charges by the fundamentalists of anti-Marxism and anti-Bolshevism. The result was a stalemate; by 1931 there was a persistent shortage of fabric and no means to rectify the situation in the foreseeable future.

In an attempt to better organize the industry and to revise the Art Council, redirecting its activities to more productive work, a conference on the topic "What Soviet Textile Design Should Be" was called in the spring of 1931 under the auspices of the newspaper of the Textile Workers Union, *Golos tekstilei* (*The Textiles' Voice*). It was attended by artists, factory artists, union workers, industry and sales representatives, and members of the Textile Association and educational institutions. The meeting began on a practical and ideologically moderate level. The keynote speech was given by David Arkin from the Academy of Artistic Sciences, who took a view considerably different from that which had been expressed by Fedorov-Davydov. Arkin maintained that it was a mistake to consider fabric similar to posters or other agitational art, because, unlike them, clothing is meant to be seen for a long time and will eventually simply bore the wearer with its social message: "From the very beginning we made mistakes when we began to produce theme designs. We approached the textile or fabric just like the poster and the picture, without taking into account its particularities and the application of each kind [of design]—for clothing, furniture, the table, the bed, and so forth. The full-scale thematic design presupposes, as a rule, the human figure (it is hard to imagine our Soviet themes in developed form without [the depiction of] a person). *Such full-scale thematic design for clothing and dress fabric should be rejected."* [24]

Nevertheless, in support of continued innovation in the development of proletarian designs, Arkin approved of the recent appearance of motifs "based on an emblem, either of the Soviet government—the hammer and sickle—or of industrial or collective-farm labor, all kinds of factory motifs, machine parts, production equipment, etc." (fig. no. 13, plate no. 567). But even in approving emblems as a motif Arkin was understandably nervous about the Art Council's tendency to extremes, and cautioned that such designs must remain "unobtrusive": "A great quantity of examples can be given where the separate elements of machines—for example, gears, pincers, tools—are depicted on the fabric. These tools or pieces of machines are depicted so that they are not essentially emblems, but illustrate the tendency of many artists and whole trends to elevate machine forms into fetishes or idols [plate no. 569]. This elevation of machine parts into some kind of divinity is not a proletarian approach to the machine."[25]

The Art Council came in for bitter criticism at the conference. A delegate from the Central Union sales agency called it a "living corpse," and even Roginskaia reproved it for "splitting hairs."[26] It was criticized for not assuming any real responsibility for the development of designs or for their general quality. It was also reproved for doing nothing to educate factory artists politically or to address any of the wider ideological issues.[27]

The apparent lack of enthusiasm for the new designs on the part of consumers was a major problem. In this era of forced collectivization the peasantry and agricultural workers were apt to regard the designs as yet another cruel joke perpetrated by the urban bureaucracy. Yet many artists and theorists found it impossible to believe that the tastes of workers and peasants did not in fact correspond to their social class, and that changing a person's preferences in printed cloth was not simply a matter of raising class consciousness. Fedorov-Davydov in his introduction to the *Soviet Textiles for Daily Life* catalogue had relied upon the masses to defend against a purely market approach to design: "Given the enormous cultural and political significance of the artistic side of the textile . . . we can't just leave the business of its artistic composition to the blind action of the market; we can't consider it only an economic problem. We have to attract social attention to this question, to interest

fig. 10
Nikitina, The Komsomol in Production, *fabric design in
OMAKhR exhibition, Moscow, 1929.*

our masses in it, to bring them nearer to an understanding of and an active influence on the art of the textile."[28] But after three years, sales records still showed that consumers, especially in the rural areas, persisted in responding more favorably to floral designs than to the new social motifs. At the conference Arkin, an aesthetic moderate who energetically opposed excessively industrial and figurative motifs on fabric, still could not bring himself to admit that buyers might recognize what was best for them. It was necessary to "study the demand of the genuine mass consumer," he told his audience, "but we mustn't go too far in this direction—[believing] that everything the consumer likes is law."[29] Roginskaia, too, tried to reconcile contradictions by implying that the wrong consumers had been consulted: "We must orient ourselves to the organized consumers, and among them to the consumer in the most advanced ranks, the shock worker among collective farmers and laborers."[30]

Far from everyone at the conference was enamored of the representational designs. The designers of weaving, although mentioned from time to time by AKhR interests, seemed to have changed little since the 1928 exhibition and simply to have ignored ideological requirements. Artists with impeccable proletarian credentials, such as the designers from the Red Rose silk factory, put up public resistance to representation. Without mincing words, Chachkhiani, herself a graduate of Vkhutein, asserted: "[In dress fabric] thematic designs are impossible . . . It is unthinkable to introduce the human face, the tractor, the factory. It is simply uncivilized."[31] Maiakovskaia, a revolutionary for more than twenty years, defended her nonrepresentational designs: "Primarily a classical type of design (stripes, spots, rings) is needed now on silk. The fabric is expensive; buyers can't make several silk dresses. They will select a neutral design, one that neither bores them nor hits them in the eye." She used thematic designs on scarves, she said, and in the future might use them for linings. Like several others, she sought to consolidate her position through organization and demanded a special "silk section" of the Art Council to address the special problems of this fabric.[32]

In spite of the statement in the concluding document of the conference that the Art Council, as it exists, "to all intents and purposes has exercised no responsibility for the artistic side of fabric design and hasn't had any effect on production, has not organized social opinion around the quality of the textile drawing, and should be immediately eliminated," this document actually expanded rather than limited the Council's powers. It was recommended that the Art Council extend its activities to the whole art side of the textile industry, that it add an executive committee to oversee the daily running of its activities, that it organize separate sections to administer different types of fabric, and that it conduct reeducation work among factory artists. The conference also went on record in favor of moving quickly toward the central design studios, advocated greater control of weaving, silk, and piece goods, and proposed research laboratories under the Council's supervision to "verify new drawings with the organized consumer."[33]

During the meeting, proponents of the agitational motifs overwhelmed all contrary opinion. More moderate forces were unable to withstand the onslaught of these young people, whose opinions were composed of a classical mixture of patriotism, class hatred, and implicit faith in a scientific theory. Although factory representatives and sales agents signed the concluding document, their opinions were not represented in it. The AKhR group backed down slightly on the question of the figurative motifs for dress fabric, but they reasserted their importance on fabric for every other type of use: *"The conference considers that the basis of {the new} design is the*

fig. 11
Zotov, Transportation, *fabric design in OMAKhR exhibition, Moscow, 1929.*

fig. 12
Grigorovich, Bikers, *fabric design in OMAKhR exhibition, Moscow, 1929.*

development of socially significant themes . . . If in the assortment for dresses these should be primarily ornamental or emblematic, then in decorative and piece goods the problem of the fully developed theme should be at the center of attention."[34]

Ultimately the conference had little effect on the AKhR designers. As if in direct defiance of Arkin's prescriptions, Nazarevskaia designed a new dress fabric with not one but many human figures—peasants helped by Red Army soldiers—picking cotton (plate no. 594). But with the onset of the Second Five-Year Plan, the country moved back to ideals that included bourgeois comforts, and the Communist Party intervened to bring the quarreling and the production of agitational designs to a halt.

On October 6, 1933, *Pravda* carried a witty but ominous article on dress fabric entitled "A Tractor in Front, A Combine Behind":

Now here is a new bright little chintz. No little flowers on it— that's petit-bourgeois. No little stripes—that's creeping Empire style. No little checks—that's an echo of feudalism. This fabric has big tractors and big combines printed on it . . .

If you want to acquaint the backward inhabitants of the city with life in the new collectivized village, don't write any articles, don't deliver any lectures. Best of all, deck yourself out in a dress of this here fabric. A multicolored picture. A very complex composition.

The big new building of the rural cooperative with a huge sign. At the entry of the cooperative there are . . . horses harnessed to a wagon.

But an exterior view alone won't do. And right here even what is going on inside the store is shown. Peasant men and women crowd at the counter. A bearded clerk sells goods. To limit oneself to just the coop building means not to present an ideologically consistent dress.

The article singles out Perepelitsyn as head of the Art Council and, employing her own brand of innuendo, turns the tables on her:

These are very "left" kids. Every drawing that is artistic yet simple, without any flourishes, they label counterrevolutionary . . . A bunch of hacks and scum, wrapping themselves in pseudorevolutionary phrases, they have sullied our fabric . . . or were there indeed some class enemies, wielding "artistic" brushes, who tried to mock us with chintz and cotton?[35]

Two months later, in December, the Council of People's Commissars issued a Resolution on the Inadmissibility of the Goods Produced by a Number of Fabric Enterprises Using Poor and Inappropriate Designs.[36] This time the rebuke was effective. Not one more agitational pattern was produced. Within a few months Nazarevskaia had created a new— floral—design (fig. no. 14), and in Russia avant-garde fabric design had come to an end.

The history of fabric decoration in the late 1920s and early 1930s demonstrates social and organizational trends that are typical of this period in the Soviet Union. The desire to enforce greater ideological control in a complex area compounded of personal taste, industrial development, and political theory set up a movement toward even greater centralization. But in the area of textiles, ideology was not the only motivation for centralization. Problems of efficiency, economy, and artistic quality—issues not of stated interest to the young activists— were similarly to be resolved by larger and more complex bureaucracies. The need for uniform political-aesthetic criteria, an idea inherited from the previous generation of avant-garde artists, went unquestioned. In spite of the fact that the AKhR textile artists repeatedly maintained that political content was the sole aspect important in design, their commitment to

fig. 13
I. I. Mitiaev
The Five-Year Plan in Four Years, *late 1920s–1931.*
State Russian Museum, St. Petersburg.

matters of form and composition—another legacy from the previous generation—is obvious from their work and from their objection to the limp naturalism of many of their colleagues in AKhR. In the end, the attempt to gain control of a seemingly intractable social situation and a fanatical belief in the correctness of their critical theory led the new artistic elite to make impossible demands on human nature, thus setting the stage for their own demise.

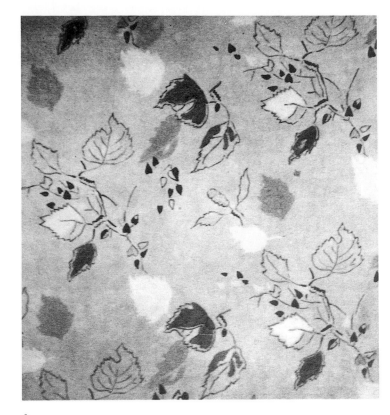

fig. 14
Mariia Nazarevskaia
Textile design, 1934.

Notes

1. The catalogue, *Pervaia khudozhestvennaia vystavka "Bytovoi sovetskii tekstil'"* (Moscow: Glaviskusstvo, 1928), lists thirty-four fabric designers and seventeen weaving students from Vkhutein.

2. N. N. Sobolev, "Itogi vystavki 'Bytovoi sovetskii tekstil','" *Izvestiia tekstil'noi promyshlennosti i torgovli* 6 (1929), pp. 111–12.

3. N. N. Sobolev, "Vystavka 'Bytovoi sovetskii tekstil','" *Izvestiia tekstil'noi promyshlennosti i torgovli* 2 (1929), p. 57.

4. A. S. Kudriavtsev, "O tsentral'noi masterskoi po sozdaniiu risunka dlia tkani," *Izvestiia tekstil'noi promyshlennosti i torgovli* 6 (1928), p. 65.

5. Ibid.

6. Ibid., p. 66.

7. Ibid., pp. 65–66.

8. A. Lobachev, "Problema sozdaniia risunka dlia tkanei," *Izvestiia tekstil'noi promyshlennosti i torgovli* 9 (1928), pp. 73–74.

9. Ibid., p. 74.

10. I. Matsa, ed., *Sovetskoe iskusstvo za 15 let. Materialy i dokumentatsiia* (Moscow and Leningrad: Ogiz-Izogiz, 1933), p. 381.

11. Anufrieva, Mitiaev, Nazarevskaia, Chachkhiani, and other textile students had taken part in the first OMAKhR exhibition in the spring of 1928. There was no designated topic for this show, however, and many of the designs exhibited were not clearly agitational.

12. F. S. Roginskaia, "Rost khudozhestvennoi smeny v tekstile," *Izvestiia tekstil'noi promyshlennosti torgovli* 7–8 (1929), p. 94.

13. "'Bytovoi sovetskii tekstil','" *Iskusstvo v massy* 1–2 (1929), pp. 36–37.

14. Quoted in [Nadezhda] Poluektova in "Bor'ba za sovetskii tekstil'," *Za proletarskoe iskusstvo* 2 (1931), p. 21.

15. *Torgovedy*—sales agents who were responsible for various districts and with whom local merchants placed their orders. They were familiar with local populations, their needs and tastes in fabric, and were consulted by the factories and trusts concerning the popularity of specific designs and the needs of the provinces. In fact, in the late twenties they formed the only group of professional "market consultants" in the textile industry.

16. "'Bytovoi sovetskii tekstil','" p. 35.

17. Roginskaia, "Rost khudozhestvennoi smeny v tekstile," pp. 91–92.

18. [Aleksei] Fedorov-Davydov, "Smysl i zadacha vystavki," *Pervaia khudozhestvennaia vystavka "Bytovoi sovetskii tekstil',"* p. 4.

19. Ibid., p. 3.

20. In practice, a few orders for piece goods were still placed with individual artists, thus bypassing the Council.

21. Poluektova, "Bor'ba za sovetskii tekstil'," p. 20.

22. Ibid. Poluektova's revolutionary credentials were impeccable. At Vkhutemas she had roomed with Varvara Armand, the daughter of the famous Inessa Armand. There, on February 25, 1921, they had entertained Lenin and Nadezhda Krupskaia.

23. I. S. Perepelitsyn, "Tvorcheskoi raboty ne bylo v khudozhestvennom biuro," *Golos tekstilei,* March 25, 1931, p. 3.

24. David Arkin, "Risunok—neotemlemaia chast' kachestva tkani," *Golos tekstilei,* March 24, 1931, p. 3.

25. Ibid.

26. Fadeev, "Nikto ne izuchaet zaprosov potrebitelia," *Golos tekstilei,* March 25, 1931, p. 3. [Frida] Roginskaia, "Provesti v zhizn' teoreticheskie ustanovki," *Golos tekstilei,* March 25, 1931, p. 3.

27. "Kachestvo tekstilia zavisit i ot risunka," *Golos tekstilei,* March 27, 1931, p. 3.

28. Fedorov-Davydov, "Smysl i zadacha vystavki," p. 7.

29. Arkin, "Risunok—neotemlemaia chast' kachestva tkani," p. 3. The emphasis by Arkin and others on the "genuine" mass consumer reflects the current effort supported by the Party to explain seeming contradictions between life and theory by making further, often spurious, class distinctions among the rural population.

30. Roginskaia, "Provesti v zhizn' teoreticheskie ustanovki," p. 3.

31. [Tat'iana] Chachkhiani, "Iz kolesa i shesterni delaiut . . . tsvetochki," *Golos tekstilei,* March 25, 1931, p. 3.

32. L. Maiakovskaia, "Risunok na shelke imeet svoi osobye zadachi," *Golos tekstilei,* March 25, 1931, p. 3.

33. "Kachestvo tekstilia zavisit i ot risunka," p. 3.

34. Ibid.

35. G. Ryklin, "Speredi traktor, szadi kombain," *Pravda,* October 6, 1933, p. 4.

36. "O rabote khlopochato-bumazhnoi promyshlennosti," *Izvestiia* 5237 (December 18, 1933), p. 3.

How Meierkhol'd Never Worked with Tatlin, and What Happened as a Result

Elena Rakitin

In a letter to his daughter Kseniia, Konstantin Stanislavskii described a work by a certain "Futurist" artist and even drew a diagram so that his daughter would have a better idea of this strange creation: an iron bucket sliced in half and mounted on yellow wallpaper.[1] Little did Stanislavskii suspect that the bucket on wallpaper had a direct connection with those new principles of stage design, employed in the productions of Vsevolod Meierkhol'd, that would so enormously impress him in the mid-1920s.[2]

A certain A. K. visited Vladimir Tatlin's studio and published a long article in the newspaper *Utro Rossii* (*Morning of Russia*). Having seen Tatlin's designs for Mikhail Glinka's opera *Zhizn' za tsaria* (*A Life for the Czar*), he praised the artist's theatrical talents, contrasting his designs with the "sickly-sweet confections and slovenly compositions" of Konstantin Korovin. And he judged Tatlin's reliefs to have "much in common with the art of the stage, the art of the director."[3] Failing to discern their self-sufficient aesthetic value, he deemed the reliefs purely the product of Tatlin's involvement with the theater.

During a discussion in 1940 of Tatlin's set designs for Aleksandr Sukhovo-Kobylin's *Delo* (*The Court Case*), the artist Vladimir Dmitriev expressed admiration for them, saying that Tatlin had "succeeded in escaping from everyday life and Naturalism." Everything was done very simply, without any superfluous ornamentation. "Were it not for [Tatlin's] counter-reliefs, these designs would never have been."[4] The teaching of counter-reliefs should, therefore, be introduced. Dmitriev, the chief designer at the Moscow Art Theater—whose statements were quite reckless for the times—had twenty years before, as a very young man, designed Meierkhol'd's production of Emile Verhaeren's *Les Aubes* (*Zori* [*The Dawns*]). He met Meierkhol'd's wishes ("We want our backdrop to be either an iron pipe or the sea or something built by the new man")[5] only halfway, suspending planes of various shapes, attached to iron cables, above the stage. Meierkhol'd was not pleased. Dmitriev, he felt, hadn't gone far enough: he "doesn't want, or perhaps lacks the ability, to leave behind aesthetic theatrical trinkets."[6] It was five years after the production's premiere, from the vantage of his Constructivist experience, that Meierkhol'd delivered this criticism of Dmitriev's failure to go beyond non-objectivity. Yet to hang a counter-relief above the stage did not mean that Tatlin's example had been followed.

No one artist, no matter how brilliant, is capable of remaking the theater on his own. "The theater is the pillar of art's decrepitude," said Kazimir Malevich, as he started work on the opera *Pobeda nad solntsem* (*Victory over the Sun,* 1913).[7] But the bomb he set did not go off. The play belongs to art history. The "Futurist" clock ran fast. The clock in the theater was set to a different time.

Tatlin's counter-reliefs contained a threat to the "painterly prosperity" of the artist working in the theater. Although Tatlin's stage designs, virtually contemporaneous with his counter-reliefs, were very much in favor with the Mir iskusstva (World of Art) group.

An answer can always be found to the question of why an artist goes into the theater. It could be said that the World of Art types, with their love for the art of bygone eras, found in the theater an opportunity to realize their dreams about the past; that the Cubist suffocated in the space of his painting but on the stage let air into his constructions; that the Constructivist in a backward and destitute country had nowhere else to turn in order to realize his dreams of the future. A widespread theory assigns the theater the role of a psychotherapeutic workshop or of a valve for "letting off steam." Everything is possible. Yet the question is improperly posed. An artist does not go into the theater. He must be summoned by it. And this occurs when the potential residing in an artist's works can be tapped to meet the needs of the theater.

History writes itself, without regard for how we later interpret it. It is a play with its own paradoxes. Though he constantly yearned to work with Tatlin, Meierkhol'd never collaborated on a single production with him.[8]

"The material of scenic production as such, devoid of any beauty, when subject to artistic reworking gives the viewer, strange as it may seem, pleasure precisely of an aesthetic order, gives beauty . . . No external conditions whatsoever affect us, for we always start from the ground, from the material (regardless of what kind it is), conquering it and organizing it."[9] These words could well have been spoken by Tatlin. They belong in fact to a student in the classes on "material stage design" conducted by Liubov' Popova at GVTM, Meierkhol'd's Higher State Theater Workshops.

Meierkhol'd had invited Popova to teach this discipline not solely because he had been impressed by her work in the 5 x 5 = 25 exhibition (Moscow, 1921) but, above all, because he had come to regard her highly during the course of their collaboration on Ivan Aksenov's *The Struggle and Victory of the Soviets,* a mass festival scheduled for Khodynskoe Field in Moscow in the spring of 1921. It was then that Meierkhol'd, in search of an artist who not only knew how to use material in three dimensions but could be an organic participant in the organization of the action onstage, made his choice.

Popova's set design for Meierkhold's 1922 production of Fernand Crommelynck's *Le Cocu magnifique* (*Velikodushnyi rogonosets* [*The Magnanimous Cuckold*], plate no. 628) is the first significant work by the Moscow Constructivists. It both influenced subsequent stage design and, to a large degree, defined a particular style of Moscow Constructivism. The "Popova canon" is easily discerned not only in Aleksandr Vesnin's maquette for G. K. Chesterton's *The Man Who Was Thursday* (*Chelovek, kotoryi byl Chetvergom*)[10]—which marked Vesnin's transition to Constructivist architecture—but in Gustav Klutsis's projects for street constructions (plate nos. 109–113) and in the way the students in Aleksandr Rodchenko's workshop at Vkhutemas (the Higher Artistic-Technical Workshops) exhibited their projects.

Beginning in 1922, the theater, summoning the Constructivists to participate in its experiments, stepped into the vanguard of artistic life. It no longer employed forms that were the prior discoveries of the other arts but created that which did not exist before. It became an inventor.

In the 1920s, young people rushed to Meierkhol'd's theater in anticipation of revelations. The young artists of Vkhutemas, writers, film directors, and musicians were hungry for the new and unprecedented. They expected from the theater not so much a celebration of feelings as much as "insights that capture the imagination and before which there are seemingly no riddles or obstacles."[11]

Exploratory productions in Meierkhol'd's workshops—conceived exclusively with the aim of making mastering the theater interesting for students (not results but the process of gaining proficiency counted) and conducted without adequate funds or performance space (which once again confirms that truism that the most intriguing and meaningful ideas are born outside theater walls)—were destined to become the manifesto of new theater in the twentieth century, launching an era in theater that to this day has not run its course. Popova's role in these productions was emphasized by Meierkhol'd numerous times.

The set design for *The Magnanimous Cuckold* was a collaborative venture. Meierkhol'd participated as an equal with Vladimir Liutse, Vasilii Fedorov, and Sergei Eizenshtein, students who, under Popova's guidance, were working out design principles for stage action unconnected with the proscenium arch. The maquette was assigned to Liutse. Popova became involved only at the final moment, "editing" the construction. A children's playground became a work of art. Popova refused until the last to add her name to the poster announcing the production—although she considered the day when she saw the construction moved from the gymnasium on Novinskii Boulevard to the stage of the former Zon Theater on Sadovo-Triumfal'naia Street to be the happiest of her life.[12] Her fear was not unwarranted. The censure came without delay. Only two days after the April 25th premiere, she read her theses—an attempt at self-justification before her colleagues, the Constructivists-Productivists—at Inkhuk (the Institute of Artistic Culture).

Popova's observations about new form—"It is still a child with only possibilities, but the main thing is that it is a 'new life' because it is a 'new form.' It is not the end but a beginning. It is simply a new way of looking at form"—were notes to herself.[13] Her theses on the design of *The Magnanimous Cuckold,* written after the fact, were lines in a play called production art. At Inkhuk, Popova deployed the notions of "production process," "work," and "utilitarian devices," and wanted to convince her listeners that she had not set out to solve any formal or aesthetic problems. Yet her theme was also guilt and repentance. "It wasn't easy to renounce outmoded aesthetic habits and criteria. A circumstance of an aesthetic order—that the action had a built-in visual character—got in the way and prevented me from considering the action solely as an ongoing working process."[14]

The word *prozodezhda* (production clothing), which for all subsequent generations was inextricably linked with Constructivism's attempt to make a worker of the actor and to turn him into the appendage of a machine, turned up in Popova's lecture. And just as quickly disappeared, remaining only in the costume sketches for *The Magnanimous Cuckold* (plate no. 629) that Popova made for an exhibition held after the premiere (although she dated the sketches 1921).

In her costume designs for Sukhovo-Kobylin's *Smert' Tarelkina* (*The Death of Tarelkin,* plate no. 626), the Meierkhol'd production that followed *The Magnanimous Cuckold* later the same year, Varvara Stepanova discarded this terminology, considering it to be nonconstructive. In fact, Popova's light and roomy blue costumes, made to Meierkhol'd's specifications,[15] were the uniform of the theater-workshop collective engaged in creating a new theater. They were the blue jeans of 1922, a democratic form of clothing much more suitable for young actors than the tails and evening dresses worn in Evgenii Vakhtangov's 1922 production of *Princess Turandot,* designed by Ignatii Nivinskii. That production was conceived as an exposé of the secrets of the theater. With the aid of multicolored pieces of fabric, a Turkish towel, a tennis racket, and so on, the young actors transformed themselves into dramatis personae in full view of the audience.

But even the costumes that Popova labeled *prozodezhda* could not deceive the vigilant orthodox Constructivist Aleksei Gan. He chastised Popova with his typical fervor: "It is preposterous for Constructivism, as the formal expression of intellectual and material production, to participate in either the performance of bucolic pastorals or new productions of theatrical October Revolutions . . ."[16]

It is preposterous to participate, yet if one is to do so, it must be with the aim of hastening the death of the theater.

In the summer of 1922, when the Actor's Theater (where

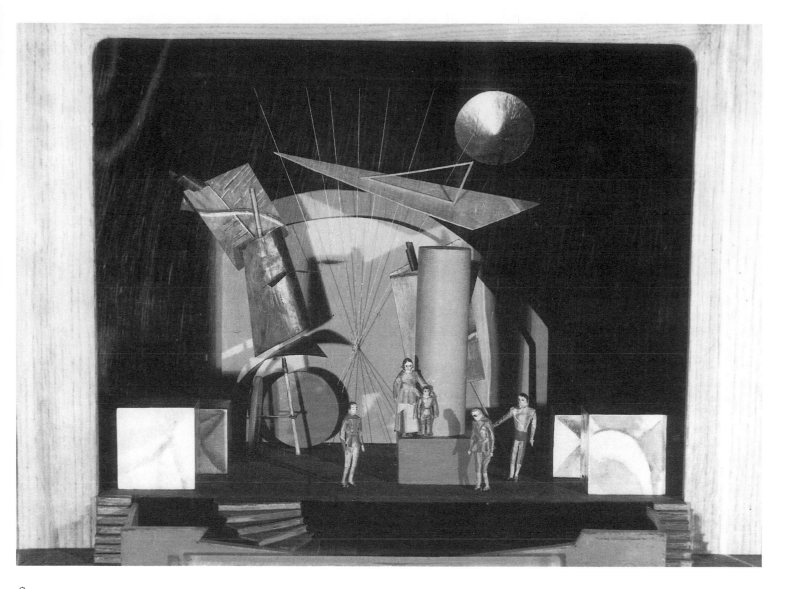

fig. I
Dmitriev's maquette for Verhaeren, The Dawns, *Moscow, 1920.*

The Magnanimous Cuckold was staged) was closed, the First Working Group of Constructivists of Inkhuk came out in support of Meierkhol'd:

Having announced a relentless war on art in general, the Constructivists were never carried away by Comrade Meierkhol'd's productions, because they understood that all his work is built, on the one hand, on the restoration of individual monuments of the theatrical culture of the past and, on the other, in accordance with the eclecticism that is the hallmark of contemporary aesthetics. Meierkhol'd's service is that he demonstrates the canons of theatrical intrigues more fully than do others and doesn't conceal the original sources of stage trickery. In this sense, his activity is revolutionary and, for as long as speculative art remains dominant, is essential. To deprive Meierkhol'd of his theater would be to strike a blow to the cause of hastening the absolute disappearance of the theater.[17]

Meierkhol'd hardly attempted to hasten the disappearance of his own theater. That was more likely the goal of the powers that be.[18] Nevertheless, he collaborated with Stepanova (who, as secretary of the group, had signed the Constructivists' statement) on his next production. Stepanova did not contribute to making *The Death of Tarelkin* a success—not because she didn't want to but because she couldn't do otherwise. Gan greeted the production's failure: "Constructivists, rejoice! Constructivism is victorious: in the present case we were witness to a lethal phenomenon in the house of the undead Tarelkin. We will work to see that the accursed Tarelkin dies at last."[19] By Tarelkin, Gan meant art.

The "uninterrupted rumbling" about the abolition of art, which in 1922 accompanied artists' intense work on new forms, deafens the contemporary researcher. He willingly swallows the bait of "production artistry" and falls into the trap of insoluble contradictions, from which he is unable to extricate himself.

From the 1910s, the vanguard artist tried on, as it were, different roles: hooligan, philosopher, scholar, and artisan. (These roles would constitute, in essence, the repertoire of twentieth-century art.) It cannot be said that the artist chose the role of Productivist without some prompting. Tatlin's production, his notion of the work of art as a real, genuine object that "doesn't reproduce reality but is itself reality,"[20] by no means led inevitably to limitation of the artist's activity to pure "applied art." "[Let there be] more art of real, tangible, audible, visible, thoroughly sniffable, and, insofar as possible, edible" things.[21] The summons is understandable. Especially in the conditions of a country torn by revolution. Just as it is understandable seventy-odd years later in Russia today. Yet this does not cancel the need for art. The essence of the Productivists' program, formulated during the discussions at Inkhuk once theorists had gained the upper hand over artists, had been spelled out by Osip Brik back in 1919:

A shoemaker makes shoes, a joiner makes tables. What does an artist make? He doesn't make anything. He creates. That sounds vague and suspicious . . . The commune has no need of either prophets or parasites. Only working people will find their place in it. If artists do not wish to share the fate of parasitical elements, they must prove their right to exist . . . Those artists who only "know how to create" and "somewhere serve beauty" will perish. Labor gives the artist the right to stand alongside the working groups of the commune: the shoemakers, joiners, and tailors.[22]

Rodchenko was the only artist working in the theater who met Brik's standards. In his sets for Anatolii Glebov's *Inga* (1929). But that was already a different historical era. The heroic days of the theater were past. The plays of Soviet authors

with their hypertrophied themes, having little in common with dramaturgy, inundated the theater. Rodchenko entitled his article on his designs for *Inga* (a play about the life of a factory director) "A Discussion of the New Clothing and Furniture—A Task for Design." It had been of paramount importance in his designs "that the bed not interfere with daily life and the dining furniture not interfere with a night's rest." "I set myself the task of creating collapsible wooden furniture, that is, furniture for which the USSR has an abundant supply of raw material."[23] Rodchenko evidently didn't do a bad job. After the play closed, the most resourceful stagehand took the furniture home and put it to good use. A reviewer also confirmed the quality of the furniture: "In each act of the play there is something of interest for our working lives—an office desk or writing table, a bed, or a chair. Showing these objects on the stage is of enormous educational significance."

The same critic was unhappy with Meierkhol'd's 1929 production of Vladimir Maiakovskii's *Klop* (*The Bedbug*), whose second part, set in the future, was also designed by Rodchenko: "The need to subordinate the design to the satirical elements of the play has deprived Rodchenko's work of practical significance for our reality. Search as they might, the leaders of our woodworking industry will not find on the stage a single object they could take away with them to produce."[24]

The word "utopia," so often used, appropriately and inappropriately, with regard to the theater of the 1920s, acquires a concrete meaning in this play. The action of its second part takes place, after all, in 1979. The play is not so simple as it seems. Maiakovskii not only shows the future through the eyes of a petit bourgeois but also parts with his own illusions as an active member of Lef (the Left Front of the Arts). His socialism is not only a *Schlaraffenland* with trees on which there are plates of oranges, apples, and bottles of perfume but also the dance of ten thousand workers, men and women practicing a new system of field work. It is radio loudspeakers instead of human voices. It is arms raised mechanically in a unanimous vote (as in Klutsis's famous poster *Rabochii i rabotnitsa, vse na perevybory sovetov* [*Workers, Everyone Must Vote in the Election of Soviets!*, 1930, plate no. 447]). It is "out of love"—that forgotten word—"one has to build bridges and bear children." In this world, the petit-bourgeois Ivan Prisypkin seems to be the only living being. It isn't surprising that the critics discerned in the languid waving of his hand a "shade of contempt for people who would dare to exhibit a person—even if he is behind the times and bourgeoisified, but, damn it, a person—in a cage along with a bedbug."[25] Maiakovskii created a dystopia.

Rodchenko made an enormous contribution to this production. The only thing not clear is the extent to which he himself was aware of it. From his comments: "The pink and light-blue costumes will show the bourgeois's conception of the future. The irony evident in Maiakovskii's depiction of the future is necessary in order to show—in such a short space of time, this entails the greatest difficulty—the surmounting of the morbid elements of our petit-bourgeois life."[26] These assertions are difficult to comprehend. Even Meierkhol'd, who normally treated artists with great respect and understanding, spoke of Rodchenko with a strange and noticeable scorn: "We're letting a certain Rodchenko, who dreams of future *prozodezhda*, etc., design the second half."[27] Be that as it may, Rodchenko perfectly expressed the intentions of Maiakovskii, whose play was one with the wicked pamphlets about socialism that had been written by bourgeois authors. The people of the future in Rodchenko's *prozodezhda* were impersonal, cold, and automatized.

In 1936, when a new production of *The Bedbug* was being discussed, it was proposed, above all, that the "elements of

fig. 2
Scene from Crommelynck, The Magnanimous Cuckold, *Moscow, 1922.*

technical preoccupation and duality" be removed. The decision was made to eliminate Maiakovskii's incomprehensible future and to move the action from 1979 back to 1938, in order to show the achievements of the Stakhanovites, collective-farm workers, and polar explorers. And naturally, suggested Brik, the extremely unsuccessful scene with the mechanical casting of votes had to be excised.[28]

In 1926, after having seen Meierkhol'd's production of Nikolai Gogol's *Revizor* (*The Inspector General*), Malevich wrote to the director. The production, in Malevich's opinion, "was very well executed." With this play, Meierkhol'd emerges from the "zone of economic revolutionary theater" and walks the line of art. "Revolutionary theater has vanished and it won't be forthcoming from the subsistence cooperative [the Productivists]. The only thing that will come out of that is grocery stores. That is the main policy of the Revolution. Art, though, has a different aim—it is not revolution . . . It's true that Marx, as people will tell you, said otherwise, yet you presented *The Inspector General* otherwise, by not even trying to show a healthy peasant spirit in Osip and the girl or bourgeois corruption in Khlestakov."[29] A staunch opponent of Constructivism, Malevich recognized the aesthetic merits of the production and urged Meierkhol'd to "go even further, to the final atrophy of the Constructivist legacy." Naturally, he did not see any connection between Meierkhol'd's masterpiece and the beginning of his "Constructivist run": *The Magnanimous Cuckold, The Death of Tarelkin,* and *Zemlia dybom* (*The Earth in Turmoil*). *The Inspector General* synthesized all the formal achievements of Meierkhol'd's analytical period. Which the proponents of "subsistence cooperatives," who had previously regarded Meierkhol'd as the sole Productivist master, also failed to realize. *The Inspector General* represented the "limit of the fall from grace since [the] October [Revolution] . . . How the hell can we take to the streets when so-called constructions are infinitely heavier and richer than the old designs?"[30]

The incisive Brik had observed as much even earlier, but phrased it more elegantly: "The dynamiter-detonators have conscientiously expended their reserves, but the result achieved was unexpected—instead of an explosion they got a brilliant fireworks display, all to the glory of that very same theatrical stronghold."[31]

The Magnanimous Cuckold was perceived primarily as a work showcasing actors' virtuosity. Joyous, deliberate, and effective virtuosity. The shroud of secrecy was removed from the actors' role playing, which was transformed into a creative activity. Intuition was placed under control, and "temperament held in check." The expedient gesture, that is, one purged of everything superfluous, chance, or ill-defined, stood in opposition to artificially "beautiful" movement. The actor's body became material that he consciously organized, laying out in space an image of his role, not identifying with it and not hiding behind a mask. By studying biomechanics, the actor learned the "ironclad truth of human nature." Biomechanical exercises were as necessary to the actor's training as the études of Czerny were to the musician's.[32] They developed consciousness of each gesture, elasticity, balance, and a precise sensation of one's body in space. Each gesture is preceded by a pre-gesture. Not even the smallest movement exists in isolation. It reverberates not only in oneself but in one's partner. Actors studied this "electric reaction." Moving to music developed an actor's sense of time, calculated to the second. Exercises with an imagined object trained his fingers to react to a material's texture, be it wood, shards of glass, water, or iron. This technique of the new actor could be labeled

Constructivist, so long as one doesn't forget that Meierkhol'd arrived at these biomechanical exercises after analyzing the work of outstanding actors worldwide.

The technique displayed by the actors in *The Magnanimous Cuckold* was truly dizzying. Their coordinated actions and sense of partnership made such a strong impression that "former critical skills for evaluating acting proved inadequate."[33] But the word "technique," in conjunction with the epithets "splendid," "brilliant," "perfect," and even "academic," was by no means indicative of a narrow technical preoccupation. "Technique" was synonymous, rather, with *mastery*. Meierkhol'd himself was called master. Tatlin was a master. The young artists who performed for the first time in *The Magnanimous Cuckold* would become masters. "Acting is shown [*igru pokazyvaiut*]," said the poster for the production, which was dedicated to Molière. Popova's identical blue costumes, with few individual details, did not hinder recognition of the types among which, as in the theater of olden times, the roles were distributed: "simple fellow," "boastful knave," "fop," and "sweetheart."

"An actor, clad in a blue coverall, metamorphosed into a mechanical robot, a mere appendage of the revolving wheels and doors of the construction."[34] These words come from a description of Meierkhol'd's *Magnanimous Cuckold* in a history of the Soviet theater compiled during Stalin's final years and published in 1954. Similar judgments can be found even today in certain Western writings, although their authors are clearly not acquainted with this Soviet publication.

Such is the description they promote of a production in which Crommelynck's rather scabrous farce—about the scribe Bruno, who suffers from unfounded jealousy and compels all the men in the village to sleep with his wife, Stella, in order to learn the identity of his rival (who does not show up)—turned into a tragic farce; in which the viewer was given a "condensed and purified image of emotion or thought that was convincing to the point of strangeness"; in which, "under cover of slapstick," images of a "frightfully naked truth" rhythmically accumulated;[35] and in which Stella (played by Babanova), "a fair-haired woman-child with a rattle in her hand and a musically deep voice ringing with the naïve purity of a silver handbell, expressed such bitter perplexity and such concealed feminine pain, that the whole theater, having just taken in the events on stage with their eyes only, shuddered from profound agitation in their hearts."[36]

The production opened with a scene that the actor Erast Garin later recalled as one of the most convincing declarations of love he had ever witnessed in the theater: "From a distance an exultant voice was heard, full of life, love, and happiness, and Il'inskii's Bruno impetuously flew, truly flew up the stairs on the wing, not stopping, to the very top of the construction and gathered in his arms Babanova's Stella, who had run to meet him. His long legs spread apart like the arms of a compass, he glided unspeakably youthfully, resiliently, and athletically down the slide, which was polished to a sheen, and lightly and inconspicuously set down his weightless burden on the floor of the stage."[37]

Popova's construction was created for action; it provoked action and was inextricably linked with it. The construction was essentially a new stage erected within the space of the old. The dernier cri in the new art—construction—turned out to be connected with the long-standing tradition of popular theater, where the designer never intervened, and at the same time directed toward the future—a model, as it were, of the theater of the future, its "original crystal."

In 1931, Meierkhol'd said—and not by accident—that the time had not arrived when constructions could be left entirely behind, since in order to do so the entire stage would have to

фоти. А. Темерина.

fig. 3
Scene from Maiakovskii, The Bedbug, *Moscow, 1929.*

be re-created.[38] For the time being, the construction—destroying one environment (Flanders, a flowering garden, or the scribe's house as the scene of the action) and disavowing everything that formerly constituted the secret and charm of the theater—elicited, by the real existence of its form, new sorts of associations in the viewer. The actor "embodied, as it were, a new man, freed from the power of things, from the power of an inert, immovable environment, [a new man] standing in a lofty, spacious world and full of that vital energy which makes it possible to calculate with utmost precision his every gesture or movement and to build anew the house of the world."[39]

"It is necessary to counter the influence of Bolshevik theater . . . We are witness to the most dangerous onslaught the theater has ever experienced. Everything in these productions—the sets, costumes, direction, and actors' interpretations—is an encroachment threatening to destroy our dramatic art, which was created by several centuries of slow evolution."[40]

These remarks would seem to refer to *The Magnanimous Cuckold*. But that is not the case. This was, rather, the reaction in the land of Racine and Cubism to the Kamernyi Theater's tour abroad in 1923. Clearly, the clocks in Paris and Moscow were set to different times. Moscow's Kamernyi Theater, affiliated with the Association of Academic Theaters, had absolutely nothing to do with Bolshevism or politics of any other sort. It was a bastion of aestheticism. André Antoine, the author of these lines, might well have been unaware that the Kamernyi production of *Phèdre* represented the culmination of the work begun by Aleksandr Tairov, with Aleksandra Ekster, in 1916 with the production of Innokentii Annenskii's *Famira Kifared* (*Thamyris the Cithara-Player*). Tairov, who enlisted artists in the theater "for the sake of the actor,"[41] was the first to see in non-objective painting possibilities for creating a new three-dimensional environment on the stage. The contradiction between the surface plane of the painting and the physical definition of the actor was erased by the means of painting itself. Ekster was the first designer "who glues together a maquette and predetermines with her fingers each protuberance, each corner of the stage box."[42] Volume was returned to the stage, and the chance to move in unison with the rhythms of the created environment restored to the actor. This environment preserved the "spirit" of painting, directing currents of painterly energy toward the viewer. Color was symbolically orchestrated (as, for example, in the complex score for the movement of color in the 1917 Kamernyi production of Oscar Wilde's *Salomé* [plate nos. 606–609]). The environment, constructed according to the laws of harmony in painting, had absolutely nothing in common with reality. The architectonics of painting, which inspired Aleksandr Vesnin's designs for *Phèdre*, transported the action to a "universal, unbounded space." The rhythmic purity of the actors' movements, the resilience of the lofty delivery of Racine's text, and the severe passion of *Phèdre* were kindred with the architectonic clarity of the stage environment. In his own way, Tairov had heeded the bidding of Edward Gordon Craig, who had urged that "so-called naturalness" be avoided, inasmuch as naturalness had appeared on the stage only because the artificial had begun to fade, had become affected and absurd. "But don't forget, there is such a thing as noble artificiality."[43]

In the consciously closed space/canvas, executed according to the laws of post-Cubist painting, the actor was a module, a unit of scale. The Cubist costume—such were the dictates of its style—turned the actor into a kind of moving colored sculpture. The space/canvas was planned with the actor in mind, but he himself was in its power. Such sets antedated

constructions, yet did not prepare the way for them. Peacefully coexisting in time and even in the oeuvre of the same artist (not to mention in the pages of monographs or on the walls of exhibitions), they nonetheless, no matter how paradoxical it may sound, belong to different eras. One is the culmination of a long historical process, which began in the Renaissance theater and gave the designer pride of place. The other inaugurated a new timetable. The critics close to the Kamernyi Theater failed to understand this, suggesting that Constructivism originated at the Kamernyi. The only difference they discerned was that, in contrast to Meierkhol'd's dry and colorless productions, the Kamernyi's were colorful and bright.[44]

Outstanding stage designers emerged from among Ekster's students at her studio in Kiev. Popova's pupils, who had studied "material stage design" with her, became directors. They thought primarily in categories of movement and aspired to penetrate to objective reality not by painting's means but by the method of construction.

For Meierkhol'd, non-objectivity in the theater was equivalent to decorativeness. He was a convinced Constructivist. He did not justify the hopes of Malevich, who had at one time believed that "Meierkhol'd will stand at the head of the movement in theater and lead it along the same path with painting and literature to non-objective form."[45]

If the set for *Phèdre* was called a machine by Jean Cocteau, who desired to praise it,[46] the set for *The Magnanimous Cuckold* suggested such a comparison itself. At the moments of greatest tension on stage, the construction's wheels and windmill sails revolved—now in succession, now in unison; now clockwise, now counterclockwise. Thus the concept of movement in stage design, which would be developed in future productions, was proclaimed. The construction's similarity to a machine frightened some, while others were delighted by it. The emphasis shifted imperceptibly, but already the chief component of theater was a moving machine and not the actor for whom it was built. "The machine—this is the main thing," wrote the poet Sergei Gorodetskii after the production of *The Magnanimous Cuckold*. "Even the stage box, stripped of decoration and with the machine in its center, brings unprecedented joy. When it becomes possible to stand at this machine and dance around it, then the joy of theater will be complete."[47] The invention of the construction suited, like nothing else, the burgeoning enthusiasm for "urbanization."

In the 1922 production, designed by Iurii Annenkov, of Georg Kaiser's *Gas* at the Great Dramatic Theater in Petrograd, the viewer was drawn into the spectacle of the mechanism on stage and forgot the existence of the actor. "The crane turned sullenly, the flywheel revolved animatedly, currents of color changed uninterruptedly, iron and steel structures appeared amid exhalations of gas, and, with a dry crackle, discharges of current pierced the whole stage; everything droned, breathed, moved."[48]

In *The Man Who Was Thursday*, directed by Tairov at the Kamernyi Theater in 1923 and designed by Aleksandr Vesnin, the metropolis was the chief protagonist. Vesnin's set was a multistoried construction with three elevators, staircases, passages, moving sidewalks, and a flashing billboard—a kind of "urbanistic extract." This architecture, which in the maquette seemed overly complicated and serious for the play for which it was intended, became almost self-sufficient in performance. It was as if the theater were trying to prove to itself that contemporaneity was a subject worthy of art. Tairov, a director who espoused beauty, had first to be convinced that engineering could be beautiful. "What previously was frightening in its complexity is now captivating in the

fig. 4
Shestakov's maquette for Faiko, Lake Liul', *Moscow, 1923.*

classical simplicity of its construction; where in the past we felt like 'lost souls,' we now experience a sense of power and dominion . . . A man simplified to the point of schematization, active and strong, thinking and feeling mathematically, moves—in rhythm with the entire mechanism—among the objects of the constructive stage. He is lord of the city, yet at the same time he is only a part of it, a lever of a powerful and well-proportioned organism, one of the columns of the urban temple," said the newspaper *7 dnei Moskovskogo Kamernogo teatra* (*Seven Days of the Moscow Kamernyi Theater*) at the production's premiere.[49] Chesterton's play did not exactly warrant such profuse enthusiasm. It was only a pretext. Many found the production "heavy and boring." They preferred Meierkhol'd's production of Aleksei Faiko's *Ozero Liul'* (*Lake Liul'*) at the Theater of the Revolution. The "metropolis" in that production, cobbled together by the young artist Viktor Shestakov, was a simple construction that couldn't compare to Vesnin's "true," durable architecture. Meierkhol'd came to Shestakov's rescue. He created such a "whirlwind" of intense onrushing action, moving it in an instant from one part of the set to another, that the quality of the set itself was lost from view. A minute into the performance, all this Russian wood began "to shudder with the pulsations of European and American skyscrapers, cafés, and shops."[50]

"The pathos of the modern age lies in simplicity . . . Realism organizes life, builds it. In the theater, such realism is based on a strict calculation of material, space, and time."[51] So spoke Tairov, fully in the spirit of Constructivism, when, with Georgii and Vladimir Stenberg, he inaugurated a new phase in 1924.

Having analyzed Popova's work in *The Magnanimous Cuckold,* Stepanova concluded that the construction in its entirety entered into the stage action only in the infrequent mass scenes. In general, the actors used individual parts alone—a bench, door, staircase, ramp, and so on—in their performance. She declared it impermissible to unite in a single construction elements serving different needs of the actors. Moreover, whereas Popova had many standards of varying "form," Stepanova wanted to reduce the construction to a single standard element. To the glory of logical Constructivist thought, the set design for *The Death of Tarelkin* embraced a number of individual "apparatuses for performance," which were united stylistically. They were all white and all made from laths.[52]

Meierkhol'd's conception was incredibly complex. He wanted to present Sukhovo-Kobylin's play as a *balagan* (fairground booth)—one where the actors flew across the stage on ropes and clapped bull's bladders, where the action began with a whistle and ended with a revolver fired into the audience and the cry "Entr-r-r-r'acte!," and whose interior had to be eerie and frightening. The theme of suspicion and mystification ran through the entire production, which was itself supposed to reveal the "mechanics of an all-Russian fistfight."[53] "The actors were to play the genial farce eccentrically yet with a profound understanding of what was occurring . . . It had to be acted humorously and cheerfully—and strike the viewer as sad."[54] The production was constructed as a sort of chain of attractions, at the intersection of the actors' performance and the performing object.

The objects constructed by Stepanova—"as instruments of the present scenic production [*proizvodstvo*] and not with a decorative goal in mind"[55]—did not fulfill their prescribed functions. That is, they did not jump, shoot, or twitch as intended. The object did not perform. "Though the word 'production'[*proizvodstvo*] is often used in the Gitis [State Institute of Theatrical Art] workshops, even the most

elementary conditions for production do not exist," Stepanova said by way of explaining her failure.[56] The objects stood still, eliciting reproaches for their "decorative illusoriness." Their associations with the furnishings of a "dacha" or "surgery" were clearly not planned. Stepanova's most successful construction resembled a hybrid cage-meat grinder, into which the enormous Aunt Brandakhlystova (played by M. Zharov) was stuffed. But this was no longer just an object in the performance. It was a metaphor.

The costumes—with which Stepanova personally was satisfied ("precisely executed, without special theatrical devices")—were taken by the audience to be either hospital gowns or artists' smocks or clowns' robes (which, incidentally, met Meierkhol'd's initial conception). Rejecting the concept of *prozodezhda* as nonconstructive and introducing several variations into her costumes, Stepanova—as Aksenov wrote (and not without irony)—"sensed [that the variations represented] a certain departure from collectivist principles and thus made a correction: she arranged the markings on the new stage clothing in such a way that when the actors stood in groups, they merged into one mass and the eye could not distinguish one actor from the other."[57] Meierkhol'd couldn't forgive Stepanova. Some years later, he said that Stepanova had "wanted to strike a blow at the late Popova. Ah, she does *prozodezhda,* and I have *prozodezhda* plus Mossel'prom. She made us this item and killed a wonderful play."[58] Meierkhol'd's mention of Mossel'prom (the Moscow Agricultural Industry) is an obvious reference to Mossel'prom's adopting for its salespeople's uniforms the hats Stepanova had designed for the creditors in *The Death of Tarelkin.* The link between her children's costumes and future athletic uniforms is also obvious.

Theater had reached a point beyond which it made no sense to go. Not just viewers but even the vanguard developed a "nostalgia for a more or less honest pavilion and even for . . . historically accurate costumes."[59]

At times, it seems that we are playing the game that amused Hemingway's characters. Mantegna? Nail holes. Rubens? A lot of meat. Constructivism in the theater? Platforms and stairways, of course.

"All Russia built constructions for a while," said Meierkhol'd in a lecture he gave on October 24, 1923.[60] The enthusiasm for constructions was universal. Naturalistic theater eagerly donned a vest adorned with a straight line. This was both fashionable and revolutionary. Constructions were a "passport to revolutionariness." Constructions, which rejected the notion of decoration, themselves became a new style of decor.

In her designs for Meierkhol'd's production of Sergei Tret'iakov's *The Earth in Turmoil* (plate nos. 630–632), Popova broke with such an interpretation of Constructivism. She returned to the initial point of departure, to material. In *The Magnanimous Cuckold,* individual elements of Popova's construction had entered into the performance; Stepanova's constructions for *The Death of Tarelkin* had been "apparatuses for performance." In *The Earth in Turmoil,* the actors performed with real objects taken directly from life. A year before, Popova was designing a geranium in a pot. Now her diagrams included not only an automobile, a machine gun, and an airplane but also a camp bed, a table, a typewriter, and a coffin upholstered in red material. This was not the old Naturalism of the early Moscow Art Theater. Objects taken from life, "shown just the way today's laborer and peasant see them in their everyday work situation,"[61] became material from which to construct the production. This constructing, as before, took place openly, in view of the audience, summoning them to

fig. 5
Scene from Ostrovskii, The Forest, *Moscow, 1924.*

participate actively in the construction-performance.

Machine guns and rifles fired, telephones rang. A cock being chased by a cook preparing soup for the generalissimo tried to flee the stage. The emperor Burbus sat on a bucket bearing an imperial monogram as if on a throne. His aide examined the contents of the bucket through binoculars and, holding his nose, carried the bucket through the audience. The doors of the theater were flung open and a truck drove in; the coffin bearing the body of the slain leader was loaded onto it.

"This is the end. Meierkhol'd the director can go no further in his self-negation and self-burial . . . Henceforth the stage of Meierkhol'd's theater might be an excellent hippodrome for motorcycle and bicycle races, for acrobats running, flying, and leaping hurdles through a most respectable audience, a training ground for the jockey, driver, and acrobat—but what scope is there for the actor's art here."[62] Meierkhol'd's analytical period, during which he had examined anew each element of the theater, came to an end with *The Earth in Turmoil*.

If in *The Earth in Turmoil* the actors performed with rifles, machine guns, and threshing machines, in Meierkhol'd's 1924 production of Aleksandr Ostrovskii's *Les* (*The Forest*), designed by Fedorov, the stage was transformed into a "moving system of things and objects, at the center of which stood the actor."[63] A piano, samovar, basins, dovecote with live pigeons, giant stride, and swing were carried on and off in view of the audience. Each character had his own milieu of things. The actors' interaction with the objects gave viewers a sense of an environment on the empty stage; and it created a hitherto unknown "resiliency of action," genuine dynamics, compared to which all the recent productions with their moving elevators seemed less theatrical. *The Forest,* according to Nikolai Chuzhak, marked the beginning of a curve leading to the "kingdom of old illusory theater"; *Mandat* (*The Mandate,* 1925) and *Bubus* (1925) were points along that curve and *The Inspector General* its culmination.[64] Yet *The Forest* and *The Inspector General* employed the same Constructivist method as *The Earth in Turmoil*.

Popova agreed with Dziga Vertov, who said, "My field of vision is life, the material of montage is life, [the stuff of] set design is life."[65] Stills from Vertov's newsreels, along with slogans and the portraits of heroes and political leaders, were projected onto the screen that Popova included in her set for *The Earth in Turmoil*. The screen played an active role. It injected itself into the action, anticipated the action or showed its result, and provided commentary on what was taking place. In short, it organized the viewer's perception of the production. The screen remained in *The Forest*. The titles of the episodes appeared on it. The montage of episodes used for the first time in *The Earth in Turmoil* was also employed in both *The Forest* and *The Inspector General*. Yet if in *The Earth in Turmoil* the screen and montage played the role of agitator and of a clamp for cementing Marcel Martinet's vague, obscure play (no stone in it was left unturned in Tret'iakov's adaptation), in *The Forest* and *The Inspector General* the same principle enhanced the multiple meaning and richness of the production's images.

"This play is crap," wrote Meierkhol'd about the play *Noch'* (*Night*). "I hate it. Why put it on? Have to."[66] A play on a contemporary—that is, Soviet—theme is a concept known to anyone even slightly familiar with the practice of Soviet theater. This was a "mandatory program," the only one that entitled the director to stage other plays. Such was the director's alibi. The interest that Meierkhol'd the Communist showed in Crommelynck's farce struck many as unseemly. "Can it really be that everything that has swept over the country and the theater in the course of five stormy years amounts to biomechanics? The fact is, all of Meierkhol'd's revolutionariness is the revolutionariness of an anklebone."[67]

The Death of Tarelkin was not universally acclaimed. There was no worthy contemporary play and no time to wait for one to be written. Thus Popova, Tret'iakov, and Meierkhol'd became the authors of a play with a "contemporary theme."

When *The Dawns* was staged in 1920, people who had just been seated in the audience found themselves the next moment leaving for the front, and the performances were punctuated with reports from the fighting. Although *The Earth in Turmoil* was labeled an agitprop production, who required converting to what cause in 1923? But how the language of art had changed in three years. It had become compressed and precise. Not a trace remained of such "aesthetic theatrical trinkets" as a counter-relief suspended above the stage. The theater "smelled of rubber and iron, military broadcloth and war." "The spectacle was perceived as equal to cinematography yet at home with the farces of Aristophanes," wrote an overly enthusiastic reviewer from Rostov-on-Don.[68]

The theater gained reliable (for the time being) patrons. This time the production was dedicated not to Molière or (as was the case with *The Death of Tarelkin*) to little Serezha Vakhtangov, the son of the late director, but to the commander in chief of the Red Army, Lev Trotskii. The dreams of the Productivists, it seemed, had come true. Ten thousand spectators saw the performance given on September 2, 1923, in Neskuchnyi Garden. Twelve thousand turned out for the show in Khar'kov. Twenty-five thousand people attended the June 29, 1924, performance in Sparrow Hills, where fifteen hundred real soldiers staged real battles. On this occasion, Popova's theses concerning her "material stage design" were written in advance of the production and were, from the Productivist point of view, irreproachable. "Rejection of any aesthetic tasks; the Red Army, electrification, heavy industry, and development of the transportation system—they provide the elements of stage scenery . . . The artist's work in selecting and joining the material elements of the production so as to create the greatest agitprop effect."[69]

Popova called her work a "machine bench-photoposter." The legacy of her collage designs for *The Earth in Turmoil* can be discerned, interestingly enough, not in the photomontage posters of the late 1920s and early 1930s, constructed so as to hammer a point home or to "attack the viewer's psyche," but in photo-frescoes, such as the photo-frieze by El Lissitzky and Sergei Sen'kin for the *Pressa* exhibition in Cologne in 1928.

From Boris Pasternak's letter of March 26, 1928, to Meierkhol'd:

Two things struck me about Cuckold. *Your attitude toward virtuosity and your attitude toward material. I saw how you accumulate virtuosity, how you store it up—better, in what forms you harbor it. You assigned it precisely the role it deserves in great and gripping art. In your work it assumed the place of a fire extinguisher or Westinghouse Co. engine brake—carried to perfection, always at hand but unobtrusive when not needed . . . You didn't become the prisoner of reborn virtuosity, you didn't furnish your home exclusively with fire extinguishers, as happened, perhaps, with Briusov and as is now being repeated (strange as that may seem, given Maiakovskii's temperament) in the Lef circle. Your train doesn't come to a Westinghouse standstill of dulled formal habit but truly catches one up and carries him away.*[70]

"We expected *The Inspector General* from Meierkhol'd, but he showed us something else," Mikhail Chekhov would say of the production. "He showed us a world that in the fullness of its creation occupied a realm of such proportions that *The Inspector General* was only a particle, only an individual sound in the larger melody—and we were frightened. We artists

fig. 6
Scene from Gogol', The Inspector General, *Moscow, 1926.*

understood that Meierkhol'd was publicly laying bare our impotence in working with only fragments. We understood that the form of a Meierkhol'd production, subordinated to the powerful content Meierkhol'd has fathomed, shapes itself anew virtually on its own and is not susceptible to rational calculation, elicits no desire to outwit this form with the cleverness of intellect."[71]

In *The Inspector General* Meierkhol'd did not retreat from the principles of economy and self-limitation. The production's space was precise, its material concrete. The small platform on which Meierkhol'd concentrated the action allowed him to accommodate a lengthy text and save time on scene changes. This platform would come to be called one for "qualified experts," because a performance on it demanded from the actor the most precise and calibrated virtuosity. Actors who had studied biomechanics possessed such virtuosity. The furnishings with which the platform was equipped were arranged according to the laws not of real life but of theatrical expediency. These objects, while seemingly accurate representations of the furniture of the age of Czar Nikolai I, were constructed to suit the lines of the actors who performed with them. All these objects were a variety of "apparatus for performance," a kind of microstage on an already tiny stage platform. The actors performed with a wardrobe. The mayor's wife entered it to make innumerable changes of dress; a flock of admiring officers fluttered out of it. Doors concealed in the bow-shaped wall and made from plywood painted red and buffed to a sheen (evoking associations with mahogany, the nineteenth century's favorite material for furniture) opened at the same time only once—for the bribe scene. Petty officials simultaneously stretched out to Khlestakov envelopes containing money. Meierkhol'd showed the Russia of Gogol' via the texture of the objects with which the actor performed. Yet a piece of antique furniture never became the object of admiration. Meierkhol'd's task was to show the "swinish" in the beautiful. He resolved a formerly insoluble problem. Symbols do not stand in opposition to life but grow out of it. A genuine material environment is superimposed on new coordinates of time and space.

Time is relative. What has transpired at various times takes place all at once in Meierkhol'd. The past alternates with the future. In *The Forest* time was speeded up; in *The Inspector General* it "froze," became immovable. Space has the ability to contract and expand. The complex associative system into which the viewer was brought "put an x" through the little square emerging from the depths of the stage platform. The spectator saw all of Russia.

There was nothing topical in the production. No one waved red flags on stage and no one sang the "Internationale." But the rhythms of the times lived in it. The young actors of *The Magnanimous Cuckold* were replaced by a "many-headed society as the single hero," a "herd driven into a confined space."

In a letter of October 2, 1928, to Meierkhol'd, Shestakov wrote:

Now about Bagdasar'ian's new play. The directors assigned to produce the play suggested the following artists as designers: Tatlin, Lavinskii, and Amosova. My opinion of the artists. Tatlin. By inviting Tatlin, they were hoping to profit from his name. Of course, Tatlin will answer for his work. It is not so much the theater as he who will have to answer to the public (which would not be the case with the work of the younger generation) . . . If you give your consent to Tatlin, I still think it necessary to have a long talk with him beforehand. First, so he won't raise another ruckus. Second, so that he'll fully understand the plans for the production and won't make overly abstract and aesthetic objects . . .[72]

By "ruckus" and "abstract and aesthetic objects," Shestakov—the stage designer of the Theater of the Revolution and a pragmatist to the core—was obviously referring to the 1923 production in Petrograd of Velimir Khlebnikov's *Zangezi,* which Tatlin had designed and directed and in which he had played the principal role (plate nos. 602–605).

Krovavaia pustynia (The Bloody Desert), fortunately, was not produced.

"Time through touch," was Tatlin's chief commandment in the theater. "We will make everything palpable so that it is felt with the eyes."[73] In his set design for *Business,* Tatlin "conjoined the hardened surface of stucco with the silken surface of the linden." This form, in his opinion, expressed Sukhovo-Kobylin. Tatlin was dissatisfied. "I am certain that if you appoint a commission, all the corners will be pronounced incorrect, crooked, slanted high or low. A strictly constructed object does not tolerate this. It turned out bad. Here it's not my fate that's being decided but Sukhovo-Kobylin's."[74] Dmitriev was delighted by the sharp effect of the material and the disposition of space in the production. "The single line for the curtain and the line of the cupboard said all that needed to be said."[75]

In 1929 Tatlin turned down an offer to design Maiakovskii's *Bania (The Bathhouse)* for the Meierkhol'd Theater. He didn't like the play. At the time he was already working on *Letatlin* (1929–32). There was no money to build a time machine for *The Bathhouse.* At the end of the play, the actors, wearing costumes designed by Aleksandr Deineka (which resembled the space suits worn by today's astronauts), exited upward along the set construction—built by the young architect Sergei Vakhtangov—carrying small suitcases and food provisions . . .

"At age fifty-six," Tatlin would say in 1941, "I still haven't once worked tranquilly in the theater, with people who would heed and wish to fulfill my intentions. This hasn't happened thus far in my life, and I don't think it ever will."[76]

—Translated, from the Russian, by Todd Bludeau

Notes

1. K. S. Stanislavskii, *Pis'ma,* vol. 7 of his *Sobranie sochinenii* (Moscow, 1960), p. 604. Stanislavskii was describing his visit to the *Khudozhniki Moskvy—zhertvam voiny* (Artists of Moscow for the Victims of the War) exhibition in late 1914.

2. After seeing Meierkhol'd's 1925 production of *Mandat* (*The Mandate*), Stanislavskii would say: "Meierkhol'd has achieved . . . what I've been dreaming of." P. Markov, *Pravda teatra* (Moscow, 1965), p. 349.

3. A. K., "U V. E. Tatlina," *Utro Rossii,* May 15, 1914.

4. Minutes of the discussion of *Delo* at the Central Theater of the Red Army, 1940, VTO Library, Moscow.

5. Vs. E. Meierkhol'd, *Stat'i. Pis'ma. Rechi. Besedy* (Moscow, 1968), pt. 2, p. 17.

6. *Teatr imeni Vs. Meierkhol'da. Muzei. Katalog vystavki "5 let"* (Moscow, 1926), p. 6.

7. *Za 7 dnei* 28 (August 15, 1913).

8. In 1916 Meierkhol'd had asked Tatlin to work as a designer on the film of Fedor Sologub's *Nav'ie chary,* but they had had differences of opinion. Tatlin designed not a "mystical tree" but one resembling his beloved ship's mast (see his set design for Richard Wagner's *Die fliegende Holländer* [*The Flying Dutchman*], plate no. 598). Tatlin's name had been suggested during a discussion of the productions of Maiakovskii's *Misteriia-buff* (*Mystery Bouffe*) and of *The Dawns.* Meierkhol'd had remarked during that discussion: "If we turn to the latest followers of Picasso and Tatlin, we can be sure of working with kindred spirits . . . We are building and they are building . . . For us, *faktura* [density or manipulation of material] is of much greater consequence than lovely little designs, patterns, and colors." Meierkhol'd, *Stat'i. Pis'ma . . . ,* p. 16.

9. Theses on the constructive stage design of *Nora,* quoted in K. Rudnitskii, *Rezhisser Meierkhol'd* (Moscow, 1969), p. 259.

10. It was evidently for this reason that a design by Vesnin for *The Man Who Was Thursday* was presented as an initial sketch for the set construction of *The Magnanimous Cuckold* in *L. S. Popova. 1889–1924. Vystavka proizvedenii k stoletiiu so dnia rozhdeniia,* catalogue for exhibition organized by the State Tret'iakov Gallery, Moscow (Moscow: State Tret'iakov Gallery, 1990), no. 259.

11. A. Matskin, *Na temy Gogolia. Teatral'nye ocherki* (Moscow, 1984), pp. 88–89.

12. See I. Aksenov, "L. S. Popova v teatre," *Novyi zritel'* 23 (1924), pp. 5–9, and "Proiskhozhdenie ustanovki 'Velikodushnyi rogonosets,'" *3 afisha TIM* (Moscow, 1926).

13. Manuscript Division, State Tret'iakov Gallery, Moscow.

14. L. S. Popova, theses on the "material set design" of *The Magnanimous Cuckold,* Inkhuk, April 27, 1922.

15. Meierkhol'd felt that light, loose-fitting clothing better revealed the actor's form than did snug costumes. The actors in his studio productions of *Balaganchik* and *Neznakomka* in Petrograd, moreover, wore identical costumes.

16. A. Gan, "Konstruktivizm. Otvet Lefu," *Zrelishcha* 55 (1923), p. 13.

17. "Iz protokola obshchego sobraniia I-i rabochei gruppy konstruktivistov," *Ermitazh* 8 (1922), p. 12.

18. "In the event of the demise of the Actor's Theater, I naturally and automatically will be compelled . . . in effect to cease my activity in the Republic, activity that evidently is deemed so injurious and loathsome that its abolition is an unalterable item on the agenda of our theatrical centers," Meierkhol'd wrote in "Komu eto nuzhno," *Teatral'naia Moskva* 46 (1922), p. 9.

19. A. Gan, "Smertel'noe iavlenie v dome neumershego Tarelkina," *Zrelishcha* 16 (1922), p. 11.

20. See N. Tarabukin, *Ot mol'berta k mashine* (Moscow, 1923), p. 8.

21. N. Chuzhak, "Ot illiuzii k real'nosti (Po povodu revizii 'Lefa')," quoted in V. Pertsov, *Za novoe iskusstvo* (Moscow, 1925), p. 125.

22. O. Brik, "Khudozhnik i kommuna," *Izobrazitel'noe iskusstvo* 1 (1919), pp. 25–26.

23. A. Rodchenko, "Diskussiia o novoi odezhde i mebeli—zadacha oformleniia," in *A. Glebov. "Inga"* (Moscow, 1929).

24. N. Lukhamanov, "Bez slov," *Zhizn' iskusstva* 22 (1929), p. 4.

25. M. Zagorskii, "Tol'ko ob akterakh," *Sovremennyi teatr* 14 (1929), p. 2 17.

26. "'Klop' Vl. Maiakovskogo v Gos. Time. Chto goroviat khudozhniki," *Sovremennyi teatr* 7 (1929), p. III.

27. "Iz vystupleniia V. E. Meierkhol'da na obsuzhdenii p'esy 'Klop' V. V. Maiakovskogo v klube imeni Oktiabr'skoi revoliutsii moskovskoi kazanskoi zheleznoi dorogi. 11 ianvaria 1929," in *Sovetskii teatr. Dokumenty i materialy* (Leningrad, 1982), pt. 1, p. 29 1.

28. *Tvorcheskoe nasledie V. E. Meierkhol'da* (Moscow, 1978), pp. 282–90.

29. Kazimir Malevich, letter to Vsevolod Meierkhol'd, January 1, 1927, Central State Archive for Literature and Art, Moscow, f. 998, op. 1, ed. khr. 1933.

30. N. Chuzhak, "Opyt revizii 'Revizora,'" *Zhizn' iskusstva* 2 (1927), p. 10.

31. O. Brik, "Ne v teatre, a v klube," *Lef* 1 (1924), p. 22.

32. On the biomechanical exercises, see E. Garin, *S Meierkhol'dom* (Moscow, 1974), pp. 28–32.

33. A. Gvozdev, "Il'-ba-zai," *Zhizn' iskusstva* 27 (1924), p. 8.

34. *Ocherki istorii russkogo sovetskogo dramaticheskogo teatra* (Moscow, 1954), vol. 1, p. 411.

35. A. Smirnov, "Problema sovremennogo teatra," *Russkii sovremennik* 12 (1924), pp. 250–51.

36. P. Novitskii, *Obrazy akterov* (Moscow, 1941), pp. 274–75.

37. Garin, *S Meierkhol'dom,* p. 50.

38. Meierkhol'd, *Stat'i. Pis'ma . . . ,* p. 250.

39. B. Alpers, *Teatr sotsial'noi maski* (Moscow, 1931), p. 28.

40. *L'Information,* March 22, 1923, quoted in *Politicheskie otkliki zapadnoi pressy na gastroli moskovskogo Gosudarstvennogo Kamernogo teatra* (Moscow, 1924), p. 31.

41. A. Tairov, *Zapiski rezhissera. Stat'i. Besedy. Rechi. Pis'ma* (Moscow, 1970), p. 295.

42. Ia. Tugendkhol'd, *Aleksandra Ekster kak zhivopisets i kak khudozhnik stseny* (Berlin, 1922), p. 18.

43. G. Kreg, *Iskusstvo teatra* (St. Petersburg, 1911), p. 31.

44. S. Ignatov, "Aki, Gitis i KAT," *Teatr* 4 (1922). Abram Efros expressed the same views in his *Khudozhniki Kamernogo teatra za dvadtsat' let* (Moscow, 1934).

45. Kazimir Malevich, letter to Vsevolod Meierkhol'd, April 8, 1932, Central State Archive for Literature and Art, Moscow, f. 998, op. 1, ed. khr. 1933. Malevich wrote to Meierkhol'd after he had learned of Meierkhol'd's plans to build a new theater. It was becoming clear to Malevich that Meierkhol'd was "still stuck in the Constructivist wheel rolling down the path of the theater's destruction." Malevich was as certain as before that Constructivism "sets itself no artistic task, only naked utility, and in the theater only pure agitprop," which is perhaps "one hundred percent consistent ideologically, yet absolutely divorced from artistic problems." In Meierkhol'd's new theater, the stage jutted far out into the hall and had seats for viewers on three sides. Platforms for the actors could be placed anywhere and at varying heights. The entire space of the theater thus became material for the designer.

46. *Nouvelles littéraires,* March 17, 1923, quoted in *Politicheskie otkliki,* p. 25.

47. S. Gorodetskii, "O trekhmernom dialekticheskom teatre," *Izvestiia VTsIK,* July 27, 1922.

48. S. Iutkevich, "Odinnadtsat' slonov," *Zrelishcha* 25 (1923), p. 10.

49. K. Fel'dman, "Chelovek, kotoryi byl Chetvergom," *7 dnei Moskovskogo Kamernogo teatra* 7 (1923), p. 2.

50. M. Zagorskii, "Chelovek, kotoryi byl Chetvergom," *Zrelishcha* 67 (1923), p. 10.

51. Tairov, *Zapiski rezhissera,* p. 295.

52. *Teatr im. Vs. Meierkhol'da,* pp. 11–13.

53. D. Zolotnitskii, *Budni i prazdniki teatral'nogo Oktiabria* (Leningrad, 1978), p. 39.

54. Vas. Sakhnovskii, "Meierkhol'd," *Vremennik RTO* 1 (1925), p. 23.

55. "Beseda s V. Stepanovoi," *Zrelishcha* 16 (1922), pp. 11–12.

56. Ibid.

57. *Teatr imeni Vs. Meierkhol'd,* pp. 11–13.

58. Meierkhol'd, *Stat'i. Pis'ma . . .,* p. 79.

59. Sadko [V. Blium], "'Smert' Tarelkina' u Meierkhol'da," *Pravda,* December 1, 1922.

60. A. Fevral'skii, *Zapiski rovesnika veka* (Moscow, 1976), p. 273.

61. Meierkhol'd, *Stat'i. Pis'ma . . .,* p. 52.

62. Ia. Braun, "Puti eksperimentatora (posleiubileinye razmyshleniia o Vs. Meierkhol'de)," *Teatr i muzyka* 11 (1923), p. 808.

63. Alpers, *Teatr sotsial'noi maski,* p. 29.

64. Chuzhak, "Opyt revizii 'Revizora.'"

65. Dziga Vertov, *Stat'i. Dnevniki. Zamysly* (Moscow, 1966), p. 71.

66. Fevral'skii, *Zapiski rovesnika veka,* p. 236.

67. "Tartiufi kommunizma i rogonostsy morali," *Teatr i muzyka* 7 (1922), p. 24.

68. "Zemlia dybom," *Sovetskii iug,* June 15, 1923.

69. Central State Archive for Literature and Art, Moscow, f. 963, op. 1, ed. khr. 324.

70. B. Pasternak, *Izbrannoe v dvukh tomakh* (Moscow, 1985), vol. 2, pp. 450–53. The letter was written after Pasternak had seen *The Inspector General.*

71. M. Chekhov, "Postanovka 'Revizora' v teatre imeni V. E. Meierkhol'da," *Gogol' i Meierkhol'd* (Moscow, 1927), p. 86.

72. *Perepiska V. E. Meierkhol'da* (Moscow, 1976), p. 286.

73. R. Zakarzhevskaia, conversation with author, December 17, 1976.

74. Minutes of the discussion of *Delo,* 1940, VTO Library, Moscow. See also F. Syrkina, "Das Theater Tatlins," in *Tatlin* (Weingarten, 1987).

75. Minutes of the discussion of *Delo,* 1940.

76. Ibid.

Nonarchitects in Architecture

Anatolii Strigalev

In the second half of the nineteenth century, and particularly in the early years of the twentieth, almost all the arts in Russia—literature, music, theater, and painting—experienced a sense of unprecedented acceleration and of creative ferment and renewal. Only architecture seemed immune.

Architects were, as a rule, competent professionals (some, of course, did possess genuine talent). At the time, architecture schools produced two types of specialists: "architect-artists"—stylistic connoisseurs, experts at monumental composition and architectural decoration—and "civil engineers" with more generalized abilities. It was common practice for an experienced "civil engineer"—the owner, say, of an established architectural firm—to invite an "architect-artist" (in most cases, a promising newcomer) to decorate the façades of a project already complete in all other respects. (New structures were awarded prizes for the "best façade" in any given year.) Thus architecture evolved in accordance with changing stylistic trends and fashions.

Russian society was, nonetheless, unhappy with the state of architecture. Inasmuch as architecture was the "mother of all the arts," its decline (whether absolute or only relative) was viewed as a brake on artistic and spiritual culture as a whole. Both the notion of a "synthesis of the arts"—which was given particularly wide currency through its promotion by Richard Wagner and which was subject in Russia to a number of distinctive interpretations—and the purposeful quest for a "style" that would be the artistic reflection and expression of the epoch made demands of architecture which its present resources were deemed inadequate to meet. What innovation there was in architecture was perceived as not radical enough. The developments in vanguard painting were not replicated in architecture.

In many countries, vanguard art exerted an extraordinary formal influence on the emergence of "new architecture" at the beginning of the twentieth century. In Russia—where this process occurred later than it did in France, Germany, Holland, or Austro-Hungary—the period of influence was quite brief (of seven or eight years' duration, from approximately 1917 to 1923) yet unusually concentrated. And it was preceded by a long period of preparation, initiated when nonarchitects, cognizant of society's displeasure with architecture, repeatedly attempted to intervene in architectural projects.

As at the end of the nineteenth century, so at the beginning of the twentieth artists—such as Mikhail Vrubel', Viktor Vasnetsov, Vasilii Polenov, Sergei Maliutin, Aleksandr Golovin, Konstantin Korovin, Nikolai Rerikh, Aleksandr Benua (Alexandre Benois), Evgenii Lansere, Ivan Nivinskii, and Sergei Vashkov—participated in architectural design (most often of façades and interiors), designed exhibitions and festive decorations, made sketches for furnishings and urban objects, and took part in architectural competitions. In most such instances, artists were not seeking to try their hand at another profession. Whether conceiving their own designs or executing a commission, they were, rather, in search of alternatives to the customary solutions of professional architects.

Arrogation of the prerogatives of the architect (or master builder) was less pronounced, yet no less consequential, in those cases where leading figures in the other arts—including Il'ia Repin, Polenov, Shcherbatov, Leonid Andreev, Maksimilian Voloshin, Vasilii Kamenskii, and Fedor Shaliapin (Feodor Chaliapin)—commissioned designs for their own homes. Repin's Penaty, his estate and studio in Kuokkala, near St. Petersburg, flouted generally accepted architectural rules and "good taste," yet demonstrated an entirely unconstrained and direct approach to architectural form (fig. no. 1). The estate was constructed to suit the individual needs of its owner, his family's style of life, and his own aesthetic preferences. The

radical formal boldness and departure from preconception evinced in Penaty put Repin in the architectural vanguard long before there was an architectural avant-garde in Russia. The "brazenness"¹ that Repin discerned in contemporary art could be labeled an almost indispensable trait of any active intervention by outsiders in architecture.

Nonarchitects were, however, most often drawn not to actual architectural practice but to the nonutilitarian and abstract "planning" of *fantastic* structures. The proliferating works of science fiction and other writing about the *future* depicted the unprecedented skyscrapers and feats of engineering, the private homes and public buildings, and the fantastic means of transportation in the mechanized city of the future. (Most of these books, it's true, were either translations into Russian or imitations of the works of Western writers, H. G. Wells foremost among them.) A distinctive fantastic and forward-looking urban "design" emerged, which combined quasi-reality (the reality of certain American and European metropolises) with unbounded imaginings.

In 1912, a certain *Sinii zhurnal* (*Blue Journal*) each month offered its readers an illustrated description of the "St. Petersburg of the future" (side by side, incidentally, with harsh gibes at "Futurism" in Russian literature and painting). The "Moscow of the future" was depicted in a 1913 series of advertising postcards as a city of contrasts, its famous architectural monuments of the past juxtaposed with imposing examples of a fantastic "Americanized" architecture. Other visions of the architecture of the future were of course put forth: the idyllic "city–garden" or the "cozy nest" hidden away in nature.

In painting and graphic art at the beginning of the century, however, the heightened interest in architecture was directed in most instances not toward the future but toward the past, toward ancient and "post-petrine" Russian architecture, above all (at the end of the nineteenth century, the latter was still not considered "Russian").² Nostalgia was the prevailing mood. Artists, as it were, boycotted contemporaneity and its accompanying architectural and urban realities.

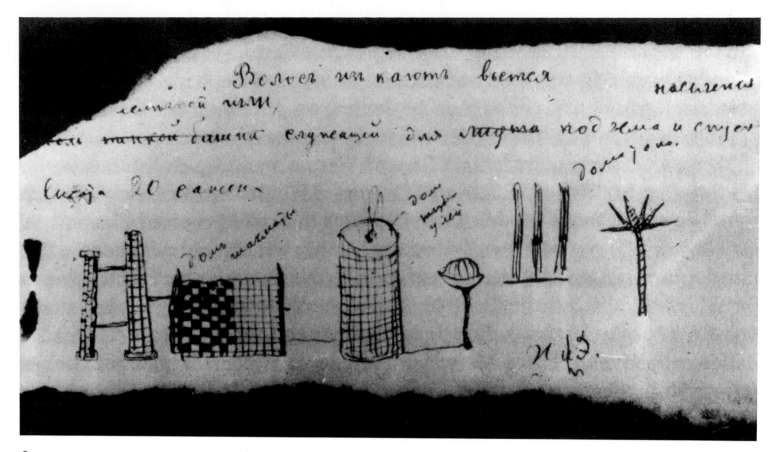

fig. 2
Manuscript with architectural fantasies sketched by Velimir
Khlebnikov, 1915–16.

Mstislav Dobuzhinskii's series *Gorodskie sny* (*Urban Dreams*)—among which one may include scattered works (fig. no. 3) dating from the late 1900s to 1922, when Dobuzhinskii left the USSR—is one of the few examples of an artistic envisioning of the "city of the future." A typical representative of the backward-looking Mir iskusstva (World of Art) group, Dobuzhinskii transformed his traditional manner in treating this subject, fusing several heterogeneous sources—Piranesi, turn-of-the-century European urban sketches, the idiom of early-twentieth-century Russian architectural Neoclassicism, and his own 1914 sketches of contemporary London (the last the fruit of his brief Cubist period). Dobuzhinskii's series exercised an undoubted influence on the plastic language of architectural projects from the early stages of the delineation of the postrevolutionary architectural avant-garde through the Palace of Labor competition in 1923[3]—a period that came to be labeled that of "revolutionary Romanticism."

Architecture was unprepared both artistically and technically to absorb the "extremes" of vanguard art, and it was only after the October Revolution that architects began to use the cityscapes of the Russian Cubo-Futurists—the paintings, dating from the 1910s, of Aristarkh Lentulov, Aleksandra Ekster, Liubov' Popova, Mikhail Le-Dantiu, Kazimir Malevich, Ivan Kliun, Ivan Puni, and others—as a "textbook" on a new spatial vision and the "aesthetics of rupture and dislocation," and as a source of certain concrete formal "motifs."

The results of acquaintance with Cubo-Futurist painting are evident in the architect Vladimir Krinskii's experimental projects from 1919–21. These are not architectural drawings but Cubist "paintings" of buildings. And the plicated or serrated dismembered architectural masses favored from 1922 by the architect Konstantin Mel'nikov were surely indebted both to Lentulov's 1919–20 series of landscapes depicting the ancient architectural ensembles of the Monastery of the Holy Trinity and St. Sergei, New Jerusalem, and Tsaritsyno as well as to Popova's architectural paintings of 1916.

In about 1910, however, when the style moderne that had prevailed at the beginning of the century had been rejected by both traditionalists and the "left," a Neoclassical movement came to the fore, buttressed by the interest in eighteenth- and early-nineteenth-century Russian culture recently awakened by Benua and World of Art. Both the "public" and architects viewed classical St. Petersburg through the works of contemporary artists and poets (such as Anna Akhmatova, Osip Mandel'shtam, and Benedikt Lifshits—the last a Classicist within Futurism). "St. Petersburg was beautiful when no one noticed its beauty and everyone dismissed it," said Aleksandr Blok. "But here we've sung St. Petersburg's praises, and now everyone knows how lovely it is, admires it, is enraptured by it!"[4]

It is interesting that both Mandel'shtam and Lifshits discerned in St. Petersburg's early-nineteenth-century architecture those spatial and temporal notions and categories whose relevance would be perceived only in the twentieth century and which would prove of particular interest to the Russian "Futurists." In poems identically entitled "Admiralteistvo" ("The Admiralty")—Mandel'shtam's from 1913, Lifshits's from 1915—the two poets declared that the architecture of this remarkable building (constructed in 1806–23) "denies the superiority of space" over time and "severs the bonds of three dimensions," "in defiance of Euclid."

Andrei Belyi's novel *Peterburg* (*St. Petersburg*, 1913–14) was an exceptionally powerful and expressive statement of a new subjective vision and perception of the metropolis. The Classical layout of St. Petersburg and the old buildings of the "era of Aleksandr"—praised for their "clarity," "simplicity," and "logic"—were in Belyi's novel a picture of spatial

irrationality, borderlessness, and existential absurdity. The critics were quick to recognize the novel as "Cubism in literary prose, equal in strength to the Cubism of Picasso" and its author as the "only true and significant Futurist in Russian literature," whose conjoining of "Cubism and Futurism . . . with true, unmediated Symbolism" made for his originality.[5]

These are the words of the philosopher Nikolai Berdiaev. Sharing the widespread belief that architecture had fallen into decline, Berdiaev not only felt that "architecture has already perished irrevocably" but (already in 1914) pinpointed the reason for its demise in the "long-standing victory in architecture of the lowest form of Futurism."[6]

For the time being, however, hopes were strong that Neoclassicism would prevail. While World War I forced a sharp cutback on new construction, planning continued unabated (this was Russia's first "architecture on paper" boom). And the artistic achievements of architectural Neoclassicism even gave rise to attempts to return vanguard painting to the "true path," to use the example of architecture to influence all of Russian art. Georgii Lukomskii, a defender of the Neoclassical revival, wrote:

While painting seeks "new" ideals, outside of any principles or traditions and with the sole end of creating art suited to the era of the automobile, telephone, and cinematograph, truly new *architecture, which meets the demands of today by erecting banks, houses of the people, car garages, markets, and telephone exchanges, finds it possible to utilize the traditions of the past beautifully and thoughtfully.*

Isn't it therefore obvious that the new aspirations in painting are strained and lifeless? . . . Doesn't it follow that it is possible *for all contemporary art to make use of old forms?*[7]

Strange though it may seem, the same argument was made by Anatolii Lunacharskii after the Revolution. People's Commissar of Enlightenment and official art-policymaker in the USSR, Lunacharskii was a both long-standing Party member and a gifted writer on public affairs, an art critic, a poet, and a widely produced playwright (though his plays were on occasion banned by the official Soviet censorship—such was the curious new situation in art). He was, moreover, the most prominent representative of the Marxist wing of Russian "Postivist aesthetics," and always approached strictly artistic—and especially formal—problems somewhat speculatively, measuring any phenomenon by sociological criteria and the theory of class struggle.

It was not only personal taste but the high value placed on the art of antiquity and the Renaissance in the writings of Marx and Engels that caused Lunacharskii's sympathies to lie unwaveringly with Classicism. He maintained that the "classics"—that is, the art of the ancient democracies and of those periods when the bougeoisie was "young and progressive"—were the most valuable cultural legacy for the proletariat. (This was somewhat difficult to square with another Marxist tenet—that each new social order is prepared within the one preceding. When in the late 1920s the architecture critic A. Mikhailov—one of the chief participants in the ideological and political persecution of Constructivist and "Formalist" Soviet architects—accordingly evinced an interest in the architecture of the capitalist period, Lunacharskii severely criticized this "mistake" and returned the "errant" Mikhailov to the summarily preferred "classics.")[8] Vanguard art (under the collective rubric of "Futurism") was, by contrast, inevitably regarded as a manifestation of "capitalist culture in the period of its decline."

Lunacharskii's outline for a monumental mass spectacle, planned for Red Square in the spring of 1921, gives some notion of his architectural utopia (as was the common practice, the

fig. 3
Mstislav Dobuzhinskii
City of the Future, *1918–19.*

spectacle presented a succession of different social epochs, symbolized by changes in architectural decoration):

Fourth act: capital . . . decorations conveying . . . a conglomeration of buildings: mills, industrial plants, prisons . . . corresponding dances (perhaps in deliberately "Futurist" style) . . .

Fifth act: . . . a group of workers . . . gradually erects the city of the future. This is a complex, gleaming with all the colors of the rainbow, of marvelous fantastic buildings (I would recommend that light aerial constructions prevail) bearing such legends as "Free School of Labor," "Temple of Science," and "Temple of Art." The most important thing is to create a bewitching tableau which would give a hint of the "promised city."[9]

The chief question for Lunacharskii was always "What kind of art do we need?"[10] And the answer he gave never varied: art kindred with the classical. In a course on the theory of art in 1921, he examined architecture as the "center of the fine arts,"[11] while in his practical work as commissar he was convinced that architecture tended least of all the arts toward change—and was least in need of any.[12] The Architecture Subsection of Izo Narkompros (the Department of Fine Arts of the People's Commissariat of Enlightenment) was, as a consequence, composed entirely of traditionalists and proponents of Classicism, and headed by Ivan Zholtovskii.[13]

The other members of Izo Narkompros—painters and sculptors for whom, it would seem, architecture should be of no concern—had quite different views. The vanguard artists under David Shterenberg in Izo Narkompros, and particularly those on Izo Narkompros's Art Board in Moscow (which was headed by Vladimir Tatlin), were advocates of innovation in architecture. Their program, calling for a radical renewal of all aspects of architecture and its "return" to the ranks of contemporary art, entailed uncompromisingly sharp criticism of the situation in architecture and rejection of its historical canons; a search for a new architecture that converged with vanguard painting and sculpture, and was understood as a new "synthesis of the arts"; a system of education oriented toward study of the contemporary construction industry and the technical side of the artist's and sculptor's craft ("artistic culture"); denial of the hierarchical ranking of "high" and "utilitarian" art; direct assistance to architects desiring additional vanguard training (Zhivskul'ptarkh [the Synthesis of Painting, Sculpture, and Architecture Commission] and Unovis [the Affirmers of the New Art]); and—most important—advancement of concrete proposals for fundamentally new buildings, structures, "minor architectural forms," and so on.

Such calls for innovation were repeated in a number of texts (sometimes almost word for word),[14] bearing witness to a certain collective conception that likely had a single source. That source was Tatlin. As no less an authority than Nikolai Punin attested, "Tatlin's influence on us . . . was, I say, boundless . . . Much of what became the program of Izo Narkompros went back to Tatlin's basic principles."[15]

Prior to the Revolution, vanguard painters had had no chance to test their formal ideas on any object of an architectural nature, yet the critics had immediately detected the architectural potential of, for instance, Tatlin's counter-reliefs. The decoration of the Café Pittoresque in the summer of 1917 afforded artists their first practical opportunity, and contemporaries viewed it as an event of fundamental significance. Georgii Iakulov, who had headed the group of artists decorating the café, considered himself as a consequence the father of Constructivism (whereas in fact he subsequently became a leading representative of the romantic line in "artists' architecture").[16]

It was Tatlin's view that the time for easel painting was past (at least for him personally) and that it was necessary to create a new art, which he first designated in 1919 as "material, volume, and construction." From the beginning of 1919, word of Tatlin's work on a project for a grand building-monument—bathed in a certain theatrical mystery—became a real factor in artistic life, influencing art's evolution toward Constructivism and production art (though they were as yet unnamed). Tatlin's model for the *Pamiatnik III-emu Internatsionalu* (*Monument to the Third International*, 1919–20) made an enormous impression on contemporaries, gained fame around the world, and was transformed into a symbol. Here, however, we will not dwell on Tatlin's Tower but, rather, examine certain of his conceptions of architecture, which were in large part shared by other artists.

Artists' intervention in architecture was a conscious, willed desire that would have to be satisfied, as they saw it, *without architects' help.* In his report on the year's work of Izo Narkompros, Shterenberg singled out the "architecture section," stating that "turning to the best architectural forces of St. Petersburg and Moscow," the Art Board "had not immediately been able to establish close contact with them, and even in the future will perhaps not entirely see eye-to-eye with them."[17] He was expressing the view of the majority of his colleagues when he said that "insofar as architects continue to start from Greek columns, from a desire to squeeze between them cars and locomotives and large buildings for meetings, libraries, and cafeterias for the broad masses, all their efforts will come to naught and artistic architecture will be entirely swept aside. Yet this doesn't mean that the greatest monuments won't be created." Shterenberg placed his hopes in "engineering construction," which "as of late . . . has far outstripped architecture and offers an array of new forms that in the future will be the cornerstone of construction."[18] Thus the stage was set for examination of architectural issues outside the Architecture Subsection of Izo Narkompros—in Izo Narkompros as a whole and in the Subsection for Artistic Labor (created, in part, to meet this need); later among the members of Zhivskul'ptarkh, Inkhuk (the Institute of Artistic Culture), and Lef (the Left Front of the Arts); and, finally, in independent vanguard architectural groups created in 1923 and 1925.

Both of the chief leaders of the avant-garde—Malevich and Tatlin—were convinced that the situation in architecture was irreparable and emphatically juxtaposed architecture with *building.* In 1920, Tatlin called those working with him on his Tower "*builders*"; in 1922, while organizing the *Obzor novykh techenii iskusstva* (*Survey of New Trends in Art*) exhibition, he endeavored "to mobilize all the artistic forces of Petrograd working in the new art—in painting, theater, music, sculpture, and *building* [emphasis added]";[19] and in 1924, he argued "against the participation of architects in the construction [of a monument to Lenin], allowing only artist-Constructivists and technician-engineers."[20] Tatlin offered a formula for the creative activity—which he labeled the "construction of materials"— that would, in his view, replace traditional architecture: "Painting + engineering − architecture = construction of materials."[21]

When working on a concrete project, Tatlin (as well as the majority of other artists in a similar position) did not seek to replace all professional specialists, only architects. In Tatlin's view, the artist, whom he regarded as the "initiating unit in the creative work of the collective," must *invent a form* suited to the task at hand; the job of various specialists was to "elaborate" and realize that form. The slogans Tatlin hung when he exhibited the model for his Tower were indicative of his stance: "We Are Inventing the Construction of Materials,"

fig. 4
Georgii Iakulov
Project for a monument, The Twenty-Six Commissars, *Baku, 1923.*

"Engineers and Bridge Builders, Base Your Computations on Invented New Form," "Metalworkers of the World, Manufacture Parts, Build New Form in Honor of the Third Communist International."[22]

Although the Tower was profoundly influential in the changes that began to occur in Russian architecture in the early 1920s, Tatlin a decade later expressed displeasure with the by then widespread functionalist-Constructivist forms of architecture: "the forms used in the construction industry (in architecture) have a certain fixed schematic character," are geometrically primitive, avoid "curved construction forms and complex curvature," and make routine use of "customary construction materials"—all of which "leads to monotony," which is "plain to see in contemporary international architectural competitions."[23] While the Constructivists deemed functionality adequate to render form artistic, Tatlin's view was that "invented" form was first artistic and then functional.

(Tatlin's later works, as well, had an impact on vanguard architects. Mel'nikov, who as a rule was indifferent to the work of others, not only promoted the model of the Tower exhibited at the *Exposition internationale des arts décoratifs et industriels modernes* [*International Exhibition of Contemporary Decorative and Industrial Art*, Paris, 1925] but was much impressed by *Letatlin* [1929–32]—a utopian and entirely nonarchitectural work.)[24]

Malevich's influence on twentieth-century architecture was even more wide-ranging than Tatlin's. His concern with architecture likely began very early on. The Suprematist paintings he showed at the end of 1915 exhibited features in principle kindred with those of architecture, and "volumetric Suprematism" dated from about 1920 (though hardly earlier).[25] Thereafter his interest in architecture only grew, reaching a peak in the early 1930s.

Immediately after the Revolution, however, Malevich contented himself with sharp and merciless criticism of the state of architecture. In a series of derisive articles published in 1918 in *Anarkhiia* (*Anarchy*) and *Iskusstvo kommuny* (*Art of the Commune*), Malevich stated categorically that "the new cannot live in the old"; that "an enormous step has been taken [in all the arts] . . . only architecture is a 'withered branch'—like cripples, the architects walk on Greek columns as if on crutches"; and that architecture insulting to contemporaneity was a "slap in the face to ferroconcrete." "We artists," he concluded, "must come to the defense of new structures."[26] Malevich's criticism was impossible to ignore.

Malevich argued the case for a transition to non-objective art ("art as such")—whose task was not to repeat (to "reflect") the forms of life but to create new forms for it—with, among other things, references to architecture and building. He cited the example of the carpenter who, while constructing a building, does not imitate "objects and things as they appear in nature" but "creates a new guise and form not known in nature."[27] This specific feature of architecture, in Malevich's view, was both a convincing justification of the expediency of non-objectivity in all the other arts ("painting as such," "poetry as such," and so on) and an aid to discerning the distortion of the essence of architecture, the subjugation of its formal principles to static and outmoded cannons, in contemporary practice. "Architecture as such" had to be restored.

Architecture was an important and integral part of Malevich's all-embracing Suprematist system. "I understand architecture as an activity outside everything utilitarian," said Malevich. With this assertion, however, Malevich was not drawing the traditional distinction between the functional art of architecture and the other arts but affirming that all the arts, architecture included, were independent from "naked utilitarianism." "Thus I understand *all the arts as activity free*

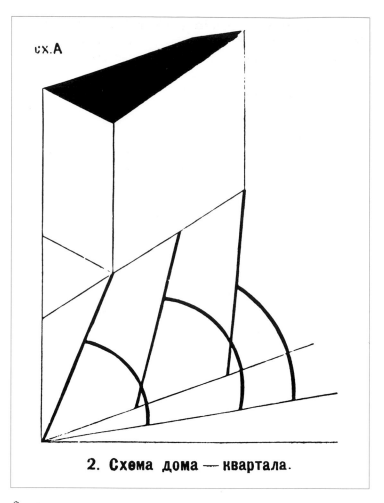

cx.A

2. Схема дома — квартала.

fig. 5
Anton Lavinskii
City on Springs: Sketch for Housing Block, *1921.*

from all economic and practical ideologies [emphasis added]."[28] Technical and utilitarian activity, according to Malevich, produced "things," whose perfection changed over time: "a cart, a carriage, a locomotive, and an airplane are a chain of unconsidered possibilities and tasks." Whereas art "can call its creations *finished works* [*proizvedeniia*], since their execution is absolute, timeless, and unchanging, hence properly considered [emphasis added]."[29]

The new (non-objective) art would not borrow its forms from nature and reality yet it would be intimately linked with reality and inspired by it. Malevich regarded Cubism, Futurism, Suprematism, and Constructivism as the inevitable art of the modern metropolis and its way of life. Though he denied the authority of utility over art, Malevich acknowledged a special, art-specific, utilitarianism ("Suprematist forms, as an abstraction, became utilitarian perfection") and "economy" ("the fifth dimension I introduced into art").[30] From 1920, Malevich methodically demonstrated various types of Suprematist architecture—in projects for speaker's rostrums (plate no. 130), living quarters, public buildings, monuments, urban complexes, and interior decorations—and persistently sought to have a hand in the training of architects.

Of all the new formal systems advanced by painting in the early twentieth century, Suprematism proved the most congenial to and influential on the worldwide movement toward "new architecture." Yet the Soviet wing of this movement—architectural Constructivism—evinced a rather strange ambivalence vis-à-vis Malevich. While in practice Malevich's forms were more widely and directly employed than were those of any other artist, the Constructivist theorists (Boris Arvatov, Aleksei Gan, and others) only partially acknowledged the significance of Malevich's formal achievements and insisted on the ideological alienness to Constructivism, and even the political enmity, of Malevich's artistic and philosophical conceptions.[31]

The vanguard artists who followed the example of Malevich and Tatlin—the nonarchitects who turned to architecture or to creative work having tasks akin to those of architecture—traveled many different paths. Works representative of what could be called the consciously utopian, maximalist trend, oriented toward unlimited scientific-technological and social progress, were intended to be powerful catalysts to development; they projected the most general formal outlines of the "architecture of the future" and were unconcerned with any "real" technical, economic, or other sort of limitations. Man's creative powers and the technology placed at his disposal were omnipotent. Such works as Anton Lavinskii's *Gorod na ressorakh* (*City on Springs,* 1921, fig. nos. 5–6) and Gustav Klutsis's *Dinamicheskii gorod* (*Dynamic City,* 1919) and series of spatial constructions (1921–22)—not to mention the great Suprematist utopia—were a continuation of "Futurism" ("The Future is our only goal") in new circumstances. The legacy of this trend may be discerned in the projects for "flying cities" executed in the late 1920s at Vkhutein (the Higher Artistic-Technical Institute) by Georgii Krutikov, Kalmykov, and Iuzefovich, as well as in certain projects by Ivan Leonidov (for a monument to Christopher Columbus [1929], a socialist settlement in Magnitogorsk [1930], and a City of the Sun [1943–59]), Mel'nikov (for a monument to Christopher Columbus [1929] and the Green City [1929]), and other architects.

Painters, naturally, regarded color as one of the most significant components of architectural form. Unfortunately, however, insuperable practical obstacles allowed only rare endeavors in this realm between 1918, when Natan Al'tman designed his decorations for Petrograd's Palace Square (plate

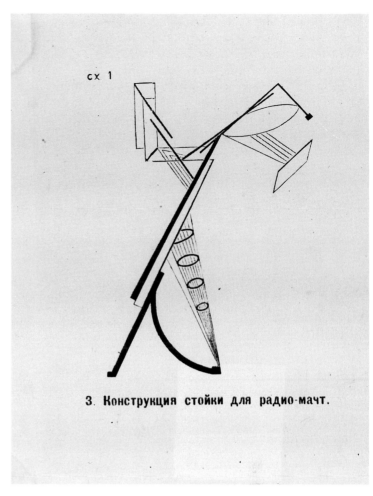

fig. 6
Anton Lavinskii
City on Springs: Construction for a Radio Tower, *1921.*

nos. 103–106), and 1932, when Georgii and Vladimir Stenberg decorated the Arbat in Moscow.

Artists such as Tatlin and Naum Gabo introduced dynamic elements into architecture, and long before architects they—along with Konstantin Medunetskii, the Stenberg brothers, Ekster, Lavinskii, Aleksandr Rodchenko, and others—attempted to integrate modern technical and constructive elements (such as towers and antennae) into architectural compositions. Professional architects had already adopted these forms by the advent of the competition for the Palace of Labor in 1922–23 (see the projects by the Vesnins, Kuznetsov and Toropov, and Il'ia Golosov, among others) and they would remain a favorite motif of the Vesnins, Leonidov, and Iakov Chernikhov.

(One has to wonder why the works of such other nonarchitects as the brilliant engineers Vladimir Shukhov [creator in 1894 of an open-work tower shaped as a hyperboloid rotation and designer of the Shabolovka Street radio tower in Moscow (1919–22)] and Tat'iana Makarova [whose hyperbolic paraboloid roofing was patented in 1928] went virtually unnoticed by the architecture of the 1920s.[32] Perhaps it was because there was no artist to serve as intermediary between engineer and architect?)

Artists' interest in such individual aspects of architecture as form and color led them logically to the next step: direct participation in architectural planning. Most of these projects (especially at first) involved "minor architectural forms": speaker's rostrums (by Il'ia Chashnik and Nikolai Suetin, 1920 and thereafter, plate nos. 140–141, 147), kiosks (by Lavinskii, Gan, and Grigorii Miller), Klutsis's agitprop constructions (1922, plate nos. 109–113), Rodchenko's reading room for a workers' club (1925), Aleksei Babichev's mobile agitprop theater (1922), the series of projects for architectural constructions displayed by the members of the First Working Organization of Artists at the *Pervaia diskussionnaia vystavka ob"edinenii aktivnogo revoliutsionnogo iskusstva* (*First Discussional Exhibition of Associations of Active Revolutionary Art*, Moscow, 1924), monuments, furnishings, exhibition pavilions (designed by Ekster [1923, fig. no. 8], Klutsis [1923], Rodchenko [1923], and by Shterenberg in collaboration with Medunetskii and Sergei Kostin [1925, fig. no. 7]),[33] and so on.

fig. 7
David Shterenberg, Sergei Kostin, and Konstantin Medunetskii Model for the Soviet Trade Center, Exposition internationale des arts décoratifs et industriels modernes, *Paris, 1925.*

fig. 8
Aleksandra Ekster with Vera Mukhina and B. Gladkov Pavilion for Izvestiia TsIK, All-Union Agricultural Exhibition, *Moscow, 1923.*

Nowhere, however, was there a more concentrated exchange between art and architecture than in Zhivskul'ptarkh, a group organized and led by the sculptor Boris Korolev. The leading representative of sculptural Cubism in Soviet Russia, Korolev did not come by this role by chance.

Korolev's Cubism was radical yet entirely unorthodox. The dominant feature of his forms, which appeared to be still in the process of assuming their final shape, was not analyticalness or constructiveness but expressiveness, an internal tension. An early commentator described Korolev as an artist who created sculptural form not by removing the extraneous but by adding parts, "modeling" one to the other.[34] The observation is partially warranted: Korolev did follow such a procedure even where it would have seemed ill-suited, for instance, in certain of his Cubist sculptures from wood. This feature of his work perhaps also goes some way toward explaining his interest in architectural form, which is always created from the conjoining of parts. Korolev's enormous works were intended for public spaces, yet they contained forms entirely without analogues in architecture: massive forms, only partially geometrized, either undifferentiated or the result of the simple placement of heterogeneous parts one on top of the other. His works not infrequently had a pear-shaped silhouette, and their vertical axis was inclined rather than straight.

Korolev was simultaneously involved in social and organizational work. After the Revolution, he was the de facto leader of the new Union of Sculptors and a member of many commissions. He later joined the Moscow Art Board of Izo Narkompros where, with Tatlin and Zholtovskii, he was part of a "troika" representing painting, architecture, and sculpture (and certainly Korolev's interest in architecture must have been fueled by this association with Tatlin and Zholtovskii).[35] He organized and headed Izo Narkompros's Subsection on Artistic Labor, was active in the reorganization of art education, and was likely the instigator and one of the chief authors of a number of documents and undertakings for the 1918 Plan for Monumental Propaganda. It was Korolev who proposed the most "Formalist" monuments, one of which—a monument to Mikhail Bakunin—was erected on a square adjoining the State Free Art Workshops. It was never, however, unveiled. Rather, in February 1920 it was destroyed as a consequence of the persistent opposition of officials of the Moscow Soviet, who labeled the work "incomprehensible to the people."[36]

In the spring of 1919, a small group of architects, recent graduates of architecture schools in Petrograd and Moscow and now participants in various arenas of the Plan for Monumental Propaganda, decided to take up architectural planning with Korolev. Nikolai Istselenov, S. Dombrovskii, Ia. Raikh, and A. Rukhliad'ev met with Korolev at the group's first session on May 6, 1919. Nikolai Ladovskii and Vladimir Fidman joined them three days later, and on June 25th so did Krinskii. Dombrovskii and Rukhliad'ev left the group for work-related reasons in August; G. Mapu joined only in late November.

The members of Zhivskul'ptarkh sought a "synthesis of painting, sculpture, and architecture" (in so doing they were part of the larger quest for a "synthesis of the arts") that would provide the basis for a new formal language of "architecture as such." They formulated their task as the "rebirth of the pure significance of the architectural construction" and as a "project for the construction of a building of pure art."[37] Their sketches for a Temple of Communion Among Nations (plate nos. 657, 659), communal homes (plate nos. 654–655, 658), and the Soviet of Deputies building did not represent "socially new types of buildings"[38] but were occasions for the elaboration of form; they were sketches, in the words of Istselenov, for a "structure freed from the utilitarian character of the latest architecture, a structure in which art would be given a chance

fig. 9
Boris Korolev
Salomé, *1922.*

to reveal its synthetic oneness."

(Inasmuch as Korolev was a sculptor by profession, the group was originally called Sinskul'ptarkh [the Synthesis of Sculpture and Architecture Commission] and defined its task as the "elaboration of principles and concrete professional questions of the linkage of sculpture and architecture as arts operating with form and space." Yet the group's members also stated that "the present . . . puts forward the question of a synthesis of the arts of spatial rhythm: painting, sculpture, and architecture." Assimilation of the formal experience of vanguard painting [which had earlier been a stimulus to vanguard sculpture, in particular to the "painterly reliefs" and other works of Russian "sculpto-painting" in the second half of the 1910s] did not require any firsthand knowledge of painting.)

Ladovskii's sketches, both as a whole and in their specific details, most fully met the aims of Zhivskul'ptarkh; they were also the most interesting and were distinguished by a particular daring and originality. It was in Zhivskul'ptarkh, moreover, that Ladovskii began to work out new pedagogical methods. In Vkhutemas's Basic Division, he promoted the teaching, to students of all specializations, of the formal bases of contemporary art. And the research laboratory he created at the school had its origins in a proposal advanced jointly with Korolev in Zhivskul'ptarkh.

The experimental Zhivskul'ptarkh projects of Krinskii and Fidman (plate nos. 660–662) also bore fruit. Whereas Dombrovskii, Rukhliad'ev, and in particular Istselenov (plate no. 663), though they shared the general aims of the group, probably found the direction taken by Korolev rather less congenial. Raikh was first and foremost an architect on the theoretical plane, while Mapu represented a type of architect—active but imitative—characteristic of the periphery of the left avant-garde.

Two painters—Rodchenko and Aleksandr Shevchenko—had joined Zhivskul'ptarkh in mid-November 1919 (six and a half months after the group's formation, and two and a half months before it ceased its activity in early February 1920).[39] Their participation should not, however, be regarded as the inauguration of a specific "painting period" in Zhivskul'ptarkh's work, for no changes occurred in the character of the sketches of the group's architect members. Shevchenko's sole known Zhivskul'ptarkh project merely borrowed from Ladovskii's idea for a dynamic communal house and endeavored to shine only in its execution. Rodchenko, by contrast, created a large series of architectural fantasies and projects during 1919–20 (plate nos. 652–653).

Zhivskul'ptarkh embodied in concentrated form the path that all of Soviet architecture would soon follow. However, during the 1920s, which witnessed the emergence of a vanguard architecture in the USSR, "nonarchitects" exercised a different sort of influence on architecture. The social standing of architecture was nominally quite high, and it attracted the more or less active interest of many Party and government figures. At the close of the decade and the beginning of the 1930s, the formal achievements of architecture would strike many of these "nonarchitects" as worthless. They would have no regrets when the direction of Soviet art and architecture was abruptly altered by an order from above.

—Translated from the Russian

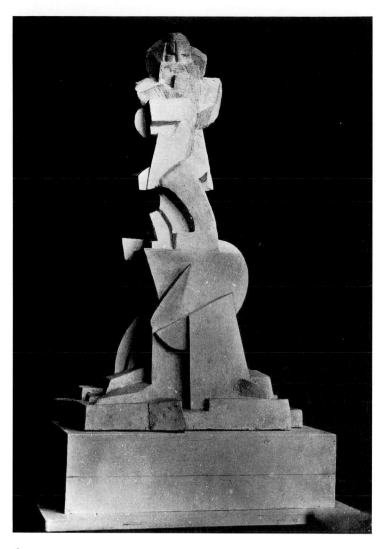

fig. 10
Boris Korolev
Project for a monument to Karl Marx, Moscow, 1919–20.

Notes

1. I. E. Repin, *Pis'ma k khudozhnikam i khudozhestvennym deiateliam* (Moscow, 1952), p. 192.

2. The first scholarly book on the history of Russian architecture (A. Pavlinov, *Istoriia russkoi arkhitektury* [Moscow, 1894]) is based primarily on the notion that "Russian" architecture ceased to be created after the beginning of the eighteenth century.

3. Many symbolic-romantic compositions depicting the construction of huge monuments or the destruction of monuments of "classical" architecture appear in revolutionary graphic works. These images were meant as signs of social change; they do not contain formal creative ideas and are for the most part imitative. In 1920, one of the leading Neoclassical architects, Ivan Fomin, proposed a project for a monument which would be based on an overturned entablature (of a particular order), and crowned with the drum of a column and crude stone frames inscribed with the slogan "We Destroy, We Finish Building—All Our Strength Lies in Ourselves."

4. Vl. Orlov, *Poet i gorod. Aleksandr Blok i Peterburg* (Leningrad, 1980), p. 148.

5. N. Berdiaev, *Krizis iskusstva* (Moscow, 1918), pp. 41–42.

6. Ibid., p. 33.

7. G. K. Lukomskii, *Sovremennyi Peterburg. Ocherk istorii vozniknoveniia i razvitiia klassicheskogo stroitel'stva 1900–1915 gg.* (Petrograd, 1917), pp. 54–55.

8. See "A. V. Lunacharskii. Neizdannye materialy," *Literaturnoe nasledstvo* 82 (Moscow, 1970), pp. 90–92, 124–125.

9. A. V. Lunacharskii, "Sstenarii dlia massovogo deistviia na prazdnike Tret'ego Internatsionala," *Literaturnoe nasledstvo* 80 (Moscow, 1971), pp. 664–66.

10. "A. V. Lunacharskii. Neizdannye materialy," p. 582. The phrase also appears in many other works by Lunacharskii.

11. Ibid.

12. A. V. Lunacharskii, "Ob Otdele izobrazitel'nykh iskusstv," *Novyi mir* 9 (1966), pp. 236–39.

13. Isolated pronouncements by Lunacharskii in support of new art, such as "the Architecture Faculty is the crown of Vkhutein" (1928), were related to peripheral factors (his gradual familiarization with the new artistic language, his unmediated aesthetic impressions, his fascination with the young students) and did not change the Commissar of Enlightenment's entrenched attachment to classicizing retrospectivism: "Back to Ostrovskii! Back to the Wanderers!"

14. See, for example, N. Punin, "O pamiatnikakh," *Iskusstvo kommuny*, March 9, 1919; D. Shterenberg, *Obzor deiatel'nosti Otdela izobrazitel'nykh iskusstv* (Petrograd, 1920), pp. 93–99 (dated by the author April 1919); *Spravochnik Otdela IZO Narodnogo komissariata po prosveshcheniiu* 1 (Moscow, 1920), pp. 37–45, 50–73 (proceedings of a conference on art education in the summer of 1920); V. Tatlin et al., "Nasha predstoiashchaia rabota," *VIII s"ezd sovetov. Ezhednevnyi biulleten'* 13 (January 1, 1921), p. 11; and B. Arvatov, *Iskusstvo i klassy* (Moscow and Petrograd, 1923), pp. 15–20, 84.

15. N. Punin, "Kvartira No. 5," *Panorama iskusstv* 12 (Moscow, 1989), p. 194.

16. Much about the work on the decoration of the Café Pittoresque remains unclear (including the individual artists and their roles). Iakulov already had experience in decorating and painting artistic cafés, but these were done in an entirely different style (one which characterized the majority of his works) than that of the Pittoresque. His sketch for the design of the stage is a notable exception. (The sketch is in the collection of the Musée national d'art moderne, Centre Georges Pompidou, Paris, where it had been labeled an "unidentified theatrical sketch." It was displayed as such in the exhibition *50 let diplomaticheskikh otnoshenii Frantsii i SSSR* [*Fifty Years of Diplomatic Relations Between France and the USSR,* Moscow, 1975], but during the preparations for the exhibition *Paris–Moscou/Moskva–Parizh,* in which the work was also shown, I identified it as Iakulov's design for the Pittoresque). The innovative aspects of the decorations for the Pittoresque (Iakulov's included) are undoubtedly related to Tatlin's active role in the work of the artistic collective.

17. Shterenberg, *Obzor deiatel'nosti Otdela izobrazitel'nykh iskusstv,* pp. 95, 94.

18. Ibid.

19. Central State Archive for Literature and Art, Moscow, f. 4340, op. 1, ed. khr. 19, l. 110b–12.

20. *Izvestiia* 46 (February 24, 1924).

21. Central State Archive for Literature and Art, Moscow, f. 4340, op. 1, ed. khr. 6, l. 43.

22. A. Strigalev, "V. E. Tatlin," *God arkhitektury* (Moscow, 1987), p. 465.

23. *Vystavka rabot zasluzhennogo deiatelia iskusstv V. E. Tatlin* (Moscow and Leningrad, 1932), p. 5.

24. Konstantin Mel'nikov, conversation with author.

25. Malevich's own dates of 1913 for the origin of Suprematism (in his set designs for *Pobeda nad solntsem* [*Victory over the Sun*]) and of 1913, 1915, 1916 for that of volumetric Suprematism (*Formula suprematizma* [*Formula of Suprematism*] and *Prostranstvennyi suprematizm* [*Spatial Suprematism*], reproduced in *Kazimir Malevich, 1878–1935* [Leningrad, Moscow, and Amsterdam, 1988, nos. 172–173] cannot be accepted. A summary view of the evidence suggests that Malevich's text (dated December 15, 1920) probably fixes with reasonable accuracy the beginning of the Suprematists' commitment to working on volumetric and architectural tasks: "Suprematism in its historical development had three stages: black, colored, and white. All periods were passed through under the conditional signs of planes; as it was expressing the plans of future volumetric bodies and truly at the present moment, Suprematism is developing in the spatial time of a new architectural construction." K. Malevich, *Suprematizm. 34 risunka* (Vitebsk: Unovis, 1920), pp. 2–3.

26. K. Malevich, "Mir miasa i kosti ushel," *Anarkhiia* 83 (June 12, 1918), and "Arkhitektura kak poshchechina zhelezo-betonu," *Iskusstvo kommuny* 1 (December 7, 1918). Malevich considered the Neo-Russian style of the Kazan' Railway Station (1912–26, designed by Aleksei Shchusev), which was then under construction, a blatant example of architectural archaism. For Tatlin, the style moderne Iaroslavl' Railway Station (1902–04, designed by Fedor Shekhtel'), which stood on the same Moscow square, was an example of architectural forms that had become "ludicrous" only a few years after construction.

27. K. Malevich, "O poezii," *Izobrazitel'noe iskusstvo* 1 (1919), p. 34.

28. K. Malevich, "Zametki o arkhitekture," reproduced in *Kazimir Malevich, 1878–1935,* p. 116.

29. K. Malevich, "Vvedenie v teoriiu pribavochnogo elementa," quoted from Kazimir Malevics, *S targynelküli vilag* (Budapest, 1986), pp. 139–140.

30. Malevich, *Suprematizm. 34 risunka*, pp. 2–3.

31. See, for example, A. Gan, "Spravka o Kazimire Maleviche," *Sovremennaia arkhitektura* 3 (1927), pp. 104, 106.

32. Several American publications (see, for example, K. P. Zygas, "Tatlin's Tower Reconsidered," *Architectural Association Quarterly* 8, no. 2 [1976], pp. 15–27) have suggested that the open-work hyperboloid defense towers on American warships (which Tatlin could have seen while he worked as a sailor on the Mediterranean Sea) were one source for the *Monument to the Third International.* Moreover, it has not yet been recognized that these towers were based on Shukhov's patent and that Tatlin undoubtedly had seen variants of Shukhov's towers (the lighthouses near Odessa and Kherson, the water towers on many railway stations and enterprises, the gun turrets of the battleship *Imperator Pavel I* [*Emperor Paul I*] in the St. Petersburg harbor) on several occasions. The prevalence in Russia of this constructive form, invented by Shukhov, only underscores the strangeness of Soviet architects' failure to employ it. It is interesting that even the memoirs of an eyewitness record that the Russian public remembered the towers of American ships, which were one of the subjects of early documentaries (see V. Kataev, *Almaznyi moi venets* [Moscow, 1990], p. 130).

33. Shterenberg, Medunetskii, and Kostin bravely competed against Mel'nikov to design the Soviet Trade Center for the *Exposition internationale des arts décoratifs et industriels modernes.* For Mel'nikov's reaction, see his *Arkhitektura moei zhizni*, comp. A. Strigalev and I. Kokkinaki (Moscow, 1985), pp. 76.

34. A. A. Sidorov, *Boris Danilovich Korolev* (Moscow and Leningrad, 1934), p. 17.

35. B. D. Korolev, *Iz literaturnogo naslediia. Perepiska. Sovremenniki o skul'ptore* (Moscow, 1989), p. 117.

36. Korolev was probably the first to make a complete break in his work for reasons of "ideology and form." The pressure on Korolev over the course of several years was so intense that, in 1923, he completely abandoned his "Formalist experiments." Yet he was blackmailed for his "Formalist past" throughout his life.

37. Citations here and below from the documents of Zhivskul'ptarkh are drawn from the B. D. Korolev files, Manuscript Division, State Tret'iakov Gallery, Moscow.

38. S. Khan-Magomedov, "Zhivskul'ptarkh," *DI SSSR* 5 (1978), pp. 32, 33.

39. Krinskii invited Rodchenko to join Zhivskul'ptarkh after the November 8, 1919, concluding meeting of the competition for the kiosk project (at which they both received awards), and Rodchenko invited Shevchenko, with whom he had worked on exhibition-related projects. Shevchenko, in turn, immediately proposed that Tatlin, who was then living in Petrograd, also be invited.

fig. 1
Vladimir Shchuko and Vladimir Gel'freikh
Competition project (reworking of Boris Iofan's scheme) for the Palace
of Soviets, Moscow; perspective of variant on square plan, 1932–33.

Mediating Creativity and Politics: Sixty Years of Architectural Competitions in Russia

Catherine Cooke

In this exhibition, as in any study of Russian avant-garde architecture, many of the most dramatic and poetic images are projects conceived for competitions. There are schemes here which have rightly entered the canon of twentieth-century architecture worldwide, as paradigms of key directions within the new discourse. As the century progresses, it has become increasingly difficult to realize how far away in time and in cultural distance the origins of these projects lie. The schemes' freshness is partly the result of the purity with which they formulated those aesthetic paradigms. It is also a consequence of the fact that the technologies on which such extraordinary formal clarity was predicated have never existed, even as imports, in Russia, and only lately have achieved enough maturity in the West to become part of the ordinary professional armory.

So radical was the constructive clarity of the frame in the Vesnin brothers' schemes for the Palace of Labor in Moscow (1922–23) and the Moscow bureau of *Leningrad Pravda* (1924), for example, that they have by now been inspirational images to many generations of architects. Even more has that technological gap postponed the realization of other visions, in particular of those to be found in Ivan Leonidov's competition schemes of the later 1920s. But as the dense traditional city to which those Vesnin projects relate has been spatially exploded in the West by the motorcar, or left as desert by economic change, Leonidov's models of a way to handle that scale, yet remain urban, have provided a starting point for the problem Peter Wilson has described as "finding a strategy to legitimise empty space." As Wilson said of Berlin, "This city is truly contemporary precisely because it is no longer continuous, connected or coherent."[1]

There arises here the whole new category of problems associated with what Bernard Tschumi has called *"la case vide"*: the empty slot, the void in the chessboard. Unique paradigms for tackling this city of emptiness were created in the Suprematist concepts of potently energized form, as developed in Leonidov's projects for the Proletarskii district Palace of Culture competition of 1930 or for the competition four years later for Narkomtiazhprom (the People's Commissariat of Heavy Industry). Thus Zaha Hadid speaks directly of "liberating the plan from the ground as did the Russian Suprematists." For Hollywood she thereby created "a new kind of urbanism which frees up the ground, programming it in with the landscape, yet being at the same time urban."[2] But these words are almost identical to those with which the Vesnins' colleague Moisei Ginzburg defended Leonidov's answer to the Lenin Library competition brief in 1927, when Leonidov's dramatic redefinition of an "urban site" was bringing politically-inspired opprobrium on the whole of avant-garde architecture.

This role in the continuing evolution of the twentieth-century city is one of the lives which these projects have led. In their own time, they played a similar role. But they also had another life, as part of a debate about the role of competitions themselves within the development of architecture. This is a debate which is as current now as it was then, focusing as it does on issues of open debate versus arbitrary, anonymous decision; of professionalism versus public participation; of innovation and the new vision versus the "realistic solution."

Like so much in that hyperintensive decade of the 1920s in Russia, this debate raised issues, characteristic of the whole Modernist epoch, with a clarity that continues to provide useful paradigms and tools for thought. But the debate also illuminates the period itself in a new way, by taking us behind the screen which the very potency of the images themselves inevitably erects between us and their provenance. Who organized the competitions, for what clients, with what motives? How was it that individual architects were competing for individual jobs in a collectivist society, where the profession seems to have been organized into vast state design offices? If competitions were part of a debate about developing a "new architecture," who were the juries, by what criteria did they judge, and how did the profession or public get feedback with which to measure architects' incremental progress? In looking at these questions alongside the projects themselves, we can take the lid off the real professional environment and the live processes within it. We can see the aesthetic issues afresh through entering the test-bed in which they were forged.

One issue of terminology needs exploring before we go further. "Competition," as the birth pangs of a post-socialist Soviet Union have for some years now been reminding us, is at one level a concept alien, even hostile, to the ideology being built in the 1920s. This is not just an observation post hoc. The duality here was reflected at the time in the use of two distinct words for the architectural "competition," with quite different meanings, and much of the battle fought by avant-gardists within the profession, as the 1920s progressed, was aimed at achieving a shift from one to the other, from an inherited word and concept to a new one, born as much of the nature of a complex modern architecture anywhere as it was of Russians' own social and ideological mission.

The traditional word for a competition was *konkurs.* Like so much else in relatively modern Russian vocabulary, *konkurs* came from abroad, from the French *concours.* This is the word we find in the professional press of the nineteenth century and through to the October Revolution. Russia was a capitalist society, albeit a socially and technically primitive one in relation to the West. Insofar as there was a market economy, its motor was the concept of *konkurentsiia* that post-Soviet *biznismeny* are now trying to get back into their bloodstreams. From old Russian roots, however, there was another word, *sorevnovanie,* which was sometimes used in Imperial Russia as a loose synonym for *konkurs,* when the reference was to the architectural competition as an event in progress. *Sorevnovanie* has connotations of a more collective process in which those with a common skill or passion "compete" with some enjoyment or celebration of pitting one talent against another. The sporting analogy would be a tournament: there is a winner, or several winners, in different categories, but the participants engage with each other directly in a mutually stimulating exercise of their skills as that winner emerges by gradual elimination. The players may indeed be teams, not individuals.

As we shall see, replacement of the *konkurs* by the *sorevnovanie* was the overriding aim of all the avant-garde groups. The differing architectural philosophies of the Constructivists and the Rationalists, for example, led them to formulate different procedural routines for the contest. As so often in these issues of the 1920s, there was in fact a firm Party-ideological line behind an apparently purely professional debate. The *sorevnovanie* was a tool specifically approved by Lenin. But no one ever mentioned that. In part, this was certainly because the notion was absorbed into the new culture architects had enthusiastically embraced. And in part, it was because the advantage to architecture was plain, in a time of design problems larger than limited professional numbers could handle by traditional ways of working. Ironically—if one looks for the conventional ironic judgment on this era—architects helped their own downfall thereby. It is a fact that the profession's own campaign to work together collectively in teams made it easier to herd architects into anonymous "studios" as fodder for the Party and the building industry in the early 1930s. But the ironic explanation does nothing to open up the sparkling vigor or creative convictions of the

extraordinary laboratory of a new architecture in the years preceding this development.

Competitions under Burgeoning Capitalism

One reason for the amount of debate provoked by the competition issue in the 1920s was the inadequacy of the regulatory and legal framework for architectural competitions inherited from the prerevolutionary regime. Superficially, prerevolutionary Russia had been a capitalist society enjoying, on the eve of World War I, the world's fastest economic growth rate. That rapid growth was accompanied by a commensurate building boom, of which a certain amount was designed through competitions, yet no universally accepted or legally reinforced procedures had been established, despite several attempts, when the war brought building to a halt for ten years. Indeed, the youthfulness of entrepreneurial culture in Russia, where serious industrialization began only in the later nineteenth century, meant that the legality and morality of professionalism as established in European and North American countries was not universally understood, and was even less consistently upheld.

This unsatisfactory situation surrounding competitions did not result from lack of effort by the upper echelons of the architectural profession who led the architectural societies of St. Petersburg, then the capital, and of Moscow. It was their last prerevolutionary draft regulations on competitions which underpinned the first architectural competitions of the Bolshevik era. Indeed, it was the prerevolutionary societies' successors, particularly in Moscow (which in 1918 again became the capital), which alternately sought to instigate better practices and were the victims of attack from the avant-gardists for their efforts.

In autocratic Russia up to the 1860s, almost all significant building—at the central or local level; whether for productive, administrative, or social purposes—was fundamentally state building. Here was a situation that would become familiar again in the 1920s. Competitions had always had an occasional role in the selection of designs for high-prestige or symbolically important buildings. Thus in St. Petersburg, the great Kazan' Cathedral on Nevskii Avenue was the subject of a competition in 1799. Andrei Voronikhin won, and building commenced in a straightforward way in 1801. When in the next decade it came to celebrating the defeat of Napoleon, however, it took twenty years of competing projects for various sites, and much political and aesthetic vituperation, before Konstantin Ton's design started on site in 1839. As cathedrals go, moreover, Ton's did not have a long life: in 1931, only seventy years after its completion, the Cathedral of Christ the Saviour was demolished by Stalin to make way for his Palace of Soviets. With suitable poetic justice, the Palace of Soviets competition, too, was, as we shall see, a long-drawn-out, multistage, and highly vituperative competition, before it finally "proved" the inapplicability of a Modernist architecture to the Bolshevik Party's aspirations.

Through the MVD (the Ministry of Internal Affairs), lesser buildings were also put out to competition. In some cases, the briefs were for "model projects" that could be used, in the tradition established in the eighteenth century, as standard designs throughout the empire. Here again was a concept, unusual in many countries, that would characterize state building in the Soviet period. In 1865, the MVD created a new Building and Technical Committee which administered virtually all state building in Russia right through to the Revolution of 1917.[3] It generally recruited from among architectural and engineering graduates of the Building College, which in 1882 became IGI (the Institute of Civil Engineers) and the sparring partner of the Imperial Academy of Arts for leadership of architectural education and dominance of professional debate. Among the Soviet avant-garde, several leaders of Constructivism were graduates of IGI. Aleksandr and Viktor Vesnin, for example, finished here in 1912. Aleksandr Nikol'skii, the Constructivist group's leader in Leningrad, was another student in their class, and Andrei Ol' had been two years their senior. As LIGI (the Leningrad Institute of Civil Engineers), the school graduated students who frequently provided teams for the intergroup *sorevnovaniia* of the later 1920s. The pioneer of concrete structures in Russia, Aleksandr Kuznetsov, who did so much to make Constructivism's formal ideas buildable, graduated from IGI in 1896; Boris Velikovskii, another of the Constructivists' mentors, graduated in 1904.

In St. Petersburg, therefore, this school was consistently a seedbed of innovative design against the more routinized canons transmitted by the Imperial Academy of Arts. By the mid-1860s, however, Moscow was beginning to go firmly its own way toward a rediscovery of Russia's own historical design roots and against the Classicism of autocracy. Back in the 1830s, the Moscow School of Painting, Sculpture, and Architecture had started to take an independent, anti-Academy stance; and in 1867, some leading Moscow architects formed Russia's first independent society to further this cause both within the profession and in the larger public consciousness.[4] The mission that the society's founder and president, Mikhail Bykovskii, outlined for MAO (the Moscow Architectural Society) was one that carried architects forward easily into the demands of an increasingly modern culture as well as the social priorities of a socialist regime. In less ponderous language, Bykovskii's assertions could have been those of any leader of the avant-garde and, in the latter part of his statement, of the Constructivists in particular:

Utilizing the whole treasure house of contemporary civilization and of science and all its newest inventions, respectfully studying the historical development of our art as manifested in its most glorious monuments, we shall be led by free analysis and our own experience. Our activity will be as far as possible independent of all the prejudices bequeathed to us by tradition. Thus we shall be enabled to work for the achievement of those benefits which architecture can bring to society through erection of buildings which satisfy the contemporary requirements of life, and answer to local climatic conditions, with solidity, hygiene, and economy.

The aesthetic implications were equally clear. The lesson of history, Bykovskii insisted, was that "imitation of forms that have no internal meaning" could produce "beauty." "Nothing which is not based on a rational, truthful application of science and experience to the requirements of contemporary life can create anything genuinely artistic."[5]

It was four years before architects in the capital created any comparable society. When POA (the St. Petersburg Society of Architects) was formed by architects from circles around IGI in 1871, it was naturally not the example of Moscow they claimed to be following. (St. Petersburg did not "follow" Moscow in anything.) POA's initiator, Viktor Shreter, had spent some time in Berlin and had seen there the effectiveness of an independent organization for furthering architectural development and protecting professional interests amid the increasingly rabid commercialism of an entrepreneurial capitalist economy.[6]

As was appropriate to a professional organization in the capital, one of POA's first initiatives was to launch a professional periodical called *Zodchii* (*The Architect*) as a vehicle for nationwide communication. It was an "architectural and technical" monthly (later weekly), more newspaper than magazine, which subsequently advertised itself as carrying "information on competitions, and full programs" for those

competitions the society itself was running.

Initially, there were not many competitions entrusted to either St. Petersburg or Moscow societies, as they had still to win a reputation for trustworthiness. A typical situation was reflected in the very first issue of *The Architect,* which carried notification of a competition announced by the MVD for a "women's correctional prison in St. Petersburg," whose full program was available in *Pravitel'stvennyi vestnik* (*The Government Courier*).[7] The MVD had a special commission responsible for working out competition programs in its field of competence, which was basically the fields where those qualified as "civil engineer," i.e., in IGI, had legal rights "to design and execute structures." This meant competitions for churches, factories, railway structures, prisons, and bridges, and later, in the absence of professional departments or training in technical aspects of town planning, competitions in this area, too.[8] The prison program suggests that the MVD's conduct of competitions was, on one hand, reliably businesslike. The jury contained representatives of the MVD as organizers, of its Building and Technical Committee, and of the Imperial Academy of Arts; all entries must be submitted under pseudonyms; there would be a ten-day exhibition of the entries to allow public discussion before jury deliberations began; two prizes would be awarded, with the winning schemes becoming the MVD's property. On the other hand, these terms did not fully satisfy the three basic conditions for jury impartiality contained in the published regulations, from 1867, of the Berlin Society of Architects, which were considered by POA an ideal model. The lawyers and technical people on the jury for the prison presumably included suitable "specialists," in order to ensure basic competence of judgment. But the "names of the judges themselves" were not given. The third key principle of the Berlin regulations was that "no judge may have any direct or indirect participation in the competition itself."[9]

During the next year, the larger issues were aired at length in a series of three articles in *The Architect* signed by M. Arnol'd. I suspect that this was a voice from Moscow— the same M. Iu. Arnol'd with whom Bykovskii was preparing a Russian translation of Viollet-le-Duc's *Entretiens.*[10] The *Architect* editors noted that they "could not agree with all the author's conclusions," but "the issue of competitions is so important that it must be fully explored before the St. Petersburg Society . . . works out formal rules as final guidance on setting and judging competitions." Certainly Arnol'd's outspokenly liberal aspirations did not sound like a voice from within the capital:

The principle of the public competition in our time cannot fail to be numbered among that series of great principles which includes, for example, free association and freedom of speech . . .

It is the essence of the competition that talent, knowledge, and labor can manifest themselves in the most favorable conditions possible.

Protectionism, influential connections, intrigues, monopoly power are eliminated.

The motivation is that most attractive of all contests—a contest {sorevnovanie} of the mind, of intellect, of talent and knowledge—a contest which powerfully moves forward science or art.

And finally, the competition benefits the public and the whole of society, exciting their interest in the subject and familiarizing them with the names and works of the practitioners.[11]

Here Arnol'd already distinguishes between the spirit of the *sorevnovanie* and the *konkurentsiia* of the marketplace. Thanks to the different motivations it engenders, he says, the architectural competition produces "a best solution that comes much closer to the best possible" than any solution that can be obtained by a direct commission, "when there are many specialists in a field and there is considerable competition among them" to get the job, just as work for their office.

Arnol'd detailed the arguments behind his "essential conditions for the success of competitions." The first condition was a certain minimum number of entries in order for a competition to be valid: he proposed "between fifteen and twenty." (Internal rules of POA, by contrast, had decreed that "the prizes announced must without fail be presented even if only one entry is received by the closing date.")[12] Secondly, there must be "high-value prizes and enough of them." This was "not a luxury" but the only way to attract good designs.

His second article dealt with the number and competence of the jury members, and the need for them to be "of such a moral quality that competitors submit their work to their judgment without apprehension."[13] He stressed that for clients, too, there is "a lot of trouble and great risk" involved in going to competition. Precisely for this reason they must be obligated "to apply to an appropriate professional society" for help. They need help not only in "understanding technical terms and drawings" but in formulating a satisfactory brief. One practice that must be banned was the issuing of "such impossibly short deadlines that there is hardly time to execute the drawings, let alone to do the necessary preliminary study and project development." And once set, the deadline must be stuck to: projects arriving after it must be automatically disqualified.

Where the first two articles echoed the tone of a lawyer, the third rang with the practical voice of a designer. The brief must indicate roughly the building costs the client has in mind, and if possible say "who is to be the builder of the structure proposed." (This latter reflects the uneven level of skills and technology available in the relatively undeveloped Russian building industry.) It must specify "what level of detailing is required in the drawings, and what type and scale of representation is required," since these must be standard for all competitors. "Drawings are the language of architectural thought," he writes, suddenly allowing himself a little poetry, but most of all do client and public need specialist help "when sparklingly effective draftsmanship conceals emptiness." Flashy graphics were therefore to be discouraged. Finally, "it should be an obligatory condition of the program that competitors provide explanatory notes. However clear and good are their drawings, these only represent the architect's thought in its final form; they do not answer the question 'why' or indicate what considerations led the author to select a particular solution." Without such notes, "judges may not grasp the advantages or disadvantages of particular aspects of [the architect's solution]."

Publishing the ten regulations of the Berlin Society in translation, Arnol'd ended by pointing out that the profession held the trump card in its own hands. "The best way to get some rational foundations under the whole competition business" would be to follow the example of the Berliners, who had "firmly agreed to a common moral obligation not to enter competitions which do not observe their basic regulations."[14]

Such was the concentration of the architectural profession in the capital that the St. Petersburg Society quickly grew to three or four times the size of the Moscow one.[15] It took a few years before the societies were recognized by the MVD or Moscow City Council as a useful professional intermediary through which to run competitions.[16] The designs of façades for two major new museums, the Polytechnical Museum and the Historical Museum, were, however, major prestige projects for which MAO helped administer competitions in 1873 and 1875, respectively.[17] The acrimony these competitions generated shows how fast Russia's still-embryonic conceptions of professional correctness were being outstripped by the ebullient energy of the rapidly growing economy in mercantile Moscow and the self-confidence of public organizations founded on this new industrial money.

By August 1875, the "multiple surprises" of these two episodes, with a "no less original" story in Odessa, produced an unsigned article in *The Architect* whose title can be roughly translated as "What the Hell Is Going On with Our Competitions?"[18]

Within a brief period we have three competitions for jobs of the highest caliber. And what do we find? For this or that reason, not one of them, as the phrase goes, has 'come off.' Here were three undertakings of vast scale, in which any architectural talent should find glory in participating, in enriching Russia with such products of the building art as all civilized nations are proud of.

Worldwide competitions were announced. Large sums of money were spent, and an even greater bounty of promises. And in the bitter end, all we have is a soap bubble . . .

We wait impatiently for the end of summer vacations at the St. Petersburg Society of Architects, which has made up its mind to work out competition regulations. Then abuse will be significantly reduced, even if not eliminated. In the present state of things, the only ways out are extreme ones: either to refuse once and for all to enter Russian competitions or forever to risk being trampled into the ground. Both are harmful and we must therefore choose the middle way—which is to establish regulations.

Both the Moscow cases were tortuous stories of winning projects deviously overturned by clients. In the case of the Polytechnical Museum, they suddenly decided the building must be in a Neo-Russian style after running a competition for one in an "Italian" style. A selective rerun on impossibly short deadline was the cloak for appointment of another architect of their own choice. In Odessa, the city announced it would build a multimillion-ruble theater, invited "architects all over Europe" to participate (but not Russians), and never announced any results. When competitors traveled to Odessa in despair, the competition committee had simply "disappeared," no one in the City Council would take responsibility, and "the poor foreigners were left to assume that Russian competitions are not at all like foreign ones."

I quote these colorful cases at some length not just as anecdotal *ekzotika* but for their extraordinary similarity to events surrounding Soviet competitions half a century later. All the key elements of the Palace of Soviets episode are here: the bombastic "international" scale of the conception; the insecure-sounding determination that Russia be seen to sit at the table of "all civilized nations"; the client's unpredictable shifts; and the closed "second stages" in pursuit of ideologically "correct" style. And European competitors retiring disillusioned.

Toward Regulations and War

This was the atmosphere in which professional societies replaced governmental bureaucracies as organizers of architectural competitions. Eventually, there were regulations. In March 1881, the St. Petersburg Society set up a drafting commission; in December of the next year, the resulting regulations were affirmed by the membership "to govern any contest conducted under [the society's] auspices"; a month later, and yet again in March 1895, the regulations were augmented further, embodying the more uncontentious elements of good practice agreed to so far.[19]

Two general statements in the regulations' preamble are interesting as reflections of the context in which architects viewed the whole competition business and as issues that would come up again in the 1920s. The first was the conception of the competition as a means for the state to achieve economic benefits through more efficient design solutions. The second was the role of competitions in the training and advancement of young architects. As POA put it here, competitions must be seen as a means of giving the "younger forces in the architectural family" a platform for demonstrating their talents. The society's own competition reports suggest this was already happening in the early 1880s. One well-established St. Petersburg architect, who participated again in the debates of the 1920s, recalled with favor in 1926 that "In prerevolutionary times, it was the habit for major masters not to enter competitions for small buildings, especially if the task was one which did not involve the devising of a new building type. There was no regulation about this, but it was not considered appropriate for the time and skill of major masters to be expended in massacring the weak."[20]

By the late 1880s, new and more commercial building types were already coming into the purlieu of POA's competitions. In 1888, POA managed the competition for a new Central Building on Russia's permanent commercial fairground at Nizhne-Novgorod, and it seems to have proceded without drama. On the other hand, in Moscow that same year, the competition announced by the Upper Trading Rows Company for a new building on Red Square (later GUM, the state department store) did not reveal the jurors' names, did not provide for an exhibition of the entries, and gave no indication of professional help in framing the brief.[21] Big money still made its own rules. Meanwhile, sheer necessity and a new social consciousness produced some attention to cheap housing for industrial workers. In 1895, MAO was asked by the city government to conduct an internal ideas-competition among its members. The next year, a major competition was run in St. Petersburg for a workers' housing complex adjoining the factory of the Russian-American Rubber Company.[22]

Early in 1899, MAO, too, published regulations to govern the growing number of competitions taking place under its auspices. Beyond the elements already established as good practice by POA, there was a clear emphasis on protecting the architects. If only one entry is received, and it fulfills the competition conditions, it must get a prize. But far more contentiously, "the final working out of the construction project must go to the architect of the premiated scheme."[23] In the city's biggest recent competition (for rebuilding the vast Hotel Metropol'), whose result was announced later that year, this was precisely and famously what did not happen: the first-prize-winning scheme was set aside for building in favor of the fourth-prize winner.[24]

From the turn of the century to the outbreak of World War I, Russia was in the grip of a building boom that raised professional life, as well as competition activity, to an unprecedented intensity. Annual industrial outputs over these years averaged 6 percent, and in 1910–13, 7.5 percent. Major construction companies, whose work was typical of the superb quality which characterized prestige capitalist architecture everywhere in that decade, were competing to build the headquarters of banks, industrial conglomerates, and learned societies; privately funded schools, hospitals, and medical research institutes; and whole new districts of middle-class apartment housing on high-density European models never previously seen in Russia.[25]

There were still scandals, and the profession sought further refinement of competition practice. To economize on professional energies and focus upon ideas, many advocates emerged for the two-stage competition, where only a selection of schemes are developed in detail. The issue of the designer's copyright was also a battleground. Fixity of the jury membership was another complaint (which scrutiny of

competition announcements and results indicates was certainly warranted). Time and again, the jury was composed of the same elderly members of POA, MAO, or the new third society of Academy-trained "architect-artists," OAKh; where tastes conflicted, many architects did not bother to enter after reading the jury members' names.[26] One innovation of programs launched by this new Society of Architect-Artists was a principle that would be much fought for by the avant-garde again in the 1920s: inclusion of a "representative of the competitors" on the jury.[27]

As 1913 was the last year of normal industrial life before ten years of hostilities and standstill, outputs of that year were the datum by which all Soviet efforts of the 1920s measured progress. "Back to 1913 levels" was the cry, and when this was achieved, mere "restoration" switched to "planned socialist reconstruction" with the First Five-Year Plan in 1927–28. The year 1913 is thus an appropriate moment to survey the scene and look forward in architectural competitions.

The research of Igor' Kazus shows that the total number of architectural competitions announced in Russia that year was forty-one. The peak of forty-nine occurred the year previously, and was not reached again till that crucial year of 1927, when the total recorded in all traceable sources was fifty-seven.[28] In fact, the 1913 index of *The Architect* shows that if competitions for town plans and for schemes of public utilities are included, the year's total rises to about sixty.[29]

Among names in the prize lists of all societies are now many which will continue to feature in such lists through the 1920s. The POA list alone contains Nakhman, who will reappear in the Tsentrosoiuz contest with Le Corbusier; Aleksandr Grinberg, with whom the Constructivist leader Ginzburg collaborated on the Palace of Labor; and Dmitrii Iofan, elder brother of Boris and his collaborator on the winning Palace of Soviets—to name just three.[30] The elder Iofan was well established on the editorial board of the *Ezhegodnik Imperatorskogo obshchestva arkhitektorov-khudozhnikov* (*OAKh Projects Annual*) with other seasoned competition winners Ivan Fomin, Vladimir Shchuko, and Aleksei Shchusev[31]—the last was already in Moscow building the Kazan' Railway Station he won in a closed competition of 1911. Going back even further to the first *Ezhegodnik* (*Projects Annual*) MAO published, in 1909, one finds that the three young Vesnin brothers already figure prominently, with a commendation in MAO's competition for a theater in Iaroslavl' and third prize for Aleksandr and Viktor, "students of the Institute of Civil Engineers," for a country church with bold, traditional high towers near Samara. Among the Vesnins' elders in the society, Antipov took a first prize for a luxurious City Tramway station. Ivan Rerberg, who would receive vitriol from the Vesnins and their Constructivist friends after another big Moscow competition in 1925, was co-victor in the competition for an extensive office development for the Northern Insurance Company, which soon started on site.[32]

Antipov thus knew what he was talking about when, in 1926, he wrote about prerevolutionary competitions. "Competitions were in no way regulated by the old legislation," he said. "In general, legislation occupied such an insignificant place in the whole operation of construction that no real necessity for such legal regulation was felt."[33] In fact, that last observation was not quite correct. By 1913, there were so many different architectural and civil-engineering societies with slightly differing codes, and so many direct "client" competitions bypassing any professional regulation at all, that OAKh took the initiative of presenting a draft for national legislation to the last prerevolutionary Congress of Russian Architects, held in Moscow in December 1913.[34] But when realistic competitions resumed again ten years later, it would

fig. 2
Aleksandr Kuznetsov
Competition project (second-prize winner) for the Palace of Labor,
Moscow; perspective, 1923.

fig. 3
Noi Trotskii
Competition project (first-prize winner) for the Palace of Labor,
Moscow; elevation, 1923.

fig. 4
Il'ia Golosov
Competition project (fifth-prize winner) for the Palace of Labor,
Moscow; elevations, 1923.

fig. 5
Moisei Ginzburg and Aleksandr Grinberg
Competition project for the Palace of Labor, Moscow; perspective, 1923.

be under very different social and technical conditions. Professionally, though, a great deal would be much the same.

Competing without Building

As war took hold, "Intensive public works began in which MAO actively participated by organizing its own lazaret for wounded soldiers . . . run by members' families under the direction of the president's wife."[35] The war was bringing Russia to its knees, and uprisings in February 1917 caused Czar Nikolai II to dissolve the quasidemocratic parliament, the Duma, and create a Provisional, or coalition, Government. By the summer, all this government could do against the growing force of a Bolshevik Party supported by masses of workers' councils, or soviets, was to ban its leader, Lenin, from the capital. But he got in, and hid for four months, awaiting the denouement which came in October. Of POA and OAKh in this period we lack records, but MAO was active: "Between the February and October Revolutions, the society continued its scholarly and professional work, and took upon itself the initiative of founding an All-Russian Union of Architects and Engineers, organized both for defense of our professional interests and with the aim of developing construction and the aesthetic bases of architecture."[36] Immediately after seizing power and declaring Russia out of the war, Lenin's government issued a decree taking all land and real estate into state ownership.[37] In one stroke, of course, this created the opportunity for entirely new forms of land use, as well as a redistribution of population and activities within the existing building stock. The key portfolio for education and propaganda, Narkompros (the People's Commissariat of Enlightenment), was given to Anatolii Lunacharskii, a trusted colleague but a cultivated man with considerable knowledge of the arts. In the spring of 1918, the new government moved to Moscow, which after two hundred years found itself again the capital city. It was now Moscow architects who were at the center of national policymaking, while those in the former capital increasingly focused on their own local affairs.

Like everyone else, architects in the capital now got a trade union. Iakov Raikh, one of the union's governing "temporary collective," proposed a commission to examine all existing sets of competition regulations, Russian and foreign, in order to devise something new.[38] Within the new Committee for State Buildings of Vesenkha (the Council of the National Economy), one department had been allocated responsibility for competition affairs, and its own documents reflected the new Party line on them: "In a proletarian state in the epoch of transition to Communism, it is evident on principle that the usefulness of competitions must be recognized, and likewise of prizes, as being measures which develop initiative, awakening energy or simply giving greater productivity of labor."[39] There should be competitions for all major building tasks, they said, preferably open ones, and the winner must get the job of executing the building. The competitions would form a "practical school for all participants."

The word used here for "competition" was the traditional *konkurs,* which remained the generic term for an architectural competition throughout the 1920s. But that socialism had a somewhat different notion of "competition" had been clearly spelled out by Lenin, soon after the Revolution, in a paper called "How to Organize the *Sorevnovanie?*" "Bourgeois writers have spent mountains of paper extolling *konkurentsiia,*" he opened, presenting *konkurentsiia* as fundamental to the "capitalist structure" and the "nature of man." That vision might have had some validity at the level of individual craft units, he said, but as mass production operates today,

it means replacement of sorevnovanie *by financial swindling, nepotism, and subservience to the top of the social ladder.*

Socialism not only does not cause sorevnovanie *to wither away; on the contrary. For the first time it creates the possibility to apply it really* widely, *on a really* mass *scale, really to draw the majority of workers into the arena of such work, where they can show their worth, develop their capacities, demonstrate the talents which are an endlessly bubbling spring in the people, but which capitalism trampled, squeezed, suppressed.*

Our task, now that a socialist government is in power, is to organize the sorevnovanie.[40]

The first competitions of the new era genuinely attempted to embrace this newly collaborative vision, and the collective research process of the *tovarishcheskoe sorevnovanie* (comradely contest) became a regular medium for developing ideas among the new artistic and professional groups.

Nothing practical could happen on the building front as resistance to the Soviets across the country turned to civil war. For several years there would be more destruction than repair, a decimation of the building industry, and nothing new erected. But in Moscow and Petrograd (as St. Petersburg was now called), parallel organizations of architectural offices emerged under Vesenkha's Committee for State Buildings and Izo Narkompros (the Department of Fine Arts of the People's Commissariat of Enlightenment), whose Moscow architectural office was headed by Shchusev and his more rigidly Classicist contemporary, Ivan Zholtovskii.[41] As teachers in the Moscow School of Painting, Sculpture, and Architecture, they gave employment in these state offices to their former students, young architects like Konstantin Mel'nikov, Vladimir Fidman, and Vladimir Krinskii. In Petrograd, too, it was a small group of the younger prerevolutionary architects who ran the new ventures: Lev Rudnev, Andrei Belogrud, Shchuko, and Shchuko's former student, Vladimir Gel'freikh. With nothing to build, they started launching competitions for the new building types of the new society, drawing a cross section of society, from Lunacharskii to workers, into discussion and judgment processes. The very first competition in Petrograd, in 1918–19, was for a "wholly new type of local cultural and educational center, a Palace of Workers." Moscow's first competitions were for a city crematorium (part of the atheism campaign) and a standard House of the People for the villages. Both had a first, closed stage to establish the viability of the brief, followed by a second, open stage. Prizes were numerous, and in a new innovation reflecting everyone's straitened circumstances, it was proposed that all competitors get a payment to cover expenses.[42]

Here the leading names of the future already started to emerge. First prize for the crematorium went to Il'ia Golosov (the younger of two brothers who qualified in the Moscow School of Painting, Sculpture, and Architecture just before the war), who submitted three massive and romantically historicist structures. The school had now been absorbed into the new network of State Free Art Workshops, whence a current student named Nikolai Kolli took third prize with a stepped pyramid of Assyrian proportions. In a similar competition in Petrograd, prerevolutionary habits returned when the grand classical project of Fomin given first prize by the jury displeased the Executive Committee of the Petrograd Soviet, which reallocated the prize to an unknown engineer.[43]

An Avant-Garde and Revival

More stimulating and rewarding territory for most of the younger architects was to be found among their artistic contemporaries in such groups as Zhivskul'ptarkh (the Synthesis of Painting, Sculpture, and Architecture Commission) or in the little "institutes" like Inkhuk (the

Institute of Artistic Culture) and "academies" like RAKhN/GAKhN (the Russian Academy of Artistic Sciences/State Academy of Artistic Sciences) that were spawning everywhere as talking shops for experiment and new ideas. Vladimir Tatlin and Kazimir Malevich remained the alternate gurus for many, and slightly younger artists like Aleksandr Rodchenko were developing new directions of their own on the foundation of what the prerevolutionary artistic avant-garde had achieved.

The very first of these groups was called Sinskul'ptarkh (the Synthesis of Sculpture and Architecture Commission), in which the seven architects Sigizmund Dombrovskii, Fidman, Nikolai Istselenov, Krinskii, Nikolai Ladovskii, Raikh, and Aleksei Rukhliad'ev met with the sculptor Boris Korolev during a nine-month period in 1919. Determined to free themselves from all control of people like Zholtovskii and Shchusev, they were united by a determination to reinvent architecture from a point completely outside existing canons.[44] Through an extended form of "comradely contest," a new concept of a mass-assembly building, a Temple of Communion among Nations, was the main vehicle of their formal explorations (see plate nos. 657, 659 for examples by Krinskii). When the painters Rodchenko and Aleksandr Shevchenko joined, the group was renamed Zhivskul'ptarkh, and through 1920 the noncompetitive comradely *sorevnovanie* continued around themes of a communal house (plate nos. 654–655, 658) and a House of Soviets or, as Rodchenko called it, Sovdep (Soviet of Deputies, plate no. 653). In the summer, the group split up and most of the members shifted their activity to the new Inkhuk, which Narkompros had set up in March, under Vasilii Kandinskii, to explore the fundamentals of all visual-art forms.

By the autumn, Kandinskii and his "fine art" ideas had gone. In the first quarter of the next year, architects and artists in the General Working Group of Objective Analysis ran another collective *sorevnovanie* on a theme so fundamental it was to establish the split of aesthetic ideology that spawned the two leading movements of the architectural avant-garde, Rationalism and Constructivism. Each member must prepare works, for communal discussion, which develop "an analysis of the concepts of construction and composition and the boundary between them." (The key portfolio of comparative pairs of analytical designs is now in the Costakis Collection [plate nos. 244–253].)[45]

Ladovskii, Krinskii, and their colleagues went one way, pursuing a notion of integral "composition" whose formal dynamics and perceptual effects they would explore and teach in their subsequent work under the banner of architectural Rationalism. Rodchenko, Aleksei Gan, Georgii and Vladimir Stenberg, and their colleagues went the other way, convinced that the zeitgeist for the new age of the machine was rooted in the principle of clear and conscious "construction," which, in Rodchenko's words, brought "utilization of material together with a predetermined purpose." The latter were joined by Aleksandr Vesnin, youngest of the three brothers. Currently working as a painter, he supported the ideas of the First Working Group of Constructivists, and was soon forming a vital bridge between these new artistic ideas and the world of professional architecture.[46]

That year, 1921, saw the end of the Civil War as Soviet forces conquered the last outposts of the old empire. From an emergency collectivism called War Communism, the government turned to a regime of partial free enterprise called NEP (the New Economic Policy) in order to restart the wheels of economic activity. Centralized bodies like the Committee for State Buildings and the architectural studios of Narkompros were dissolved, to be gradually replaced by a free-for-all of design and construction offices. Some were agencies of local

municipalities; others were effectively profit-and-loss "companies" or, increasingly, cooperatives. NEP recreated a world not so different, for a professional, from that of before, but in an economy now in standstill rather than boom. Both human and technical aspects of the construction industry had been decimated by the hostilities.

There was a role for the architectural societies again, and during 1922, first MAO was revived, then POA and OAKh. Shchusev was MAO's new president; Ivan Ryl'skii and the oldest Vesnin, Leonid, were his deputies; and Antipov was one of two Board secretaries.[47] "Before us lies a ruined Moscow, a new social and legal environment, in which the architect's work must move in new directions," declared the Board to the membership. Yet, as Antipov reported a year later, "the halt in building activity has created a burdensome state of unemployment among architects." Amid all this, "the organization of architectural competitions is the issue of most burning importance in the society's activity."[48]

Thus MAO sent a circular letter to all relevant industrial and local and central government agencies in August 1922 urging the use of architectural competitions "in order to obtain the very best possible solutions to the rebuilding and planning problems across the whole country . . . and to ensure the rational application of scarce building materials." The letter immediately brought invitations to run two competitions for the Moscow Soviet: for model workers' housing of a new kind, and for "the creation in Moscow of a grandiose Palace of Labor."[49]

With the housing competition, architects resumed pioneering work from the turn of the century, but this was now a genuine attempt to define and explore what "socialist" housing for working people might be. The brief was highly realistic, with detailed schedules of accommodation for small family and single-person apartment housing—with such model amenities as a central laundry, pharmacy, and common meeting room for residents—on two green-field sites on the southern edge of the city. Management of the competition, however, with a jury of ministerial representatives, was highly conventional. Il'ia and Panteleimon Golosov figured in prize lists for both sites. The experienced Leonid Vesnin won one of them. The most original entry, spatially and conceptually, came from the young Mel'nikov. A second stage was aimed at real building, but that was still too optimistic.[50]

The Palace of Labor, of course, was even less likely to get built. Its main spaces were auditoriums for 8,000 and 2,500 people, and a dining hall to seat 1,500. The brief, listing but not dimensioning the rooms, defined the concept of the new organism as a "palace" for great assemblies of workers' representatives. The site was just off Red Square and products of other competitions faced it front and back: the Hotel Metropol', now a government headquarters, to the north, and the Historical Museum to the south. Beyond a general respect for context, the brief specified quite modestly that "In the treatment of its façades and its interiors, the Palace must have a rich feeling corresponding to its purpose, but expressed in simple contemporary forms, not in the specific style of any particular past epoch." A couple of months before the closing date, however, the political charge was intensified in a speech by Sergei Kirov, one of the leading Party activists, to the First All-Union Congress of Soviets which gathered in an improvised accommodation to ratify unification of the country into the USSR. Said Kirov, "These exceptional parliaments of ours will soon need more spacious accommodation . . . let us gather all the riches of our Soviet land, invest all the creativity of our workers and peasants in this monument, to show our friends and foes that we 'semi-Asiatics,' whom they continue to look down upon, are capable of adorning this sinful earth with

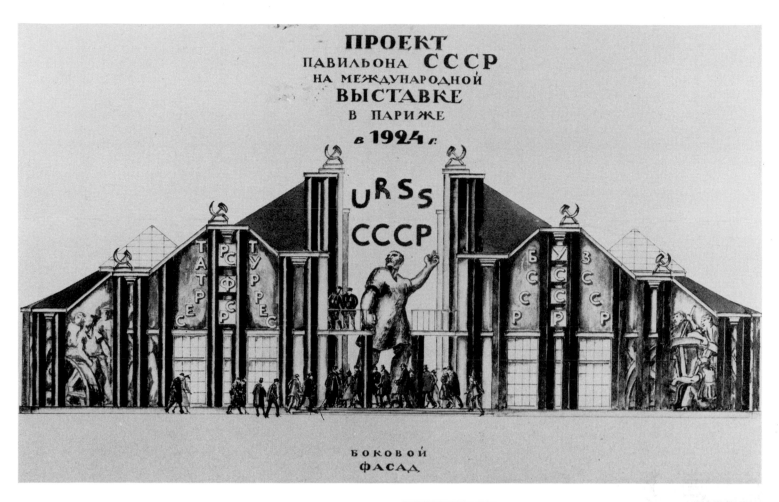

фиг. 6
Konstantin Mel'nikov
Competition project (first-prize winner) for the Russian pavilion,
Exposition internationale des arts décoratifs et industriels
modernes, *Paris; elevation, 1924.*

фиг. 7
Vladimir Shchuko
Competition project for the Russian pavilion, Exposition
internationale des arts décoratifs et industriels modernes, *Paris;
perspective, 1924.*

фиг. 8
Ivan Fomin
Competition project for the Russian pavilion, Exposition
internationale des arts décoratifs et industriels modernes, *Paris;
elevation, 1924.*

фиг. 9
Konstantin Mel'nikov
Russian pavilion, Exposition internationale des arts décoratifs et
industriels modernes, *Paris; completed building.*

such works of great architecture as our enemies never dreamed of."[51]

The Palace of Labor competition was to prove seminal to the future of Soviet architecture, in particular through the impact of the Vesnin brothers' third-prize-winning entry.

Forty-seven projects were entered. Faced with handling such massive volumes, but instructed to abandon the "historical styles" with which most of them were trained to articulate such scale, many architects resorted to structurally inarticulate "masses" of masonry in lumpy, indeterminate, and generally romantic compositions. Il'ia Golosov, who came in fifth, gave some of these volumes the profile of gear wheels, others the form of a grid of pilasters (fig. no. 4). The entry of the experienced Belogrud, from Petrograd, still had the air of a medieval Italian fortress. Ginzburg, a new young member of MAO, had teamed up with the experienced Grinberg, but their industrial-scale blocks were presented with Piranesian drama (fig. no. 5). The second-prize-winning scheme from another experienced Muscovite, Kuznetsov, was clearly the work of someone who understood the concrete frame imaginatively (fig. no. 2). Mel'nikov had made the building more spatial than solid by exploiting the passages and routes across the site. The winning scheme, by a newly qualified Academy student from Petrograd named Noi Trotskii, was like Hagia Sophia in external profile, but without the towers (fig. no. 3).

In this company the immaculately crisp structure and volumetric articulation of the Vesnins' scheme was unique and extraordinary (plate nos. 679, 681–682). It resulted from a synthesis of experience and ruthlessly fresh thinking. As their notes in the Constructivist literary journal *Lef* (*Left Front of the Arts*) explained: "We set ourselves the task of solving all requirements of the competition according to the principles of constructiveness, utility, rationality, and economy. All forms derive from the most rational distribution of the accommodation and how it is used, from the volumetric dimensions of it, and from the most constructive use of the materials selected, namely, iron, reinforced concrete, and glass."[52] A few years later, the Vesnins' colleagues looked back to this project as a "landmark for Constructivism in its first real architectural manifestation," "for the first time embodying the essential principles of the new approach . . . attempting the creation of a new social organism, whose inner life flowed as a whole not from stereotypes of the past but from the novelty of the job itself." For its synthesis of social innovation and the new architecture, the Vesnins' Palace of Labor was contrasted to Walter Gropius's externally rather similar Chicago Tribune Tower, of the same date. Gropius's building was "a brilliantly executed, radically constructed object, designed with a new simplicity, but its inner content is the typical American conception of the 'business house,' while the Vesnin 'palace' originates from a new social conception of the fundamental organism of a building, so establishing the most essential characteristic of Constructivism."[53] With this scheme so dramatically representing the new movement, one conspicuous feature of the competition was the total absence of the Constructivists' rivals, the Rationalists like Ladovskii and Krinskii. This was no accident. The Rationalists had taken the stand advocated by Arnol'd, "following the example of the Berlin architects," back at the beginning of the competitions debate in Russia, in 1872: they would not enter a competition whose conditions they found in any way unacceptable. Their protest was against the presence on the MAO jury not just of Zholtovskii but also of the aged Fedor Shekhtel', doyen of art nouveau in Moscow at the turn of the century and president of MAO until Shchusev took over during the previous summer.[54] These two embodied everything the young Rationalists were seeking to eliminate from architecture. This was to be the start

of a campaign of radical activism to reform competition practice that they maintained throughout the decade.

MAO itself had two provincial competitions running, and was currently framing the program for another in Moscow, for a vast national sports complex called the Red Stadium.[55] It was not alone in the competition-running business: according to Kazus's figures, the annual total of competitions nationwide during 1920–24 ranged between thirteen and fifteen. But MAO was at center stage, and many members recognized that their regulations were "somewhat out-of-date, having last been revised in 1912."[56] But before their special commission reported back, the Rationalists were raising another protest, demanding changes to the brief for the Red Stadium, in which they and their Vkhutemas (the Higher Artistic-Technical Workshops) students were already somewhat involved. In a later letter to El Lissitzky, Ladovskii reported how "we won the sympathy of comrade Podvoiskii, chairman of the Society for Building the Red Stadium, whose attitude toward Shchusev and MAO was highly skeptical."[57]

In an attempt at peacemaking, the Section of Technical Engineering Cadres in the Trade Union of Builders took the initiative of convening a meeting for all concerned about competitions, but as the Section's chairman Rozhanovich later regretfully admitted, "this discussion did not produce any concrete results."[58]

MAO, however, was getting ever stronger. It was proudly back in publishing with a substantial journal called *Arkhitektura* (*Architecture*). The journal lasted only two issues, but these provide a useful close-up on the period. The production editor was Ginzburg, who had lately returned to Moscow after building some villas and researching vernacular architecture in the Crimea during the Civil War. He was a talented designer, scholarly and widely read, and in touch with new European ideas through having done his first degree in Milan just before the war. Having had time to think, he was now talking and writing prolifically on architectural theory.[59] His editorials for *Architecture* brought the ideas of Le Corbusier and *L'Esprit nouveau* boldly but diplomatically into the Russian context.[60] Papers he read to MAO and to the research institute RAKhN took these ideas further, connecting them with the Constructivism of the artist-designers Rodchenko and Gan and with the architectural principles demonstrated by the Vesnins in their Palace of Labor scheme.

Tired of MAO's monopoly in professional affairs, the Rationalists formed their own society in the summer of 1923, the first officially constituted new society since the Revolution. They called it Asnova (the Association of New Architects). Ladovskii and Krinskii were the leaders, and Lissitzky an active if often absent participant, who gave them a prestigious "European" link.[61] In 1924, Ginzburg's earlier papers to MAO and RAKhN came out as the book *Stil' i epokha* (*Style and Epoch*). In his clear theory of architectural history and through his useful, analytical analogies between the problems of designing machines and those of designing socially new building types, Ginzburg gave a clear profile and agenda to the emerging concept of a Constructivist architecture, and a rallying point for its adherents.[62] Meanwhile, all the "new" architects were increasingly active in competitions.

Takeoff at Home and Image Abroad

The year 1924 saw architects' takeoff into confident new architectures, and with building only just starting again after its "ten years' sleep," competitions were the main medium for developing these approaches and languages. There were five major competitions during this year, three run by MAO, one by a Party newspaper, and one—for the new country's first official building abroad—by the government. The extensive

House of Soviets for Briansk was won by Ginzburg's elder colleague on the Palace of Soviets, Grinberg, who went on to build it with his contemporary, Velikovskii.[63] The Moscow headquarters of Arkos, a cooperative venture running Anglo-Russian trade, was won by the Vesnins with a dramatically bold exposed frame, but remained unbuilt.[64]

The *narodnyi dom* or House of the People required for the cotton-industry city of Ivanovo-Voznesensk was a new type explored back in that very first postrevolutionary competition in Petrograd. Since Lenin had died in January 1924, this one was now "named for Lenin." Like the Palace of Labor, these buildings were largely comprised of major auditoriums, and were equally difficult, therefore, to handle convincingly. Il'ia Golosov's scheme (plate no.699) has some of the same vestigial classical elements he used for the Palace of Labor. It was one of several schemes "commended and recommended to be acquired"; others were by Raikh, Grinberg, Daniil Fridman, and Asnova members Krinskii and Rukhliad'ev. Panteleimon Golosov came in fifth, the Vesnins third, and first prize went to a slightly older member of their generation, Grigorii Barkhin, who graduated from the Imperial Academy of Arts in 1907 and worked for several of the progressive Moscow architects before the war.[65] In its planning, his building had the clarity of the Vesnins' Palace of Labor, and essentially established the "type" for the *narodnyi dom* for the rest of the decade, but it did not share the Vesnins' confident replacement of wall by frame.

This competition was an open one, run by MAO, and would have been typical of the material which a correspondent of the May issue of the journal *Stroitel'naia promyshlennost'* (*The Building Industry*) had in mind when he begged for the best of non-prizewinning competition material to be acquired by some central agency for circulation to the provincial schools, "which are in extreme need of teaching textbooks on architectural design":

When architectural circles in the capitals are discussing contemporary trends in architectural composition with ever greater breadth and subtlety, students who are also future builders have little but albums of railway structures or total trash in their libraries.

Meanwhile, MAO competitions have produced dozens of talented and well-worked-out schemes for various new types of building . . . which we are too poor to publish. Mounted on pinup walls . . . as the basis for group discussions and seminars . . . they would also cease to be 'wasted work' in the designers' portfolios.[66]

Whether or not this was done, the request indicates the great gulf which existed between the center and the provinces in these formative years.

The competition for a little Moscow headquarters for the newspaper *Leningrad Pravda* must rank in world records for the highest ratio of innovation to entries in any contest. It was a closed competition, launched on July 16, 1924, with only three invitations issued: to Mel'nikov, Il'ia Golosov, and the Vesnin brothers (only Aleksandr and Viktor eventually worked on it). Each competitor would receive 170 rubles, with a further 100 for the winner. The jury expressed a slight preference for the Vesnins' scheme, but deemed their entry and Mel'nikov's to deserve equal prizes.[67] Nothing was built, and no information remains on this competition beyond two sets of competitors' notes and the project drawings.

So powerful are the images, particularly the Vesnins' (plate no. 684), that it is hard to realize these buildings are hardly more than multistoried kiosks. The site allocated, on Strastnaia (now Pushkin) Square in central Moscow, measured six-by-six meters. As the Vesnins' plans show, the accommodation comprised a ground-level reception and sales desk, with room for the caretaker, a public reading room, and work space for a few correspondents with essential utilities.[68] For the rest, as all of the competitors saw, the building was an advertisement.

For Golosov's scheme (plate no. 685) no notes remain. However, having had access to archival material, Selim Khan-Magomedov has suggested that Golosov was treating the project as "the application of a device he had worked out as an exercise for his students in the next academic year. It involved the generation of a building volume around the plan form of 'two squares rotated through forty-five degrees, so that from any direction the viewer can perceive the system.'"[69] Four elevational images are preserved which slightly clarify the result, but its overweaning complexity is the best evidence that Khan-Magomedov is right about its conceptual origins.

Mel'nikov's scheme (plate no. 683) also had doubtful realism in its time, given the level of Soviet technology, though it was less unrealistic than the only other Soviet project to propose rotating volumes: Tatlin's model for the *Pamiatnik III-emu Internatsionalu* (*Monument to the Third International*) of five years before. These are the notes accompanying Mel'nikov's project:

I have provided a five-storied building in a lightweight steel structure, in order to give realism to the idea which I had, and became fascinated by, of 'an architecture that is alive.' The pavilion must undoubtedly have an element of advertising, and here it occurred to me to include the advertising within the organism of the actual building.

Onto a static circular pivot-core (containing staircases and elevators) are threaded the floors, which rotate freely in any direction: an endless fairy-tale spectacle of diverse architectural silhouettes—using the force of architectural dynamics that has not yet been put to the test.

The elevational drawing shows each floor rotated to its maximum extension.[70]

The Vesnins' project is, of course, no less keenly pursuing a "concept," but it is built up by different means:

The fundamental task in designing this building was to distribute as rationally as possible, within the six-by-six-meter area for the building foundations, all accommodation necessary for the productive process specified, and to express the productive and agitational character of the building in the façades.

The building is designed, in five stories, of steel, glass, and reinforced concrete. The ground floor contains the newspaper kiosk and caretaker accommodation; first floor—public reading room; second floor—general office and advertising section; third and fourth—editorial staff. Basement—heating.

On the façade facing Strastnaia Square are located: a plate-glass window for current information; apparatus for illuminated advertisements; a clock, loudspeaker, and projector.[71]

Beyond this, human movement covers much of the outer surface—on balconies, in two glazed elevators, on the glazed staircase—and all working activity inside is visible across the square. It was a microcosm of the modern city as the Vesnins reinterpreted it from photographs from abroad, from night shots of Broadway and so on. Two years later, when one of their young colleagues reviewed Erich Mendelsohn's photo album *Amerika,* he wrote: "You are suddenly hit by the realization of an idea that was formerly only vaguely coalescing in your mind . . . the idea of the urbanistic city turns from an abstract concept into a reinforced concrete reality."[72]

The third competition of 1924 represented in the present exhibition was for the building which for the first time would represent the USSR to the world. In January, the Second Congress of Soviets had approved the country's first constitution. One after another, foreign countries then

fig. 10
Viktor Pashkov
Vkhutemas diploma project: Lenin Library, Moscow; perspective, 1927.

fig. 11
Aleksandr, Leonid, and Viktor Vesnin
Competition project (second, closed stage) for the Lenin Library,
Moscow; perspective, 1928.

fig. 12
Aleksei Shchusev
"Modernized" competition project (second, closed stage) for the Lenin
Library, Moscow; perspective, 1928.

fig. 13
Vladimir Shchuko and Vladimir Gel'freikh
Lenin Library, Moscow, as built 1930–41 (a much retouched "official"
montage with subway entrance pavilion later demolished).

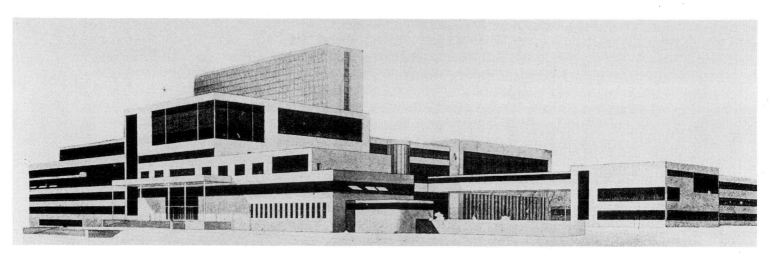

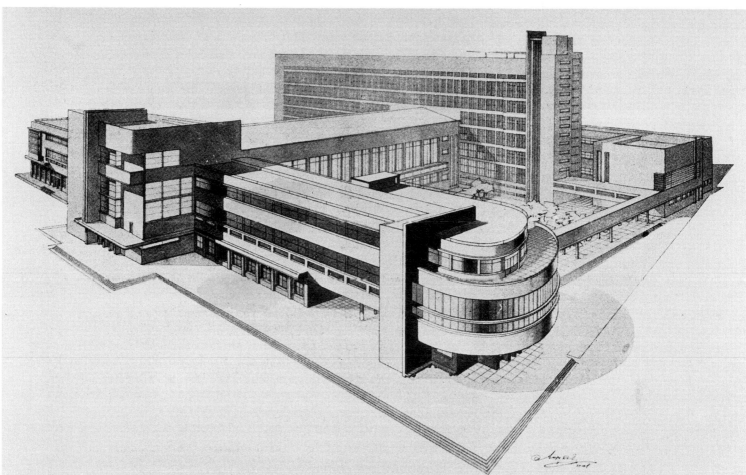

recognized the new state and one of the last to do so was France, on October 28th. Within three days, the Soviet government received a telegram from the French prime minister inviting the USSR to participate in the next year's *Exposition internationale des arts décoratifs et industriels modernes* (*International Exhibition of Contemporary Decorative and Industrial Art*), opening in Paris in May. Narkompros put the task in RAKhN's hands. Vladimir Maiakovskii was to plan the catalogue, Rodchenko to handle design exhibits, and a Soviet diplomat in Paris cabled back, "Have chosen site between pavilions of Great Britain and Italy. Area not great so need to build upward."[73]

On November 15th, as all this got going, a meeting of MAO affirmed the new set of competition regulations finally produced by their commission.[74] Still highly traditional, the regulations would do nothing to prevent more protest later by Asnova and others. Nor did any such regulations apply to this uniquely prestigious and accelerated contest to represent the nation in Paris.

The "invitation to participate in a closed *sorevnovanie* for a sketch project" was rapidly issued to ten names representing all trends in the competition-winning fraternity: the Vesnins, Ginzburg, Il'ia Golosov, Mel'nikov, Ladovskii, Krinskii, Nikolai Dokuchaev, Shchuko, Fomin, and a group of recent Vkhutemas graduates. The brief stipulated that "The pavilion must above all give an impression of the uniqueness of the USSR, while being characteristic of its architectural achievements. Therefore it must be designed in the spirit of a purely contemporary architecture and, ideologically, must reflect the idea of the USSR as a state of laboring workers and peasants and a brotherly union of different nations."[75] It must be wooden, cheap, and "allow the greatest possible flow-through of people, with a broad staircase easy to ascend and good ventilation." It had also to be designed at speed.

The students and the Vesnins did not submit, but other projects were first looked at by a committee of architects and others, including Lunacharskii and Maiakovskii, on December 18th. On December 28th, they announced that Mel'nikov's project (fig. no. 6) was "best," followed by Ladovskii's and Ginzburg's. Golosov's scheme (plate no. 697) was not placed. Nor was Fomin's (fig. no. 8), which had most literally sought to embody the synthesis specified by the brief.

Mel'nikov had to redesign so that the rain could not penetrate the central passageway, and be back at 1:30 P.M. the next day for further instructions from Lunacharskii, who would now be the final arbiter of detail. Mel'nikov's reworking of the project in light of those instructions must be brought by 8 P.M. the day after that. The construction schedule was going to be similar, and it was well understood that "best," in the committee's eyes, meant the project that could most satifactorily be modified for prefabrication and rapid assembly.[76] The rigor which the Western audience so admired in the final building (fig. no. 9) owed as much to those disciplines as to Mel'nikov's initial conception.[77] But the result put Soviet avant-garde architecture in the spotlight of international attention.

How Should Competitions Be Run? 1925–26

In 1925, the fruits of NEP were becoming apparent throughout the Soviet economy and, in particular, in building. New cooperative mechanisms throughout the production and service sectors were creating a middle way between the old private enterprise and the fully socialized, planned systems toward which the government was working. According to Kazus's count, there were twenty-nine architectural competitions announced that year, twice as many as in 1924;[78] even without searching rigorously across the building press, I have identified

fifteen. Not surprisingly, tensions and arguments were growing in parallel.

The two poles of this competition activity were neatly juxtaposed in January. First came a suitably extraordinary competition procedure for the unique task of enshrining the body of "the founder of the Soviet state." In the year since Lenin died, Shchusev had built two temporary timber mausoleums for his body on Red Square. Now a permanent structure was needed. After a speech from Lunacharskii "On Working Out the Competition Conditions," politicians and senior members of the profession announced on January 9th a procedure not of two stages but of three. The first stage was an open competition, in widest possible pursuit of what was essentially a suitably "monumental" image for the structure, and this was launched immediately.[79] The eventual building was not completed until 1930.

Descending, in Soviet terms, from the sublime to the ordinary, the real national problem was housing. Virtually no cheap workers' housing had been inherited from the old regime. Until resettled in bourgeois housing by the building nationalization of 1917, industrial workers lived in dosshouses, or several families to a room in basements and primitive barrack blocks. Practically as well as symbolically, housing construction was now at the top of the agenda for every local government and industrial concern. As MAO's first competition in this area had stressed, it was a new problem for a new social task, but it needed practical solutions from people with building experience, rather than obscure geometry.

This theme was publicly reinforced in January 1925 by an article in the main periodical of construction and municipal affairs, *The Building Industry*. Velikovskii, author of the article, was an IGI-trained man, a slightly older colleague of the Vesnins. Just starting on his drawing board was the Gostorg building in central Moscow, which Alfred H. Barr, Jr. would describe soon after its completion as "easily the finest modern architecture in Moscow, very Gropius in style with all glass sections, steamboat balconies, etc."[80] Velikovskii was already deeply involved in the new house-building cooperatives.[81] He was thus well placed to see that "the character of the construction work that is starting to take place now is entirely different from those forms and tasks which we had in the previous epoch," and that beyond the social change, architects faced a change in the nature of design itself.

As a process, said Velikovskii, building design could no longer move by a slow evolution, "developing by stages from one case to the next"; it required the generating of organisms that were entirely new. On the ground, likewise, development could no longer be incremental: new settlements had to be conceived as an integrated whole in one go, "according to a single plan." These tasks were too complex even for "an architect of special and unusually diverse erudition," and design of the new integrated residential areas must become a "public process." "A competition of projects would be such a process," whereby all sections of society, as well as young and old from all relevant professions, could be drawn into discussions, "continuously expanding the range of participants in the process." It must be forbidden to finance any development not proceeding in this way. "Competitions themselves must be modified, to bring them down from the quasi-artistic clouds and get them firmly onto earth-based rails" with real construction and costing details, and clear, simple drawings "that do not distract judges from the essential ideas."[82]

When the Moscow Soviet announced its first two housing competitions later that year—one for family housing, the other for semi-communalized housing—they were aimed at, and attracted, quite a different section of the architectural profession from those who succeeded with the prestige public buildings. MAO representatives on the jury were swamped by people from eleven technical and housing organizations, and the brief included such unprecedented requirements as "the serviceable life span of the building must correspond to the amortization period of the capital invested," and "materials and equipment must be those available through the local market and production."[83] At a larger scale, Velikovskii's combination of the radical and the practical was typical of the role his slightly older generation could play. More open, participatory processes of this kind abounded over the next few years, though typically (as now) not producing high architecture.

In the explosion of competitions, their subject matter was widening. New big public-assembly buildings—under various names, such as House of Labor or Palace of Culture—were needed as catalysts of new consciousness in towns across the country.[84] The new industrial and cooperative banks needed buildings. The Moscow House of Textiles competition typified the central business house sought by the central administrations of different industries. As the hub of the country's affairs, Moscow also needed a new Central Telegraph, Telephone, and Post Office, for which another competition ran this year. Even industrial plants became the subjects of competition in November, when Tsugprom (the Central Administration of State Industry) launched the country's first competition in this field, for a textile mill in Ivanovo-Voznesensk.[85] In December, with great success in restoration of industry achieved under NEP, the Fourteenth Party Congress launched the country on the first step toward central planning. The new official policy was a "socialist industrialization of the USSR" that would be led by heavy industry. Amid all this, the unsuspecting Erich Mendelsohn became the focus of a new row about competitions.

In the spring of 1925, managers of Leningrad's Textile Trust had visited Germany and commissioned Mendelsohn, known to them as a designer of several textile plants, "as a consultant to present an alternative design to the project produced by their own architects" for a large new complex for Leningrad. It was plainly his visit in October, "with a preliminary scheme and model," which brought the situation to public attention.[86] Someone seems to have alerted *The Building Industry* to a "scandal," on which their editors then sought various views. Thus their December issue carried three "statements" expressing various degrees of indignation. Shchusev and Antipov, president and secretary of MAO, expressed the society's "bewilderment at the issuing by one of our largest industrial trusts of a personal commission to an architect from Germany," for "architects of the USSR are hardly to be pushed aside for any lack of technical adequacy in such tasks." In their opinion, any such commissioning of foreigners "must take place only as a result of a competition, which Soviet architects consider to be the only correct approach [to commissioning a building]." MAO was confident that competitions would show "our architects are closer to understanding our new social priorities than Westerners are."

The Circle of Civil Engineers thought it much better "to bring in from abroad whole teams of relevant specialists from established bureaus, who are accustomed to working on the same project together." Given the gulf in technical standards, Asnova thought it was "more rational to seek organizational means" through which Soviet and Western architects "could conduct work collaboratively."[87]

This did not end the attacks on Mendelsohn: over a year later, he was still publicly defending himself in the Soviet architectural press.[88] After the Fourteenth Party Congress launched the national industrialization drive in December 1925, building and design work were increasingly distributed among specialized offices "according to a plan," like everything else. Thus as building began to take off, with architectural competitions continuing to double each year and with an ever greater consciousness of the need for Western technical help, the Mendelsohn row provided timely clarification of principle on how foreign architects were to be used and selected. In the same month, the Constructivists entered all aspects of public debate with new force as they formed an officially registered group, OSA (the Union of Contemporary Architects). The founders were the growing number of architects and students in the circle around Ginzburg and the Vesnins.[89] During the next year, 1926, they launched a substantial bimonthly architectural journal, *Sovremennaia arkhitektura* (*Contemporary Architecture*). During that next year, the issue of architectural competitions was continuously under debate.

"The Organization of Competitions Is Intolerable"

With so many views already in the air, a senior member of the Technical Cadres department of the Trade Union of Builders, Rozenberg, an OAKh member before and after the Revolution, took several pages of *The Building Industry* in February 1926 to lay out the issues. As his boss Rozhanovich said in a preamble, "there is unanimity only on one fact: that the existing position with the organization of competitions is intolerable under conditions of the Soviet state." The reason was clear, as Rozenberg put it: "Competitions are one of the most advanced and sophisticated methods of creating designs for a building, [but] the culture of competitions that was carefully devised over several decades in czarist times has been transplanted into the new social and political conditions without any questioning of how far it might be appropriate to it." As a systematic exposition of current issues and problems in competition practice, Rozenberg's paper was comparable to that of Arnol'd back at the beginning of the first expansion of competitions, in 1872. Rozenberg examined competitions systematically, as "stimuli to creative design work," and then from legal, economic, professional, and public points of view.

Many of his observations were by now well rehearsed, but he cited new points of great potential importance to the whole competition policy, and some figures that later were to be much used to vindicate the importance of competitions.

As "stimuli to creativity" and as a form of legal contract between designer and client, competitions were not much changed by the new political structure, Rozenberg said. The most profound consequences for the type of competition appropriate in Soviet conditions arose, as he saw it, from "the fact that most buildings are now state property, and that the economic interests of owners and the state therefore now coincide." The real contibution of a competition, he said, was to generate options for "correct utilization of the site allocated for the building, in such a way that the processes which the building serves to organize will be given the most economical and efficient organization possible, for the given volume of construction."

In the nature of design, these issues are the ones "being primarily solved at the level of the basic sketch scheme." "The difference between a good solution and a bad one at this level," he said, "is usually not more than 5–10 percent of building costs, but is sometimes significantly higher, whereas a client's outlay on a competition may be about 1 percent of building costs." Since nothing in the later detailing-up of a building influences this figure significantly, the preference for the competition method is a "simple economic calculation." But more significantly, it indicates that, as a general rule,

fig. 14
Hector O. Hamilton
Competition project (reworked scheme) for the Palace of Soviets,
Moscow; perspective of riverward side, 1932.

fig. 15
Hector O. Hamilton
Competition project (reworked scheme) for the Palace of Soviets,
Moscow; section, 1932.

fig. 16
Boris Iofan
Competition project (selected as basis of final scheme) for the Palace of
Soviets, Moscow; perspective, 1932.

it is more appropriate to limit the competition to just sketch-stage solutions, requiring a creative concept, since the greater the number of designers attracted into the process, the greater the field of search, and thus the greater probability of finding a successful solution.

This is the viewpoint from which it is necessary to approach the drawing up of the competition program.

This was already a widely held opinion. More contentious was the proposal that competitors should present "not a final set of drawings but an economic and constructional analysis of a series of variants with comparative calculations, derived from what will inevitably have been, as every designer knows, dozens of sketches that precede the finally resolved idea." With this in mind, he said, "it follows that it is better not to set a very exact program which confines creativity, for a very tightly defined program often predetermines one variant of the general solution, reducing creativity to the solution of some geometrical charades."[90] This view was to be robustly reinforced by OSA in their new journal.

Rozenberg's conclusion was a logical preference for the two-stage competition: the first for sketch schemes; the second, with a fuller brief, to work these into detail. In the new circumstances this was also a far more responsible use of scarce architectural manpower. This led him to the vexed question of inviting foreigners, where his view followed MAO's: wherever "technical intervention" is necessary, "the international competition is the very best form of it." To sort out the competition business and regulate it, there should be a central Competitions Committee, combining state agencies with "representatives of the professional and technical societies" who would have a hierarchy of "commissions" operating in each republic and region.

Much of this was very favorable to the position of the avant-gardists. But this last proposal inflamed another row. In May, a major congress on construction took place in Moscow. As the Constructivists reported it in their new journal, *Contemporary Architecture:* "Rozenberg's proposals for a central bureaucratic organization of competitions met with unanimous rejection by architects attending the congress. It was significant that all differences of view between Muscovites and Leningraders on aspects of detail were set aside, and representatives spoke out as a united front for defense of the slogan 'the free competition, organized by representatives of the competitors.'"[91] There were numerous heated exchanges over questions of "the competitor's interests." Shchusev, for instance, insisted that two-stage "sketch" competitions were disastrous for architects, as ordinary people could not read such drawings: "If we permit small-sketch competitions, they will not be properly understood. The public needs to have large-scale detailed drawings."[92] The most powerful blast came from Asnova just after the congress in a short statement "In Defense of Competitors." Asnova, too, started a journal, modest and short-lived compared to OSA's, but as ever with a fresh, designerly view aimed at maximizing the positive exploitation of design creativity and of advancing architectural innovation.

One side of Asnova's thinking was aimed at achieving a far richer and better informed dialogue between the competitors and the client and jury. Competitors must play a part in shaping the brief that went beyond the usual ritual of questions and answers. More significantly, the whole manner in which jury members "spoke for" entries at the first sifting must be changed, to follow the model of law courts. The mediators between projects and jurors should be specialists, speaking for and against projects in front of the jury, with the competitor having the right "to send in his comments on the experts' conclusions" up to the final judging, in order to guarantee judgments were not made "on the basis of a misunderstanding about the considerations which have motivated the design." The jury in this model would be akin to a legal jury: not specialists but people to balance the evidence for and against as presented to them by the advocates.

This was interesting and radical, but most fundamental to the question of what competitions were (or are) for were Asnova's proposals on prizes. "The practical fact that only one design is required for actually building" meant that one significant prize should be given to "the scheme which best answers the requirements of the brief." But then "another prize must be given for the project which, though not necessarily following the brief literally, contains in itself an *extraordinary proposal.* Remaining monies should be divided into as many small prizes as possible, to recompense entrants for labor and materials expended."[93]

Both these proposals have as many ramifications now as then for the terms of judgment, the conduct of a public-professional debate on architecture, and the role of competitions. The issue of the "extraordinary proposal" was one of the most powerful ideas emerging in this entire debate. It led to some of the most vexatious cases raised by competitions of the next few years, in particular as the young Vesnin student, Leonidov, started making his mark. It also goes to the very heart of the larger issue of competitions which I touched on at the beginning, that of their longer-term contribution to developing the collective resources of architecture as a whole.

Leonidov was still very much a student when his teachers launched *Contemporary Architecture,* though his work soon started to appear in it. The first issue, which came out about the time of the Builders Congress, showed OSA increasingly heading for confrontation with MAO. The immediate conflict was over two MAO competitions recently concluded.

The prize list for the House of Textiles competition was well filled with OSA members: of the eight prizes given, Il'ia Golosov took the first, Ginzburg the third, and three other founding members, students and recent graduates, the sixth.[94] Their complaints about the brief therefore carried some authority, and they precisely exemplified Rozenberg's criticisms of a brief so specific that design was reduced to a "geometrical charade." "The program written by MAO on behalf of the Textile Syndicate already gave 90 percent of the solution." Not only did it go into "the exact floor area for every secretary in the building" but, "as has become typical of our programs," it specified the number of floors the building must have (ten) and, worse still, laid down precisely which activity was to be located on which floor. This building was another multifunctional complex akin to Arkos in its conception. All such complexes were based on the traditional Moscow concept of the *delovyi dvor* or "business house," a trading base that included everything from warehousing to hotel accommodation for visitors. The old business district near Red Square where these new headquarters were being located was full of buildings conceived on this model. As the OSA author (probably Ginzburg) put it in relation to the House of Textiles, "any healthy-thinking architect knows that all these different functions like housing, banking, etc., require different conditions and, in particular, different block depths, so what is the rationality of arranging them thus on the vertical?" By their brief, "the competition organizers cut off at the root any possibility for the emergence of interesting solutions. Briefs like this cannot be the arena for any kind of creative contest." It was merely a "colossal squandering of forty architects' energies."[95]

The story of the Central Telegraph was even more juicy, much of it redolent of prerevolutionary practice. *Contemporary Architecture* headed its attack by reproducing the relevant press cutting from *Pravda*. In this MAO competition, six prizes were awarded. (Grinberg was first, Leonid and Aleksandr Vesnin second.) The Postal Department had simultaneously commissioned two projects, from Shchusev and Rerberg, *hors concours*. Overturning the competition result, the department had decided Rerberg's was best "for daylighting, construction, and use of site, giving maximum possibilities for future expansion." *Contemporary Architecture* was almost speechless: "Certainly the Postal Department's engineers are not obligated to know anything about architecture. Nonetheless, it would be worth getting them to understand that a building cannot have 'good daylight' when . . ."—and they enumerated the building's absurdities with respect to all claims of its merits, as well as its distinctly retro style.[96] By a timely accident, Bruno Taut passed through Moscow with Mendelsohn and publicly supported OSA's critique, leaving them happily "convinced that the international front of modern architecture is becoming a practical reality."[97] In his lecture to MAO, Taut explained the German system of jury decision by secret ballot.[98]

The waste of professional energies was a theme to which Rozenberg returned again in *The Building Industry* in August. Figures from fourteen competitions run by MAO showed eight hundred submissions for the eleven principal ones. Whatever the competitions' value as training for young architects and students, "eighty prizes went to old and distinguished architects, who took between one and eleven prizes each." He recalled the prerevolutionary practice of established architects holding back in favor of the young. The other problem of MAO's dominance was the routinized judgment resulting from "their jury members too zealously manifesting their own tastes." The prerevolutionary situation was returning, when no Muscovite bothered to enter a competition announced by the St. Petersburg society, and vice versa. (Leningraders had far less enthusiastically rejected classical elements in favor of total modernity.) Many of the other old problems were recurring: too short a submission period, so that serious design studies were impossible and entry was reduced to "a kind of lottery." How many entries should constitute a "valid" competition? How to prevent juries full of "specialists and representatives" being so large that "no one felt any real personal responsibility?" Just at the moment when "we need a way to handle the oncoming avalanche of project work," Rozenberg said, "we have competitions that increasingly satisfy nobody: not competitors, client, the public, or the state."[99]

MAO's secretary, Antipov, came back shortly with what was essentially the society's defense, still totally opposed to any "central bureaucracy." But he recognized that Asnova's ideas on "the system of premiation and jury work . . . deserved attention." The one thing worth centralizing (as others had proposed back in 1924) was a publication of good entries "to popularize contemporary architectural trends, especially for the provinces, which are completely cut off from this." In a further plug for his society, he previewed the volume of competition schemes they had in press for precisely this purpose.[100]

Boom Years for the New Architecture, 1926–27

Meanwhile, the avant-garde groups went their own ways internally, following their own principles. The Constructivists in OSA started research on the most urgent problem— housing—through organizing their own internal contest, a "comradely socialist *sorevnovanie*," "entirely free, and without program."[101] The results of this work, from both the Moscow and Leningrad branches, were highly fruitful, producing new apartment types more relevant to current family structure and new spatial configurations for housing blocks. It formed the starting point of all their well-known housing research

thereafter, in the Stroikom RSFSR (the Russian State Building Committee) and in their Narkomfin and other model projects. Though increasingly opposed to MAO now, the Constructivists were effectively the legatees of the freethinking, scientifically-based approach which MAO had made characteristically Muscovite when it was founded.[102]

Equally focused on housing, Asnova used a commission it had from the Moscow Soviet for a site at Shabolovka in southern Moscow to demonstrate its concept of a competition. Each participant in the first stage received money commensurate with his contribution, with the highest reward going to the *chrezvychainyi* or "extraordinary" proposal. After all participants had discussed the body of work together, and after they had examined the criticisms which came back from the client, the best variants formed the basis for a final project which was worked out together by the authors of those best variants.[103] The result was genuinely the collective product of group work, and offered, as they saw it, a model for the socialist competition.

As this work proceeded through 1926 and 1927, the number of competitions rose to thirty-five and fifty-seven, respectively,[104] with major public complexes all over the Soviet Union going to competition and with a sharp rise in industrial schemes.

In one notable confrontation, Ginzburg fought a battle of ideologies with Zholtovskii over "how to respond to local traditions" in the House of Soviets competition for Makhachkala in Dagestan; Ginzburg ridiculed Zholtovskii's "stylization" in relation to the results of objective climatic and social study conducted through the Constructivist "functional method of design."[105] By winning a similar competition for the House of Government in Alma-Ata the next year, Ginzburg got his own back and the chance to demonstrate the power of the new approach to handle these Central Asian contexts. In 1926, his Orgametal building was another distinguished "business house" project unrealized for Moscow.[106] A similar design task from that year was the Elektrobank scheme by Il'ia Golosov (plate no. 700). It has become traditional in Soviet literature to call the scheme a "competition project," though to my knowledge no one has produced documentation on the competition itself or other entries. Golosov had designed a housing block for Elektrobank earlier,[107] and this may have been some small contest by invitation. Whatever its origins, the scheme itself is a perfect example of the gulf between "impractical" proposals and the current state of the Soviet building-materials market which had inflamed "realists" at the Builders Congress when they saw the MAO display of competition entries.[108]

In 1927, Golosov's elder brother Panteleimon had significant successes. A middle-of-the-road Modernist in MAO and not allied with Constructivism, he took first prize in the spring for the Khar'kov Central Postal Depot, which he then built, and second prize three months later, in another MAO competition, for the Sovkino moviemaking complex outside Moscow.[109] Talented students were following close behind: a group from MVTU (the Moscow Technical School) came in second for Khar'kov; Ginzburg took the first prize for the new Polytechnic in Ivanovo-Voznesensk together with one of his students, Ignatii Milinis, who increasingly figured in the lists on his own. With the spring months dominated by Party decrees on industrialization and rationalization, Leningrad became something of a center for competitions in this field. With the Engineers Association, LAO and OAKh formed a special Bureau for Industrial Competitions, which announced eight of them, and all competitions announced in Leningrad that year were industrial ones.[110] One of the very few Iakov Chernikhov designs we have for real buildings appears to have

fig. 17
Ivan Fomin
Competition project for Narkomtiazhprom, Moscow; elevation onto Red
Square, 1934.

fig. 18
Panteleimon Golosov
Competition project for Narkomtiazhprom, Moscow; perspective of Red
Square side, 1934.

fig. 19
Ivan Fomin
Competition project for Narkomtiazhprom, Moscow; north elevation
closing square toward Bol'shoi Theater, 1934.

been for one of these competitions.[111] In another response to this government campaign, OSA urged Vesenkha to set up a systematic series of competitions for better constructional detailing in buildings. Their international survey of flat-roof detailing conducted by questionnaire to leading Soviet and European architects in the previous year, 1926, had set a "comradely" model here.[112]

Sovkino, Alma-Ata, and the first moves toward the Lenin Library competition marked the debut in competitions of Leonidov. Though he was an active and increasingly central member of OSA, his highly individual and radical approach to competitions was the best vindication of Asnova's conception of the "extraordinary." In the first of these three contests, he was unplaced; in the second, he was third; and the Lenin Library scheme was his Vkhutemas final diploma project based on a reinterpretation of the Library committee's brief. In its organization and language, the Alma-Ata scheme was closer to Ginzburg's manner than to Leonidov's own more Suprematist spatiality. Hence it was more acceptable to a jury than were his other schemes.[113] Yet the others were the breakthroughs that have lasted as architectural paradigms.

Sovkino was one of the few competition projects in which Leonidov stuck correctly to the brief's requirements. It was a careful response to the technical needs, but organized with enormous power on the site. One long volume was played off against freestanding "location" areas, embracing them all into one synthesis of landscape flowing into building.[114] The diploma project had more complex origins.

Early in 1927, the Lenin Library administrators wanted to conduct explorations prior to a new building competition, and they asked the Architecture Faculty of Vkhutemas if any diploma students would like to explore the task. Some did, and we have the projects of Viktor Pashkov (fig. no. 10) and Leonidov.[115] Leonidov did nothing to help the Library by redefining the brief as an Institute of Library Sciences (which was only one small part of the Library's requirement) and moving it from the north side of the Kremlin out to the open spaces of the Lenin Hills on the city's edge (there had long been a utopian notion of erecting some educational memorial to Lenin there).

He treated the site and its volumes in a manner far removed from the logical plan linkages and tight volumes which characteristically resulted from applying the Constructivist "method." But he produced a new image of urbanity enormously potent then as now.[116] The scheme came into the spotlight when Leonidov's superb model was displayed in OSA's *Pervaia vystavka sovremennoi arkhitektury* (*First Exhibition of Contemporary Architecture*) at Vkhutemas that summer (see plate no. 418 for Gan's poster for the show).[117] Being clearly beyond Soviet building resources of the time, this scheme became the Achilles' heel of Constructivism vis-à-vis politicians and the growing number of fellow professionals tiring of the Constructivists' assumed hegemony over Modernism. For students throughout Moscow schools, it became the seductive touchstone of what was ultimately, as so often, no more than a fashionable stylization.[118] Recognizing the danger of this, and likewise the truth of the technical critique, Ginzburg spelled out precisely those merits of the project which have attracted attention again some sixty years later:

This work is especially valuable to us as a categorical break with that whole system of techniques, schemas, and elements which have inevitably become common and habitual {in our design} . . .

Leonidov's Library results in a purely space-oriented architectural treatment which leads away from the traditional conception of a building and toward a reorganization of the very concept of the public space and the city in which such a building might stand . . .

Leonidov's design in a sense constitutes a landmark and reference point for our future work.[119]

Confronting Monumentality, 1928–29

While issuing the challenge to the students, the Library also commissioned an exploratory project from a team under a senior MAO member, Dmitrii Markov, plainly seeking by these two means to make all approved preliminary moves to ensure a viable brief. On January 1, 1928, the open competition for the Lenin Library was announced, conducted by MAO for Narkompros and closing in April. A closed competition was run simultaneously, with schemes invited from the Vesnins, Shchusev, Shchuko, and Rerberg.[120] The brief was a rich one, for a building of genuine technical and organizational complexity, and in the course of its two stages the competition produced a range of interesting and buildable schemes from the Constructivists and the Rationalists, as well as some stylistically lame attempts at modernity from the older guard. The perspective of the Vesnins' first scheme (plate no. 711) is an extraordinarily elegant design which today's Western technology could realize with stunning crispness.

As the Lenin Library was a state building of symbolic and geographical importance, the brief included specifications of monumentality which had not been much heard in competitions since the early postrevolutionary years but which would soon start to ring out again loudly. Given its role as a memorial to Lenin and its landmark status in the city, the building should reflect "the character of the epoch, incarnating the will of the workers for the building of socialism." It must fit in with the historical architecture of its surroundings, not set itself up in contrast to them. Elevations should be monumental but undecorated and simple. Practically, the Library must function as "a powerful hothouse of knowledge and enlightenment," and overall, give a "harmonious and joyful impression." The jury was a suitable mix of library specialists, relevant Moscow Soviet specialists (including the city's chief planner), two MAO representatives, and Lunacharskii.

At this stage, Markov entered the open competition with two Rationalists, Fridman and Fidman. One historical merit of competitions in this period is the perspective they give on the Rationalists' work. As the members of this group did not build much, and ran no continuing publication, their achievements in building design have been unfairly overpowered in most records by those of the prolific Constructivists. This competition provides good examples of their capacity to produce stunningly powerful and subtle volumetric compositions in a concrete situation with buildings that are also very well planned. The team, which was certainly dominated by Fridman and Fidman, won the open competition from an entry of ten schemes. As for the commissioned schemes, the jury issued a note that Shchusev, Shchuko, and Rerberg had suffered a "relapse into the old styles." Nonetheless, Shchuko and Shchusev, with the Vesnins and the Rationalist team, were asked to redesign and resubmit in November. The guilty parties reclad their schemes in stripped Modernist clothes.[121] Narkompros announced that Shchuko had won, as his scheme had the potential for reworking to greater monumentality.[122] The noise about that was to come later.

Meanwhile, this competition was running simultaneously with another, of equal complexity, for the large administrative center of Soviet cooperative organizations called Tsentrosoiuz, further north in the capital. This was conducted not by MAO but by VOGI (the Civil Engineers Society). Here foreigners were to be involved, and in approved manner they came in through competition. From April to June 1928, an open competition of Soviet architects produced thirty-two projects

704

for the very high rewards of twelve prizes and three commendations—surely enough even to satisfy Asnova. Velikovskii won; Kapustina and other young Constructivists were second; and Trotskii, Leningrad winner of the Palace of Labor competition in 1923, was back in the Moscow prize lists. The foreigners invited simultaneously, but with more time, were Le Corbusier, Max Taut, and the Londoners Tait and Burnet, all competing with Tsentrosoiuz's own architects Anatolii Samoilov and Nakhman. Le Corbusier's scheme was preferred, but he was then taken a stage further against Peter Behrens, Zholtovskii, and a mass of Constructivists: the Vesnins, Leonidov, and Aleksandr Pasternak from the Moscow group, and Nikol'skii and Ol' as leaders in Leningrad. A foreigner was clearly heading for this job, yet was not getting it easily. Indeed, more time was spent, with Kolli assisting revisions in Le Corbusier's Paris office before a final scheme was affirmed in April 1929. The story has been told in detail elsewhere.[123] It is interesting here as a follow-up to the saga of Mendelsohn, and as a prelude to another saga of foreign invitations for the Palace of Soviets.

Just as Tsentrosoiuz was starting, a very constructive article by Barkhin, a good Modernist and regularly successful competition entrant himself, appeared in *The Building Industry*. (Barkhin was, of course, architect of the famous *Izvestiia* building, completed in 1927.) Barkhin was not a member of either younger group, but what he proposed is interesting as a halfway house toward embracing the priority for design and designers underlying Asnova's proposals for competitions. The issue had been brought alive again by another series of meetings called by the Builders Union in pursuit of some "short basic legal statute" to regulate all matters that "are not highly contenious."[124]

Barkhin had been a MAO member since before the Revolution, but without hesitation declared MAO's regulations "in need of significant reworking." He was highly favorable to creation of a central organization, "for example, under Gosplan," but its powers must be strictly limited to deciding which buildings were obligatorily to be the subject of competitions and what monies were to be made available, and to handling publicity, central records, and any legal adjudications necessary. All design-related matters, including the juries, must remain with the various professional societies and be conducted according to the societies' internal regulations, with clients choosing among societies as they preferred. "Virtually unchanging composition of juries" must cease. This was "a major cause of competition failure" and "harmful to free development of architectural thought." Barkhin therefore proposed, first, that "no one jury member can serve on more than two consecutive competitions." Secondly, that this professional part of the jury "must be chosen from among people who have themselves competed in recent competitions with some success," in order to ensure they are up-to-date with "current trends and architectural concerns." Thirdly, in order to guarantee competitors' confidence in a jury, some part of it should be elected by secret ballot of the competitors, who would send their vote for members of a candidate list when they submitted their schemes. In the process of judgment, not one but two jury members should be scrutineers and spokesmen for any given project, and they should examine its merits according to a standard questionnaire of points established by the whole jury in their initial discussions together. At the preliminary public exhibition, those questionnaire comments must be on display, for public and competitor to comment and respond factually as they wish. Eventual voting according to these criteria should be done by the secret ballot method (as Taut had described from German practice). By this means, the judgment is "maximally objective, even almost automatic," as schemes are premiated in order of aggregate votes cast for them. When everything is concluded, all records are deposited with the central competitions office. This plan may not be ideal, said Barkhin, and it may need modifications, "but if we start to talk along such lines, these things may more rapidly cease to be a bugbear."[125]

Under the same stimulus of renewed debate, MAO was itself preparing new draft regulations for the overall legalities of competitions, which were sent to Narkompros by MAO's vice president, Leonid Vesnin, in late May. For all Barkhin's determination to distance himself from MAO's position, these draft regulations in no way conflicted with his proposals. Indeed, as conceived in his own paper, they were essentially complementary, being effectively that "short legal statute of the uncontenious" which the Builders Union had sought. For their own contests, they also modified the detail to include two aspects of Barkhin's proposals: numerical voting by jurors, and a statement of the principles which had guided their judgment.[126] That autumn, a competition for a local department store for the Bauman district of Moscow, for which young Milinis did a crisp scheme, was the first competition judged in that way.[127]

Various other societies also framed new internal regulations for themselves at about the same time. Aru (the Association of Urban Architects), a planning-oriented offshoot of Asnova, carried forward much the same system, except that authors of the best initial schemes would consent to work together later, not be compelled into it: perhaps they had experienced too many comradely rows. In Leningrad, OAKh now had a thriving competition program of its own and also updated its regulations. While MAO, seeking as ever to lead the whole operation, trundled its draft "Decree of a Directional Character" through various bureaucractic stages until overtaken by centralization of the profession—first locally, then nationally—from 1929 onward.[128]

In new government measures of June 1928 "to get construction in industry in order," the figure of "22.5-percent potential cost savings through design" was being widely bandied about as furthering the argument for competitions. Six months later, in January 1929, Vesenkha was instructing the People's Commissariats, the Narkomats, to use competitions whenever possible.[129] On the other hand, the same processes of increased economic pressure and centralization were making competitions' very slowness, unpredictability, and high usage of manpower ever less attractive. Annual numbers started dropping, but the central prestige competitions were increasingly becoming stylistic and ideological battlegrounds. The Lenin Library competition, for one, was not closing peacefully.

Modes of Protest, 1929–30: Words or "Extraordinary Proposals"?

In early May 1929, a nationwide assembly of the Constructivist group OSA was gathered in Moscow at their First Congress, when the government commission responsible for the Lenin Library gave the go-ahead for construction of Shchuko's final reworked project. "PROTEST" read the headline inside the front cover of *Contemporary Architecture*'s June–July issue. In bold typography were statements from its own Congress Presidium, the Aru Presidium, the Council of Asnova, the Architectural Club of Vkhutein (the Higher Artistic-Technical Institute), and the Bureau of the new "proletarian" architectural society, Vopra (the All-Union Association of Proletarian Architects); a note across the bottom stated that "The editors have also received a series of protests from other architectural organizations."

OSA expressed its "decisive and categorical protest." The "reactionary design . . . weakest of all submitted," had been "very negatively received by the broad Soviet public in all meetings and debates, as well as in government and party newspapers." (*Izvestiia*, *Pravda*, and *Komsomol'skaia Pravda* had spread the debate nationwide.) "Soviet public opinion cannot be so rudely ignored": the government must radically reexamine its decision. For Aru, this case reinforced its members' view that "public opinion must be organized around questions of quality in new buildings of state importance." The open competition was a failure because the loading of the jury with members of MAO predetermined the group of architects for whom it was "worth entering." The closed competition failed because "the organizers confused building experience with architectural talent." Both factors served to exclude the young. A new Library competition should take place "on a different organizational basis, with the *konkurs* transformed into a socialist *sorevnovanie* between teams from all existing architectural groups and societies." To Asnova, this decision was another in the line that had started with the Central Telegraph. Only public involvement could stop "bureaucratic departments inviting chosen individuals" like this. Vopra echoed this, and the Vkhutein people had "already protested when preliminary projects emerged in the first competition." Four perspectives from Shchuko and Shchusev schemes were featured in suitably retro frames at the top of the page. In the groveling patois of prerevolutionary domestic servants, the caption sarcastically asked: "How may we oblige you, sir? People like us are not too proud for anything."[130]

Shchuko's former student and long-time partner, Gel'freikh, came from Leningrad to work with him, and the building went slowly ahead (fig. no. 13). But the episode no doubt contributed to the proposal OSA published on the page opposite the protests, a proposal for "all progressive forces" in Soviet architecture to come together in a Federation of Revolutionary Architects. They would be stronger together than apart, "for fighting the eclectic and unprincipled in Soviet architecture, for reorganization of competition affairs," and much else.[131] The Vesnins' second Library scheme followed as the main building feature of that *Contemporary Architecture* issue (fig. no. 11).

The differences between groups went too deep for any such federation to be formed, but various factors were favoring team design within the groups. One factor was the increasingly aggressive Party hostility to assertions of individual identity over the collective. Another was the increasing complexity and pressure of the building tasks themselves. In January 1929, as I have mentioned, Vesenkha instructed the Narkomats to use competitions wherever possible. In December of that year, the Narkomats' own supreme body, Sovnarkom, forbade them "from handing out design work to individual persons."[132] The combined implications were clear: competitions should be used to raise standards, but they must be competitions of teams, not of individuals. Though fueled by different motivations, cries for replacement of "competitions" by teamwork in intergroup *sorevnovaniia* were moving this hitherto most individualistic aspect of professional practice in the same direction. After Asnova's long propaganda for that approach, it was finally used in two major Moscow competitions during 1929–30. Some groups fielded one person, others fielded a team after intragroup exploration of the task, but entries were submitted in the group name. In both these competitions, Leonidov was OSA's representative. In both, he was pilloried for rewriting the brief, but he had devised potent new architectural paradigms in the process.

The first contest, in late 1929, was for another example of the integrated "business house" or *delovyi dvor*, again in the old business district of Moscow alongside Red Square, whose monuments must be respected. This so-called House of Industry was a headquarters for Vesenkha, which invited teams or representatives from Asnova, Aru, VOGI, Vopra, MAO, OSA, and the architecture faculties of Vkhutein and MVTU to compete. Seven projects were eventually submitted and Panteleimon Golosov took first prize for MAO with a conventionally organized nine-storied office building on an F-shaped plan, forming two deep, dull courts.[133]

Leonidov completely rethought the activity of "working in an office" and produced a building concept akin to the best Western office-building practice of the 1980s or 1990s: open-plan working areas for all, with integral green-planted areas everywhere for frequent brief periods of indoor or fresh-air relaxation; integral feeding and health facilities; a rooftop running track and summertime swimming pool. With great political correctness, all this was aimed at "economy" and "rationalization": by "raising the individual's energy and vitality," the building would "increase labor productivity"—and all that had been achieved with a floor area 40,000 square meters less than the brief had specified. To open up the city and liberate ground space, all accommodation was drawn up into a single Miesian tower of some forty stories.[134] "Buildings of the tower type are not permitted," said the brief.[135] So this truly "extraordinary" and forward-looking new paradigm for the office building was disqualified.

As this competition closed in March 1930, another began, for a Palace of Culture to serve the Proletarskii district on Moscow's southern edge, where employment was mainly in the AMO car plant. The competition was run by the main trade union at the plant, the Union of Metalworkers, and was exemplary in being an intergroup *sorevnovanie* for both Moscow and Leningrad, with maximum worker participation in debate, and openly published judgments.

Leningrad organizations did not distinguish themselves. The LOA entry was "very detailed, but crude in its architecture." LIGI had "lovingly executed the program" but created "a series of small courtyards that would disorient the visitor." "The work of the Leningrad Vkhutein has no interest whatever." (Coming from the former Academy of Arts, this scheme may have been classical.)[136] MAO, OAKh, the Moscow Vkhutein, and MVTU got no further. Vopra, LIGI, Aru with Asnova, and, somewhat surprisingly, OSA in the person of Leonidov were invited to a second stage. The exquisite little white-on-black drawings with collage which are in the present exhibition (plate nos. 714–716) formed part of Leonidov's first-stage submission.

On the site, Leonidov marked out a line of four grid-squares containing, in sequence, a physical-culture area of soccer and other outdoor pitches around a square pyramidal sports pavilion; an open-air terrain with one small building in the corner, for mass parades; a park area with large and small lightweight hemispherical domes for theatrical and other mass performances; and a scientific and historical study center, with one long building and an outdoor screen and projection area.[137] It is an essentially Suprematist composition of subtly placed prismatic structures, whose three-dimensional tensions, on hilly riverside land looking back over the city, demand a model. As in any scheme of Leonidov's, or any in this genre, the overall spatial system created by built volumes in the landscape is ill-conveyed by plan and elevation.

Public opinion might not have liked Shchuko, but most of it was a long way from seeing any "architecture" in Leonidov's submission. So, indeed, was most of the profession. The whole thing "lacks the high emotional power which workers demand as the materialized expression of the power of their class." The architect was "talented, but an anarchist, a petit-bourgeois," "cut off from reality." The long building was a "barrack of

Nikolai I." The site was a "desert." "The chessboard device may organize the drawings, but it does nothing to organize the Palace of Culture." Though obscured by this detailed comment, the real essence of what Leonidov had done was in fact recognized by both sides. As the report in *Stroitel'stvo Moskvy* (*Construction of Moscow*) said, "Workers in their speeches drew attention to a profoundly individualistic attitude toward the program, which led to a total ignoring of its demands, producing an irrelevant experimentalism."[138]

More specific was the Asnova and Aru man Georgii Krutikov, in *The Building Industry*: "The OSA project by Leonidov stands apart from all the others" because it was "based on a reorganization of cultural provision for the whole Proletarskii district." He had "evenly dispersed" all elements of mass catering, activities for children, and classrooms for adult education around the district, so that only the really "mass" activities remained to be accommodated on this site. Again, there were no marks to be gained for a radical rethinking of the problem which produced a new paradigm. It was another example of what Asnova called the "extraordinary project." But in late 1930, times were increasingly conformist. Thus the same Krutikov who once did the *Gorod na vozdushnykh putiakh soobshcheniia* (*A City on Aerial Paths of Communication*, 1928, plate nos. 688–692) was careful. Leonidov had been a fellow student only one year his senior in Vkhutemas. Krutikov merely reported that "The project was rejected because there is no real basis for implementing a cultural combine on this model."[139]

Leonidov's second scheme brought many elements back onto the site and was more compact, but still "cut off from reality."[140] The eventual building by the Vesnins, though only partly executed, was extensive. But it was an entirely conventional Modernist complex.

Earlier that year, hard realism won Panteleimon Golosov the commission for *Pravda*'s new printing plant and publishing center (plate no. 713). This was a closed competition with a three-week deadline, the projects coming from a team in Gosproekt, Shchusev and Leonid Teplitskii, Golosov with Aleksandr Kurovskii, and a somewhat schematic one from Lissitzky.[141] (He was currently working for the Soviet press on foreign exhibitions.) Golosov's was a thoroughly professional modern building that could have served similar purposes in Europe or North America. Started the next year and completed in 1935, it still houses the whole *Pravda*-related publishing empire today.

"To Show Our Friends and Foes"

The Lenin Library and Palace of Culture competitions of 1928–30 gave clear indications of a social atmosphere in which the practical performance of a public building was becoming of less interest to official clients than something communicating a sense of achievement, in a conventional way symbolic of success and power, or "monumental." As ever in such symbol-building, the client, whether individual or collective, could not visualize what that "symbolic object" looked like; in the nature of the artistic process, clients define their "right" form by successive rejections from the range of alternatives generated by artists. Even more explicitly than in the Lenin Library case, the competition for the Palace of Soviets, in 1931–33, was a tortuous process of elimination in pursuit of a form rich enough in resonances to become a "monument" or "symbol." Ironically, the building being demolished for it was another official statement of government self-congratulation. Itself the product of fierce battles over the relationship of ideology and style, Ton's Cathedral of Christ the Saviour set no precedents for a smooth ride here.

The Palace of Soviets competition was explicitly launched by the Party in early 1931 as a resumption of the Palace of Labor idea of 1922–23. As the Palace Construction Council declared in its publicity, "The First Congress of Soviets in 1922 decreed that a building be erected in Moscow for the Union of Soviet Socialist Republics: a Palace for meetings of the soviets of the Union. Only now, though, with the great successes of socialist construction achieved and the First Five-Year Plan completed in four years . . . are all preconditions fulfilled for realizing the First Congress's decision."[142] The numbers of delegates forming these soviets meant a building with auditoriums for 15,000 and 8,000 people. Beyond that significant technical challenge was another, which, as the Council pointed out, "posed for designers a somewhat unusual task" of generating a symbolic concept or "image" for a building that must "characterize our epoch, as a physical manifestation of the will of the workers for the building of socialism."[143] For these symbol-making tasks, as had been said when the Lenin Mausoleum competition was planned in 1924–25, the more widely the net is cast, the greater the probability of someone, somewhere, generating a form capable of evoking and bearing the necessary symbolic loading.

In this as in other respects, the Palace of Soviets competition procedure was well framed in relation to earlier experience and critiques. A first "consultation stage was aimed at further refinement of the basic brief,"[144] and was in part conducted as an intergroup *sorevnovanie* with fifteen schemes, twelve commissioned and three sent as personal initiatives. This stage later became known as the "preliminary closed competition," but the Construction Council was at pains to stress it was noncompetitive. On the basis of lessons learned, a brief was then issued for a competition open to all Soviet architects and the workers at large.[145] Certain foreigners were also invited: Le Corbusier, keen for more work in Moscow, "accepted enthusiatically," as did Perret, Lamb, and Urban from the United States; Mendelsohn, Gropius, and Poelzig from Germany; and Boris Iofan's former teacher in Rome, Brazini, from Italy. Ostberg, the Swede, "stated his price for a sketch project would be 39,000 gold rubles, so discussions with him were dropped."[146] Some other foreigners entered, too, notably the emigré Russians Naum Gabo and Antoine Pevsner, and Lubetkin with his friends Blum and Sigalin. Hector Hamilton from New York was likewise an uninvited entrant; I suspect he was attracted by the challenge after visiting Moscow in "a group of American architects . . . who are building a radio-city in New York and who lectured on their work, and saw the preliminary Palace projects" in admiring amazement at their scale.[147]

The schedule of accommodation issued was not absurdly detailed for such a task. Precise specifications were given of the drawings required. There were clear statements of priority and organizational principle. After review of the preliminary projects, a full table of their performances against various functional criteria was published; a similar table was published for the better projects of the open competition. Drawings from each of the preliminary schemes were published, with detailed comments on their merits and failures, in journals and in six thousand copies of a second *Biulleten' Upravleniia stroitel'stvom Dvortsa sovetov pri prezidiume TsIK SSSR* (*Bulletin of the Central Committee's Special Administration for the Palace of Soviets*), which included answers to competitors' questions with discussions of the accoustic and servicing tasks. There were public exhibitions and extensive public discussions in workers' clubs and other forums around the city, after both the preliminary submission in July 1931 and the full open submission that December. Virtually every project submitted to the vast second stage was published in a special issue of the main architectural journal, with a brief paragraph of comment.[148] At this level, the openness could hardly be faulted. On the ever-crucial matter of jury membership, however, the situation was ominously different. It was naturally a question asked by competitors: "Who is the jury?" It was question no. 37 of 38 which were answered in the first *Bulletin* in September: "In accordance with the general conditions applying in this competition, there will not be a jury in the usual form. Scrutiny and preliminary evaluation of the projects will be carried out for the Construction Council by technical experts whom the Council will designate. Final evaluation of the projects and distribution of the prizes will be done by the Construction Council in accordance with requirements, as well as evalution of the schemes by the broad mass of workers and by elements of the Government." A couple of years before, that statement would have led to a mass professional boycott. The calls to national duty surrounding this event made that no longer an option. Architects' real freedom to choose would have been no greater if they had known that the jury chairman was Central Committee member Gleb Krzhizhanovskii and that the jury's two leading cultural figures were the key theorists of emerging Socialist Realism, Lunacharskii and Maksim Gor'kii. Amid all the pressures of the Five-Year Plan, employers of architects were under government instruction to "relieve them of other burdens . . . so they may participate in this task of such enormous political importance."[149]

The saga of the many stages that ensued, as the jury and Party edged their way toward defining a "truly proletarian architecture" and a building that would be a "product of the great art of Bolshevism," is not our interest here. Nor are the theories of Bolshevik aesthetics and Socialist Realism reflected in the decisions. I have discussed them elsewhere.[150] It was a saga that ran to four main stages, and on into extensive discussions and redesignings thereafter. The projects in the present exhibition derive from three of those four main stages. Of the schemes here, four were commissioned for the exploratory first stage during February–July 1931; one, Gabo and Pevsner's, was submitted to the open competition of July–December 1931 (plate nos. 719–720); the last, Ginzburg's, was commissioned at the first of two more closed stages which followed during 1932 and early 1933 (plate nos. 723–724). The avant-garde emphasis of the present exhibition means that the projects here are in no way a balanced sample of the overall body of submissions. No non-Modernist drawings serve to indicate the weight of classical and eclectic historicism that opposed them. Only Gabo and Pevsner's scheme, ironically, is "monumental." Indeed, it predicts with some accuracy (though less hypertrophy) the profile that would emerge from later stages, as Boris Iofan's second scheme was developed under Party guidance into a "final design" (fig. nos. 1, 16); his officially co-opted assistants were Shchuko and Gel'freikh, and his architect his elder brother Dmitrii, all in different ways now considered "reliable."

With good procedures and well-prepared, carefully presented brief, how did this competition become an international "scandal" from which so many retreated disillusioned?

Blame on the jury is misplaced. They were entirely consistent, and there was plenty in the brief to indicate their aspirations. Quantitatively, the key statements may have been dominated by technical detail, but they were clear to those in tune with the current atmosphere. "The building must be given an aesthetic treatment of the maximum ideological clarity, which clearly expresses its essence" and "corresponds to its importance as an artistic and architectural monument of the capital of the USSR." In the abstract, these statements could be interpreted variously. But by mid-1931—indeed, at any time after the Lenin Library confrontation—their implications were unambiguous. So much so that the invitations to avant-

gardists seem in retrospect intended as invitations to hang themselves: on any other basis it is surprising that people like the Vesnins and Ginzburg were being invited to later stages at all. "Facing materials must be appropriate," and samples of exotic Soviet marbles were already going on public display.[151] On the other hand, barriers of cultural and linguistic distance gave the Westerners every excuse. (Jean-Louis Cohen has noted that Le Corbusier received "very bad" translations.)[152] The indicative document was the second *Bulletin*. Its printing dates indicate no one would have got it much before submission on December 1st, but if we look at its critiques of the projects in the present show, the perceived shortcomings and connotations of the Modernist projects become ruthlessly clear.

The project of Nikolai Beseda, Krutikov, Vitalii Lavrov, and Valentin Popov (plate no. 718) was the team entry of Aru. They had moved part of the complex onto an adjacent site, "unnecessarily carving up the district," and had destroyed any atmosphere in "the great auditorium by making it like a stadium." Above it, "as the Palace's main external feature," rose "a great glazed tower providing things the Palace does not need"; this and "mechanical means of changing the space" were "superfluous mechanization." Throughout the project they had thus "taken the line of least resistance rather than solve real problems." The final punch line condemned them thus: "By ignoring the aesthetic aspects of the building, the authors have produced a solution that derives from the abstract fantasizing of the intelligentsia"—there was by now, in the Soviet government's eyes, no more anti-proletarian class.

Ladovskii was the leader of Aru, but his was a one-man submission (plate no. 725). His combination of dome and tower had produced "the most compact and economical scheme in terms of site use" among them all. On the other hand, his treatment of the great halls was "spatially abstract and a very academic constructive expression." Almost alone (except for Hamilton later), he had embraced the proposed subway station in the building's circulation, but the movements of people were so concentrated as to be "catastrophically dangerous and impermissible." The external appearance was "abstract, schematic" and "totally neglects the role of the spatial arts."

Nikol'skii was the leader of the Constructivist group in Leningrad, but he, too, had been invited as an individual. In the critics' eyes, his scheme (plate nos. 721–722) was very confused in its imagery. It "resembles an industrial building squashed flat" through which rises "a form like an Eastern hat." In approved Constructivist fashion, he presented the "flow diagrams" around which the building was planned. The critics knew about this stuff, however: "Automatic derivation of the form from the functions without architectural or artistic treatment leads to a typical Constructivist solution of the task, ignoring the aesthetic element in architecture and having nothing to do with the 'monumental building . . . fitting in with the monuments of Moscow' specified in the brief."

To the juries' justifiable and ill-concealed fury, several schemes had placed the building on another site. Even Shchusev was guilty of this, though his building was "realistic" (and still thoroughly Modernist). Fidman, in a dramatically simple non-invited submission "with the wholly unsuitable form reminiscent of an airship," had taken the references to 1923 literally and placed the building on the Palace of Labor site at the far end of the Kremlin. The team entry from the Constructivists (now called SASS [the Sector of Architects of Socialist Building], not OSA) was even more insubordinate.

In this case, the scheme was not by Leonidov: he was working in the Crimea with Ginzburg. The team comprised two of Leonidov's students, Pavlov and Mikhail Kuznetsov, who were well versed in his approach. In the critics' words, they had *removed from the site everything except the great hall. All other accommodation has been distributed in a circle around the map of Moscow and forms no part of the project. This is done in order to create around the hall a vast public plaza for 'mass actions' and physical-culture exercises in the open air . . .*

All this leads the authors to create vast lifting walls, roofs that open back, a staircase 170 meters wide, and a vast overload of superfluous mechanization of 'dynamic' parts of the hall . . . With its glass and steel construction, this is a model example of technological fetishism . . . Businesslike architectural design has been given up for graphic exercises that have no real content . . . It represents the bourgeois tendency in architecture, ideologically hostile to proletarian architecture.[153]

If the foreigners could have read this when their copies of the second *Bulletin* arrived, the final jury verdict would have surprised them less. In one quasi-official commentary, Barkhin, on the "committee of experts," described the projects collectively as "disappointing."[154] Some were, by any standards. Others, notably Le Corbusier's "factory-like hangar," were magnificent answers to a problem of crazy scale for the site, yet were objectively "disappointing" in relation to those key phrases of the brief.

The three equal first prizes in this open competition went to an eclectic, basically classical scheme by Boris Iofan; to Hamilton, for reasons about which there are various speculations[155]; and to Zholtovskii, for a sprawling but typically literate "Classical Palace" complex of mammoth scale. This last, in particular, was an example of the ironic general critique made of the preliminary schemes: that they "repeated the mistake made by the architect Ton, author of the Cathedral that is being demolished, who mechanically enlarged a little five-domed church to the grandiose dimensions of a cathedral." None of them had produced a "proletarian, Bolshevik architecture, born of the battle for building socialism." Through the pencils of their loyal adherents in the profession, the Palace Construction Council eventually devised that for themselves, in accordance with their notions of a realism that was Socialist, if definitely not practically realistic. With much energy invested in the Tsentrosoiuz, but construction near a standstill and no fees forthcoming, Le Corbusier kept his correspondence civil, and at the level of Lunacharskii.[156] CIAM (the Congrès internationaux d'architecture moderne), on the other hand, in the persons of Giedion, van Esteren, and the suitably named Bourgeois, sent two letters to Stalin, telling this heir of Lenin that his chosen project was "a direct insult to the spirit of the Russian Revolution" and that "The world, which has its eyes fixed on the development of the great Soviet construction effort, will be stupefied by it."[157] If the letters ever arrived, they no doubt provoked a gleeful toast. "Stupefying our enemies" was, after all, precisely the competition's real agenda.

Using Competitions Sparingly

During the months of March to July 1932, while Ginzburg was doing the third-stage Palace of Soviets scheme, the dramatic changes took place which had threatened the profession for several years. On April 23rd, the Party issued a Decree on the Restructuring of Literary and Artistic Organizations, which abolished independent professional groups and societies in all creative fields. On July 18th, a central and official Union of Soviet Architects was formed and all the familiar groups like MAO, Asnova, Aru, OSA/SASS, and OAKh were dissolved.[158]

The years of freedom to group and regroup, to debate and protest—over competition practices or anything else—were finished. Ginzburg was on the Board of the new Union, as were Viktor Vesnin, Ladovskii, and Fridman, but in company with Zholtovskii and Vopra's Karo Alabian. The official "method" of the Union, as of all creative activity, was now Socialist Realism, a synthesis of "critically assimilated" (i.e., politically "correct") elements of the heritage and a new content and new technologies, all geared to creating optimistic Party- and class-reinforcing imagery. I have discussed the development and meaning of this in architecture elsewhere.[159]

During 1932, with the Second Five-Year Plan of economic reconstruction just starting, the new priorities were reinforced by the creation of Narkomtiazhprom. Heavy industry was the leading sector of the economy in its battle "to catch up with and outstrip capitalism," and Narkomtiazhprom's administration was thus symbolically the main engine of the country's revolutionary reconstruction. It was obvious that Narkomtiazhprom should be located at the symbolic center of the state. More than that, it should literally trample underfoot the old regime's center of business and financial power in Kitaigorod, the Wall Street of capitalist Moscow, where we have seen lesser unbuilt competition projects for "industrial headquarters," such as Arkos and the House of Industry, being sited during the 1920s. Kitaigorod is separated from Red Square by the great galleria structure of the Upper Trading Rows (GUM), the competition for which had caused quarrels back in the 1890s. These would be demolished to place Narkomtiazhprom on the suitably enlarged central space of the nation, and the vast four-hectare site could be further enlarged as the architects chose.[160]

After another lengthy series of competitions, involving Germans, Le Corbusier, and innumerable Soviet professionals, strategic planning studies were under way in the Moscow Soviet for a socialist restructuring, and a rescaling to twentieth-century needs, of the whole medieval and capitalist city. On two sides of the Narkomtiazhprom site was the tightly-knit fabric of eighteenth- and nineteenth-century commercial development. On its other two sides stood some of Russia's greatest architectural monuments, like the Kremlin and St. Basil's, the Bol'shoi Theater and Teatral'naia Square, quite apart from such products of more recent contests as the Historical Museum, the Hotel Metropol', or the Lenin Mausoleum.

In this delicate and still unresolved planning situation a closed competition was launched in 1934, apparently by the all-powerful Narkomtiazhprom itself, and plainly without professional advice of appropriate caliber or vision. "What reflection did this exceptional architectural and planning task find in the competition brief?" asked the main commentary on resulting projects in *Construction of Moscow* at the end of the year. As the author himself answered: "Almost none. Along with the paragraphs relating to interdepartmental links in offices and supplementary accommodation, to the need for elevators and hot-water central heating, there was just a small mention of architecture: 'of the need for the most careful attention to the complex around it . . . to choice of entrance axis . . . to application of various facing marbles, and of sculpture, painting, etc., inside and out.' That's all. Not a single word on the overall compositional solution of the new architectural ensemble for the entire nation around Red Square." Some of the twelve entrants had indeed "involved themselves in the task far more deeply than was suggested in the brief." But general opinion was reflected in Aranovich's judgment that "as a whole, the competition must be considered to have failed." It had been entirely the wrong kind of competition. "The brief demanded that competitors focus on internal planning and technical equipment instead of working on site plans and sketch projects with schematic indications of building masses—which at this stage of the design would have been appropriate."[161] Behind the superficial megalomania, the great Narkomat's vision had been totally self-centered and myopic. Hence the competition process itself had got paralyzed in detail. But so, too, more surprisingly, had some of the architects.

More than any earlier competition, this one revealed the limitations of orthodox Constructivism and what Ginzburg had earlier called "that whole system of techniques, schemas, and elements which have inevitably become habitual with us." Yet again it was Leonidov (plate nos. 729–732) who had "taken a bold leap out of ordinariness" and produced a "purely space-oriented architectural treatment which leads away from the traditional conception of a building toward a reorganization of the very concept of the public space and the city in which such a building might stand."[162] As the commentator Aranovich reported, a range of distinct paradigms had emerged. In one of them, exemplified by Abram Zaslavskii and Avraam Faifel''s project, a high building looked over the Kremlin to addresss the other new insertion of the Palace of Soviets at its far end, producing a longitudinal symmetry and a ninety-degree reorientation of Red Square's "main" axis. Others, notably Boris Korshunov and Fomin (both experienced urbanists), had continued but enlarged the fabric of hollow courtyards characterizing the old city, enclosing traditionally resolved urban spaces with the monuments around the great complex itself. A third type, exemplified by Aleksandr and Viktor Vesnins' project, said Aranovich, was "solved in quite another way." But "the main difference does not lie in the fact that Fomin as ever is classical, and the Vesnins, also as ever, are Constructivist in orientation. The difference is deeper: while Fomin's project [fig. nos. 17, 19] is a proposal for the reconstruction of Red Square, the Vesnins' project has approached [the task] only as a building for Narkomtiazhprom." As the jury had put it, "in the Vesnins' project, Red Square is reduced to being just the adjacent area, and does not acquire any specific form defined by architectural masses. Sverdlov Square [to the north] is not architecturally completed." A look at the Vesnins' perspective (plate no. 733) confirms the judgment that "Their tall composition is completely cut off from Red Square. It ignores requirements for any relationship of scale with the mausoleum or the Kremlin, categorically refusing to engage in any ensemble with any other buildings whatever. This is not a spatial organization of the city center but an object which individualistically distinguishes itself from the space of the center." Ginzburg's almost identical scheme "also proceeds not from an architectural reconstruction of Red Square but from a literal reading of the design task set."[163]

As with the Palace of Soviets competition a few years before, the client/jury combination was engaged in a learning process, but here it was not stylistic. Mere solution of the brief as set by the client quickly revealed its limitations. The strange way that the Vesnins' and Ginzburg's schemes got "stuck," despite several "redesigns," on a single identical model, showed that there was no indicator to a larger conceptual solution from within the brief itself. All the lessons laboriously learned in the 1920s—about the merits of two-stage, exploratory competitions, about the dialogue that produced about a problem's real nature—had been ignored.

Mel'nikov's literalness was of another order (plate nos. 727–728). His plan was built on two Roman "fives"—intersecting Vs—for the two Five-Year Plans. "Technology" and the "heritage" were collaged together as vast moving staircases rising through great shaft-bearings to a monstrous compilation of heroic sculptural figures, all doubly dramatized by the gulf down to sixteen partially exposed floors to which Red Square's ground surface suddenly descended. The message he sought to convey is a matter for speculation. As

contemporaries well understood, it was certainly neither civil nor sympathetic to the new official definition of what constituted "architecture."

In one sense, Mel'nikov's was the "extraordinary proposal" of this competition, but it was not one that offered any new paradigm. Conceptually, it differed little from the Vesnins' scheme. On the other hand, the official commentary bracketed his entry with Leonidov's as "the two frankly utopian and formalistic schemes."[164] Of Mel'nikov one might agree with the criticism that here he had "misused his outstanding talents for artistic and spatial invention," but on Leonidov one must unquestionably disagree.

To the jury, Leonidov's "overall architectural conception" was "pretentious," "the placing of the three very tall vertical volumes is too close, and appears accidental."[165] (In the new canon as written by the Palace of Soviets jury, anything asymmetrical was "accidental" and manifested "unplannedness.") As I have written elsewhere, the cluster of three towers, in my view, certainly refers to the traditional three towers in the *pogost* or symbolic heart of the Russian village, and is but one of numerous appropriate historical references which Leonidov has subtly reworked into a new, highly contextual, synthesis. Low buildings around the site are addressed with low building, forming richly but simply resolved new urban spaces to north and south, as well as viewing terraces onto Red Square and its parades. The polychrome drum marking the Narkomtiazhprom workers' club refers to, but focally supercedes, the religious monument of St. Basil's. A crossroute from the heart of Kitaigorod focuses dramatically on the Lenin Mausoleum. Lissitzky was the only official commentator to concede that while Mel'nikov's scheme was merely "embarrassing," Leonidov's "series of sketches," with St. Basil's, the Kremlin river frontage, Red Square, and the Bol'shoi Theater, showed evidence of "trying to find a unity for the new complex."[166]

Leonidov's own accompanying notes indicated an entirely different level of thinking beyond this local resolution of the site. Here was a consideration of process: of the process of rebalancing that takes place when a massive new element enters a historically evolved context or "ensemble." "The role of some buildings within the central Moscow complex will change . . . with construction of a colossal new building." Leonidov's formal response to this was clear. The only possible "new instrument" in the delicate "symphony" which Red Square and the Kremlin create is one "that will lead the orchestra." The new composition must be founded not on "details . . . but on simplicity, severity, harmonious dynamism . . . on the principle of aesthetic contrast."[167]

As I noted in relation to Leonidov's Palace of Culture project, these schemes which recompose a whole landscape, be the landscape natural or man-made, need three-dimensional representations which embrace the whole canvas that is being conceived. Here a model of the complex alone cannot show how this new "instrument" sounds in the symphony. Nor can it show the subtlety of a synthesis of historical memory and new technology which was as far removed from the jury's (and, I suspect, his contemporaries') experience as was the technology it posited. Having now achieved the technology, and being ourselves confronted with these scaleless masses and *cases vides* in the matrix of historic cities, the subtlety and the method itself have something to say to us.

The method of problem resolution appropriate at that scale, as the Vesnins' and Ginzburg's failure here indicates, is not conventionally Constructivist. It requires a radicalism which the Constructivists themselves recognized, as editors of *Contemporary Architecture,* back in 1930. It depends on precisely that feature in Leonidov's work which overrides its shortcomings, as they said, to "make it in certain respects better and more valuable than the work of his competitors": "This is the fact that Leonidov speaks in his projects as an architect who is a social activist, who is a thinker, who does not slavishly execute the architectural task posed to him but socially redirects it, sometimes drawing up another program, introducing into it everything which from his point of view will help speed up the reconstruction of our daily life."[168] The "reconstruction" here was "onto socialist principles," but that is of no significance for the relevance of the method. The method which combines "simplicity" with "harmonious dynamism" at this scale is essentially Suprematist. The "forms" are "units of energy" in a perceptual space, in what Malevich called "the space inside the skull."[169]

As I have already observed, one valuable result of looking at Russian avant-garde architecture through competitions is the new light it throws on a traditionally OSA-centered view of the period. Mainstream Constructivists were very successful, and rightly so, as designers of immediately useful new buildings and building types, but these are contributions to their own time, not to the future. By looking more closely into the competitions, we see Asnova's capacity to produce formally and spatially very powerful buildings. But we also see their contribution to discussions of the larger architectural agenda. They in particular raised questions of the organizational means by which creative work can be most fruitfully fostered; of what "competition" means—mutual stimulus or mutual "defeat"— in creative fields; of its aim when formalized into a discrete event. Is it for consolidating and reinforcing established prototypes, or setting markers for the future?

Their answer to that was embodied in the concept of the two parallel prizes, for the "best answer to the task in the brief" and for the "extraordinary proposal." That distinction remains a very valuable clarifier of underlying architectural intentions. It also provides an answer to the argument against competitions raised by their Dutch contemporary J. J. P. Oud, in his time extensively published in *Contemporary Architecture*, who all his life refused to enter competitions as "hopelessly inadequate" for producing architecture. Twenty years after the Narkomtiazhprom contest, Oud wrote: "It is precisely the incessant to-and-fro between the wishes of the sponsor and the ideas of the architect which make building into a living embodiment of society's needs. It is in this respect that competitions are hopelessly inadequate; because of this permanent lack of contact they lead to a cut-out architecture . . . Because the contact between life and design is so minimal in competitions, it is best to use them sparingly."[170] The lesson of the 1920s is that "useful" results depend on clear thinking about intentions. As the contest of Iofan versus Leonidov continues, however, the paradigms established by "extraordinary proposals" remain important as clarifiers of architectural thought, long after their own time.

Notes

1. Peter Wilson, "Berlin—The Forum of Sand," in A. Papadakis, C. Cooke, and A. Benjamin, eds., *Deconstruction: Omnibus Volume* (New York: Rizzoli, 1989), p. 253.

2. Zaha Hadid, "The project for Kurfürstendamm 70, Berlin," and "The project for West Hollywood Civic Center," in Papadakis, Cooke, and Benjamin, *Deconstruction*, pp. 209, 219.

3. N. A. Smurova, "Organizatsiia konkursnogo dela v Rossii," in A. Strigalev, ed., *Problemy istorii sovetskoi arkhitektury. Sbornik*, Moscow, 1983, pp. 14–21; pp. 14–15, quoting material in the Central State Archive for Literature and Art, Moscow.

4. On the formation and early history, including competitions activity, of MAO, see *Istoricheskaia zapiska o deiatel'nosti Moskovskogo arkhitekturnogo obshchestva 1867–1897*, Moscow, 1897.

5. Bykovskii, speech in MAO, November 24, 1868, in *Ezhegodnik MAO* 5 (1928), p. 9, and *Istoricheskaia zapiska*, pp. 7–9.

6. *Zodchii* 1 (1872), pp. 4–7 surveys the formation and early origins of POA.

7. Advertisement in *Zodchii* 1 (1872), p. 65; 3 (1872), p. 166; and 5 (1872), p. 79.

8. Smurova, "Organizatsiia," p. 14.

9. M. Arnol'd, "K voprosu o konkursakh," *Zodchii* 6 (1872), pp. 80–84 gives these regulations in full (p. 84).

10. *Istoricheskaia zapiska*, p. 6.

11. M. Arnol'd, "K voprosu o konkursakh," *Zodchii* 4 (1872), pp. 60–63, and editors' note, p. 60.

12. "Ustav i dopolnitel'nie k nemu pravila POA," *Zodchii* 6 (1872), pp. 99–100, para. 28 "O konkursakh."

13. M. Arnol'd, "K voprosu o konkursakh," *Zodchii* 5 (1872), pp. 65–68.

14. Arnol'd, "K voprosu," *Zodchii* 6 (1872), pp. 80–84.

15. Within months, POA already had 126 architect members (*Zodchii* 1 [1872], p. 7) and it continued to rise, whereas MAO membership quickly leveled off around 50 actual architects (*Istoricheskaia zapiska*, pp. 7, 11, 20, etc.), and they were constantly short of resources for their public ventures.

16. On the earliest MAO competitions, see *Istoricheskaia zapiska*, pp. 10–16. Early POA competitions are recorded in *Zodchii*.

17. *Istoricheskaia zapiska*, pp. 22–28.

18. "Chto takoe nashi konkursy?," *Zodchii* 7–8 (1875), pp. 83–86. Historical Museum announced in *Zodchii* 1 (1875), p. 12. On the Polytechnical Museum, see "Po povodu konkursa na proekt fasada Muzeiia v Moskve," *Zodchii* 6 (1875), pp. 32, 46, and 70.

19. *Pravila dlia arkhitekturnykh konkursov, utverzhdennykh S-Peterburgskim obshchestvom arkhitektorov dlia svoego rukovodstva, v sobraniakh 14 dek. 1882, 11 ianv. 1883 i 28 marta 1895*, St. Petersburg, 1896. For summary, see Smurova, "Organizatsiia," pp. 16–17.

20. A. V. Rozenberg, "Sovremennaia praktika konkursnogo dela," *Stroitel'naia promyshlennost'* 8 (1926), pp. 564–66.

21. "Konkurs na proekt zdanii vysochaishi utverzhdennogo Obshchestva verkhnikh torgovykh riadov na Krasnoi ploshchadi v Moskve," *Nedelia stroitelia* 44 (1888), p. 228.

22. On Moscow venture, see *Istoricheskie zapiski MAO*, pp. 66–67; St. Petersburg competition noted in William Craft Brumfield, *The Origins of Modernism in Russian Architecture* (Berkeley: University of California Press, 1991), p. 302 n. 2, from *Stroitel'* 9–10 (1897), pp. 321–54.

23. "Pravila konkursov MAO," *Nedelia stroitelia* 4 (1899), p. 29. For summary, see Smurova, "Organizatsiia," p. 19.

24. For notes on the Hotel Metropol' saga in English, see Brumfield, *Origins of Modernism*, pp. 85, 87.

25. Brumfield, *Origins of Modernism*, discusses housing and some other building types.

26. Announcements, juries, and results can be found in *Zodchii, Nedelia stroitelia*, and in the *Ezhegodnik* of the architectural societies OAKh and MAO; grievances about the system are frequently under discussion in *Zodchii*, particularly from 1904–5 onward.

27. OAKh's loose flyers distributed in *Zodchii*, for example, with 4 (1914) for Tashkent City Summer Theater. In bound volumes these have usually been lost, but they may still sometimes be found in loose issues.

28. I. A. Kazus, "Arkhitekturnye konkursy 1917–1933 godov. Opyt sravnitel'nogo statisticheskogo analiza," in A. Strigalev, ed., *Problemy istorii sovetskoi arkhitektury. Sbornik,* Moscow, 1980, pp. 5–15; graphs p. 11.

29. "Konkursy," *Oglavlenie zhurnala Zodchii za 1913 god,* pp. vii–viii.

30. "Konkursnye proekty," *Oglavlenie zhurnala Zodchii za 1913 god,* p. iv.

31. *Ezhegodnik Imperatorskogo obshchestva arkhitektorov-khudozhnikov* 9 (1914), p. 3.

32. *Ezhegodnik Moskovskogo arkhitekturnogo obshchestva* 1 (1909).

33. P. Antipov, "K voprosu organizatsii arkhitekturnykh konkursov," *Stroitel'naia promyshlennost'* 12 (1926), pp. 885–87.

34. Lecture of A. Tamanian to Fifth Congress of Russian Architects, "Proekt pravila dlia konkursov, ob"iavliaemykh arkhitekturnymi obshchestvennymi organizatsiiami," *Zodchii* 3 (1914).

35. I. Mashkov, "Moskovskoe arkhitekturnoe obshchestvo 1867–1927gg," *Ezhegodnik MAO* 5 (1928), pp. 9–14.

36. Ibid., p. 12.

37. "Dekret o zemle," *Izvestiia*, October 28, 1917, p. 1.

38. I. A. Kazus, "Organizatsiia konkursnogo proektirovaniia v sovetskoi arkhitekture (diskussii i praktika)," in Strigalev, *Problemy istorii,* 1983, pp.21–34; p.23, from sources in the Central State Archive for Literature and Art, Moscow.

39. Ibid., p. 23, from sources in TsGANKh.

40. V. I. Lenin, "Kak organizovat' sorevnovanie?," December 1917, in his *Polnoe sobranie sochineniia,* 5th ed., Moscow, 1962, vol. 35, pp. 195–96.

41. Documents in V. Khazanova, comp., *Iz istorii sovetskoi arkhitektury 1917–1925. Dokumenty i materialy* (Moscow: Nauka, 1963) and I. Kazus, "Pervye arkhitekturno-proektnye masterskie sovetskoi Rossii," in *Problemy teorii i istorii arkhitektury. Sbornik,* Moscow, 1973, pp. 65–71; pp. 65–66.

42. For documents on these competitions, see Khazanova, *Iz istorii sovetskoi arkhitektury 1917–1925,* pp. 134–38 (from *Iskusstvo kommuny* 7 [January 19, 1919], *Zhizn' iskusstva,*

May 10–11, 1919, etc.) and p. 214; V. Khazanova, *Sovetskaia arkhitektura pervykh let Oktiabria,* Moscow, 1970, p. 122 (from Norvert in *Khudozhestvennaia zhizn'* 1 [1919]); and Khazanova, *Iz istorii sovetskoi arkhitektury 1917–1925,* pp. 214–17.

43. These results from Khazanova, *Iz istorii sovetskoi arkhitektury 1917–1925,* pp. 138, 217.

44. On Sinskul'ptarkh, etc., see Selim O. Khan-Magomedov, *Pioneers of Soviet Architecture: The Search for New Solutions in the 1920s and 1930s,* ed. Catherine Cooke, trans. Alexander Lieven (London: Thames and Hudson, 1987), pp. 67–69.

45. S. O. Khan-Magomedov, "Diskussiia v Inkhuke o sootnoshenii konstruktsii i kompozitsii (ianv.–apr. 1921 goda)," in *Tekhnicheskaia estetika,* Trudy VNIITE, sbornik no. 20 (Moscow: VNIITE, 1979) pp. 40–78. For verbatim transcripts of part of the discussion, see Selim O. Khan-Magomedov, *Rodchenko: The Complete Work,* ed. Vieri Quilici, trans. Huw Evans (London: Thames and Hudson, 1986), pp. 83–89; for Inkhuk portfolio, see Angelica Zander Rudenstine, ed., *Russian Avant-Garde Art: The George Costakis Collection* (London: Thames and Hudson, 1981), pp. 110–27.

46. For discussion of the key ideas of Rationalism and Constructivism, with buildings and translated documents, see C. Cooke and J. Ageros, eds., *The Avant-Garde: Russian Architecture in the Twenties,* London and New York, 1991; on the development of Constructivist ideas, see also C. Cooke, "Form is a function, X," in Cooke, ed., *Russian Avant-Garde Art and Architecture* (New York: St. Martin's Press, 1983), pp. 34–49, enlarged in Papadakis, Cooke, and Benjamin, *Deconstruction,* pp. 21–37. For an account of this whole period which complements the present study by focus on theoretical and stylistic positions of leading figures, see Catherine Cooke, "Images in Context," in *Architectural Drawings of the Russian Avant-Garde* (New York: The Museum of Modern Art, 1990), pp. 10–48.

47. For details on dates of re-formation, membership, etc., see V. Khazanova, comp., *Iz istorii sovetskoi arkhitektury 1926–1932. Dokumenty i materialy* (Moscow: Nauka, 1970), pp. 7–9 (MAO), 26–27 (POA and OAKh). On MAO, see Mashkov, "Moskovskoe," p. 13; P. Antipov, "Khronika," *Arkhitektura* 1–2 (1923), pp. 47–49.

48. Antipov, "Khronika," pp. 47–49.

49. Ibid.

50. Brief, etc., in Khazanova, *Iz istorii sovetskoi arkhitektury 1917–1925,* pp. 51–55; projects and review, in *Arkhitektura* 3–4 (1923), pp. 34–45; second stage, in Antipov, "Khronika," pp. 68–69.

51. Brief, site plan, and longer extract from Kirov's speech, in Khazanova, *Iz istorii sovetskoi arkhitektury 1917–1925,* pp. 146–49. Competition announced in September 1922, closed February 5, 1923.

52. Khazanova, *Iz istorii sovetskoi arkhitektury 1917–1925,* p.151n, reprinted from *LEF* 4 (1924), pp. 59–62.

53. M. Ia. Ginzburg, "Itogi i perspektivy," *Sovremennaia arkhitektura* 4–5 (1927), pp. 112–18.

54. Khazanova, *Iz istorii sovetskoi arkhitektury 1926–1932,* p. 40 gives essentials; see also Kazus, "Organizatsiia," p. 25 on further protest over brief.

55. Antipov, "Khronika."

56. Report on Norvert lecture of May 2, 1923, in Antipov, "Khronika."

57. Kazus, "Organizatsiia," pp. 25, 33 n. 19, from sources in the Central State Archive for Literature and Art, Moscow. On student involvement, see Khazanova, *Iz istorii sovetskoi arkhitektury 1926–1932,* p. 58, and I. Kokkinaki, "Gradostroitel'nyi proekt . . . 1-i etap proektirovaniia Krasnogo stadiona," in A. Strigalev, ed., *Problemy istorii sovetskoi arkhitektury. Sbornik,* Moscow, 1985, pp. 68–79.

58. Khazanova, *Iz istorii sovetskoi arkhitektury 1926–1932,* p. 8; A. Rozhanovich, "K voprosu ob organizatsii konkursnogo dela," *Stroitel'naia promyshlennost'* 2 (1926), p. 139.

59. On Ginzburg's early career, see Anatole Senkevitch, introduction to Moisei Ginzburg, *Style and Epoch,* trans. Anatole Senkevitch (Cambridge, Mass.: MIT Press, 1982).

60. "Estetika sovremennosti," *Arkhitektura* 1–2 (1923), pp. 3–6; "Staroe i novoe," *Arkhitektura* 3–4 (1923), p. 3.

61. Khazanova, *Iz istorii sovetskoi arkhitektury 1926–1932,* pp. 39–40; Khan-Magomedov, *Pioneers,* pp. 141–42.

62. For English translation, see Ginzburg, *Style and Epoch.*

63. Photographs of completed House of Soviets, Briansk, in *Ezhegodnik MAO* 5 (1928), pp. 41–43.

64. Arkos project published in *Sovremennaia arkhitektura* 1 (1926), pp. 5, 7–8.

65. On the *narodnyi dom* in Ivanovo, see Khazanova, *Sovetskaia arkhitektura pervykh let,* pp. 132–34; A. G. Barkhina, *G. B. Barkhin* (Moscow: Stroi-izdat, 1981), pp. 40–41, which also gives prize list; fully published in *Konkursy MAO 1923–1926,* Moscow, 1927, pp. 5–16.

66. N. Sheviakov, "K voprosu ob ispol'zovanii rezul'tatov arkhitekturnykh konkursov," *Stroitel'naia promyshlennost'* 5 (1924), p. 360.

67. Notes by Kazus, in C. Cooke and I. Kazus, *Soviet Architectural Competitions, 1920s–1930s,* London, 1992, p. 19. On prize money, see A. Strigalev and I. Kokkinaki, eds., *K. S. Mel'nikov* (Moscow: Iskusstvo, 1985), p. 262 n. 31.

68. Elevations, plans, section, and perspective published in *Sovremennaia arkhitektura* 1 (1926), pp. 1–3.

69. S. O. Khan-Magomedov, *Il'ia Golosov* (Moscow: Stroi-izdat, 1988), p. 114, from material in the Central State Archive for Literature and Art, Moscow; four elevations, p. 115.

70. Strigalev and Kokkinaki, *Mel'nikov,* p. 158; also incompletely in M. G. Barkhin, ed., *Mastera sovetskoi arkhitektury ob arkhitekture* (Moscow: Iskusstvo, 1975), vol. 2, p. 163.

71. Vesnin project notes, *Sovremennaia arkhitektura* 1 (1926), p. 1.

72. A. L. Pasternak, "Amerika," *Sovremennaia arkhitektura* 4 (1926), pp. 92–93.

73. Telegrams published in M. Astaf'eva-Dlugach, "K istorii sooruzheniia pervykh sovetskikh vystavochnykh pavilionov," in V. A. Tikhanov, ed., *Voprosy sovetskogo izobrazitel'nogo iskusstva i arkhitektury,* Moscow, 1973, pp. 391–407. Allocation of tasks, etc., from documents in Khazanova, *Iz istorii sovetskoi arkhihtektury 1917–1925,* p. 190.

74. Kazus, "Organizatsiia," pp. 25, 33 n. 21.

75. Full brief published in Astaf'eva-Dlugach, "K istorii," pp. 401–2.

76. Minutes of meeting of exhibition committee, December 28, 1924, in Astaf'eva-Dlugach, "K istorii," pp. 402–3. Some other material, including Fomin text, in Khazanova, *Iz istorii sovetskoi arkhitektury 1917–1925,* pp. 187–88, 190.

77. On details of building and Western responses, see S. Frederick Starr, *K. Melnikov. Le Pavillon sovietique Paris 1925,* Paris, 1981. On role of Rodchenko, builders, etc., see Jean-Louis Cohen, "Il padiglione di Melnikov a Parigi: Una seconda riconstruzione," *Casabella,* November 1986, pp. 40–51.

78. Kazus, "Arkhitekturnye konkursy," p. 11.

79. On permanent Lenin Mausoleum, see Khazanova, *Iz istorii sovetskoi arkhitektury 1917–1925,* pp. 227–29.

80. Alfred H. Barr, Jr., "Russian Diary" (of a trip in the winter of 1927–28), in I. Sandler and A. Newman, eds., *Defining Modern Art: Selected Writings of Alfred H. Barr, Jr.* (New York: Abrams, 1986), p. 116. In this entry, Barr calls it the "trade union building."

81. Velikovskii housing of 1925, see *Ezhegodnik MAO* 5 (1928), p. 26.

82. B. Velikovskii, "Arkhitekturnye konkursy v zhilstroitel'stve," *Stroitel'naia promyshlennost'* 1 (1925), pp. 3–4.

83. Competition briefs in Khazanova, *Iz istorii sovetskoi arkhitektury 1917–1925,* pp. 61–64.

84. An accessible source of many such projects is Khan-Magomedov, *Pioneers.*

85. Kazus, "Arkhitekturnye konkursy," p. 9.

86. Mendelsohn's defense, "Pis'mo Erika Mendel'sona," *Sovremennaia arkhitektura* 3 (1927), p. 108, gives full chronology of events and work done.

87. "O privlechenii inostrannykh spetsialistov k stroitel'stvu SSSR," *Stroitel'naia promyshlennost'* 12 (1925), pp. 822–23.

88. "Pis'mo Erika Mendel'sona."

89. On the formation of OSA, see Khazanova, *Iz istorii sovetskoi arkhitektury 1926–1932,* pp. 65–68.

90. A. V. Rozenberg, "Osnovnye polozheniia organizatsii konkursov v sovremennykh usloviiakh," and introductory note, A. Rozhanovich, "K voprosu ob organizatsii konkursnogo dela," *Stroitel'naia promyshlennost'* 2 (1926), pp. 139–43.

91. Ia. A. Kornfel'd, "Arkhitektura na pervom s"ezde po grazhdanskomu i inzhenernomu stroitel'stvu," *Sovremennaia arkhitektura* 2 (1926), p. 58.

92. *Trudy Pervogo vsesoiuznogo s"ezda po grazhdanskomu i inzhenernomu stroitel'stvu,* Moscow, 1928; some of this particular discussion is summarized in Kazus, "Organizatsiia," p. 28.

93. "V zashchitu konkurentov," *Izvestiia ASNOVA* 1 (1926), n. pag.

94. Full prize list in "Nedavnye konkursy," *Stroitel'naia promyshlennost'* 2 (1926), pp. 143–44, and *Konkursy MAO 1923–1926.*

95. "K konkursu Doma tekstilei," *Sovremennaia arkhitektura* 1 (1926), p. 12. Contents of building also in Khazanova, *Iz istorii sovetskoi arkhitektury 1926–1932,* p. 38.

96. "Khronika. K predstoiashchemu ukrasheniiu Moskvy," *Sovremennaia arkhitektura* 1 (1926), p. 16.

97. "Sobesedovanie v VOKSe," *Sovremennaia arkhitektura* 2 (1926), pp. 60–62.

98. Reported in Kazus, "Organizatsiia," p. 29, from *Stroitel'naia pro.myshlennost'* 6–7 (1926).

99. A. V. Rozenberg, "Sovremennaia praktika."

100. P. Antipov, "K voprosu organizatsii"; the forthcoming volume was *Konkursy MAO 1923–1926.*

101. "Tovarishcheskoe sorevnovanie OSA," *Sovremennaia arkhitektura* 4 (1926), p. ii; 4–5 (1927), p. 158. The jury was the "OSA collective," i.e., all members together; for another on communal housing, see *Sovremennaia arkhitektura* 4 (1929), pp. 121–22.

102. On their method of work, housing research, and the link to prerevolutionary theory, see Cooke, "Form is a function, X"; Irina Kokkinaki, "The first exhibition of modern architecture in Moscow," *Architectural Design* 5–6 (1983), pp. 50–59; and C. Cooke, "Roots of a method: pre-Revolutionary architectural thought," *A&V: Monografias de arquitectura y vivienda* 29 (1991).

103. V. Lavrov, "Uchastie ASNOVA v zhilishchnom stroitel'stve Mossoveta," *Stroitel'stvo Moskvy* 1 (1928), pp. 14–17.

104. Kazus, "Arkhitekturnye konkursy," p. 11.

105. Ginzburg project published in *Sovremennaia arkhitektura* 4–5 (1927), pp. 113, 115; fully illustrated in Anatole Kopp, *Constructivist Architecture in the USSR* (New York: St. Martin's Press, 1985), pp. 88–89. Zholtovskii project published in *Ezhegodnik MAO* 5 (1928), pp. 51–52, and ridiculed by OSA in "Nasha deistvitel'nost'," *Sovremennaia arkhitektura* 2 (1927), pp. 47–50.

106. Ginzburg's Alma-Ata project in *Sovremennaia arkhitektura* 3 (1928), pp. 75–77 and *Ezhegodnik MAO* 6 (1930), pp. 130–31. Numerous drawings also in Kopp, *Constructivist Architecture,* pp. 90–91. Ginzburg's Orgametal scheme in *Sovremennaia arkhitektura* 2 (1927), pp. 62–63.

107. Golosov Elektrobank housing block in *Sovremennaia arkhitektura* 2 (1926), p. 59.

108. "Steklo v sovremennoi arkhitekture," *Sovremennaia arkhitektura* 3 (1926), pp. 63–64.

109. Panteleimon Golosov projects in *Ezhegodnik MAO* 5 (1928), pp. 102–3 (Khar'kov), 116 (Sovkino).

110. Quoted from *Izvestiia* and Party decisions in Kazus, "Arkhitekturnye konkursy," p. 9.

111. Chernikhov Red Nailer factory project in *Ezhegodnik OAKh* 13 (1930), p. 134.

112. "Nasha deistvitel'nost'," pp. 47–50, and "Anketa o ploskoi kryshe," *Sovremennaia arkhitektura* 4 (1926), pp. 98–103.

113. Leonidov's Alma-Ata project in *Ezhegodnik MAO* 6 (1930), pp.134–35; *Sovremennaia arkhitektura* 2 (1928), pp.63–65, and in Andrei Gozak and Andrei Leonidov, *Ivan Leonidov: The Complete Works* (New York: Rizzoli, 1988), pp. 53–55.

114. Leonidov's Sovkino in *Sovremennaia arkhitektura* 1 (1928), pp. 5–8, and Gozak and Leonidov, *Leonidov,* pp. 50–52.

115. On early history, see Kazus, in Cooke and Kazus, *Soviet Architectural Competitions,* p. 23. Pashkov's project in *Sovremennaia arkhitektura* 6 (1927), p. 185.

116. Leonidov project in *Sovremennaia arkhitektura* 4–5 (1927), pp. 119–24, and Gozak and Leonidov, *Leonidov,* pp. 42–49.

117. On this exhibition, see Kokkinaki, "The first exhibition."

118. For typical critique in *Stroitel'naia promyshlennost',* see Gozak and Leonidov, *Leonidov,* p. 42.

119. Ginzburg, "Itogi i perspektivy," partially translated in ozak and Leonidov, *Leonidov,* p. 42.

120. Markov preliminary project published in *Ezhegodnik MAO* 5 (1928), pp. 70–71. Details of the competition from note by Kazus, from archives, in Cooke and Kazus, *Soviet Architectural Competitions,* p. 23.

121. Certain projects in *Ezhegodnik MAO* 6 (1930); for others, in color and with discussion of stages of redesign, see Cooke, in Cooke and Kazus, *Soviet Architectural Competitions,* pp. 14–15.

122. Kazus, archival notes, in Cooke and Kazus, *Soviet Architectural Competitions.*

123. Jean-Louis Cohen, *Le Corbusier et la mystique de l'URSS: Théories et projets pour Moscou* (Paris: Pierre Mardaga, 1987), with full bibliography of Russian sources. See also archival notes by Kazus, in Cooke and Kazus, *Soviet Architectural Competitions,* and Gozak and Leonidov, *Leonidov,* pp. 56–57.

124. Editorial preface to G. Barkhin, "K voprosu ob arkhitekturnykh konkursakh (v diskussionom poriadke)," *Stroitel'naia promyshlennost'* 4 (1928), p. 304.

125. Barkhin, "K voprosu ob arkhitekturnykh konkursakh," pp. 304–6.

126. Full text of draft *polozhenie* and Vesnin letter, from archival materials in the Central State Archive for Literature and Art, Moscow, published in Khazanova, *Iz istorii sovetskoi arkhitektury 1926–1932,* pp. 22–25.

127. On competition, see Kazus, "Organizatsiia," p. 30 (no references given); Milinis project illustrated in Khan-Magomedov, *Pioneers,* fig. 1336.

128. Archival material on Stroikom STO and MOVANO, from the Central State Archive for Literature and Art, Moscow, in Kazus, "Organizatsiia," p. 31.

129. Decree of Sovnarkom SSSR, June 1, 1928, "O merakh k uporiadocheniiu kapital'nogo stroitel'stva promyshlennosti i elektrostroitel'stva"; Decree of VSNKh SSSR, January 13, 1929, "Organizatsiia izyskatelskikh i proektirovochnykh rabot v prommyshlennom stroitel'stve."

130. "Protest," *Sovremennaia arkhitektura* 3 (1929), inside front cover.

131. "Sozdadim federatsiiu revoliutsionnykh arkhitektorov," *Sovremennaia arkhitektura* 3 (1929), p. 89.

132. Decree of Sovnarkom SSSR, December 26, 1929, "O merakh k ozdorovleniiu stroitel'stva," *Pravda,* December 29, 1929.

133. N. Dokuchaev, "Konkurs na Dom promyshlennosti," *Stroitel'stvo Moskvy* 3 (1930), pp. 31–33.

134. Leonidov's project and description in *Sovremennaia arkhitektura* 4 (1930), pp. 1–2, and Gozak and Leonidov, *Leonidov,* p. 69.

135. Extracts from brief in Dokuchaev, "Konkurs," p. 31.

136. Jury comments published in *Stroitel'stvo Moskvy* 8–9 (1930), p. 24.

137. Leonidov's project and description in *Sovremennaia arkhitektura* 1 (1930), pp. 1–6, and Gozak and Leonidov, *Leonidov,* pp. 72–76.

138. A. Karra and V. Simbirtsev, "Forpost proletarskoi kul'tury," *Stroitel'stvo Moskvy* 8–9 (1930), p. 22; partial English translation in Gozak and Leonidov, *Leonidov,* p. 77.

139. G. Krutikov, "Voprosy prostranstvennoi organizatsii kul'turnogo kombinata," *Stroitel'naia promyshlennost'* 10 (1930), p. 794; partial English translation in Gozak and Leonidov, *Leonidov,* p. 77.

140. Illustrated in *Stroitel'stvo Moskvy* 1–2 (1931), p. 29, and Gozak and Leonidov, *Leonidov,* p. 78.

141. Lissitzky's model and drawing are illustrated in Khan-Magomedov, *Pioneers,* figs. 1145–46.

142. From Decree (*Postanovlenie*) of the Construction Council on Launching the Competition for a Palace of Soviets Design, quoted in *Biulleten' Upravleniia stroitel'stvom Dvortsa sovetov pri prezidiume TsIK SSSR* 1 (September 1931), p. 3 (hereafter cited as *Biulleten'*).

143. "Delo vsekh tvorcheskikh sil sovetskoi obshchestvennosti," *Biulleten'* 1 (September 1931), p. 5, and "Utochnennoe zadanie," *Biulleten'* 1 (September 1931), p. 7.

144. *Biulleten'* 1 (September 1931), p. 16.

145. Competition announced in *Izvestiia,* July 13, 1931. Brief published in *Stroitel'stvo Moskvy* 7 (1931), pp. 8–10 under heading "Vse na konkurs." In *Biulleten'* 1 (September 1931), submission deadline extended from October 20th to December 1st, and modifications to brief published that "take into account lessons of the preliminary design stage," ibid., p. 2.

146. *Biulleten'* 1 (September 1931), p. 16, and *Biulleten'* 2–3 (October 1931), p. 56.

147. *Biulleten'* 2–3 (October 1931), p. 56.

148. "Pervye proekty Dvortsa sovetov," *Stroitel'stvo Moskvy* 8 (1931), pp. 2–7. They were more systematically presented in *Biulleten'* 1 (September 1931), where p. 2 gives dates for the final exhibitions, etc. *Biulleten'* 2–3 (October 1931), p. 56 gives reports on preliminary exhibitions. One of the biggest public discussions, on November 18, 1931, was held in the AMO factory, for which the Proletarskii district Palace of Culture was being built; reported in *Stroitel'stvo Moskvy* 11 (1931), pp. 4–5.

149. *Biulleten'* 1 (September 1931), on jury see p. 16; on time off, see p. 12. Later jury members were named, though Cohen, *Le Corbusier,* p. 228, gives different names from those supplied from archives by Kazus, in Cooke and Kazus, *Soviet Architectural Competitions,* p. 59.

150. Cooke, "Images in Context," pp. 25–28, 40, and in more detail in C. Cooke, "The theory and practice of Socialist Realism in Soviet architecture," in B. Taylor and M. Cullern Bown, eds., *The Art of the Soviets,* forthcoming.

151. *Biulleten'* 1 (September 1931), pp. 5, 7; on marbles, etc., see *Biulleten'* 2–3 (October 1931), p. 56.

152. Jean-Louis Cohen, *Le Corbusier and the Mystique of the USSR: Theories and Projects for Moscow, 1928–1936,* Princeton, 1992, p. 169.

153. *Biulleten'* 2–3 (October 1931), pp. 6–8 (Beseda, etc.), 28–30 (Ladovskii), 33–35 (Nikol'skii), 42–45 (Shchusev), 39–41 (Fidman), 13–15 (Pavlov and Kuznetsov).

154. G. B. Barkhin, "Inostrannye arkhitektory na konkurse Dvortsa sovetov," in *Dvorets sovetov. Vsesoiuznyi konkurs 1932g* (Moscow: Union of Soviet Architects, 1932), pp. 83–84. For foreign entries, see *Architectural Review,* May 1932, pp. 196–200.

155. Cohen, *Le Corbusier,* p. 198 (from documents in the Fondation Le Corbusier, Paris), attributes Hamilton's success to "intrigues of Albert Kahn," who was building Soviet factories. The best American source on Hamilton, etc., is "Soviet Palace Competition," *Architectural Forum,* March 1932, pp. A–D.

156. On this, see Cohen, *Le Corbusier,* pp. 188–95.

157. Letters of March 1932, CIRPAC in Barcelona to Stalin, and April 1932, CIAM officers to Stalin, in CIAM Archives, ETH-Zurich.

158. Decree of TsK VKP(b), April 23, 1932, "O perestroike literaturno-khudozhestvennykh organizatsii," *Pravda,* April 24, 1932; reproduced in Khazanova, *Iz istorii sovetskoi arkhitektury 1926–1932,* p. 163; in English in C. Vaughan James, *Soviet Socialist Realism: Origins and Theory* (London: Macmillan, 1973), p. 120. Notice, "Soiuz sovetskikh arkhitektorov," *Izvestiia,* July 18, 1932, in Khazanova, *Iz istorii sovetskoi akhitektury 1926–1932,* p. 163.

159. Cooke, "Theory and practice of Socialist Realism."

160. Brief outlined in D. Aranovich, "Arkhitekturnaia rekonstruktsiia tsentra Moskvy. Konkurs proektov doma Narkomtiazhproma," *Stroitel'stvo Moskvy* 10 (1934), pp. 20–29; further details by Kazus from archival sources, in Cooke and Kazus, *Soviet Architectural Competitions,* p. 85.

161. Aranovich, "Arkhitekturnaia rekonstruktsiia," pp. 20–21.

162. Ginzburg, "Itogi i perspektivy."

163. Aranovich, "Arkhitekturnaia rekonstruktsiia," p. 23.

164. Editorial introduction to publication of Narkomtiazhprom projects in *Arkhitektura SSSR* 10 (1934), pp. 4–5; partial English translation in Gozak and Leonidov, *Leonidov,* p. 115.

165. Jury quoted in Aranovich, "Arkhitekturnaia rekonstruktsiia," p. 28.

166. Catherine Cooke, "Ivan Leonidov: Vision and Historicism," *Architectural Design* 6 (1986), pp. 12–21; Cooke, "Images in Context," pp. 42–45. L. Lisitskii [El Lissitzky], "Forum sotsialisticheskoi Moskvy," *Arkhitektura SSSR* 10 (1934), pp. 4–5.

167. Leonidov's description from *Arkhitektura SSSR* 10 (1934), pp. 14–15; in English in Gozak and Leonidov, *Leonidov,* p. 75.

168. "Ot redaktsii," *Sovremennaia arkhitektura* 5 (1930), pp. 2–3; English translation in Gozak and Leonidov, *Leonidov,* p. 75.

169. "Having established the specific features of the Suprematist system, I charge the young architects, in the broadest sense, with the further development of a specifically architectural Suprematism . . . I myself have entered a remote and for me new realm of thought; as best I can I give an account of what I perceive in the infinite space of the human skull." Kazimir Malevich, *Suprematizm. 34 risunka* (Vitebsk: Unovis, 1920), as translated in K. S. Malevich, *Essays on Art, 1915–1933,* ed. Troels Andersen, trans. Xenia Glowacki-Prus and Arnold McMillin (Copenhagen: Borgen, 1969), vol. 1, p. 126. On Suprematism as "units of energy," see C. Cooke, "Malevich: from theory into teaching," in A. Papadakis, ed., *Malevich,* London, 1989, pp. 6–27, especially pp. 11, 14, 17–19.

170. J. J. P. Oud, from unspecified text of 1954, quoted in H. de Haan and I. Haagsma, *Architects in Competition,* New York, 1988, p. 18.

Index of Artists and Works

Plate numbers are indicated after each work.

Decorative design on a dark-red background, *1924–26.*
State Tret'iakov Gallery, Moscow.
335

Non-Objective, *1920s.*
State Lunacharskii Museum of Fine Arts, Krasnodar.
330

Vasilii Ermilov
Composition No. 3, *1923.*
The Museum of Modern Art, New York. The Riklis Collection of McCrory Corporation (fractional gift), 1983.
88

Relief, *1924.*
Galerie Dr. István Schlégl, Zurich.
122

Composition, *early 1920s.*
Collection L. Zhadova Family, Moscow.
87

Exhibition project, Kanatka, 1928.
Museum Ludwig (Collection Ludwig, Cologne).
121

Vera Ermolaeva
Set design for Aleksei Kruchenykh,
Victory over the Sun, *Vitebsk, 1920.*
Private collection, Germany.
152

Suprematist Construction, *sketch for festive decoration of Vitebsk, 1920.*
State Russian Museum, St. Petersburg.
127

Suprematist Construction, *sketch for festive decoration of Vitebsk, 1920.*
State Russian Museum, St. Petersburg.
128

Suprematist Construction, *sketch for festive decoration of Vitebsk, 1920.*
State Russian Museum, St. Petersburg.
129

Woman with Child, *1933.*
State Russian Museum, St. Petersburg.
406

Woman with Rake and Child, *1933.*
State Russian Museum, St. Petersburg.
405

Vladimir Fidman
Architectural Fantasy No. 9; *elevations, 1919.*
State Tret'iakov Gallery, Moscow.
662

Architectural Fantasy No. 6; *plan and perspective sketches, 1919.*
State Tret'iakov Gallery, Moscow.
660

Pavel Filonov
White Painting, *1919.*
State Russian Museum, St. Petersburg.
340

Formula of the Petrograd Proletariat, *1920–21.*
State Russian Museum, St. Petersburg.
342

Untitled, *1923.*
State Russian Museum, St. Petersburg.
341

Man in the World, *1925.*
State Russian Museum, St. Petersburg.
343

Naum Gabo
Constructed Head No. 2, *1916.*
Collection Nina Williams, England.
300

Study for an Outdoor Construction, *1917.*
Galerie de France, Paris.
304

Study for a Tower, *1917.*
Berlinische Galerie, Museum für moderne Kunst, Photographie und Architektur, Berlin.
305

Maquette for Constructed Torso, 1917–18, reassembled 1985.
Berlinische Galerie, Museum für moderne Kunst, Photographie und Architektur, Berlin.
301

Design for a Construction, *1918.*
Collection Nina Williams, England.
303

Study for a Square in Moscow, *1919.*
Collection Thomas P. Whitney.
306

Column, *ca. 1923, reconstruction 1937 by the artist.*
Solomon R. Guggenheim Museum, New York.
307

Naum Gabo and Antoine Pevsner
Competition project for the Palace of Soviets, Moscow; plan and section, July–December 1931.
State Shchusev Museum, Moscow.
720

Competition project for the Palace of Soviets, Moscow; section and main elevation, July–December 1931.
State Shchusev Museum, Moscow.
719

Aleksei Gan
Cover for his Long Live the Demonstration of Everyday Life!, *ca. 1923.*
Collection Helix Art Center, San Diego.
500

Poster, First Exhibition of Contemporary Architecture, 1927.
Collection Merrill C. Berman.
418

Ivan Gavris
Violin (Cubism), *1920.*
State Lunacharskii Museum of Fine Arts, Krasnodar.
203

Moisei Ginzburg, Gustav Hassenpflug, and Solomon Lisagor
Competition project for the Palace of Soviets, Moscow; axonometric and perspective, March–July 1932.
State Shchusev Museum, Moscow.
723

Competition project for the Palace of Soviets, Moscow; situational plan, axonometric, March–July 1932.
State Shchusev Museum, Moscow.
724

Il'ia Golosov
Competition project for the Lenin House of the People, Ivanovo-Voznesensk; elevation, 1924.
State Shchusev Museum, Moscow.
699

Competition project for the Moscow bureau of Leningrad Pravda; axonometric section, 1924.
State Shchusev Museum, Moscow.
685

Competition project for the Russian pavilion, Exposition internationale des arts décoratifs et industriels modernes, Paris; elevations, 1924.
State Shchusev Museum, Moscow.
697

Competition project for the Elektrobank building, Moscow; perspective, 1926.
State Shchusev Museum, Moscow.
700

Panteleimon Golosov
Competition project for the Pravda *printing plant and publishing center, Moscow (variant); perspective, 1930–35.*
State Shchusev Museum, Moscow.
713

Georgii Iakulov
Set design for Charles Lecocq, Giroflé-Girofla, *Kamernyi Theater, Moscow, 1922.*
State Bakhrushin Museum, Moscow.
622

Boris Ignatovich
Brass Band of the Dynamo Factory, *1926.*
Galerie Alex Lachmann, Cologne.
460

Demonstration, *1927.*
Galerie Alex Lachmann, Cologne.
459

In the Harbor of Leningrad, *1929.*
Galerie Alex Lachmann, Cologne.
463

Mechanical Piling of Wood in the Harbor of Leningrad, *1929.*
Galerie Alex Lachmann, Cologne.
465

The Hermitage, Leningrad, *1929.*
Galerie Alex Lachmann, Cologne.
461

Factory, *1931.*
Galerie Alex Lachmann, Cologne.
466

Smokestacks and Factories of an Industrial Plant in Leningrad, *1931.*
Galerie Alex Lachmann, Cologne.
467

Karl Ioganson
Composition, *1921.*
Art Co. Ltd. (Collection George Costakis).
248

Construction, *1921.*
Art Co. Ltd. (Collection George Costakis).
249

Nikolai Istselenov
Architectural Fantasy No. 2; *elevation and perspective, 1919.*
State Tret'iakov Gallery, Moscow.
663

Architectural Fantasy No. 2; *general plan and elevation, 1919.*
State Tret'iakov Gallery, Moscow.
661

Lev Iudin
Composition, *1920–21.*
State Tret'iakov Gallery, Moscow.
199

Cubism, *1920–21.*
State Lunacharskii Museum of Fine Arts, Krasnodar.
201

Composition, *1921.*
State Tret'iakov Gallery, Moscow.
198

Composition (Head), *1921.*
State Tret'iakov Gallery, Moscow.
200

Valentin Iustitskii
Painterly Easel Construction, *1921.*
State Radishchev Art Museum, Saratov.
84

Painterly Easel Construction, *1921.*
State Radishchev Art Museum, Saratov.
85

Painterly Construction with Wire, *early 1920s.*
State Radishchev Art Museum, Saratov.
86

Textile sample, late 1920s or early 1930s.
Mukhina College Museum,
St. Petersburg.
579

Textile sample, late 1920s or early 1930s.
Mukhina College Museum,
St. Petersburg.
577

The Five-Year Plan in Four Years!,
late 1920s or early 1930s.
Ivanovo State Museum of History and
the Revolution.
580

Transmission, *late 1920s or early 1930s.*
Collection T. K. Strizhenova, Moscow.
569

Tunnel, *late 1920s or early 1930s.*
Mukhina College Museum,
St. Petersburg.
563

Guggenheim Museum

Conservation
Gillian MacMillan, Associate Conservator
Elizabeth Estabrook, Assistant Conservator
Nancy Heller, Assistant Conservator, Sculpture
Stephanie Hornbeck, Conservation Coordinator

Exhibitions/Design/ Technical Services
Pamela Myers, Administrator for Exhibitions and Programming
Cara Galowitz, Graphic Designer
Charles Bryan, Assistant Designer
Laura Antonow, Museum Technician, Lighting
Peter Hendrick, Museum Technician, Planning

Photography
David Heald, Photographer
Lee Ewing, Assistant Photographer
Samar Qandil, Photography Coordinator

Installation and Collection Services
Scott Wixon, Manager of Installation and Collection Services
Anibal Gonzalez-Rivera, Manager, Collection Services
Peter Read, Jr., Manager, Fabrication Services
Joseph Adams, Senior Museum Technician
Peter Costa, Senior Museum Technician
David Veater, Senior Museum Technician
Andrew Roberts-Gray, Technical Specialist
Timothy Ross, Technical Specialist
Lisette Baron Adams, Museum Technician
Robert Attanasio, Museum Technician
William Smith, Museum Technician
Guy Walker, Museum Technician
David Johnson, Museum Technician/Carpenter
Josh Neretin, Museum Technician/Carpenter
Hubbard Toombs, Technical Services Coordinator

Visitor Services/Facilities
Taylor Miller, Administrator for Facilities and Visitor Services

Visitor Services
Suzette Sherman, Manager for Visitor Services
Pia Licciardi, Assistant Manager for Visitor Services
Ernest Rodriguez-Naaz, Tour and Group Associate
Jennifer Farrell, Visitor Services Assistant
Esther Wahl, Visitor Services Assistant
Kelly Williams, Admissions Desk Supervisor, Part-time

Facilities
John Kahrs, Facilities Manager
Gerald Catanzaro, Assistant Facilities Manager
Michael Lavin, Electronic Systems Technician
Michael Yu, Electronics Technician
Gary Karjala, Maintenance Foreman
Walter Christie, Maintenance Consultant
Alfred Bracci, Watch Engineer
Garrett Comba, Administrative Assistant
Austin Bertand, Shift Custodian
Peter Donnolo, HVAC Mechanic
Abraham Edwards, HVAC Mechanic
Robert Ranieri, HVAC Mechanic
Raymond Taylor, Sr., Maintenance Mechanic
Raymond Taylor, Jr., Maintenance Mechanic
Arturo Tumboken, Maintenance Mechanic
Loretta Zidzik, Day Matron

Security
Marie Bradley, Assistant Manager for Administration
Winston Campbell, Security Supervisor
Janeen Lipchik, Security Supervisor
James Bessetti, Security Guard
Salvatore Bessetti, Security Guard
Wendi Carlock, Security Guard
Daniel Dixon, Security Guard
Michael Evans, Security Guard
Robert Fahey, Security Guard
Adina Ferber, Security Guard
Nigel Freeman, Security Guard
Rachel Hansen, Security Guard
Michael Heffernan, Security Guard
Lawrence Jenzen, Security Guard
Natalie Johnson, Security Guard
Patricia Keating, Security Guard
Robert Keay, Security Guard
John Mahoney, Security Guard
Mario Martini, Security Guard
Geneveva Munoz, Security Guard
Todd Murphy, Security Guard
Macs McAree, Security Guard
Eric McDougall, Security Guard
Kevin McGinley, Security Guard
Felix Padilla, Security Guard
Lyonel Pierre-Antoine, Security Guard
Scott Redden, Security Guard
Sandro Rodorigo, Security Guard
Carlos Rosado, Security Guard
Eric Simpson, Security Guard
Timothy Stock, Security Guard
Fred Taylor, Security Guard
James Thacker, Security Guard
Caroline Walker, Security Guard
Carol Warner, Security Guard
Chet Washington, Security Guard
Gregory Weinstein, Security Guard
Leonard Wilson, Security Guard

Learning Through Art
Mary Foster, Executive Director
Debbie Uyar, Public Relations and Assistant to the Executive Director
Beth Rosenberg, Museum Education and School Programs Associate
Andrea Pedersen, Development Associate
Luigi Gasparinetti, Program Development Associate
Ellen Leerberger, School Programs Associate
Maria Cuomo, Bookkeeper
Kim Rozzi, Education Assistant

Peggy Guggenheim Collection
Philip Rylands, Deputy Director
Fred Licht, Curator
Paul Schwartzbaum, Conservator
Renata Rossani, Assistant to the Deputy Director
Claudia Rech, Development and Public Affairs Coordinator
Annarita Fuso, Public Affairs Assistant
Laura Micolucci, Accountant
Gabriella Andreatta, Accounting Assistant
Chiara Barbieri, Assistant
Alessandro Claut, Security
Giorgio Lucerna, Security
Franco Pugnalin, Security
Emilio Trevisan, Security
Siro De Boni, Maintenance